The Carolingian Wo

At its height, the Carolingian empire spanned a million square kilometres of western Europe – from the English Channel to central Italy and northern Spain, and from the Atlantic to the fringes of modern Hungary, Poland and the Czech Republic. As the largest political unit for centuries, the empire dominated the region and left an enduring legacy for European culture. This comprehensive survey traces this great empire's history, from its origins around 700, with the rise to dominance of the Carolingian dynasty, through its expansion by ruthless military conquest and political manoeuvring in the eighth century, to the struggle to hold the empire together in the ninth. It places the complex political narrative in context, giving equal consideration to vital themes such as beliefs, peasant society, aristocratic culture, and the economy. Accessibly written and authoritative, this book offers distinctive perspectives on a formative period in European history.

MARIOS COSTAMBEYS is Senior Lecturer in the School of History at the University of Liverpool. His previous publications include *Power and Patronage in Early Medieval Italy: Local Society, Italian Politics and the Abbey of Farfa, c.700–900* (Cambridge, 2007).

MATTHEW INNES is Professor of History at Birkbeck, University of London. His previous publications include *State and Society in the Early Middle Ages: The Middle Rhine Valley, 400–1000* (Cambridge, 2000).

SIMON MACLEAN is Senior Lecturer in the School of History at the University of St Andrews. His previous publications include *Kingship and Politics in the Late Ninth Century: Charles the Fat and the End of the Carolingian Empire* (Cambridge, 2003).

Cambridge Medieval Textbooks

This is a series of introductions to important topics in medieval history aimed primarily at advanced students and faculty, and is designed to complement the monograph series *Cambridge Studies in Medieval Life and Thought*. It includes both chronological and thematic approaches and addresses both British and European topics.

For a list of titles in the series, see
www.cambridge.org/medievaltextbooks

THE CAROLINGIAN WORLD

MARIOS COSTAMBEYS
University of Liverpool

MATTHEW INNES
Birkbeck, University of London

SIMON MACLEAN
University of St Andrews

CAMBRIDGE
UNIVERSITY PRESS

CAMBRIDGE
UNIVERSITY PRESS

University Printing House, Cambridge CB2 8BS, United Kingdom

Cambridge University Press is part of the University of Cambridge.

It furthers the University's mission by disseminating knowledge in the pursuit of education, learning and research at the highest international levels of excellence.

www.cambridge.org
Information on this title: www.cambridge.org/9780521564946

© Marios Costambeys, Matthew Innes and Simon MacLean 2011

First published 2011
3rd printing 2012

A catalogue record for this publication is available from the British Library

Library of Congress Cataloguing in Publication data
Costambeys, Marios.
The Carolingian world / Marios Costambeys, Matthew Innes, Simon MacLean.
p. cm. – (Cambridge medieval textbooks)
Includes bibliographical references and index.
ISBN 978-0-521-56366-6 (hardback)
1. Carolingians – History. 2. France – History – To 987. 3. France – Civilization.
4. Europe, Western – History. 5. Europe, Western – Civilization. 6. Europe – History –
476–1492. 7. Civilization, Medieval. I. Innes, Matthew. II. MacLean, Simon.
III. Title. IV. Series.
DC70.C67 2011
944'.014 – dc22 2010054602

ISBN 978-0-521-56366-6 Hardback
ISBN 978-0-521-56494-6 Paperback

For Rosamond McKitterick and Jinty Nelson

CONTENTS

———— · ————

ILLUSTRATIONS

— · —

MAPS

———————— · ————————

ACKNOWLEDGEMENTS

Our initial thanks are due to Rosamond McKitterick and to Jinty Nelson, for first presenting each of us with the challenge of teaching the history of the early Middle Ages. As many of the references in this book testify, the work of these two scholars has fundamentally influenced the development of this field over the last few decades, and during our PhD research and since we have also been privileged to learn from them in person. We also owe warm thanks to Elina Screen. Her contribution extends well beyond the formal aspects to which we initially asked her to pay attention; both form and content would have been much the poorer without her diligent work. We would like too to thank Sally Lamb, on whose work Maps 15, 17 and 18 are based, and all those who read parts of the book in draft, or discussed particular problems or issues with us. All offered useful comments, though of course none is responsible for the views we have expressed. From the start we envisaged that undergraduates would form an important part of our readership, and indeed the idea for this book first arose when two of the authors covered some of Rosamond McKitterick's lecturing duties at the University of Cambridge during a period of research leave. Teaching and writing history are genuinely interconnected activities, and we are grateful to our friends and students at the Universities of Liverpool, Birkbeck London and St Andrews not just for road-testing drafts of some chapters, but also for helping us form and clarify our ideas. We are also indebted to successive commissioning editors at CUP for their encouragement, efficiency and patience: Bill Davies, Simon Whitmore, Michael Watson and Liz Friend-Smith. Our most profound gratitude goes, of course, to our families, for support, encouragement, and welcome distraction: to Greg and Joe, and Naomi and Evan, and to Charlotte, Jayne and Claire.

ABBREVIATIONS

—————— · ——————

AB	*Annales Bertiniani* [Annals of St Bertin], ed. F. Grat, J. Vielliard, S. Clémencet and L. Levillain (Paris, 1964), trans. J. L. Nelson, *The Annals of Saint-Bertin* (Manchester, 1991)
AF	*Annales Fuldenses* [Annals of Fulda], ed. F. Kurze, *MGH SRG in usum scholarum separatim editi* IX (Hanover, 1891), trans. T. Reuter, *The Annals of Fulda* (Manchester, 1992)
AL	*Annales Laureshamenses* [Annals of Lorsch], ed. G. H. Pertz, *MGH SS* I (Hanover, 1826), pp. 22–39
AMP	*Annales Mettenses priores* [Earlier Annals of Metz], ed. B. von Simson, *MGH SRG in usum scholarum separatim editi* X (Hanover and Leipzig, 1905)
Annales HSS	*Annales. Histoire, Sciences Sociales*
ARF	*Annales regni francorum* [Royal Frankish Annals], ed. F. Kurze, *MGH SRG in usum scholarum separatim editi* VI (Hanover, 1895), trans. B. Scholz, *Carolingian Chronicles* (Ann Arbor, MI, 1970)
AV	*Annales Vedastini* [Annals of St Vaast], ed. B. von Simson, *Annales Xantenses et Annales Vedastini*, *MGH SRG in usum scholarum separatim editi* XII (Hanover and Leipzig, 1909); extract (*a*.844–62)

	trans. P. E. Dutton (ed.), *Carolingian Civilization: a Reader*, 2nd edn (Peterborough, ON, 2004), pp. 347–50
AX	*Annales Xantenses* [Annals of Xanten], ed. B. von Simson, *Annales Xantenses et Annales Vedastini, MGH SRG in usum scholarum separatim editi* XII (Hanover and Leipzig, 1909); extract (*a*.882–6) trans. Dutton (ed.), *Carolingian Civilization*, pp. 507–12
Bede, *HE*	Bede, *Historia Ecclesiastica*
Capit. I, II	A. Boretius and V. Krause (eds.), *Capitularia regum francorum, MGH Leges sectio* III, 2 vols. (Hanover, 1883–97)
CC	*Codex epistolaris Carolinus*, ed. W. Gundlach, *MGH Epp.* III (*Epistolae merovingici et karolini aevi* I) (Berlin, 1892), pp. 476–657
CCCM	*Corpus Christianorum, continuatio medievalis*
CCM	*Corpus consuetudinum monasticarum* (Siegburg, 1963–)
CCSL	*Corpus Christianorum, series Latina*
CDL	L. Schiaparelli, C. Brühl and H. Zielinski (eds.), *Codice diplomatico longobardo*. 5 vols. Fonti per la storia d'Italia 62–6 (Rome, 1929–86)
Chron. Moiss.	*Chronicon Moissiacense* [Moissac Chronicle], ed. G. Pertz, *MGH SS* I (Hanover, 1829), pp. 282–313; extracts trans. in P. D. King, *Charlemagne: Translated Sources* (Kendal, 1987), pp. 145–9
CL	K. Glockner (ed.), *Codex Laureshamensis*, Arbeiten der historischen Kommission für den Volksstaat Hessen 3. 3 vols. (Darmstadt, 1929–36)
Conc. I, II	A. Werminghoff (ed.), *Concilia aevi Karolini* II.1 and II.2 (Hanover, 1906–8)
DA	*Deutsches Archiv für Erforschung des Mittelalters*
Dipl.	Diplomata
Dipl. Kar. I	E. Mühlbacher *et al.* (eds.), *Die Urkunden der Karolinger* I: *Die Urkunden Pippins, Karlmanns und Karls des Großen. MGH Diplomata Karolinorum* I (Hanover, 1906)

Dipl. LG	P. Kehr (ed.), *Die Urkunden Ludwigs des Deutschen, Karlmanns und Ludwigs des Jüngeren.* MGH Diplomata Regum Germanie ex stirpe Karolinorum I (Berlin, 1934)
Dipl. Loth II	T. Schieffer (ed.), *Die Urkunden Lothars I und Lothars II. MGH Diplomata Karolinorum* III (Berlin, 1966)
DNB	H. C. G. Matthew, B. H. Harrison, L. Goldman (eds.), *Oxford Dictionary of National Biography* (Oxford, 2004)
EHD	D. Whitelock (ed.), *English Historical Documents,* 2nd edn (London and New York, 1979) I: *c.500–1042*
EHR	*English Historical Review*
Einhard, *VK*	Einhard, *Vita Karoli* [Life of Charlemagne], ed. O. Holder-Egger, *MGH SRG* xxv (Hanover, 1911), trans. P. Dutton, *Charlemagne's Courtier: The Complete Einhard* (Peterborough, ON, 1998), and D. Ganz, *Two Lives of Charlemagne* (Harmondsworth, 2008)
EME	*Early Medieval Europe*
Ep., Epp.	*Epistola, Epistolae* [Letter(s)]
Fred., *Cont.*	Fredegar, *Continuations,* ed. and trans. J. M. Wallace-Hadrill, *The Fourth Book of the Chronicle of Fredegar with its Continuations* (London, 1960)
HL	Paul the Deacon, *Historia langobardorum* [History of the Lombards], ed. L. Bethmann and G. Waitz, *MGH SRL* (Hanover, 1878), pp. 12–187
HZ	*Historische Zeitschrift*
LHF	*Liber historiae francorum* [Book of the History of the Franks], ed. B. Krusch, *MGH SRM* II (Hanover, 1888), pp. 215–328
LP I, II	*Liber pontificalis* [Book of the Popes], ed. L. Duchesne, *Le Liber pontificalis. Texte, introduction et commentaire,* 2 vols. (Paris, 1886 and 1892); amplified 3 vol. edn ed. C. Vogel (Paris, 1955–7), trans. in three books by R. Davis, *The Book of Pontiffs* (Liber Pontificalis), revised edition (Liverpool, 2000); *The Lives of the Eighth-Century Popes* (Liber Pontificalis)

UBF

E. E. Stengel (ed.), *Urkundenbuch des Klosters Fulda*. Veröffentlichungen der historischen Kommission für Hessen und Waldeck 19 (Marburg, 1936)

UBMR

H. Beyer, L. Eltester and A. Goerz (eds.), *Urkundenbuch zur Geschichte der jetzt die Preußischen regierungsbezirke Coblenz und Trier bildenden mittelrheinischen Territorien* 1: *Von den ältesten Zeiten bis zum Jahre 1169* (Koblenz, 1860)

VMPIG

Veröffentlichungen des Max-Planck-Instituts für Geschichte

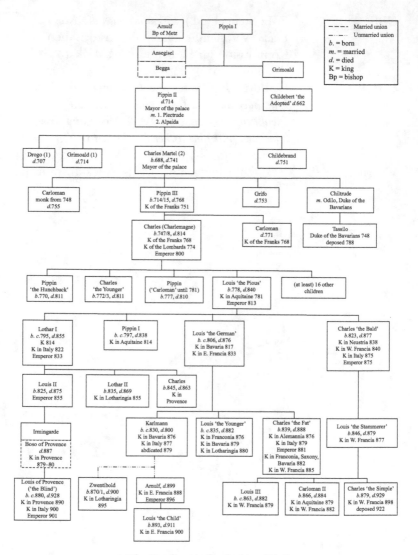

The Carolingian family (simplified)

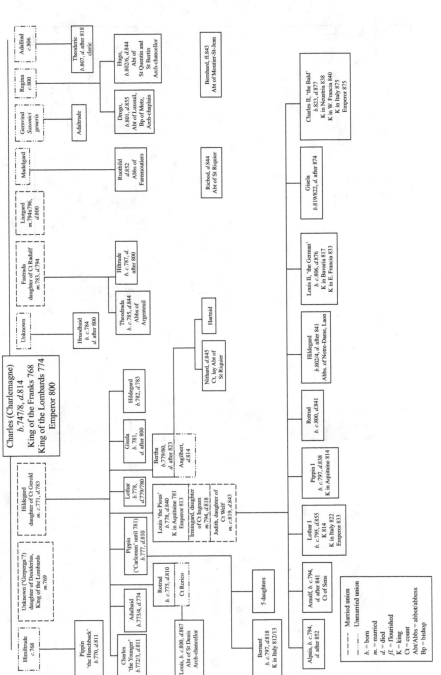

The children and grandchildren of Charlemagne

Charles (Charlemagne)
*b.*747/8, *d.*814
King of the Franks 768
King of the Lombards 774
Emperor 800

Himiltrude
*c.*768

Unknown ('Gerperga'?)
daughter of Desiderius,
King of the Lombards
*m.*769

Hildegard
daughter of Ct Gerold
*m. c.*771, *d.*783

Unknown

Fastrada
daughter of Ct Radulf
*m.*783, *d.*794

Luitgard
*m.*794x796,
*d.*800

Madelgard

Gersvind
*Saxonici
generis*

Regina
*c.*800

Adallind
*c.*806

Pippin
'the Hunchback'
*b.*770, *d.*811

Pippin
('Carloman' until 781)
*b.*777, *d.*810

Rotrud
*b. c.*775, *d.*810
Ct Rorico

Lothar
*b.*778,
*d.*779/780

Louis 'the Pious'
*b.*778, *d.*840
K in Aquitaine 781
Emperor 813

Gisela
*b.*781,
d. after 800

Hildegard
*b.*782, *d.*783

Bertha
*b.*779/80,
d. after 823

Hruodhaid
*b. c.*784
d. after 800

Theodrada
*b.*785, *d.*844
Abbs of
Argenteuil

Hiltrude
*b. c.*787, *d.*
after 800

Ruodhild
*d.*852
Abbs of
Faremoutiers

Adaltrude

Drogo,
*b.*801,
Abt of Luxeuil,
Bp of Metz,
Arch-chaplain

Hugo,
*b.*802/6, *d.*844
Abt of
St Quentin and
St Bertin
Arch-chancellor

Theoderic
*b.*807, *d.* after 818
cleric

Adalhaid
*b.*773/4, *d.*774

Charles
'the Younger'
*b.*772/3, *d.*811

Lothar I
*b. c.*795, *d.*855
K 814
K in Italy 822
Emperor 833

Pippin I
*b.*797, *d.*838
K in Aquitaine 814

Rotrud
*b.*800, *d.*841

Hildegard
*b.*802/4, *d.* after 841
Abbs. of Notre-Dame, Laon

Louis II, 'the German'
*b. c.*806, *d.*876
K in Bavaria 817
K in E. Francia 833

Gisela
*b.*819/822, *d.* after 874

Charles II, 'the Bald'
*b.*823, *d.*877
K in Neustria 838
K in W. Francia 840
K in Italy 875
Emperor 875

Angilbert,
*d.*814

Nithard, *d.*845
Ct, lay Abt of
St Riquier

Hartnid

Richbod, *d.*844
Abt of St Riquier

Bernhard, fl.843
Abt of Moutier-St-Jean

Louis, *b. c.*800, *d.*867
Abt of St Denis
Arch-chancellor

Bernard
*b. c.*797, *d.*818
K in Italy 812/13

5 daughters

Alpais, *b. c.*794,
d. after 852

Arnulf, *b. c.*794,
d. after 841
Ct of Sens

— — — — Married union
· · · · · · · Unmarried union

b. = born
m. = married
d. = died
fl. = flourished
K = king
Ct = count
Abt/Abbs = abbot/abbess
Bp = bishop

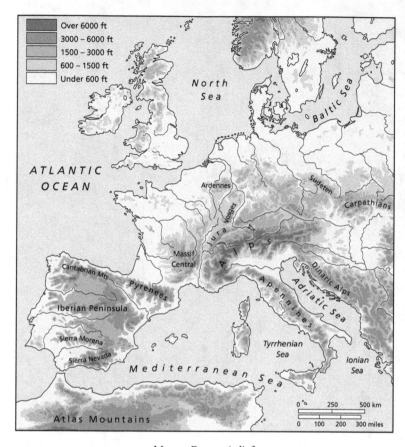

Map 1. Europe (relief)

—————— I ——————

INTRODUCTION

—————— . ——————

Late in the year 753, Pippin, king of the Franks, heard news that the pope had left Rome and was coming to visit him. This journey – the first time a pope had ever crossed the Alps – presented the king with both a problem and an opportunity. On the one hand, he may have known that what Pope Stephen II wanted was military protection, with all the risk and expense that that entailed, against an opponent in Italy, the king of the Lombards, whose predecessor had been Pippin's own godfather. On the other hand, the pope was just the kind of politically neutral and prestigious figure from whom Pippin could seek endorsement for the radical move he had made two years earlier, when he had usurped the throne of the Franks from the Merovingian dynasty that had held it for the previous two and a half centuries.

Neither Pippin nor Stephen quite appeciated the impact that their actions that winter would have but, in a process that typifies the problems faced by historians of this period, political significance was quickly heaped onto their meeting and within a few years the circumstances surrounding it were being intensively rewritten. Thus Stephen II's biographer, a clerk in the papal bureaucracy, reports that Pippin sent his young son Charles to meet the pope 100 miles from his destination and to escort him to the king, who knelt in homage before him. A Frankish source, on the other hand, has the pope and his attendant clergy kneeling before the king.[1] Other Frankish sources assert that Pippin had already sought the approval of Stephen's predecessor for his usurpation; a claim apparently unknown to papal writers.[2] It was certainly true that each could help the other. Frankish and papal sources concur that the pope anointed Pippin and his family.[3] Pippin then secured the approval of the Frankish aristocracy[4] and despatched campaigns in successive years which forced the Lombard king Aistulf to sue for peace. Returning home, Stephen reinforced his attachment to the Franks by granting buildings near St Peter's in Rome to the Parisian monastery of St Denis, the Frankish royal saint under whose auspices he had secured his alliance with Pippin.[5]

In the short term the effects of this alliance were not decisive for either party. The popes remained relatively weak and for the next two decades the Lombards continued to menace their interests in and around Rome, while the Franks were generally reluctant to fulfil their newly acquired obligation to protect the papacy by committing themselves to military action hundreds of miles away across the Alps. In a longer perspective, however, these events represent what has long been interpreted by historians as an epochal turning point in the history of western Europe. For some historians of the first half of the twentieth century the change of ruling dynasty was regarded as 'the most momentous act of the entire Middle Ages', either because it inaugurated the pope's involvement in the legitimation of kingship, or because of the break it signalled between Rome and the surviving 'Roman' empire in the east – the Byzantine empire that covered the Balkans and Asia Minor.[6] These views were crystallised in the 1920s in the work of the famous Belgian historian Henri Pirenne,

---

[1] See *LP* I, c. 25, p. 447, trans. Davis, *Lives of the Eighth-Century Popes*, p. 62, and *Chron. Moiss.*, *s.a.* 741, pp. 292–3.

[2] McKitterick, *History and Memory*, pp. 137–8.

[3] *LP* I, c. 27, p. 448, trans. Davis, *Lives of the Eighth-Century Popes*, p. 63; Fred., *Cont.*, c. 33.

[4] As even the papal biographer in the *Liber pontificalis* tells us: *LP* II, c. 29, p. 448; Davis, *Lives of the Eighth-Century Popes*, p. 64.

[5] M. Costambeys and C. Leyser, 'To be the neighbour of St Stephen: patronage, martyr cult and Roman monasteries, *c.*600–900', in K. Cooper and J. Hillner (eds.), *Religion, Dynasty and Patronage in Early Christian Rome, 300–900* (Cambridge, 2007), pp. 262–87, at pp. 273–4.

[6] See R. Schieffer, '"Die folgenschwerste Tat des ganzen Mittelalters"? Aspekte des wissenschaftlichen Urteils über den Dynastiewechsel von 751', in M. Becher and

who saw this break as only one component of a structural shift in the political and economic geography of Europe, as the lands of the western Mediterranean separated decisively from the eastern empire and struck up a more intense relationship with the kingdoms of the north, thus permanently fixing the shape of a new, specifically western, European civilisation.[7]

Pippin did not see himself as standard bearer of a new age in these terms. Indeed, he was motivated above all by a sense of his own vulnerability. As we shall see in greater detail in Chapter 2, by having himself proclaimed king in 751 in place of the reigning king Childeric III, Pippin had defied a strong sense among the Franks that the aura of legitimacy rested upon Childeric's family, the Merovingians. Pippin's need to legitimise his action and to undermine the opposition of those hostile to his new royal status, including some members of his own family, lay behind his acquisition of papal blessing not only for himself but for his wife and sons as well.[8] Nonetheless, the novelty of these rituals did reflect a self-conscious attempt to mark off and announce the beginning of a new political era. It was successful in ways that those present in 753–4 could not have foreseen: Pippin was born an aristocrat; his descendants would be kings and emperors of western Europe.

Thanks to their monopoly on royal power in the Frankish realms between 751 and 888, the Carolingians ('the family of Charles' (Latin: *Carolus*) – named for Pippin's father Charles Martel) are remembered as one of European history's great dynasties. The first phase of their tenure witnessed a breath-taking territorial expansion. Seeking to consolidate their tenuous position, Pippin and his sons embarked on a spectacularly successful series of campaigns pursued in equal measure through extreme violence and ruthless political manoeuvring. Within fifty years of Stephen's visit to Paris, they had doubled their territory and accumulated an empire spanning approximately one million square kilometres, stretching south from the English Channel

J. Jarnut (eds.), *Der Dynastiewechsel von 751. Vorgeschichte, Legitimationsstrategien und Erinnerung* (Münster, 2004), pp. 1–14.

[7] See Chapter 7 below, pp. 326–8, and H. Pirenne, *Mahomet et Charlemagne* (Brussels, 1937), trans. as *Mohammed and Charlemagne* (London, 1939).

[8] See P. Fouracre, 'The long shadow of the Merovingians', in Story (ed.), *Charlemagne*, pp. 5–21; Becher and Jarnut (eds.), *Der Dynastiewechsel von 751*; McKitterick, *History and Memory*, pp. 133–55; M. J. Enright, *Iona, Tara, and Soissons: The Origin of the Royal Anointing Ritual* (Berlin and New York, 1985).

to central Italy and northern Spain, and east from the Atlantic to the fringes of modern Hungary, Poland and the Czech Republic: easily the largest European political unit for many centuries. On Christmas Day 800 Pippin's son Charles 'the Great' (or Charlemagne as he is known to posterity, the same boy who as a five-year-old had reportedly been sent to receive Pope Stephen in 753) was crowned emperor in Rome, the first man to bear this title in the West since the deposition of the last Roman emperor in 476. Five of his immediate successors were to be emperors and many more ruled as kings as generations of Carolingians maintained and dominated this huge empire through most of the ninth century, during which the territory was often formally divided between members of the family, but always remained a dynastic unit. The territorial integrity of the empire was definitively ended only in 888, hastened by a succession crisis within the family.

Imperial aggrandisement was the basis, but not the end, of the dynasty's achievement. Inspired by court circles filled with scholars and spiritual advisers of international repute, the Carolingians also declared their aspiration to reform the social and moral behaviour of the peoples under their dominion. They sought to achieve this imaginative goal by exploiting to their limits the technologies of government available in the early Middle Ages. Pippin and his successors constructed a hierarchical political system which could allow the word of the king to penetrate to the furthest reaches of his realms; and they managed to do so in large part because of advances in the production, dissemination and preservation of knowledge. To some extent these advances were down to royal initiative. The foundation or revival by Carolingian rulers and aristocrats of institutions for which the written word was a central raison d'être – particularly, but not exclusively, the institutions of the Church – is a cardinal fact of the age.[9] This is of the utmost importance for historians because those institutions' ability to copy existing works, to produce new ones, and to preserve both, has fundamentally shaped the record not just of the Carolingian period but of every preceding century back to the dawn of western history. We owe a good proportion of what we know of every century before 900 to the hands of Carolingian scribes. Their work attests a fusion of economic vitality (manuscripts

---

[9] Generally, capital-C 'Church' refers to the institution, while small-c 'church' refers to the building: thus we can write of the Anglo-Saxon (or Roman or Catholic) Church, but the church of St Peter's, cathedral church at Tours, etc.

were very expensive), political will and intellectual ambition which confirms that the Carolingians were distinctive for much more than the novelty of their relationship with the popes.

The Carolingians thus left an indelible mark on the historical record, but they also bequeathed an ideological legacy which dominated the imaginations of their successors. The heroes of the dynasty did not take long to pass into the realm of mythology, and posterity quickly canonised Pippin's family as a benchmark for dynastic prestige. It was this aura which, in 1000, drew the German emperor Otto III to Charlemagne's palace chapel at Aachen where, as an act of piety and political theatre, he exhumed and re-interred the great emperor's body, eyewitnesses reporting that apart from overlong fingernails and a touch of decay on the nose he remained bodily incorrupt and upright on his throne. In the twelfth century Suger, abbot of St Denis, built a new church to house the bodies of his patrons alongside the Carolingians already buried there, and thus to create a sense of dynastic continuity that flattered the great Capetian dynasty of his own day. Meanwhile, the German emperor Frederick I 'Barbarossa' sought to outdo the Capetians, and assert unmediated control of the Carolingian past, by translating Charlemagne's remains to a new casket in 1165, and having him recognised as a saint.[10] Post-medieval imperialists have also looked to the eighth and ninth centuries to anchor their sense of themselves: the memory of the Carolingians was appropriated, for instance, by Napoleon, who visited Charlemagne's tomb to contemplate the great emperor prior to his own coronation in 1804. He has also found a place in the ideologies of modern regimes of various hues including those of the Nazis (whose army contained a unit named after Charlemagne) and the European Union (which sponsors a prize for European unity named after him).[11]

---

[10] Respectively, see: G. Althoff, *Otto III* (University Park, PA, 2003); L. Grant, *Abbot Suger of St-Denis: Church and State in Early Twelfth-Century France* (London, 1998); J. Petersohn, 'Saint-Denis – Westminster – Aachen. Die Karls-Translatio von 1165 und ihre Vorbilder', *Deutsches Archiv für Erforschung des Mittelalters* 31 (1975), pp. 420–54. In general see M. Gabriele and J. Stuckey (eds.), *The Legend of Charlemagne in the Middle Ages. Power, Faith and Crusade* (New York, 2008).

[11] R. J. Morrissey, *Charlemagne and France: A Thousand Years of Mythology* (Notre Dame, IN, 2003); J. Story, 'Introduction: Charlemagne's reputation', in Story (ed.), *Charlemagne*, pp. 1–4; R. D. McKitterick, *Charlemagne: The Formation of a European Identity* (Cambridge, 2008), pp. 1–3.

It is, then, not surprising that modern historians, whose work is never uncontaminated by the wider ideological atmosphere in which it is written, continue to reinvent the contemporary relevance of the Carolingians by casting them in the role of 'a family who forged Europe', and seeing in their empire 'the scaffolding of the Middle Ages'.[12] Some of the most prominent debates about the origins of modern Europe have revolved around the significance of key events in Carolingian history. The defeat by Pippin's father Charles Martel of a Muslim army near Tours was traditionally seen as decisive in halting the northward spread of Islam;[13] Charlemagne's imperial coronation in 800 was, centuries later, recast as the founding event of the 'Holy Roman Empire'; the Treaty of Verdun in 843, by which the empire was divided into three parts, two of which corresponded roughly to France and Germany, has been seen as 'the birth certificate of Europe';[14] and the end of the empire in 888 was the focus for an intensely ideological debate about the origins of the kingdom of Germany coloured by a barely concealed mid-twentieth-century political agenda.[15] The modern baggage loaded on to these distant moments hints at how the period has been quarried as a source of material for highly charged controversies about modern national identities, particularly those of France and Germany.[16] To some extent this way of thinking was hard-wired into the field from the start: sustained critical study of the period was inaugurated in 1819 by the founding of the *Monumenta Germaniae historica* (Historic Monuments of Germany), an institution whose purpose was explicitly framed as a patriotic attempt to raise German national consciousness through the publication of all texts relating to the medieval history of a country that was at that point still over fifty years from emerging as a full nation-state.[17] Conversely, mid-twentieth-century French historians like Louis Halphen, haunted by the cataclysm of World War

---

[12] The quotations are from P. Riché, *The Carolingians: A Family who Forged Europe*, trans. M. I. Allen (Philadelphia, PA, 1993) and Pirenne, *Mohammed and Charlemagne*, p. 235.

[13] P. Fouracre, *The Age of Charles Martel* (Harlow, 2000), pp. 86–7; I. Wood, *The Merovingian Kingdoms, 450–751* (London, 1994), p. 283.

[14] Riché, *The Carolingians*, p. 168.

[15] C. Brühl, *Deutschland–Frankreich. Die Geburt zweier Völker*, 2nd edn (Cologne and Vienna, 1995), pp. 7–17.

[16] P. Geary, *The Myth of Nations* (Princeton, NJ, 2002), esp. pp. 1–14.

[17] D. Knowles, *Great Historical Enterprises* (London, 1963), pp. 65–97.

II, wrote the Carolingian story as a great tragedy of failed European unity; while some more recent authors have sketched a very different narrative arc by explicitly claiming the empire as a foreshadowing of contemporary Europe, united in diversity.[18] All these views find support in the sources because the empire was always united (as an ideal) and often divided (in reality): contemporaries saw themselves as simultaneously members of regional or national groupings and of an imperial community, emphasising one or the other depending on who they were talking to or about. Because contemporary Franks argued about their identity in recognisable terms, the contested history of the Carolingian empire is useful for writing any one of a number of modern stories about the past.[19]

It is not the aim of this book to take issue with or propound any one of these possible narratives. Rather, its writing has been prompted by the fact that the most recent general surveys of Carolingian history published in English are now over twenty-five years old, and since they were written there has been a dramatic surge in research that has subjected many aspects of the field to new levels of scrutiny.[20] As is proper, this work has not led to the incremental formation of consensus on all topics, but has opened up new questions by identifying the parameters and paradoxes within which debate about eighth- and ninth-century society can be framed. Thus this often appears to be a world very alien to our own, one in which the ruling class was simultaneously pious and violent (with no sense of dissonance between the two); in which officials fulfilled functions we call 'governmental' and yet had little concept of the state; in which peasants, though legally free, could be bound by complex obligations to landlords and rulers; and in which increasing efforts to define and prescribe Christian belief were made against a background

---

[18] L. Halphen, *Charlemagne and the Carolingian Empire* (Amsterdam, 1977); J. L. Nelson, *The Frankish World, 750–900* (London, 1996), pp. xiii–xiv; A. Barbero, *Charlemagne: Father of a Continent* (Berkeley, 2004). On the writing of European history across specific periods, see S. Woolf, 'Europe and its historians', *Contemporary European History* 12 (2003), pp. 323–37.

[19] K. Leyser, 'Concepts of Europe in the early and high middle ages', *P&P* 137, pp. 25–47, repr. in Leyser, *Communications and Power in Medieval Europe: The Carolingian and Ottonian Centuries* (London, 1994), pp. 1–18.

[20] The most recent English-language surveys of a specifically defined Carolingian period are Rosamond McKitterick's *The Frankish Kingdoms under the Carolingians, 751–987* (London and New York, 1983) and Riché, *The Carolingians*, which also first appeared in 1983.

of enormously varied religious practices. The last twenty-five years have witnessed huge advances in historical comprehension of most of these areas, stimulated in part by increasing interest in the Carolingian period in the Anglophone scholarly world. Our aim is therefore not only to introduce the main features of the period to readers who may not be well acquainted with it, but also to synthesise and engage with the issues debated in the latest research. Working out how to fit all this together involves making difficult decisions, especially in a book aimed primarily at newcomers to the period. Political narrative is an essential framework for modern readers, as it was for contemporary authors. However, one of our aims in this book is to suggest that developments in social structures, rural and elite society, economic forces, religious beliefs and aspects of culture were inextricably tied up with political events, and with each other, in a complex multilateral relationship. One way we have chosen to emphasise this (since writing three-dimensional 'total history' is impossible) is by playing down the political narrative that dominates most textbooks and weaving it throughout the book, mainly restricted to chapters at the beginning, middle and end. Nevertheless, the interleaved thematic chapters do broadly follow a chronological arc so that, for example, it makes sense to know about Charlemagne's wars of conquest before discussing the establishment of structures of religious belief during his reign; but it is also sensible to analyse the main features of elite society before turning to the role of the aristocracy in the years leading up to the end of the empire. We hope that the book therefore not only serves to synthesise the recent flourishing of Carolingian studies, but also reflects scholars' increasing awareness of the complex interrelationships between political, social and economic phenomena that are often regarded as discrete.

At the same time, we have had to decide what to leave out. By focussing on broad themes such as belief, communications, village society and elite culture, we draw on examples that come from a range of geographical areas. Naturally, we are drawn more regularly to some areas than others – those for which sources survive most abundantly, and those that we know best. An inevitable consequence of this is that some important areas are under-represented in this book, for instance northern Spain, southern Gaul and the eastern frontiers. Other very important topics have receded into the background because comprehensive introductory accounts are readily available elsewhere. In this category we might place art, literature and other high cultural aspects of the Carolingian reform; the role of law and law-making; and warfare.[21] Still others which could have been placed centre-stage, such as the political role of women, the structures of the institutional Church and the workings of government, we have tried to fold into our thematic discussions. We cannot claim comprehensiveness, and the bibliography at the end of the book should be used by readers wishing to learn more about particular subjects.

WAS THERE A CAROLINGIAN WORLD?

Listing some of the topics that do not appear in this book means that we are obliged to try to justify the coherence of those that do. Self-evidently, the book rests on the proposition that the 'Carolingian world' in the eighth and ninth centuries constitutes a discrete historical time and place that deserves analysis; and in doing so it could be seen as privileging a narrative of European history defined by the deeds of a single powerful family that focusses disproportionately on the geographical areas where they owned their greatest estates (in particular the Seine basin, the Rhineland and the Po valley). An important critique along these lines was published in 1989 by the American historian Richard Sullivan, who argued that by underplaying the importance of regionalism and screening out underlying continuities, historians were guilty of overemphasising the distinctiveness and significance of the Carolingian empire and era.[22] He was certainly correct to stress the significance of regionalism in the eighth and ninth centuries. The geographical coherence of the empire is artificially enhanced by modern cartography, which can create the illusion of political boundaries as firm and uncontested lines. Contemporary thought did have a place for precisely defined borders – Carolingian kings thought they could impose restrictions on the passage across their frontiers of some commodities, particularly weapons

---

[21] Both McKitterick, *Frankish Kingdoms* and Riché, *The Carolingians* have very good discussions of culture; see also R. McKitterick (ed.), *Carolingian Culture: Emulation and Innovation* (Cambridge, 1994); on law see P. Wormald, *The Making of English Law: King Alfred to the Twelfth Century* I: *Legislation and its Limits* (Oxford, 1999) (which despite the title contains much on continental history); on warfare, G. Halsall, *Warfare and Society in the Barbarian West* (London and New York, 2003). On all these areas, see *NCMH* II.

[22] R. Sullivan, 'The Carolingian age: Reflections on its place in the history of the Middle Ages', *Speculum* 64 (1989), pp. 267–306.

and coins, which suggests a significant level of confidence in their ability to fix and police borders, as does Charlemagne's imposition of a trade embargo in a dispute with King Offa of Mercia around 790.[23] However, the varying degree of royal control in different parts of the Frankish realms means that our maps' sharp edges begin to look frayed under close inspection. Some areas were at times nominally part of the empire but in practice not fully integrated, such as northern Spain, central Italy and Brittany.[24] Other parts of Europe, including the kingdoms of Anglo-Saxon England, were clearly beyond the frontier but through regular contact and cultural pressure absorbed many of the characteristics of Carolingian political culture.[25] Nor was the empire cleanly defined against outsiders as a religious entity: while Charlemagne's campaigns against the pagan Saxons are talked about in some sources in terms that suggest religious justifications were used, he also fought Christians in Brittany and Aquitaine, and his attacks on Muslim Spain were initiated not against an enemy defined by its different religion, but on behalf of one faction within the Caliphate against another. By the same token, Frankish Christian elites in the ninth century often pursued internal political and military interests by allying with non-Christian Scandinavians and Slavs. Concepts of religious difference overlapped with, and could be superseded by, a different set of assumptions concerning the cultural difference or similarity of the Franks' neighbours.[26]

Since the Carolingians found it impossible to impose or adhere to rigid geographical boundaries in their world, we have not sought to

---

[23] On frontiers, see W. Pohl, I. Wood and H. Reimitz (eds.), *The Transformation of Frontiers from Late Antiquity to the Carolingians* (Leiden, Boston and Cologne, 2001) and W. Pohl and H. Reimitz (eds.), *Grenze und Differenz im frühen Mittelalter* (Vienna, 2000). On Charlemagne and Offa, see Alcuin, *Epistolae*, ed. E. Dümmler, *MGH Epp.* IV (*Epp. Karolini aevi* II) (Berlin, 1895), pp. 1–493, no. 7, trans. S. Allott, *Alcuin of York: his Life and Letters* (York, 1974), no. 31; J. Story, *Carolingian Connections: Anglo-Saxon England and Carolingian Francia, c.750–870* (Aldershot, 2003), p. 186.

[24] See respectively R. Collins, *Early Medieval Spain: Unity in Diversity, 400–1000* (2nd edn, Basingstoke, 1995); M. Costambeys, *Power and Patronage in Early Medieval Italy* (Cambridge, 2007), Chapters 7 and 8; J. M. H. Smith, *Province and Empire. Brittany and the Carolingians* (Cambridge, 1992).

[25] J. Story, 'Charlemagne and the Anglo-Saxons', in Story (ed.), *Charlemagne*, pp. 195–210; Story, *Carolingian Connections*.

[26] I. Wood, 'Missionaries and the Christian frontier', in Pohl, Wood and Reimitz (eds.), *Transformation of Frontiers*, pp. 209–18.

do so in this book. Our coverage is of course partly dictated by that of the primary sources, which survive more thickly from some areas than from others. Even the focus of many of the narrative sources on the Carolingians themselves lends little geographical consistency to the picture, both because rulers were itinerant and because, after 840, the division of the realm produced multiple simultaneous foci. It is certainly possible to distinguish regions such as the Rhineland or the Po valley, but what can be said about them varies according to the concerns of the source material. Overall, the reader will find that most of the evidence discussed in the following chapters is drawn from the core Frankish realm – modern France, Belgium, Luxembourg, Switzerland, the Rhineland and southwestern Germany – and from northern and central Italy, where the Carolingians became dominant after 774. But other areas will come into focus when the book turns to topics on which their material makes especially significant contributions: the English and Irish in the discussion of Christianisation; Brittany when we turn to village life; Scandinavia and the Arab world in relation to long-distance exchange. Most of these experienced the strength of Carolingian political power only slightly, if at all. But they all made vital contributions to the shaping of the Carolingian world, and were themselves directly or indirectly influenced by it.

Carolingian influence fluctuated in intensity within the empire's borders as well as beyond them. Despite the rhetoric of unity persistently transmitted by Carolingian rulers and their religious advisers, we have to be constantly aware of the empire's great regional diversity in social and cultural terms. The huge and powerful monasteries of the middle Rhine or western Gaul, for instance, dominated landscapes defined by very different social, political and religious conditions from those surrounding the rather more impoverished churches of newly conquered Saxony.[27] Similarly, not only did many peoples in the regions of the empire have their own lawcodes, but close study of how law operated in particular local societies has sharpened our appreciation of how different were the experiences of people who lived in a place like Catalonia from those of their,

---

[27] See respectively M. Innes, *State and Society in the Early Middle Ages: The Middle Rhine Valley, 400–1000* (Cambridge, 2000) and C. J. Carroll, 'The bishoprics of Saxony in the first century after Christianization', *EME* 8 (1999), pp. 219–45.

say, Bavarian contemporaries.[28] Linguistic variety was almost equally kaleidoscopic.[29] Acknowledging this variety does not, though, lead inevitably to the conclusion that the idea of a coherent Carolingian world is an illusion concocted to satisfy the fantasies of nineteenth-century nationalists or late-twentieth-century Europeanists; or that the persistence of internal differences is simply a sign that the Carolingian drive for unity and hierarchy should be judged a failure. Unity and diversity are not mutually exclusive – indeed, outside the totalitarian and absolutist states of the more recent past, large polities had to be built precisely through the acknowledgement of local identities by the central authority.[30] The Carolingian empire was not like the British empire with a clearly defined centre-to-periphery political economy, nor a centralised state on the model of the Roman empire, but rather an agglomeration of regions with their own identities and greater or lesser degrees of autonomy.[31] In writing this book we have tried to keep in mind as much as possible the fact that there were many Carolingian worlds, each of which adapted in different ways to being part of a larger political entity, and readers should keep this in mind before reaching general conclusions.

---

[28] On Bavaria, see W. Brown, *Unjust Seizure: Conflict, Interest and Authority in an Early Medieval Society* (Ithaca, NY, 2001); on Catalonia, see C. J. Chandler, 'Between court and counts: Carolingian Catalonia and the aprisio grant, 778–897', *EME* 11/1 (2002), pp. 19–44; see also the essays in W. Davies and P. Fouracre (eds.), *The Settlement of Disputes in Early Medieval Europe* (Cambridge, 1986), for discussion of regions including Brittany, Spain and Italy.

[29] On language see M. Banniard, 'Language and communication in Carolingian Europe', in *NCMH* II, pp. 695–708 and P. Kershaw, 'Laughter after Babel's fall: misunderstanding and miscommunication in the ninth-century west', in G. Halsall (ed.), *Humour, History and Politics in Late Antiquity and the Early Middle Ages* (Cambridge, 2002), pp. 179–202.

[30] See R. McKitterick, 'Unity and diversity in the Carolingian church', in R. Swanson (ed.), *Unity and Diversity in the Church*, Studies in Church History 32 (1996), pp. 59–82; M. Innes, 'Danelaw identities: ethnicity, regionalism and political allegiance', in D. M. Hadley and J. D. Richards (eds.), *Cultures in Contact: Scandinavian Settlement in England in the Ninth and Tenth Centuries* (Turnhout, 2000), pp. 65–88.

[31] On typologies of polity, see the essays by W. Pohl, 'Staat und Herrschaft im Frühmittelalter: Überlegungen zur Forschungsstand', H.-W. Goetz, 'Die Wahrnehmung von "Staat" und "Herrschaft" im frühen Mittelalter', M. de Jong, '*Ecclesia* and the early medieval polity' and P. Wormald, 'Premodern "State" and "Nation": definite or indefinite?', all in S. Airlie, W. Pohl and H. Reimitz (eds.), *Staat im frühen Mittelalter*, Forschungen zur Geschichte des Mittelalters 11 (Vienna, 2006), respectively pp. 9–38, 39–58, 113–32 and 179–89.

The chronological limits we have chosen to define the book are those which constitute the period during which the empire was united through rule by members of the same family, but these dates are also potentially porous. It is possible that political structures conventionally associated with the Carolingian takeover of the mid-eighth century are actually continuations of older phenomena for which we simply lack the sources.[32] The ideological novelty of Pippin's anointing in 754 can certainly be played down using this sort of argument.[33] At the other end of the period, despite the territorial disintegration of the empire in 888, members of the dynasty intermittently held royal status in parts of west Francia and Italy for another century. The Carolingian period neither began nor ended with a social revolution. Most historians would agree that most forms of change during the period were significant but gradual, governed by slow transformation rather than abrupt shifts or collapses that might have created the clean edges useful to those interested in defining historical eras. On the other hand, the step change in the number of surviving written sources (which we will consider more fully in the next section) from around the time of Pippin's usurpation could be seen as a significant historical fact in itself. It might indicate a shift in contemporary consciousness as people and institutions responded to the new political circumstances – in this case by taking up writing with new enthusiasm. It would be possible to explain the jump in the number of surviving documents recording donations to monasteries in, for instance, the Rhineland, Alsace and Bavaria in the reigns of Pippin and Charlemagne, by casting these institutions as prominent markers of shifts in the organisation of local society prompted by

---

[32] See P. Fouracre, 'Conflict, power and legitimation in Francia in the late seventh and early eighth centuries', in I. Alfonso, H. Kennedy and J. Escalona (eds.), *Building Legitimacy: Political Discourses and Forms of Legitimacy in Medieval Societies*, The Medieval Mediterranean: Peoples, Economies and Cultures 400–1500 53 (Leiden, 2004), pp. 3–26.

[33] See Y. Hen, 'The Christianisation of kingship', in Becher and Jarnut (eds.), *Der Dynastiewechsel von 751*, pp. 163–77; R. Le Jan, 'Die Sakralität der Merowinger oder: Mehrdeutigkeiten der Geschichtsschreibung', in Airlie, Pohl and Reimitz (eds.), *Staat im frühen Mittelalter*, pp. 73–92. The notion that Pippin's usurpation in 751 included his anointing by bishops has been called into question by the reconsideration of the sources by R. McKitterick, 'Kingship and the writing of history', in *History and Memory*, pp. 133–55.

the rise of the Carolingians.[34] Yet this point itself indicates that the change of dynasty cannot be given sole responsibility for every major development. Donations to monasteries also survive in increasing numbers from areas beyond the Carolingians' writ (at least initially), like Lombard Italy.[35] What is more, the proliferation of monasteries at around this time itself affected the historical record. While it is an open question whether monastic houses were better at producing written texts than were previous groups of scribes, it is certain that they were better at producing texts that would last, and better at preserving both their own and earlier texts, partly because they themselves proved durable as institutions.[36] The relationship between patterns of source survival and changes in the social and political world they reveal is, in other words, something of a chicken-and-egg problem.

What defined the Carolingian world above all was the ruling dynasty itself.[37] The dynasty thought of itself as such even when (as after 840) the territories of the empire were divided between multiple and competing kings: responding to a belittling jibe from the Byzantine emperor Basil I in 871, who had patronisingly observed that being ruler of Italy alone did not make him much of an emperor, Louis II fumed that the western empire was exactly that because of the common blood shared by all of its Carolingian rulers.[38] This was not just ideological froth. The dynasty's identity was not an incidental feature of the period; their longevity rested in part on their success in creating and imposing ways of thinking that self-consciously redefined the Frankish world *as* Carolingian. The rewriting of the past

---

[34] On these regions, see respectively Innes, *State and Society*; H. Hummer, *Politics and Power in Early Medieval Europe: Alsace and the Frankish Realm, 600–1000* (Cambridge, 2005); Brown, *Unjust Seizure*.

[35] See M. Costambeys, 'The laity, the clergy, the scribes and their archives: the documentary record of eighth- and ninth-century Italy', in W. Brown, M. Costambeys, M. Innes and A. Kosto (eds.), *Documentary Culture and the Laity in the Early Middle Ages* (forthcoming).

[36] See the introduction to Brown, *et al.* (eds.), *Documentary Culture*.

[37] For the following, see above all S. Airlie, *Carolingian Politics* (Oxford, forthcoming).

[38] *Epistola ad Basilium I.*, ed. W. Henze, *MGH Epp.* vii (*Epp. Karolini aevi* v) (Berlin, 1928), pp. 386–94; S. Fanning, 'Imperial diplomacy between Francia and Byzantium: the letter of Louis II to Basil I in 871', *Cithara* 34 (1994), pp. 3–15. For western attitudes to Byzantium more generally, see C. Wickham, 'Ninth-century Byzantium through western eyes', in L. Brubaker (ed.), *Byzantium in the Ninth Century: Dead or Alive?* (Aldershot, 1998), pp. 245–56. For the context, see below, Chapter 8.

that became, as we shall see, such a feature of the cultural output of the age was shot through with a concern to locate the Carolingians in history. Contemporary intellectuals sought both to write the history of the Franks in terms of the deeds of Carolingian (and proto-Carolingian) rulers, and to find a place for the 'Carolingian' era itself in the schemes provided by established models of long-term historical development – and ultimately, therefore, to make the empire's rise seem inevitable and its continued existence natural. Thus, writing in the middle of the 880s, Notker of St Gallen conceived of Charlemagne's Frankish empire as a divinely ordained successor to the great empires of the past: a new, discrete and coherent entity ready to be loaded with religious and political significance.[39]

Texts like this could influence the thought-processes of the Frankish elite, but could not control them. Fragments of alternative discourses allow us to glimpse contemporaries imagining the possibility of a world not dominated by Carolingians.[40] Yet even authors writing away from court in the ninth century were usually party to the same assumptions and modes of thought as those who enjoyed more regular contact with the king.[41] By the time of Charlemagne's grandsons, and certainly by Notker's day, the court's cultural and reform agendas had been internalised by provincial bishops and monks.[42] Such ways of thinking could filter down to ordinary lay people in a variety of ways: through the courts of the counts regularly convened in the king's name; through daily use of coins bearing his name and image;

---

[39] Notker, *Gesta*, 1.1, trans. Ganz, p. 55.

[40] See S. Airlie, '*Semper fideles?* Loyauté envers les carolingiens comme constituant de l'identité aristocratique', in Le Jan (ed.), *La Royauté et les élites*, pp. 129–43; K. Brunner, *Oppositionelle Gruppen im Karolingerreich* (Vienna, 1979); and M. Innes, 'Kings, monks and patrons: political identities and the abbey of Lorsch', in Le Jan (ed.), *La Royauté et les élites*, pp. 301–24, on St Nazarius.

[41] See S. Airlie 'The aristocracy in the service of the state in the Carolingian period', in Airlie, Pohl and Reimitz (eds.), *Staat im frühen Mittelalter*, pp. 93–111; R. Collins, 'Charlemagne's imperial coronation and the Annals of Lorsch', in Story (ed.), *Charlemagne*, pp. 52–70; H. Reimitz, 'The art of truth. Historiography and identity in the Frankish world', in R. Corradini *et al.* (eds.), *Texts and Identities in the Early Middle Ages* (Vienna, 2006), pp. 87–104.

[42] See Hummer, *Politics and Power*, pp. 130–54; J. L. Nelson, 'Charles le Chauve et les utilisations du savoir', in D. Iogna-Prat, C. Jeudy and G. Lobrichon (eds.), *L'École carolingienne d'Auxerre* (Paris, 1991), pp. 37–54, repr. as no. VII in J. L. Nelson, *Rulers and Ruling Families in Early Medieval Europe: Alfred, Charles the Bald and Others* (Aldershot, 1999).

through the prayers said for his soul in church on Sunday.[43] An idea
of the political implications of this can be gleaned from the fact that,
of the many rebellions in the period between 785 and 888, only one
was led by an outsider against the dynasty – that of Boso of Vienne –
while the rest sought only to replace one Carolingian with another.[44]
Little wonder, then, that contemporary authors commenting on the
dynastic crisis of 888 perceived it as the end of an era: with the
accession of non-Carolingian kings and the consequent territorial
division of the empire between different dynasties, something had
very definitely finished.[45] We can, in other words, describe this world
as Carolingian because that is how contemporaries perceived it.

THE SOURCES FOR THE CAROLINGIAN WORLD

The most striking aspect of the historian's evidence for the Carolingian world is simply its quantity: as we have already noted, far
more texts survive from this era than from earlier ones. Only 1,800
manuscript books or fragments of books survive that were written in
the continental west before AD 800, and many of those were copied
in the eighth century. From the same part of the world, we possess
over 9,000 manuscript books or fragments produced by scribes in
the century from 800 to 900.[46] These dramatic figures require some

---

[43] Patzold, 'Die Bischöfe im karolingischen Staat. Praktisches Wissen über die politische Ordnung im Frankenreich des 9. Jahrhunderts', in S. Airlie, W. Pohl
and H. Reimitz (eds.), *Staat im frühen Mittelalter* (Vienna, 2006), pp. 133–62';
I. Garipzanov, *The Symbolic Language of Authority in the Carolingian World
(c.751–877)* (Leiden and Boston, 2008).

[44] See Airlie, *'Semper fideles?'*; S. Airlie, 'Charlemagne and the aristocracy: captains
and kings' in Story (ed.), *Charlemagne*, pp. 90–102.

[45] *AF, s.a.* 888 and Regino, *Chronicle, s.a.* 888; for discussion see S. Airlie, '"Sad
stories of the deaths of kings": narrative patterns and structures of authority in
Regino of Prüm's *Chronicle*', in E. M. Tyler and R. Balzaretti (eds.), *Narrative and
History in the Early Medieval West* (Turnhout, 2006), pp. 105–31.

[46] This calculation has been cited, with minor differences, by J. R. Davis and
M. McCormick, 'The early Middle Ages: Europe's long morning', in Davis
and McCormick (eds.), *The Long Morning of Medieval Europe*, pp. 1–10, at p. 2;
D. Ganz, 'Book production in the Carolingian empire and the spread of Carolingian minuscule', in *NCMH* II, pp. 786–808, at p. 786; G. Brown, 'Introduction:
the Carolingian Renaissance', in McKitterick (ed.), *Carolingian Culture*, pp. 1–51,
at p. 34; and R. McKitterick, *The Carolingians and the Written Word* (Cambridge,
1989), pp. 163–4. See also B. Bischoff, *Latin Palaeography. Antiquity and the Middle
Ages*, trans. D. Ó Cróinín and D. Ganz (Cambridge, 1990), p. 208.

explanation. Only a minority of the 9,000 ninth-century manuscripts contained works composed in that century. Mostly they were copies of texts that had been written many years earlier: Latin classics like Virgil, early Christian literature, or books of the Bible. We are dealing here with an increase in copying, quite as much as a rise in literary creativity. But is the increase itself a real one, or an accident of survival? Does it signify a genuine quantum leap in the rate of production of written texts? A number of developments of the Carolingian age may inadvertently have affected the rate of survival. This period saw the development of a new script in which most books came to be written. Caroline (or Carolingian) minuscule is easily legible to us – indeed, it is the forerunner of the font in which this book is printed. This standardisation was evidently important in a contemporary context, though it is far from certain that its familiarity to modern eyes favoured the survival of books using the new script. More importantly, the Carolingian age benefited from long-term changes in the construction and materials of books that made them easier to preserve. Where in the ancient world the main writing material was papyrus, made from reeds, and books were scrolls of sheets of papyrus stitched together, by the Carolingian period writing was generally done on parchment, made from the skins of sheep, cows and goats and therefore far more durable than papyrus. Parchment leaves were stacked in quires and stitched together between hard or soft covers to form a codex – or what we would recognise as a book. Where papyrus scrolls were apt to rip and rot, parchment books could last for centuries – and have.[47]

These changes in the technology of the written word themselves suggest that the Carolingian age placed new emphasis on knowledge and its dissemination. Scribes before that time may not have been quite as scarce as the paltry survivals of their work suggest, but they were working in contexts and with techniques that had changed since the Roman period only in the dwindling amount of resources devoted to them. The growth of Carolingian literate culture was largely the product of patronage directed at new institutions – principally monasteries – that were especially concerned to foster

[47] On book production and the development of scripts, see Bischoff, *Latin Palaeography*. On the factors involved in the preservation of books, see P. J. Geary, *Phantoms of Remembrance: Memory and Oblivion at the End of the First Millennium* (Princeton, NJ, 1994).

writing and learning. It is these which produced and preserved the very large documentary residue of the Carolingian world, including the original compositions of the time: histories, laws, land transactions and a host of other textual genres. Overall, we possess many more sources about the Carolingian period than about any previous era of comparable length.[48]

One area where the Carolingian impact on culture can be observed very easily is in the production of historical writing. In the eighth and ninth centuries, remembrance of the past was a matter both of *memoria* – the commemoration of the dead, especially in books of the names of the deceased whose souls were the subject of prayer (*Libri vitae, libri memoriales*)[49] – and of *historia* – the relating of past deeds,[50] and the form of the latter was changing as the annals, which started as by-products of liturgy, evolved into free-standing literature. Annals were one part of the outpouring of history, which sought (as mentioned earlier) to explicate the present and the recent past with reference to more distant times. Historical works written after 800 reveal constant debate about the place of the Carolingians in relation to past empires and the place of the empire in God's plans for the future as hinted at in the Bible. Contemporary historians and annalists tacked accounts of their own times on to versions of the more distant past that modelled the present variously as a continuation of the Roman past, a reinvention of it, a Christian empire that was distinct from the Roman, or the final age of the world in the eschatological scheme popularised by St Augustine.[51] Often they did so by rewriting or suppressing uncomfortable memories of the more recent Merovingian past, anxious to mask the sour taste of usurpation and resistance.[52] The fact that this debate existed at all suggests that whichever model they chose, contemporaries regarded

---

[48] Davis and McCormick, 'Europe's long morning', pp. 1–5.

[49] J. Raaijmakers, 'Memory and identity: the *Annales necrologici* of Fulda', in Corradini, *et al.* (eds.), *Texts and Identities*, pp. 303–22.

[50] For an influential early medieval definition of *historia*, see Isidore of Seville, *Etymologiae*, 1.41, ed. and trans. S. A. Barney, *et al.*, *The Etymologies of Isidore of Seville* (Cambridge, 2006), p. 67.

[51] M. Innes and R. McKitterick, 'The writing of history', in McKitterick (ed.), *Carolingian Culture*, pp. 193–220; I. H. Garipzanov, 'The Carolingian abbreviation of Bede's World Chronicle and Carolingian imperial "genealogy"', *Hortus Artium Medievalium* (2005), pp. 291–7; McKitterick, *History and Memory*, esp. pp. 218–64; see also the studies in Y. Hen and M. Innes (eds.), *The Uses of the Past in the Early Middle Ages* (Cambridge, 2000).

[52] Fouracre, 'Long shadow', pp. 5–21.

the Carolingian period as a distinct historical era.[53] The spill-over of this concern into continuous histories of the present makes even more obvious the role of numerous contemporary annalists and chroniclers in the 'Carolingianising' of the Frankish world. An initial model was established by the authors of the *Royal Frankish Annals*, which presented an account of history between 741 and 829 that defined the history of the Frankish people in terms of the deeds of Carolingian kings: their wars, assemblies, and itineraries were the scaffolding used to construct a narrative of the times. This way of thinking was obviously part of the court's ideological armoury, but it also had a wider impact. The *Royal Frankish Annals* were copied, excerpted and reused many times during the ninth century to the extent that they became part of a canon that influenced both subsequent writers and the consciousness of the Frankish elite.[54]

The extent to which Carolingian political success had itself shaped the historical record becomes clear when we consider the contrast between the material produced before and after around 750. The only contemporary narrative history from the late seventh and early eighth centuries is the *Liber historiae francorum* ('Book of [the] History of the Franks': hereafter referred to as the *LHF*).[55] Completed in 727, probably in Soissons and perhaps by a woman, the *LHF* traces the history of the Franks from their legendary beginnings, drawing on and summarising earlier sources until the last of them, the fourth book of the *Chronicle* of Fredegar, ends in 642, from which point it provides an original, if rudimentary, account of events up to 721, seen from the perspective of the Neustrian – that is, the west Frankish – aristocracy.[56] There are, in addition, a number of saints' lives that

---

[53] Cf. P. Magdalino, 'The distance of the past in early medieval Byzantium (VII–X centuries)', in *Ideologie e pratiche del reimpiego nell'alto medioevo*, Settimane 46 (Spoleto, 1999) I, pp. 115–46.

[54] McKitterick, *History and Memory*, pp. 120–32; Reimitz, 'Art of truth'.

[55] *LHF*, ed. B. Krusch, *MGH SRM* II (Hanover, 1888), pp. 215–328; commentary and Eng. trans. of cc. 43–53 (covering 638–726) in P. Fouracre and R. Gerberding, *Late Merovingian France. History and Hagiography 640–720* (Manchester and New York, 1996), pp. 79–96, and of cc. 1–4 and 43–53 in R. Gerberding, *The Rise of the Carolingians and the* Liber historiae francorum (Oxford, 1987); for a complete translation, see B. S. Bachrach, *Liber historiae francorum* (Lawrence, KS, 1973).

[56] Gerberding, *Rise of the Carolingians*, pp. 146–72; for the suggestion of female authorship, see J. L. Nelson, 'Gender and genre in women historians', in J.-P. Genet (ed.), *L'Historiographie médiévale en Europe*, Éditions du CNRS (Paris, 1991), pp. 149–63, repr. in Nelson, *Frankish World*, pp. 183–97, at pp. 194–5. On Fredegar see J. M. Wallace-Hadrill (ed. and trans.), *The Fourth Book of the Chronicle*

have been mined for the snippets of information that they give on political events and personalities, especially when those lives related events within the living memory of their intended audiences. Such matters were not their main concern, however: when approached with due regard to their original purpose, they allow us to glimpse the complexity of Merovingian culture and belief and to sample the mood prevalent in aristocratic society.[57]

Although they depend on the *LHF*, the two other major narratives of the period from 687 to 721 post-date Pippin III's takeover of the Frankish kingship in 751. Continuations of the *Chronicle* of Fredegar were most likely added after Pippin's death in 768. Comparison with other sources reveals the tendency of these continuators, and especially the first, to garble events that had occurred only a generation earlier. This indicates the extent to which they were writing with their eyes on the present, and sought precedents for their current situation in the relatively recent past. In this case we know that the continuations to Fredegar's chronicle were written under the auspices of Pippin III's uncle Childebrand, and of the latter's son Nibelung.[58] The way in which the continuators reworked the text of the *LHF* is very evident. Reporting the death of the Merovingian Childebert III (694–711), the *LHF* states 'then the famous and just lord King Childebert of good memory, passed away unto the Lord'.[59] The first continuator of Fredegar is significantly more laconic at this point: 'it was now that King Childebert died'.[60]

Equally rooted in their time of composition are the *Annales Mettenses priores* (Earlier Annals of Metz), a set of annals first put together

---

of Fredegar with its Continuations (London, 1960); R. Collins, *Fredegar*, Authors of the Middle Ages 13 (Aldershot, 1996).

[57] For insights into the value to the historian of Merovingian hagiography, see P. Fouracre, 'The origins of the Carolingian attempt to regulate the cult of saints', in J. Howard-Johnston and P. A. Hayward (eds.), *The Cult of Saints in Late Antiquity and the Middle Ages. Essays on the Contribution of Peter Brown* (Oxford, 1999), pp. 143–66; P. Fouracre., 'Merovingian history and Merovingian hagiography', *P&P* 127 (1990), pp. 3–38; Fouracre and Gerberding, *Late Merovingian France*, pp. 37–52.

[58] Cf. R. Collins, 'Deception and misrepresentation in early eighth-century Frankish historiography: two case studies', in J. Jarnut, U. Nonn and M. Richter (eds.), *Karl Martell in seiner Zeit*, Beihefte der Francia 37 (Sigmaringen, 1994), pp. 227–47, esp. pp. 241–6; McKitterick, *History and Memory*, pp. 138–9.

[59] *LHF*, c. 50, trans. Fouracre and Gerberding, *Late Merovingian France*, p. 94.

[60] Fred., *Cont.*, c. 7, p. 86, trans. (rather freely) Wallace-Hadrill, p. 86.

in a surviving version in 805.[61] This work seeks, from its beginning
at 688, to portray the history of the late seventh and eighth centuries
as the history of the Carolingians.[62] Its demonstrable use of an earlier
source at least for events up to 751 might only reinforce the view that
its account is unreliably 'pro-Carolingian'.[63] Nevertheless, that earlier source, in so far as it can be discerned, can be set alongside other
sources – letters written outside Francia, charters and coins – which
seem to attest considerable power in the hands of earlier Carolingians,
Pippin II and Charles Martel, before the 750s. Historians still debate
the extent to which that power was exaggerated by later authors like
those of the *Annales Mettenses priores*. The most succinct example of
the latter's perspective is in the biography of Charlemagne by his
courtier Einhard, who claimed that the last Merovingians possessed
no more than a single estate, and travelled in an ox-cart.[64] Annals of
a more conventional kind were written at various centres in Francia throughout the eighth and ninth centuries. Relating events to a
particular year is a practice that dates back to antiquity, but it was
given a new context by the organisation of time that the Christian
Church gradually imposed. The production of Easter tables, necrolo-
gies and martyrologies encouraged the recording of events annually,
and this was made easier by the adoption from the beginning of
the eighth century of dating by the incarnation of Christ.[65] These
yearly entries appear in eight early Carolingian annals.[66] Interrelated,
with often identical entries, and becoming ever fuller through the
eighth century and into the ninth, they pursue a 'pro-Carolingian'

---

[61] *AMP*, ed. B. von Simson, *MGH SRG in usum scholarum separatim editi* x (Hanover
and Leipzig, 1905); Eng. trans. of Section I (to 725) with commentary in Fouracre
and Gerberding, *Late Merovingian France*, pp. 330–70; see also McKitterick, *Charlemagne*, pp. 52–3, 60–2.

[62] Wood, *Merovingian Kingdoms*, pp. 257–9.

[63] R. Collins, 'Pippin III as mayor of the palace: the evidence', in Becher and Jarnut
(eds.), *Der Dynastiewechsel von 751*, pp. 75–91. Compare R. McKitterick, 'Political
ideology in Carolingian historiography', and Y. Hen, 'The Annals of Metz and
the Merovingian past', in Hen and M. Innes (eds.), *Uses of the Past*, pp. 162–74
and 175–90 respectively.

[64] Einhard, *VK*, c. 1, and trans. Dutton, *Charlemagne's Courtier*, pp. 16–17.

[65] On this form of writing in the Carolingian age, see R. McKitterick, 'Constructing
the past in the early Middle Ages: the case of the Royal Frankish Annals', *TRHS*
6th ser. 7 (1997), pp. 101–29, and Innes and McKitterick, 'The writing of history',
esp. pp. 199–202.

[66] *Annales Sancti Amandi, Annales Tiliani, Annales Laubacenses, Annales Petaviani,
Annales Laureshamenses, Annales Alamannici, Annales Guelferbytani, Annales Nazariani*, all ed. G. H. Pertz, *MGH SS* I (Hanover, 1826), pp. 6–12, 22–60.

agenda by relating only the deeds of the Carolingians, especially their military victories. They therefore sometimes transmit unique snippets of information that are less difficult to interpret than the narratives of the continuations of Fredegar and the *Annales Mettenses priores*.

As a form of writing about the past, annals were taken up energetically in some areas beyond Francia, not least in the British Isles, where the later ninth century saw court-centred annalistic works take shape in several Anglo-Saxon kingdoms (the origins of the later *Anglo-Saxon Chronicle*) and in Wales (the *Annales Cambriae*).[67] Other regions preferred different historiographical forms. In Italy, just before Charlemagne's imperial coronation, Paul the Deacon completed a history of his own people, the Lombards, that proved to be an important foundation for subsequent Italian historians.[68] Nonetheless, it can be read as using the Lombard past as a vehicle for comment on what was for Italy by the 790s a Frankish present.[69]

The images of the past that Paul wrote into his *History of the Lombards* seem to have been aimed principally at a circle of courtiers, either those of Duke Arichis of Benevento or those of Charlemagne's son Pippin, king of Italy under his father from 781. Many of the other writings about the past in this period seem similarly to have been intended, at least initially, for a fairly exclusive audience, whether courtiers of a ruler, an aristocratic entourage, or a monastic community *(familia)*. Many may never have permeated beyond these

---

[67] See P. Stafford, 'The Anglo-Saxon Chronicles, identity and the making of England', *Haskins Society Journal* 19 (2008), pp. 28–50; M. Miller, 'Final stages in the construction of the Harleian *Annales Cambriae*', *Journal of Celtic Studies* 4 (2004), pp. 205–11; *Annales Cambriae*, ed. and trans. D. N. Dumville, *Annales Cambriae, AD 682–954, texts A–C in parallel* (Cambridge, 2002).

[68] On Paul the Deacon see above all W. Pohl, 'Paulus Diaconus und die "Historia langobardorum": Text und Tradition', in A. Scharer and G. Scheibelreiter (eds.), *Historiographie im frühen Mittelalter*, Veröffentlichungen des Instituts für Österreichische Geschichtsforschung 32 (Vienna and Munich, 1994), pp. 375–405; P. Chiesa (ed.), *Paolo Diacono. Uno scrittore fra tradizione longobarda e rinnovamento carolingio* (Università di Udine, 2000); on Paul's continuators, including Andreas of Bergamo, see J. Ferry and M. Costambeys, *Historians of Ninth-Century Italy* (Liverpool, forthcoming), and A. Berto, *Testi storici e poetici dell'Italia carolingia* (Padua, 2002).

[69] R. McKitterick, 'Paul the Deacon and the Franks', *EME* 8 (1999), pp. 319–39; A. Plassmann, 'Mittelalterliche *origines gentium*. Paulus Diaconus als Beispiel', *QFIAB* 87 (2007), pp. 1–35.

immediate audiences. Nevertheless, in conveying messages to powerful social groups these writers had the opportunity to influence opinion and attitudes among the political community.

The decade after Charlemagne's death in 814 seems to witness a change in the historical perspective of Frankish writers. Their concern was now not merely to offer 'Carolingianised' views of the past, but also to comment on recent events in ways charged with the language of contemporary controversies. Thus both of the extant biographies of Louis 'the Pious' give voice to opinions on Louis's sons' revolt against their father in 833–4: in Thegan's *Life*, written in 836, we can detect the views of the circle of Rhenish aristocrats who were his chief contacts; while the author known to us only as 'the Astronomer' (because of his interest in celestial objects) wrote just after 840 from the perspective of the court itself, and probably making use of its archive.[70] After 843, with the formal division of the empire, the multiplication of royal courts and the frequency of conflict between kingdoms gave a further boost to the writing of contemporary history, most notably in the *Annals of Fulda* from the east Frankish realm, and the *Annals of St Bertin* from the West. We can get an impression of how such works might have been read by looking at the manuscripts which contained them. The biographies of Louis, for example, circulated principally alongside Einhard's *Life of Charlemagne* and often with versions of the *Royal Frankish Annals*, and were edited and amalgamated to produce composite works of Frankish history with a distinctly Carolingian flavour. The texts of many annals, however, circulated piecemeal, meaning that they could be used as a form of news and comment, and might be tinged with traces of local colour. The *Annals of Lorsch*, for example, preserved its very particular, east Frankish, memory of the revolt against Charlemagne by members of that region's aristocracy under Hardrad.[71]

Historical writing is only one index of an increasing attention to literature in the decades following the accession of Charlemagne in 768. The emergence at that time of a group of men of letters, working initially at the royal court, has seemed one of the best indications that

---

[70] Innes and McKitterick, 'The writing of history', pp. 209–10; on the revolt of 833–5 and subsequent events, see below, pp. 218–22.

[71] R. McKitterick, *Perceptions of the Past in the Early Middle Ages* (Notre Dame, IN, 2006), pp. 68–81.

Charlemagne's age witnessed a renaissance of learning: a return to classical standards of intellectual life after a slump in the later sixth, seventh and earlier eighth centuries. The apparent void may, however, be due in part to the vagaries of manuscript loss, and in any case the standard of work of the great literary figures of the late eighth and early ninth centuries must owe something to a pre-existing tradition of Latin letters. These men employed a variety of genres, but one with which they evidently liked to play was poetry: the 'final phase of a thorough education' at the time.[72] The sheer quantity of poetry preserved, as well as the number of surviving manuscripts including verse, shows that contemporaries saw poetry as neither unusual nor arcane as a medium for all sorts of ideas and sentiments. Slender threads of the Latin poetic tradition can be traced through the late seventh century and into the eighth, especially in Italy, where its range of uses – from theology to civic identity to commemoration – serves as a warning not to underestimate how important a literary form it was to contemporaries.[73] If it was partly the influx of Italians into the royal court, alongside other scholars from beyond Francia, that turned it into the centre of intellectual activity in Charlemagne's kingdom, it is the surviving poetry that stands testimony to their conversations. In the Carolingian age, Latin verse was a vehicle not only for the dedications and epitaphs for which it would remain popular throughout the Middle Ages, but for reflections on the lives and relationships of the poets, their nicknames, their friendships and their flytings. The surviving poems seem to have been very immediate in their aims. As Mary Garrison has noted: 'apparently verse was intended to address and entertain contemporaries, not posterity'.[74] Most prominently, the verses of these new poets were aimed at the king himself. Numerous lines of often extravagant praise were addressed to Charlemagne in particular. Epic set-pieces such as the so-called *Paderborn Epic*, purporting to depict the king's encounter with Pope Leo III at that town in 799, present Charlemagne as the terrible scourge of his pagan enemies, as well as the generous patron of

---

[72] M. Garrison, 'The emergence of Carolingian Latin literature and the court of Charlemagne (780–814)', in McKitterick (ed.), *Carolingian Culture*, pp. 111–40 at p. 114.

[73] On poetry in inscriptions from Lombard Italy, see N. Everett, *Literacy in Lombard Italy, c.568–774* (Cambridge, 2003), pp. 244–7.

[74] Garrison, 'The emergence of Carolingian Latin literature', p. 128.

the pope.[75] Poems of this sort mirrored the classical form of the praise poem or panegyric, albeit with new tones and emphases.[76] Imitation of the classics continued as an ideal in later generations, growing in ambition as authors sought consciously to echo the epics and elegies of Roman poets like Virgil and Ovid. But such works were not merely imitative: they served all the various purposes that historians have identified in the works of Carolingian cultural protagonists.

While the writing of *historia*, recording the deeds of the past, whether distant or very immediate, responded to the needs of discrete, often elite, groups, the culture of *memoria* had a wider impact. As we shall see in Chapter 3, memorialisation of the dead came to be bound up with patronage of churches and monasteries, and that patronage was generally enacted by or recorded in legal documents. Indeed, so great was the number of such documents, and so good were churches and monasteries at preserving them, that for some regions there is an impression that ecclesiastical patronage was the *only* reason to produce documents. This was clearly not the case, but it does point to the need to bear in mind that the documentary legacy of the early Middle Ages has been shaped by the way in which documents have been transmitted down the centuries; and that process has been dominated, until the modern era, by the Church. The early medieval legal documents that we now possess survive in clusters associated with particular archives across the Carolingian world, mostly those of monasteries and episcopal churches. Some of them – those which embody the pronouncements of rulers – fit quite well into the 'Carolingianising' of the record that we have noted in narrative histories: legal decrees divided into chapters (*capitulae*, and hence known as capitularies) provided the framework for the actions of those to whom power was delegated in the localities, while collections of them transmitted this fundamentally Carolingian structure to successive generations.[77] In simple numerical terms, however, the great majority of surviving legal documents are charters, the single sheets of papyrus or (more usually) parchment with which business of all sorts was conducted (see for example Figure 1). We possess these

---

75 A partial translation of the *Paderborn Epic* is in P. Godman, *Poetry of the Carolingian Renaissance* (London, 1985), pp. 197–207; original text, *Karolus magnus et Leo papa*, ed. E. Dümmler, *MGH Poet.* 1 (Berlin, 1881), pp. 366–79.

76 P. Godman, *Poets and emperors: Frankish Politics and Carolingian Poetry* (Oxford, 1987), p. 184.

77 For more on capitularies, see Chapter 4.

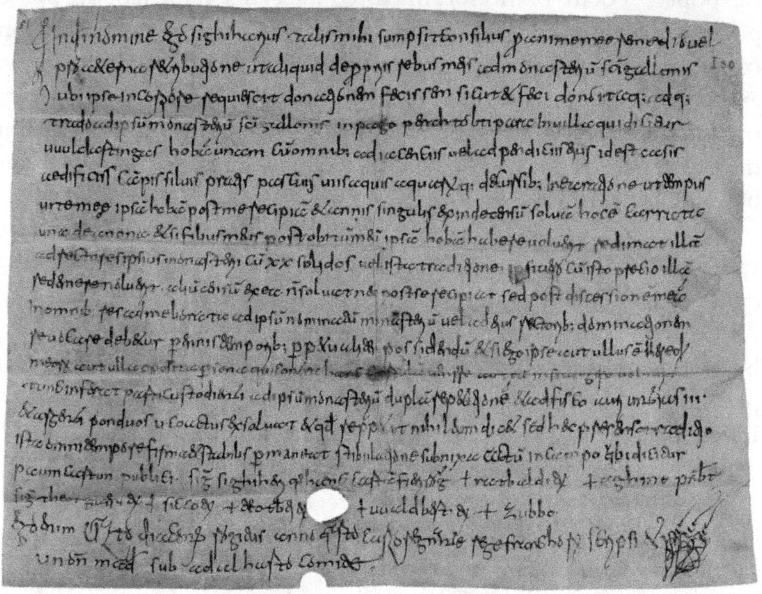

Figure 1. A charter from the abbey of St Gallen, modern Switzerland, which retains 750 original charters and contemporary copies written between the eighth century and 920. This example, issued on 2 May 775 by one Sighiharius, was written by the abbey's deacon, and later abbot, Waldo, who made a note on the dorse (reverse), summarising its contents: one of the first signs of systematic record management at St Gallen.

in sufficient numbers to see that their subject matter extended well beyond the interests of particular church institutions, and down to the most small-scale and mundane activities: not only conveyances of property through gift, sale and exchange, but also testaments, judicial and extra-judicial dispute settlements, leases, inventories and many others.

The Carolingian period witnessed changes in society's awareness of these documents. Charters survive in increasing numbers from about the middle of the seventh century, giving some insight into literate culture and patterns of production, landholding and power in a few localities, and providing the skeleton of a political chronology.[78]

---

[78] See below, Chapter 4. Original surviving charters dating before 800 are published in *Chartae Latinae Antiquiores*, ed. A. Bruckner, R. Marichal, *et al.* (Zurich, 1954–1998), and those dating to the ninth century are in the course of publication in

In many of the lands that came to form the Carolingian realm, the number of survivals increases markedly through the eighth century. This cannot be ascribed to a dramatically higher level of their production: those that do survive from the Merovingian period concerned business that was just as routine as the Carolingian examples, and as legal documents in the late Roman period.[79] But in that earlier time, there had been reliable ways not only to preserve documents, but also to validate, re-affirm and re-record the legal business they contained. The network of Roman public legal offices – *gesta municipalia* – may not have been quite so extensive, elaborate or reliable as has sometimes been maintained, but it did ensure that documents were a crucial part of the framework of social regulation. The continued appearance of references to parts of this framework – to the *gesta* as public centres of legal validation and record, with attendant officials – in the Merovingian and early Carolingian periods indicates two things. First, that at least in some regions the framework persisted after the end of Roman rule, and second, that it had disappeared by the mid-eighth century, while some of its functions had been taken up by those institutions – overwhelmingly, it would seem, churches and monasteries – capable of the regular production and, perhaps, the retention of relatively standardised documents.[80] Legal record-keeping no longer depended on organs of government in the way that it had done. Moreover, attitudes to archiving were changing. Those institutions that could preserve records – not just of their own legal business but of those who had entrusted documents to them – began to sift and shape their archives to help construct their institutional memory. Often, in fact, what was in their archives (and also,

Chartae Latinae Antiquiores, 2nd ser., ed. G. Cavallo, G. Nicolaj, *et al.* (Olten and Lausanne, 1997–); principal among the many editions, which also include texts not surviving as originals, are T. Kölzer with M. Hartmann and A. Stieldorf (eds.), *Die Urkunden der Merowinger*, 2 vols. (Hanover, 2001) and J. M. Pardessus, *Diplomata, chartae, epistolae, leges ad res Gallo-Francicas spectantia*, 2 vols. (Paris, 1843–9; repr. Aalen 1969); for comment, see Fouracre and Gerberding, *Late Merovingian France*, pp. 28–9 and 36.

[79] D. Ganz and W. Goffart, 'Charters earlier than 800 from French collections', *Speculum* 65 (1990), pp. 906–32.

[80] W. Brown, 'Lay people and documents in the Frankish formula collections', and Brown, 'On the *Gesta municipalia* and the public validation of documents in Frankish Europe', both in Brown, *et al.* (eds.), *Documentary Culture* (forthcoming); A. Rio, *The Formularies of Angers and Marculf: Two Merovingian Legal Handbooks* (Liverpool, 2008), pp. 255–8.

therefore, what had been lost) dictated the way they viewed their own past. Thus, monasteries not only produced cartularies into which their scribes laboriously copied the sheaves of documents in their archives, but also cartulary chronicles, in which selected documents formed a framework for a narrative history of their institution – and in particular a very partial (in both senses) account of its acquisition of its properties.[81]

Careful consideration of the ways in which our record was created allows us to glimpse beyond it a world of document-users, both lay and clerical. Even as it stands, the record includes evidence for substantial engagement with documents by the laity: dossiers of documents involving only lay men and women were preserved in a number of monastic archives in the eighth and ninth centuries, such as those of St Gallen in Alemannia and Monte Amiata in Tuscany. That their protagonists possessed widely varying social statuses, and often also appear alongside churchmen conducting similar legal affairs, indicates both that document use by the laity was in many areas absolutely routine and that in any case a strict demarcation between lay people and clerics in this context is not really necessary. Although preserving documents for long periods may gradually have become the preserve of ecclesiastics, the use of documents at the time was certainly not.

Charters offer insights well beyond levels of engagement with writing, or the bald mechanics of the landholdings that are the principal subjects of the majority of the survivals. Because they were redacted at assemblies of local people, some of whom attested them as witnesses, and because they often describe not only the extent of landed properties, but their agricultural uses and the names and, often, conditions of the people living on them, these documents constitute invaluable witnesses to many aspects of the everyday life of the mass of the population. These emerge best when a number of charters from a particular locality and a relatively restricted period can be studied together, as is increasingly possible thanks to a steady increase in modern editions. Cumulatively these bodies of documents reveal the composition, and some of the dynamics, of groups of local

---

[81] Geary, *Phantoms of Remembrance*, pp. 81–133; A. Sennis, 'The power of time: looking at the past in medieval monasteries', in A. Müller and K. Stöber (eds.), *Self-Representation of Medieval Religious Communities: the British Isles in Context*, Vita Regularis, Abhandlungen 40 (Münster, 2009), pp. 307–26.

people, sometimes extending quite far down the social hierarchy. For these reasons, the charter evidence forms much of the basis of the observations on rural life and social structure in Chapters 5 and 6.

While today's historian theoretically enjoys a quantity of written sources for the Carolingian world barely higher than that available to previous generations, in practice he or she has readier access to much of it and is better able to appreciate the implications of its transmission, and so to place it in an appropriate context. Moreover, written sources can be set alongside a growing volume of material data, revealing hitherto hidden features of eighth- and ninth-century existence. The sustained attention that archaeologists have paid to the early Middle Ages over the last thirty years or so has produced a rising tide of data on aspects of life that our written sources mention only tangentially, if at all. Archaeology can give a much more three-dimensional view of the physical realities of early medieval life – not only of such things as dwellings, implements, ornaments and diet, but also of the physical condition of the people themselves. Such evidence is not a simple complement to the written sources; often, it challenges historians' long-standing interpretations of their texts. Thus, the charters' terminology for settlements, such as *villa* or *fundus*, in many areas remained relatively constant, while archaeology reveals dramatic changes taking place in the actual shape of human communities, such as the emergence of nucleated villages in many parts of Europe between the sixth and eighth centuries.[82] New techniques of investigating the past also take us beyond material culture to movements of people themselves. Both recovered ancient DNA and samples taken from modern populations can be analysed to determine the movements, and the coming together, of biologically distinguishable populations in the past.[83] The problem of mapping this data on to the historical sources is difficult: medieval ethnic and cultural labels cannot be applied straightforwardly to genetic profiles.

---

[82] For full discussion, see Chapter 5.
[83] For introductions to the application to early medieval history of techniques drawn from the biosciences, and especially from genetics, see M. McCormick, 'Molecular Middle Ages: early medieval economic history in the 21st century', in Davis and McCormick (eds.), *The Long Morning of Medieval Europe*, pp. 83–98; M. McCormick, 'Toward a molecular history of the Justinianic pandemic', in L. K. Little (ed.), *Plague and the End of Antiquity. The Pandemic of 541–750* (Cambridge, 2007), pp. 290–312. For a cautionary note see G. Halsall, *Barbarian Migrations and the Roman West, 376–568* (Cambridge, 2007), pp. 451–2.

Nonetheless, this new and rapidly developing science holds out the possibility of a much better understanding of human migrations, a crucial issue for our period, flanked as it is by the 'barbarian' migrations of the fifth and sixth centuries and the Viking settlements of the late ninth and tenth.

The growth in archaeological and biological data has been rapid, and their integration into the written history of the early Middle Ages is a significant preoccupation of students of the period. This drawing together of diverse and often fresh sources holds out the possibility that what has hitherto been frustratingly obscure or at least opaque might become clearer in the future. This is perhaps especially the case with aspects of everyday life – diet, for instance, or housing – that are only glancing concerns for the major genres of written text. Our more complex and subtle appreciation of the meanings in these latter sources is a necessary corollary of the effort to read them alongside the new stories related by material culture and biology. As a result, at the start of the twenty-first century, the Carolingian world has never appeared with sharper definition, and greater scope for understanding.

2

THE CREATION OF
CAROLINGIAN KINGSHIP TO 800

REPLACING THE RULING DYNASTY

We began Chapter 1 with the elevation of the Carolingian Pippin, generally known as Pippin III, or Pippin 'the Short', to the kingship of the Franks.[1] Almost everything about this event is uncertain. The best evidence for Pippin's accession comes from his charters – the single-sheet documents through which legal business like property transactions were habitually enacted. A charter of 20 June 751 was issued in the name of 'the illustrious man Pippin, mayor of the palace'. By the time of another court case on 1 March 752, Pippin was styled 'king of the Franks' (*rex francorum*).[2] At some point between these dates, therefore, Pippin had replaced Childeric III, last king of the Merovingian family that had ruled the Franks for over 250 years. That Pippin and his brother Carloman, jointly mayors of the palace (the most senior non-royal office in the Frankish kingdom) had themselves established Childeric as king just four years earlier gives

---

[1] Pippin I (*d.*640), an Austrasian Frankish magnate, had a daughter named Begga. Her marriage to one Ansegisel is not well attested, but they are nevertheless generally held to have been the parents of Pippin II (*d.*714), the father of Charles Martel (*d.*741), whose second eldest legitimate son is therefore counted as Pippin 'III' (*d.*768).

[2] Respectively, *Die Urkunden der Arnulfinger*, ed. I. Heidrich (Bad Münstereifel, 2001), no. 22, and *Dipl. Kar.* I, no. 1, pp. 3–4. In *Die Urkunden der Arnulfinger*, nos. 23 (which, on the basis of the properties it lists, probably dates from before 20 June 751) and 24 (which has no formal date clause, but is assigned by Heidrich to '741–751'), Pippin was still styled *maior domus* (mayor of the palace).

some indication of the strong position from which Pippin could launch this bid for the throne. But the precise mechanics of the takeover are entirely unknown. Although our texts are often difficult to date precisely, the strongest likelihood is that, the charters apart, all our Frankish sources for the events of 751 were written after 768, when Pippin died and his sons succeeded to the kingship. In other words, these texts probably formed part of a deliberate and retrospective attempt to establish the ease and propriety of Pippin's succession in order to make that of his sons (who were, after all, not Merovingians but children of a usurper) seem routine.

A cluster of texts containing one or other version of a narrative about Pippin's acquisition of the kingship were written in a context in which the Carolingians were already dominant. The most famous rendition of the story is that of Einhard in his *Vita Karoli* (Life of Charlemagne), probably written around 817, who claims that by 751 the Merovingian family 'had in fact been without any vitality for a long time and had demonstrated that there was not any worth in it except the empty name of king'.[3] But Einhard was simply echoing the various sets of annals compiled in the last years of the eighth, and first decades of the ninth, century. The most influential, and probably the earliest, of these are the so-called *Annales regni francorum* (Royal Frankish Annals), according to which legates (they are named as Bishop Burchard of Würzburg and Fulrad the chaplain) were sent to Rome to gain Pope Zacharias's sanction for the replacement of Childeric III with Pippin. This the pope duly gave, commenting, in the words of the annalist, that 'it was better to call him king who actually possessed royal power'. Pippin was therefore anointed king (the annalist says that this was performed by the renowned English missionary Boniface) and Childeric III was tonsured and sent to a monastery.[4] Reports along these lines also appear, with less detail, in

---

[3] Einhard, *VK*, c. 1, trans. Dutton, *Charlemagne's Courtier*, p. 16. The *Vita* has been dated variously between 814 and 830. For arguments in favour of an early date see Innes and McKitterick, 'The writing of history', pp. 203–8; McKitterick, *Charlemagne: The Formation of a European Identity*, pp. 7–30. For a date in the later 820s see M. Tischler, *Einharts Vita Karoli. Studien zur Entstehung, Überlieferung und Rezeption*, MGH Schriften XLVIII, 2 vols. (Hanover, 2001), esp. pp. 163–4, 587–9.

[4] *ARF*, s.a. 749 and 750, trans. Scholz, *Carolingian Chronicles*, p. 39. For discussion of the annals as a genre, see McKitterick, *History and Memory*, pp. 84–119 (esp. pp. 101–19, together with 141–2, for the *Annales regni francorum*); McKitterick, *Perceptions of the Past*, pp. 65–8.

the Continuations to the *Chronicle* of Fredegar, and in a text known as the *Clausula de unctione Pippini regis* (the clause on the anointing of King Pippin). Each of these has periodically been dated as roughly contemporary with the events of 751, but the argument for a later date is stronger in both cases: the Continuations were most likely added to the *Chronicle* of Fredegar in the period 768–86, while the *Clausula* looks certain to have been written in the ninth century.[5] Their composition after the kingship had been passed successfully to a second generation of Carolingians makes it highly unlikely that they could have presented an objective record of 751, even if one could be recalled. Moreover, their partisanship looks all the more striking if we compare them to texts written in Rome, which are the only ones, apart from the charters, that may be roughly contemporary. Despite the growing general interest of papal biographers in the papacy's contacts with Francia, the *Life* of Pope Zacharias, part of the collection of papal biographies known as the *Liber pontificalis*, breaks off its narrative in 749, while the collection of letters between the popes and the Carolingians, the *Codex Carolinus*, includes no letter between 747 and 753.[6] It may be that the Roman authors placed no great importance on Pippin's elevation; alternatively, these apparent oversights may point to a deliberate attempt to restrict or manipulate the memory of 751. Either way, the silence from Rome casts doubt on the later version of events contained in Frankish sources, and in particular on the notion that Pippin's seizure of the kingship was sanctioned beforehand by the pope.

---

[5] *Clausula de unctione Pippini Regis*, ed. B. Krusch, *MGH SRM* 1 (Hanover, 1885), trans. B. Pullan, *Sources for the History of Medieval Europe from the Mid-Eighth to the Mid-Thirteenth Century* (Oxford, 1966), pp. 7–8; repr. in Dutton, *Carolingian Civilization*, pp. 13–14. The dates given here are those proposed – to our minds convincingly – by McKitterick, *History and Memory*, pp. 137–42; see also McKitterick, *Charlemagne: The Formation of a European Identity*, pp. 7–20. Many alternatives have been put forward for both: for the *Continuations* of Fredegar see in particular Collins, *Fredegar*. The *Clausula's* attribution of regnal dates to his sons Charles (Charlemagne) and Carloman before Pippin's death in 768 argue strongly against its contemporaneity.

[6] The last narrative chapter of Zacharias's *Life* is c. 23, *LP* 1, pp. 433–4, trans. Davis, *Lives of the Eighth-Century Popes*, pp. 47–8. The only letter from Zacharias to Pippin dates from 747: *CC*, no. 3; the next ones in sequence are *CC*, nos. 4 and 5, which can be dated to 753 by reference to *LP* 1, pp. 433–4, trans. Davis, *Lives of the Eighth-Century Popes*, p. 59.

As we saw in Chapter 1, papal backing for Pippin's elevation came not before the event, but after it, and involved not Pope Zacharias but his successor Stephen II. It is significant that texts mostly written in the reign of Pippin's son Charlemagne still felt the need to justify Pippin's takeover by supposing prior papal approval. This suggests very strongly that what actually took place was, and was recognised as, a usurpation whose controversial nature required special explanation. It has implications for the pope too: in so far as he came to be recognised as possessing the kind of authority that could be used to legitimise secular kings – which had not previously been the case – it was because he had become involved in the effort to justify Pippin's usurpation. In other words, it was an authority with which he was invested by Carolingian apologists, and not something already regarded as a natural part of his remit. The texts written by these apologists also retrospectively inflated the power of members of the Carolingian family in the era before they attained formal kingship, while diminishing that of the Merovingian kings, and especially the later scions of the dynasty in the seventh and early eighth centuries. They thus painted a picture of Merovingian ineptitude, incapacity and obsolescence that has proved very durable.[7]

THE MEROVINGIAN WORLD AND CAROLINGIAN ORIGINS

If we mentally take ourselves back to the later seventh century itself, the Merovingian kings look far less vulnerable than they do in later texts, and Carolingian success very far from inevitable. The Carolingians originated in the eastern part of the Frankish realm and first emerge into the historical record as one of a number of aristocratic families who figure in sources describing the many succession crises of the Merovingian dynasty in the seventh century. Pippin I had been mayor of the palace – the premier aristocratic office under the king – in the eastern Frankish sub-kingdom of Austrasia in the 620s and 630s. Pippin's son Grimoald seems to have risen to even greater power there, to the extent that his son Childebert was 'adopted' by the Merovingian king of Austrasia Sigibert III, and succeeded him as king, even though Sigibert had a son of his own, Dagobert. None of this was accomplished without opposition from other factions

---

[7] See e.g. Hen, 'Annals of Metz'; E. Peters, *The Shadow King. Rex inutilis in Medieval Law and Literature, 751–1327* (New Haven, CT, 1970), pp. 8–14.

within the Austrasian, and wider Frankish, aristocracy, however, and in 657 or 661/2 this 'Pippinid' (an alternative name for the earlier Carolingians) King Childebert was ousted from the Austrasian throne and replaced by Childeric II, a Merovingian from the western sub-kingdom of Neustria.

This narrative immediately reveals the highly fragmented nature of Merovingian Francia. There was, first, a distinction between the kings and aristocrats of the different Frankish sub-kingdoms (*regna* in Latin). The basic structure of the Frankish realm had been established by the 530s, with the conquest of the lands of the Alemans (*c.*506) and of the Burgundians (534) and the cession by the Ostrogoths of most of Provence (536) (see Map 2). Thereafter, it encompassed all of modern France, with the exception of Septimania (between the Rhône delta and the Pyrenees), held by the Visigoths until the early eighth century, and it also included most of modern Switzerland, central and southwestern Germany, the Rhineland and the Low Countries as far north as the lower Rhine.[8] It has even been argued that at this time the Franks exercised some sort of rule over southern England, although the evidence for this is circumstantial, at best.[9] England apart, the shape of this vast area enjoyed remarkable stability for nearly four centuries, partly because other peoples buffered it from potential invaders from the east and south (though not from the north, as we shall see). This stability is all the more remarkable because the whole realm was united under one ruler for less than half of this period, and intermittently at that.[10] Almost from its inception, the Frankish realm had been divided among different members of the Merovingian dynasty. The kingdom's effective creator, Clovis (*d.*511), reportedly set the precedent by providing for its division between his four sons on his death, although his reasons for doing so and the precise nature of the division are hard to see clearly through

---

[8] Wood, *Merovingian Kingdoms*, pp. 51–4.
[9] I. N. Wood, *The Merovingian North Sea* (Alingsås, 1983), pp. 12–13. Bishops from Kent attended the council held by King Chlothar II at Paris in 614: *Concilia Galliae a.511–695*, ed. C. de Clercq, *CCSL* 148A (Turnhout, 1963).
[10] These were 558–61 (Chlothar I), 613–23 (Chlothar II), 629–32 (Dagobert I), 656–7 (Clovis II), 673–5 (Childeric II), 687–91 (Theuderic III), 691–741 (the last Merovingians and Charles Martel), 748–68 (Pippin III after the 'retirement' of Carloman), 771–840 (Charlemagne and Louis the Pious) and 884–8 (Charles the Fat): a total of 166 of the 377 years from 511 to 888, of which only thirty-nine fell before 700. These figures can only be a rough guide since the precise nature of some divisions is open to debate.

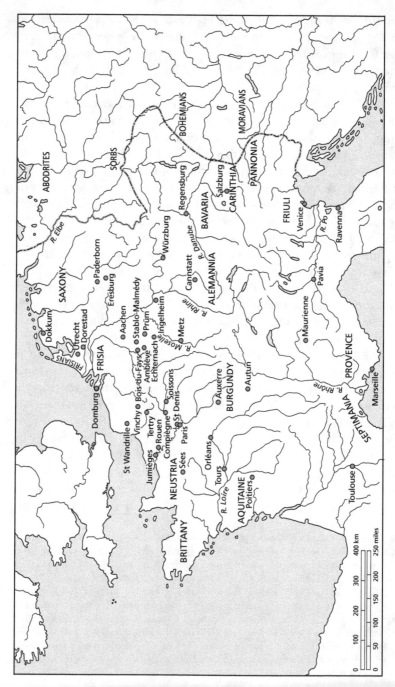

Map 2. Places mentioned in Chapter 2: 'The creation of Carolingian kingship to 800'

our highly political sources.[11] Because the rules of inheritance were at no time well defined, rivalries within the Merovingian family, exacerbated by the uxoriousness of most of its male members in the sixth century, ensured that no simple pattern was ever established to govern the royal succession. The repeated divisions of the realm gradually encouraged the coalescence of three kingdoms within it: Neustria in the northwest, Austrasia in the east and Burgundy in the centre and south. Frequently these kingdoms were ruled over by different Merovingian kings, though by the mid-seventh century Neustria and Burgundy usually had the same king. Aquitaine, in the southwest, was in the seventh century generally carved up between the different kings, but by the early eighth century its elite was increasingly independent of any Merovingian control.

Some measure of the fractures in the Merovingian world at this time can be taken from the account of the travels of the Anglo-Saxon ecclesiastic Wilfrid by his biographer, Stephen of Ripon. Travelling through Austrasia in 680 on his way back to England from Rome, Wilfrid was waylaid by a bishop 'with a great army', who berated, and nearly killed, him for having sent back to Austrasia the Dagobert who had been ousted by Grimoald and Childebert 'the Adopted' back in 656. The rule of this Dagobert (II) had proved oppressive, according to the bishop, and he had been murdered.[12] This story reveals something of the factionalism of the Frankish aristocracy at this time.[13] According to Stephen of Ripon, a group of Frankish, presumably Austrasian, aristocrats had asked Wilfrid to arrange for the return of Dagobert II from exile in Ireland. On his outward journey to Rome in 679 Wilfrid had therefore been warmly welcomed by Dagobert and offered the bishopric of Strasbourg (an offer perhaps also prompted by his connections within the Burgundian aristocracy).[14] But only a year later, as the wheel of Austrasian factional fortune turned against the king, these same connections were what placed Wilfrid's life in danger. Fortunately for him, Wilfrid was

---

[11] M. Widdowson, 'Merovingian partitions: a genealogical charter?', *EME* 17 (2009), pp. 1–22.

[12] Stephen of Ripon, *Vita Wilfridi*, c. 33, ed. and trans. B. Colgrave, *The Life of Bishop Wilfrid by Eddius Stephanus* (Cambridge, 1927; repr. 1985), pp. 68–9.

[13] The term 'faction' (Latin *factio*) is used in contemporary sources: e.g. Fredegar, *Chronicle*, ed. and trans. J. M. Wallace-Hadrill, *The Fourth Book of the Chronicle of Fredegar with its Continuations* (London, 1960) IV, c. 40.

[14] Stephen of Ripon, *Vita Wilfridi*, cc. 4, 6 and 28.

a formidable operator and he managed to talk his way out of trouble. Nonetheless, the episode highlights the highly partisan and volatile nature of Merovingian politics.

Dagobert II's short reign in fact exemplifies a period of particular instability that followed the murder in 675 of Childeric II, the king who had supplanted the Pippinid Childebert 'the Adopted' on the throne of Austrasia. Childeric had assumed the kingship of Neustria and Burgundy as well as Austrasia in 673, but was killed by a faction of Neustro-Burgundian aristocrats who apparently thought his government tyrannical. It may be that he had been over-dependent on the support of Austrasian aristocrats. The murder split the aristocracies of both sub-kingdoms. The dominant faction in the years following 675 was one that drew support from both Neustria–Burgundy and Austrasia, and was headed by the mayor of the Neustrian palace Ebroin. This faction was opposed by others in both sub-kingdoms. A Neustro-Burgundian faction led by Bishop Leudegar of Autun was dealt with by Ebroin in a bloody series of killings culminating in that of the bishop himself – his death would later be painted as a martyrdom. In Austrasia, there may in fact have been a number of factions. A group of aristocrats opposed to Ebroin had sought Wilfrid's help in bringing the exiled Dagobert II back to the throne; it was a group aligned with Ebroin who, in their turn, killed him three years later. Some power also resided in the hands of a third group, who supported neither the murdered king nor Ebroin, and were led by the ancestor of the Carolingians, the mayor of the Austrasian palace Pippin II. This Pippin's origins are not entirely clear, since the association between his father Ansegisel, and the earlier 'Pippinids', Pippin I and Grimoald, is attested only in later sources,[15] but a faction under his co-leadership came to blows with that of Ebroin in 679 at a battle at Bois-du-Fays (also known as 'Lucofao'), from which Ebroin emerged the victor. Nevertheless, he was himself murdered in the following year, and, after further in-fighting, a peace was brokered between Pippin and a new dominant group in Neustria. This faction in turn splintered in 686–7, and a part of it sided with Pippin, who won a victory with its support at Tertry in 687.

These episodes clearly demonstrate the centrality in Frankish aristocratic society of warfare, albeit often on a limited scale. Nevertheless, victory at Tertry did not bring Pippin immediate control

---

[15] See Fouracre, *Charles Martel*, pp. 33–40, and n. 1 above.

of Neustria: non-military factors like marriage and court intrigue were also important in building political support.[16] The mayor of the Neustrian palace, Berchar, survived the battle, only to be assassinated shortly afterwards at the behest of his mother-in-law, Ansfled. She represented a Neustrian faction that was prepared to ally with the Pippinid family, an alliance sealed by the marriage of Ansfled's daughter (Berchar's widow) to Pippin's son Drogo. This allowed Pippin to take over the office of mayor of the Neustrian palace. But he could not yet exercise power there in the same way as in Austrasia. The best evidence for Pippinid power in Austrasia comes from contemporary charters preserved in the archives of monasteries. This material suggests a precocious association with or control of monasteries as a significant element in early Carolingian power. That said, we must remember that monastic documents are more likely to survive than other sources, and that even then we do not have them in great numbers. What's more, most of the individuals that appear in these charters are not otherwise known. The considerable efforts made by historians to reconstruct from this evidence the composition of contemporary factions thus remains highly speculative, especially when it is dependent on such questionable methods as assuming a family relationship between two individuals simply because they had similar names.[17]

Despite these problems, it is possible to see that Pippin's power in Austrasia was centred on two principal areas: the valley of the Sambre (in present-day Belgium), where there were a number of Pippinid-controlled monasteries; and the area around Cologne and in the valleys of the Moselle and Meuse, where the family of Pippin's wife Plectrude had extensive lands. The main monastic house in this area was Echternach, founded in 697/8 and taken under Pippin's protection in 706.[18] As Austrasian mayor of the palace Pippin also seems to have been able to acquire fiscal (i.e. royal) lands in the turmoil surrounding Dagobert II's death: another important resource for winning support from his peers.[19] Pippin's power in Austrasia was effectively sovereign, as shown by grants of immunity he made to

---

[16] Fouracre, *Charles Martel*, pp. 41–8.
[17] Further on this, see Fouracre, *Charles Martel*, pp. 41–5.
[18] For the minimalist and maximalist views of Pippinid lands and connections around the time of Tertry, see Fouracre, *Charles Martel*, pp. 41–54.
[19] Fouracre, *Charles Martel*, p. 47.

the church of St Arnulf in Metz and to the monastery of Stablo-Malmédy.[20] These actions reflect the potency of the office of mayor of the palace: participation in, if not power over, the exercise of royal rights like the issuing of diplomas stemmed from the mayor's traditional role in controlling access to the king. The mayoralty of Neustria had been the most important non-royal position in the Frankish kingdoms throughout the seventh century, especially after 675 when the sole remaining Merovingian king seems to have been permanently based in that kingdom.

It is thus significant that, having gained the mayoralty of Neustria through his alliance with Ansfled, Pippin II relinquished it almost immediately to a certain Nordebert. Although Nordebert was a follower, and although Pippin's son Grimoald took over the office on Nordebert's death, probably in 696, this act suggests that Pippinid power in Neustria was as yet limited.[21] True, Pippin did exercise some control in the region of Rouen, where he was able to install supporters as bishop of Rouen and as abbot of the important monastery of St Wandrille; and about the same time, his son Drogo was made duke in Champagne on the frontier between Neustria and Austrasia.[22] But charters from the reign of Childebert III (694–711) show the king's court upholding the rights of monasteries, including the Merovingians' principal abbey of St Denis, against the encroachments of Drogo and Grimoald; and reveal that his court still attracted magnates from across the Merovingian realm, including some (like Antenor, *patricius* of Provence, and Savaric, bishop of Orléans) who would be remembered as opponents of the Pippinids.[23] Evidently, Pippin's power was restricted in Neustria, and resisted especially in the Seine–Oise region where King Childebert himself was based, and where St Denis lay. We should therefore take seriously our only contemporary Neustrian narrative, the *Liber historiae francorum*, when it describes Childebert as 'the famous and just lord . . . of good memory', and conclude that the battle of Tertry was not the decisive turning point it was claimed to be by later Carolingian apologists like the compiler of the *Annales Mettenses priores*.[24]

---

[20] Kölzer (ed.), *Urkunden der Merowinger*, no. 7 (Metz) and no. 125 (Stablo-Malmédy), and see Gerberding, *Rise of the Carolingians*, p. 100, n. 55.
[21] *LHF*, cc. 48, 49.   [22] Wood, *Merovingian Kingdoms*, p. 264.
[23] Kölzer (ed.), *Urkunden der Merowinger*, nos. 149, 156, 157.
[24] *LHF*, c. 50. On the *LHF* and the *AMP*, see above, Chapter 1, pp. 19–21.

After Childebert's death, though, there are signs that the core Frankish elite was beginning to disintegrate. It was probably at this point that Antenor rebelled in Provence, and Savaric built up his independent power base in the region of Orléans and Auxerre.[25] And already before that, outlying regions that had once fallen under Merovingian hegemony were responding to the centrifugal pull generated by the turmoil within that core aristocracy from 675 onwards. A ninth-century source asserts that the duke of the Alemans stopped obeying the Franks because he was 'no longer able to serve the Merovingian kings as [he] had been accustomed to do before'.[26] Though written a century after the events it describes, this statement may reflect a real shrinking, starting even before Childebert's accession, in the scope of the king's personal effectiveness. For all that he could not call the shots unhindered in Neustria, in the kingdom writ large it was now Pippin who led Frankish armies against peoples traditionally tributary to the Merovingians. He responded against the Alemans with annual campaigns between 709 and 712, and took the army to Frisia, also independent of the Franks by the 670s, in 690 and 695, when he seems to have seized territory as far north as Utrecht, thus bringing under Frankish control the important trading centre of Dorestad.[27] Ultimately, Pippin was able to make peace with the Frisian leader Radbod, whose daughter married Pippin's son Grimoald some time after 711. In the meantime, these wars show Pippin directing the Frankish military machine even while Childebert III was on the throne. Leadership in war — that most powerful attracter of political support — had passed out of the hands of the Merovingians. But there was as yet no thought of doing without them: even if he no longer played general to his aristocratic warriors, Childebert III was still an effective political force, as were his successors in the decade following his death.

If the political balance, which had been maintained to good effect while he was alive, tilted slightly away from the Merovingians on Childebert III's death (as indicated by the revolts of Antenor and Savaric), the death of Pippin in December 714 reset the political agenda by tipping the Frankish heartlands into civil war. Within a year

---

[25] Fouracre, *Charles Martel*, p. 66.
[26] Erchanbert, *Breviarium regum francorum annis 715–827*, ed. G. Pertz, *MGH SS* II (Hanover, 1829), p. 328.
[27] On Dorestad, see below, Chapter 7.

the Pippinids had come close to extinction. Pippin's two sons with Plectrude had died – Drogo in 707 and Grimoald just a few months before his father in 714 – leaving Grimoald's young son Theudoald as nominal mayor in Neustria. After Pippin's death, the Neustrians rebelled, defeated Theudoald's forces at Compiègne and drove him from the kingdom. At the same time, Pippin's only surviving adult son, Charles, had been imprisoned by his stepmother Plectrude. The absence of any sign that this Charles, who had acquired the nickname 'Martel' ('the Hammer') by the ninth century, featured in his father's plans up to this point makes it ironic that it was to be he who rescued Pippin's legacy.[28] The lack of continuity from father to son – with the eventual eradication of what historians have tended to regard as the 'legitimate' Pippinid line of Drogo and Grimoald – is the main reason why from this point on posterity knows the family not after Pippin but after Charles. The Pippinids were becoming the Carolingians.

But in late 715 the prospects did not look bright for either branch of the family. With the expulsion of Theudoald, the Neustrians appointed their own mayor, Ragamfred, and made an alliance with the Frisian leader Radbod. The Merovingian king Dagobert III now died, and Ragamfred replaced him with a monk called Daniel, a son of Childeric II, who was crowned with the name Chilperic (II). Charles Martel, having managed to escape from Plectrude's custody, tried to stop Radbod's attack on Austrasia but was beaten, and the Neustrians and Frisians forced Plectrude to pay them off with a good deal of Pippin's treasure. When Ragamfred and Chilperic II were returning to Neustria in April 716, however, Charles Martel met and defeated them at Amblève. Quite how this table-turning victory was achieved is not known. Our sources for all these events are decidedly sparse, consisting principally of the *Liber historiae francorum* and deductions about dates made from the few surviving charters. The elaborations made by later, Carolingian-era, narratives, are less than reliable. However, it seems fair to suggest that many Austrasians would have supported Charles Martel simply because they were in a very tight spot – beset not only by the Neustrians and Frisians but from the north-east by the Saxons – and he was the only

---

[28] The only reference to him before this point might suggest that he was well educated: this, at least, is one meaning of the adjective *elegans*, which the *LHF* attaches to him in its first mention of him: *LHF*, c. 49.

surviving adult male representative of the Pippinid family. His victory is nonetheless remarkable, and began a sequence that bears out the *Liber historiae francorum*'s comment that he was 'effective in battle'.[29] By the following spring Charles had attracted enough support to be able to attack and beat the Neustrians at Vinchy near Cambrai. This was not, however, a decisive defeat; nor should we imagine the political conflict in terms of a simple Neustria–Austrasia split. Charters of Chilperic II dating from after the battle demonstrate his continued, and very far-flung, power, and the willingness of at least some of the Austrasian aristocracy to associate with him.[30] Charles Martel remained excluded from the Merovingian palace – still in theory the fount of sovereign authority – and turned instead to securing his position in his heartland by travelling to Cologne where he forced Plectrude to surrender the rest of his father's treasure. That he also at this time established another Merovingian, Chlothar IV, in rivalry to Chilperic II demonstrates the continued necessity of having a Merovingian stamp on the exercise of power, even in Austrasia. Ragamfred and Chilperic now allied with the duke of the Aquitanians, Eudo, and their army met that of Charles in battle at Soissons in the spring of 718. This seems to have been a more decisive encounter than Vinchy: Charles won, and pursued his enemies across Neustria until they took refuge in Orléans. He was now able to take control in Neustria. Over the next few years, we find a number of his supporters, including laymen, in possession of many of the bishoprics of that kingdom. Most prominent among them was Charles's nephew Hugo, a product of that marriage of Drogo that had first introduced Pippinid power into Neustria. Quite contrary to canon law, Hugo was simultaneously abbot of the prominent Neustrian abbeys of St Wandrille and Jumièges, as well as bishop of no fewer than five different sees, including Paris and Rouen. Chlothar IV having died in 718, by about 720 Charles had come to terms with Eudo and secured the return of Chilperic II, along with his treasure. Chilperic died in 721 and was replaced by Theuderic IV, now truly merely a cipher. Theuderic reigned, but it was now Charles who ruled over the core of the old Merovingian realm, a power amply demonstrated by his imprisonment in 723 of the two surviving sons of Drogo (one of

---

[29] *LHF*, c. 49; for Charles's possible supporters at this time, see Fouracre, *Charles Martel*, pp. 61–3.

[30] Fouracre, *Charles Martel*, pp. 64–6.

whom died). The Pippinid branch of the family had now decisively given way to the Carolingians.[31]

The reasons for Charles Martel's astonishing success between 715 and 723 must ultimately have lain in his ability to attract the support of his fellow aristocrats. This was presumably achieved through a combination of material inducements in the form of treasure and land, but it also reflects the centrality of participation in warfare to the identity of the ruling class. Whether Charles started off with enough moveable and landed wealth to attract the following needed to secure his first victories, or whether it was those successes, perhaps especially at Amblève and Vinchy, that enabled him to offer rewards to his followers, is an ultimately unanswerable chicken-and-egg question. But his own prowess as a warrior must have some bearing on the answer, and the rest of his career leaves the strong impression that this was a man who was most at home, and most successful, when at the head of an army. This was fortunate for the Franks, because if the intermittent turmoil of the previous fifty years had fractured the old Merovingian hegemony, the civil warfare of the previous nine, 714–23, threatened to split it wide open.

CHARLES MARTEL AND THE EXTENSION OF CAROLINGIAN POWER

Merovingian rule was a hegemony, so had not operated in the same way everywhere. This means that we need to distinguish different levels of relationship between the Frankish heartland and the different areas in which Charles and his sons had to fight. Some places that were essentially part of that heartland had broken off under independent rulership during the civil war of 714–19: Orléans, Auxerre and the surrounding region under Savaric, and Angers, where Ragamfred took refuge after his defeat at Soissons. These had been brought under Charles's control by 721 (though Ragamfred made a final abortive bid to assert himself in 724). There were also regions more geographically distant from the centre, but where the aristocracy was closely bound by family and social ties to the ruling class in Neustria and Austrasia. This was especially true of central-southern Burgundy and Provence. The former area is very hard to see through the

[31] Fouracre, *Charles Martel*, pp. 74–5.

confused source material, most of it written long after the event.[32] Our most reliable source reports that Charles began in the early 730s to establish within Burgundy trustworthy and able men as a counterweight to the rebellious and unfaithful. He handed over the Lyonnais to his followers, and made written legal agreements to shore up his rule there.[33]

That there was a major upheaval in the area in the later 730s is evident too in the sources for Provence. We have seen that the *patricius* there, Antenor, who was connected to northern aristocratic families, had rebelled after Pippin II's death. His dominance in Provence seems to have extended well into the period of Charles Martel's rule in Francia, during which time he despoiled the lands of local monasteries. We do not know the precise state of Provence when Charles invaded in 735 following his successful campaign in Burgundy, but we do know that he found there both friends and enemies.[34] He was opposed by a certain Maurontus, titled *dux* ('duke', but literally 'leader'), who may have been a member of a recently ousted Burgundian aristocratic family. Contemporary chronicles assert that Maurontus enlisted the help of Muslim contingents based in Septimania. Charles had to send another army in 736, headed by his half-brother Childebrand, to deal with this threat, following it up himself. The combined Muslim and Provençal enemy seems finally to have been subdued after a further campaign in 739. That Charles also drew on local support in this effort is clear from a document drawn up in that latter year, the will of Abbo, who was by then *patricius* of Provence. Earlier in his career in 726 we can see him as *rector* (roughly, administrator) of the crucial Susa-Maurienne region that straddled the main Alpine pass into Italy. Abbo's will reveals that he had subsequently benefited from gifts by Charles (and, so the document says, King Theuderic IV: evidently the veneer of Merovingian rule was still necessary) of land confiscated from rebels. The patriciate must have been the crowning reward for support in an area where Charles badly needed it. Abbo's will also suggests the severity of the long series of wars in Provence: it tells of Abbo's dependants

---

[32] Reviewed fully by Fouracre, *Charles Martel*, pp. 89–93.
[33] We are reliant here on Fred., *Cont.*, cc. 14 and 18, the Latin of which is not entirely clear: see Fouracre, *Charles Martel*, p. 92, for the most likely interpretation.
[34] The following account draws heavily on P. Geary, *Aristocracy in Provence. The Rhône Basin at the Dawn of the Carolingian Age* (Stuttgart, 1985).

having been 'dispersed by necessity' because of the depredations of the Muslims. The evident decline of the formerly important port of Marseille, and of trade in the western Mediterranean in general, in this period must also be in part connected with political disorder in the south.[35]

On a different, more distant, level of detachment from the Frankish heartland were the duchies of Alemannia and Bavaria, whose rulers (usually termed *duces* in our sources) had traditionally owed allegiance to the Merovingians. The *Laws of the Alemans* reissued by Duke Lantfrid in the 720s even stressed the ultimate authority of the (Frankish) king. But as the Frankish mayor's power increased, so also did the enmity of the Aleman duke towards him. Charles first waged war in Alemannia in 730, and in 734 expelled Lantfrid's successor as *dux*. Of more direct impact on the Carolingian family were his dealings with Bavaria, where the dukes were intent on increasing their power. In 716, for instance, Duke Theodo exploited his connections with Italy, where the Lombard kings were members of the same, extensive Agilolfing clan (as indeed were the dukes of the Alemans), to seek papal help in restructuring the Bavarian Church. The strong suggestion in the sources that at this time Theodo married a sister of Plectrude reflects equally the increasing prominence of both the Agilolfing and Pippinid families. The stakes were high, then, when on Theodo's death in 717 or 718 conflict broke out between his son Grimoald and grandson Hugbert. In 725, after Grimoald was murdered, Charles Martel invaded Bavaria in support of Hugbert. He strengthened the new Bavarian duke's dependence on him by marrying one of his relatives, Swanahild.[36] Bavaria remained quiescent even after Hugbert's death in 735 or 736, which brought the direct line of Agilolfing dukes to an end. The new duke, Odilo, from the Aleman ducal family, was chosen with Charles's permission, according to one Carolingian annalist.[37] When Odilo was expelled from Bavaria in 740, for reasons which can only be guessed at, he took refuge at the Frankish court, where he formed a relationship with Charles's daughter Chiltrudis, who followed him back to Bavaria

---

[35] S. Loseby, 'Marseille and the Pirenne thesis II: "ville morte"', in Hansen and Wickham (eds.), *The Long Eighth Century*, pp. 167–94. See also below, Chapter 7.
[36] Fred., *Cont.* 12; Fouracre, *Charles Martel*, pp. 108–9; J. Jarnut, 'Untersuchungen zur Herkunft Swanahilds, der Gattin Karl Martells', *Zeitschrift für bayerische Landesgeschichte* 40 (1977), pp. 254–9.
[37] *AMP*, p. 33.

when he was restored in the following year. Charles's involvement in Bavaria therefore produced two children who, as we shall see, were to prove deeply troublesome to his successors over the next two generations: Grifo (his own son with Swanahild), and Tassilo (the son of Odilo and Chiltrudis).[38]

Aquitaine was another of the duchies traditionally subordinate to the Merovingians. Very little is known about this area before the second decade of the eighth century. It seems to have been governed in the later seventh century by dukes: we know the names of Felix in the 660s and Lupus in the 670s. How far its aristocracy was independent of those in Neustria, Austrasia and Burgundy is a matter of debate among historians.[39] We can say little more than that northern monasteries had lands in Aquitaine. For how long and by what means Eudo had been duke before his first appearance in the sources is impossible to know. That first appearance, as we have seen, was in 718, when he allied with Chilperic II and Ragamfred against Charles Martel. By 720, however, he had concluded a treaty with Charles. By this time, the Muslims who had conquered Visigothic Spain with lightning speed from 711 were raiding north of the Pyrenees. Eudo defeated a contingent near Toulouse in 720 or 721, and the sources suggest that by this time he was both militarily successful and prestigious. He was certainly sufficiently strong for Charles Martel to put off campaigning in Aquitaine until two raids in 731. Eudo may at this time have been increasingly distracted by Muslim pressure.[40] The claim of our main Frankish source, the Continuations of the *Chronicle* of Fredegar, that Eudo invited the Muslims into Aquitaine after Charles's attacks, has been recognised as a fabrication by a highly partisan pro-Carolingian writer – Eudo was in fact attacked and defeated by the Muslim leader 'Abd ar-Rahman before he called on Charles for aid.[41]

The result of this appeal was what history generally knows as the battle of Poitiers, 732 (which in fact took place nearer Tours,

---

[38] See in general K. L. R. Pearson, *Conflicting Loyalties in Early Medieval Bavaria: a View of Socio-Political Interaction, 680–900* (Aldershot, 1999); C. I. Hammer, *From Ducatus to Regnum: Ruling Bavaria under the Merovingians and Early Carolingians* (Turnhout, 2007).

[39] Compare, for instance, Fouracre, *Charles Martel*, pp. 81–9 and Wood, *Merovingian Kingdoms*, pp. 281–4.

[40] Note the account of his defeat on the Garonne by the *Chron. Moiss.*, p. 291.

[41] Collins, 'Deception and misrepresentation', pp. 35–41.

and probably in 733).[42] This victory has come to define Charles's posthumous reputation: it regularly features in lists of history's most significant battles, and gained the mayor a heroic place in numerous romantic paintings. Yet this reputation is based more on the epigrammatic but misplaced judgements of Enlightenment historians like Edward Gibbon (who thought the battle was all that prevented Europe falling completely to Islam) than on contemporary sources. Although the combined forces of Charles and Eudo were victorious, and 'Abd ar-Rahman was killed, the Muslim army was a raiding party rather than the vanguard of a religiously motivated invasion from Spain. And while further attacks by the Muslims on Aquitaine were deterred, they simply turned their attention to Provence instead, as we have seen. Charles does not seem to have gained any permanent influence in Aquitaine from the victory. Though he raided there again just after Eudo's death in 735, and may have exerted some control of the succession of the latter's son Hunoald to the duchy, he is recorded as fighting 'the sons of Eudo' in the following year, and Hunoald was certainly among the sternest opponents of Charles's sons after his death.

Some peoples on the edges of the Frankish realm had only been occasionally tributary to the Merovingians, and remained distinct in both their leadership and culture: in particular, they resisted straightforward Christianisation. This was the case with the Frisians, who were an important influence on Frankish politics in the 710s, as we have already seen. Though Pippin II had gained some measure of control as far north as Utrecht in the 690s, and had allied with the Frisian ruler Radbod through Grimoald's marriage to the latter's daughter, on his death Radbod had attacked Austrasia in synchrony with the Neustrians, and had given a distinctly hostile reception to incoming Anglo-Saxon missionaries who were supported by Pippin.[43] Only after Radbod's death in 719 was Charles able to resume some sort of influence. But a new Frisian leader, Bubo, had arisen by the 730s, and Charles campaigned against him in 734.[44] The fact that this was at least partly a naval campaign indicates two points:

[42] Fouracre, *Charles Martel*, pp. 86–7; Wood, *Merovingian Kingdoms*, p. 283.

[43] LHF, c. 52; Alcuin, *Vita Willibrordi*, ed. W. Levison, MGH SRM VII (Hanover, 1920), pp. 81–141, trans. C. H. Talbot, *Anglo-Saxon Missionaries in Germany* (London, 1954), pp. 9–10. See further Chapter 3 below.

[44] Fred., *Cont.*, c. 17.

first, what the Franks really coveted in that region was unquestionably the trade that ran through the important emporia of Dorestad and Domburg; secondly, the terrain of fens, dunes and coastal islands was extremely hard to penetrate.[45] After 734 Frankish rule theoretically extended as far north as the river Lauwers (in the modern province of Groningen); in practice, as the murder of the missionary Boniface at Dokkum in 754 suggests, it remained very hard to impose.[46]

Most distinctively and steadfastly pagan of the Franks' neighbours to their north and east were the Saxons, whose apparently expansionist activity was disturbing the whole region in the early eighth century. It may be for this reason that Charles had found time even in 718 to campaign against them, and waged war in Saxony again in 720, 724, 728 and 738. These were not, apparently, wars of conquest: at least, if that had been their object, they were entirely unsuccessful, though Fredegar's Continuator does report that in 738 Charles ordered the Saxons in the region of the river Lippe to pay tribute.[47] These Frankish claims to tribute from the Saxons dated back at least a century to the high Merovingian era and were to continue to feature in Carloman's and Pippin III's campaigns against them.[48] By consistently couching Saxon activity in terms of rebellion and infidelity, Frankish sources suggest that throughout this period the Franks retained some sense of hegemony over the Saxons, and from Carloman's time, at least, this was accompanied by the ambition to convert them to Christianity. Before the reign of Charlemagne, however, these efforts made little headway.

Charles Martel's campaigns allowed the coagulative quality of aristocratic warfare in the early Middle Ages to have its full effect, bringing on to his side the aristocracy of the Frankish heartland. For them the prospect of victory held the promise of plunder, office and land. Crucial to his success at the time, this patronage has also contributed to Charles's traditional reputation, both positive and negative. Earlier historians credited Charles not only with saving Christendom from Islam, but also with inventing a new type of cavalry warfare which, because of its expense, was funded with church property seized to

---

[45] See below, Chapter 7, pp. 349–51.
[46] For Boniface, see below, Chapter 3, pp. 102–4.
[47] Fred., *Cont.*, c. 19. For Martel's Saxon campaigns in general see Fouracre, *Charles Martel*, pp. 117–18.
[48] See below, pp. 52, 64.

reward his followers. In fact, none of these points really stands up. Not only is the significance of 'Poitiers' much overrated (as we saw), but there is no good contemporary evidence that Frankish military success was based on mastery of cavalry. Horses were indeed used by the Franks, but so they were also by their opponents, and in truth success in warfare depended on a variety of strategies and tactics.[49] Meanwhile, Charles's reputation as an oppressor of churches was largely a retrospective invention of ninth-century hagiographers. While we do have charters recording temporary grants of church lands ('precarial grants') to his lay followers, this was not an unusual practice – especially given the disputes over ownership created by the turbulence of the times – and it cannot be seen as a co-ordinated programme.[50] What Charles definitely achieved was the attraction of a significant following among the Frankish aristocracy, so much so that after the death of Theuderic IV in 737 he felt no immediate need to put another Merovingian on the throne, though he did not, on the other hand, raise himself to the kingship. Among those who now permanently attached themselves to the Carolingians we can identify the family of Rotbert, *dux* in the Hesbaye region (in modern Belgium), who seems to have been given some power in the county of Sées in Neustria: he may in fact have been a distant relative of the Carolingians.[51] The loyalty of such men reveals the strength of Carolingian power in the Franks' Neustrian and Austrasian heartland. We see no real rivals to them there after the end of the civil war in which Charles had come to power.

Links could arise, however, between potential opponents further afield and those closer to home. The principalities on the periphery of that heartland – Thuringia, Alemannia, Bavaria, Provence, Aquitaine – had never been part of the core Frankish realm, and were bound into Frankish politics first and foremost by loyal attachment to the Merovingian dynasty. It is perhaps a sign of their sense of superiority to the rulers of these principalities that the Merovingians never allied themselves to them through marriage. The Pippinids, by contrast, had not been so remote. The family of Pippin II's wife Plectrude seems to have been connected by marriage to the family that

[49] B. Bachrach, 'Charles Martel, mounted shock combat, the stirrup and feudalism', *Studies in Medieval and Renaissance History* 7 (1970), pp. 49–75; see also Halsall, *Warfare and Society*, pp. 185–6.

[50] See Fouracre, *Charles Martel*, pp. 137–45; Halsall, *Warfare and Society*, pp. 72–7.

[51] Fouracre, *Charles Martel*, pp. 72–3; Innes, *State and Society*, pp. 178–9.

provided the dukes of both Alemannia and Bavaria, the Agilolfings. This relationship with Charles's rivals within the Pippinid family, added to the Agilolfings' loyalty to the Merovingians, meant that the latter were a powerful potential enemy for Charles. It may have been a need to neutralise this threat that had led to his marrying Swanahild.[52] This marriage proved of great significance in the years following the death of Theuderic IV in 737, not least because it produced a son, Grifo. The lateness of our sources means that historians have had to work hard to discern not just Grifo's true role, but also the general course of events at this time.[53] The succession to Charles was far from assured in his last years: Grifo was still a minor in 737, and of Charles's two legitimate sons with his first wife, only the elder, Carloman, had a son; Pippin was still unmarried.[54] Our main narrative of events comes from a continuator of the *Chronicle* of Fredegar, who reports that in 740 Charles provided for the division of the kingdom between Carloman and Pippin, implicitly excluding Grifo.[55] But this source, remember, was written with hindsight after Pippin had become king. There are in fact indications that Charles intended to make, or even did make, provision for Grifo alongside his other sons in a geographical division of responsibility of the Frankish realm.[56] Squinting at this complex picture of alliances and relationships, we can see that the defining feature of Frankish politics, gradually obscuring the role of the Merovingians and subsuming relations with the frontier principalities, was now the competition for power between members of the Carolingian family.[57]

SECURING CAROLINGIAN HEGEMONY: PIPPIN III

That Charles could hope to make such a division between his sons illustrates how crucial the mayor's own prestige and personality had

---

[52] See above, pp. 46–7.

[53] See S. Airlie, 'Towards a Carolingian aristocracy', in Becher and Jarnut (eds.), *Der Dynastiewechsel von 751*, pp. 109–28.

[54] M. Becher, 'Drogo und die Königserhebung Pippins', *Frühmittelalterliche Studien* 23 (1989), pp. 131–53.

[55] Fred., *Cont.*, c. 23.

[56] Collins, 'Pippin III as mayor of the palace', in Becher and Jarnut (eds.), *Der Dynastiewechsel von 751*, pp. 75–91, esp. pp. 84–5; Fouracre, *Charles Martel*, pp. 161–5.

[57] As argued by Airlie, 'Towards a Carolingian aristocracy'.

become to holding together the Frankish hegemony; and what happened on his death shows how fragile a construction such power was.
In the years that followed, his two eldest legitimate sons, Carloman
and Pippin, worked closely together to win for themselves as much of
Charles's legacy as they could. Moving quickly after Charles's death
in October 741, they had Theudoald, the last descendant of Pippin II
and Plectrude, killed, made Grifo captive, and confined his mother
Swanahild to a nunnery. The latter is held responsible by a continuator of Fredegar's *Chronicle* for encouraging their sister Chiltrudis to
marry her lover Odilo, the duke of Bavaria, a match that we are told
Carloman and Pippin strongly opposed.[58] In the following year, 742,
Carloman and Pippin struck a deal to divide up the Frankish realm
between them. Having first dealt with their rivals within the family,
their over-riding challenge became the opposition that now made
itself fully evident throughout the principalities on the periphery of
the Frankish core. Although a ninth-century source identifies Odilo
of Bavaria as ring-leader, it was against Duke Hunoald in Aquitaine
that the brothers turned first, in 742.[59] That same year they fought the
Alemans, and in 743 raised a new Merovingian, Childeric III, from
obscurity to the kingship – a measure that points up their insecurity
at this time. In that year they also attacked Odilo, whose marriage to
Chiltrudis had obvious potential to prejudice Carloman and Pippin's
position because it united the Carolingian line with the Agilolfings.[60]
In the following year, Carloman fought the Saxons and Pippin the
Alemans.[61] In 745 they campaigned together in Aquitaine.[62] It was
the turn of the Alemans again in 746 in a battle at Cannstatt (modern
Stuttgart) where Carloman's army inflicted slaughter on the Aleman aristocracy. Along with this came wholesale expropriation: in
the next generation, a high proportion of the known property in
Alemannia was in the hands of Franks (see Map 3).[63]

In the midst of this campaigning, both brothers held councils
of bishops to promulgate rules on religious matters: Carloman in
742, 743 and (probably) 747, and Pippin in 744.[64] The staging by

---

[58] Fred., *Cont.*, c. 25.
[59] *AMP, s.a.* 742; Fred. *Cont.*, c. 25. For a more equivocal reconstruction, see Collins,
'Pippin III as mayor of the palace', p. 79.
[60] Fred., *Cont.*, c. 26.   [61] Fred., *Cont.*, c. 27.   [62] Fred., *Cont.*, c. 28.
[63] T. Reuter, *Germany in the Early Middle Ages 800–1056* (London and New York,
1991), pp. 59–60.
[64] For details, see below, Chapter 3.

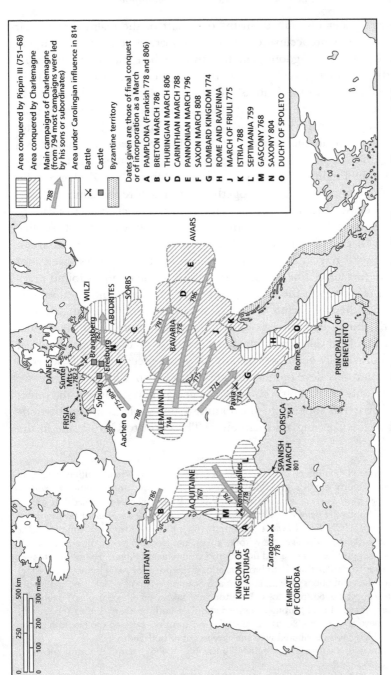

Map 3. The expansion of the Carolingian empire. Although the arrows suggest a primarily military expansion, many of the regions incorporated into the empire were taken without fighting.

each brother of councils in his own part of the realm shows their overlapping preoccupations: to consolidate a sense of identity in their new sub-kingdoms, and to reinforce the ecclesiastical structure, with better-organised personnel and tighter rules, to cement their kingdoms' common Frankish, Christian culture. That the need was greater in Carloman's sub-kingdom, which, being more easterly, bordered yet unchristianised lands, is explanation enough for his greater involvement in such activity at this time: we need not take it as a sign that Pippin was any less devout than his brother.[65] Letters both from the English missionary Boniface and from Pope Zacharias refer to the two brothers acting together to restructure the Church,[66] and Pippin also requested that the pope send to Francia copies of canons (ecclesiastical laws) from earlier councils.[67] It was from texts like these that Pippin later drew phrases that appear in his charters, about the moral responsibilities of the Christian ruler.[68] These were not mere formulae. The moral exhortations of the councils found practical reflection in the efforts of the Englishman Boniface, alongside many others, to bring the full apparatus of the Christian Church, with church buildings, priests, monasteries, monks and the regular round of liturgical practices, to areas east of the Rhine where it had previously been known only very imperfectly, if at all. We shall examine this development in greater detail in Chapter 3; here we need only say that little could have been achieved without the direct and material support of the Frankish upper class, and in particular of the Carolingians themselves. The effort to Christianise in the

---

[65] *Contra* H. Schüssler, 'Die fränkische Reichsteilung von Vieux-Poitiers (742) und die Reform der Kirche in den Teilreichen Karlmanns und Pippins', *Francia* 13 (1985), pp. 45–111; see also Collins, 'Pippin III as mayor of the palace', p. 91.

[66] In Boniface, *Epistolae, Ep.* 57 (ed. M. Tangl, *Die Briefe des Heiligen Bonifatius und Lullus*, MGH *Epp. selectae* 1 (Berlin, 1916), pp. 102–5, trans. E. Emerton, *The Letters of Saint Boniface* (New York, 1940), no. xlv, pp. 72–4), Boniface praised the support he had received from both Carloman and Pippin. *Ep.* 58 (pp. 105–8) refers to a letter from both brothers asking the pope for *pallia* (symbols of office) for the archbishops of Sens, Rheims and Soissons – two of which were in Pippin's territory; *Ep.* 60 (pp. 120–5; Emerton, no. xlviii, pp. 85–9, at p. 86) refers to a recent synod held 'through the mediation' of both brothers; *Ep.* 61 (pp. 125–7; Emerton, xlix, pp. 89–91), a general letter from the pope to the Frankish clergy and laity, was distributed with the agreement of both brothers.

[67] Boniface, *Epistolae, Ep.* 77, ed. Tangl, pp. 159–61, trans. Emerton, no. lxi, pp. 112–13.

[68] See e.g. Pippin's charter for Prüm, *Dipl. Kar.* 1, no. 16.

east was a telling practical result of very genuine Christian belief among powerful lay people. Another instance, of more immediate and dramatic significance for the Carolingians, occurred in the year after Cannstatt, 747, when Carloman abdicated his position and went off to Rome. It is not known if this was simply a pilgrimage, or whether from the start he intended it as the first step on a path towards the monastic habit in which he ended up, but he was certainly not the only such figure to become a monk in this period: others include the brothers' erstwhile opponent Hunoald, duke of the Aquitanians, as well as several Anglo-Saxon kings.[69]

It looks certain that on his abdication Carloman intended and expected his part of the Frankish realm to be given over to his son Drogo.[70] At first, in fact, this is precisely what happened: there is some evidence that Drogo was able to enjoy his father's inheritance for a short time.[71] Pippin had delayed marrying until three years after his father's death, and had then taken as his wife Bertrada, member of a family who were prominent landowners in Carloman's part of the kingdom. By 747 Bertrada had still borne no children, so Drogo remained the only direct heir of both Carloman and Pippin.[72] Initially, therefore, Carloman's abdication meant for Pippin not greater power, but more uncertainty. Very unusually, the Frankish army does not seem to have assembled in 747, and in that year too Pippin's half-brother Grifo was released, or escaped, from his captivity, and travelled to Bavaria.[73] As the product of a union between the Carolingians, in the person of Charles Martel, and the Agilolfings, in

[69] C. Stancliffe, 'Kings who opted out', in P. Wormald, D. Bullough and R. Collins (eds.), *Ideal and Reality in Frankish and Anglo-Saxon Society* (Oxford, 1983), pp. 154–76; for Hunoald, see *AMP*, p. 36. One set of annals suggests that Carloman took up the religious life in remorse for the slaughter at Cannstatt: *Annales Petaviani*, *s.a.* 746, ed. Pertz, *MGH SS* I, p. 11.

[70] Since it was written after Pippin was firmly established as king, the report of Fred., *Cont.*, c. 30 that on abdication Carloman 'handed over his rule together with his son Drogo' to Pippin has been widely and rightly mistrusted: e.g. Collins, 'Pippin III as mayor of the palace', p. 86.

[71] Boniface, *Epistolae, Ep.* 79, ed. Tangl, pp. 171–2, trans. Emerton, no. LXIII, pp. 119–20; Becher, 'Drogo und die Königserhebung Pippins'.

[72] J. L. Nelson, 'Bertrada', in Becher and Jarnut (eds.), *Der Dynastiewechsel von 751*, pp. 93–108.

[73] We are dependent for the news of Grifo's release on a later source: *AMP, s.a.* 747, pp. 39–40, which credits it to Pippin, 'moved by mercy'; see also Airlie, 'Towards a Carolingian aristocracy', pp. 116–17, and Fouracre, *Charles Martel*, pp. 172–3.

the person of Swanahild, he presented a powerful alternative focus of loyalty for the aristocracy, with potentially wider reach than Pippin. Duke Odilo having recently died, Grifo was able to make himself duke in Bavaria in 748, but Pippin managed to recapture him, restored Odilo's son Tassilo as duke and gave Grifo twelve counties in Neustria as recompense.[74] This was evidently not enough to satisfy his ambition, and he fled again, this time to Aquitaine.

In the meantime, Pippin's situation changed fundamentally when, in April 748, Bertrada finally gave birth to his son, Charles (the future Charlemagne).[75] It may have been this that prompted Pippin now single-mindedly to aim at hegemony for himself and his bloodline. Exterminating, rather than accommodating, Grifo was part of this. His other rival, Carloman's son Drogo, had now probably reached maturity. Concern for his son may lie behind Carloman's departure from his monastery to intervene again in Frankish politics, though one source says that rather than supporting his son Drogo, he delivered 'words of concord and peace' to Pippin and their half-brother Grifo.[76] If there is uncertainty whether Pippin considered as his chief opponent his half-brother or his nephew, it is at least clear that by the late 740s both were regarded as rivals rather than potential co-rulers.

Carloman's intervention shifts the focus to Italy, the affairs of which now impacted directly and momentously on Francia. The fact that it was the natural destination for Carloman following his abdication illustrates the attractive influence that Italy, and especially its cultural and religious connotations, exerted not just on the Franks, but on all western Christian peoples. Rome may have held particular fascination: by the end of the eighth century, it accommodated hostels specifically designated for Lombard, Frankish, Frisian and 'Saxon' (that is, Anglo-Saxon) pilgrims.[77] But Frankish relations had for generations also been cordial with the Lombards, who ruled most of the north and centre of Italy. This is attested most clearly by the adoption in 737 of Charles Martel's son Pippin by the Lombard king Liutprand, an act which forged a strong personal bond between the

---

[74] *ARF*, s.a. 748, trans. Scholz, p. 39.

[75] M. Becher, 'Neue Überlieferungen zum Geburtsdatum Karls des Großen', *Francia* 19 (1992), pp. 37–60.

[76] *Epistolae aevi Merowingici collectae*, no. 18, ed. W. Gundlach, *MGH Epp.* III (*Epp. Merovingici et Karolini aevi* I) (Berlin, 1892), p. 467.

[77] On the *scholae peregrinorum* (pilgrim hostels), see R. Schieffer, 'Charlemagne and Rome', in J. M. H. Smith (ed.), *Early Medieval Rome and the Christian West* (Leiden, 2000), pp. 279–95, at pp. 291–3.

two families.[78] The fact that Charles chose to secure it through his second son Pippin suggests that marriage with a daughter of Liutprand may have been mooted. Nothing came of this, but it might also be argued that the adoption of a Carolingian as a king's son was the first step towards the family's adoption of the kingship itself.[79] This kind of venture into Italian politics was never straightforward, however, as Pope Gregory III's response on this occasion indicates: he twice wrote to Charles seeking help against precisely the Lombard king to whom the Frank had so recently become related.[80] Conflict between the Lombards and the Byzantines, still then in control of large parts of central Italy, including Rome, had been a feature of Italian politics for generations. In the early eighth century, with the emperor making heavy fiscal demands on his Italian subjects, but with Byzantine strength in Italy simultaneously looking increasingly uncertain, indigenous Romans, and specifically the pope (their bishop), were prompted to explore other sources of help against Lombard pressure. The Franks were the obvious choice, and Gregory III's reported gifts to Charles, the keys to St Peter's tomb and a link from his chains, were certainly valuable.[81] Charles, though, resisted the pope's blandishments. Given the choice, he preferred the ability to treat with the Lombards as equals to an unpredictable entanglement with a new ally – the kudos arising from Liutprand's adoptive paternity over Pippin should not be underestimated.

Gregory III's failure did not discourage his successor, Pope Zacharias, from continuing to pursue closer relations with the Franks. The exchange of a string of letters with Boniface shows that Zacharias appreciated the opportunity that the Englishman's activities in northern Europe presented for extending papal authority among Christians there.[82] But what really brought the papacy, and Italian affairs, into the secular politics of the Franks was Carloman's arrival in Italy

---

[78] Paul the Deacon, *HL* VI, c. 53; see also next note.
[79] J. Jarnut, 'Die Adoption Pippins durch König Liutprand', in J. Jarnut, U. Nonn and M. Richter (eds.), *Karl Martell in seiner Zeit* (Sigmaringen, 1994), pp. 217–26; see also B. Kasten, *Königssöhne und Königsherrschaft. Untersuchungen zur Teilhabe am Reich in der Merowinger- und Karolingerzeit*, MGH Schriften 44 (Hanover, 1997), esp. p. 111.
[80] *CC*, nos. 1 and 2, pp. 476–8.   [81] Fred., *Cont.*, c. 22.
[82] Boniface, *Epistolae*, *Epp*. 50, 51, 52, 53, 57, 58, 59, 60, 61, 68, 77, 80, 82, 83, 86, 87, trans. Emerton, nos. XL, XLI, XLII, XLIII (pp. 56–69); XLV–XLIX (pp. 72–91); LIV (pp. 100–1); LXI (pp. 112–13); LXIV (pp. 120–7); LXVI–LXVII (pp. 128–32); LXX–LXXI (pp. 135–42).

following his abdication. Zacharias proved very adept at negotiating his way between interests and opinions in both the Frankish and the Lombard kingdoms. He handled Carloman carefully, giving him his monastic tonsure and apparently also bestowing on him the monastery on Monte Soracte, where he seems to have spent some time between 747 and 750 before entering the recently restored abbey of Monte Cassino, but he did not or could not prevent Carloman from continuing his interest in Frankish politics with the intervention that we have just noted.[83] Whether Carloman's journey back to Francia indicates that Zacharias had had him tonsured against his will is a much-debated, but ultimately unanswerable, question. The suggestion may underestimate the extent to which continued engagement with the secular world was possible in a cosmopolitan institution like Monte Cassino, for all its ascetic ideals. Carloman could return there, probably in 751, only to embark on a second mission north a few years later, as we shall see. Zacharias's dealings with the Lombards were equally astute. He was able to agree peaceful settlements with successive kings – Liutprand (712–44) and Ratchis (744–9) – even if on each occasion part of the price was a loss of Byzantine territory.[84] (See Figure 2 for the altar that Ratchis had made when he was duke of Friuli.) Among the Lombards themselves there were conflicting tendencies, aspiring on the one side towards peaceful co-existence with Byzantine territories in Italy, and on the other towards their conquest. While there were some Lombard aristocrats who were unwilling to risk themselves in war, there must certainly have been others who coveted the wealth, in both land and moveables, of the Byzantine lands.[85] It may have been this tension that lay behind the ousting in 749 of Ratchis, who was himself then sent to Monte Cassino, and his replacement by his brother Aistulf.

---

[83] For Carloman at Monte Soracte, see *CC*, no. 23, pp. 526–7, though note that the date of this letter is highly uncertain. For Carloman's monachisation and entry into Monte Cassino, see *LP* I, p. 433, trans. Davis, *Lives of the Eighth-Century Popes*, pp. 46–7.

[84] W. Pohl, 'Das Papsttum und die Langobarden', in Becher and Jarnut (eds.), *Der Dynastiewechsel von 751*, pp. 145–61, at pp. 148–51.

[85] For apparent reluctance among some Lombard aristocrats, see *CDL* I 114, *CDL* V 52; for wavering loyalty towards the kings on the part of some Lombard bishops, Pohl, 'Das Papsttum und die Langobarden', p. 155; S. Gasparri, 'Roma e i longobardi', in *Roma nell'alto medioevo*, Settimane di Studio del Centro italiano di studi sull'alto medioevo 48 (Spoleto, 2001), pp. 219–53, at pp. 246–7.

Figure 2. The altar of Duke Ratchis, commissioned 734–7 before he became king of the Lombards (744–9), is now in the Museo Cristiano del Duomo in Cividale del Friuli. While incompetence is one possible explanation for its obvious disproportions, it may be that the figures are abstractions, emphasising what were considered the most spiritual parts of the body – the head and hands – and so focussing attention on Christ's divinity.

The campaigns that Aistulf launched against the Byzantine territories in central Italy were certainly not unprecedented – Zacharias's desperate diplomacy with his predecessors Liutprand and Ratchis would hardly have been necessary if they had not been exerting similar pressure – but what made them significant was simply their success. By the summer of 751 he had conquered the whole of the Byzantine exarchate of Ravenna and the duchy of the Pentapolis, attacked Istria, and made a separate peace with Venice. In central Italy only Rome and its surrounding duchy remained outside his control.[86] These powerful actions provoked strong reactions in our key sources, though close analysis shows that they do not wholly justify the poor reputation from which the Lombard king has suffered in subsequent history. The ninth-century Ravennate chronicler Agnellus, for instance, certainly portrayed Aistulf as an oppressor, but overall he leaves the impression that he preferred Lombard to papal

[86] *Pauli continuatio cassinese*, c. 4, ed. G. Waitz, *MGH SRL* (Hanover, 1878).

domination.[87] Our principal contemporary sources for these years, papal letters and the *Liber pontificalis* biography of Pope Stephen, heap abuse onto Aistulf's head: in one letter this Catholic king is even called 'a devourer of the blood of Christians'.[88] Amid the hyperbole, though, Pope Stephen's biographer cannot avoid admitting that Aistulf actually renewed the peace treaty that Liutprand had made with the Romans, and indeed extended it to forty years. And while he says that Aistulf tried to exact 'tribute' from the Romans,[89] his emphasis on the pope's frequent diplomatic overtures, gifts and promises of peace to Aistulf, on the consent of the Romans for the pope's actions, and on divine favour, reads very much like a retrospective justification for Stephen's approach to Pippin, perhaps in reaction to direct criticism of the pope's actions, either within Rome or further afield. Yet on the ideological, if not the political, level, there was no question that the king and the pope were contesting control of the same ground. Aistulf's statement, in the prologue to his first set of laws, that the Roman people had been 'given to us by the Lord',[90] precisely conflicts with the papal claim to represent the whole of Byzantine Italy, advanced first categorically in Stephen II's pontificate: in 752 Stephen approached Aistulf 'for the entire exarchate of Ravenna and for the people of the whole of this province of Italy'.[91] The pope, that is, was asserting that he was representative of these 'Roman' people: not just the citizens of the city, but all those who still, in some way, regarded themselves as subjects of the 'Roman' (that is, Byzantine) emperor in Constantinople. Although this was a role apparently assigned to him by that emperor, the pope knew

---

[87] Agnellus, *Liber pontificalis ecclesiae Ravennatis*, ed. D. M. Deliyannis, *CCCM* 199 (Turnhout, 2006), *Vita Sergii*, cc. 155–6, trans. D. M. Deliyannis, *Agnellus of Ravenna. The Book of Pontiffs of the Church of Ravenna* (Washington, DC, 2004), pp. 279–80; for discussion of Agnellus, see J. M. Pizarro, *Writing Ravenna. The Liber pontificalis of Andreas Agnellus* (Ann Arbor, MI, 1995).

[88] *CC*, no. 11 ('devorator sanguinum Christianorum').

[89] *LP* I, pp. 441–2, trans. Davis, *Lives of the Eighth-Century Popes*, pp. 54–5.

[90] '...traditum nobis a Domino': *Leges Ahistulfi* [Laws of Aistulf], prologue, ed. F. Beyerle, *Leges langobardorum, 643–866. Die Gesetze der Langobarden* (Weimar, 1947; repr. Witzenhausen, 1962), p. 194; the translation by Fischer-Drew, *The Lombard Laws*, p. 227, is unfortunately and misleadingly wide of the mark here.

[91] *LP* I, c. 15, p. 444, trans. Davis, *Lives of the Eighth-Century Popes*, p. 58 ('pro universo exarchato Ravennae atque cunctae istius italiae provinciae populo...'); see further Pohl, 'Das Papsttum und die Langobarden', p. 157. That this statement is roughly contemporary seems confirmed by similar claims made in papal letters: see *CC* nos. 10 and 11 (probably dating from 756 and 757 respectively).

that, with the Byzantines looking increasingly unable to give practical help, he needed to turn elsewhere for a strong military ally. It was in this context that Stephen decided to leave Rome in October 753 and to head north, to the kingdom of the Franks.

While Aistulf was winning territory in Italy, Pippin had become king of the Franks. At the start of this chapter we looked at the difficulties in establishing precisely how this came about, difficulties which show that it was controversial – indeed, we have references to disloyalty among the aristocracy which suggest that the coup of 751 had not sealed the Carolingian victory.[92] Pippin therefore seized the opportunity presented by Pope Stephen's arrival in the winter of 753 to gain some endorsement for his takeover. The *Royal Frankish Annals* report that 'Pope Stephen confirmed Pippin as king by holy anointing and with him he anointed as kings his two sons, the Lords Charles and Carloman.'[93] The *quid pro quo* was not straightforward, however, because in seeking his support Pope Stephen was asking Pippin – and the Frankish aristocracy – to abandon a generations-long alliance with the Lombards, one which, as we have seen, in Pippin's case extended to his own spiritual paternity. It was a radical departure for the papacy too. Stephen's biographer works hard to present precedents for the alliance, but in reality no contemporary report before 753 gives the Franks any role in papal political diplomacy.[94] Named Frankish envoys to Rome appear in our sources only after Pope Stephen's initial soundings with Pippin.[95] The anointing of 753–4 carried enormous ideological implications for the future, since, as we have seen, apologists for the dynasty later celebrated papal endorsement as a crucial element in legitimising Carolingian kingship, and backdated it to coincide with the coup itself. But it also had immediate consequences for the last of Pippin's family rivals, who now found themselves marginalised even further. Not coincidentally, it was in 753 that Grifo was finally caught and killed by two of Pippin's counts while en route from Aquitaine to Italy – that this was a fully fledged battle indicates that he had retained

---

[92] *CC* no. 5.   [93] *ARF*, s.a. 754, trans. B. Scholz, *Carolingian Chronicles*, p. 40.

[94] Pohl, 'Das Papsttum und die Langobarden', p. 160: which is not to say that there had been no *contacts* between the Franks and the popes, just that they had not operated on the level of political negotiation.

[95] Abbot Droctegang was the first such envoy, with Bishop Chrodegang, Abbot Fulrad, and the dukes Autchar and Rothard subsequently involved: see *LP* I, c. 16, p. 444, c. 18, 20, p. 445, c. 24, p. 447, trans. Davis, *Lives of the Eighth-Century Popes*, pp. 59–62 (*Vita Stephani II*, cc. 16, 18, 20, 24).

substantial support to the last.[96] What's more, around the same time Carloman's sons (Drogo and an unnamed brother) were sent to a monastery. It was probably on their behalf that their father left his monastic retreat for a second time and travelled to Francia, but, whatever he thought he could achieve, he was swiftly detained and died soon after.[97] One may suspect, indeed, that Pippin's decision to risk all by seizing the throne, and by breaking the Lombard alliance in search of papal endorsement two years later, was prompted less by a desire to underline Carolingian superiority over the Merovingians than by a pressing need to make a decisive move in the fight for dominance within his own family: the birth of his first son Charles in 748 had given him an urgent incentive to push Drogo, Grifo and his other male relatives out of the picture for good.[98] Thirteen years after the death of Charles Martel, the junior branch of the Carolingians had established itself as unchallenged rulers of the Franks.

The papal anointing went hand in hand with Pippin's effort to convince the Frankish aristocracy to launch war against the Lombards. But persuading the warrior class to attack their erstwhile allies may have taken some time, even after the anointing: it was probably not until 755 that the Frankish army set out for the Alpine passes into Italy.[99] Defeating the Lombards there, Pippin then besieged Aistulf in his capital of Pavia, and forced him into an accommodation which essentially acknowledged his subordination to the Franks.[100] Yet this seems simply to have encouraged the Lombard king to go

---

[96] Fred., *Cont.*, c. 35.

[97] Compare *ARF*, s.a. 753 with the revised version of the same annal (trans. Scholz, p. 40), and *LP* I, c. 30, pp. 448–9. The *LP* says that Carloman was put into a monastery in Francia by Pippin and Pope Stephen, where he died after a few days; see further M. de Jong, 'Monastic prisoners or opting out? Political coercion and honour in the Frankish kingdoms', in de Jong and Theuws with van Rhijn (eds.), *Topographies of Power*, pp. 291–328.

[98] Becher, 'Drogo und die Königserhebung Pippins'; Fouracre, *Charles Martel*, pp. 171–4.

[99] Charter evidence for the summoning of the Lombard army in 754 has been taken to indicate that Pippin's campaign took place in that year; but this is not necessarily the case, and the sum of the evidence is consistent with a date for the first campaign of 755, as argued by T. F. X. Noble, *The Republic of St Peter. The Birth of the Papal State, 680–825* (Philadelphia, PA, 1984), p. 88, n. 113.

[100] This is often called the First Peace of Pavia, the terms of which are reported variously by Stephen's biographer and Frankish annalists: see *LP* I, p. 451, trans. Davis, *Lives of the Eighth-Century Popes*, pp. 67–8; *ARF*, s.a. 755; *AMP*, s.a. 754, pp. 46–7; *Pauli continuatio tertia*, c. 39, ed. G. Waitz, *MGH SRL* (Hanover, 1878), p. 210.

to the brink, and he besieged Rome early in 756. This in turn provoked a second Frankish campaign, a second siege of Pavia, and a
second peace treaty.[101] Once again the Franks had shown their military superiority over a neighbour. But almost since the day itself
doubts have circulated about the settlement that Pippin was thereby
able to impose. It looks certain that he deputed Fulrad of St Denis
to oversee Aistulf's relinquishing of a roster of cities in central Italy.
These, it seems, were to be transferred to St Peter, or rather to his
representative, the pope. But whether by this Pippin intended the
establishment of a papally governed 'state' seems more doubtful. This
was an age in which such matters were thought of in terms not of
territorial sovereignty, but of rights, about the definition of which
our evidence is very vague. Whatever Pippin tried to stipulate in
756, however, neither Aistulf nor his successor Desiderius (king from
757) did much to fulfil their part of the settlement, and control of
central Italy was once more contested in the reign of Charlemagne,
as we shall see.

After a hiatus under the later Merovingians, the ruler of the Franks
came back into the reckoning of other powerful rulers following Pippin's intervention in Italy. His contacts with the Byzantine emperor
Constantine V underline how uncertain the settlement of Italy still
was. It was shortly after his second successful Italian campaign – in 756
or 757 – that Pippin exchanged embassies with Constantine V, and,
according to the Continuator of Fredegar's *Chronicle*, 'through their
representatives each swore friendship and fidelity to the other'.[102]
Other sources tell us that Pippin and Pope Paul I sent a joint embassy
to Constantinople in 763, which returned three years later with a
reciprocal legation from the emperor. Among the subjects of discussion were certainly the theological innovations introduced by
Constantine V in Byzantium, reinterpreting the Trinity and denying
the validity of images of Christ and the saints in worship, and Pippin
attended a debate between the Byzantine envoys and Greek-speaking
Romans at Gentilly just outside Paris in 767.[103] But other points of
contact were more amicable: it was proposed that Pippin's daughter

---

[101] *LP* I, pp. 452–4, trans. Davis, *Lives of the Eighth-Century Popes*, pp. 70–2.
[102] Fred., *Cont.*, c. 40.
[103] For the despatch of the embassy in 763, *CC*, nos. 28 and 29; for the debate
at Gentilly, *CC*, nos. 36 and 37, convincingly interpreted by M. McCormick,
'Textes, images et iconoclasme dans le cadre des relations entre Byzance et
l'occident', *Testo e immagine nell'alto medioevo*, Settimane di Studio del Centro
italiano di studi sull'alto medioevo 41 (Spoleto, 1994), pp. 95–162.

Gisela might marry Constantine V's son, the future emperor Leo IV (reigned 775–80).[104] And the fact that Frankish envoys in turn accompanied the Byzantine legation back to Constantinople indicates that both sides saw the value of continued negotiation. All this shows how Pippin's military success was bringing him into contact with more distant rulers. He also despatched envoys to Baghdad in 763 or 764 and received a return embassy from the caliph in 767–8. Though our sources do not reveal it, the amicable nature of the contacts – gifts were exchanged and the Muslim envoys were escorted back as far as Marseille – and the strategic situation at the time suggest that one major subject of discussion would have been the situation in Spain and Aquitaine.[105] In these regions too things were changing: the Carolingians were not the only new (usurping) dynasty on the scene in the mid-eighth century. In the Muslim world the Abbasids had seized the caliphate from the Umayyad dynasty, one of whose last representatives had, however, managed to take power in Muslim-controlled Spain. Thus the Abbasid caliph al-Mansur faced in Spain a similar danger to that confronting Pippin in neighbouring Aquitaine; and thus, perhaps, the tentative contacts between the two.[106]

Aquitaine was in fact the overriding military concern of Pippin's reign as king. Although he also campaigned against the defiant Saxons in 753 and 758, a sustained Frankish effort there had to wait. As we have seen, it was the Aquitanian duke Hunoald who was the first regional leader against whom Pippin and Carloman had had to fight after their father's death, and while their campaigns in Aquitaine in 742 and 745 succeeded in pacifying the region temporarily, Pippin was called back there in 759 and thereafter had to make war against Hunoald's son Waifar in every year but one until 768. The annalistic record of these campaigns reveals that they were destructive affairs, a matter of small-scale raiding and counter-raiding, of the systematic ravaging of territory and, occasionally, of siege warfare.[107] By 768

---

[104] For the diplomatic to and fro of these years, see McCormick, *Origins of the European Economy. Communications and Commerce AD 600–900* (Cambridge, 2001), pp. 873–4; for the marriage proposal, *ARF, s.a.* 767.

[105] Fred., *Cont.*, c. 51.

[106] For this line of argument, see M. McCormick, 'Pippin III, the embassy of Caliph al Mansur, and the Mediterranean World', in Becher and Jarnut (eds.), *Der Dynastiewechsel von 751*, pp. 221–41.

[107] Halsall, *Warfare and Society*, pp. 136–8. For a sustained narrative, see McKitterick, *Frankish Kingdoms*, pp. 50–3.

Duke Waifar was a hunted man, and while on the run from his Frankish pursuers he was assassinated by his own men. Despite his death, Aquitanian resistance continued under Hunoald II, probably his son. But Pippin's own son, the twenty-year-old Charles, was now well placed to batter down the doors his father had cracked open.

CHARLEMAGNE AS KING

When Pippin died in September 768, therefore, the Aquitanians' continuing rebellion was the first problem confronting his sons Carloman and Charles (hereafter to be known by the name he has borne through subsequent history: Charlemagne – Charles 'the Great'). The brothers marched into Aquitaine together in 769, but for some reason, perhaps a quarrel over the division of the duchy between them, Carloman soon returned home, and it was left to Charles to chase down Hunoald. His capture marked the end of Aquitanian resistance. The wars there from 759 to 769 demonstrate how solid was the Carolingians' control now of the resources and manpower of their heartlands. In the end the Aquitanians were ground down by relentless, year-after-year campaigning. The ability to do this allowed the Carolingians to inflict a new level of defeat on their enemies. They used the same technique in Saxony, as we shall see, and it must be significant that, once subdued, neither the Saxons nor the Aquitanians seriously challenged Carolingian rule thereafter.

The falling out of Charlemagne and Carloman in 769 was the first sign of difficulties between the two brothers that played themselves out over the next two years, chiefly in the context of continued uncertainty in Italy. The brothers were made fully aware of papal anxieties in a letter from Pope Stephen III (768–72) in 770, urging them to help the pope to secure what he saw as his rights.[108] At about that time, their mother Bertrada travelled to Italy with a rather different object in mind: the marriage of her elder son Charlemagne to the daughter of the Lombard king Desiderius, who was probably named Gerperga. There was some strategic sense in this: Desiderius was in a strong position, having married other daughters to the rulers of Bavaria and Benevento – a significant proportion of the

---

[108] *CC*, no. 44.

'independent' Christian rulers in continental western Europe.[109] Nonetheless, it seems clear that Bertrada's initiative was an act beneficial to one son (Charlemagne) and prejudicial to the other (Carloman). Charlemagne's marriage meant that Carloman was encircled, by his brother, by King Desiderius, and by Tassilo, duke of the Bavarians and husband of another of the Lombard king's daughters.[110]

The political logic changed utterly, however, with Carloman's premature death in December 771.[111] Charlemagne's priority now was to weld his brother's sub-kingdom, and especially its aristocracy, to his own. The need to create unity within the Frankish realm necessitated a change of stance toward those beyond it. Thus Charlemagne now sought in marriage Hildegard, a descendant of the ducal house of Alemannia, in order to secure that part of Carloman's former kingdom. This, of course, meant the repudiation of the Lombard princess and, inevitably, the enmity of her father. At the same time, in Rome, Pope Stephen III, who had been in favour of the Franco-Lombard alliance (it at least helped him get the disputed towns that he wanted), died and was replaced by Hadrian I, who was far more inimical towards the Lombards. With Charlemagne intent on taking over his late brother's kingdom, and members of the latter's following deserting to his side – among them Fulrad, the abbot of St Denis, and his eventual successor Maginarius – Carloman's wife and children fled for refuge to Desiderius. The Lombard king now reversed his policy and once more began to threaten Rome. This prompted an appeal for help from Pope Hadrian to Charlemagne. The latter initially offered Desiderius money if he would restore captured towns, but he refused. So, very late in the campaigning season in 773, Charlemagne launched a two-pronged attack on Italy, over the Mont Cenis and Great St Bernard Passes. Desiderius, perhaps thinking that

[109] The only others being the king of Asturias (then Silo), and the duke of the Bretons.

[110] On this marriage, see J. L. Nelson, 'Making a difference in eighth-century politics: the daughters of Desiderius', in A. C. Murray (ed.), *After Rome's Fall: Narrators and Sources of Early Medieval History. Essays presented to Walter Goffart* (Toronto, 1998), pp. 171–90, at pp. 178–84; on the name Gerperga, p. 183.

[111] For the events of this paragraph, see Noble, *Republic of St Peter*, pp. 99–137; R. Collins, *Charlemagne* (Basingstoke, 1998), pp. 38–9; Costambeys, *Power and Patronage*, Chapter 8; J. Jarnut, 'Ein Bruderkampf und seine Folgen: die Krise des Frankenreiches (768–771)', in G. Jenal and S. Haarländer (eds.), *Herrschaft, Kirche, Kultur: Beiträge zur Geschichte des Mittelalters. Festschrift für Friedrich Prinz zu seinem 65. Geburtstag* (Stuttgart, 1993), pp. 165–76.

the Franks would return home at the end of the season as Pippin had done in 755 and 756, took refuge behind the walls of his capital, Pavia. However, in another sign of the step change in Frankish military capability under the Carolingians, Charlemagne kept his army before the walls of Pavia throughout the winter of 773–4. The siege was sufficiently secure for Charles to be able to travel to Rome to celebrate Easter in 774. By June, Desiderius was ready to surrender. He was taken into exile in Francia, his son Adelchis having fled to Constantinople. Carloman's children, meanwhile, vanished from history: once more, there is a suspicion that the outward expansion of Carolingian power was driven partly by a need to eliminate the threat represented by members of the dynasty itself.

Charlemagne's assumption of the title 'King of the Lombards' (*rex langobardorum*) in the summer of 774 was an act without parallel. No west European king had taken another's kingdom and title by force for over 200 years.[112] The relative ease with which Charlemagne accomplished the transfer indicates two things. First, it suggests that the bulk of the Lombard aristocracy submitted to Charlemagne's rule in the first half of 774: certainly, he was initially willing to let them keep their offices. And secondly, it points to a radically more ambitious attitude on the part of the Frankish king. The aim now was not merely to pacify or to dominate through the exaction of tribute, but to rule. This shows the degree to which Charlemagne now felt secure in his government of the Frankish kingdom proper. In northern Italy, Lombard resistance to the Carolingian takeover was a piecemeal and half-hearted affair. Charlemagne had to return to Italy in 776 to suppress a rebellion launched the previous year by the dukes of Friuli and Treviso. Although the rebels may have harboured the aspiration that other Lombard dukes would join them, there is no evidence that any did so, and the revolt ended with the killing of Duke Hrodgaud of Friuli.[113] Frankish counts now replaced Lombard dukes in those cities that had resisted. Charlemagne returned to Italy twice in the next ten years. A trip to Rome in 780–1 saw the anointing and crowning by the pope of his two younger sons, Pippin

---

[112] See Collins, *Charlemagne*, p. 62. The point applies only to kings: note that both Merovingians and Carolingians had at times replaced lesser rulers, in, for example, Aquitaine and Alemannia.

[113] The only evidence of the aspiration is a letter of Pope Hadrian, who had an interest in talking up the hostility of some Lombard dukes to Frankish rule: *CC*, no. 57, pp. 582–3.

and Louis. Charles clearly already had an eye on the future: Pippin was to be king of the Lombards, Louis of the Aquitanians (both nominal appointments at first, since the boys were children); we must assume that he intended his elder son Charles to succeed to the Frankish kingdom proper.[114] In 786 Charlemagne entered Italy with the express purpose of bringing to heel the Lombard duchy of Benevento, which covered most of southern Italy and had always been a separate entity from the Lombard kingdom in the north. After the deposition of Desiderius, Arichis II, the duke of Benevento, had begun to style himself 'prince'. Charlemagne was rapidly successful, receiving hostages, including Arichis's younger son Grimoald, and oaths from both the prince and his leading men, though he did not attempt to rule Benevento directly.

The Frankish conquest of northern Italy and, in particular, Pope Hadrian's decisive commitment to a Frankish alliance, radically affected relations with the dominant power in the east, the Byzantine empire. The city of Rome itself was the key to this change, for Byzantium was simply the continuation of the eastern portion of the old Roman empire, and as long as it held Rome – however nominally – that continuity was real. Once the city had fallen under Frankish 'protection' (which in practical terms meant military and political domination), Byzantium was a Roman empire without Rome. Yet Byzantine weakness, which had caused the popes to look to the Franks as alternative protectors in the first place, meant that Constantinople harboured few realistic hopes of military action to recover Italian lands. Their attitude to the Franks was therefore ambivalent. They could entertain, as they did in the 780s, secret negotiations with Prince Arichis of Benevento, while at the same time pursuing a plan hatched in 781 for the marriage of the young emperor Constantine VI to Charlemagne's daughter, Rotrud. That this potentially momentous match did not come about seems to have been due to reluctance on the part of Charlemagne, who refused to send Rotrud to Constantinople. In 788 he allowed his Beneventan hostage Grimoald to return to the principality, to become a ruler with what he hoped would be a pro-Frankish stance. As a result, the Byzantines sent an army to southern Italy. It is significant,

[114] J. L. Nelson, 'Charlemagne – Pater Optimus?', in P. Godman, J. Jarnut and P. Johanek (eds.), *Am Vorabend der Kaiserkrönung: das Epos "Karolus Magnus et Leo papa" und der Papstbesuch in Paderborn 799* (Berlin, 2002), pp. 271–83.

however, that this was opposed, and heavily defeated, by Grimoald of Benevento and Duke Hildeprand of Spoleto, both still nominally independent Lombard rulers. This did not, however, indicate complete Carolingian domination of Benevento, which had to wait until after 800. In the meantime, Byzantine policy towards the Frankish kingdom remained changeable. The Byzantine dowager empress and regent Irene may have pleased the pope by her attempts to undo the previous emperors' religious policy of iconoclasm, particularly at the Synod of Nicaea in 787, but among north European theologians (using a faulty translation of that synod) it prompted only further condemnation of Byzantine practices as now constituting the veneration of images.[115] It did not help relations that Constantine VI then lost a violent power struggle with his mother Irene, who blinded him (causing wounds from which he subsequently died). Following this, it could be considered by the Franks that the imperial throne in Constantinople, occupied by a woman, was effectively vacant.

The successful conclusion of the Beneventan campaign in 787 allowed Charlemagne to deal with the last of the quasi-independent duchies bordering Francia itself – Bavaria. Much mystery surrounds the background to the fate of Bavaria. Its duke, Tassilo, had been in exile at the Frankish court until his reinstallation in 748, as we have seen.[116] According to the *Royal Frankish Annals*, Tassilo not only owed the recovery of his duchy to Pippin, but went on to swear formal loyalty to the Frankish kings in 757 and 781. Then, in the later 780s, Charlemagne took a series of increasingly stringent measures with the clear object of eradicating the Bavarian duchy's independence: a disagreement between Charlemagne and Pope Hadrian on one side, and Bavarian envoys on the other, led in 787 to a three-pronged Frankish invasion of Bavaria, which the duke fended off only by swearing further oaths of loyalty and handing over hostages. The following year Tassilo attended an assembly at Charlemagne's palace of Ingelheim, was accused of disloyalty (some of the charges relating to events almost three decades in the past) and apparently helplessly submitted. He was tonsured and sent to a monastery, in what the Carolingian sources claim, with jaw-dropping cynicism, was an act of mercy (the original sentence having been death).

---

[115] See T. F. X. Noble, *Images, Iconoclasm and the Carolingians* (Philadelphia, PA, 2009); and below, Chapter 3.
[116] See above, pp. 55–6.

Not surprisingly, we have to take this account with a strong pinch of salt. The first section of the *Royal Frankish Annals* is thought to have been compiled around this very time (late 780s), and it is therefore hardly surprising to find that it presents a carefully manufactured retrospective argument against Tassilo. The details of this account have been exposed as extremely tendentious, and in places demonstrably inaccurate – indeed, the text itself has to be seen as part of the process mobilised against Tassilo, rather than a detached description of it.[117] All this gives the strong impression that Charlemagne had already made up his mind that he wanted to be rid of the duke, and that the annexation of Bavaria was unprovoked. That he succeeded may seem inevitable with hindsight, but in truth it was anything but: Tassilo was a powerful and independent ruler and the scion of a long-established ducal dynasty. (See Figure 3 for the Tassilo Chalice, the inscription of which shows the Bavarian duke's desire to assert his own leadership credentials, in the face of the growing power of his Carolingian neighbours.) He was also considerably older and more experienced than the Frankish king – his downfall, engineered without significant bloodshed, testifies to Charlemagne's astonishing political sagacity as well as his overwhelming military resources. When considering Charlemagne's motives, we should recall that Tassilo was a grandson of Charles Martel and therefore a member of the Carolingian family; and that the duke's son was also taken into Frankish custody and tonsured. Once more, we have to ask whether territorial expansion was conceived with one eye on the family tree. Bavaria was carved up into counties on the Frankish model and entrusted to the overall supervision of Charlemagne's brother-in-law, Count Gerold.

The principal charge against Tassilo in 788 was that he had been plotting with the Avars. The latter were an originally nomadic, Asiatic people who had in the sixth century taken control of a huge swathe of land along the middle Danube and its tributaries. From there they posed a perennial threat to north-eastern Italy, and thus became a concern for Charlemagne after his invasion across the Alps in 774. One of the first recorded clashes between Franks and Avars took place in northern Italy in 788; the two sides also came

---

[117] M. Becher, *Eid und Herrschaft. Untersuchungen zum Herrscherethos Karls des Großen* (Sigmaringen, 1993); S. Airlie, 'Narratives of triumph and rituals of submission: Charlemagne's mastering of Bavaria', *TRHS* 6th ser. 9 (1999), pp. 93–119.

Figure 3. The Tassilo Chalice was given by Tassilo III, duke of the Bavarians (748–88) and his wife, the Lombard princess Liutperga (here 'Liutpirc'), to the monastery of Kremsmünster, probably at the time when Tassilo founded it in 777. Cast in bronze, and depicting Christ and saints, its inscription reads 'TASSILO DVX FORTIS + LIVTPIRC VIRGA REGALIS' (brave Duke Tassilo + Liutperga royal scion).

to blows in Bavaria at the same time.[118] There then seem to have been some diplomatic contacts, apparently concerning the frontier between the territories of Charlemagne and the Avar ruler, the *khagan*. Then, at an assembly in Regensburg in 791, Charlemagne

[118] *ARF, s.a.* 788.

organised a two-pronged attack on the Avar lands, with an army including Saxon and Frisian contingents. Accounts of this campaign reveal a strong religious element: the army spent three days in penitential fasting and prayer before entering the territory of the pagan Avars.[119] The Avars' response to this attack was far more feeble than their fearsome reputation had promised, and Charlemagne's armies returned home having ravaged the western part of their lands with impunity. For the next few years he was occupied with fighting elsewhere, but the Avars proved quite capable of damaging their cause for themselves, as the evidence points to the outbreak of a civil war among them. It fell to Eric, duke of the north-east Italian frontier region of Friuli, to take advantage of this. In 796 he launched an expedition that attacked and successfully plundered the Avars' *Hringum* or 'Ring', their main royal residence and collection point for the tribute and treasure that they had accumulated over many generations. Charlemagne's son Pippin, king of Italy, launched a second expedition in the same year to complete the destruction. The weakness of the Avars in the face of these attacks suggests that, however militarily powerful the Franks may have been, the Avar confederation was collapsing in any case, and the Franks were simply fortunate enough to be in the right position to benefit from its fall. The extent of that benefit is clear from the evidence that Charlemagne sought, successfully, to enhance Carolingian prestige by lavishly distributing gifts from the Avar treasure hoards to his neighbours, such as King Offa of Mercia, and to the Church.[120] Some of the Avar leaders seem to have accepted baptism before their defeat in 796 (indeed, this may have contributed to fractures in the confederacy and hence to the Carolingian victory), but in its wake were sent missionaries directed by Arno, bishop of Salzburg. The next phase of the history of that region was to be that of Christianisation, but it is a story that belongs to the ninth century, and does not really feature the Avars, who disappear from the record within a generation of the Frankish victory: their last appearance comes in 822, when they are recorded as having sent gifts and envoys to Louis the Pious.[121]

[119] *ARF, s.a.* 791.
[120] For the gift to Offa, see Alcuin, *Ep.* 100, trans. Loyn and Percival, *Reign of Charlemagne*, no. 28, trans. King, *Charlemagne: Translated Sources*, pp. 312–14. For the general impact of the treasure: Einhard, *VK*, c. 13.
[121] *ARF, s.a.* 822.

Warfare and religion were far from inseparable: after all, the Franks sometimes fought other Christians, and habitually conducted peaceful relations with non-Christian neighbours. Yet they merged nowhere more clearly, more protractedly and more bloodily than in the Frankish campaigns against the Saxons. Their sheer duration, lasting thirty years, makes them the most prolonged and, probably, most costly of Charlemagne's military activities. It is unlikely, however, that he anticipated their importance from the start. After all, the Franks had fought intermittent campaigns against the Saxons for the previous 250 years – Charlemagne's father and grandfather had done so, as we have seen – without ever getting bogged down. Several reasons conjoined in Charlemagne's reign to make the Saxons a more difficult problem. First, they seem unquestionably to have been expanding their territory south from the Lippe valley where Carloman and Pippin had tried to limit it in their campaigns of the 740s. Secondly, the tendency of Frankish sources to describe Saxon aggression in terms of 'rebellion' and 'infidelity' was not mere rhetoric. For while successful campaigns normally concluded with the soldiers of the losing side swearing oaths *en masse* to respect agreed peace terms, in the case of the pagan Saxons, their difference in religion with Christian Franks meant that their oaths were insecure. Already, therefore, Carloman in 744 and Pippin in 747 had made efforts to Christianise the Saxons, baptising those whom they captured.[122] Christianisation was plainly one motivation behind Charlemagne's initial campaign too. In 772, having captured the fortress of Eresburg, his army proceeded to destroy the Irminsul, an idol or shrine that was clearly a place of religious significance to Saxon paganism.[123] Retaliation by the Saxons in 773 was followed, in the winter of 774 and still more in 775, by concerted Frankish efforts to subdue them. These were successful in extracting formal submissions and hostages from some of the major sub-groups into which the Saxons were divided. Frankish suspicions about the value of such deals were confirmed in the following year, however. While Charlemagne was suppressing Hrodgaud's revolt in Italy, the Saxons attacked Frankish-held fortresses. Marching north late in 776, Charlemagne now for the first time forced one group to be baptised. Significantly, he held the Franks' annual assembly

---

[122] Fred., *Cont.*, cc. 27 and 31.
[123] *ARF*, *s.a.* 772. For a full narrative of the Saxon wars, Collins, *Charlemagne*, pp. 47–56, and see *ARF*, *s.a.* 772–802.

the next year at the new fortress that he had established in Saxony, Paderborn. But not all were subdued: a Saxon leader called Widukind remained in revolt and fled to the north at this time. Any thoughts of Saxon submission once again proved temporary, for in the next year the Saxons raided the Frankish Rhineland, provoking, in 779 and 780, renewed Frankish campaigns and further mass baptisms. The indecisiveness of all this warfare reflects not just the insecurity of oaths and treaties due to religious differences, but also the lack of a shared political culture between the antagonists: the Saxons, most importantly, had no king, and decisions were apparently made at gatherings of lesser leaders.[124] Would-be invaders therefore faced a many-headed hydra, and could not hope for a decisive victory by capturing an identifiable political centre.

In 782 Charlemagne issued what is known as the First Saxon Capitulary, outlining thirty-four new laws to be applied to the Saxons, many of them of Christianising intent, from the prohibition of human sacrifice to the death penalty for eating meat during Lent. These provisions were unprecedented – the Franks had never before tried to impose Christianity on a conquered population in so systematic a way. Most significant was the imposition of tithe (a payment of a tenth of the moveable wealth and produce of all free men for the support of the Church), which shows that 'Christianisation' implied not just strictures about religious belief, but involved forced adjustment of social structures, ways of life, and even economic behaviour. Such measures provoked hostility not just from the Saxons themselves but also from Charlemagne's own advisers. The Northumbrian Alcuin, a leading scholar at Charlemagne's court, wrote to Arno of Salzburg and to Charlemagne, declaring tithes to be an impediment to Christianisation: how could new converts be genuinely brought to God through such oppression?[125] This kind of stringency on the part of the Franks must have contributed to the almost immediate, and serious, uprising of the Saxons. A contingent of Franks was heavily defeated in the Süntel mountains, provoking dramatic retribution from Charlemagne: according to one annalist, 4,500 Saxons were summarily executed.[126] Yet even this did not bring an end

---

[124] D. H. Green and F. Siegmund (eds.), *The Continental Saxons from the Migration Period to the Tenth Century: an Ethnographic Perspective* (Woodbridge, 2003).

[125] Alcuin, *Ep.* 107 (to Arno) and 110, 174 (to Charlemagne); P. E. Dutton (ed.), *Carolingian Civilization: a Reader*, 2nd edn (Peterborough, ON, 2004), pp. 125–7.

[126] *ARF*, s.a. 782.

to what had become a general rebellion, and the Franks had to fight intensively in Saxony in the next few years, even campaigning through the winter of 784–5. This seemed to have achieved its objective when Widukind surrendered and received baptism, with Charlemagne standing as godfather. But peace was not to last long. In 793, perhaps attempting to capitalise on Pippin 'the Hunchback's' revolt against Charlemagne, the Saxons once more rebelled. The king retaliated in 794, and the next few years saw tit-for-tat rebellions and punitive campaigns. In contrast to the wars of the 770s and 780s, fighting is now reported to have taken place mostly in northern Saxony, and the Franks enlisted the support of the Saxons' neighbours to the east, the Abodrite Slavs. Despite a further setback in 798 when a number of Frankish nobles are reported as having been killed, the Saxons' gradual subjugation was brought about by a combination of the Abodrite alliance, constant campaigning (Charlemagne wintered in Saxony again in 797–8) and increasingly repressive measures against recalcitrants. The latter included mass deportations, recorded in 799 and, more extensively, in 804. The Chronicle of Moissac reports that 'the emperor sent his *scarae* [armies] . . . into Wihmodia [part of northern Saxony] . . . to take the people there away, out of their homeland; and he also removed the Saxons beyond the Elbe from their homes, and he dispersed them within his kingdom where he saw fit'.[127]

Charlemagne's campaigns against the Lombards, Avars and Saxons were essentially wars of expansion that took the Frankish empire beyond its traditional frontiers. The reconstruction by military means of the old Merovingian hegemony had really been completed slightly earlier with the defeat of the duke of Aquitaine. This achievement, in 769, saw the end of nearly a century of faction-fighting and fractioning of kingdoms that had begun, as we have seen, in 675. A mere glance at this history, which was being written up so busily in the later eighth century by the continuators of Fredegar's *Chronicle* and the compilers of the *Royal Frankish Annals*, made palpably clear to Pippin III and Charlemagne what were the keenest dangers to their rule: on the one hand competition for dominance within the Carolingian dynasty, and on the other the centrifugal tendencies among the ruling class which continually encouraged the pursuit by individuals, families and factions of goals that were detrimental to

[127] *Chron. Moiss.*, s.a. 802, pp. 306–7, trans. King, p. 146.

Carolingian kingship. The political history of this century is thus a story not just about 'the rise of the Carolingians', but equally one about the rise of some Carolingians at the expense of others – and the two stories are inextricably linked. Following them has taken us on a body-strewn path through late-seventh- and eighth-century history, at whose end we find the triumphant figure of Charlemagne. Yet while he was unquestionably more powerful than any of his predecessors, his position would not have been possible without their efforts. Nor was that position ever totally secure: he had to keep running just to stand still. Once the 'peripheral' provinces of Alemannia, Bavaria and Aquitaine had been conquered, their elites had to be tied into a new, king-centred, system. How, in the eighth century, was this to be achieved?

The first, earliest and principal means was, as we have already pointed out, to wage war. The eighth century was a century of aggressive warfare; much more so, as far as the Franks and their neighbours were concerned, than the seventh (and especially the second half of the seventh). To our annalists, it was a surprise when a year passed without a campaign.[128] And as the eighth century progressed, that aggression was increasingly, and then routinely, led by the king. It can hardly be coincidental, then, that the seventh century witnessed the gradual diminution of royal power, while the eighth saw it steadily increase. In order to fight alongside the king (or, initially, the mayor of the palace) one had to pledge loyalty to him, and back up that pledge with action; in return, one qualified for the king's gratitude, usually by sharing in the resources or position of his vanquished foes. This links to the second means of binding together the potentially fractious aristocracy: the distribution by the ruler of office, or what in the early Middle Ages were called *honores*. In most places government seems to have continued at a local level through the upheavals of the earlier eighth century. The Carolingians were fortunate that the old Merovingian structure of counts and bishops had survived. These offices were still valued; they still bestowed real advantages on their holders. Reconnecting them to the kingship meant providing, or reinvigorating, central places that allowed physical access to, and personal contact with, the king, as well as with other officeholders. Thus in Pippin III's reign, and still more in Charlemagne's, we see a renewed emphasis on the court as a forum for aristocratic activity. As under the Merovingians, this court was at first itinerant, travelling

---

[128] E.g. *ARF*, s.a. 792.

between a number of royal villas spread out across the heartland. The choice of a particular estate at any given time was determined by the resources available there and by political or military necessity. The Avar campaign thus necessitated a protracted stay for Charlemagne at Regensburg from the winter of 791 to the spring of 793. Yet at this very period we can also see a desire for greater stability, as work began on a more permanent palace complex at Aachen, which became Charlemagne's principal, though still not his only, residence from 796. Excavation has revealed something of the plan of this site, as also at Ingelheim, where he stayed in 787 and 788, and which became a favourite of Louis the Pious. Perhaps the most prominent building in both was the chapel – that at Aachen still surviving as part of the later cathedral. It was here that, throughout the Carolingian era, the king's most ritualised acts were performed.[129] Less formal, but of equal importance, was the personal contact that took place between the king and his aristocracy, contact that reaffirmed the bonds of the battlefield through communal activities like hunting and feasting and reinforced loyalty through conspicuous generosity of lands, material goods and offices. Among those who benefited from such activity we can mention Gairefred and Gairhard, who were successively counts of Paris, an office that their family held consistently from 753, if not earlier, to 858.[130] Their example shows the constant tension between this society's strong propensity towards heritability, and the ideal of *ministerium* – service in an office for which one had to show oneself worthy. Families like that of Gairhard sought to pass their *honores* down through the family because they were secure from the vagaries of partible inheritance. The strong competition for position that this situation created was perfectly manageable while the realm was expanding and the kings were stern enough occasionally to replace the incompetent and the disloyal. Thus in Pippin III's and Charlemagne's reigns, the traffic in *honores* maintained a low hum that denoted the operation of healthy, king-centred government.[131]

[129] J. L. Nelson, 'The Lord's anointed and the people's choice: Carolingian royal ritual', in D. Cannadine and S. Price (eds.), *Rituals of Royalty* (Cambridge, 1987), pp. 137–80; repr. in Nelson, *Frankish World*, pp. 99–131.

[130] R Hennebicque-Le Jan, 'Prosopographica neustrica. Les Agents du roi en Neustrie de 639 à 840', in H. Atsma (ed.), *La Neustrie: les pays au nord de la Loire de 650 à 850*, Beihefte der Francia 16, 2 vols. (Sigmaringen, 1989), I, pp. 231–69, at pp. 236–7; also Fouracre, *Charles Martel*, pp. 163–4.

[131] For more on these themes see below, Chapter 4.

Yet there remained tension not far below the surface. Even the strongly pro-Carolingian sources cannot hide from us a major rebellion east of the Rhine in 785–6 which expressed outright opposition to the dynasty's authority – the rebels said they wanted to kill the king. Charlemagne prevailed, but only by mutilating and murdering the ringleaders – an extreme penalty that smacks uncomfortably of royal insecurity.[132] The peoples incorporated into the Frankish empire did not necessarily take it lying down. Be that as it may, dissent within the Carolingian family itself remained a more serious threat to the ruler. Since his marriage to the Lombard princess in 770, Charlemagne had increasingly marginalised his eldest son with Himiltrude, Pippin (known, on the basis of a report by Einhard, as 'the Hunchback'). That he did not figure in his father's plans for the future must have been plain when the king had his second son with Hildegard, hitherto called Carloman, renamed Pippin after his baptism by the pope.[133] Little wonder, perhaps, that Pippin 'the Hunchback' eventually instigated a conspiracy against Charlemagne. The plot was uncovered by a Lombard called Fardulf (later made abbot of St Denis for his trouble), and Pippin was packed off to the monastery of Prüm. His co-conspirators were executed. The fact that Pippin seemingly attracted substantial support – that his plot was not confined within the family – points to the dangers and responsibilities that had been thrust upon Charlemagne as king. Even his virtually boundless success could not give satisfaction to every aristocrat in his expanding realm. By rewarding some he was automatically denying opportunity to others, who might find in disenchanted members of the royal family a convenient focus for their resentments.

What is more, the principal response to these two conspiracies, a royal capitulary (edict) issued at Regensburg in 789, indicates that those who acquired office did not always use it as the king might wish.[134] Men had complained, it says, that 'they do not have their law maintained'. The king was forced to affirm that if anyone had suffered anything contrary to their law, it was certainly not by his command: 'indeed, if a count or *missus* or any man has done this, let it be reported to the lord king, for he wishes to set such matters

---

[132] For this paragraph see J. L. Nelson, *Opposition to Charlemagne* (German Historical Institute, London, 2008).

[133] Nelson, 'Pater optimus' discusses the shifting succession arrangements.

[134] Capitularies are discussed more fully in Chapter 4.

most fully to rights'.[135] The law, then, did not reside with the king: it belonged to each man, and it was the king's responsibility to uphold it. But how effectively he could do so – how effective Carolingian government ultimately was – depended in large part on his agents: on their debt to, and loyalty to, the king. Through their own actions, or lack thereof, royal agents could make enemies for the king. They, as much as Charlemagne, could provide ammunition for hostility among other aristocrats, and there might be little to balance this out. After all, as the rebels of 785–6 had pointed out when questioned, they had sworn no oath of fidelity to the king. Hence the major provision of that same 789 capitulary was to require the king's envoys to ensure that all the more important of Charlemagne's subjects swore an oath of loyalty to him. But the king required a *quid pro quo*. Stipulations about the oath are followed by a requirement from the elite of something even more crucial: participation in the army.[136] In this capitulary, then, the oath was the preliminary, if not the prerequisite, for service in the army, that most significant badge of aristocratic identity. The first step on the road to elite status could now not be made without sworn loyalty to Charlemagne.

---

[135] *Capit.* I, no. 25, trans. King, *Charlemagne*, p. 223.
[136] *Capit.* I, no. 25, c. 6, trans. King, *Charlemagne*, p. 223.

3

BELIEF AND CULTURE

In the first two chapters we have made regular references to the Christian character of the Frankish court, which acted as a powerful patron associated with the founding of monasteries, the patronage of holy men and intellectuals, and the production and standardisation of religious texts. Well before the end of the eighth century, where we left Charlemagne demanding comprehensive oaths of loyalty from his elite male subjects, and indeed before the anointing of 753–4, kingship itself was conceived as an office with religious responsibilities. Christianity was part of the very identity of elite Franks, who increasingly came to see themselves as a people chosen by God, and thus to define themselves in distinction to the non- and imperfectly Christian peoples that surrounded them. These ideologies played a part in the Franks' justifications to each other and to themselves of their conquests. As victorious Carolingian armies withdrew they were often – as we have seen – replaced by missionaries, charged with winning the hearts and souls of the conquered, and with establishing their obedience to the Frankish Church (and, therefore, empire). Even if we find it to be outlandish or distasteful, we should not be surprised that Frankish kings thought themselves to have a moral responsibility to save the souls of those under their dominion, nor should we write this off as moral posturing designed to justify territorial expansion – after all, given the long decades of virtually unblemished military success, how could they not believe they were doing God's work? These themes represent central aspects of Carolingian politics and society which have been touched on earlier in this book, but which take centre stage in this chapter – here we hope to explain the mentalities and intellectual attitudes that informed the actions of those involved in the high politics of the previous chapter.

Yet placing Carolingian Christianity under the spotlight complicates matters more than one might expect. The closer we look at the concepts of religion, paganism, the Church, and Christianity itself, as they operated in early medieval Europe, the more they start to fall apart under our gaze. By placing Carolingian Christianity in a broad context, the chapter is therefore intended to shake the foundations of some commonly held modern assumptions about the early Middle Ages, as well as to offer some reorientation. The discussion is divided into three main sections: the problem of Christianisation; the problem of sin; and the role in society of Christian kingship and learning. But to understand the place of these phenomena in eighth- and ninth-century Europe, we must first define our terms of reference, and ask what we mean when we talk about paganism, Christianity and the Church. We can begin exploring these questions by visiting the Carolingian court itself.

THE PROBLEM OF CHRISTIANISATION

Defining Christianity

When, towards 860, Lothar II, king of the Franks, wanted to get divorced, some of his bishops wrote to Archbishop Hincmar of Rheims to ask him whether 'it can be true, as many men say, that there are women who can create with their evil-doing irreconcilable hatred between man and wife, or join together a man and woman with uncontrollable love'.[1] The archbishop's reply comprised a long and vivid enumeration of the demonic powers that he detected at work in Lothar's court:

there are magi, who are commonly called evil-doers because of the enormity of their sins ... there are necromancers, whose incantations seem to understand the dead as if revived and to reply to their questions ... there are soothsayers, who utter evil prayers and offer sacrifices to the dead around the altars of idols ... there are augurs who observe the flights and songs of birds ...

---

[1] Hincmar of Rheims, *De divortio Lotharii regis et Theutbergae reginae*, ed. L. Böhringer, *MGH Concilia* IV, supp. I (Hanover, 1992), p. 205.

and many others besides.[2] But it opened with more pointed observations, including that 'certain men are debilitated by witches or by
feminine wiles, and certain women are found to have committed
sexual intercourse with harpies in the guise of men, with whom
they fall in love'.[3] The bishops would not have mistaken Hincmar's
intended target. Lothar was seeking the dissolution of his union with
his wife Theutberga so that he could marry his long-standing mistress
Waldrada. Witchcraft and devilry, Hincmar was hinting, lay behind
the latter's hold over the king.

Hincmar's depiction of a Carolingian court beset by soothsayers,
sorcerers and witches is a troubling one on a number of levels. At first
sight, it seems to reveal a society that was incompletely Christian,
even at the very top. Five and a half centuries after the conversion to Christianity of the Roman emperor Constantine, and some
three hundred years after that of the first Christian Frankish king
Clovis, Hincmar depicts a Frankish Church in daily battle with distinctly unchristian beliefs and practices that apparently held sway
even among the elite. This is surprising not least because most other
indications, and the accounts historians have built from them, tell of
the complete Christianisation of the Franks by this time. The eighth
century in particular was in fact, according to the traditional view, the
period when the Franks sponsored missions aimed at converting to
Christianity other peoples living to their immediate north and east:
Frisians, Saxons, Hessians and Thuringians. The missionisers themselves, in a neat and often-noticed progression, were drawn from
among the Anglo-Saxons so recently Christianised themselves by a
mission sent by a pope from Rome. According to this view, when
that pope's successors consecrated English 'missionary bishops', and
when those bishops allied with the Franks' rulers both to extend
Christianity and to reform it within the kingdom, Rome-rooted
mission had come full circle.[4] This section, then, will re-assess the
idea of the extension of Christian belief in this period, while subsequently we will look at the condition of Christianity itself, and the
development of the Christian Church.

---

[2] *Ibid.*, p. 207.   [3] *Ibid.*, p. 206.
[4] The best detailed account along these relatively traditional lines is still W.
Levison, *England and the Continent in the Eighth Century* (Oxford, 1946), the
poignancy of which book might be detected in Levison's understated preface,
pp. v–vii.

The difficulty of this task is immediately evident from a second level of disquiet about our source: Hincmar was not a neutral observer but a partisan of a king, Charles the Bald, who had a vested interest in ensuring his nephew Lothar's childlessness for the leverage it gave him in inter-kingdom politics.[5] What is more, Hincmar's long description of the various kinds of magic-makers and malefactors is actually taken, almost verbatim, from a much earlier work, the *Etymologies*, a kind of encyclopedia written by Bishop Isidore of Seville in the seventh century.[6] It looks as if Hincmar wanted to project a particular picture of Lothar's court, for political reasons, by reproducing recognisable images of unacceptable practices. The one passage from this section of the work that does not parrot an earlier text is precisely the one about wanton, bewitched and bewitching women which was aimed, undoubtedly, at the 'adulterous' Waldrada. That said, Hincmar's description must have 'rung true' to himself and his intended audience (most immediately, the bishops of Lothar's kingdom who had prompted his letter in the first place). It would have had little impact if it had amounted entirely to fantasy. So even if Hincmar and his colleagues did not think that dark spiritual forces *were* at work at Lothar's court, they admitted the possibility that they *could* be.

It is not immediately clear where such forces stood in relation to Christianity. Some historians have suggested that these demons were the distinctive residue of a pre-Christian world of magic and superstition that survived uncleansed despite centuries of attentive opposition by Christian activists; that, in other words, such texts offer direct evidence for non-Christian belief.[7] It is very probable, however, that Hincmar himself would have thought nonsensical the very notion of 'pre-Christian', since Christ was Alpha as well as Omega, and that in his mind these forces were understood in very

---

[5] On the possible motivations behind Hincmar's polemic, see S. Airlie, 'Private bodies and the body politic in the divorce case of Lothar II', *P&P* 161 (1998), pp. 3–38; and for context see below, Chapter 8.

[6] Hincmar, *De divortio*, p. 207, n. 14, identifying Isidore, *Etymologiae* VIII.9.9–29. As first pointed out by W. Boudriot, *Die altgermanische Religion* (Bonn, 1928), Hincmar was not the only ninth-century writer to borrow descriptions of unChristian practices from earlier authors – not only Isidore but, in particular, Caesarius, bishop of Arles (*c.*470–542). All ultimately go back to Biblical texts, e.g. Deuteronomy 18:10–11.

[7] V. Flint, *The Rise of Magic in Early Medieval Europe* (Oxford, 1991), pp. 155–7.

Christian terms, as earthly representatives of the Biblical devil, the perennial tempter, and foe, of the aspirant Christian. As such, they were coded symbols for the human moral corruption which was the root of Lothar's personal crisis. Hincmar may simply have been noting that the Carolingian elite languished in the same sinful condition as every human since Adam's fall from grace. In this sense Hincmar's reply to the bishops, like many early medieval Christian texts, is more useful for telling us what Christianity was not – that is, for revealing what those who called themselves Christians thought were the *wrong* beliefs and practices – than for enumerating the correct doctrines and actions that we could put in a pigeonhole marked 'Christian'.

Prejudiced and derivative, then, Hincmar's letter illustrates how difficult it is for us to access belief in this period. By foregrounding actions like chanting and sacrificing, it is one among many texts that have encouraged the view that in the earlier Middle Ages belief was largely a matter of external practices rather than of internal mentality – that what mattered was what one did, not what one thought or felt – and that these practices were generally communal rather than individual or personal. But we need to remember that the kinds of sources we have condition our view of early medieval beliefs. After the end of the period covered by this book, a number of texts began to emphasise individual rather than collective piety, to an extent that has sometimes been seen as marking a radical break with early medieval practice; but the change may reflect the adoption of new genres and styles of writing at least as much as actual or generalised shifts in what people believed. It would be wrong, and unfair, to deny to the inhabitants of early medieval Europe the capability of reflective belief, just because they articulated it in different ways from their later medieval counterparts, ways perhaps no longer recoverable.

It has been crucial to the long-term success of Christian doctrine that it is very flexible, the result of its origins among Greek-speakers in the Roman empire steeped in the philosophical tradition of the eastern Mediterranean. In these first generations, what came to be called Christianity amalgamated the cult of a Jewish prophet with the concerns of Hellenistic philosophy. In particular, the latter's interest in the nature of God and the divine relationship with the physical universe became central issues of emerging Christian doctrine, and arguments in early councils of bishops duly focussed on Jesus's relationship with God (Christology) and on the idea of salvation for humans through him (soteriology).[8] From the mid-fifth century, however, Christian apparatchiks – the priests, bishops and monks of the Church hierarchy – began to seek, and to gain, access to aspects of life of only tangential interest to earlier Christian leaders, and into which the priests of pagan Roman cults had never even dreamt of intruding: sexual relations, for instance, and marriage. In speculative theology, there is no mistaking the decline in an interest in the precise *nature* of the divine, and a stress instead on the *presence* of the divine in this world, and on the practical steps believers might take to touch it, in both the here-and-now and the hereafter.[9]

The spread of this attitude signalled a reorientation of the way in which people viewed their relationship with an institution, the Church. ('The Church' in this sense is a problematic concept in itself, since it is questionable whether at this period the community of Christians was organised into any kind of institution sufficiently coherent to deserve the title; as we shall see, the argument in favour of its existence is stronger towards the end of the period we are covering than at the beginning.)[10] Crucially for us, it also involved a radical change in the way in which people discussed that relationship. Emerging genres of writing, such as hagiography, stressed that belief was revealed through practice: actions displayed the heart and mind of the actor.[11] Such texts make it as hard to arrive at any detailed definition of Christianity as it is to get a clear view of non-Christianity. At the start of our period, around 700, self-professed Christians would very probably accept the possibility of eternal life after death for those who believed that God had become man in the person of Jesus. Many might further have accepted that public profession of this belief should be made through the initiation ritual of baptism.

---

[8] This characterisation draws on G. Vermes, *Jesus the Jew. A Historian's Reading of the Gospels*, 5th edn (London, 1994); *Jesus and the World of Judaism* (Philadelphia, PA, 1984); *The Changing Faces of Jesus* (London, 2001).

[9] On the 'eclipse of theology', see A. Angenendt, *Das Frühmittelalter. Die abendländische Christenheit von 400 bis 900* (Stuttgart, 1990), p. 155; also P. Brown, 'Vers la naissance de purgatoire. Amnistie et pénitence dans le christianisme occidental de l'Antiquité tardive au Haut Moyen Âge', *Annales HSS* 6 (1997), pp. 1247–61 at pp. 1260–1.

[10] G. Macy, 'Was there a "Church" in the Middle Ages?', in R. Swanson (ed.), *Unity and Diversity in the Church*, Studies in Church History 52 (Oxford, 1996), pp. 107–16.

[11] See J. Arnold, *Belief and Unbelief in Medieval Europe* (London, 2005), pp. 1–26 and 143–90.

Beyond that, though, all was variety. Holy writ – the Bible – was by no means universally known, and there were in any case numerous interpretations of it. In short, there was not one Christianity, but many Christianities, not one Church, but many churches.[12] It is instructive to compare this definition with that implicit in Hincmar's condemnation of Lothar's court, which, as we have noted, is really a list of what Christianity was not. It excludes a whole raft of practices and beliefs which some earlier writers had slated as 'rustic', most of which go back not just to Isidore of Seville in the seventh century, but to the writings of the sixth-century bishops Caesarius of Arles and Martin of Braga.[13] But it also assumes a more rigid definition of what Christianity actually was. By Hincmar's time, Christianity in the eyes of churchmen was increasingly thought of as constituting the rules of an institution as much as a code of moral practice. These uncertainties about the very nature of Christianity, and the emergence of increasingly confident definitions in the ninth century, are important to keep in mind.

Defining non-Christianity

If Christianity in the early Middle Ages is difficult to define, then so too are other concepts that are habitually used when discussing beliefs. Terms such as 'paganism', 'religion', 'magic' and 'superstition' imply to the modern ear concepts that were recognisable and well-defined in practice. What is more, ancient and medieval writers were just as seduced by them as modern authors: in the early fifth century, for instance, St Augustine of Hippo optimistically declared that superstitions were merely the tenuously surviving beliefs that Christianity would abolish.[14] The problem is that none could agree on which practices belonged in which category, and therefore on which were unacceptable and which tolerable. In practice, concepts

---

[12] Peter Brown has characterised Christianity's development up to the seventh century as the emergence of a series of 'Micro-Christendoms': P. Brown, *The Rise of Western Christendom*, second edn (Oxford, 2003), pp. 355–79.

[13] Caesarius of Arles, *Sermones*, ed. G. Morin, 2 vols., *CCSL* 103–4 (Turnhout, 1953) (e.g. nos. 13, 15, 62); Martin of Braga, *On the correction of the rustics* (*De correctione rusticorum*), ed. and trans. C. W. Barlow, *Iberian Fathers* 1: *Martin of Braga, Paschasius of Dumium, Leander of Seville* (Washington, DC, 1969) (e.g. cc. 8, 9).

[14] Y. Hen, *Culture and Religion in Merovingian Gaul* (Leiden, 1995), pp. 158–9, esp. n. 25.

like 'religion', 'superstition' and 'magic', as well as 'paganism', can be defined only in relation to each other: that is, what might constitute 'religion' to one person might look like 'magic' to another, and 'superstition' to a third.[15] Those who sought to foretell the future might be demonic to Hincmar, but it is hard to see what really separated them from the Christian heroes who were praised for their prophetic powers.[16] The difficulty is evident in the *Indiculus superstitionum et paganiarum*, a brief list of (presumably proscribed) practices produced in the context of the Church councils in the east Frankish kingdom instigated by St Boniface in the 740s, of which there will be more to say shortly. The *Indiculus* was clearly composed for a society familiar with Christianity: it mentions 'sacrilegious acts in churches', 'sacrifice which is made to any of the saints', 'the improper places which they [the unnamed religious miscreants] tend for the saints'.[17] Yet its authors were happy to lump these practices – which really come under the heading of 'bad Christianity' – together with 'amulets', 'incantations', 'sacred rites of woods', 'sacred rites of Mercury and Jupiter', 'auguries using either the dung or utterances of birds, horses or cattle', and 'the pagan dance which they call "yrias", with torn cloaks or shoes', among others.[18] In part, these evidently belong to the same tradition as Hincmar's litany of sorceries; both authors were drawing on that series of common models of 'wrong' religious behaviour, some of them quite venerable, that we have already identified. It is surely this that accounts for the reference to Mercury and Jupiter, rather than the Roman re-casting of

---

[15] For a definition of 'magic' that subsumes many of the characteristics of 'superstition', see Flint, *Rise of Magic*, esp. p. 3.

[16] As was, for example, St Cuthbert: Bede, *Vita Cuthberti*, trans. B. Colgrave, *Two Lives of Saint Cuthbert. A Life by an Anonymous Monk of Lindisfarne and Bede's Prose Life* (Cambridge, 1940), pp. 142–307; see also C. Stancliffe, 'Cuthbert and the polarity between pastor and solitary', in G. Bonner, D. Rollason and C. Stancliffe (eds.), *St Cuthbert, his Cult and his Community to AD 1200* (Woodbridge, 1989), pp. 21–44.

[17] *Indiculus superstitionum et paganiarum*, ed. R. Rau, *Briefe des Bonifatius; Willibalds Leben des Bonifatius* (Darmstadt, 1968), pp. 444–8, nos. 5, 9, 18, trans. J. T. McNeill and H. A. Gamer (eds.), *Medieval Handbooks of Penance* (New York, 1990), pp. 419–21, and repr. in Dutton (ed.), *Carolingian Civilization*, pp. 3–4 (from which the translation given here differs slightly).

[18] *Indiculus superstitionum et paganiarum*, nos. 6, 8, 10, 12, 13, 24. The full list runs to thirty clauses.

Germanic gods that we shall examine shortly, still less a centuries-long continuity of cult from antiquity.[19]

Moreover, while modern definitions sometimes try to distinguish 'magic' (categorised as the attempt to bend nature to one's will), from 'religion' (defined as appealing to a higher power), the *Indiculus* prefers to blur such categories.[20] Amulets (which might constitute 'magic') and idols (which are more straightforwardly 'religious') are equally condemned, and thrown together with some fairly rustic superstitions, like shouting 'triumph, moon!' ('vince, luna!') during an eclipse.[21] Charlemagne's close adviser Alcuin, writing in the heyday of Carolingian Church formation, combined these elements when he described the whittling down of the company of his fellow Englishman St Willibrord, as a pagan king selected victims by lot in punishment for their violation of an island dedicated to the god Fosite, with its temples, spring and sacred cattle.[22] 'Religion', 'magic' and 'superstition' are not, in fact, neatly distinct, and neither Alcuin nor the writers of the *Indiculus* tried to make them so.

Things might be clearer if we had writings left by non-Christians about their beliefs, but since none survive we have to look at this lost world from the hostile and often clichéd perspectives of contemporary learned Christians. But these Christian authors were not primarily concerned with drawing a boundary between religious and non-religious belief – they were looking at themselves, using non-Christian practices to help develop a new, narrow and rigorist definition of 'true' Christianity. This has to be borne in mind even when we are reading letters, or the reports of church councils. These texts' purposes were not so much to report the real practices of lay people as to define them in relation to the emerging Christian Church. When, for example, Pope Gregory III exhorted peoples in Germany to 'reject absolutely all divination, fortune-telling, sacrifices to the dead, prophecies in groves or by fountains, amulets,

---

[19] See now J. Palmer, 'Defining paganism in the Carolingian world', *EME* 15 (2007), pp. 402–25.

[20] See e.g. A. Meaney, 'Magic', in M. Lapidge, *et al.* (eds.), *The Blackwell Encyclopedia of Anglo-Saxon England* (Oxford, 1999), pp. 298–9, and, in general, Flint, *Rise of Magic*.

[21] *Indiculus superstitionum et paganiarum*, no. 21; and compare Hrabanus Maurus, *Homilia* XLII ('Contra eos qui in lunae defectu clamoribus se fatigabant'), PL CX, coll. 78–80.

[22] Alcuin, *Vita Willibrordi*, trans. Talbot, p. 10.

incantations, sorcery (that is, witchcraft) and all those sacrilegious practices', he was echoing late antique canon law, replicated in turn in the acts of the councils that Boniface organised, as well as, in its fullest form, in the *Indiculus*.[23] Whether or not people in Germany actually did those things, by the eighth century the traditions of the Church said that they *might*. The authors of the *Indiculus* were therefore drawing on the same traditions as Hincmar, and with the same result: an increasingly rigid definition of Christianity among the learned elite, pointing towards the condemnation of anything else as unbelief and, ultimately, heresy.[24] Not for nothing was the term *correctio* often used to describe these currents of thought.

The fact that contemporaries were arguing intensely about where to fix the boundaries between Christianity and non-Christianity makes it more difficult for us to decide where the lines actually were – the reality is hard to see through their discourse. The tenets and practices that each community held before its profession of Christianity differed from region to region. In lands with direct cultural continuity from Rome, we sometimes find references to the Greco-Roman gods – Jupiter, Mercury and the rest of the Olympian pantheon. It is difficult to know, however, whether these attest real continuity, or simply authors using the *interpretatio romana* – the drawing of parallels between Roman and non-Roman gods, and attributing to the latter the names of the former – which dates back to classical Roman writers.[25] Since, as we shall see, such references are found well into Germany, in lands that never fell into the Roman empire, it is in fact impossible to draw a neat line between areas where beliefs and practices had been essentially Roman, and those areas where they were something else. The term 'religion' itself is problematic here, because earlier sets of beliefs and practices did not have a number of features that we find in Christianity and other monotheistic faiths:

---

[23] Boniface, *Epistolae*, *Ep.* 43, ed. Tangl, pp. 68–9, trans. Emerton, no. XXXIII, pp. 69–71 (from which the translation given here differs slightly). The language seems to be lifted from the canons of the fourth-century Council of Laodicea (PL LXVII, p. 168), replicated in later councils (e.g. Council of Agde 506, *Concilia Galliae a.314–a.506*, ed. C. Munier, *CCSL* 148 (Turnhout, 1953)).

[24] R. I. Moore, 'Literacy and the making of heresy *c.*1000–*c.*1150', in P. Biller and A. Hudson (eds.), *Heresy and Literacy, 1000–1530* (Cambridge, 1994), pp. 19–37, repr. in L. K. Little and B. H. Rosenwein (eds.), *Debating the Middle Ages. Issues and Readings* (Oxford, 1998), pp. 163–75.

[25] Tacitus, *Germania*, c. 9, trans. M. Hutton, *Agricola, Germania, Dialogus* (London, 1970), pp. 143–5.

sacred texts, a prophetic or historical tradition, abstract theology.[26] There was a consciousness that Christianity had a more substantial identity – perhaps it was this that led Louis the Pious's moneyers to strike coins with the legend *Christiana religio*.[27] The search for the 'old gods' in different parts of northern and western Europe is also hampered by the dating of the available evidence. A good deal is said about supposedly pre-Christian deities and their veneration in much later literature, but its distance in time from the genuinely pre-Christian era makes irrecoverable the real beliefs of that earlier era, which are transformed, through layers of accretion, into something more like folklore.[28]

The religious tenets and practices that preceded Christianity in many of the more northerly parts of the Carolingian world, and are generally labelled 'Germanic', are a good example of this bleeding of religion into mythology. The most elaborate accounts of those beliefs survive only in the writings of authors in twelfth- and thirteenth-century Iceland, creating their distant past through the filter of the Christianity which had been adopted there over two hundred years earlier.[29] In any case, it is very difficult to say what the religion of the Icelanders' tenth-century ancestors shared with that of eighth-century Saxons, or seventh-century Frisians. Their languages, and therefore their names for gods, were related (thus, in Old English, Old High German and Old Norse respectively, Woden/Wodan/Odin, and Thunor/Donar/Thorr), but this does not mean they shared common religious beliefs: the 'Germanic' culture of the period is a modern invention. In general, eighth- and ninth-century north European sources provide far more information about practices than they do about beliefs. For example, burial practices, both cremation and inhumation, might evince belief in an after-life – and burial with a means of transport, whether a horse or the Sutton Hoo ship, seems to indicate the notion of a journey towards it – but we can say nothing about how it was imagined, or how it was thought

---

[26] On definitions of religion and superstition, see Hen, *Culture and Religion*, pp. 157–61.

[27] See S. Coupland, 'Money and coinage under Louis the Pious', *Francia* 17/1 (1990), pp. 23–54.

[28] For the apposite example of Ireland in this context, see T. Charles-Edwards, *Early Christian Ireland* (Cambridge, 2000), pp. 200–2.

[29] See P. Meulengracht Sørensen, 'Religions old and new', in P. Sawyer (ed.), *The Oxford Illustrated History of the Vikings* (Oxford, 1997), pp. 202–24.

attainable.[30] Similarly, while there is evidence for the celebration of non-Christian festivals and even cattle sacrifice, it is less often clear what they signified.[31] Some people east of the Rhine in the eighth century may even have practised human sacrifice, if Pope Gregory III's complaint to Boniface about Christians who sold their slaves to pagans for sacrifice was at all well informed; and we have evidence of ritual drownings taking place in Frisia at around the same time.[32] But what any of this effusion of blood was for, or to whom the deaths were offered, is far from clear.

Pre-Christian gods feature as weakly in our evidence as does their capacity to withstand Christianity. Boniface's mentor, Bishop Daniel of Winchester, knew that they could be demystified simply by pointing to their supposed genealogies, and therefore to their very biological, non-divine, need for procreation.[33] It is straightforward to put names to some of these gods, since they occur in the days of the week (in both medieval and modern languages, and in both England and Germany): Tîw, Woden, Thunor, Freya. They appear also in place names (especially in England), and in some contemporary written sources: a baptismal formula apparently used for converting Saxons required them to renounce Donar, Woden, and Saxnot, and one of the intriguing Old High German charms refers to Woden and Freya.[34] By referring also to gods that are not otherwise

[30] For Sutton Hoo, see M. Carver, *Sutton Hoo: Burial Ground of Kings?* (Philadelphia, PA, 1998).

[31] For festivals accompanied by drinking, see I. Wood, 'Pagan religion and superstitions east of the Rhine from the fifth to the ninth century', in G. Ausenda (ed.), *After Empire* (Woodbridge, 1995), pp. 253–68, at p. 259. Sacrifice: Alcuin, *Vita Willibrordi*, trans. Talbot, p. 10; *Pactus legis Salicae*, ed. K. A. Eckhardt, *MGH Legum sectio* I, *Leges Nationum Germanicarum* IV (Hanover, 1962) 2, 16, trans. K. Fischer-Drew, *The Laws of the Salian Franks* (Philadelphia, PA, 1991).

[32] Boniface, *Epistolae*, *Ep.* 28, trans. Hillgarth, *Christianity and Paganism*, p. 175: 'Among other difficulties which you face in those parts, you say that some of the faithful sell their slaves to be sacrificed by the heathen. This, above all, we urge you to forbid, for it is a crime against nature'; see also trans. Emerton, no. XX, pp. 57–9; Altfrid, *Vita Liudgeri* 1.6–7, ed. W. Diekamp, *Die Vitae Sancti Liudgeri* (Münster, 1881). Christian priests performing pagan sacrifice: Boniface, *Epistolae*, *Ep.* 80, trans. Emerton, no. LXIV, pp. 142–9.

[33] Boniface, *Epistolae*, *Ep.* 23, trans. Emerton, no. XV, pp. 48–50.

[34] Saxon baptismal formula: H. D. Schlosser (ed.), *Althochdeutsche Literatur* (Frankfurt, 1970), pp. 251–60, and W. Lange, *Texte zur Bekehrungsgeschichte* (Tübingen, 1962), p. 176. Second Merseburg Charm: Knight Bostock, *Handbook on Old High German Literature*, pp. 26–7, and W. Braune, *et al.*, *Althochdeutsches Lesebuch* (Tübingen,

known, several texts reveal the patchiness of our knowledge: the
Lives of Willibrord and Liudger show both saints encountering the
cult of the otherwise obscure Fosite;[35] and an Anglo-Saxon spell
refers to an 'earth mother' named Erce, not attested anywhere else.[36]
As to cult places themselves, our sources for continental Germany
point to the importance not of religious buildings, firm evidence for
which is entirely lacking, but to natural sites: as we have seen, Fosite was culted especially at a sacred spring, while Boniface chopped
down an oak at Geismar in Hesse which evidently served as an idol.[37]
The attribution of spiritual power to places connects with a belief in
the existence of animate spirits, which might also take physical form.
This is most apparent in the evidence from Anglo-Saxon literature
for dragons, giants, elves and dwarves, who intruded mischievously
or menacingly into human affairs.[38] The monsters in the Anglo-
Saxon poem *Beowulf* – Grendel, Grendel's mother, and the dragon
that was the hero's nemesis – are only the most famous of these.[39]
Nonetheless, it is worth repeating, these creatures are known to us

1958) XVI, 2, II (p. 86). On both, see C. Edwards, 'German vernacular literature:
a survey', in McKitterick (ed.), *Carolingian Culture*, pp. 141–70.

[35] Alcuin, *Vita Willibrordi*, trans. Talbot, p. 10; Altfrid, *Vita Liudgeri* 1.22. See further
R. Bartlett, 'Reflections on paganism and christianity in medieval Europe', *PBA*
101 (1998), pp. 55–76.

[36] 'Erce, eorðan modor', in *Æcerbot*, ed. and trans. G. Storms, *Anglo-Saxon Magic*
(The Hague, 1948), no. 8.

[37] Alcuin, *Vita Willibrordi*, trans. Talbot, p. 10; Willibald, *Vita Bonifatii*, ed.
W. Levison, *MGH SRG in usum scholarum separatim editi* LVII (Hanover, 1905)
c. 6, trans. Talbot, pp. 45–6. There may have been some temples in England, but
the Anglo-Saxons may here have been re-using or mimicking the Roman and/or
Christian religious buildings that they found there: Wood, 'Pagan religion', p.
261. Some Slav peoples of the later ninth and early tenth centuries certainly
had temples: see the description by Thietmar of Merseburg, *Chronicon*, ed. R.
Holtzmann, *MGH SRG, n.s* IX (Berlin, 1935), VI.23–5, trans. D. Warner, *Ottonian Germany: The* Chronicon *of Thietmar of Merseburg* (Manchester, 2001), and L.
Słupecki, *Slavonic Pagan Sanctuaries* (Warsaw, 1994).

[38] For spells or charms, see G. O. Cockayne (ed.), *Leechdoms, Wortcunning, and Starcraft
of Early England*, 3 vols. Rolls Series 35, reprint rev. C. Singer (London, 1961),
vol. II. See also *Beowulf*, ed. E. van K. Dobbie, *Beowulf and Judith*. Anglo-Saxon
Poetic Records 4 (New York and London, 1953), ll.111–13, trans. R. M. Liuzza,
Beowulf (Peterborough, ON, 2000), p. 56: 'From thence arose all misbegotten
things,/ trolls and elves and the living dead,/ and also the giants . . .' ('Þanon
untydras ealle onwocon,/eotenas ond ylfe ond orcneas,/ swylce gigantas . . .').

[39] On these monsters and their interpretation see, classically, J. R. R. Tolkien,
'Beowulf: the monsters and the critics', *PBA* 22 (1936), pp. 1–53; repr. in J. R.
R. Tolkien, *The Monsters and the Critics and Other Essays* (London, 1983). As we

almost entirely in stories written in Christian contexts. Grendel's genealogy in *Beowulf* leads back not to some pagan figure but to the Old Testament's aboriginal fratricide Cain.[40] The persistence of these figures troubled some churchmen – 'what has Ingeld to do with Christ?' complained the Anglo-Saxon scholar Alcuin, referring to a figure we know only from an oblique reference in *Beowulf*; but others, evidently, saw no incompatibility between their Christianity and belief in such beings.[41] It is decidedly moot whether many of them should be labelled 'pagan' at all. All pre-Enlightenment cultures (including Christianity) developed explanations of the world around them that involve what we would call the supernatural. It would be wrong then, as some of the more optimistic readings of these texts have done, to see references to such phenomena as tip-of-the-iceberg evidence for a fully coherent pagan religion.[42]

Extending the Church

By suggesting that non-Christian religion was insubstantial and adaptable we are also undermining the traditional notion of conversion to Christianity (from something else, equally well defined) as a result of 'mission'. Contemporary narratives made much play of the idea of missions to the pagans, thus presenting the development of Christianity as a black-and-white conflict. Until recently modern histories have followed suit, to the extent that they often tell the story of the Christian Church's spread through the lives of a series of Christian heroes – missionaries – whose triumphant struggle was

---

have it, *Beowulf* is probably a composition of the late ninth or tenth centuries: best initial guides to the poem are R. E. Bjork and J. D. Niles (eds.), *A Beowulf Handbook* (Lincoln, NE, 1997), and A. Orchard, *A Critical Companion to 'Beowulf'* (Woodbridge, 2004).

[40] *Beowulf*, ll. 104–10, trans. Liuzza, p. 56; Brown, *Rise of Western Christendom*, pp. 482–5.

[41] Alcuin, *Ep.* 124, ed. Dümmler, p. 183: 'quid Hinieldus cum Christo?', see D. Bullough, 'What has Ingeld to do with Lindisfarne?', *Anglo-Saxon England* 22 (1993), pp. 93–125, and now M. Garrison, 'Quid Hinieldus cum Christo?', in K. O'Brien O'Keefe and A. Orchard (eds.), *Latin Learning and English Lore: Studies in Anglo-Saxon Literature for Michael Lapidge*, 2 vols. (Toronto 2005), I, pp. 237–59. Ingeld appears in *Beowulf*, l. 2064, trans. Liuzza, p. 116.

[42] The notion was dismissed effectively by E. G. Stanley, *The Search for Anglo-Saxon Paganism* (Cambridge, 1975).

aimed at winning large numbers of direct, pagan-to-Christian, converts. These heroes' efforts to extend Christianity are seen as working
in parallel with the drive to define it more closely.[43] This narrative
portrays conversion not just as the adoption of a faith, but as induc-
tion into an institution, with definite administrative and geo-political
boundaries: the Church. As we have already noted, though, it was
only in our period that the Church began to emerge with any kind of
solid institutional profile, and much diversity persisted. The Church
has looked most concrete and tangible in the acts of church councils
(meetings of bishops), which gradually built up into a formidable
body of canon law, applying in theory not only to churchmen but
to anyone involved in issues that the Church claimed as its own, like
marriage. Accumulating into a body of legal rules, these have tended
to encourage the notion of a unified Church, since the series begins
with the acts of the universal or 'ecumenical' councils of the fourth
century. But before the eighth century, councils in the former western empire had generally been restricted to, at best, single realms,
Frankish, Visigothic or Lombard, with no aspiration to apply beyond
that particular kingdom. The mistaken complaint that even these had
not been held in Francia for more than eighty years by the 740s is a
sign that when new councils were summoned at that time, it was at
the initiative of Christian leaders of a different stripe.[44] These were
Anglo-Saxons with their unique, rigorous and expansionist vision of
the institutional Church, and the new Carolingian dynasty, eager for
an ideology to underpin their rulership. The writ of these councils
ran as far as that of the Carolingians themselves, traversing the old
political boundaries. At the same time, the identity of the western
Church was firming up in relation to that of the east. This is already
evident in the acts of the council of Pavia, held under the auspices of
the Lombard king Cunincpert in 698, which presented a specifically
Lombard, and therefore western, solution to the Three Chapters dispute, an argument over eastern ideas that had split the north Italian
churches.[45]

---

[43] See e.g. R. Fletcher, *The Conversion of Europe: From Paganism to Christianity, 371–
1386* (London, 1997), pp. 271–84.

[44] In Boniface, *Espitolae, Ep.* 50 (trans. Emerton, no. XL, pp. 78–83), datable to 742,
Boniface complains that 'the Franks have not held a council for more than eighty
years'. In fact, we possess acts of Frankish synods in the Merovingian period up
to at least 695.

[45] *Acts of the Council of Pavia*, ed. G. Waitz, *MGH SRL* (Hanover, 1878), pp. 189–
91; on the Three Chapters (or Tricapitoline) schism, see R. Markus, *Gregory the*

The traditional narrative, then, tends to see the religious history of these centuries in terms of the extension to new peoples of the institution governed by the rules of canon law, membership of which was acquired primarily through submitting to the initiation ritual of baptism. At the opening of our period, the community of Christians so defined extended no further than the writ of the rulers who had formally accepted Christianity: the kings of the Lombards, Franks and Visigoths, the dukes of the Bretons, Alemans and Bavarians, and the various rulers of the British Isles. In the latter, the last Anglo-Saxon people formally to accept Christianity – those on the Isle of Wight – had done so only in the years after 686,[46] while most of Visigothic Spain would pass into the hands of Muslims very suddenly in 711. 'Christendom' (a later concept of strictly limited applicability here) was restricted, even embattled. By 900, however, Christianity had been accepted in some sense in the Germanic-speaking lands as far east as the Elbe and as far north as the North Sea and the Jutland peninsula. The first sustained attempts at evangelisation in Scandinavia were made in the ninth century, though they put down no long-term roots at that time.[47] By the end of that century too, concerted efforts at Christianisation were being aimed at the Slavic-speaking peoples, both those immediately to the east of Frankish territory – the Carantanians, Bohemians and Moravians – and those to the north of the Byzantine empire, principally the Bulgarians.[48]

Mapping onto this geography, it has been the growth of the Church's institutional profile – its buildings, its personnel, their organisation – that has most often captured the attention of historians. Our period was one in which this aspect of Christianity became far more complex and concrete. While it needs to be noted that these aspects of the Church are of course very imperfect means of measuring Christianisation – they tell us little of the social impact of Christianity, let alone of changes in actual belief – they do indicate the spread of the institution of the Church. It was generally this, rather than the more intellectual and psychological features of 'mission', like preaching, that was the first concern when trying to

---

Great and his World (Cambridge, 1997), pp. 125–40; J. Herrin, *The Formation of Christendom* (Oxford, 1987), pp. 119–27.

[46] Bede, *HE* IV.16.

[47] I. Wood, *The Missionary Life: Saints and the Evangelisation of Europe, 400–1050* (Harlow, 2001), pp. 123–41.

[48] *Ibid.*, pp. 168–244; Fletcher, *Conversion of Europe*, pp. 327–68.

extend Christianity geographically. In particular, it was important to set up bishops with cathedral seats and delineated dioceses. From the conversion of the emperor Constantine in the early fourth century, the late Roman period had seen this skeletal structure of bishops and dioceses established across most, if not all, of the western empire.[49] Subsequently the hiatus of imperial collapse and the establishment of 'barbarian' kings seems to have erased this network in some places, especially Britain and northern Gaul. In most provinces, though, there was a good deal of continuity. It was a bishop seated as far north as Rheims, Remigius, who, around 500, persuaded the first great Frankish king Clovis of the benefits of Christian baptism.[50] Even in the heart of the empire, in Italy, where the written records for Christianity are very sparse in the years of turmoil between the mid-fifth and the mid-sixth century, the archaeology of some episcopal centres shows disruption, hiatus and retrenchment.[51] Yet Christianity never disappeared. Its presence had been felt among barbarian groups even before they entered the empire, when many adopted the Arian form of the faith at a time when it was coming to be regarded by leaders of the Church within the empire as heretical:[52] this was itself a sign that religious discussion in the later Roman empire was already coming to take place entirely in Christian terms. The prevalence of Christianity in the empire's successor states is affirmed for the historian by evidence from the late sixth, and above all from the seventh, century which reveals the level of veneration of Christian saints by this time. While Gregory, the late-sixth-century bishop of Tours, could write of the numerous, already venerable (and distinctly legendary) martyrs and confessors of the Gaul of two or more hundred years previously, seventh-century Frankish writers

[49] See A. Cameron, *The Later Roman Empire* (London, 1993), pp. 66–84, esp. pp. 71–4. The exception here may have been parts of Britain, which may have had as few as three bishops during the Roman period: see A. S. Esmonde Cleary, *The Ending of Roman Britain* (London, 1989), p. 121.

[50] Dating Clovis's baptism has provoked a long debate: see most recently D. Shanzer, 'Dating the baptism of Clovis: the Bishop of Vienne vs the Bishop of Tours', *EME* 7 (1998), pp. 29–57.

[51] See for example V. Gaffney, H. Patterson and P. Roberts, 'Forum novum (Vescovio): a new study of the town and bishopric', in H. Patterson (ed.), *Bridging the Tiber: Approaches to Regional Archaeology in the Middle Tiber Valley* (London, 2004), pp. 237–48.

[52] P. Heather and J. Matthews, *The Goths in the Fourth Century* (Liverpool, 1991), pp. 124–43.

turned to the task of sanctifying the Christian leaders of their own day in pristine hagiographies. These leaders were saints, according to such texts, because they had demonstrated their supernatural power through the unimpeachably Christian method of performing miracles, usually those which improved the human condition, for example by healing.[53] The point of writing about them was to reveal their holiness,[54] and it was in that context that apparently Christianising activities should be read. His anonymous hagiographer could write of St Audoin that

> strengthened in the practice of his faith, with the Lord as protector, he turned the most savage ferocity of the Franks into gentleness, and from the holy font he so tempered them with the sweetness of honey, and so consecrated his parishes with the divine practice, that they abandoned the rite of the heathen and voluntarily placed themselves under the yoke of Christ and their necks under his service.[55]

But he tells us this immediately after relating Audoin's consecration as bishop of Rouen. Seen in the light of Gregory of Tours's descriptions, from a hundred years previously, of a highly Christianised Merovingian Gaul, we are forced to read this passage as describing what its author thought a bishop – especially the ideal, or the best, bishop – *ought* to do.[56]

---

[53] Such thaumaturgical miracles – rooted in, and improving, the physical world – are a hallmark of Merovingian hagiography. Elsewhere, hagiographers sometimes revealed saints' divine powers operating transcendentally, for instance in prophecies. For the categorisation and characterisation of miracles, see Fouracre and Gerberding, *Late Merovingian France*, pp. 134–5, and Brown, *Rise of Western Christendom*, pp. 161–3, 214, and their references.

[54] See J. McNamara, 'A legacy of miracles: hagiography and nunneries in Merovingian Gaul', in J. Kirshner and S. Wemple (eds.), *Women of the Medieval World. Essays in Honour of John H. Mundy* (Oxford, 1985), pp. 36–52, at p. 38: 'Miracles are the whole point of the *vitae* . . .'

[55] *Vita Audoini episcopi Rotomagensis*, ed. W. Levison, *MGH SRG* v (Hanover, 1910), pp. 536–67, c. 4, trans. Fouracre and Gerberding, 'Life of Audoin', *Late Merovingian France*, p. 156.

[56] Yitzhak Hen has noted how relatively incidental the theme of conversion is in the Merovingian *Lives*, including that of Audoin, and how it is stressed to a far greater degree in Carolingian, ninth-century, versions of the same hagiographies: *Culture and Religion*, pp. 189–97. For a slightly different slant on the *Life of Audoin* from the one taken here, see P. Fouracre, 'The work of Audoenus of Rouen and Eligius of Noyon in extending episcopal influence from the town to the country in seventh-century Neustria', *Studies in Church History* 16 (1979), pp. 77–91.

Audoin's position as a bishop in fact indicates where the priorities of historians diverge from those of hagiographers. Audoin was a particularly important bishop less because of his miracles than because he had been a prominent, high-born and powerful aristocrat before he became a cleric.[57] His career neatly demonstrates the extent to which the history of Christianity throughout western Europe in the seventh century can be sketched as the history of bishops and their dioceses: the delineation of their extent, and their powers. Audoin's elevation to the see of Rouen was a reward for royal service and a mark of his membership of the Frankish ruling class at least as much as a sign of his holiness, although in his case it was probably also that.[58] These earlier associations with the kingship and aristocracy may have lain behind his foundation of no fewer than four important monasteries, but the fact that when he moved across into the clerical profession it was more or less immediately into a bishopric nonetheless indicates the dominance of that office within the clerical hierarchy, as well as the importance of this institutional aspect of the wider Christian community.[59] It is perhaps not surprising, given the relatively systematic nature of the Anglo-Saxons' Christianisation, that the episcopal office and diocesan structure were among their chief concerns, as they gradually turned in the seventh century to a Christianity that was partly inherited from their British predecessors, but received more concretely, and more or less simultaneously, from the Irish, Roman and Frankish churches. Differences between the organisation of these latter explains the century-long controversy in England over Christian structures and the powers of bishops, which reached its culmination with the career of the argumentative bishop Wilfrid of York, whose power provoked opposition from both kings and fellow bishops.[60] Wilfrid's mistake, it has been argued, was to aspire to be, and to behave like, a bishop of Frankish Gaul.[61] That is,

---

[57] Fouracre and Gerberding, *Late Merovingian France*, pp. 133–52, esp. 147–52.

[58] Early and independent evidence for Audoin's reputation for holiness is provided by Fredegar, *Chronicle*, IV, c. 78, p. 66, ed. and trans. Wallace-Hadrill.

[59] On Audoin's influence on monasticism, see Fouracre and Gerberding, *Late Merovingian France*, pp. 147–8.

[60] On the conversion of the Anglo-Saxons, see now J. Blair, *The Church in Anglo-Saxon Society* (Oxford, 2005), pp. 8–51. On Wilfrid, A. Thacker, 'Wilfrid', *Oxford Dictionary of National Biography*, s.n.

[61] H. Mayr-Harting, *The Coming of Christianity to Anglo-Saxon England* (3rd edn, London, 1991), pp. 130–9; ecclesiastical magnates of similar scope and power

he was an extensive landowner who aspired to control every aspect of Christian life in his diocese (the extent of which was, in any case, a major cause of dispute): in particular, he combined his episcopal role with being head of monastic communities at Ripon and Hexham.[62] In fact, the complexion of Wilfrid's Christian leadership, while it found some parallels in the kingdom of the Franks, was coloured even more intensely by the special circumstances of the early Anglo-Saxon Church, which left him the only bishop in the Northumbrian kingdom, a prominent monastic leader, and a significant influence elsewhere. Wilfrid lacked the local saints – earlier bishops and martyrs – whose cults were an important adjunct of Frankish bishops' power. He himself became such a figure after his death, though for centuries his cult was strictly limited, especially to his foundations at Ripon and Oundle.[63] Rather, he had to channel his episcopal power through imported relics, and his biographer stresses the care he took on his visits to Rome to collect the remains of martyrs, and notes his particular devotion to the apostle Andrew, venerated at important sites in Rome.[64] This is one witness among many of the significance widely attached to the tradition of Rome as a centre of early martyrdom.[65]

Rome was more than a source of relics for Wilfrid; it was also the seat of the bishop of Rome – the pope – and Wilfrid's journeys there were above all quests for a source of authority as his unprecedented

---

existed also at this time in Ireland: Charles-Edwards, *Early Christian Ireland*, pp. 416–40. So in the character of his rule as well as in practices like calculating the date of Easter, to label Wilfrid as 'Roman' and to oppose him to an 'Irish' party is too simplistic.

[62] D. P. Kirby (ed.), *Saint Wilfrid at Hexham* (Newcastle-upon-Tyne, 1974); R. N. Bailey, 'St Wilfrid, Ripon and Hexham', *American Early Medieval Studies* 1 (1990), pp. 3–25.

[63] Thacker, 'Wilfrid'.

[64] Stephen of Ripon, *Vita Wilfridi*, cc. 35 and 55, pp. 66–8 and 120 (note that modern scholars agree that the name 'Eddius Stephanus' arises from a misinterpretation: his biographer, a monk of Ripon, was called just 'Stephen'). See also A. Thacker, 'In search of saints: the English Church and the cult of Roman apostles and martyrs in the seventh and eighth centuries', in Smith (ed.), *Early Medieval Rome and the Christian West*, pp. 247–77 at pp. 258–61. Andrew was dedicatee of a chapel at the Vatican and, most significantly here, of Gregory the Great's monastery on the Caelian hill, home to Augustine and his companions before their mission to England.

[65] J. M. H. Smith, 'Old saints, new cults: Roman relics in Carolingian Francia', in Smith (ed.), *Early Medieval Rome and the Christian West*, pp. 317–39.

power as an ecclesiastical leader meant that he crossed swords with secular rulers. Deposed from his see of York in 678 by King Ecgfrith of Northumbria, Wilfrid appealed for reinstatement to the pope.[66] It is hard to imagine a Frankish bishop doing the same. Although the pope's judgement in favour of Wilfrid was pointedly ignored by King Ecgfrith, the fact that it was thought worth making at all illustrates how the convergence of differently originating trends served to build up both the ideological and the administrative structures of the western Church. Pre-existing reverence for Rome as a centre of early Christianity in the west; recognition of the succession of its bishops from St Peter, the prince of the apostles (in an as yet loosely defined way); the Roman and papal roots of one of the currents that evangelised the Anglo-Saxons; the increasing emergence of ecclesiastical leaders on a par with each other and hesitating to submit to single secular authorities – as we shall see, all these circumstances led to more frequent recourse to the papacy as arbiter, the firming up of an administration built around bishops, and better-defined lines of authority.

Creating Christians in northern Europe

Wilfrid has traditionally been seen as a pioneer in 'mission' to the pagans. But behind this rhetorical status, it looks to have been his particular configuration of episcopal power, and his insistence on lines of authority culminating in St Peter, that were his most important contributions to future generations of Christianisers. His 'mission' was really a chance by-product of his first journey to Rome. According to his biographer Stephen of Ripon, political circumstances forced him away from the shortest route across the Channel, and towards the land of the Frisians instead. There he 'preached the word of God daily to the people', so that 'with a few exceptions all the chiefs were baptised by him in the name of the Lord, as well as many thousands of the common people'.[67] In a slightly later account, Bede is if anything even keener to stress this aspect of Wilfrid's activity.[68] But these tales clash rather abruptly with stories of continued, and quite strongly held, paganism among the Frisians in the next generation. Wilfrid's

---

[66] Stephen of Ripon, *Vita Wilfridi*, c. 24. On this episode see above, Chapter 2, p. 37.
[67] Stephen of Ripon, *Vita Wilfridi*, c. 26.   [68] Bede, *HE* v.19.

impromptu 'mission' turned out to be the first of many attempts by Anglo-Saxons to make new Christians on the continent, and as such looks to have been rather less deliberate or successful than writers with their own missionising agendas would suggest.

Reports of active paganism among the Frisians arise in connection with the figure of Willibrord, himself formerly a member of Wilfrid's monastery at Ripon. On Wilfrid's fall in 678 Willibrord had gone to Ireland, to a monastery established by another Englishman, Ecgberht, who, according to Bede, wished to travel to the continent to try to convert peoples from whom he knew that the Anglo-Saxons derived their origin.[69] Prevented from doing this himself, and after false starts by others, he sent Willibrord, who first won the support of the Frankish mayor of the palace Pippin II, and then went to Rome 'in order to begin the missionary task he wished to undertake with the pope's permission and approval'.[70] Willibrord's mission to the Frisians encountered some serious obstacles, to judge by the account of his biographer Alcuin, writing some hundred years later.[71] Alcuin was evidently keen to create an impression of obdurate Frisian pagans, who proved ultimately unmoved by Willibrord's teaching. This image of strong Frisian paganism is painted too in another hagiography, the *Life* of Bishop Wulfram of Sens, written in response to Alcuin's *Life* of Willibrord and set in the same period as the latter's career. It describes contemporary Frankish efforts to Christianise in Frisia, directed from the monastery of St Wandrille, and stresses that their success depended not, as in Alcuin's narrative, on a preaching 'mission', but on miracles.[72] These, it suggests, were a more reliable method of counter-acting non-Christian religious feeling which, while not as coherent as Christianity, may have become more solid under threat from it. It seems likely, in fact, that the first Frisians to adopt Christianity did so in Francia, and Willibrord certainly enjoyed more success where the writ of the Frankish rulers ran.[73] There 'many

[69] Bede, *HE* v.9.
[70] Bede, *HE* v.11. For what follows, see M. Costambeys, 'Willibrord', *Oxford Dictionary of National Biography, s.n.*
[71] Alcuin, *Vita Willibrordi*, trans. Talbot, pp. 3–22; Wood, *Missionary Life*, pp. 79–99.
[72] *Vita Vulframni*, ed. W. Levison, *MGH SRM* v (Hanover, 1910), pp. 657–73; see Wood, *Missionary Life*, pp. 92–4 and idem, 'Saint-Wandrille and its hagiography', in I. N. Wood and G. A. Loud (eds.), *Church and Chronicle in the Middle Ages* (London, 1991), pp. 1–15.
[73] Altfrid, *Vita Liudgeri* i, cc. 1–3, ed. Diekamp, pp. 6–8.

began in their zeal for the faith to make over to the man of God their hereditary properties'.[74] Among them were Pippin himself, and members of his own family, one of whom founded the monastery of Echternach, and gave it over to Willibrord as its first abbot. With this secure base well within the Frankish heartland, Willibrord attracted patronage from far afield, including from landowners who may have been inimical to, or at best neutral towards, the Pippinids. He did so because he was able to act as an honest broker, a figure who rose above the petty and competing interests in orbit around late Merovingian kingship.[75]

The notion among some Anglo-Saxons of 'mission' to pagans on the continent cannot simply be dismissed as a chimaera, however, especially in the light of what we know about the man usually seen as Willibrord's successor in his 'mission field', Boniface. Originally called Wynfreth, he journeyed first from Wessex to Frisia in 716, but found himself in the middle of a war between Charles Martel and the Frisian leader Radbod and quickly returned home.[76] He set off for a second time in 718 and this time went to Rome, where he was given the name Boniface (Latin: *Bonifatius*) and commissioned by the pope to 'go forth with His [i.e. God's] guidance to those peoples who are still in the bonds of infidelity'.[77] The pope specifically mentioned 'the work of beneficial preaching'.[78] At first this was undertaken alongside Willibrord, who had been given the former Roman fortress at Utrecht as his see by Pippin II, and consecrated archbishop of the Frisians by Pope Sergius I.[79] But Boniface felt called to strike out on his own and in 721 went to Hesse, where, according to his biographer Willibald, he encountered the local rulers, 'two twin brothers named Dettic and Devrulf, whom he converted from the sacrilegious worship of idols which was practised under the

---

[74] Alcuin, *Vita Willibrordi*, trans. Talbot, p. 11.

[75] See above, Chapter 2, and M. Costambeys, 'An aristocratic community on the northern Frankish frontier', *Early Medieval Europe* 3/1 (1994), pp. 39–62.

[76] See above, Chapter 2.

[77] Boniface, *Epistolae*, *Ep.* 12, trans. Emerton, no. IV, pp. 32–3. The best short account of Boniface's career is now I. Wood, 'Boniface', *DNB*, *s.n.*

[78] Boniface, *Epistolae*, *Ep.* 12: '. . . in laborem salutiferae praedicationis'; Emerton translates this as 'to missionary work' at p. 33, which assumes a little too much, to my mind.

[79] Costambeys, 'Willibrord'; *LP* I, p. 376, trans. R. Davis, *The Book of Pontiffs* (Liber pontificalis), revised edition (Liverpool, 2000), p. 89.

cloak of Christianity'.[80] Though these words suggest syncretism (the juxtaposition of different or opposing religious practices), Willibald is also happy to call their religion straightforward 'paganism'; he credits Boniface with much success in turning these people to Christianity. In 722 Boniface returned to Rome to receive consecration as a bishop, with no fixed see: the pope's letter of introduction mentions vaguely 'some peoples in the regions of Germany and on the eastern side of the Rhine'.[81]

Willibald goes on to credit Boniface with successful evangelisation further into Hesse – where he felled a great oak dedicated, in an apparent example of *interpretatio romana*, to Jupiter – and in Thuringia.[82] Throughout this region Boniface, from 732 invested with the authority to consecrate other bishops, also founded monasteries at Ohrdruf, Fritzlar, Tauberbischofsheim, Ochsenfurt and Kitzingen. Fleeting military success by Charles Martel against the Saxons even raised in him the hope, attested in his letters, that he might extend his mission into their lands. But the tide of war flowed back in the Saxons' favour and he journeyed instead to Bavaria, to whose Christian community Willibald credits him with bringing both organisation and doctrinal orthodoxy.[83] Returning to Hesse, in 742 Boniface was able to establish what proved to be his most important monastic foundation, at Fulda, thanks to a gift from Charles Martel's son Carloman.[84] In that year also he could write to Pope Zacharias to announce his creation of three new dioceses in central Germany, at Würzburg, Erfurt (soon transferred to Eichstätt) and Buraburg.[85] Finally receiving a settled see at Mainz in 746, he used it to lay claim to the legacy of Willibrord: he appointed a bishop to the see of Utrecht, and made plans himself to take a campaign of preaching far into northern Frisia. There, on 5 June 754, his party was attacked and Boniface killed along with many companions.

The reaction to Boniface's death, which quickly came to be treated as a martyrdom, demonstrates the breadth of his influence. It was soon commemorated far and wide: in annals in Northumbria, and in the prayers of the monks of Monte Cassino in southern Italy (joined in

---

[80] Willibald, *Vita Bonifatii*, c. VI, trans. Talbot, p. 42.
[81] Boniface, *Epistolae*, *Ep.* 17, trans. Emerton, no. IX, pp. 42–3 (from which the translation given here differs slightly).
[82] See above, n. 37.   [83] Willibald, *Vita Bonifatii*, c. VII, trans. Talbot, p. 42.
[84] For Carloman's authority, see above, Chapter 2.
[85] Boniface, *Epistolae*, *Ep.* 50, trans. Emerton, no. XL, pp. 78–83.

confraternity with the monks of Fulda).[86] But his impact continued
to be felt most deeply in and around his mission field, through the
band of enthusiastic architects of an organised Church among his
disciples. His designated successor was Lull, who became archbishop
of Mainz. Others of his followers succeeded to the abbacy of Fulda
and the bishopric of Utrecht. Each furthered Boniface's work in
their own area, but this inevitable fragmentation of his legacy also
led to tensions, not least over his own remains. Hagiographical texts
written some years later point to disagreement over where the saint
should be laid to rest. Mainz, Fulda and Utrecht each had good
reason to want to be the centre of the cult of the immediately sainted
missionary hero, not least because of the patronage it might bring
for their institution. But the contest also partly reflected the differing
priorities of some of Boniface's heirs. While Lull was concerned with
his place, as archbishop, in the emerging Church hierarchy, and so
was seeking to bolster his archiepiscopal church at Mainz, at Fulda
the priority was to build the most successful monastic community
east of the Rhine.[87] Boniface was therefore portrayed there as first
and foremost a monk and monastic founder: missionising was not
high on the agenda at Fulda.[88]

England continued to provide personnel and materials to support the new continental churches. In letters to English contacts
both Boniface and Lull requested books.[89] People, too, continued to
come. Like Willibrord before him, from Northumbria came Willehad, who about 770 began to work among the Frisians.[90] It was
here, more than anywhere else, that the earlier English churchmen's
sense of mission – of deliberately seeking the conversion of non-
Christians – would be taken forward by their successors. This is
especially evident in the career of Liudger, himself from a family

[86] See the *Northern Annals*, ed. T. Arnold, *Symeonis monachi opera omnia*, 2 vols.,
Rolls Series 75 (London, 1882–5), II, pp. 30–66, trans. Whitelock, *EHD*, no. 3(a),
p. 266, and the *Continuation* of Bede, *Historia Ecclesiastica*, trans. Whitelock, *EHD*,
no. 5, p. 286, *s.a.* 754; for Monte Cassino, see Boniface, *Epistolae*, Ep. 106.

[87] On Lull, see J. Palmer, 'The "vigorous rule" of Bishop Lull: between Bonifatian
mission and Carolingian church control', *EME* 13/3 (2005), pp. 249–76.

[88] For Boniface's heirs, see Wood, *Missionary Life*, pp. 57–73.

[89] See e.g. Boniface, *Epistolae*, *Epp.* 30, 35, 75, 124, 142, trans. Emerton, nos. XXII,
XXVI, LIX, pp. 60–1, 64–5 and 132–3 (124 and 142 not translated).

[90] *Vita Willehadi*, ed. A. Röpke, *Das Leben des heiligen Willehad* (Bremen, 1982),
trans. T. F. X. Noble and T. Head, *Soldiers of Christ* (University Park, PA, 1995),
pp. 279–91.

of Frisian converts to Christianity, who was sent to reinforce the Christian Church first in eastern Frisia and then, by Charlemagne himself, across the river Lauwers in Saxon Westphalia, where his work inevitably became entangled in the Frankish–Saxon contest.[91] Though forced to withdraw by Saxon attacks in the late 770s, he eventually established in that territory both a bishopric, at Münster, and a monastery, at Werden. Dependence on Frankish military power was constantly evident: when Liudger ventured from his Frisian base at Deventer to smash pagan shrines, he gave two-thirds of their treasure to Charlemagne: this, surely, was the *quid pro quo* for the force, or threat of it, that allowed Liudger so brusquely to overturn traditional Frisian religion. Hagiographers wove into their stories of Christian heroism the Frankish campaigns against the Saxons that began in 772: another English evangeliser, Leofwine (known as Lebuin), stepped boldly into an assembly of Saxons to warn them that if they were unwilling to accept Christianity 'there is a king in a neighbouring country who will invade your land, who will despoil and lay waste, will tire you out with his campaigns, scatter you in exile, dispossess or kill you . . .'[92] Writing in the mid-ninth century, the *Life's* author knew perfectly well how accurate this prophecy would prove. In between the Franks' military activities among the Saxons and their legal attempts to impose Christianity, the job of evangelisers was less that of winning hearts and minds and more of building in bricks and mortar. Liudger built a monastery and episcopal seat at Münster, Willehad a cathedral at Bremen, Charlemagne himself one at Paderborn. These were the foundations for a Christianity in Saxony, which by the tenth century was among the most vibrant in Europe.

As we have seen, however, our sources for this apparently triumphant progress have their shortcomings. Where their descriptions of organised paganism turn out to be unreliable, or their references to real preaching missions frustratingly scant, we can question the black-and-white narrative of Christian victory over paganism. These texts were not, after all, of a kind intended to give an objective view of religious life in western Europe. They were predominantly hagiographies, meant to vindicate the claims to sanctity of their subjects. Willibrord's slaughtering of the sacred cattle of Fosite and

---

[91] On Liudger's career, see the summary in Wood, *Missionary Life*, pp. 100–17.
[92] *Vita Lebuini*, c. 6, ed. A. Hofmeister, *MGH SS* xxx.2 (Leipzig, 1934), pp. 789–95, p. 794; translation based on Talbot, p. 232.

Boniface's felling of the oak of Jupiter are portrayed as miraculous, and the miracle lay in the fact that they were allowed to get away with such deeds in what their hagiographers were keen to stress were viperous nests of pagans. But these interpretative problems are not limited to saints' *Lives*. Letters in the Boniface collection could misrepresent the situation in Germany, exaggerating the robustness of paganism, or other difficulties faced: Fulda was not, as Boniface claimed in a letter to Pope Zacharias, 'in the midst of a vast wilderness'.[93] A related point is that the Anglo-Saxon 'missionaries' belonged to a limited network of prominent religious. As Alcuin said himself, he was in fact related to Willibrord, as was the man for whom he wrote his biography, Willibrord's successor-but-one as abbot of Echternach, Beornrad.[94] Boniface received close support not only from his blood relative Leoba, who became abbess of Tauberbischofsheim, but from others with whom he corresponded: his old diocesan bishop Daniel of Winchester; a Mercian network that included his successor Lull and the bishop of Würzburg Burchard; and a number of abbesses and nuns in England.[95] These interconnections remind us that early medieval societies worked and interacted most often on personal levels. They also suggest that the rhetoric of 'mission' was not the only, or even the dominant, motivation for travel to the continent. It often looks more like a social and family enterprise, which reinforces the impression that expectations of bold encounters with inveterate pagans quickly gave way to the more prosaic business of the assimilation of immigrants: 'far more had been achieved by the Frankish clergy than Boniface and his compatriots realised when they set out'.[96] The notion of 'mission' was at least as much about the English as about the continental situation, for it was born out of the very particular circumstances of the English conversion: the deliberate 'mission', we might almost say 'embassy', despatched to King Æthelberht by Pope Gregory, and its subsequent spread in

---

[93] Boniface, *Epistolae*, *Ep.* 86, trans. Emerton, no. LXX, pp. 157–9; Eigil follows the same *topos* in the *Vita Sturmi*, ed. G. Pertz, *MGH SS* II (Hanover, 1829), pp. 365–77, cc. 5–12: see Wood, *Missionary Life*, p. 70.

[94] Wood, *Missionary Life*, p. 91. Beornrad was also archbishop of Sens.

[95] R. McKitterick, *Anglo-Saxon Missionaries in Germany: Personal Connections and Local Influences*, Vaughan Paper 36 (Brixworth, 1991), repr. in McKitterick, *Books, Scribes and Learning in the Frankish Kingdoms, 6th–9th Centuries* (Aldershot, 1994), no. IV.

[96] Wood, *Missionary Life*, p. 92.

like manner to other kings. Subsequent generations owe this reconstruction in particular to one man, Bede. Writing while Willibrord
was still alive, and Boniface was at his most active, Bede saw these
enterprises through the intellectual prism he had constructed, using
materials above all from Canterbury, over a lifetime's work at the
monastery at Jarrow which he never left as an adult.[97]

We need also to take account of the evidence for what we might
call the background noise of religious life in the seventh to ninth
centuries. Some of it points to paganism, avowed as such, present
in the heart of the Frankish kingdom: in the Merovingian era
St Amandus cured a woman of blindness by making her cut down
the tree where she had venerated an idol.[98] On the other hand, there
was the behaviour of which Boniface complained in letters to the
pope, of fornicators and drunkards among the Frankish priesthood,
and even among the bishops, of prelates who hunted, and entered
into bloodfeuds, and of pagan revelries practised (and here, it seems,
his tact wholly deserted him) even in the heart of Rome, 'in the
neighbourhood of St Peter's'.[99] Somewhere between the apparently
pagan practices which his biographer has Amandus combat in the
Frankish heartland of the 640s, and the earthily secular behaviour
of the Frankish bishops of the mid-eighth century condemned by
Boniface, there was room for practices that were neither transparently
non-Christian nor obviously contrary to the ancient rules of the institutional Church. Rather, they arose through interpreting Christian
precepts in singular, unconventional ways. We know, for example,
that in parts of England in the eighth century people were taking
their communion wine not from a special, ecclesiastically sanctioned
vessel, but from an ordinary drinking-horn: an English Church council condemned them for doing so.[100] Similarly, Charlemagne complained that many had adopted the Christian practice of lifting a child
from the baptismal font, without having the basic Christian knowledge – of the Lord's Prayer, for example, and the Creed – that was

---

[97] On Bede's notion of mission, see Wood, *Missionary Life*, pp. 44–5.
[98] *Vita Amandi*, c. 24, ed. B. Krusch, *MGH SRM* v (Hanover, 1910), p. 448, trans.
Hillgarth, *Christianity and Paganism*, p. 147.
[99] Boniface, *Epistolae*, *Epp.* 50 and 60, trans. Emerton, nos. XL and XLVIII, pp. 78–83
and 107–11. See also J. M. Wallace-Hadrill, The *Frankish Church* (Oxford, 1983),
p. 137.
[100] As the Council of 786 reported to Pope Hadrian: Alcuin, *Ep.* 3, c. 10, ed.
Dümmler, pp. 19–29 at p. 23.

expected of properly Christian godparents.[101] What these examples indicate is that Christianisation constituted a spectrum of activities. Combating a 'pagan' religion might be one of them, though there are question marks against even our most detailed depictions of these (such as in the *Life* of Willibrord). Very often, though, the Church must have been filling a vacuum, where nothing nearly as sophisticated, in spiritual and theological terms, had existed before its arrival. Indeed, where no organised, institutionalised pagan religion existed, Church promoters may have felt the need to invent the appearance of one, in comparison with which Christianity would look a more coherent spiritual proposition.

The problem appears especially starkly in the case of the Frankish encounters with the Avars and the Saxons. In Charlemagne's reign these were, as we have seen, decidedly violent. But both peoples had in fact had long contact with the Franks and experience of their Christian religion: archaeology reveals thriving Frankish–Saxon commerce, for instance.[102] Frankish churchmen worried not that Christianity was entirely alien to their foes, but that they understood it incompletely, or practised it poorly. Hence, the conquest of the Avar kingdom in 796 was the occasion for an exceptional meeting of Frankish bishops on the banks of the Danube, where correct practices, and baptism in particular, dominated discussion;[103] and Alcuin, in letters to his friend Arno, bishop of Salzburg, and to Charlemagne, argued in favour of preaching and baptism as the right way to deal with both the Avars and the Saxons.[104] Revolts of both peoples were due to 'negligence' on the Franks' part.[105] However, these recommendations, which recognised the complexities of belief on and across the Frankish frontier, had minimal practical effect on Frankish activity there, where the concern was above all military subjugation. Carolingian reports of these wars tend to by-pass the

---

[101] *Capit.* I, no. 122, p. 241; and see J. Lynch, *Godparents and Kinship in Early Medieval Europe* (Princeton, NJ, 1986), pp. 285–332.

[102] I. Wood, 'Before or after mission. Social relations across the middle and lower Rhine in the seventh and eighth centuries', in Hansen and Wickham (eds.), *The Long Eighth Century*, pp. 149–66.

[103] *Conventus episcoporum at ripas Danubii* (a.796), in *Conc.* II/1, no. 20, pp. 172–6; de Jong, 'Charlemagne's Church', in Story (ed.), *Charlemagne*, pp. 126–7.

[104] Alcuin, *Epp.* nos. 107, 110, 112, 113, trans. Allott, nos. 59, 56, 137. For context on the Avars and Saxons see above, Chapter 2, pp. 70–2, 73–5.

[105] Alcuin, *Ep.* 184, trans. Allott, no. 65.

conciliatory concerns of the leading ecclesiastics, detailing slaughter by the Franks, and equating the Saxons' stubbornness directly with their paganism.[106] After another 'revolt' – or continued resistance to conquest – even Alcuin questioned the point of 'toiling over the accursed tribe of the Saxons'.[107] As we have seen, the baptismal formula that the Franks imposed on the Saxons stressed renunciation of the old gods.[108] But the suspicion remains that this image of paganism attests a Frankish desire for self-justification as much as a real, deep-rooted, non-Christian religion.

The repeated injunctions of kings and ecclesiastics against them are sufficient testimony that across the Carolingian world practices unsanctioned by the ecclesiastical hierarchy never disappeared. To counteract them, the process of Christianisation put stress on outward activities, on the rituals and symbols that made religious change visible. We should not think that this emphasis detracted from or excluded deepening inward understanding of the Christian message. Moreover, both ritual and word may often have been less important in the process of initial conversion than social and political bonds, but both worked in harness, miracle and message together, in deepening the Christian experience thereafter.[109] Nevertheless, the concern to define, interpret and standardise rituals, which we will see most pertinently in the case of the eucharist, related problematically to the fundamental message that the more sophisticated Christian thinkers wanted to project: that Christian belief involved not simply the performance of ritual practices, but wholesale self-improvement. The goal was certainty of salvation, reached through moral 'perfection'. The right rituals might help, but the target remained dauntingly challenging, and naturally gave rise to the language of negativity and complaint about the moral state of this world that we have seen in Archbishop Hincmar's letter. Some in this world were so imperfect that they could be characterised as 'non-Christians'; others, self-professed Christians, were still nothing like perfect enough. What

---

[106] E.g. Chapter 2.   [107] Alcuin, *Ep.* 184, trans. Allott, no. 65.
[108] See above, p. 91.
[109] For the relationship between miracle and word in a slightly earlier context, see K. Cooper, 'Ventriloquism and the miraculous: conversion, preaching, and the martyr exemplum in late antiquity', in K. Cooper and J. Gregory (eds.), Signs, Wonders, Miracles. Representations of Divine Power in the Life of the Church, *Studies in Church History* 41 (Woodbridge, 2005), pp. 22–45.

stood in the way of perfection in this world, and so guaranteed continuing pessimism about it, was, in a word, sin.

THE PROBLEM OF SIN

Hincmar's apparent anxiety about non-Christian practices among Carolingian courtiers masks his deeper concern for the sins of particular individuals: the incestuous sodomy, resulting in abortion (*sic*), of which Lothar II's queen Theutberga was accused, and the adultery of the king himself. Theutberga's enemies could point both to her sins themselves and to the penance required for her absolution – her confinement to a nunnery – as making her unfit to be a wife and queen, while the other side could allege that Lothar had transgressed the morality required of a Christian king.[110] Paganism existed in Hincmar's world less as a reality than as an image in which to cast a preoccupation with the human moral failings which stood between the believer and heaven. This concern was a vital pulse, impeccably Christian, yet so basic and insistent as to be almost subconscious among Christians of Hincmar's generation. Christianity's central teaching was to tackle sins in this world by appealing to the next: Jesus had taken the sins of humanity to the cross, and in his resurrection offered the prospect of redemption for them, in a life of bliss after death. This message therefore focussed the attention of Christians on sin and death together.

Christian death and giving to the Church

By 700, Christianity was already beginning to influence the treatment of the dead. Between *c.*400 and *c.*700, many across western Europe deposited in their burials goods ranging from pots to swords alongside the corpses of their dead, earning the gratitude of modern archaeologists for the invaluable insights into their society's material culture that they thus provided. The gradual disappearance of this practice from *c.*700 cannot be taken as direct evidence for the Christianisation of the act of burial, however: Christian writers had not complained about the practice, and some excavated graves contain distinctly Christian artefacts (for example, votive crosses), while other

---

[110] Airlie, 'Private bodies'.

furnished burials are found in churches.[111] Rather, it is a sign of a change in a variety of social actions that accompanied death. In some places, old strictures about the location of burials broke down as families began to bring clergymen into the burial process.[112] Everywhere, lavish deposition rituals which had affirmed the status and wealth of the deceased clashed against an increasing recognition of the need to help the inevitably sinful souls of the dead after death. Families continued to spend publicly on their dead, but rather than displaying their wealth at the point of inhumation by ostentatiously furnishing graves, they were encouraged to sponsor the rituals that Christian belief increasingly emphasised as effective remedies for the soul's sinful condition.[113] Chief among these was the mass – the re-enactment, enjoined apparently by Christ himself, of the Last Supper, which immediately became a commemoration of his sacrifice.[114] The mass would gradually acquire a great weight of meaning, as it came to be regarded as a miracle, a daily instance of divine power working in the world, and we will see shortly how and when this came about. Its development in the early Christian centuries was evidently a response to the centrality of sacrifice in some sense to nearly all religions at that time. But it also developed as part of a wider body of liturgical practices, in particular of prayers, which emerged as the Church deepened its involvement with everyday society. Eloquent testimony to the importance of these practices in the Christianising societies of the post-Roman west is provided by some of the many hundreds of single-sheet documents (charters) on which much legal business, especially transactions of all kinds, was set down. The ones that survive mostly concern ecclesiastical institutions, because they themselves lasted often through many generations, and so were best able to preserve documents down the centuries.

[111] Innes, *State and Society*, pp. 34–40 with references; G. Halsall, 'Burial ritual and Merovingian society', in J. Hill and M. Swan (eds.), *The Community, the Family and the Saint* (Turnhout, 1998), pp. 325–38, and G. Halsall, 'Female status and power in early Merovingian central Austrasia: the burial evidence', *Early Medieval Europe* 5/1 (1996), pp. 1–24. In general, see F. S. Paxton, *Christianizing Death: The Creation of a Ritual Process in Early Medieval Europe* (Ithaca and London, 1990).

[112] M. Costambeys, 'Burial topography and the power of the Church in fifth- and sixth-century Rome', *PBSR* 69 (2001), pp. 169–89.

[113] C. La Rocca, 'Segni di distinzione. Dai corredi funerari alle donazioni "post obitum" nel regno longobardo', in L. Paroli (ed.), *L'Italia centro-settentrionale in età longobarda* (Florence, 1997), pp. 31–54.

[114] See Matt. 26:26–8, Mark 14:22–4, Luke 22:19–20; also I Cor. 11:23–7.

One such institution was the monastery of St Bartholomew, built in Pistoia in Lombard northern Tuscany in the early eighth century, and the recipient of a smaller monastery of Sts Peter, Paul and Anastasius from the latter's founder, Ratpert. He had established it with an endowment of half of his property in a charter of 748. In this document we can detect the voice of Ratpert himself, standing at the scribe's shoulder, instructing the monastery's abbot

to pray day and night to almighty God and to Mary, the mother of the same almighty God, and to the most blessed saints Peter, Paul and Anastasius, in whose honour the church is founded, for my soul and for the heavy burden of my sins, so that I, a great sinner, may be worthy to break the chains of my punishments . . . [115]

Ratpert's evident anxiety arose in part from the grave illness from which he was then suffering. In his case, endowing ecclesiastical institutions was relatively uncomplicated because he had no sons, and even required that his female relatives – mother, wife, sister and daughter – take up a monastic life in the new foundation or forfeit any right to enjoy the family property. When male heirs existed account had to be taken of their rights to inherit – and when our charters record disputes in this period, they very often involved lay heirs trying to vindicate claims to properties that churches and monasteries had or claimed through gifts of their owners. But such problems did not deter patronage of the Church: we have only to look at St Bartholomew's itself for an example of a patron transmitting property to an institution in addition to, rather than instead of, a bequest to his son. It had been established by the long-standing royal doctor Gaidoald, who even stipulated that his son and later heirs should defend the monastery in any dispute and ensure that its property was not diminished; property which, it is worth underlining, would have passed to the son himself had the monastery not been established. [116]

---

[115] *CDL* I 96: 'pro anima mea grauata ponderibus peccatis meis die noctuque omnipotentem Deum et eiusdem omnipotentis Dei genitrice Maria uel beatissimi sancti Petri et Pauli seu Anastasii, in cuius honore ecclesia est fundata, exorare, ut me nimis peccator de uinculis penarum eripere dignetur'; the passage continues: 'et inter sanctis et electis suis aliqua parte uel societas tribuere iubeas, quia scriptum est per eloquium et minestrationem domini nostri Iesu Christi: "petite et dabitur uobis, querite et invenietis, pulsate et aperietur uobis"' (Matthew 7:7).

[116] *CDL* II 203; on Gaidoald *medicus* see C. Wickham, *Framing the Early Middle Ages. Europe and the Mediterranean, 400–800* (Oxford, 2005), p. 215.

Gaidoald, it seems, was engaging in a common practice, 'using the end of life as a pretext for arranging relations during life'.[117]

Gaidoald, like Ratpert, was endowing monks 'who by their works offer alms and do not cease to pray to the Lord day and night for our sins'.[118] Theirs were acts and attitudes by no means confined to Lombard Italy, but found across the Christianising west. Charters from the mid-eighth century like these represent the culmination of important stages in the development of a distinctively Christian and distinctly post-Roman western culture. Spreading from the British Isles was the notion that individual sins could be atoned for by precisely calibrated penances usually in the form of periods of prayer and fasting.[119] Sins and their requisite penances were set out in detailed tariffs – penitentials – that first emerged in Ireland in the sixth century. From there in the seventh century they spread along with peregrine Irish monks to England and to Francia.[120] In the latter in particular, these individual or 'secret' penances, as they were sometimes called, sat comfortably next to the liturgical practices of communities of monks, who were seen as specialist purveyors of activities for purging the soul – their monasteries were 'powerhouses of prayer', in Peter Brown's vivid phrase.[121] Everywhere, establishing these institutions chimed with a culture routinely animated by donation and counter-donation. Making over one's property to communities of monks and nuns prompted the reciprocal gift of their expertise for atonement, honed for themselves, but offered also to others – to material patrons, to distant kings, to 'ordinary' lay associates. By the ninth century, many monasteries had 'books of commemoration' (*libri memoriales*) recording the names of those for whom the monks

---

[117] C. La Rocca, 'La legge e la pratica. Potere e rapporti sociali nell'Italia dell' VIII secolo', in C. Bertelli and G. P. Brogiolo (eds.), *Il futuro dei Longobardi. L'Italia e la costruzione dell'Europa di Carlo Magno* (Brescia, 2000), pp. 45–69 at p. 52.

[118] *CDL* II 203.

[119] R. Meens, 'The frequency and nature of early medieval penance', in P. Biller and A. Minns (eds.), *Handling Sin: Confession in the Middle Ages* (Woodbridge, 1998), pp. 35–61.

[120] S. Hamilton, 'The unique favour of penance: the Church and the people *c.*800–*c.*1100', in Linehan and Nelson (eds.), *The Medieval World*, pp. 229–45, esp. 232–3.

[121] Brown, *Rise of Western Christendom*, p. 226. On the meaning of such prayers for the dead, see A. Angenendt, 'Theologie und Liturgie der mittelalterlichen Totenmemoria', in K. Schmid and J. Wollasch (eds.), *Memoria. Der geschichtliche Zeugniswert des liturgischen Gedenkens im Mittelalter* (Munich, 1984), pp. 80–199.

prayed, which they could not recite individually since they now ran into thousands.[122] Individual penance, monastic prayer and patronage of the Church had been coalescing throughout the post-Roman period in the west. By the eighth century they had integrated to produce a culture in which pious gifts were commonplace.

In his charter, the ailing Ratpert makes clear enough his pressing concern with 'the heavy burden of my sins' and suggests a belief that prayer could help to wash it away. But behind that concept lay a number of tensions, the resolution of which remained at the centre of debate among Christians for centuries – up to, and indeed beyond, the Reformation.[123] One of these is evident if we look at particular passages in charters like that of Ratpert just quoted (a passage called a proem or *arenga*, which set down the motives for the legal act embodied in the charter). While some express a certainty that a pious gift would result in definite benefits to the soul, others acknowledge the need to have in addition the mercy or grace of God: 'certainty' faded into 'hope'. This ambiguity, still at the heart of Christian doctrine, can be traced back at least to the pre-eminent western theologian of earlier centuries, St Augustine, bishop of Hippo, who in the early fifth century taught that human sin was ultimately ineradicable because of Adam and Eve's original sin in Eden, but affirmed nonetheless that penances were a necessary part of human life, so that what he called the 'minor' sins (*peccata levia*) of an individual could and should be atoned for through such daily penances as prayer and almsgiving.[124] The tension between this view and the rather less nuanced idea behind 'tariffed' penances that were thought to wash away carefully enumerated sins was not one on which early medieval Christians generally chose to dwell, however. Augustine had focussed their attention rather on the notion that the

---

[122] See the controversy between Althoff and Hoffmann, the most recent salvo in which is G. Althoff and J. Wollasch, 'Bleiben die *Libri Memoriales* stumm? Eine Erwiderung auf H. Hoffmann', *Deutsches Archiv für Erforschung des Mittelalters* 56 (2000), pp. 33–53, and D. Geuenich, 'A survey of the early medieval confraternity books from the continent', in D. Rollason (ed.), *The Durham Liber Vitae and its Context* (Woodbridge, 2004), pp. 141–7.

[123] D. MacCulloch, *Reformation. Europe's House Divided, 1490–1700* (London, 2003), pp. 11–14.

[124] P. Brown, *The End of the Ancient Other World: Death and Afterlife between Late Antiquity and the Early Middle Ages*, Tanner Lectures (New Haven, CT, 1996), pp. 51–3. It should be noted that the distinction between 'venial' and 'mortal' sins, still current in Catholic theology, comes later.

process of cleansing the stain of minor sins crossed the threshold of death; 'the geography of the hereafter' became of central concern to Christians as they continued to atone for sin beyond the grave.[125] With hindsight, this is an idea that points directly to purgatory, although the absence of the term itself until the twelfth century has made it hard to trace its development as a coherent doctrine.[126] Before the seventh century, in the works of figures like Augustine, the emphasis was on intercession on behalf of believers' souls by an emperor-like God mercifully disposed to amnesty, or by the great heroes of Christianity who had direct access to him – the saints. But in the seventh century there developed a more practical, hands-on approach to individual salvation, which happened in conjunction with the first signs of interest in what the after-life might actually look like. In tales that began to be told of the soul's voyage after death, souls eternally damned and those temporally purged mingled in the same space: in his terrifying Vision, the flames of an unpurged sinner burnt the cheek of the Irishman Fursa, while in a similar text angels and demons contested the soul of the Frankish aristocrat Barontus.[127]

As Christian belief absorbed and disseminated these terrible possibilities, Christians were increasingly prompted to make provision in their lifetime for the good of their own souls, and of those of their families, encouraged by the idea that sins could still be purged, and divine mercy appealed to, even after death. Hence in the seventh, and increasingly through the eighth, century, a rising tide of gifts to churches and monasteries – property, people and possessions, intended to sponsor the prayers of priests, monks and nuns – effected a massive transfer of wealth to Church institutions. Later in the Middle Ages, the salvific benefit of such prayers would be quantified on an individual basis, each 'unit' of intercession measuring with scholastic determination a specific subtraction from the soul's spell in

---

[125] P. Brown, 'Vers la naissance de purgatoire'.

[126] Compare e.g. Brown, *Rise of Western Christendom*, pp. 258–65 with C. Watkins, 'Sin, penance and purgatory in the Anglo-Norman realm', *P&P* 175 (2002), pp. 3–33.

[127] *Visio Fursi* [Vision of Fursa], 16.5, ed. C. Carozzi, *Le Voyage de l'âme dans l'au-delà*, Collection de l'EFR 189 (Rome, 1994), p. 691, and see in general pp. 99–186; *Visio Baronti*, ed. W. Levison, *MGH SRM* v (Hanover, 1910), pp. 386–94, 12, trans. Hillgarth, *Christianity and Paganism*, p. 199; see also Y. Hen, 'The structure and aims of the *Visio Baronti*', *Journal of Theological Studies*, n.s. 47 (1996), pp. 477–97; Brown, *Rise of Western Christendom*, pp. 258–60.

purgatory.[128] But at this stage the sponsorship of prayer was neither so organised nor so institutionalised. Family and monastery were not distinct entities, and indeed overlapped to the point of identity in cases such as Ratpert's own foundation in Pistoia. In larger monastic houses, monks and nuns were drawn from numbers of different sponsoring families, but the gifts of each were made less for the discrete benefit of a specific individual than to bind each family to a community whose penitential activities benefited their entire collection of patrons – their *familia*, in the contemporary Latin.[129]

The complications of the relationship between families and the monasteries they sponsored are evident in the case of the abbey of Lorsch, founded by Cancor under the influence of his kinsman Chrodegang, his era's most creative shaper of the religious life (see Figure 4a).[130] By 772, its ownership was the subject of a dispute, submitted to Charlemagne's judgement in Easter of that year, between Cancor's son Heimerich and his kinsman, the then abbot Guntland. Cancor's death late in 771 had provoked the tussle, but what provided Guntland with the opportunity to win it was the death around the same time of Carloman, who until that time had divided rule over the Frankish realm with his brother Charlemagne.[131] At this particular juncture, the dispute over Lorsch offered Charlemagne the opportunity to assert his authority over a religious institution, and by extension over a family that had formerly maintained a careful equidistance between himself and his brother; equally, Guntland's success depended on his ability to make real the prospect of Charlemagne's control. It is no surprise, then, that when Charlemagne duly ruled in Guntland's favour and against Heimerich, the abbot immediately placed Lorsch under royal protection, turning it into what Carolingian historians tend to call a 'royal monastery'.[132] We

---

[128] See Watkins, 'Sin, penance and purgatory', pp. 14–15.

[129] M. McLaughlin, *Consorting with Saints: Prayer for the Dead in Early Medieval France* (Ithaca and London, 1994); P. Geary, 'Exchange and interaction between the living and the dead in early medieval society', in Geary, *Living with the Dead in the Early Middle Ages* (Ithaca, NY, and London, 1994), pp. 77–94; and D. Iogna-Prat, 'The dead in the celestial bookkeeping of the Cluniac monks', in Little and Rosenwein (eds.), *Debating the Middle Ages*, pp. 340–62.

[130] Innes, *State and Society*, pp. 18–19. On Chrodegang: M. Claussen, *The Reform of the Frankish Church. Chrodegang of Metz and the* Regula canonicorum *in the Eighth Century* (Cambridge, 2004), pp. 19–57.

[131] *Dipl. Kar.* I, no. 65. For the political background, see above, Chapter 2.

[132] Innes, *State and Society*, pp. 55–7 and 180–2; Innes, 'Kings, monks and patrons', pp. 308–10.

Figure 4a. Abbey of Lorsch, Germany, gatehouse. Lorsch was patronised by several kings, and two – Louis the German (*d*.876) and his son Louis the Younger (*d*.882) – were buried there. The gatehouse was probably built in the time of the latter.

are fortunate that the details of this case have survived, because it demonstrates how a family's beliefs were made concrete by the establishment and patronage of an institution, and how that institution was inescapably bound to the world that had created it.

The objects of patronage: masses, priests and monks

This connection between abbey and aristocracy demonstrates an essential paradox at the heart of the monastic enterprise. Monasticism had arisen out of the belief, not unique to Christianity, which identified virtue, and ultimately the purification or perfection of the soul, with the rejection of all things associated with 'the world': material wealth, power over fellow men, the concupiscence of the flesh. For Christians, who drew on the New Testament's repeated emphasis on self-denial, to pursue the ascetic ideal of renunciation was to seek to imitate in some way the sacrificial life of Christ. Monasticism was the conduct of such asceticism communally (as that of the disciples in Jerusalem after the resurrection),[133] rather than as a hermit. But since monks and nuns were themselves drawn from 'the world' and

[133] Acts 2: 44–6.

depended upon it for sustenance, and since that world recognised, and wanted to harness, the spiritual power of these ascetics, they could never break entirely free from it. Monastic practitioners therefore faced the inescapable problem of what degree of compromise with the material world was acceptable. The battle to keep the world out of the monastery required that monks and nuns keep in mind constantly the need for reform: both on a personal level – reform of the individual's lifestyle and soul – and on that of the institution – reform of the practices of the monastery and of its personnel. And what was good for monasticism was good for the Christian Church generally: the ever-present nagging fear of compromise engendered pressure for reform; and though ever-present, in historical terms that pressure for reform has ebbed and flowed.[134]

Enthusiasm for reforming religious life drew on the basic notion that the activities that were most effective for the good of the soul were those performed by the purest actors, least blemished by the world of sin. Attention to the activities of the clergy, monastic and secular, grew only slowly, and the eighth century was still a period in which the prayers that they offered took many forms.[135] In the charters quoted above, neither Ratpert nor Gaidoald was especially precise about the form of the prayers they were sponsoring. Prayers were of course incorporated into the service of the mass, and many donations similar to those of these Italian benefactors were made 'for the mass and for lights' (*pro missa et luminaria*): the expense of illuminating churches was a central concern of patronage.[136] Already in the Merovingian period in Francia, the mass, as high point of the liturgy, was also becoming the convergence point for the ideas of commemoration and of gift that we have just noted. What had once been seen as a ritual re-enactment of the Last Supper was therefore itself coming to be thought of as a gift to God, or even as a sacrifice, if in symbolic form: it was a particularly privileged form of that mediation between man and God that was the common concern of

---

[134] See initially G. Ladner, *The Idea of Reform: Its Impact on Christian Thought and Action in the Age of the Fathers* (Cambridge, MA, 1959).

[135] For the diversity of liturgy in Merovingian Francia in this context, see Hen, *Culture and Religion*, pp. 61–81 and 143–4.

[136] *CDL* I 54, 59; II 188, 190, 234, 291; on lighting in this context, see P. Fouracre, 'Eternal light and earthly needs: practical aspects of the development of Frankish immunities', in W. Davies and P. Fouracre (eds.), *Property and Power in the Early Middle Ages* (Cambridge, 1995), pp. 53–81.

Augustine, Fursa, Barontus and Ratpert.[137] As such, and as writers of the ninth century emphasised, it reaffirmed the identity of every Christian within the community of the faithful.[138]

By the ninth century, the centrality of the mass to the efficacy of Christian practice, the daily experience of it by legions of priests and monks, and the increased production of liturgical texts that this necessitated, led many scholars to explore what the mystery of the eucharist signified, and what exactly was the nature of the 'miracle' that it enacted.[139] The abbey of Corbie in northern Neustria emerged as a centre of the lively debates that sometimes ensued. (Although nothing from this era survives at Corbie, Figure 4b shows the Carolingian *Westwerk* of its daughter house of Korvey in Germany.) There at the end of the eighth century an anonymous monk had set down an apparently straightforward perception of the mass:

> For what reasons is the mass celebrated? For many reasons. First so that they may frequently address the Lord. Second, so that God may receive prayers and offerings. Third, for offerants and for the dead. Fourth, for the kiss of peace. Fifth, so that the offering may be sanctified. Sixth, so that the offering may be confirmed through the Holy Spirit in the body and blood of Christ. Seventh, so that the Our Father may be sung...[140]

But this sixth reason, in particular, proved in fact to be very problematic: the question of the 'real presence' in the eucharist – that is, in what sense the bread and wine are, or become, or represent, the body and blood of Jesus – has been in contention in Christianity

---

[137] In the preface to the *Expositio antiquae liturgiae Gallicanae*, for example, the mass 'is sung in commemoration of the death of the Lord . . . that by being offered it may bring about the salvation of the living and the rest of the dead': *Expositio antiquae liturgiae Gallicanae*, ed. E. Ratcliff, Henry Bradshaw Society 98 (London, 1971), pp. 3–16, here p. 3, trans. Hillgarth, *Christianity and Paganism*, pp. 186–92, here p. 186. The text is convincingly dated to the Merovingian period by Hen, *Culture and Religion*, pp. 47–9. Noting this development in the eighth and ninth centuries makes conceptions of the mass in the twelfth century look less original; for the latter, see M. Rubin, *Corpus Christi: the Eucharist in Late Medieval Culture* (Cambridge, 1991), esp., in this context, pp. 13–14.

[138] R. McKitterick, *The Frankish Church and the Carolingian Reforms, 789–895* (London, 1977), pp. 115–55; D. Ganz, 'Theology and the organisation of thought', in *NCMH* II (Cambridge, 1995), pp. 758–85, at pp. 777–80.

[139] Rubin, *Corpus Christi*, p. 16.

[140] A. Wurnburger (ed.), *Über eine ungedruckte Kanonensammlung aus dem 8. Jahrhundert* (Munich, 1890), p. 60 (taken from Paris, BN lat. 12444), quoted in McKitterick, *Frankish Church*, p. 148.

Figure 4b. Abbey of Korvey, Germany, *Westwerk*.

ever since; but a heightened concern for it in the eighth and ninth centuries must be seen as a direct response to the mass's emerging importance at the centre of Christian ritual. Thus in 844 Corbie's then abbot, Paschasius Radbertus, stepped into the debate by sending to Charles the Bald a detailed work in which he averred that in the eucharist 'Christ's real flesh and blood is truly created'.[141] His claims were countered by a monk of his own monastery, Ratramnus, who argued that he had taken too literal an interpretation of the Last Supper. Ratramnus preferred to see the sacraments as visible words, distinct from the matter that they signified.[142] Similar

---

[141] Paschasius Radbertus, *De corpore et sanguine Domini*, ed. B. Paulus, *CCCM* 16 (Turnhout, 1969), p. 23.
[142] Ratramnus of Corbie, *De corpore et sanguine Domini*, PL cxxi, cols. 169–70.

arguments unfolded at Lyon in response to the ideas of Amalarius of Metz. Amalarius had put forward detailed allegorical explanations for every part of the liturgy, including the eucharist, and attempted to implement his resulting scheme for new liturgical practice in the episcopal church at Lyon when, between 835 and 837, he replaced the exiled archbishop Agobard.[143] Agobard and his deacon Florus both responded with vigorously critical works, and Amalarius was hauled before a synod at Quierzy in 838 and his opinions condemned as heretical.[144]

Anxiety in the Amalarius affair focussed around the effect his ideas might have on the priesthood.[145] Most priests were not members of the highly educated circle among whom texts like Amalarius's circulated. Growing emphasis on the mass cast steadily more insistent attention on the office of priest, for only he could dispense the sacraments. This task, it was increasingly felt, demanded a certain moral purity on the part of the celebrant, and this only added to a list of requirements for priests that lengthened through our period as the Church became better defined as an institution. It is very hard to discover much about the range of Christian and Christianising activities that come under the heading of 'pastoral care' in the years around 700: we know very little about who precisely dispensed communion, administered baptisms and officiated at funerals in the early eighth century – and, with exceptions, about where they did so. Rural churches and their accompanying priests do appear sometimes in donations of landed estates to monasteries. In Italy, for instance, where Christianity was relatively deeply embedded, the abbey of Farfa received in this manner at least sixteen churches during the eighth century.[146] This at least indicates that alongside the

---

[143] Amalarius of Metz, *De officiis*, ed. J. Hanssens, *Amalarii opera liturgica omnia* II, Studi e Testi 138–40 (Vatican City, 1948–50), pp. 13–543.

[144] Agobard of Lyons, *De Antiphonario*, ed. L. van Acker, *CCCM* 52 (Turnhout, 1981), pp. 335–51; Florus of Lyon, *Adversus Amalarium*, PL 119, cols. 74–6; Synod of Quierzy: *Concilium Carisiacense*, Conc. II/1, pp. 768–82; see further Ganz, 'Theology and the organisation of thought', pp. 777–8.

[145] McKitterick, *Frankish Church*, pp. 150–5.

[146] Costambeys, *Power and Patronage*, Chapter 2 (this figure includes, however, four churches in or just outside local towns). On the 'extreme flexibility of religious geography in the early middle ages', see P. Toubert, *Les Structures du Latium médiéval: Le Latium méridional et la Sabine du IXe siècle à la fin du XIIe siècle*, 2 vols., Bibliothèque des écoles françaises d'Athènes et de Rome 221 (Rome, 1973) II, pp. 855–6.

existence of proprietary monasteries (*Eigenklöster*) we need to posit that of proprietary churches (*Eigenkirche*) – in other words, institutions effectively owned by powerful churches or aristocrats. But it is not clear whether these ever extended their functions much beyond those of family chapel and/or the commemoration of a saint's cult.

Although texts relating to priests gradually increase through our period, they were mostly produced by their superiors. The Carolingian kings' capitulary legislation envisaged that the collectivity of priests within a diocese would be formally subordinate to the bishop,[147] and slightly later indicated to bishops their responsibility for educating priests in their duty of care over their flock.[148] Structurally, though, the Church was still rudimentary. In the Carolingian empire the only definite units of ecclesiastical administration were the 180 episcopal sees, which nearly all followed boundaries of the now long-departed Roman secular administrative structure. These were being grouped into metropolitan archbishoprics following the pattern established for the English Church and brought to the continent by English evangelisers.[149] A formal structure of parishes did not appear until the tenth century or, mostly, even later.[150] Priests themselves were very far from a uniform group. Some might be rural representatives of the communities of canons that came into being around many episcopal cathedrals in the eighth and ninth centuries.[151] Priestly office could also be held by professed monks, either inmates of the great houses that large-scale patronage had created, or from the many small *cella* – some of them, as we have seen, essentially family owned – that dotted parts of western Europe. The latter were mostly in the same position as the priests of the proprietary churches (*Eigenkirche*) that we have already noted, beholden to their lords and receiving from them, perhaps, only a portion of the income that their church received through the tithe.

[147] E.g. *Capit.* I, nos. 138, c. 9, 140, c. 5.

[148] *Admonitio ad omnes regni ordines*, c. 5, *Capit.* I, p. 304.

[149] On development of the metropolitan structure, see R. Reynolds, 'The organisation, law and liturgy of the western church, 700–900', in *NCMH* II, pp. 587–621 at pp. 599–600.

[150] For a relatively upbeat assessment of the extent of parish organisation in Francia by the time of Hincmar, see McKitterick, *Frankish Church*, p. 64; see also C. Treffort, *L'Église carolingienne et la mort* (Lyon, 1996), p. 188.

[151] C. van Rhijn, *Shepherds of the Lord. Priests and Episcopal Statutes in the Carolingian Period* (Turnhout, 2007).

The involvement of lay lords and great abbots meant that leadership of this motley group was still contested. Those who asserted it most explicitly were the bishops, who at the same time set out the ideals to which they hoped priests would aspire, in *capitula episcoporum* – directives sent by bishops to the clergy of their dioceses. Priests worthy of the 'blessed people' of the Franks[152] should have clean hands when they administered the sacraments, unpolluted by sex and violence; they should be distinguished, socially and hierarchically, from their flock and, as a corollary, freed from economic dependence on any secular lord; and they should be literate, and in possession of the texts needed to do their job.[153] Although it took centuries for the western Church's priesthood even to come close to fulfilling the first of these requirements, its persistence is striking. The insistence on clerical celibacy was one sign among many that the preoccupations of the monastery – of personal holiness, of living according to a Christian code of morality – were invading the world of secular priests. Who those priests were is not easy to discern, but efforts to ensure their economic self-sufficiency were an early preoccupation of the Carolingians, with Pippin III's measures to enforce the payment of tithe for the upkeep of priests.[154] As for the literate capabilities of the priesthood, two surviving manuscript codices that were evidently used as handbooks by rural priests give an encouraging picture of a priesthood that both knew and regularly used canon law and the standard liturgies, though both seem to have originated in the Carolingian heartland, where we might expect closest conformity to the ideal.[155] Manuscript illustrations, too, may have been designed partly with the education of priests in mind. (See Figure 5.)

The prescriptiveness of so much of our evidence for priests generates a certain tension in the way we interpret it. When bishops set

---

[152] Alcuin, *Ep.* 228, trans. Allott, no. 91; see M. Garrison, 'The Franks as the new Israel? Education for an identity from Pippin to Charlemagne', in Hen and Innes, *Uses of the Past*, pp. 114–61, esp. pp. 159–60 and de Jong, 'Charlemagne's church', p. 113 ('the expression *novus Israel* was never used').

[153] M. de Jong, 'Religion', in R. McKitterick (ed.), *The Early Middle Ages: Europe 400–1000* (Oxford, 2001), pp. 131–66, at pp. 155–6.

[154] There is still scope for a detailed study of Carolingian tithe. Pippin III's concern to enforce it seems evident from a letter to Archbishop Lull: Boniface, *Epistolae*, *Ep.* 118 (not translated in Emerton); see further G. Constable, *Monastic Tithes from their Origins to the Twelfth Century* (Cambridge, MA, 1964).

[155] Y. Hen, 'Knowledge of canon law among rural priests', *Journal of Theological Studies* 50 (1999), pp. 117–34.

Figure 5. The Stuttgart Psalter, now Stuttgart, Württembergische
Landesbibliothek, Bibl. fol. 23, but probably produced at the monastery of
St-Germain-des-Prés *c.*820–30, includes on fol. 55r this illustration for Psalm 43:5:
'Why art thou cast down, O my soul?' David plays a cithara, a biblical instrument,
while 'Anima' (soul) is personified on a hilltop, reflecting Carolingian Christianity's
emphasis on measures that Christians could take to benefit their souls.

down in their *capitula* the detailed canonical rules that they wanted
priests to follow, does this indicate, as our two handbooks suggest,
that those orders flowed out through a widespread network of educated, responsive Christian ministers? Or was it a case, more often,
of a rarefied learned elite trying to impose its agenda on a haphaz-
ard patchwork of grudging and independent priests? Although the
question has sometimes been posed in this starkly oppositional way,
it should be pointed out that in a realm of the size that the Carolingians' had attained by the early ninth century, both scenarios, and
most points on the spectrum between them, may have co-existed.
Tension of a similar intensity is present too when we try to interpret
the development of penance in this period. As we have seen, individual or 'secret' penance – the performance of specific numbers of fasts
or prayers to atone for specific sins – grew on the continent in parallel with the sponsorship of intercessory prayers and masses. As with
the mass, penance involved the priesthood materially, for only they
could hear the confession and prescribe the correct penitential action.
The evidence of penitential books, liturgies, and episcopal statutes,
while ambiguous about the involvement of ordinary priests in the

administration of penance, at least before the tenth century, does show a consistent aspiration to control it on the part of bishops.[156] How far they actually did so, however, is moot: when we have bishops complaining about priests accepting money from those seeking to avoid penances, this could indicate that lay people either had fully absorbed the ideas behind penance, and were trying to manipulate them, or that they still found such rules alien and elitist.[157] The ninth century's new concern to distinguish these more everyday 'secret' penitential activities from penances that were performed in public for sins committed in public certainly reveals how the notion was elaborated among the powerful. Louis the Pious experienced both the benefits and drawbacks of this development. As will be seen in Chapter 4, his penance in 822 was a means of reconciling discontents from a position of strength, casting himself in the role of a late Roman emperor, whereas that which he was forced to perform at Soissons in 833 risked endangering the entire political order, so severely did it humble the emperor. Royal penance, a subset of the penitential mentality that lasted throughout the Middle Ages, would never again threaten kingly status itself.[158]

Uncertainties within the hierarchy of the secular clergy about their responsibilities and capabilities were mirrored in monastic communities. Here the main root of anxiety was the entanglement of monasteries and their patron families that we noted earlier.

In early-eighth-century Northumbria, Bede complained of 'laymen in charge of monks', founding so-called monasteries where they lived with their families like secular lords.[159] Changes in the practice of monasticism in the course of the eighth century might be seen as in some measure responses to these worries. It is in this era that we

---

[156] Hamilton, 'The unique favour of penance', pp. 240–2. See further C. van Rhijn and M. Saan, 'Correcting sinners, correcting texts: a context for the *Paenitentiale pseudo-Theodori*', *EME* 14/1 (2006), pp. 23–40.

[157] Hamilton, 'The unique favour of penance', p. 231.

[158] M. de Jong, 'Power and humility in Carolingian society: the public penance of Louis the Pious', *EME* 1 (1992), pp. 29–52; M. de Jong, 'What was public about public penance? *Poenitentia publica* and justice in the Carolingian world', *La giustitia nell'alto medioevo (secoli IX–XI)*, Settimane di Studio del Centro italiano di studi sull'alto medioevo 44 (Spoleto, 1997), pp. 863–902; M. de Jong, 'Transformations of penance', in Theuws and Nelson (eds.), *Rituals of Power*, pp. 184–224; Hamilton, 'The unique favour of penance', pp. 234–5.

[159] Bede, *Epistola ad Egbertum*, ed. C. Plummer, *Venerabilis Baedae opera historica* (Oxford, 1896), pp. 405–23, esp. 414–16.

get the first signs of a concern physically to segregate monks from secular society: in Lombard Italy, the duke of Spoleto specifically forbade women from walking near or approaching the abbey of Farfa;[160] and monastic buildings increasingly included a *claustrum* (cloister) – a secluded inner space accessible only to members of the community, and to a few privileged guests.[161] In addition, greater attention began to be paid to the way of life of monks: their prayers would be effective only if they were rigorous in their pursuit of holiness for themselves. Moreover, increasing focus on the mass meant that growing numbers of monks sought ordination as priests: no prayer was more powerful than a votive mass, and the monks' asceticism was some sort of guarantee of the purity of the celebrant. This did not entirely disadvantage nunneries, whose virgin inmates retained a prized spiritual status. Another response was the institution of canons: clerics organised into a community, usually around a cathedral. The first rule for such canons was composed in 742 by Chrodegang, bishop of Metz and co-founder of Lorsch.[162]

Gauging the motivation behind the patronage of monasteries is not as straightforward as the pious declarations of surviving charters suggest. We need to note, first, that these documents survive precisely because they benefited monasteries: only there would they be preserved down the centuries. So we are ignorant, for the most part, of how far this culture of gift-giving extended to other targets, and even to the non-religious. The earliest charters preserved by the monastery of Echternach were often addressed not to the institution, but to its abbot, Willibrord, who was also bishop of Utrecht. Evidently, patronage did not *have* to be directed at a monastic institution. Secondly, these gifts very often had consequences other than the purely spiritual. Through such patronage, Lorsch became the most extensive landowner in the middle Rhine;[163] Echternach was made the vehicle for drawing an entire local elite – that of Toxandria, the hazy, low-lying frontier zone between Franks and Frisians – into the

---

[160] *CDL* IV/1 8.
[161] On the development of the cloister, see W. Braunfels, *Monasteries of Western Europe. The Architecture of the Orders*, trans. A. Laing (London, 1972), pp. 27–9. For the cloister at Farfa and, by comparison, at other eighth-century abbeys, see C. McClendon, *The Imperial Abbey of Farfa* (New Haven, CT, 1987), pp. 8, 64–6, 70–4, 116.
[162] Claussen, *The Reform of the Frankish Church*, pp. 19–57.
[163] Innes, *State and Society*, pp. 51–9.

Figure 6. Mosaic, apse of the chapel at Germigny-des-Prés, France, commissioned *c.*793 by Theodulf, bishop of Orléans, reflects both his response to Byzantine image veneration in his *Opus Caroli regis*, and his beliefs about the eucharist. Angels gesture towards an empty ark of the covenant – no longer housing for the divine or exemplar of religious imagery – and below it, to the altar, where Christ was present in the eucharist.

Frankish orbit;[164] Reichenau and St Gallen came to play pivotal roles in the extension of Carolingian power into Alemannia;[165] and Farfa attained a crucial mediating position between the secular rulers of northern Italy and formerly Byzantine Rome.[166] All these monasteries had been established at the end of the seventh or in the first decades of the eighth century, and all were by 800 more or less securely under Carolingian control. Many others found themselves in similarly politically and socially influential positions. (See Figure 6.) Landed patronage had turned them into powerful corporations, with substantial disposable wealth: lands that could be leased to secular lords, and had the potential to provide significant

[164] Costambeys, 'An aristocratic community'.
[165] McKitterick, *The Carolingians and the Written Word*, pp. 83–4, 178–85; *Frankish Kingdoms*, pp. 42–4.
[166] Costambeys, *Power and Patronage*, pp. 250–352.

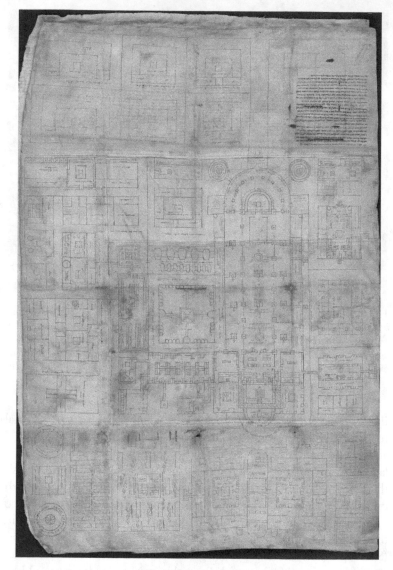

Figure 7. Plan of St Gallen.

military retinues. The ability of the Carolingians yearly to collect an effective military force was based partly on their granting to military men as 'benefices' lands attached to monasteries under their control. What was good for the kings was good for the rest of the aristocracy, and even abbots themselves could be found granting monastic land in order to build a military retinue.[167] Abbeys thus offered practical, military support as well as prayers for the soul as return gifts to their royal patrons: Louis the Pious had a list drawn up of these gifts, of all kinds.[168]

The political, economic, and cultural status of monasteries in the Carolingian age is underlined by the remarkable 'Plan of St Gallen'. (See Figure 7.) Now in the Monastic Library of St Gallen (Switzerland), the Plan was actually created at the monastery of Reichenau (in modern southern Germany) at some point between 819 and 826. It is drawn on five pieces of parchment stitched together, measuring 112 cm × 77.5 cm, and depicts the ground plan of a monastic complex, including scriptorium, dormitory, privy, laundry, refectory, kitchen, bake and brew houses, guest house, abbot's residence, and an infirmary. We cannot be certain why it was created, but the monastery's actual main church, built in the 830s, does not closely follow the design on the Plan; and in any case the Plan's overall complex could not have fitted into the actual site of St Gallen. We should therefore see the Plan not as a practical blueprint but as a generic image of the ideal monastery, at a time when monasteries' wealth made them sources of valuable economic and military, as well as spiritual, power.

How far such a position was desired or planned for on the part of the monasteries' lay benefactors is questionable. But it meant that control over them became a political issue of great significance. Many of these seventh- and eighth-century foundations, even if they had originally been established by a single aristocratic family, soon began to attract donations from others. In some cases these were families, perhaps of lower status or wealth, keen to associate themselves with the founding family, as seems to have been the case, for example, at Hornbach.[169] In others, power relations between the various

---

[167] Halsall, *Warfare and Society*, pp. 72–6; J. L. Nelson, 'The Church's military service in the ninth century: a contemporary comparative view?', in W. J. Shiels (ed.), *The Church and War*, Studies in Church History 20 (1983), pp. 15–30, repr. Nelson, *Politics and Ritual* (1986), pp. 117–32; Innes, *State and Society*, pp. 13–34; Fouracre, *Charles Martel*, pp. 137–45.

[168] *Notitia de servitio monasteriorum* (a.819), ed. P. Becker, *CCM* 1 (Siegburg, 1963), pp. 493–9.

[169] A. Doll, 'Das Pirminskloster Hornbach. Gründung und Verfassungsentwicklung bis Anfang des 12. Jahrhunderts', *Archiv für mittelrheinische Kirchengeschichte* 5 (1953), pp. 108–42.

donors are far less clear. Monasteries could be used to pool the resources of local elites, or they could broker contests over wealth and influence between different families. They could also mediate between such elites and kings. Indeed, rulers had in their gift legal privileges, grants of immunity, that helped to strengthen many monasteries' institutional identity and in some cases to move them decisively away from the control of one family or faction. Beginning with the seventh-century Merovingians, kings could grant to an abbey freedom from tolls on its goods – like that which survives exempting St Denis, near Paris, from levies on the oil that was transported up from the south to light the church.[170] They could go further and exclude their own officials from any jurisdiction over the buildings and lands of the monastery. Bishops too could be excluded, or could exclude themselves, from interference in the monastery's affairs.[171] This untouchability sometimes had a paradoxical effect: while monasteries enhanced their holiness by thus distancing themselves from the sullying influence of worldly government, they thereby became all the more attractive as nodes of peculiar status, both to elites looking to by-pass royal power structures, and to rulers looking to enhance them. The acts by which Pippin II, ancestor of the Carolingians, took Echternach under his protection before giving himself the right to confirm its abbot and requiring that the latter remain loyal to his family, reveal that there was a short distance between exempting a monastery from old impositions and exacting new ones.[172] By the time he took these measures, in 706, Pippin was effective ruler of the region in which Echternach lay; over the next fifty years, he and his descendants would use control of monasteries as an important weapon in the extension of their power. We have seen how Charlemagne used the dispute over its ownership to take over Lorsch. His action was one in a series by which the Carolingians overrode the rights of bishops to control monasteries, bringing significant numbers under their own protection.[173]

---

[170] See Fouracre, 'Eternal light', pp. 70–1.
[171] B. Rosenwein, *Negotiating Space: Power, Restraint and Privileges of Immunity in Early Medieval Europe* (Manchester, 1999), esp. pp. 74–96.
[172] C. Wampach (ed.), *Geschichte der Grundherrschaft Echternach im Frühmittelalter* I.2: *Quellenband* (Luxemburg, 1930), nos. 14 and 15.
[173] M. de Jong, 'Carolingian monasticism: the power of prayer', in *NCMH* II, pp. 623–7.

CHRISTIAN LEADERSHIP AND LEARNING

Regulating Christianity under the Carolingians

Royal moves to control monasteries highlight a feature of Carolingian religious culture that we can also see behind the letter of Hincmar with which we began. Asking whether Lothar II's marriage was lawful, or whether he should be allowed a divorce, and on what grounds such a decision could be made, were components of a much broader quest for more authoritative rules and more secure structures in belief and practice that preoccupied western religious culture in the eighth and ninth centuries. The new emphases of the period – on gifts to churches and monasteries, on the spiritual benefits of masses and prayers, on the moral distinctiveness of priests, monks and nuns – all contributed to the growth and strengthening of the Church as an institution. This was one of the great religious developments of the age. But it would be wrong to think that the emergence of the Church opened up a gap between the ecclesiastical and the secular. One of the most striking features of this period – remarkable because it goes against traditional distinctions between ecclesiastical and lay, Church and state – is that the more robust the Church's hierarchy became, the more prominent its buildings in the landscape, the better defined its hierarchy, and the more explicit its rules, then the more intertwined it became with the dominant culture among the laity.[174] This meant that moral questions, which in much later centuries the Church would claim for its own, were in this period decided by clerical and lay elites together.

This symbiosis of the secular and the ecclesiastical is clear in the case of Lothar II's divorce. His marital situation was unexceptional in the context of the traditional attitude to sexual relationships. Both Roman and post-Roman law allowed for a variety of types of marriage, varying according to the requirements for the consent of the parties and their families, the payments between the parties at the point of marriage, the legal status of the wife, the inheritance rights of the children, and the ease of dissolubility. They allowed for sexual relationships outside marriage – chiefly when a high-born man took a lower-status woman as a concubine – and the possibility of multiple simultaneous partnerships of different levels. Already in the Merovingian period we can perceive a growing distance between

---

[174] De Jong, 'Charlemagne's Church', p. 106.

such arrangements and developing Christian thinking on marriage. Church doctrine in the later Roman period may have been based on secular Roman law – and therefore recognised concubinage – but Christian thinkers had from the beginning a fairly rigorous approach to human sexual relations. In passages later inspirational to the ascetic movement, though of questionable representativeness of his own views, St Paul suggested a strict list of moral priority: 'It is well for a man not to touch a woman. But because of cases of sexual immorality, each man should have his own wife and each woman her own husband.'[175] As asceticism crystallised, so the attitudes of some towards sex and marriage in lay society hardened: Columbanus pointedly denied the legitimacy of the Merovingian Theuderic II's children by his concubines, and in his vision the danger to Barontus's soul was prompted by his multiple marriages and adulteries.[176] Beginning with a synod in Rome in 721, successive church councils sought to refine the definition of marriage. Non-biological kinship acquired at the baptismal font had already achieved a significant status, proving very useful in Christianising societies in promoting and strengthening Christian identity within groups of families, and bishops were keen to close the gap between biological and spiritual kin further by bringing the latter into the group within which marriage would constitute incest.[177] There were even moves to extend the definition of prohibited, consanguineous relations from the traditional four generations to seven (i.e. prohibiting marriage to any descendant of one's great-great-great-great-great grandfather).[178] It

---

[175] I Corinthians 7:1–2 (NRSV). For comment, see P. Brown, *Body and Society. Men, Women and Sexual Renunciation in Early Christianity* (New York, 1988), pp. 53–5 ('Paul left a fatal legacy to future ages').

[176] Jonas, *Vita Columbani*, 1.19, ed. B. Krusch, *MGH SRM* IV, p. 87, trans. E. Peters, *Monks, Bishops and Pagans* (Philadelphia, PA, 1975), p. 94; see J. L. Nelson, 'Queens as Jezebels: Brunhild and Balthild in Merovingian history', in D. Baker (ed.), *Medieval Women: Essays Dedicated and Presented to Professor Rosalind M. T. Hill*, Studies in Church History: Subsidia 1 (Oxford, 1978), pp. 31–77 at p. 29, repr. in Little and Rosenwein (eds.), *Debating the Middle Ages*, pp. 219–53, and in J. L. Nelson, *Politics and Ritual in Early Medieval Europe* (London, 1986), pp. 1–48. *Visio Baronti*, c. 12, ed. Levison, p. 386, trans. Hillgarth, *Christianity and Paganism*, p. 199.

[177] Lynch, *Godparents and Kinship*.

[178] M. de Jong, 'To the limits of kinship: anti-incest legislation in the early medieval west (500–900)', in J. Bremmer (ed.), *From Sappho to De Sade: Moments in the History of Sexuality* (London and New York, 1989), pp. 36–59.

was also stipulated that weddings be public, that Christian marriage was indissoluble, and that simultaneous sexual relationships should be avoided.[179] Yet, although he may have found it harder than did the Merovingians to pursue relationships with both his queen and his concubine simultaneously, it was not really these developments of which Lothar II was the victim. What necessitated his divorce was rather his desire to make his concubine his queen, a desire born not of dynastic or religious considerations, but of love. Early medieval sources are frustratingly silent on the subject of love and, though the argument once put forward that romantic love did not even exist before the twelfth century is easily disproved, such emotional attachments are rarely explicit, and more often have to be inferred, as in the evidence for Lothar's divorce.[180] Lothar's case at least shows that when it came to love and marriage, in the early Middle Ages you could have one without the other.

What made Lothar's divorce so difficult was that it was proposed at a time when authority was particularly hotly contested, between factions comprising both laymen and ecclesiastics, and between essentially secular powers and ecclesiastical institutions. Among the latter was especially the pope, Nicholas I, who intervened to invalidate the divorce in 863. Though this did not make the case a straightforward contest between Church and state, as some conflicts between pope and emperor later in the Middle Ages might better be described, it does indicate that the central problem was competing claims to authority over moral issues. Lothar's case was judged by various bodies: a secular court, employing trial by ordeal (which he lost); a council of bishops, hearing the evidence of a new witness (favourable to Lothar); and the pope, who as we have seen ruled against the king.[181] Lothar was accorded no authority to adjudicate his own case. Paradoxically, it had been weakened by his own plea, which showed him to be vulnerable either to his own passions or, as we

---

[179] P. Toubert, 'The Carolingian moment (eighth–tenth century)', in A. Burguiere, et al. (eds.), *A History of the Family* (Cambridge, 1996), pp. 379–406, at 396–406.

[180] On the elusiveness of early medieval love, on which further study is certainly needed, see C. Larrington, 'The psychology of emotion and study of the medieval period', *EME* 10/2 (2001), pp. 251–6.

[181] The progress of the case is summarised in Airlie, 'Private bodies', pp. 8–9. For a similar marital problem also accessible to us through Archbishop Hincmar's writings, see Smith, *Europe after Rome: A New Cultural History* (Oxford, 2005), pp. 131–3.

have seen Hincmar hint at the outset of this chapter, to others' unholy malefactions.[182] As king, Lothar II was in fact almost uniquely vulnerable in the ninth century to the evolving Christian agenda for marriage, which took centuries to impose itself on wider society. But it was precisely the ideology developing around kingship that increased the attention on the Carolingians' moral rectitude.

The entire Frankish elite, lay and ecclesiastical, approved and supported each new king, who in return offered leadership and office. The duties of office, from the king downwards, were conceived of as a *ministerium* (literally, ministry), which encompassed leadership not only in worldly affairs, but also in spiritual ones. Part of the responsibility of *ministerium*, then, was leadership of a Christian people to salvation, and on none did this responsibility fall more heavily than on the king. This notion that the ruler should lead both secular polity and Christian institution naturally looked back to Constantine and his successors as late Roman Christian emperors, but followed the lead also of barbarian kings who had presided over synods – Chlothar II (614), the Visigoth Sisenand (633), the Bernician Oswiu (664) – as well as drawing on the model of Christian leadership by a *rector* propounded by Pope Gregory I (590–604).[183] Thus, throughout our period, by far the strongest role in legislating on religious as well as on secular matters was taken by the king. And this was not only true of the Carolingians: the emergence of a culture of religious patronage in the eighth century is a feature of Lombard Italy as much as of Francia, and the Lombard king Liutprand legislated in response to it.[184] The close attention Liutprand paid to regularly promulgating and disseminating written laws finds an echo in the activity of the Carolingian kings after 754. But unlike in the Lombard kingdom, Carolingian legislation was bound up with ecclesiastical authority from the very first.

Sources of authority: kings, popes and bishops

The Franco-papal alliance that came about in the fraught circumstances of 753–4 has traditionally been viewed as politically expedient

---

[182] Airlie, 'Private bodies', pp. 29–33.

[183] Markus, *Gregory the Great*, pp. 28–9.

[184] E.g. *Leges Liutprandi* 6, ed. F. Beyerle, *Leges langobardorum, 643–866. Die Gesetze der Langobarden* (Weimar, 1947; repr. Witzenhausen, 1962), pp. 99–182, trans. Fischer-Drew, *The Lombard Laws*, p. 146. On Liutprand's legislating, see La Rocca, 'La legge e la pratica'.

for both parties. Each side made attempts to put its own slant on the meeting between Pope Stephen II and Pippin III.[185] Papal sources, for instance, agree that on Pope Stephen's arrival in Francia Pippin prostrated himself before the pontiff;[186] in Frankish texts, it was the pope who was on his knees before the king.[187] What this episode, and especially the anointing of Pippin and his sons, certainly achieved was to bind the new regime to the bishops of Rome in an unprecedented way. The Carolingians' fortunes were from then on entangled with events in Italy: a point fully appreciated by Charlemagne, and which must go some way to explaining his own decision to invade the Lombard kingdom in the autumn of 773. But if he entered the Lombard kingdom as a conqueror, Charlemagne came to Rome principally as a pilgrim.[188] Our picture of the Rome that he visited is shaped fundamentally by the papal biographies, kept up apparently by papal clerks intermittently through each pope's lifetime and collected in a work known to posterity as the *Liber pontificalis*.[189] The long lists of papal building projects included in these *Lives* portray a Rome in the process of transformation by successive popes in the later eighth century.[190] But, extensive though they are, we can tell from other sources that these omit many instances of construction and other material patronage, by no means all of which were papal.[191] Literal readings of the *Liber pontificalis* give a one-sided impression of Rome, and this is true too when we try to see how the implications of the Franco-papal alliance were worked out in the pontificate of

---

[185] Different manuscripts of collections of papal biographies transmit different texts of Stephen II's *Life*, among which two contrasting versions have been identified (one more and one less 'pro-Frankish' or 'anti-Lombard'): see Davis, *The Lives of the Eighth-Century Popes*, pp. 51–2; but all versions agree that Pippin was at the pope's feet, not *vice versa*.

[186] *LP* I, pp. 447, trans. Davis, *Lives of the Eighth-Century Popes*, p. 63.

[187] E.g. *Chron. Moiss.*, p. 293.

[188] De Jong, 'Charlemagne's Church', p. 116.

[189] Translated in three books by R. Davis, *The Book of Pontiffs* (Liber Pontificalis), rev. edn (Liverpool, 2000); *Lives of the Eighth-Century Popes*; *The Lives of the Ninth-Century Popes* (Liber pontificalis) (Liverpool, 1995).

[190] T. F. X. Noble, 'Paradoxes and possibilities in the sources for Roman society in the early middle ages' in Smith (ed.), *Early Medieval Rome and the Christian West*, pp. 55–83, at pp. 58–73 (construction) and pp. 73–83 (other gifts); see also C. Goodson, *The Rome of Pope Paschal I. Papal Power, Urban Renovation, Church Rebuilding and Relic Translation, 817–824* (Cambridge, 2010).

[191] R. Coates-Stephens, 'Byzantine building patronage in post-Reconquest Rome', in M. Ghilardi, *et al.* (eds.), *Les Cités de l'Italie tardo-antique (IVe–VIe siècle)* (Rome), pp. 149–66.

Hadrian, both in his *Life* in the *Liber pontificalis* and in his correspondence, as preserved in the so-called *Codex Carolinus*. The latter in particular, however, clearly lifts phrases from earlier letters, suggesting that its authors were very deliberately drawing on the papal bureaucracy's literary traditions to build a case for the maximum possible freedom of manoeuvre for the papacy, addressed to Charlemagne's 'Italian experts': the handful of prominent Frankish magnates and ecclesiastics who dominated his dealings there in the first generation after 774. Other evidence shows how different was those experts' perspective from that of papal authors. In Rome, the Franks found what Anglo-Saxon missionaries had already discovered: a city of martyrs that stood as a new pinnacle to their hierarchy of holiness, and a source of relics, the bones of the martyrs, which would be taken north to bring new sanctity into the heart of their realm. For northern Christian peoples, therefore, the city of Rome's authority derived from its past associations, not from any current power. The Carolingians knew that contemporary Rome was 'incessantly poisoned by feuds'.[192] What attracted them to it was precisely what the Romans were themselves beginning to emphasise as they redefined their own identity, falling back on the indigenous as they cut loose the ties to Constantinople: that is, the traditions peculiar to the city itself, built above all around the magnetism of Rome's martyrs and pre-eminently around St Peter.

For the Carolingian elite this authority was transmitted through particular texts in various genres. Pope Zacharias had already sent to Pippin III a small collection of canon law in around 747;[193] when Charlemagne celebrated Easter at Rome in 774, while his army besieged Desiderius in Pavia,[194] Pope Hadrian presented him with a revised version of the famous compilation of canon law made by Dionysius Exiguus in the sixth century (and so generally called the *Dionysio-Hadriana*). Large parts of this were then formally promulgated across his kingdom by Charlemagne in the *Admonitio generalis* of 789, and passages from it were read aloud at the synod of Aachen in 802.[195] Rome's ability to supply authoritative texts may have encouraged the request for a copy of the service-book, or sacramentary,

[192] Alcuin, *Ep.* 245, ed. Dümmler, pp. 393–8, trans. Dutton, *Carolingian Civilization*, p. 131, trans. Allott, no. 114.
[193] *CC*, no. 3.   [194] See above, Chapter 2, pp. 66–7.
[195] Y. Hen, *The Royal Patronage of Liturgy in Frankish Gaul to the death of Charles the Bald (877)*, Henry Bradshaw Society Subsidia 3 (London, 2001), pp. 65–95.

thought by the Franks to have been composed by Pope Gregory the Great. Knowledge that no such thing existed did not deter Pope Hadrian from despatching a mass-book known as the *Hadrianum*, containing a text with Gregorian associations that was no longer followed in Rome itself. Further, in 787, Charlemagne sought the set of monastic regulations known as the *Rule of St Benedict*, which was coming to be seen as the most authoritative such collection of rules, and asked for a copy from the manuscript thought to be Benedict's autograph, which had been preserved at Rome and then taken to Benedict's abbey of Monte Cassino after its refoundation *c*.717.[196] This demand for authoritative texts which might set a uniform standard arose both because of the desire for points of authority – whether at the Frankish court or the papal palace – and as a reaction, conscious or not, to what we can now see was a situation of great diversity. There had been no single *Rule of St Benedict*, but instead, within a few decades of the great monastic saint's death around 550, many lists of rules bearing his name, each more or less different in wording from the next.[197] Similarly, we can see that much of the liturgy that supposedly originated in Rome, and especially the sacramentary attached to Pope Gregory's name, was concocted from texts produced in many of the post-Roman kingdoms, including the Frankish.[198] The true, complex, origins of these texts – canon law, liturgy, monastic Rule – mattered less than the image that they helped to create of a single authority under the Roman brand. The texts themselves were often adapted to suit Frankish requirements – thus Benedict of Aniane had to write a long supplement to the *Hadrianum*, to cover the diverse liturgical needs across the Frankish empire.[199]

---

[196] Theodemar of Monte Cassino, *Letter to Charlemagne*, ed. K. Hallinger and M. Wegener, *CCM* I (Siegburg, 1963), pp. 157–75, and *MGH Epp.* IV (*Epp. Karolini aevi* II), ed. E. Dümmler (Berlin, 1895), no. 13, pp. 509–14. According to Paul the Deacon, the autograph copy of the *Rule of St Benedict* had been taken from Monte Cassino to Rome when the former was sacked by the Lombards in the 570s (*HL* IV.17), and returned by Pope Zacharias in the 740s following Petronax's refoundation of the abbey (*HL* VI.40).

[197] K. Zelzer, 'Von Benedikt zu Hildemar. Zu Textgestalt und Textgeschichte der *Regula Benedicti* auf ihrem Weg zur Alleingeltung', *Frühmittelalterliche Studien* 23 (1989), pp. 112–30.

[198] Hen, *Royal Patronage of Liturgy*, pp. 72–8.

[199] Hen, *Royal Patronage of Liturgy*, pp. 75–6.

Responding to holiness in the way most familiar to them, what the
northern ecclesiastical aristocrats whom Charlemagne sent south to
pursue his interests sought to acquire in Rome was not mere tourist
souvenirs but actual ownership of holy sites.[200] The popes' perspective, though founded on the same emphasis on Rome's traditional
Christian aura, was rather different: only in papally produced texts –
the letters they sent north, the biographies that their clerks produced
of them – is there any durable sense that the spiritual aura of Rome's
past imbued its present bishop with an authority that was not simply
doctrinal or ecclesiastical, but secular and political; that is, that by dint
of the city's past, its bishop could be a secular ruler. There are signs of
uncertainty in the Frankish elite's response to the wave of ideological
implications that followed their military success, especially over the
Lombards. There was, as we shall see in Chapter 4, lively debate over
the meaning, and even the desirability, of Charlemagne's coronation
as emperor by the pope on Christmas Day 800. To some extent there
still is, though it has proved impossible reliably to recover contemporary intentions on either side. On the one hand, 800 has been claimed
as a defining point in the establishment of a separate polity centred
on Rome and headed by the pope. On the other, Frankish writers
even at the time were pretty consistent in their belief that Rome
was part of Charlemagne's empire. On the level of ideology, Alcuin
argued that the king not only had to defend the Church, but also
had to act to strengthen the faith within the Christian community:
the pope's role was simply to pray for the king's victory.[201] Lothar
I, sub-king in Italy under his father Louis the Pious, enshrined this
attitude in his definition of the political position of the city of Rome
in 824, known as the *Constitutio romana*, which among other things
required that the emperor approve papal elections. Only when the
imperial office was weakened by political divisions later in the ninth
century did the fractiousness of Rome's local aristocracy make the
Constitutio's written provisions less viable in practice.

Another crucial component in the Franco-papal relationship was
the establishment of close ties with the figures who were taking
control of, and building to new strength, the Church in Francia.
First among these was Boniface, who as we have seen found that
east of the Rhine there was at least as often weak or incomplete
Christianity as there was outright paganism. He himself had a striking
conviction in the rightness of his own conception of Christianity,

[200] Costambeys and Leyser, 'Neighbour of St Stephen'.   [201] Alcuin, *Ep.* 93.

such as could come only from a society but freshly Christianised itself. But he needed the authority to put that conception into practice, and here the popes could certainly help him. This explains his frequent visits to Rome, and the stress placed by him and others on the innovative titles and offices awarded to him by successive popes, themselves stepping unsurely into an unfamiliar world of Church-building. Gregory II referred to Boniface's *ministerium*, and appointed him a bishop 'consecrated to the duty of preaching';[202] Gregory III made him an archbishop with metropolitan powers 'to ordain bishops where the multitude of the faithful has become very great';[203] and Zacharias finally allowed him a fixed see to go with his metropolitan status, first intended to be Cologne but ultimately established at Mainz.[204] These offices, each in response to requests or hints from Boniface, were innovations, because the pope had not previously played any part in the appointment of Frankish bishops. They drew, rather, on the example of the Gregorian mission to England. Nor was there any necessary conflict between the pope as a source of authority and the other power on which Boniface relied, the Carolingian mayors and kings. It was Carloman who instigated the first of a series of church councils organised by Boniface and usually seen as the first chapters in a programme of church reform under Carolingian rule.[205] The first, called simply the *Concilium germanicum* because its place of meeting is unknown, set the tone. Its concern above all was the moral fitness and correct behaviour of the clergy: all clerics were forbidden to carry arms or to hunt; priests had to wear distinctive clerical dress, and be subject to their bishop, rendering to him an annual account of their activities, and penances were prescribed of flogging and imprisonment for transgressors; bishops should make the rounds of their diocese, taking particular care, 'with the help of the count', to prevent pagan practices.[206] Reference to the latter, we have already seen, was a stylised literary convention as well as, or as much as, an

---

[202] Boniface, *Epistolae, Ep.* 19, ed. Tangl, p. 33 ('Ministerio quoque praesentis fratris karissimi Bonifatii, quem ad vos episcopum consecratum in sorte praedicationis distinavimus...'), trans. Emerton, no. XI, pp. 44–5. The translation given here differs slightly from Emerton's.

[203] Boniface, *Epistolae, Ep.* 28, p. 50, trans. Emerton, no. XX, pp. 57–9.

[204] Boniface, *Epistolae, Epp.* 60 and 80, trans. Emerton, nos. XLVIII and LXIV, pp. 107–11 and 142–9.

[205] Boniface, *Epistolae, Ep.* 51, trans. Emerton, no. XLI, pp. 83–8, a letter from Zacharias to Boniface of 1 April 743, brings out Carloman's role.

[206] Boniface, *Epistolae, Ep.* 56, trans. Emerton, no. XLIV, pp. 91–4; 'Karlmanni principis capitulare', *Capit.* I, pp. 24–7.

indication of real opposition to Christianity. Either way, it was the strengthening of the Church, especially through improvements in its personnel, that was the key priority. A council in the following year at Les Estinnes reiterated these points, as well as trying to regulate the leasing of Church land for military purposes, and including the first of many rulings forbidding adultery and incestuous marriage.[207] Subsequent councils – at Soissons in 744, an unknown location in 747, Ver in 755, Verberie in 756, Compiègne in 757 and Attigny in 762 – continued to reflect these concerns. The meeting at Soissons was the first to be held under the auspices of Carloman's brother Pippin, king from 751, and this and subsequent councils cannot be separated from other efforts to bolster his rule after his usurpation of the Merovingians' crown: in them we see 'a new king affirming his control of the sacred by creating clear hierarchical structures'.[208]

The council of Soissons is the first to give us a precise idea of the difficulties facing those seeking a stricter definition of the Christian Church. The bishops there condemned for heresy a certain Aldebert, who claimed to possess a letter from heaven and had had written a saint's life of himself. He was sent to Rome and there stripped of his priesthood and anathematised, as was an Irish priest named Clemens who denied the teachings of the Church Fathers.[209] Opposing such men was a relatively straightforward task since all within the Church hierarchy could agree on the unsoundness of their doctrine; indeed, Aldebert may even have proved useful, as a negative image of sanctity (claimed, arrogantly, by himself) to set against the positive image of the humble saint (recognised as such by others, through his works).[210] Once the Frankish rulers were on side, Boniface also found that he could persuade them to take measures against contemporary bishops who he felt were too prone to typical aristocratic behaviour, such as hunting: we find, for instance, a certain Bishop Gewilib dashing off to Rome to contest (unsuccessfully) his deposition from the

---

[207] 'Capitulare Liptinense', *Capit.* I, pp. 27–9.

[208] De Jong, 'Charlemagne's Church', p. 111.

[209] Boniface, *Epistolae, Ep.* 59, trans. Emerton, no. xlvii, pp. 98–107; see further N. Zeddies, 'Bonifatius und die zwei nützliche Rebellen: die Häretiker Adelbert und Clemens', *Ordnung und Aufruhr im Mittelalter: historische und juristische Studien zur Rebellion*, Ius Commune. Sonderheft 70 (Frankfurt, 1995), pp. 217–63.

[210] This seems to be the implication of Pope Zacharias's decision to keep Aldebert's unholy documents: Boniface, *Epistolae, Ep.* 60, trans. Emerton, no. xlviii, pp. 107–11.

see of Mainz.[211] A more difficult opponent was Virgilius, probably originally Ferghil, abbot of Aghaboe in Ireland, who had established himself at Salzburg where he incurred Boniface's displeasure by, apparently, holding the unorthodox view that there was 'another world and other men, and also a sun and moon' below the earth.[212] The pair also came into conflict when Virgilius challenged Boniface's insistence on rebaptising those baptised by an illiterate priest.[213] Pope Zacharias was inclined to leniency towards this minor transgression, and was rather more concerned that Boniface's rebaptism of the people in question was itself heretical. Virgilius proved, in fact, at least as successful a promoter of the Church as Boniface. His career shows that we should not over-concentrate on the figure who left the most prominent legacy to posterity.

The dependence of churchmen and women like Boniface and his followers on the Carolingians, as a source of authority as well as of effective power, only increased after Pippin III's seizure of the Frankish throne. Lacking the legitimacy bestowed by blood or tradition, Pippin turned to Christian ideology to sanction his rule. His anointing by the pope was of critical significance, and, as we have seen, helps to explain his dramatic interventions in Italy in 755 and 756. The next decades saw the crystallisation of an ideology portraying the king as 'rector of the kingdom of the Franks and devout defender and humble adjuvant of the holy Church'.[214] This heightening of the king's responsibility for the spiritual welfare of his people led to yet further emphasis on correct clerical practice: as noted already, masses would be most effective where those who conducted them were most correct. There was therefore a more concerted attempt both to define the correct liturgy, and to ensure its performance throughout the kingdom. Texts were sought from Rome, and schools of chant established. This stress on correct liturgy continued under Charlemagne. The key theme of the capitulary known as the *Admonitio generalis* (General Admonition), issued in 789, was the conduct of the

---

[211] Boniface, *Epistolae, Ep.* 60, trans. Emerton, no. XLVIII, pp. 107–11.
[212] Boniface, *Epistolae, Ep.* 80, trans. Emerton, no. LXIV, pp. 143–9, at p. 147.
[213] Boniface, *Epistolae, Ep.* 68, trans. Emerton, no. LIV, pp. 122–3. The ignorant Bavarian priest had apparently said 'Baptizo te in nomine patria et filia et spiritus sancti' (I baptise you in the name fatherland and daughter and holy spirit), instead of 'Baptizo te in nomine patris et filii et spiritus sancti'.
[214] *Admonitio generalis*, preface, *Capit.* I, no. 22, p. 53, trans. King, *Charlemagne: Translated Sources*, p. 209.

episcopate and priesthood. They were to introduce no innovations into the liturgy. Rather, the emphasis was on preaching according to a strictly defined programme of doctrine and moral exhortation. The message was repeated in further capitularies and letters throughout the reign, and finds its natural reflection in the *capitula episcoporum* mentioned earlier, with their concern for episcopal oversight of priestly behaviour.[215] The aim was nothing less than control over the moral conduct of the laity. The *Admonitio* was the first great expression of this unprecedented ambition, though it had been adumbrated in Carloman's councils, which explicitly delegated royal authority by assigning to the bishops responsibility for 'moral' crimes like adultery and incest. The theme became a keynote of ninth-century royal legislation: in 846, for example, Lothar I outlined bishops' responsibility to investigate and punish 'public shameful acts', including homicide and theft, as well as incest, adultery, and the ravishing of nuns.[216] But bishops were not alone in this moral duty: other capitularies required the royal *missi* – secular and ecclesiastical officials – to safeguard correct ways of life so that 'all are to live in perfect charity and peace one with another'.[217]

Christian rulership and the promotion of culture

That such measures were the natural results of a Christian ideology of kingship became properly apparent in legislation issued by Charlemagne. The impetus began with a concern for what was happening in church. In the *Epistola de litteris colendis* ('Letter on the cultivation of letters'), addressed by Charlemagne to Baugulf, abbot of Boniface's foundation of Fulda, ecclesiastical communities were instructed to teach literacy, 'so that those who seek to please God by right living may not neglect to please Him also by right speaking'.[218] This view was elaborated in the *Admonitio generalis*. Its logic was straightforward. The king had responsibility for the salvation of his people: he

---

[215] Perhaps not coincidentally, the one letter of Charlemagne to dwell on the preaching of the priesthood was addressed to Bishop Gerbald of Liège, also closely associated with surviving examples of the *capitula episcoporum*: the letter is *Capit.* I, no. 122.

[216] *Capit.* II, no. 203, c. 6, p. 66.

[217] *Capitulare missorum generale* a.802, *Capit.* I, nos. 33–4, pp. 91–102, trans. King, *Charlemagne: Translated Sources*, pp. 233–42.

[218] *Epistola de litteris colendis*, *Capit.* I, no. 29, pp. 78–9, trans. King, *Charlemagne: Translated Sources*, pp. 232–3.

had to follow the example of the biblical king Josiah, who 'strove to recall the kingdom which God had given him to the worship of the true God'.[219] This was to be achieved by trying to ensure that moral and religious conduct was both correct and uniform. To establish correctness required authoritative texts, above all. As we have seen, the majority of the *Admonitio* consists of canons copied from the collection that Charlemagne had recently received from Rome. These, the traditional rules of the Church, were only one of a set of texts of which authoritative copies were needed. Selection, edition and dissemination were paramount. Thus in Chapter 72 of the *Admonitio*, Charlemagne required that monasteries and cathedral churches should set up schools to teach the psalms, musical notation, singing, computation and grammar: the skills required to save the souls of his people through prayer. 'Correct properly the catholic books', he exhorted, 'for often, while people want to pray to God in proper fashion, they yet pray improperly because of uncorrected books'.[220]

The focus of Charlemagne and his advisers, then, was on books. The period also produced frescoes, church architecture, sculpture and jewellery, examples of all of which survive, if in small quantities. But the main artistic medium – for pictorial as well as literary art – was the parchment of the book.[221] By this time the codex had fully replaced the scroll, and it was inscribed with the new script developed in this period, Carolingian minuscule.[222] What a Christian kingdom needed above all, of course, was Bibles. Scriptoria often only copied sections of the Bible – the gospels, or the psalter – rather than the whole book, depending on what was required, although two of the intellectual luminaries of Charlemagne's court, Alcuin and Theodulf, both produced editions of the full Bible (pandects). A fair proportion of the other books produced in this period were also those necessary for Christian worship. Sacramentaries set down the order of the mass, antiphonaries contained its music, and the requirement for correct preaching led Charlemagne to commission from the Italian scholar Paul the Deacon a new homiliary – a book of approved

---

[219] II Kings 22, 23: cited in *Admonitio generalis*, prologue, *Capit.* I, no. 22, pp. 52–62 at 54, trans. King, *Charlemagne: Translated Sources*, p. 214.

[220] *Admonitio generalis*, c. 72, *Capit.* I, no. 22, pp. 52–62 at 60, trans. King, *Charlemagne: Translated Sources*, p. 217.

[221] For a good introduction to the visual art and architecture of the period, see D. Bullough, *The Age of Charlemagne* (London, 1965), pp. 131–59.

[222] R. McKitterick, 'Script and book production', in McKitterick (ed.), *Carolingian Culture*, pp. 221–47. See also above, Chapter 1, p. 17.

sermons, taken from the writings of the Church Fathers – which was disseminated along with a covering letter in or just after 786.[223] Although the primary concern of Carolingian copyists was what was read and said in churches and monasteries, they also copied works on more secular subjects, notably an approved collection of the laws of post-Roman rulers, together with a digest of Roman law, produced by a designated scriptorium.[224]

Historians have dubbed this efflorescence of learning 'the Carolingian Renaissance'. How apt is this tag? The term 'renaissance' implies a marked improvement in cultural quality – an estimation that is ultimately rather subjective. As we said in Chapter 1, many more sources survive from the Carolingian than from the earlier Merovingian period, but that contrast may or may not reflect fundamental cultural change.[225] It is also the case that cultural activities in the Carolingian period have been fundamentally influential on modern culture, not only by preserving the culture of antiquity for posterity, but also because the script forms developed then form the basis for those in use today. What is more, as the examples of the *Admonitio generalis* and the *De litteris colendis* demonstrate, writings emanating from the Carolingian court consistently promoted the dynasty as cultural improvers, combining the ideas of renewal (*renovatio*) and correction (*correctio*).

How seriously can we take this rhetoric? There is certainly better evidence for direct *royal* involvement in culture under the Carolingians than under the later Merovingians. But there were nevertheless ample precedents for this kind of royal patronage, both historical and contemporary. Earlier Merovingians like Chilperic and Dagobert I had shown their interest in culture, as had sixth-century rulers like the Byzantine emperor Justinian or the Ostrogothic king Theoderic, and the Carolingians' contemporaries – the Lombard kings Liutprand and Desiderius, the Byzantine emperor Theophilus, or the English kings Offa and Alfred – all sponsored cultural production of a high order.

---

[223] *Epistola generalis, Capit.* 1, no. 30, pp. 80–1, trans. King, *Charlemagne: Translated Sources*, p. 208.

[224] R. McKitterick, 'Some Carolingian law-books and their function', in B. Tierney and P. Linehan (eds.), *Authority and Power. Studies in Medieval Law and Government Presented to Walter Ullman* (Cambridge, 1984), pp. 13–27, and McKitterick, 'Carolingian book production: some problems', *The Library*, 6th ser., 12 (1990), pp. 1–33; both repr. in her *Books, Scribes and Learning in the Frankish Kingdoms* (Aldershot, 1994).

[225] See above, Chapter 1, pp. 16–17.

If there is no sign of such a concern among the later Merovingians, this might be accounted for partly by their relative emasculation, and by the youth at accession and early deaths of many of them. What is unquestionable is the increase in the sheer number of texts that survive from the Carolingian era compared with the Merovingian. We have already seen the bald figures: while only 1,800 books or fragments survive from the entire period to 800, there are 9,000 from the ninth century alone.[226] It is overwhelmingly Carolingian scribes whom we have to thank for copying and transmitting the writings of classical antiquity: in the period between 750 and 900 the earliest copies were made of most of the classical works that we know today, of some seventy authors.[227] Some of the authors thus transmitted were pagan, but many more were Christian: the early Fathers of the Christian Church were as, if not more, important to the readership of these books than authors like Virgil and Ovid, whose paganism was problematic for Christian readers. That works such as the latter came to be defined as 'the classics' at all, distinct from other categories of literature, resulted from a movement for Christian reform that nonetheless allowed room for scholarship, even if its dangers were appreciated: Ermenric of Ellwangen told the story of his haunting by the ghost of Virgil because of his love for the pagan classics.[228]

The sheer volume of copying indicates a sincere desire in the Carolingian age to preserve and transmit Christian texts and the learning of the past. The original compositions of the period have, in general, been less easily esteemed. Yet the eighth and ninth centuries saw the writing of numbers of important new works not only in what seem to have been the most popular genres (at least among the monastic scribes who wrote most of them), like Biblical commentary or poetry, but also in grammar, spelling, philosophy and theology. Perhaps most strikingly, writers of the Carolingian period explored new genres, including (as we saw in Chapter 1) innovative ways of writing about the past, not least in annals and royal biography.[229] Some new types of text reflect the concerns of the monasteries in which they were, for the most part, produced: confraternity books that recorded the names of the many thousands of patrons and associates for whom the monks prayed; and cartularies into which were

---

[226] See above, Chapter 1.   [227] For this calculation, see Chapter 1.
[228] Ermenric of Ellwangen, *Epistola ad Grimaldum Abbatem*, ed. E. Dümmler, *MGH Epp.* v (*Epp. karolini aevi* III) (Berlin, 1899), pp. 561–2.
[229] See above, Chapter 1, pp. 18–23.

copied the documents by which some of those patrons donated their wealth, mostly lands, for the support of the monks. But there were also, as we have seen, handbooks for ordinary priests to guide them in their pastoral work.

Many of the most authoritative texts – sacramentary, canon law, monastic rule – came from Italy. Travelling in the same direction was a movement of scholars to the king's court in the wake of Charlemagne's conquest of the Lombard kingdom. The poet and grammarian Paulinus, later patriarch of Aquileia, was followed by Peter of Pisa, who according to Einhard taught grammar to Charlemagne himself, and the all-round intellectual Paul the Deacon, to whose work as historian, poet and liturgist we have already referred.[230] Signalling that the royal court would be the focus of intellectual and cultural achievement in the Frankish kingdom for that generation, these men were joined by scholars from all over western Europe. The most prominent of them for posterity was Alcuin, the Anglo-Saxon monk and scholar (and relative of Willibrord), who came to Francia at Charlemagne's invitation in 782 and whose hand has been detected behind many of the king's pronouncements on cultural and religious activity.[231] From England also came Beornrad, who became abbot of Echternach and archbishop of Sens, Cathwulf, who wrote a letter of advice to Charlemagne in 775,[232] the theologian Hwita, known as Candidus, the nickname that Alcuin, as was his custom, bestowed on him,[233] and Fridugisus (or Frithugils, in Old English), another theological writer who became close to the royal family, witnessed Charlemagne's will in 811 and was archchancellor to Louis the Pious from 819 to 833.[234] From Ireland there came the deacon Joseph, a poet who was employed by the king as one of his Italian envoys,[235] the philosopher Dúngal,[236] and Dícuil, who wrote

---

[230] For the Italian scholars, see D. Bullough, '*Aula renovata*: the Carolingian court before the Aachen palace', *PBA* 71 (1985), pp. 267–301, repr. in Bullough, *Carolingian Renewal*, pp. 123–60.

[231] L. Wallach, *Alcuin and Charlemagne*, 2nd edn (Ithaca, NY, 1968), pp. 198–226; Bullough, '*Aula renovata*', p. 284.

[232] See now J. Story, 'Cathwulf, kingship and the royal abbey of Saint-Denis', *Speculum* 74 (1999), pp. 1–21.

[233] J. Marenbon, 'Candidus', *Oxford DNB, s.n.*

[234] M. Garrison, 'Fridugisus', *Oxford DNB, s.n.*

[235] M. Garrison, 'Joseph Scottus', *Oxford DNB, s.n.* (for most of the Middle Ages, the epithet 'Scottus' meant 'Irishman').

[236] D. Ganz, 'Dúngal', *Oxford DNB, s.n.*

on astronomy and computus (the reckoning of time, involved especially in the calculation of the date of Easter).[237] Another Irishman, known as Cadac-Andreas, was a writer of exegesis (commentary on the Bible) so pedantic as to arouse the ire of this scholarly circle's great poetic eulogist, Theodulf, who had come to the court from the last vestige of Visigothic Spain. The latter was a poet and theologian, who composed the *Opus Caroli regis* (also known as the *Libri Carolini*), an extensive and learned discussion of the place of art in Christian worship (see Figure 6 above). This was intended as a riposte to the Byzantine rejection of images of Christ and the saints in worship ('iconoclasm'), though it seems to misunderstand the acts of the Byzantines' second council of Nicaea of 787, which were in fact intended to restore the use of images.[238] After his appointment to the bishopric of Orléans in 800 Theodulf became assiduous in his concern for the education of the local clergy. From the 790s the so-called 'court school' dispersed to such posts around the kingdom, spreading their ideas wherever they went. Alcuin became abbot of St Martin's in Tours in 796 and continued to be pivotal as the teacher of many of the next generation of Carolingian scholars.[239]

The cultural effort was therefore continued under Charlemagne's successors, though subtle differences emerged. Only after Charlemagne's death was literature used as a vehicle for political criticism, however guarded.[240] Only from that time, too, were attempts made to demarcate the education of the monastic and the secular clergy, the synod of Aachen of 817 restricting entry into monastic schools to oblates.[241] This is symptomatic of a wider shift in emphasis, for as

---

[237] J. J. Contreni, 'Dícuil', *Oxford DNB, s.n.*
[238] See Godman, *Poetry of the Carolingian Renaissance*, no. 15, ll. 213–33 (with trans.), for Theodulf's verses against Cadac-Andreas, and pp. 6, 10–16 on Theodulf's poetry and rivalry with Cadac-Andreas, with references. *Opus Caroli regis contra synodum (Libri Carolini)*, ed. A. Freeman with P. Meyvaert, *MGH Conc.* II (Hanover, 1998); on this text see T. F. X. Noble, *Images, Iconoclasm and the Carolingians*, esp. pp. 158–206. The usual term for the struggle over images in the Byzantine empire – 'iconoclasm' (literally, 'image-breaking') – is misleading because there is very little evidence for the actual destruction of images. On the whole issue, see J. Haldon and L. Brubaker, *Byzantium in the Iconoclast Era, c. 680–850* (Cambridge, 2010).
[239] D. Bullough, 'Alcuin', *Oxford DNB, s.n.*
[240] P. E. Dutton, *The Politics of Dreaming in the Carolingian Empire* (Lincoln, NE, 1994).
[241] Aachen, 817, c. 5, *CCM* I (Siegburg, 1963), p. 474.

the institutional Church became an ever more secure and widespread presence, so attention moved from the foundational work of Charlemagne's reign, with its emphasis on basic authoritative texts, to a more managerial concern with running a large and supremely important institution. Education was beginning to aid social mobility – both the scholar Walahfrid Strabo and the archbishop of Rheims Ebo came from humble backgrounds – and the proliferating clergy in general needed to be properly directed. Hence the need for the handbook for trainee clerics (*De institutione clericorum*) composed by Hraban Maur (*c.*780–856), whose *On the Nature of Things* (*De rerum naturis*), a kind of encyclopedia, is the epitome of the high Carolingian urge to classify and to organise.[242] Hence too demarcation became a major preoccupation of Hincmar of Rheims. In several works he tried to define the responsibilities of the different grades of the clergy,[243] while his 'On the Governance of the Palace' sought to idealise a similar level of organisation at the heart of the secular world.[244] Indicative of the same institutional context are Hincmar's efforts, involving appeals to the authority of the pope, to depose bishops consecrated by his rebellious predecessor Ebo, or later to impose his superiority on his own nephew, Hincmar, bishop of Laon.[245]

With the fading of the generation after Boniface, there was also a change in the way in which the Christian Church conceived of its heroes. In the eighth century it was still possible for Christians to revere as saints the only recently dead among their leaders. This was precisely what had happened to Boniface, in fact: we have already noted the rather unseemly struggle for possession of his recently dead corpse between his episcopal foundations of Utrecht and Mainz and his monastery at Fulda.[246] But even this contest might be taken as a sign of the increasing stress being laid on corporeal relics as the centre of devotion. The holy man was now not a living role model,

[242] Hrabanus Maurus, *De institutione clericorum libri tres. Studien und Edition*, ed. D. Zimpel (Frankfurt, 1996), and Hrabanus Maurus, *De rerum naturis*, PL 111, cols. 9–614.

[243] Hincmar of Rheims, *Collectio de ecclesiis et capellis*, ed. M. Stratmann, *MGH Fontes iuris germanici antiqui* XIV (Hanover, 1990); also *Capitula quibus de rebus magistri et decani singulas ecclesias inquirire*, PL CXXV, cols. 777–92.

[244] Hincmar of Rheims, *De ordine palatii*, ed. T. Gross and R. Schieffer, *MGH Fontes iuris germanici antiqui* III (Hanover, 1980), trans. D. Herlihy, *A History of Feudalism* (London, 1970), pp. 209–27; see J. L. Nelson, 'Kingship, law and liturgy in the political thought of Hincmar of Rheims', *EHR* 92 (1977), pp. 241–79.

[245] P. McKeon, *Hincmar of Laon and Carolingian Politics* (Urbana, IL, 1978).

[246] Wood, *Missionary Life*, pp. 57–73.

but a dead saint. The ninth century produced no new saints. Rather, increasing effort was directed at identifying, translating and venerating the bodies of those whom tradition revered. The process is epitomised by the transfer from the suburban catacombs of Rome into the city's churches of the bones of long-dead 'martyrs', which began under Pope Paul I (757–67), and the subsequent removal of many of them to churches in Francia. Both Hraban and Hincmar exemplify the centrality of the cult of relics to the structure of the Carolingian Church: the former arranging the procurement of the bones of Roman martyrs for his abbey of Fulda, the latter devoting considerable energy to promoting the cult, and ultimately composing the hagiography, of his fifth-century predecessor at Rheims, St Remigius.[247]

This kind of activity demonstrates the reach of the Christian culture that grew to fit into the Carolingian empire: traffic between Rome and Germany was normal; the single rulership of Charlemagne and Louis the Pious giving the appearance of unity as much to the Church as to the empire. But we should resist the temptation to read into the break-up of this empire a deterioration also in the Church, and in the culture that had grown in parallel with it. The later ninth century has often seemed a time of fragmentation, and not only in politics. Culturally, what has been seen as an exclusive commitment of resources to Christian uses in the heyday of the Carolingian renaissance looks diluted when we observe in the later ninth century the growth of a lay vernacular culture exemplified by the Old High German poem *Ludwigslied*, whose tale of a Frankish king battling the Vikings seems to characterise the age. But vernacular poems and stories never really stood in opposition to Latinate, Christian culture. The *Ludwigslied* is a resolutely Christian text, a praise-poem for a ruler in a long tradition with both Germanic and Latin exemplars.[248] What happened to Carolingian culture as Louis the Pious's rule gave way to that of his sons was less fragmentation than diversification.

The cultural artefacts of the later ninth century were in general just as diverse as they had been earlier: law, history, hagiography,

---

[247] Smith, 'Old saints, new cults'; Hincmar of Rheims, *Vita Remigii episcopi Remensis*, ed. B. Krusch, *MGH SRM* III (Hanover, 1896), pp. 239–349, trans. D. Herlihy, *A History of Feudalism* (London, 1970), pp. 122–4.

[248] P. Fouracre, 'The context of the OHG *Ludwigslied*', *Medium Aevum* 54 (1985), pp. 97–103.

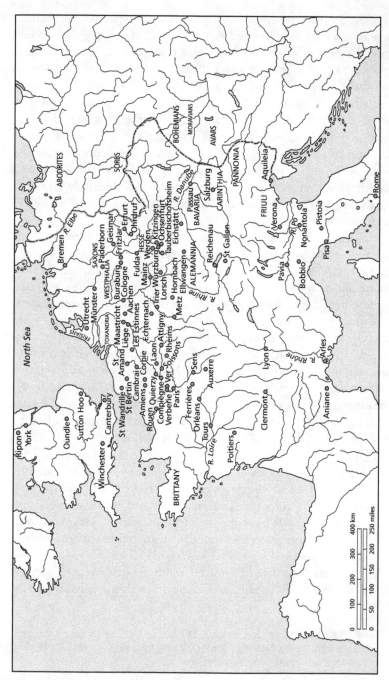

Map 4. Cultural centres in Carolingian Europe

poetry, theology, grammar, computus. What changed was that the forces motivating their production, which had previously come first and foremost from the royal court and palace, became more numerous, as more than one royal court existed at the same time, and as monasteries, bishoprics and aristocrats more often stepped forward as cultural patrons in their own right. The process had begun, as we have seen, in Charlemagne's day, as the learned figures of the initial court school distributed themselves around the kingdom. Their pupils, and their pupils' pupils, gradually spread out to form a dense network of cultural centres across the empire (see Map 4). What we can see of it now is attested by the books which survive from that era, copies both of classics and of original compositions. Library catalogues are extant from a number of centres, and reveal important facets of the organisation of knowledge at the time. Since, in common with much else, we lack catalogues or inventories from the Merovingian period, it is hard to see the immediate precedents for Carolingian practice, but by the first decades of the ninth century the surviving catalogues reveal the emergence of a roughly defined canon of intellectual literature, and display a certain consistency in their organisation, listing first works for use in church (especially the Bible or parts of it), then works of wider relevance to the institutional Church (monastic rules, canon law, hagiographies), and finally school books (grammar, rhetoric, history). Among the remnants of early medieval libraries, very few have remained together (the best example is the collection of manuscripts at the monastery of St Gallen in modern Switzerland).[249] Mostly, the books of a particular early medieval institution have to be identified among manuscripts scattered through modern libraries, usually on the basis of palaeographical and codicological characteristics. In this way, for example, we can piece together the surviving books of the library of the important monastery of St Amand in northern Francia. This continued to be a thriving intellectual centre throughout the ninth century, producing figures like Hucbald, whose works of poetry, music, logic, computus and hagiography encompass a polymathic output which, like those of Hraban Maur and Hincmar of Rheims in previous generations, shows that although Carolingian intellectuals took pains to arrange

[249] McKitterick, *The Carolingians and the Written Word*, pp. 182–5.

material according to genres, they did not find them restrictive.[250] Hucbald's work reaches across the end of this book's period – he died in 930 – throughout which time St Amand remained a major producer of books. Nearly half of the books in its own library were copied there, a relatively high proportion, but it also demonstrably exported its work: it was a major source of gospel books and sacramentaries for other centres.[251] This kind of production necessitated consistent cooperation between intellectual centres, a traffic in books and a workforce of competent copyists to sustain Carolingian culture. The figure of Lupus of Ferrières (805–c.862) exemplifies this empire-wide network. Trained initially at Ferrières and then at Fulda, where he compiled a corpus of secular law and a hagiography, his correspondence with many of the major intellectuals of the ninth century is peppered with requests for books to copy, and a number of these, bearing Lupus's own hand, are extant.[252]

One of St Amand's most notable products takes us back to Lothar II, and in doing so demonstrates that although this cultural activity was dispersed across the realm and remained resolutely intellectual, it was never detached from the nitty-gritty of Frankish political life. Lothar never did manage to get his divorce from Theutberga formalised, and so when he died in 869 he lacked a legitimate heir. Immediately, one of his uncles, Charles the Bald, made a grab for his 'middle' kingdom, and had himself crowned as its king that September in Metz. It was almost certainly for that occasion that the scribes of St Amand produced a carefully chosen compilation of writings on Frankish history, rounded off with a three-page summary of the codex's narrative that portrayed Carolingian rulers fitting seamlessly into a continuous line of succession over the west Frankish lands – Charles the Bald's original kingdom – stretching back to the seventh-century Merovingians (and from there ultimately back to the legendary Priam, king of Troy, whence, one legend said, the Franks had originally come).[253] The book would have made an elegantly apt

---

[250] For Hucbald of St Amand, see initially J. M. H. Smith, 'A hagiographer at work: Hucbald and the library at Saint-Amand', *Revue bénédictine* 106 (1996), pp. 151–71.

[251] McKitterick, *Frankish Kingdoms*, pp. 207–10.

[252] On Lupus, see T. F. X. Noble, 'Lupus of Ferrières in his Carolingian context', in A. C. Murray (ed.), *Rome's Fall and after. Narrators and Sources of Early Medieval History* (Toronto, 1998), pp. 232–50.

[253] H. Reimitz, 'Ein fränkisches Geschichtsbuch aus Saint-Amand und der Codex Vindobonensis palat. 473', in C. Egger and H. Weigl (eds.), *Text-Schrift-Codex*.

addition to Charles the Bald's already substantial court library which, together with other surviving books dedicated to him, reveal him to have been a notable patron of book production and literate culture. The projection from the king or emperor of a deliberate programme for fostering education and culture is an aspect of Carolingian rule that is often emphasised, and seems to set the dynasty apart from both its predecessors and its successors. The systematic approach to cultural and intellectual patronage, the specific attention to schools, the use of the court as a magnet for talent, and the dissemination from it of approved texts are all distinctive features of Carolingian kingship.[254] The reasons for this have already been mentioned: at root, the promotion of learning was seen as a necessity for the proper Christianisation of the people and the purging of sin from the realm and, therefore, an obligation on the king. Two further points need to be made about this extraordinary effort. The first is that, despite the emphasis in much of the rhetoric on uniformity of texts and doctrines, it is striking how much variety there still was in the cultural and scholarly products of the age. Partly this was itself due to the variety in the sources and models that writers and artists of the period used, drawn from previous post-Roman kingdoms, late antique Christianity and the pagan classical tradition. One of the results, and this is the second point, was that the Carolingian cultural effort did not eradicate disagreement. Controversies still occurred, for instance over baptism or, as we saw earlier, over the eucharist;[255] they would break out with new vigour in succeeding periods. But what the Carolingians bequeathed to the future was a sense that rulers *should* concern themselves with such matters; that they had a duty to sponsor art and foster learning. This was done through the medium of the book, which found its essential form in this period; and it was done to bring about reform of society in the direction of Christian ideals. This was a need felt too in successive ages – through the Ottonian tenth, the reform movement of the eleventh, and the renaissance of the twelfth century – and contemporaries responded to it by recourse to the means that the Carolingians had given them.

Quellenkundliche Arbeiten aus dem Institut für Österreichische Geschichtsforschung, MIÖG Ergänzungsband 35 (Vienna and Munich, 2000), pp. 34–90; Reimitz, 'Art of truth'.

254 R. McKitterick, 'The Carolingian renaissance of culture and learning', in Story (ed.), *Charlemagne*, pp. 151–66.

255 See above, pp. 119–21.

4

INVENTING THE CAROLINGIAN EMPIRE: POLITICS AND GOVERNMENT, 800–840

INTRODUCTION

Very early in the year 814, having endured a winter of fevers and pains in his side, Charlemagne took to his deathbed. Abstaining from food, as he was accustomed to do when sick, the sixty-five-year-old ruler tried to fight off his illness armed with 'nothing more than an occasional drink'. A week later, on 28 January at 9 o'clock in the morning, he died.[1] Charlemagne's friend and biographer Einhard tells us that without delay, the emperor's body was washed and prepared for burial. Later that same day he was placed in a late antique imperial sarcophagus obtained from Italy and interred under the west entrance of the church in his principal palace at Aachen while all present wept.[2] To judge by a lavish lament written shortly afterwards by a monk from the Italian monastery of Bobbio, their tears were shared by mourners across the empire: 'Francia has endured

---

[1] Einhard, *VK*, c. 30 (who wrongly thought that Charles was seventy-two). On the literary constructions of emperors' deaths see E. Tremp, 'Die letzten Worte des frommen Kaisers Ludwig. Von Sinn und Unsinn heutiger Textedition', *DA* 48 (1992), pp. 17–36.

[2] Einhard, *VK*, c. 31. See A. Dierkens, 'Autour de la tombe de Charlemagne: considérations sur les sépultures et les funérailles des souverains carolingiens et des membres de leur famille', *Byzantion* 61 (1991), pp. 156–80; J. L. Nelson, 'Carolingian royal funerals', in Theuws and Nelson (eds.), *Rituals of Power*, pp. 131–84, at pp. 145–53.

awful wounds / But never has suffered such great sorrow as now / Alas for miserable me.'[3]

The hyperbole used to describe his people's grief should probably be taken with a pinch of salt, and serves as an index of how quickly after his death Charlemagne passed into the realms of mythical greatness. Nonetheless, people taking stock of his final achievements in the immediate aftermath of his death would probably have been inclined to dwell on three major landmarks. One was Charlemagne's most famous act, his coronation as emperor on Christmas Day 800 in Rome. This resonant event seems in retrospect to represent the highpoint of his reign, setting the seal on the territory he had acquired, reinforcing his alliance with the papacy and opening a new imperial epoch in European history. Another was the winding down of the wars of expansion in the early years of the ninth century, drawing to a successful close the annual cycles of war and aggression that had characterised Frankish politics since the age of Charles Martel. Thirdly and finally, shortly before his final illness Charlemagne bequeathed the Frankish empire, secured, stabilised and ennobled by the lustre of Rome, to his last surviving son Louis ('the Pious') with the consent of all the leading men.[4]

According to the trajectory of this rosy narrative, Louis could hardly have taken over the reins of the empire in a better position. Nevertheless, in the view of posterity, he blew it. If Charlemagne is the archetypally heroic medieval emperor, Louis is the hapless failure from central casting. He has long been seen as a pale reflection of his magnificent predecessor, as weak and feckless a ruler as his father was great. The story of his lengthy reign (814–40) is usually written as a tragic tale of disaster and crisis in which the emperor is cast as a weak cipher, dominated by his churchmen and his wife, aloof and uninterested in worldly affairs, and overdependent on particular favourites.[5] Writing in 837 one of his two biographers, Thegan of

[3] *Planctus de obitu Karoli*, ed. E. Dümmler, *MGH Poet. Latini aevi Karolini* I, pp. 435–6, trans. Dutton, *Carolingian Civilization*, pp. 157–9.

[4] Einhard, *VK*, c. 30; *ARF, s.a.* 813.

[5] For a recent example see I. Gobry, *Histoire des rois de France: Louis Ier, Premier successeur de Charlemagne* (Paris, 2002); critiqued by C. Booker, 'The demanding drama of Louis the Pious', *Comitatus: A Journal of Medieval and Renaissance Studies* 34 (2003), pp. 170–5. See also P. Depreux, 'Louis le Pieux reconsidéré? À propos des travaux récents consacrés à l'héritier de Charlemagne et à son règne', *Francia* 21

Trier, sketched a Louis who was detached and imperious and 'never even allowed his white teeth to be bared in laughter'.[6] The other, an anonymous author known as the Astronomer, wrote shortly after Louis's death that he had had the fault of being 'all too mild'; and that at times he had considered abandoning secular responsibility to enter a monastery.[7] Both biographies were attempts to grapple with the causes and consequences of the great events of the reign, in particular the massive rebellions raised against the emperor by his three eldest sons in 830 and 833–4, which attracted considerable aristocratic support and for a time achieved his deposition. The success of the rebellions was unprecedented in living memory and their deeply unsettling consequences reverberated through Carolingian politics for decades: even forty years later they were still invading the dreams of the emperor's son King Louis the German, who saw a troubling vision of his father in hell and ordered all the churches in his kingdom to organise prayers for his soul's redemption.[8] Modern historians have been similarly shocked by the turmoil of the early 830s, sometimes defining it as the first chime of the empire's slow decline.[9] As a result, accounts of Louis's reign are often compressed into a search for clues as to the personal and political flaws that lay at the root of the disintegration.

These two caricatures (Charles as Great, Louis as Weak) form a diptych which until recently structured almost all accounts of Frankish politics in the first half of the ninth century. Since the 1990s,

---

(1994), pp. 181–212, and M. de Jong, *The Penitential State: Authority and Atonement in the Age of Louis the Pious, 814–840* (Cambridge, 2009).

[6] Thegan, *Gesta Hludowici imperatoris*, ed. E. Tremp, *Die Taten Kaiser Ludwigs, MGH SRG in usum scholarum separatim editi* LXIV (Hanover, 1995), c. 19, trans. Dutton, *Carolingian Civilization*, p. 165.

[7] Astronomer, *Vita Hludowici imperatoris*, ed. E. Tremp, *Astronomus. Das Leben Kaiser Ludwigs, MGH SRG in usum scholarum separatim editi* LXIV (Hanover, 1995), prologue and c. 32.

[8] *AF*, s.a. 874; Flodoard, *Historia Remensis ecclesiae*, ed. J. Heller and G. Waitz, *MGH SS* XIII (Hanover, 1881), pp. 405–599, III.20; Dutton, *Politics of Dreaming*, pp. 219–22. For the enduring memory of the rebellions see also D. Ganz, 'The *Epitaphium Arsenii* and opposition to Louis the Pious', in P. Godman and R. Collins (eds.), *Charlemagne's Heir: New Perspectives on the Reign of Louis the Pious (814–840)* (Oxford, 1990), pp. 537–50.

[9] See now C. Booker, *Past Convictions: the Penance of Louis the Pious and the Decline of the Carolingians* (Philadelphia, PA, 2009).

however, there have been significant attempts to write more nuanced accounts of Louis's reign which rehabilitate his personal capabilities.[10] The most common mitigating plea is that Charlemagne's last years, far from being the glorious culmination described in our opening paragraphs, in fact witnessed a phase of decline and disintegration, and that some of Louis's problems were therefore inherited from his frail father. Images of age suffuse early-ninth-century descriptions of Charlemagne's imperial years, during the final four of which he was ill.[11] Compare the flickering images of the bellicose and perpetually moving eighth-century Charlemagne provided by Einhard and the *Royal Frankish Annals*, a ruler unable even to sleep through the night without getting up to deal with affairs of state, with the poet Ermold the Black's stately tableau of the old emperor on his throne in 813, white hair flowing over his pale neck and quavering that 'my war-like right hand, once famous throughout the world, now shakes as my blood grows cold'.[12] In the months before he died, omens symbolising the decay of the aged emperor were reported. The word *princeps* (ruler) faded from the inscription identifying him as the builder of the church at Aachen: the emperor's personal decline was seen as connected to the dwindling of what he had created.[13] Historians have also detected the frustrations of an old man in the exasperated tone of some of Charlemagne's governmental decrees from late in the reign, which rage about the shortcomings of various royal agents.[14] These hints of underlying political decline have suggested to some historians that the last decade of Charlemagne's reign should be seen as a political twilight, and that the slow fade of this once-great conqueror rendered him unable to construct an impersonal governmental apparatus that could survive without his

---

[10] Godman and Collins (eds.), *Charlemagne's Heir*; de Jong, *The Penitential State*. E. Boshof, *Ludwig der Fromme* (Darmstadt, 1996) is more traditional.

[11] Einhard, *VK*, c. 22.

[12] Ermold, *In honorem Hludowici imperatoris*, ed. E. Faral, *Ermold le Noir. Poème sur Louis le Pieux* (with French trans.) (Paris, 1964), p. 52, trans. Dutton, *Carolingian Civilization*, p. 152. On images of age in Carolingian sources see P. E. Dutton, *Charlemagne's Mustache and Other Cultural Clusters of a Dark Age* (New York, 2004), pp. 151–67.

[13] Einhard, *VK*, c. 32.

[14] J. L. Nelson, 'The voice of Charlemagne', in R. Gameson and H. Leyser (eds.), *Belief and Culture in the Middle Ages: Studies Presented to Henry Mayr-Harting* (Oxford, 2001), pp. 76–88.

own unique personality – that, in effect, his failure left his successor
running to stand still.[15]

These issues – Louis's weakness, and the extent to which he inherited a malaise incubated during his father's dotage – are central to
traditional versions of Carolingian history written as 'magnificent
tragedy'.[16] But before accepting the terms of this debate we should
pause to acknowledge the problematic assumptions inherent in their
foregrounding of great or inadequate personalities as major historical forces. Arguing about the relative personal qualities of individual
rulers requires us to engage in a kind of retrospective psychoanalysis
for which the sources are much less useful than they may seem. In an
era when the personal was highly political, the gestures, expressions
and comportment of kings could be seen as profoundly symbolic.
Louis's reported monastic inclinations and refusal to smile, therefore, have to be read as pointed literary constructions that tell us
more about contemporary discussions of political ideas than about
the emperor's sense of humour or dedication to secular affairs.[17]
The nickname *pius* represented a positive attribute that did not carry
with it modern overtones of other-worldliness.[18] Care is also needed
with the Astronomer's rueful reflection on the emperor's excessive
mildness, which is undermined several times by his own account, in
which for example Louis decides to blind an opponent whom the

---

[15] F. L. Ganshof, 'Louis the Pious reconsidered', 'The last period of Charlemagne's
reign: a study in decomposition', and 'Charlemagne's failure', all in Ganshof,
The Carolingians and the Frankish Monarchy (London, 1971), pp. 261–72, 240–55,
256–60 respectively. See also J. M. Wallace-Hadrill, *The Barbarian West, 400–1000*
(London, 1952), pp. 87–114. For a recent appraisal see Collins, *Charlemagne*,
pp. 171–4.

[16] J. L. Nelson, 'Rewriting the history of the Franks', in Nelson, *Frankish World*,
p. 170.

[17] T. F. X. Noble, 'The monastic ideal as a model for empire: the case of Louis the
Pious', *Revue Bénédictine* 86 (1976), pp. 235–50; Noble, 'Louis the Pious and his
piety reconsidered', *Revue Belge de Philologie et d'Histoire* 58 (1980), pp. 297–316;
M. Innes, '"He never even allowed his white teeth to be bared in laughter": the
politics of humour in the Carolingian renaissance', in G. Halsall (ed.), *Humour,
History and Politics in Late Antiquity and the Early Middle Ages* (Cambridge, 2002),
pp. 131–56; de Jong, *Penitential State*, pp. 83–4.

[18] R. Schieffer, 'Ludwig "der Fromme". Zur Entstehung eines karolingischen
Herrscherbeinamens', *Frühmittelalterliche Studien* 16 (1982), pp. 58–73; P. Depreux,
'La *Pietas* comme principe de gouvernement d'après le *Poème sur Louis le Pieux*
d'Ermold le Noir', in Hill and Swan (eds.), *Community*, pp. 201–24.

author himself considered 'worthy of mercy'.[19] Although the personalities of early medieval kings could be very important in shaping
their reigns, contemporary texts rarely open transparent windows
onto their inner feelings or defining characteristics – much more
often they have to be read as carefully crafted polemical presentations which were constructed to suit the agendas of their authors
and audiences, and offer only an indirect view of the public image
adopted by the ruler at court.[20]

Instead of distilling the political history of this period into a story
of kingly strength and weakness, of rise and decline, this chapter will
try to show the underlying complexities of the political situation by
focussing on the two main problems facing Charlemagne and his
son after 800: the management of power within the royal/imperial
dynasty; and the need to establish a pattern of politics that would
tie the regional elites of the empire to the political centre. We will
see that, ironically, the very success of the strategies developed to
meet these challenges helped create the preconditions for the crises
of the early 830s. These twin problems were perennial conundrums
for early medieval dynasts (they featured prominently, after all, in
Chapter 2), but they loomed over the early-ninth-century empire
with particular immediacy owing to the end of territorial expansion.
Eighth-century soldier-kingship was structured around an annual
cycle of assemblies, campaigns and redistribution of booty which
bound the Frankish elite to their Carolingian leaders and created a
political culture with the war-trail at its centre. The tailing-off of
the wars of conquest in the 790s, and their cessation in the very
early 800s, catalysed a dramatic shift in this culture which meant the
roles of every member of the elite from the royal family downwards
had to be redefined.[21] The elites of regions recently incorporated
by force had to be persuaded to become willing participants in the

---

[19] Astronomer, *Vita Hludowici imperatoris*, c. 21.
[20] For discussion see S. Hamilton, 'Early medieval rulers and their modern biographers', *EME* 9 (2000), pp. 247–60; D. Ganz, 'Einhard's Charlemagne: the characterization of greatness', and J. L. Nelson, 'Charlemagne the man', both in Story
(ed.), *Charlemagne*, pp. 38–51 and 22–37 respectively; G. Koziol, 'Is Robert I in
Hell?', *EME* 14 (2006), pp. 233–67.
[21] On the shift see above all T. Reuter, 'Plunder and tribute in the Carolingian
Empire', *TRHS* 5th ser. 35 (1985), pp. 75–94; Reuter, 'The end of Carolingian
military expansion', in Godman and Collins (eds.), *Charlemagne's Heir*, pp. 391–
405. Both are repr. in Reuter, *Medieval Polities and Modern Mentalities*.

new political order. The empire had been cobbled together, now it had to be made to fuse: in other words, it had to be invented in the imaginations and mentalities of its elites.

THE IMPERIAL CORONATION

At first sight, it seems natural to assume that the imperial coronation of Charlemagne in Rome on Christmas Day 800 must have played a major part in this process, by setting a seal on the spectacular conquests of the preceding decades and creating the idea of the empire as a single entity. The revival of the imperial title was a novelty: there had been no emperor in the west since the deposition in 476 of the last Roman to hold the title. Despite the breathtaking audacity of the move, hindsight has made it look almost inevitable, a natural sequel to the Franco-papal alliance established in the 750s. European rulers looked back to the event centuries later and identified it as the founding moment of the 'Holy Roman Empire'. Oppressed by our inability to ignore the knowledge of what happened later, it is easy to forget that Charlemagne was not a prophetic architect of the European future. When we look at the contemporary circumstances in detail, it becomes clear that the coronation itself was the result of a period of serious political conflict, rather than the culmination of a smooth and assured rise to imperial power, and that it may have had a much more limited significance to contemporaries than it did to the ideologues of later centuries.[22]

The immediate context was a dispute within the city of Rome.[23] Long-simmering tensions surrounding the pontificate of Leo III (795–816) came to a head on 25 April 799 when the pope was attacked during a public procession by enemies including senior members of the papal entourage and relatives of his predecessor. He was charged with perjury, simony (the buying of ecclesiastical office) and sexual impropriety, and an attempt was made to incapacitate him by cutting out his eyes and tongue (successful but miraculously reversed, according to papal sources). After undergoing what may have been formal deposition proceedings, Leo came to meet

---

[22] There are many discussions of the coronation: see for example R. Folz, *The Coronation of Charlemagne, 25 December 800* (London, 1974); Collins, *Charlemagne*, pp. 141–59; M. Becher, *Charlemagne* (New Haven, CT and London, 2003), pp. 7–17.

[23] For what follows the key sources are *ARF*, s.a. 799–801 and *LP* II, pp. 1–8, trans. Davis, *The Lives of the Eighth-Century Popes*, pp. 176–89.

Charlemagne in the autumn at the palace of Paderborn where the
king had been campaigning against the Saxons.[24] Having heard representations from the pope and (again, according to papal sources)
his enemies, the king sent Leo back to Rome accompanied by royal
legates under instructions to investigate further and to reinstate him.
That, for the time being, seemed to be the end of the matter. Charles's
itinerary over the subsequent year (see Maps 5 and 6) gives few obvious clues that he was gearing up for a journey to the eternal city,
being taken up largely by tours of the northern coastline, apparently
to oversee the construction of a fleet against the Danes, and visits
to the holy shrines of Neustria. However, in August 800 the king
announced his departure for Italy and at the end of his journey was
received by Leo at Mentana, at the twelfth milestone from Rome.
Entering the city itself at the end of November, he 'made it clear
to all why he had come to Rome'.[25] At the same time, an assembly
was staged at which Leo swore that he was innocent of all that had
been alleged against him in the previous year. Finally, Charles was
acclaimed and crowned as emperor on Christmas Day.

Although this basic outline of events is relatively clear, their meaning and precise contours are frustratingly opaque, which has given
rise to a veritable historical cottage industry dedicated to the issue.
Our sources are relatively plentiful but very partial, and almost all of
them were written several years later – they deceive us in appearing
to provide clear journalistic windows onto the events of 799–800.
Their information should be inspected as the fossilised remains of an
after-the-fact and politically charged debate about the significance of
what had happened; these texts were subtly argumentative, and were
written as part of a contemporary struggle to control interpretation of
the encounter between Charles and Leo. This means that we should
resist the temptation to create a composite account of events that
draws apparently complementary details from different sources, and
undermines our attempts to discover what really happened.[26] Firstly,
there is an obvious difference of emphasis between the Frankish and

[24] J. Fried, 'Papst Leo III. besucht Karl den Großen in Paderborn oder Einhards
Schweigen', *HZ* 272 (2001), pp. 281–326; P. Godman, J. Jarnut and P. Johanek
(eds.), *Am Vorabend der Kaiserkrönung: das Epos "Karolus Magnus et Leo papa" und
der Papstbesuch in Paderborn 799* (Berlin, 2002).

[25] *ARF*, s.a. 800.

[26] J. L. Nelson, 'Why are there so many different accounts of Charlemagne's imperial
coronation?', in J. L. Nelson, *Courts, Elites and Gendered Power in the Early Middle
Ages: Charlemagne and Others* (Aldershot, 2007), no. XII.

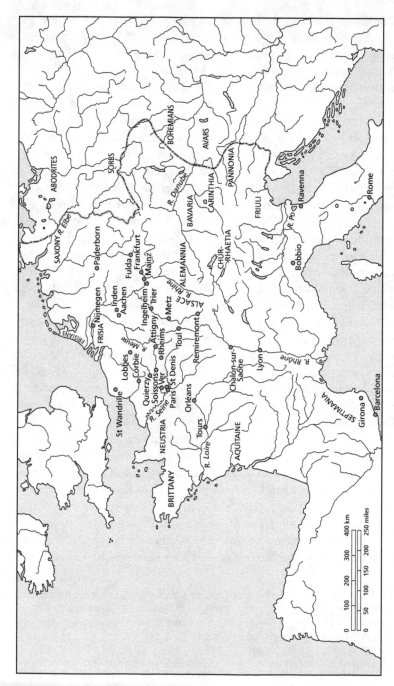

Map 5. Places mentioned in Chapter 4: 'Inventing the Carolingian empire: politics and government, 800–840'

Map 6. Places on Charlemagne's itineraries, 768–814. Plotting the places known to have been visited by Charlemagne shows how far he travelled, but not how many times he stayed in one place, nor for how long. In fact, his most frequent stops almost all lie in the area between the Seine and the Rhine, and visits to Saxony, Italy and Bavaria were connected with exceptional military or political expeditions.

papal sources as to the relationship between the main protagonists. The author of this section of the *Royal Frankish Annals*, working around 807, depicts Charles as a saviour riding into Rome to save the pope from his enemies, while Leo's biographer (writing after the pope's death in 816) downplays his problems and places him in the driving seat.

The *Royal Frankish Annals* projects an image of Charlemagne claiming his rightful place at the head of the world order, confirmed by propitious omens and exotic gifts sent by respectful eastern rulers (including the Patriarch of Jerusalem, who reportedly sent him the keys to the Holy Sepulchre). A mosaic installed in the Lateran Palace by the pope conveys a rather different set of messages. (See Figure 8.) It shows Leo and Charlemagne kneeling together at the

Figure 8. Mosaic of Charlemagne and Pope Leo III, Rome.

feet of St Peter, and the identifying inscriptions above or next to
each figure reveal the work to have been dedicated by the pope
to the king: 'St Peter, the most holy lord pope Leo, to the lord
king Charles'. St Peter sits with the keys to the kingdom of heaven
in his lap, indicating his power over the fate of every human soul

(Matt. 16:19). To Pope Leo he gives a pallium, symbol of the jurisdictional rights of the bishop; to Charlemagne, a banner, indicating
his responsibility to protect the Church; and this message is reinforced by the inscription below the figures: 'Blessed Peter give life
to Pope Leo; give victory to King Charles.' The image was mirrored
on the left of the apse by a mosaic in which Christ gives the keys
to heaven to an unknown pope (Peter or Sylvester), and a banner to
Constantine, the first Christian Roman emperor (r.306–37). In the
apse itself, Christ exhorts the apostles, in the words of the so-called
Great Commission (Matt. 28:19–20): 'Go ye therefore, and teach all
nations, baptising them in the name of the Father and of the Son and
of the Holy Spirit.' Although the mosaic (now on an exterior wall)
that the modern visitor to Rome sees is a reconstruction, the original
decorated an interior wall of the so-called *triclinium maius*, the greater
of two banqueting and reception halls begun by Pope Leo III in 797
or 798, and demolished in the 1580s. The mosaic was certainly completed before Charlemagne's coronation as emperor on 25 December
800, since the Frankish ruler is there still styled 'king'. The deco-
rative scheme conveyed several linked messages: it stressed the role
of the Church, and particularly the papacy, in Frankish military victory, especially over pagans like the Saxons, whom Charlemagne was
fighting at that time, and the Avars, whom he had recently defeated;
it linked that victory with Christianisation; it implied an association between Charlemagne's rule and that of the Roman emperors
of antiquity; and it promoted the idea that legitimate Carolingian
rulership depended on St Peter, and therefore on the pope.[27] The
gist of papal claims around this time is also reflected in the *Donation of
Constantine*, an influential text which claims (falsely) that the powers
and resources of the western empire had been handed over to the
papacy by the eponymous emperor in the fourth century.[28]

Secondly, the respective biases of the sources make the balance
between planning and opportunism difficult to establish. For example, Einhard's famous assertion, written down at least seventeen years
after the fact, that Charles had no idea what was going to happen

---

[27] For the mosaic, which has been heavily restored but which was also recorded
in an early modern sketch, see Dutton (ed.), *Carolingian Civilization*, pp. 58–62;
M. Becher, 'Die Kaiserkrönung im Jahr 800. Eine Streitfrage zwischen Karl dem
Großen und Papst Leo III.', *Rheinische Vierteljahrblätter* 66 (2002), pp. 1–38, at
pp. 21–2.
[28] See Dutton (ed.), *Carolingian Civilization*, pp. 14–22.

on Christmas Day in St Peter's before he entered the church, is sometimes taken at face value but must surely be read as a literary attempt to highlight the emperor's virtuous humility.[29] Conversely, on the basis of references to the realm as the *imperium christianum* in letters written by his close adviser Alcuin, it has been argued that members of Charlemagne's circle were already thinking in imperial terms in 798–9; but we must also acknowledge that the concepts to which this terminology referred were as much eschatological as political.[30] While Einhard's claim seems implausible, and Alcuin's dangerously ambiguous, the important thing is to understand why authors made such claims at all: in the end, we probably have to be satisfied with trying to understand the ways contemporaries argued about the coronation rather than hoping to excavate the precise details of its stage-management from the mass of rhetoric under which they are buried.

This is not, however, to say that we can know nothing. When we tighten our perspective to the sources written closest in time to events, the role of another party to this argument suddenly swims into focus. A manuscript from Cologne apparently written in 798 refers obliquely to an occasion 'when messengers came from Greece to hand over the empire [to Charles]'.[31] Discussions with the Byzantines, who considered their empire to be an uninterrupted continuation of the Romans', may have been thought by Charlemagne more important than those with Leo, whose authority after all was weak even in Rome. As with the events of 753–4 discussed in Chapters 1 and 2, we should not let the novelty of the papacy's involvement in the making of secular rulers, nor its ability to make its views stick in the historical record, mislead us into overestimating its contemporary influence. When Charles met the pope at Paderborn in 799, there were probably Byzantine legates in attendance too. The weight given by the Franks to the position of Byzantium is confirmed in backhanded fashion by the account in the *Annals of Lorsch*, which justified the coronation with reference to the fact that the Byzantines were ruled by a woman (the dowager empress Irene), and argued

[29] Einhard, *VK*, c. 28.

[30] Folz, *Coronation of Charlemagne*, pp. 118–31; M. Alberi, 'The evolution of Alcuin's concept of the *Imperium Christianum*', in Hill and Swan (eds.), *Community*, pp. 3–17.

[31] Fried, 'Papst Leo III.'; D. Bullough, 'Charlemagne's men of God: Alcuin, Hildebald and Arn', in Story (ed.), *Charlemagne*, pp. 136–50, at pp. 145–6; Nelson, 'Why are there so many different accounts?', pp. 16–18.

that the position of emperor was therefore implicitly vacant. This is almost certainly the earliest of our narrative sources, and probably represents a version of the official line developed by the court upon Charlemagne's return from Italy.[32]

Acknowledging the importance to the Franks of Byzantine sensibilities may also help us get closer to the contemporary meanings of the coronation. It has been argued that Charlemagne's imperial status was devised as a way of making his rule acceptable to the Saxons, whose pre-conquest society had no kings, but since Saxony had not been in the Roman empire it is hard to see on what basis an emperor would have been any more welcomed.[33] In parts of Italy, on the other hand, the imperial title had more immediate resonance. Southern and central Italy (including Rome itself) were long accustomed to an imperial presence either directly or mediated through the Byzantine exarchates, so the gradual retreat of Byzantine power from the peninsula during the eighth century may have created something approaching a crisis of authority for its elites. Charlemagne's bid to acquire imperial status may have been designed in large part to answer that crisis by appealing to Italian models of authority; and hence to bolster his claims to govern parts of that realm which had hitherto remained beyond his reach. In this context it is significant that a Sicilian embassy visited Aachen in 799, that an official from the island is known to have defected to Charlemagne in 800 and that, according to the Byzantine chronicler Theophanes, Constantinople's greatest worry about the Frankish king's trip to Rome was that he intended to take over Sicily and the south.[34] The events of 800 may thus be viewed in part as the result of a fortuitous alignment of Charlemagne's desire to justify his Italian ambitions through appropriation of a traditional and appropriate form of authority, Leo's need to prop up his position in Rome by making powerful friends and recasting himself as a maker of monarchs, and the Byzantines' inability to maintain active influence over their far-off Italian possessions. In the era of Charles's grandsons and for centuries after that, the title of emperor became a *de facto* adjunct to the kingship of Italy – and as

---

[32] *AL, s.a.* 801; Collins, 'Charlemagne's imperial coronation'.

[33] H. Mayr-Harting, 'Charlemagne, the Saxons and the imperial coronation of 800', *EHR* 111 (1996), pp. 1113–33.

[34] *ARF, s.a.* 799, 811; Theophanes, *Chronographia*, ed. C. de Boor, 2 vols. (Leipzig, 1883–5), a.m. 6293, trans. C. Mango and R. Scott with G. Greatrex, *The Chronicle of Theophanes Confessor. Byzantine and Near Eastern History AD 284–813* (Oxford, 1997), p. 653.

already a primarily Italian affair is perhaps the best way to interpret the dynamics that led to the events of Christmas Day 800.

This does not mean that the emperor's new status could not also have had wider resonances. There are some hints that the coronation coincided with a shift in the way that he expressed his authority. In the last twenty years of Charlemagne's reign, a new palace at Aachen was erected and gradually became the centre of a more sedentary style of Frankish rulership that could be described as imperial. Charlemagne's visit to Italy in 800–1 afforded him the opportunity to collect antique adornments for the palace which enhanced its symbolic references to the classical past: one contemporary source even refers to Aachen as a 'new Rome', and another reveals that part of the complex was known as 'the Lateran'.[35] The seriousness with which Charlemagne regarded the title is also demonstrated by the valuable territorial concessions he was prepared to make in 812 to acquire renewed Byzantine recognition of his status – only after this was secured did he put the title on his coins.[36] Being emperor clearly mattered to him. In other respects, Charles wore his new status lightly. It is important to remember that contemporary Rome was a religious and not a political centre, a place of pilgrimage rather than a source of jurisdiction.[37] The coronation endowed the emperor not with a new set of constitutional powers, but rather an enhanced prestige, the nature of which drew on the powerful religious and classical–imperial resonances of the city but remained ill defined: ancient Rome was not a direct template for Alcuin's *imperium christianum*. After 801 Charlemagne declined to intervene directly in Rome's affairs, and the fact that he never went back there hints that his relationship with the pope was rather tense – although his subordinates took an interest in the city and its relics, their activities did not require them to pay much heed to papal claims to power there.[38] The imperial dignity became part of his titulature, but did not supersede its other parts. Charles retained his traditional status as 'king of the Franks and Lombards' and continued to comport himself as a Frankish king rather than as a neo-Roman emperor – and, tellingly, the wording of the additional title he adopted (the

[35] J. L. Nelson, 'Aachen as a place of power', in de Jong and Theuws with van Rhijn (eds.), *Topographies of Power*, pp. 217–41; McKitterick, *Charlemagne: The Formation of a European Identity*, pp. 157–70.

[36] Collins, *Charlemagne*, p. 153; S. Coupland, 'Charlemagne's coinage: ideology and the economy', in Story (ed.), *Charlemagne*, pp. 211–29, at pp. 223–7.

[37] Schieffer, 'Charlemagne and Rome'; Smith, *Europe after Rome*, pp. 268–77.

[38] Becher, 'Die Kaiserkrönung'; Costambeys, *Power and Patronage*, Chapter 8.

rather lukewarm 'governing the Roman empire') owed more to the terms of Italian charter formulas than it did to the conventions of ancient Rome or contemporary Byzantium.[39] The coronation did not change the character of the empire as a territorial unit. Nobody tried to pretend that internal regnal boundaries had been erased, and the empire remained an agglomeration of smaller units each with its own laws and customs. 'Kingdom' and 'empire' were not distinct constitutional concepts, and the Latin words *regnum* and *imperium* are much more ambiguous than their English counterparts (hence their general interchangeability in this book).

If the title did not radically change the way Charlemagne ruled, or the nature of what he ruled, nor did it transform the character of his dynasty. In a plan made in 806 for a posthumous division of the realm between his three sons, Charlemagne made no mention of the imperial title, though he implied that Rome was a special place outwith the main territory of the empire and was to be protected corporately by all the Frankish kings.[40] When in 813, after the deaths of his two elder adult sons, he eventually did crown the third, Louis, as emperor, he staged the ceremony in Aachen and without reference to the pope. It is significant that Einhard, however sceptically we view the details of his account, felt able tacitly to claim that this event was *more* important than the coronation of 800.[41] After 800, triumphal histories of the Carolingian dynasty such as the *Earlier Annals of Metz* (*c.*806) did not reconfigure their heroes as proto-emperors, but continued to root their narratives in the Merovingian Frankish past, starting with Pippin II and eulogising him and his successors as great conquerors and defenders of the Church.[42] Twenty years later, even after Louis the Pious had been re-crowned by another pope, the poet Ermold the Black listed the predecessors of Louis's son Pippin of Aquitaine in exactly the same terms and sequence as had the Metz annalist – traditional ways of characterising the dynasty were not effaced.[43] Empire and *Romanitas* were resonant concepts, ringing

---

[39] On titles see I. H. Garipzanov, 'Communication of authority in Carolingian titles', *Viator* 36 (2005), pp. 41–82; Garipzanov, *Symbolic Language*.

[40] *Divisio regnorum*, ed. A. Boretius, *Capit.* I, cc. 3–4 establish the sons' shared access to Italy.

[41] Einhard, *VK*, c. 30.

[42] Fouracre and Gerberding, *Late Merovingian France*, pp. 330–70; Hen, 'Annals of Metz'; Fouracre, 'Long shadow'.

[43] Ermold, *Ad eundem Pippinum*, ed. E. Faral, *Ermold le Noir. Poème sur Louis le Pieux* (with French trans.) (Paris, 1964), pp. 228–30.

with echoes of Rome's great secular past and its current identity
as a holy city. Yet these concepts were slippery and contemporary
observers clearly disagreed about their significance – they meant
different things to different audiences.[44] To Charles himself, as far
as we can tell, being emperor was an extremely important badge of
prestige, but perhaps no more than that. To all intents and purposes
he already ruled an empire, and it remained more or less what it
already was: neither a reinstitution of ancient Rome nor a newly
minted 'Holy Roman Empire', but something all of its own – an
'empire of the Franks'.

GOVERNING THE EMPIRE

A nearly simultaneous but unrelated development of the early ninth
century had a far more profound influence on the politics of the
empire than did events in Rome at Christmas 800 – namely, the end
of Frankish military expansion. After the defeat of the Avars in the
mid-790s, thirty years of Franco-Saxon conflict finally ground to a
halt in 804 with the forced immigration to Francia of the people
beyond the river Elbe.[45] The decision to bring to an end nearly
a century of territorial aggrandisement seems to have been made
consciously and was presumably based on a combination of factors including geography, limitations on resources and the extension
of the empire to the traditional limits of Frankish influence. Military activity by no means stopped completely. The last few years
of Charlemagne's reign, for example, saw the Franks assert themselves as an influential naval power in the Mediterranean, scoring
victories over Byzantines and Arabs alike in Corsica, the Balearics
and elsewhere.[46] However, the establishment at this time of 'marks'
(*marca*), military commands designed to control the frontiers in the
east and south, illustrates the conscious shift away from expansionary
warfare in favour of a more regularised frontier structure.[47]

---

[44] Garipzanov, *Symbolic Language*, pp. 277–82.
[45] Einhard, *VK*, c. 7; I. Wood, 'Beyond satraps and ostriches: political and social
structures of the Saxons in the early Carolingian period', in D. H. Green and
F. Siegmund (eds.), *The Continental Saxons from the Migration Period to the Tenth
Century: An Ethnographic Perspective* (Rochester, NY, 2003), pp. 271–97.
[46] *ARF*, s.a. 799, 806, 807, 809, 812, 813. See below, Chapter 7, pp. 372–3.
[47] Reuter, 'End of Carolingian military expansion'; H. Wolfram, 'The creation
of the Carolingian frontier system, *c*.800', in Pohl, Wood and Reimitz (eds.),
Transformation of Frontiers.

These arrangements were not purely defensive, but also served as platforms for attempts to impose tributary status on the Slavs to the east and Danes to the north.[48] Frankish interference in these regions had a variety of unintended consequences which could affect patterns of cross-border interaction, as exemplified by the case of the Abodrites. This grouping of Slavs, found to the east of the Elbe river, had become allies of the Franks during the Saxon campaigns, and by dealing with and bolstering sympathetic elements within the Abodrite elite Charlemagne encouraged the formation of a much clearer political hierarchy with a single leader, where previously there had been several.[49] In the case of the Abodrites and other Slavic peoples, this form of pervasive cultural and political pressure created an impulse to social change which was hard to resist and which allowed the regularisation of relations with neighbouring peoples without the need for territorial incorporation or even persistent evangelisation.[50] The effects of these dynamics were not always benevolent for the Franks – for example, the destabilising pressure placed on the Danes by Charlemagne's conquest of Saxony played a material role in creating the preconditions for the Viking raids of the ninth century.[51] The consolidation of the frontiers nevertheless clearly symbolises a fundamental shift in the orientation and temperament of the Frankish polity.

The metronomic listing of conquests and frontiers in ninth-century descriptions of the empire suggests that the memory of the Franks' past victories lived on in their imaginations and constituted a central pillar of the elite's political identity.[52] At the same time,

---

[48] J. M. H. Smith, '*Fines imperii*: the Marches', in *NCMH* II, pp. 169–89.

[49] *ARF*, *s.a.* 804, 808, 809; Collins, *Charlemagne*, p. 164.

[50] P. Heather, 'Frankish imperialism and Slavic society', in P. Urbańczyk (ed.), *The Origins of Central Europe* (Warsaw, 1997), pp. 171–90; M. Innes, 'Franks and Slavs, 700–1000: European expansion before the millennium', *EME* 6 (1997), pp. 201–14; P. M. Barford, *The Early Slavs. Culture and Society in Early Medieval Eastern Europe* (London, 2001), pp. 89–113; T. Reuter, 'Charlemagne and the world beyond the Rhine', in Story (ed.), *Charlemagne*, pp. 183–94.

[51] For arguments along these lines see B. Myhre, 'The archaeology of the early Viking age in Norway', in H. B. Clarke, M. Ní Mhaonaigh and R. Ó Floinn (eds.), *Ireland and Scandinavia in the Early Viking Age* (Dublin, 1998), pp. 3–36. See also below, Chapter 7, pp. 355–6.

[52] H. Reimitz, 'Conversion and control: the establishment of liturgical frontiers in Carolingian Pannonia', in Pohl, Wood and Reimitz (eds.), *Transformation of Frontiers*, pp. 188–207 discusses such lists as a strategy of 'positive affirmation'.

the end of expansion had potentially negative implications for the Frankish aristocracy, which was by nature geared for war and for its reward, booty.[53] Charlemagne's attempt to ease his aristocracy into a new 'peacetime' mentality is visible in a series of decrees from the first decade of the ninth century which aimed to redefine the military obligations of the nobility. Whereas previously, leading members of the secular aristocracy would have turned up every year at the start of the campaigning season together with their warrior followings, ready to fight in the king's army and share in the prestige and proceeds of war, the lessening of the opportunities for expansionary campaigning meant that the emperor now had to regularise and limit their duty to serve – only in the case of invasion from without were all expected to take up arms and defend the patria.[54] The sheer size which the empire had now attained also had profound implications for how it was ruled. After the conquest of Saxony the total area of Frankish dominion extended to some one million square kilometres, a huge and rapid increase from the days of Pippin III. Einhard commented that the empire nearly doubled in size during Charlemagne's reign.[55] An informed estimate suggests that there were approximately 600–700 pagi (basic geographical units used to describe administrative or political jurisdiction); 700 royal estates; 150 royal residences, of which twenty-five were major palaces; 180 bishoprics (not counting around forty-five subject directly to Rome); and about 700 monasteries.[56] By any standards, all this would take some governing. In an age before the bureaucratic state and in the absence of mass communications, this meant that the aristocracy, habituated to annual campaigning, now had to be bound into the life of the polity by other means (see Figure 9).

The Carolingians' response to this imperative is discernible in the gradual institutionalisation of Frankish politics which gained

[53] Reuter, 'Plunder and tribute'.
[54] Reuter, 'End of Carolingian military expansion'; T. Reuter, 'Carolingian and Ottonian warfare', in M. Keen (ed.), Medieval Warfare: A History (Oxford, 1999), pp. 13–35. For additional nuances see Innes, State and Society, pp. 143–53; J. France, 'The composition and raising of the armies of Charlemagne', Journal of Medieval Military History 1 (2002), pp. 61–82; Halsall, Warfare and Society, pp. 71–110.
[55] Einhard, VK, c. 15.
[56] K. F. Werner, 'Hludovicus Augustus: gouverner l'empire chrétien – idées et réalités', in Godman and Collins (eds.), Charlemagne's Heir, pp. 3–123, at pp. 82–3. Cf. the figures cited by M. Stansbury, 'Early medieval biblical commentaries, their writers and readers', Frühmittelalterliche Studien 33 (1999), pp. 49–82: 312 cathedrals, 1,254 monasteries, 129 palaces.

Figure 9. The Utrecht Psalter, probably produced in the Rheims area *c*.850, includes this illustration to Psalms 149 and 150, texts about God's glory and inflicting punishment on nations and kings. Although taking such images as reflecting the artist's world is sometimes problematic, it is possible that, for instance, the seated men talking in the structure towards the top left were drawn with a royal assembly in mind.

pace after 800. One crucial aspect of this process was the stabilisation of the political centre through the establishment of a system of government structured around palaces. Charlemagne's rule became increasingly sedentary from the 790s, coinciding with the Aachen building project, and palaces on a similar scale were built at other sites including Frankfurt, Ingelheim and Nijmegen.[57] These complexes provided forums for regular assemblies of the great and the good. The practical benefits of such a system are illustrated by the Astronomer's description of the young Louis the Pious rotating his court around four winter palaces in Aquitaine in order to spread the burden of provisioning a large and hungry royal entourage.[58] The regularity and predictability of this circular progress, with the venue for the next assembly announced at the end of the previous, was its central virtue: access to the ruler was made possible for all those who mattered, and the king was made available in different parts of his kingdom at different times. The effects of this on the royal itinerary are clear from the full reign of Louis the Pious, whose movements can be studied in some detail. Louis was a relatively static ruler, able to govern without making endless circuits of the empire. This is not to say he was immobile, but his itinerary was contained within relatively tight borders. He never visited Italy and rarely went west of Paris, south of Chalon-sur-Saône, north of Nijmegen or east of Remiremont or Paderborn. His general assemblies (two or three a year in the period 816–28) were almost always held in the three major palace complexes centred on Aachen, the Seine–Oise region (Ver, Quierzy etc.) and the Middle Rhine (Frankfurt, Mainz and Ingelheim).[59] In other words, Louis ruled effectively from the heartlands of the empire, maintaining political influence in more far-flung regions by bringing the nobles in to court and sending his agents out to regulate their behaviour.[60] Another indication of this style of government is the huge number of royal charters surviving from his reign: around 500, compared with only about twenty for

---

[57] R. Samson, 'Carolingian palaces and the poverty of ideology,' in M. Locock (ed.), *Meaningful Architecture: Social Interpretations of Buildings* (Woodbridge, 1994), pp. 99–131; Nelson, 'Aachen as a place of power'; McKitterick, *Charlemagne: The Formation of a European Identity*, pp. 157–70.

[58] Astronomer, *Vita Hludowici imperatoris*, c. 7.

[59] Werner, 'Hludovicus Augustus', p. 8.

[60] On royal and aristocratic landscapes see M. Innes, 'People, places and power in the Carolingian world: a microcosm', in de Jong and Theuws with van Rhijn (eds.), *Topographies of Power*, pp. 397–437. On assemblies see S. Airlie, 'Talking heads: assemblies in early medieval Germany', in P. S. Barnwell and M. Mostert (eds.), *Political Assemblies in the Earlier Middle Ages* (Turnhout, 2003), pp. 29–46.

the last twelve years of Charlemagne's reign.[61] Charters, documents recording grants of land and privileges to churches and loyal followers, are the visible remains of royal patronage, clever deployment of which allowed rulers to intervene directly in distant regional politics and create bonds of mutual obligation between granter and recipient, shoring up aristocratic loyalty. The dramatic increase in the number of these documents hints at both the growing geographical centralisation of Louis's regime and the developing need to replace the diminishing flow of war booty with alternative forms of royal patronage.

These palaces were not simply administrative centres, but served to translate the political capital built up by the successful but ephemeral campaigning of the eighth century into the permanence of stone. The construction of 'public' buildings was an act for which classical and late antique emperors were often praised, and Einhard discusses Aachen, Ingelheim and Nijmegen in this context as indicative of Charlemagne's greatness (see Figures 10a and 10b).[62] The architecture itself also conveyed the prestige of the ruler. The palaces were monumental rather than defensive or strategic, and were usually sited in rural locations not far from major towns (Ingelheim, for instance, was close to Mainz). Their multi-storey frontages rising from the surrounding countryside were intended to inspire awe in those who viewed and visited them, and their complex layouts, with halls, chapels and living quarters linked by walkways surrounding public courtyards and balconies, as at Aachen, provided monumental settings for the pronouncements of the emperor.[63] The paraphernalia of late antique rulership adorned the rooms and open spaces of Aachen: an imperial eagle on the dome of the roof, pillars of rare black stone, and the statue of a mounted ruler believed by contemporaries to be the great sixth-century king Theoderic of the Ostrogoths.[64] An

---

[61] Werner, 'Hludovicus Augustus', pp. 7–8. Unfortunately, Louis is the only Carolingian whose charters are still not available in a modern critical edition.

[62] Einhard, *VK*, c. 17.

[63] T. Zotz, 'Carolingian tradition and Ottonian–Salian innovation: comparative observations on Palatine policy in the empire', in A. Duggan (ed.), *Kings and Kingship in Medieval Europe* (London, 1993), pp. 69–100; U. Lobbedey, 'Carolingian royal palaces: the state of research from an architectural historian's viewpoint', in C. Cubitt (ed.), *Court Culture in the Early Middle Ages* (Turnhout, 2003), pp. 129–54; Samson, 'Carolingian palaces'.

[64] Nelson, 'Aachen as a place of power'; J. Story, *et al.*, 'Charlemagne's black marble: the origins of the epitaph of Pope Hadrian I', *PBSR* 73 (2005), pp. 157–90.

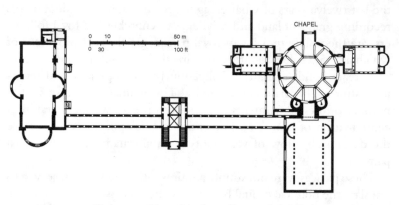

Figure 10a. Plan of Aachen palace and chapel.

Figure 10b. Reconstruction of palace at Ingelheim.

organ received from the Byzantines and an elaborate water-clock from Baghdad represented cutting-edge technology, advertising the regime's modernity and its imperial reach. Game parks and orchards in the grounds were home to exotic peacocks and at least one middle-aged elephant, whose presence was a reminder of Charlemagne's relationship with the Abbasid caliph Harun al-Rashid from whom he had received it.[65] Historians have even detected religiously significant number-symbolism in the dimensions of the chapel, whose octagonal shape also echoed ancient templates in Ravenna.[66] It is debatable whether all this can be read as part of a carefully designed and unified ideological programme encoded into the design of the buildings, or whether it should be seen as a mish-mash of souvenirs and ideas stuffed into sacks as passing Frankish armies looted Ravenna and other Italian cities – but either way, these palaces and their furniture were unmistakable as concrete expressions of Carolingian prestige.[67]

It is important to realise that these buildings were not passive and silent embodiments of imperial status, but were actively used as a way of staging and building up the authority of the ruling dynasty. Ermold the Black provides a famous and detailed description of the paintings on the walls of Ingelheim, which he had visited in the mid-820s. The chapel was lined with images from the Bible, from the Garden of Eden to the Crucifixion, and the hall of the palace was decorated with a picture cycle celebrating the deeds of great kings. Down one side were depicted the exploits of legendary classical kings and Roman emperors, and facing them were the military achievements of the Carolingians: Charles Martel conquering the Frisians, Pippin III bringing law to Aquitaine, and Charlemagne mastering the Saxons.[68] These images of conquest served as the backdrop for magnificent state occasions like the baptism of the Danish king Harald Klak in 826, but also, as Ermold points out, for the more mundane routines of daily government.[69] Regardless of whether

---

[65] Ermold, *In honorem Hludowici imperatoris*, pp. 136–42; Einhard, *VK*, c. 16; Dutton, *Charlemagne's Mustache*, pp. 43–68; McKitterick, *Charlemagne: The Formation of a European Identity*, pp. 279–91.

[66] J. L. Nelson, 'Charlemagne's church at Aachen', *History Today* (Jan. 1998), pp. 62–3.

[67] Samson, 'Carolingian palaces', argues against the ideological coherence of palace architecture. See now M. de Jong, 'Charlemagne's balcony: the solarium in ninth-century narratives', in Davis and McCormick (eds.), *The Long Morning of Medieval Europe*, pp. 277–90.

[68] Ermold, *In honorem Hludowici imperatoris*, pp. 157–65, trans. Godman, *Poetry of the Carolingian Renaissance*, pp. 250–5; and Dutton, *Carolingian Civilization*, pp. 252–4.

[69] Ermold, *In honorem Hludowici imperatoris*, pp. 166–93 on Harald; p. 166 for the reference to governmental business in the hall. Trans. Godman, *Poetry of the*

contemporaries saw in these images the same nuances as do modern historians, the basic message behind pictures of kings smashing their enemies is hard to mistake: at Ingelheim, memories of the dynasty's triumphs and conquests were kept alive and made permanent, given a place at the culmination of sacred and imperial history. In this way they were domesticated and channelled into the service of a new type of governmental regime through being hard-wired into the perceptions and memories of those who participated in it.[70] Narrative sources written in the late eighth and earlier ninth centuries increasingly refer to royal palaces as special places, at times even employing the reverential expression *sacrum palatium* (sacred palace).[71] The spectacular return on the symbolic capital invested in their residences by Charlemagne and Louis is indicated in back-handed fashion by a poem written by the courtier and monk Walahfrid Strabo in 829.[72] Seeking to evoke the political tensions and recriminations of that year (to which we shall come shortly), the poet could do no better than to invert the symbolism of Aachen: the statue of Theoderic became a dark and brooding presence, while the Byzantine organ exuded decadence rather than prestige.[73] By 829, the palace system had become so entrenched in the mentality of the Frankish elite that one could drape a critique of the entire political regime over the architecture and furniture of its flagship buildings.

Carolingian Renaissance, p. 255: 'With these and other deeds that place shines brightly / those who gaze on it take strength from the sight.'

[70] S. Airlie, 'The palace of memory: the Carolingian court as political centre', in S. R. Jones, R. Marks and A. J. Minnis (eds.), *Courts and Regions in Medieval Europe* (York, 2000), pp. 1–20; see also J. L. Nelson, 'The Lord's anointed'.

[71] M. de Jong, '*Sacrum palatium et ecclesia*. L'Autorité religieuse royale sous les carolingiens (790–840)', *Annales HSS* 58 (2003), pp. 1243–69.

[72] M. Herren, 'The *De imagine Tetrici* of Walafrid Strabo: edition and translation', *The Journal of Medieval Latin* 1 (1991), pp. 118–39; M. Herren, 'Walafrid Strabo's *De imagine Tetrici*: an interpretation', in R. North and T. Hofstra (eds.), *Latin Culture and Medieval Germanic Europe* (Groningen, 1992), pp. 25–41.

[73] Cf. Ermold, *In honorem Hludowici imperatoris*, p. 192, which dwells on the organ as a symbol of prestige; and de Jong, *Penitential State*, p. 95 for a different interpretation. Theoderic was an ambiguous figure in the culture of the Frankish court: see F. Thürlemann, 'Die Bedeutung der Aachener Theoderich-Statue für Karl den Großen (801) und bei Walahfried Strabo (829). Materialien zu einer Semiotik visueller Objekte im frühen Mittelalter', *Archiv für Kulturgeschichte* 59 (1977), pp. 24–65; M. Innes, 'Teutons or Trojans? The Carolingians and the Germanic past', in Hen and Innes (eds.), *Uses of the Past*, pp. 227–49.

As they rarely ventured outside the northern heartlands of their empire after 800, Charlemagne and Louis needed reliable agents to carry out their will in the provinces. The archetypal secular officials were counts, whose most important local responsibilities included the enforcement of justice and the gathering of those eligible to serve in the army.[74] There were probably around 400 counties north of the Alps, but since they were not cleanly defined territorial units the power enjoyed by different counts could vary considerably – blocks of several counties were sometimes committed to a single man in strategically important areas, especially on the frontiers.[75] Bishops and abbots, drawn from the same aristocratic families as the counts, were also regarded as royal representatives, appointed by the ruler and expected to cooperate with the count and to contribute contingents to the army (as we saw in Chapter 3, the sense of 'the Church' as something separate from 'the state' is anachronistic before the late eleventh century at the very earliest).[76] Local conditions determined the precise roles of these men: whereas the establishment of a network of counties was used by the Carolingians as a key technique of control in annexed kingdoms like Italy, other regions such as Alsace were ruled more through royal monasteries than secular officials.[77] A kaleidoscopic array of lesser figures also flits across the sources, among their number estate managers, gamekeepers, vice-counts and palace officials.

Overseeing all of these people were agents known as *missi* – literally, 'the sent men'. Before about 800 the term was applied to men sent out from the palace on a variety of *ad hoc* missions, but from the early ninth century the system became increasingly regularised as pairs of *missi* (often a bishop and a count) were despatched to check up on the conduct of affairs in carefully defined territories (*missatica*). A document issued by Louis the Pious in 825 gives a sense of what

---

[74] F. L. Ganshof, *Frankish Institutions under Charlemagne* (Providence, RI, 1968), pp. 26–34; K. F. Werner, 'Missus–marchio–comes: entre l'administration centrale et l'administration locale de l'empire carolingien', in W. Paravicini and K. F. Werner (eds.), *Histoire comparée de l'administration (ive–xviiie siècle)* (Sigmaringen, Munich and Zurich, 1980), pp. 191–239; Innes, *State and Society*, pp. 118–24; M. Innes, 'Charlemagne's government', in Story (ed.), *Charlemagne*, pp. 71–89.

[75] Ganshof, *Frankish Institutions*, p. 28 for the estimate of 400.

[76] De Jong, '*Ecclesia* and the early medieval polity', and Patzold, 'Die Bischöfe im karolingischen Staat'.

[77] Hummer, *Politics and Power*, pp. 56–75.

their duties might include, by telling them to hold meetings with local functionaries (counts, abbots and so on) in the middle of May to find out if they were doing their jobs properly, and, if not, to correct them on royal authority and to settle any cases that had been left unresolved through their negligence.[78] Another document, from 802, charges the *missi* with investigating and rectifying anything that was being done 'against written law' and instructs them to refer difficult cases to the emperor.[79] We should resist the temptation to look at such arrangements simply as an administrative hierarchy governed by formal checks and balances. Almost without exception (except in conquered regions like Italy), counts, bishops and abbots were members of families whose local dominance predated their acquisition of these titles, local bigwigs whose influence was bolstered through their acquisition of official status.[80] The *missi* were no more impartial. Indeed, the areas designated as *missatica* in the 825 document were dioceses, and many of the *missi* appointed were the bishops of those very dioceses. Contemporaries saw no paradox in this – if local officials were to have any clout in the regions where they were assigned influence, they had to have family, friends and contacts in the area already.[81] The ruler could distribute these offices to the people with most integrity and aptitude – the 802 document claims that the *missi* were chosen on the basis of their superior 'good sense and wisdom' – but the range of candidates in a given locality would be severely limited by the need to spread this form of favour around a restricted group of leading families who expected a share in power.

Beyond such general observations, it is actually quite difficult to define how these royal agents were regulated by the ruler and

---

[78] *Capit.* I, no. 151; cf. no. 152.

[79] *Capit.* I, no. 33, c.1, trans. King, *Charlemagne: Translated Sources*, pp. 233–4.

[80] J. Hannig, 'Zentrale Kontrolle und regionale Machtbalance. Beobachtungen zum System der karolingischen Königsboten am Beispiel des Mittelrheingebietes', *Archiv für Kulturgeschichte* 66 (1984), pp. 1–46; J. Hannig, 'Zur Funktion der karolingischen *missi dominici* in Bayern und in den südöstlichen Grenzgebieten', *Zeitschrift der Savigny-Stiftung für Rechtsgeschichte, Germanistische Abteilung* 101 (1984), pp. 256–300. The classic demonstration (originally published in 1965) of the antiquity of prominent Carolingian-era noble families is K. F. Werner, 'Important noble families in the kingdom of Charlemagne', in Reuter (ed.), *The Medieval Nobility*, pp. 137–202, first published in W. Braunfels and P. E. Schramm (eds.), *Karl der Große: Lebenswerk und Nachleben*, 4 vols. (Düsseldorf, 1967).

[81] J. L. Nelson, 'Dispute settlement in Carolingian west Francia', in Davies and Fouracre (eds.), *Settlement of Disputes*, pp. 45–64, at pp. 47–8; Fouracre, *Charles Martel*, pp. 13–15.

how they operated in their regions. Our 825 document on the *missi* is one of few that state explicitly what was expected of local officials – although thousands of sources obliquely testify to a relatively high level of organisation and regulation of early-ninth-century society, contemporaries hardly ever felt the need to write nuts-and-bolts descriptions of how that worked. Historians are now gradually reconstructing the regional impact of Carolingian rule through painstaking analysis of the rich but opaque charter material that survives in quantities from certain monasteries, and we will return to this matter in Chapters 5 and 6.[82] For now, however, we will keep our attention on the political centre and try to catch a flavour, from a fairly large surviving body of legislative material, of how Carolingian government was meant to work. There was no single set of laws for all the peoples of the empire, which was founded on the acknowledgement and even encouragement of ethnic distinctions within its frontiers and not on the ideological imposition of a single uniform identity. Accordingly, the Franks, Bavarians, Saxons, Lombards and other regnal groups had separate and sometimes quite old lawcodes (*leges*) which were systematically revised, and in some cases written down for the first time, during the reign of Charlemagne.[83] These *leges* (which derived from late Roman provincial law rather than – as was once thought – from the norms of pre-migration barbarian society) contained rules to do with social status, landholding, criminality and other areas in which disputes were likely to arise. On the face of it, they appear to provide a framework for the running of local affairs, but matters are made more complicated by the fact that it is very hard to find clear examples of the written texts being cited or applied in practice. In truth, the small worlds of Carolingian Europe were regulated primarily by bodies of custom transmitted orally and refracted through local power relations. While the resulting norms bore similarities to the written provisions of the *leges*, they rarely corresponded exactly and the latter are perhaps best seen not as cast-iron rules but as starting points for negotiation in the process of disputes.[84]

---

[82] Innes, *State and Society*; Brown, *Unjust Seizure*; Hummer, *Politics and Power*; Costambeys, *Power and Patronage*.

[83] McKitterick, *The Carolingians and the Written Word*, pp. 23–75; Wormald, *Making of English Law*, pp. 45–9.

[84] H. Nehlsen, 'Zur Aktualität und Effektivität germanischer Rechtsaufzeichnungen', in P. Classen (ed.), *Recht und Schrift im Mittelalter* (Sigmaringen, 1977), pp. 449–502; A. Rio, 'Freedom and unfreedom in early medieval Francia: the evidence of the legal formularies', *P&P* 193 (2006), pp. 7–40; M. Costambeys,

For governing the empire, on the other hand, the fundamental royal documents were the legislative texts known as capitularies. Capitularies can be defined in the most general terms as texts which recorded the will of the ruler in consultation with his leading men (though rarely as the direct product of an assembly); which were organised into chapters (*capitula*); and which were intended to be disseminated to, and acted upon by, the counts, bishops and *missi*. Their precise character and legal force are, however, debated by historians, with much discussion about whether they gained legal force through being written down as documents or through oral pronouncement by the ruler.[85] Part of the problem arises from the fact that the texts confidently classified as capitularies by nineteenth-century editors are really quite diverse in both form and content. They cover a wide and ambitious range of topics including the regulation of weights and measures, precise stipulations about the form, timing and nature of military service, amendments to the *leges*, and instructions to counts and *missi*. Some had very particular regional audiences, while others served as general statements of intent or exhortation on behalf of a ruler. Ideally, therefore, they should be read as individual texts rather than as a coherent genre about which we can safely generalise. But as long as we bear in mind these caveats, for present purposes we need not worry too much about splitting hairs, particularly because Carolingian writers themselves did not hesitate to generalise about royal legislation. *De ordine palatii* ('On the Governance of the Palace'), written in 882 by Archbishop Hincmar of Rheims but based on an earlier work probably composed during the reign of Charlemagne, and one of the very few Carolingian texts directly concerned with the mechanics of government, contains a detailed description of how reports from the regions were received at court, pondered and processed into capitulary form.[86] Ninth-century commentators

'Disputes and courts in Lombard and Carolingian central Italy', *EME* 15 (2007), pp. 265–89; A. Rio, *Legal Practice and the Written Word in the Early Middle Ages: Frankish Formulae, c.500–1000* (Cambridge, 2009).

[85] For discussion and further references see J. L. Nelson, 'Literacy in Carolingian government', in R. McKitterick (ed.), *The Uses of Literacy in Early Medieval Europe* (Cambridge, 1990), pp. 258–96; C. Pössel, 'Authors and recipients of Carolingian Capitularies, 779–829', in R. Corradini, R. Meens, C. Pössel and P. Shaw (eds.), *Texts and Identities in the Early Middle Ages* (Vienna, 2006), pp. 253–74.

[86] Hincmar, *De ordine palatii*, c. 34. For discussion of the date, see now McKitterick, *Charlemagne: The Formation of a European Identity*, pp. 149–55.

like Hincmar, blissfully unencumbered by the intellectual baggage of nineteenth- and twentieth-century scholarship, betray no angst when talking about the capitularies as a specific genre relating to a particular sphere of royal activity.

After the turn of the ninth century there is a marked increase in the number and quality of these documents, which cannot be put down to mere accident of survival. For the first thirty-two years of his reign Charlemagne is known only to have issued twelve capitularies, while between 800 and 814 there are over fifty. The high rate of output continued well into the reign of Louis the Pious. Although statistical analysis is not really possible owing to the nature and quantity of the evidence, there is a clear trend here which appears to indicate a genuine intensification of Charlemagne's ambitious governmental programme. It has been argued that this gear-change was informed in part by Charles's perception of his imperial status as something which gave him an enhanced responsibility for the religious integrity of his realms, and thus demanded of him a redoubled effort in his programme of *renovatio*.[87] But the more important factor was surely the new peace-time footing of the empire and the need to establish more regularised relations between the political centre and the provinces – to give, in short, the warrior aristocracy something else to do now that regular opportunities to demonstrate their power and social status through offensive warfare had been taken away. Historians have, therefore, understandably approached these documents as integral parts of an effort to construct institutions and procedures, and hence to streamline and unify governmental structures.[88]

The problem is that, as with the *leges*, normative sources tell us much less about what happened than about what was *meant* to happen, and it is frustratingly difficult to prove that the capitularies' prescriptions were actually followed in practice. Despite the survival of many records of formal courtroom proceedings presided over by Carolingian *missi*, counts and bishops, not one of them provides a

---

[87] For example F. L. Ganshof, 'Charlemagne's programme of imperial government', in Ganshof, *Carolingians and the Frankish Monarchy*, pp. 55–85, at p. 70. On *renovatio* see above, Chapter 3.

[88] The archetype of this approach is usually taken to be the work of the great Belgian historian François Louis Ganshof (1895–1980), whose essays are translated and collected in *The Carolingians and the Frankish Monarchy* and *Frankish Institutions under Charlemagne*. McKitterick, *Charlemagne: The Formation of a European Identity*, pp. 228–63 offers a new interpretation.

concrete example of a capitulary being consulted or cited. Moreover, their status as an official record of governmental decision-making is open to question. Capitularies were often copied into manuscripts alongside works from disparate genres including history and theology, which suggests that they were not always seen as having practical legal uses. Despite occasional references to a palace archive, there is little evidence for the existence of an authoritative central storehouse of governmental documents: when Abbot Ansegisus of St Wandrille made a collection of capitularies in 827 that was subsequently taken up as a standard reference work, he misattributed several texts and was apparently unable to find many others that are known today.[89] Arguments have therefore been made that the capitularies were actually more ideological than practical, issued principally to conform with the long European tradition that saw law-giving in writing as a characteristically royal or imperial act.[90] All this leaves us with a spectrum of possibilities for understanding the contemporary function of capitularies: as evidence primarily for the Carolingians' ideological preoccupations; as a source for their ambitions and aspirations, but not necessarily their effectiveness; or, most optimistically, as practical governmental tools used in their duties by agents of the king.

We can attempt to weigh up these possibilities by looking at a single example. The so-called 'Programmatic Capitulary' (the title is modern), promulgated by Charlemagne along with a range of other legal codifications upon his return to Aachen from Italy in 802, is one of the most lavish pieces of Carolingian legislation.[91] Its forty articles cover a very wide range of subjects. After an opening statement about the supremacy of justice and the necessity that it be maintained through respect for written law and the correct behaviour of the *missi*, the text dwells for eight chapters on the nature and implications of the loyalty oath that everyone over the age of twelve was required

---

[89] G. Schmitz, 'The capitulary legislation of Louis the Pious', in Godman and Collins (eds.), *Charlemagne's Heir*, pp. 425–36; S. Airlie, '"For it is written in the law": Ansegis and the writing of Carolingian royal authority', in S. Baxter, *et al.* (eds.), *Early Medieval Studies in Memory of Patrick Wormald* (Aldershot, 2009), pp. 219–36.

[90] P. Wormald, '*Lex scripta* and *verbum regis*: legislation and Germanic kingship from Euric to Cnut', in P. H. Sawyer and I. N. Wood (eds.), *Early Medieval Kingship* (Leeds, 1977), pp. 105–38, at pp. 107–10.

[91] Text: *Capitulare missorum generale*, *Capit.* I, no. 33, trans. King, *Charlemagne: Translated Sources*, pp. 233–42. Context: Einhard, *VK*, c. 29; *AL*, *s.a.* 802. Commentary: Ganshof, 'Charlemagne's programme'.

to swear to the emperor, and then spells out the qualities demanded of different sections of society – the purity of monks, the probity of clerics and the justice of counts. The *missi* were to be given assistance and not hindered, the exemptions of the poor were to be respected, and the crimes of incest and homicide were condemned. This text encapsulates some of the genre's apparent paradoxes. Although it was seemingly intended as something like a definitive statement of the Carolingian agenda, very little of its content corresponds with what modern observers might expect of governmental legislation, and what there is of that (declarations about criminality, for example) comes towards the end. Hardly any of it is specifically interested in procedural matters and how exactly things should be done. The key sanction was the oath, and personal fidelity was seen as the social glue that would hold the empire together. The universal oath to the ruler had been introduced in something like this form in 789 (as we saw at the end of Chapter 2), but the 802 document expanded it by specifying that it implied acceptance of various obligations beyond remaining faithful, including service in the army, acting honestly in court and respecting the emperor's property. Even passive failure to act against threats to the emperor's interests became an act of treason. This oath, taken solemnly and publicly on holy relics, underwrote a hierarchy in which people had to promise to do more or less whatever they were told.[92] Yet despite the all-encompassing nature of these obligations, the emperor's claims to authority were expressed in quite abstract and rhetorical terms. Instead of the contract jargon familiar from modern managerial government, or indeed from old-fashioned concepts of 'feudal' oaths, Charlemagne's demands are couched in the language of moral exhortation. The moral tone in which obligations and sanctions were set out pervades the text and explains how a document that begins with a statement about the significance of written law ends with an instruction to the *missi* to check up on the behaviour of other royal officials, 'and above all how each is striving to keep himself in God's holy service'.

It is not hard to see how a text like this might contribute to a view of capitularies as impractical. The rather generalising moral tone might suggest a ruler who had only a slender grasp on the way his representatives actually ruled their localities, and a governmental

---

[92] Becher, *Eid und Herrschaft*, esp. pp. 211–12; Innes, 'Charlemagne's government', pp. 80–2.

mentality obsessed with theological posturing and grand statements of majesty. Certainly, the emphasis on moral probity fits with Carolingian understandings of the ruler's role in the 'correction' of his people: to rule (*regere*) was to correct (*corrigere*).[93] This is why criticisms of royal government in the ninth century lingered less on accusations of inefficiency or mismanagement than on kings' failure to ensure political stability by maintaining the moral integrity of their households and agents.[94] We might well be tempted to interpret this attitude as primarily ideological, telling us a lot about how the ruler and his advisers understood their mission but having little to do with the nuts-and-bolts running of affairs in the empire.

On the other hand, it is also possible to interpret such documents as practical governmental instruments. Although the 'Programmatic Capitulary' itself was preserved in only one manuscript, it has been seen as a kind of statement of intent, meant to instruct those charged with ruling the Italian kingdom under Charlemagne's son Pippin.[95] Other capitularies are known to have been disseminated more widely and although (as noted earlier) their impact on legal proceedings cannot be observed directly, their provisions very occasionally left traces elsewhere. The 802 oath, for example, appears not just in capitularies like the one we have been examining, but quickly turned up in documents written in places as distant as Freising in Bavaria.[96] There was certainly a presumption that capitularies were to be used somehow: the texts cross-reference each other, counts were instructed to keep copies against which their actions could be judged, and kings threatened penalties against royal agents who ignored their 'letters'.[97] Surviving manuscripts containing collections of capitularies suggest that some royal agents obeyed these injunctions by keeping reference books of the king's commands.[98] A legal compendium owned

---

[93] See above, Chapter 3.

[94] For example, Paschasius Radbertus, *Epitaphium Arsenii* (hereafter *Life of Wala*), ed. E. Dümmler, *Abhandlungen der kaiserlichen Akademie der Wissenschaften zu Berlin, phil.-hist. Klasse* (1900), trans. A. Cabaniss, *Charlemagne's Cousins. Contemporary Lives of Adalard and Wala* (New York, 1967), bk. II, c. 2.

[95] McKitterick, *Charlemagne: The Formation of a European Identity*, pp. 261–2.

[96] T. Bitterauf (ed.), *Die Traditionen des Hochstifts Freising* I (Munich, 1905), no. 186. For context see now W. Brown, 'The idea of empire in Carolingian Bavaria', in Weiler and MacLean (eds.), *Representations of Power*, pp. 37–55.

[97] *Capit.* I, no. 85, c. 7; no. 139, c. 16.

[98] R. McKitterick, 'Zur Herstellung von Kapitularien: Die Arbeit des Leges-Skriptoriums', *Mitteilungen des Instituts für Österreichische Geschichtsforschung* 101

by *marchio* (margrave) Eberhard of Friuli, one of the era's greatest magnates, shows signs of having been updated and therefore, presumably, used.[99] It may have been with this kind of collection in mind that an exasperated Charlemagne, confronted with a list of detailed questions from a count, snapped back impatiently that he should already know the answers, referring him not just to his capitularies but also to Frankish (Salic) law and to instructions received in person.[100] The existence of letters like this one, combined with the rarity of evidence for the capitularies' direct use, might lead us to the conclusion that capitularies were intended to be followed and that they were widely distributed, but that much to the court's chagrin they were rarely consulted and their injunctions hardly ever acted upon.

The evidence does not, then, tell a single story. One way out is simply to make a choice between the two main interpretations outlined so far, and decide either that these texts were ideological statements of authority or that they were intended to make specific demands on royal agents but that they were often ineffective. However, we can also ask whether these views can be reconciled. A more subtle and comprehensive interpretation is possible if we take seriously the exhortatory rhetoric of the capitularies and think about how it might have served to shape the identities and actions of those for whom it was intended – the king's agents. Despite the scolding administered by the emperor to the hapless character mentioned at the end of the last paragraph, we should not regard his apparent lack of knowledge as the only significant aspect of the exchange. The fact that counts like him made enquiries to the court at all is also interesting, and suggests that some kind of two-way dialogue existed between the ruler and his representatives. The capitularies can be seen as a fragmentary remnant of this dialogue, engagement in which bolstered the local authority of counts and *missi* by legitimising their claims to act on the ruler's behalf.

If the texts did not always furnish counts and *missi* with precise procedural instructions, that is probably because they were already

---

(1993), pp. 3–16; Wormald, *Making of English Law*, pp. 53–70; McKitterick, *Charlemagne: The Formation of a European Identity*, pp. 263–6.

[99] P. Kershaw, 'Eberhard of Friuli, a Carolingian Lay Intellectual', in Wormald and Nelson (eds.), *Lay Intellectuals*, pp. 77–105 at pp. 85–6.

[100] *Capit.* I, no. 58, cc. 2, 4, 6, trans. King, *Charlemagne: Translated Sources*, pp. 267–8.

expected to know how to administer justice according to local laws and customs. Moral exhortation was not some kind of conceit concocted to cover up an embarrassing lack of power – this rhetoric was itself the language of politics, referring to codes of behaviour that royal agents implicitly understood and were repeatedly reminded of. Capitularies and narrative sources alike are full of the language of 'admonition': Charlemagne's great capitulary, the *Admonitio generalis*, issued in 789 but distributed widely thereafter, refers to the ruler's role as 'visitation, correction and admonition'.[101] This view of government was inspired by the Bible, but these codes also pervaded the vocabulary of contemporary office-holding. The responsibilities of counts and other office-holders were generically referred to as *honores* ('honours') or, from the 780s onwards, *ministeria* ('ministries').[102] These terms betray the notions of honour and responsibility that coloured contemporary perception of these roles – to be removed from office was not simply to lose one's job but to be literally 'dishonoured'.[103] Such ideas were not, obviously, new, but were insisted upon by the Carolingians with increasing coherence and intensity. By the reign of Louis the Pious at the latest these concepts had been internalised by men like Orendil, a count in Bavaria who described his own position in terms of *ministerium*.[104] The capitularies' vocabulary of honour, justice and moral probity helped to mould the identities of counts like Orendil – to influence the way they saw themselves. They created parameters for such men's activities, defined by the court but acted upon locally, and reinforced regularly by attendance at palace assemblies and interaction with the *missi*.

To evaluate the efficiency of Frankish government by combing the capitularies for evidence of a self-standing institutional structure, and to measure their effectiveness by enumerating hard examples of their practical use, is therefore an enterprise that rests on potentially

---

[101] De Jong, *Penitential State*, pp. 112–47, esp. pp. 131–5.

[102] T. Zotz, 'In Amt und Würden. Zur Eigenart "offizieller" Positionen im früheren Mittelalter', *Tel Aviver Jahrbuch für deutsche Geschichte* 22 (1993), pp. 1–23. On *honores* see also below, Chapter 6, pp. 313–20.

[103] Jonas of Orléans, *De institutione regia*, ed. J. Reviron, *Les Idées politico-religieuses d'un évêque du IXe siècle: Jonas d'Orléans et son* De institutione regia (Paris, 1930), pp. 119–94, Admonitio line 156 and c. 9.

[104] Bitterauf (ed.), *Traditionen*, no. 313; Zotz, 'In Amt und Würden', pp. 12–13. On Orendil see also below, Chapter 6, pp. 314–15.

anachronistic questions.[105] Although they could be very precise in their stipulations, in general they were not definitive lists of rules and regulations so much as guides to how royal agents should behave and conceive of their actions. Men like Eberhard of Friuli and Orendil were powerful not because they held positions delegated by kings, but because of the lands and regional influence held by their families – they and their ilk had to be convinced to see themselves primarily as royal subordinates. The capitularies offer us glimpses of this process of persuasion, and represent one of the means by which it was furthered. They reveal not a pre-existing political hierarchy, but a constant effort on the part of the Carolingians to create one.

This is why the capitularies rarely had much to say on procedure but were obsessed with structure and establishing chains of command.[106] Repeated injunctions to counts and *missi* to refuse bribes, to hold courts in appropriate settings and not in their vassals' houses, and to refrain from cutting short judicial hearings to go hunting, are back-handed evidence not for corruption but for the Carolingians' drive to persuade their aristocratic followers to consider themselves royal agents and to follow certain codes of behaviour when they were on the king's business.[107] The urgency of these attempts to mark off boundaries between its agents' public functions and their membership of local aristocratic culture shows that Carolingian government was not something that existed external to society, but was rather deeply enmeshed in pre-existing social structures. In the previous generation, these sorts of men would have participated in the political system by bringing their armed followers and dependants to the annual assembly and riding with the king on campaign. In the new post-expansion world the court's need to stabilise and routinise their power into predictable roles became increasingly pressing. This was not just, or even mainly, about satisfying an urge to create administrative efficiency – it was about giving these powerful men a stake in the polity from which they could profit without having to reach for their swords.

---

[105] For historiographical discussion of these issues see Innes, *State and Society*, pp. 1–12.
[106] E.g. *Capit.* I, no. 150, c. 8.
[107] E.g. *Capit.* I, no. 20, c. 1; no. 139, c. 13; no. 189; see also Theodulf of Orléans's characterisation of Carolingian judges: *Carmina* 28, ed. E. Dümmler, *MGH Poet.* I (Hanover, 1881), pp. 493–517; and the selection trans. Godman, *Poetry of the Carolingian Renaissance*, pp. 162–6.

None of this should be taken to mean that counts became more just in practice. Far from it – by bolstering the authority of local aristocrats this ideology probably increased rather than diminished the oppressiveness of village and county society.[108] Not everyone was equal before the law. The Carolingians vigorously legislated against the formation of horizontal social bonds (branding them as *coniurationes* – conspiracies) and insisted on the primacy of vertical bonds of obligation based on sworn fidelity and lordship.[109] While 'men of good family who act[ed] wickedly or unjustly' were to receive the benefits of due process through being tried before the king and could expect a firm request to mend their ways, lesser men were told to put up with anything their lord decided they deserved short of attempted murder, rape, or land-theft – a resounding endorsement of the brutal structures of lordship.[110] The official rhetoric of justice, wisdom and correction cannot hide the fact that *missi* must often have acted less like chairs of public enquiries than as the ruler's strong-men, and that adjudication and investigation could easily be euphemisms for intimidating and loading local meetings – such was the case in 781 when Charlemagne's *missi* orchestrated a judgement which removed some strategic land in Thuringia from a local aristocrat and placed it instead in the hands of a trusted royal agent, the abbot of Fulda.[111] But we do not have to approve of strong kingship to recognise it. All this helped to strengthen the idea that authority descended from the king. Occasionally, as in the surviving letters written by Bishop Frothar of Toul (*c*.813–47), we have a source that lets us glimpse the king's servants responding to specific orders (for example Frothar organised a cull of wolves in his diocese), and therefore acting directly as the ruler's instruments.[112] The dispossessed elements of the Thuringian aristocracy may not have enjoyed their experience of Carolingian

---

[108] P. Fouracre, 'Carolingian justice: the rhetoric of improvement and contexts of abuse', *Settimane di Studio del Centro italiano di studi sull'alto medioevo* 42 (Spoleto, 1995), pp. 771–803.

[109] E.g. *Capit.* I, no. 19, c. 31; no. 20, cc. 14, 16; no. 44, c. 10. O. G. Oexle, '*Coniuratio* und Gilde im frühen Mittelalter', in B. Schwineköper (ed.), *Gilden und Zünfte: kaufmännische und gewerbliche Genossenschaften im frühen und hohen Mittelalter* (Sigmaringen, 1985), pp. 151–213; McKitterick, *Perceptions of the Past*, Chapter 3.

[110] *Capit.* I, no. 77, cc. 12, 16, trans. King, *Charlemagne: Translated Sources*, p. 245.

[111] Nelson, *Opposition to Charlemagne*, pp. 18–19.

[112] Frothar of Toul, *Letters*, ed. K. Hampe, *MGH Ep.* v (*Epp. Karolini aevi* III) (Berlin, 1899), pp. 275–98; French trans. M. Parisse and J. Barbier, *La Correspondance d'un*

rule any more than did the wolves of Toul, but such glimpses at least prove that the moral language of office did map onto relationships of hierarchy, accountability and obligation that actually made things happen.

All these tendencies represented an intensification rather than a complete transformation of politics. All the post-Roman kingdoms including those of the Merovingians and Lombards inherited a language of office-holding that helped shape the way they were governed, and the Merovingians also commanded counts and issued documents resembling capitularies. The distinctiveness of Carolingian government in the earlier ninth century was less of kind than of degree, thrown into sharp focus by contrast with the preceding phase of military expansion. This intensification could not have been achieved simply by top-down *Diktat*. As we have seen, the evidence suggests that local elites embraced it, sometimes enthusiastically. By accepting a redefinition of their status in terms of delegated office, they bought into a political system that not only opened up to them the prospect of access to the ruler and promotion to a wider imperial stage, but also helped to legitimise and reinforce their existing influence. This calculation of advantage explains why we sometimes see counts actively soliciting royal interference in their affairs: aristocrats wanted strong kings.[113] By the 820s, an ethos of service can be discerned as part of the identity of the more prominent nobles who served as Carolingian *missi*. Through meeting at court and being despatched on missions in royal service, men from divergent family and geographical origins got to know each other, formed common memories of important events, and developed a sense of themselves as a group distinguished in part by their participation in royal government.[114] This oligarchic understanding of government means that we cannot reduce our view of the effectiveness of the king's power to his ability to convince each of his agents to do what they were told. The capitularies' repetitive insistence on particular patterns of 'public' activity for counts and *missi* helped create a system that was more than the sum of a vast number of individual personal

---

évêque carolingien: Frothaire de Toul (ca. 813–847). Avec les lettres de Theuthilde, abbesse de Remiremont (Paris, 1998). Airlie, 'The aristocracy in the service of the state', pp. 107–8.

[113] Innes, 'Charlemagne's government', p. 79.

[114] Airlie, 'The aristocracy in the service of the state', esp. pp. 100–9.

relationships. The establishment of ideas in the minds of counts like Orendil (and, indeed, their ecclesiastical counterparts) about the correct ways to exercise office was central to the project of creating social roles patterned on repetitive and predictable behaviours: the state was the aggregate of these roles and mentalities.[115]

The elusiveness of the sources and the obvious differentness of Carolingian government when set against modern expectations do not, then, mean that it was inefficient or that the rulers lacked power. In the few places where its operation can be discerned in any kind of detail, Carolingian government looks surprisingly effective and intrusive. The ability of the Frankish state to sustain itself by taxing its subjects had dwindled by the seventh century at the latest, but the Carolingians were nevertheless very successful at gathering revenues, influencing the circulation of currency, raising armies and standardising aspects of religious and judicial culture.[116] Close study of monastic charters has revealed the extent to which the emperor's *missi* succeeded in establishing Frankish understandings of property rights in areas like Alsace and Bavaria, in the process transforming previously dominant local norms and instigating political and social change.[117] The evidence also suggests that the court had a pragmatic governmental mentality, implicit in its obsession with lists. Although only a few survive (of, for example, military obligations owed by monasteries and of people who had sworn the oath of fidelity before an Italian *missus*) that is perhaps because such practical texts had little long-term value and were less likely than capitularies to be preserved.[118] We should probably place in the same category the deceptively small number of documents that contain attempts to micro-manage specific situations.[119] Royal authority was a powerful

---

[115] Pohl, 'Staat und Herrschaft', p. 35. On episcopal office as *ministerium* see S. Patzold, 'Redéfinir l'office épiscopal: les évêques francs face à la crise des années 820/30', in F. Bougard, L. Feller and R. Le Jan (eds.), *Les Élites au haut Moyen Âge. Crises et renouvellements* (Turnhout, 2006), pp. 337–59.

[116] On the significance of the shift from tax to land see Wickham, *Framing the Early Middle Ages*. On coinage see Coupland, 'Charlemagne's coinage'.

[117] Innes, *State and Society*, pp. 193–5; Brown, *Unjust Seizure*, pp. 73–123; Hummer, *Politics and Power*, pp. 76–129.

[118] *Capit.* I, nos. 171, 181. No. 80 demands lists of fiscal estates and benefice holders, among other things. For discussion of one such list see J. L. Nelson, 'Charlemagne and empire', in Davis and McCormick (eds.), *The Long Morning of Medieval Europe*, pp. 223–34.

[119] *Capit.* I, nos. 152, 155.

enough agency to send high aristocrats to offices in all corners of the empire, sometimes within the course of a single career. Charlemagne's cousin Wala, for example, started out as a count in Francia, but by the time he died in 836 he had also served as abbot of the important monastery of Corbie and done two stints in Italy as guardian and adviser to Louis the Pious's son Lothar.[120] His brother Adalard, also abbot of Corbie, covered a similarly impressive amount of territory in royal service: from acting as close adviser to Charlemagne in Aachen, he went on to serve as regent in Italy after the death of the emperor's son Pippin in 810, and performed various functions at assemblies in Francia after that.[121] As members of the royal family these two men are unusually well documented, but the trajectory of their careers in royal service was not atypical of the very highest stratum of the aristocracy.

Early medieval government was not like Roman, later medieval or modern government, but it existed and it worked. Its effectiveness depended as much on underlying social structures as on formal institutions: even by the end of our period the idea of a clear distinction between the public and private identities of the king's agents was far from being cut and dried. Nevertheless, contemporaries implicitly understood royal government as an entity in itself. While not using terms that can be easily translated as 'state', and hardly ever devoting direct attention to its operations, they still thought of the political order as a coherent whole, and they had a vocabulary for discussing it in the abstract.[122] The renewal of the state across the generations depended on the continuity of the aristocratic families and elite culture with which it was bound up – these underlying social structures changed too slowly to be fundamentally affected by the frailty and even death of any individual king, however great. Charlemagne complained in a capitulary of 811 that he had heard about

---

[120] P. Depreux, *Prosopographie de l'entourage de Louis le Pieux (781–840)* (Sigmaringen, 1997), pp. 390–3.

[121] B. Kasten, *Adalhard von Corbie: die Biographie eines karolingischen Politikers und Klostervorstehers* (Düsseldorf, 1986); Depreux, *Prosopographie*, pp. 76–9.

[122] H.-W. Goetz, 'Regnum: zum politischen Denken der Karolingerzeit', *Zeitschrift der Savigny-Stiftung für Rechtsgeschichte, Germanistische Abteilung* 104 (1987), pp. 110–89; de Jong, '*Ecclesia* and the early medieval polity'; Airlie, 'The aristocracy in the service of the state', pp. 97–100; Wormald, 'Pre-modern "state" and "nation": definite or indefinite?'. For the view that such a vocabulary was lacking, see J. Fried, 'Der karolingische Herrschaftsverband im 9. Jahrhundert zwischen "Kirche" und "Königshaus"', *HZ* 235 (1982), pp. 1–43.

too many people misbehaving in the counties, being disobedient to their counts, and 'having more frequent recourse to the *missi* than was previously the case'.[123] This has been used as prime evidence for corruption, decay and decline at the end of the old emperor's reign. Surely, though, what it actually reveals is the canny manoeuvring of people who had become familiar enough with the hierarchy and functions of royal officials to play the system – and that, therefore, there was some sort of system in place for them to play.

DYNASTIC POLITICS, C. 806–827

The establishment of these governmental routines and structures meant that the political system was not exclusively dependent on the will or personal qualities of any given ruler. The king had a unique role, but no individual king was indispensable. Not even Charlemagne was immune from the plottings of the discontented, as in 792 when his eldest son Pippin ('the Hunchback') felt himself being marginalised and attracted enough support to unsettle the king seriously. Afterwards Charles rewarded those who had *not* rebelled and had it put about that Pippin was illegitimate and physically imperfect (both questionable claims) in an attempt to 'un-person' him – these measures show how vulnerable Charlemagne had been made to feel.[124] To stop such situations before they arose, early medieval rulers had to manage their families: when disgruntled aristocrats joined forces with a king-worthy member of the royal family, as they had in 792, the possibility of usurpation became real and the stability of the whole realm could start to unravel.[125] Kings' sons were conditioned to expect not only a share in the succession but also a role in the government of the kingdom while their fathers still lived. Because they tried to exclude all but their legitimate sons from these arrangements, the Carolingians were even more interventionist and aggressive than the Merovingians (whose dynastic definitions were more flexible) in their efforts to prune the family tree.[126] As their

---

[123] *Capit.* I, no. 73, c. 9, trans. King, *Charlemagne: Translated Sources*, p. 265.

[124] *AL*, s.a. 793. See above, Chapter 2, pp. 78–9.

[125] Airlie, 'Charlemagne and the aristocracy'.

[126] On the general issues see Kasten, *Königssöhne und Königsherrschaft*; S. Kaschke, *Die karolingischen Reichsteilungen bis 831. Herrschaftspraxis und Normvorstellungen in zeitgenössischer Sicht* (Hamburg, 2006). On the Merovingian family see I. Wood, 'Deconstructing the Merovingian family', in R. Corradini, M. Diesenberger

stakes in the empire were defined and negotiated, the complex dance of competing interests engaged in by kings with their sons, nephews and cousins became the engine driving political events in the early decades of the ninth century.

Charlemagne was a serial monogamist and a prolific parent: his five wives and many concubines bore him around twelve children in total. After the death of his last wife Liutgard in 800 he made a conscious decision not to remarry. With Pippin safely confined to a monastery, the emperor was left with three legitimate sons, all with his third wife Hildegard. Charlemagne seems to have begun thinking seriously about the succession at the latest during his trip to Rome in 800, when he had his eldest son, also Charles, crowned and perhaps anointed as king.[127] Since the others, Louis and (another) Pippin, had been granted this status already in 781, this meant all three of his sons were now kings, and in 806 the emperor set out a division and succession plan to regulate relations between them. Charles the Younger was to receive Francia proper (the land between the Seine and Meuse) as well as various outlying lands in Bavaria, Burgundy, Thuringia, Frisia and Neustria; Pippin was to get Italy, Alemannia and Chur-Rhaetia (the latter covering roughly the east-ernmost part of modern Switzerland); and for Louis the Pious were earmarked Aquitaine, the Auvergne and other areas in the southwest. The project was about the present as much as the future (it confirmed the two younger sons in possession of some territories that they had in truth controlled for some time), and claimed to place all three heirs on an equal footing. To this end it set out a long series of safeguards to ensure they continued to cooperate, including provisions for what should happen to their kingdoms and children when one of them died, and rules for dealings between uncles and nephews.[128] However, Charles the Younger's share was marginally superior to those of

---

and H. Reimitz (eds.), *The Construction of Communities in the Early Middle Ages* (Leiden and Boston, 2003), pp. 149–71.

[127] *LP* II, pp. 7–8, trans. Davis, *Lives of the Eighth-Century Popes*, pp. 187–8; Alcuin, *Ep.* 217. For the proposition that an earlier succession plan was conceived in the early 780s see W. Goffart, 'Paul the Deacon's *Gesta episcoporum Mettensium* and the early design for Charlemagne's succession', *Traditio* 42 (1986), pp. 53–87; and the critique by Nelson, 'Charlemagne the man'. See also P. Classen, 'Karl der Große und die Thronfolge im Frankenreich', in *Festschrift für Hermann Heimpel* (Göttingen, 1972), III, pp. 109–34.

[128] *Divisio regnorum.*

his brothers, containing as it did the Frankish heartlands which were traditionally divided between the ruler's sons. It is quite possible that this inequality of prestige, if not of formal authority, would have led to serious tensions upon Charlemagne's death had he not been pre-deceased by Pippin of Italy in 810 and Charles the Younger in 811. The loss of his children 'deeply disturbed' the emperor, as one might well imagine, but it made things look politically straightforward for the youngest and only remaining legitimate son, Louis the Pious.[129] On 11 September 813, Charlemagne called a general assembly at Aachen and 'established Louis as the co-ruler of the entire kingdom and the heir to the imperial title'.[130]

The *Royal Frankish Annals* and Einhard's *Life of Charlemagne*, both most likely written up some time after the fact, suggest that upon Charlemagne's death in January 814 Louis's succession pro-ceeded straightforwardly 'with the full consent and support of all the Franks'.[131] As with the coronation of 800, however, things may not have been as simple as these authors chose to remember. The historian Nithard, who was Charlemagne's grandson and presum-ably drew on personal memories, refers darkly to 'those [at Aachen] whose loyalty seemed doubtful'.[132] Even the annals note that the new ruler (who was some distance away) took thirty days to arrive at the palace, long enough for any doubts about the prospect of Louis's rule to harden into discussions about the alternatives. If we bear in mind that Louis was in many ways an outsider at Aachen, the suggestion of opposition is not so surprising. Almost all of his thirty-six years had been spent in Aquitaine and on campaign on the Spanish March, far from the main centres of Frankish power. In contrast, Charles the Younger seems to have been groomed for rule in the Frankish heartlands: although he was given the title of king much later than his brothers, he was given responsibilities that kept him close to his father at the political centre.[133] While Louis was occasionally summoned to his father's court, Charlemagne is said to have snubbed his son when requested to make a return trip to Aquitaine, perhaps hinting at a frosty edge to their relationship.[134] After Charles the Younger's death

---

[129] Einhard, *VK*, c. 19.   [130] Einhard, *VK*, c. 30; *ARF*, s.a. 813.

[131] *ARF*, s.a. 814.

[132] Nithard, *Historiarum Libri IV*, ed. P. Lauer, *Histoire des fils de Louis le Pieux* (Paris, 1926), I.2.

[133] M. Innes, 'Charlemagne's will: piety, politics and the imperial succession', *EHR* 112 (1997), pp. 833–55, at pp. 841–5; Nelson, 'Pater optimus?'.

[134] Astronomer, *Vita Hludowici imperatoris*, c. 12.

the really influential people at Aachen were in fact the women of the dynasty: Charlemagne's daughters, for whom the emperor reportedly had such fondness that he refused to let them marry or even leave his side, and other female members of court.[135] It may well have been his daughters who made the decision to bury Charlemagne at Aachen on the same day as his death, thus over-riding the emperor's own earlier plans to be interred at St Denis next to Pippin III and other great Frankish kings of past ages. By making an instant pitch to be seen as the custodians of the dead ruler's last wishes they asserted their control of the palace during the transitional period and staked a claim to have a say in his succession.[136]

Could Charlemagne's daughters have orchestrated an attempt to have someone other than Louis take the throne in January 814? There were certainly other candidates close at hand. Wala, Charlemagne's cousin, was 'greatly feared' at Aachen in this period according to the Astronomer, his tongue loosened by Louis's own death: 'it was thought that he might plot something sinister against the new emperor'.[137] Wala's sisters had been close to Charlemagne, and his position was therefore strong – he was listed first among the secular magnates in the emperor's will.[138] Pippin of Italy's son Bernard was another contender: his sisters had also been living in Aachen since their father's death in 810, and a list of names entered in the confraternity book of the monastery of St Gallen c.812 shows that Bernard had extensive networks of kin and contacts north of the Alps as well as south, and particularly in Alemannia.[139] Little wonder

---

[135] Einhard, *VK*, c. 19; J. L. Nelson, 'Women at the court of Charlemagne: a case of Monstrous Regiment?', in J. C. Parsons (ed.), *Medieval Queenship* (New York, 1993), pp. 43–61, repr. in Nelson, *Frankish World*, pp. 223–42; J. L. Nelson, 'La Cour impériale de Charlemagne', in R. Le Jan (ed.), *La Royauté et les élites*, pp.177–91; repr. in Nelson, *Rulers and Ruling Families*.

[136] Nelson, 'Carolingian royal funerals', pp. 145–53.

[137] Astronomer, *Vita Hludowici imperatoris*, c. 21, trans. A. Cabaniss, *Son of Charlemagne: A Contemporary Life of Louis the Pious* (Syracuse, NY, 1961), p. 54. On Wala see L. Weinrich, *Wala. Graf, Mönch und Rebell. Die Biographie eines Karolingers* (Lübeck, 1963); H. Mayr-Harting, 'Two abbots in politics: Wala of Corbie and Bernard of Clairvaux', *TRHS* 5th series 40 (1990), pp. 217–37; Depreux, *Prosopographie*, pp. 390–3.

[138] Paschasius Radbertus, *Vita Sancti Adalhardi*, ed. Dom J. Mabillon, PL cxx, 1507–1556c, c. 33; Einhard, *VK*, c. 33; J. L. Nelson, 'Gendering courts in the early medieval west', in L. Brubaker and J. M. H. Smith (eds.), *Gender in the Early Medieval World. East and West, 300–900* (Cambridge, 2004), pp. 185–97, at p. 191.

[139] J. Fried, 'Elite und Ideologie, oder die Nachfolgeordnung Karls des Großen vom Jahre 813', in Le Jan (ed.), *La Royauté et les élites*, pp. 71–109, at pp. 90–5.

that pro-Louis authors went out of their way to minimise Bernard's claim by insinuating that he was illegitimate (when in fact he may have inherited Carolingian blood, legitimately, from both parents); and that he had been made king of Italy in 813 only as a kind of subordinate to Louis (when in fact he had been an independent king since 812, before Louis was designated emperor – a decision which, according to the *Annals of Lobbes*, had been approved by both Louis and Charles the Younger).[140] The multiplicity of serious candidates and the potential for conflict between them may have been what lay behind the appeals for peace and unity in the face of an anticipated but unspecified threat to the stability of the realm that featured in a major series of Church councils held under imperial patronage in 813.[141] These exhortations uncover Charlemagne's own concerns about the fragility of the political situation, which were disguised by subsequent authors anxious to minimise the memory of opposition to the new regime. Potential crisis was an ever-present consideration in early medieval dynastic politics, even in the reign of a powerful ruler like Charlemagne, and successful rulership was about managing and containing it. In this context the manipulation of historical memory was one way that sympathisers like Einhard sought to erase political tension in the present.

As we saw at the beginning of this chapter, Louis the Pious has traditionally been seen as the archetype of an unsuccessful king, the antithesis of his war-like and powerful father. Historians often portray him as unsmiling, puritanical and dominated by his episcopal advisers, in stark contrast to the all-action war-leader Charlemagne. There is good reason, however, to cast serious doubt on the validity of this polarised comparison between Louis and his father. Louis's public political piety was not unusual, and only came to be seen as a mark of weakness when placed in the value systems of eighteenth- and nineteenth-century historians (the nickname which eventually stuck was only one of a number of imperial virtues applied to him by contemporaries).[142] When we read between the lines, we see fundamental continuities between Charlemagne's and Louis's practice of rulership. Charlemagne was just as ardent a reformer of religious practice and social morality as his son, and pursued these ends with

---

[140] P. Depreux, 'Das Königtum Bernhards von Italien und sein Verhältnis zum Kaisertum', *QFIAB* 72 (1992), pp. 1–25; Fried, 'Elite und Ideologie', p. 84.
[141] *Conc.* II, nos. 34–8; Fried, 'Elite und Ideologie', pp. 71–5.
[142] Schieffer, 'Ludwig "der Fromme"'.

palpable urgency and energy: 'are we really Christians?' he anxiously pondered in one of his later capitularies which ordered a seminar on a Biblical text that he believed would reveal some eternal verities about how to govern.[143] By the same token, Louis was just as much a traditional Frankish ruler as was his father: both his biographers stress his love of hunting, an archetypally masculine elite activity. Louis's imperial postures as expressed in iconography and texts looked to the same sorts of political models as had his father's: not only Biblical rulers like David and Solomon, but also Frankish kings like Clovis and Roman emperors such as Constantine and Theodosius (see Figure 11).[144] To dismiss Louis's personality and political style as pale shadows of his father's is to be misled by the foreknowledge that he was to suffer serious rebellions in the 830s. His reputation for severe religiosity does not explain the outcome of his reign, nor why those rebellions happened.

In fact, we get closer to the truth if we invert this proposition: it is the politics of the reign which help us understand Louis's image. Louis the puritan reformer was a political persona consciously created by the emperor in the first few months of his reign. In early 814, the new emperor set out to establish himself in control of the palace by banishing his sisters from court and placing them in nunneries. He also expelled Wala and his brother Adalard, and replaced many of his father's advisers with his own.[145] To justify this palace revolution, Louis denounced Aachen as a den of sexual permissiveness and corruption and presented himself as a righteous and pious reformer, riding into town to cleanse the court and the empire of impurity. The houses of officials and their servants were to be searched for hidden 'whores' and 'men', who once discovered were to be publicly flogged.[146] Removing his actual or potential opponents from the palace was an obviously political move, but we cannot rule

---

[143] *Capit.* I, no. 71, trans. King, *Charlemagne: Translated Sources*, pp. 263–4. For discussion see Nelson, 'Voice of Charlemagne', pp. 80–1; and for broader context see de Jong, '*Sacrum palatium*'; T. F. X. Noble, 'From brigandage to justice: Charlemagne, 785–794', in C. M. Chazelle (ed.), *Literacy, Politics, and Artistic Innovation in the Early Medieval West* (Lanham, MD, 1992), pp. 49–76.

[144] Werner, 'Hludovicus augustus', pp. 56–69.

[145] Depreux, *Prosopographie*, pp. 46–7.

[146] *Capit.* I, no. 145, trans. Nelson, 'Aachen as a place of power', pp. 238–9. See Nelson, 'Women at the court of Charlemagne', repr. in Nelson, *Frankish World*, pp. 239–41; R. Collins, 'Charlemagne and his critics, 814–29', in Le Jan (ed.), *La Royauté et les élites*, pp. 193–211, at pp. 204–5.

Figure 11. Portrait of Louis the Pious, from 'On praising the Holy Cross' by Hraban Maur. The letters form a dedicatory epistle, with subsidiary verses made up of just the letters within the cross, the halo, the shield, and Louis's body. These blend Roman and Christian influences in praising Louis as both a warrior (dressed in Roman war-gear) and a 'soldier of Christ'.

out the possibility that Louis did actually disapprove of his unmarried sisters' sexual conduct, especially in view of his closeness to a group of Aquitanian monastic reformers. The king's household and the palace already had religious associations, encouraged by Charlemagne's stance as a moral reformer – as mentioned earlier, texts from the 790s onwards sometimes referred to it as the *sacrum palatium* (sacred palace).[147] Louis developed this identity into a more concrete and explicit form of political ideology. In 817, after ordering an enquiry into the monasteries of the empire with a view to establishing the Benedictine Rule as the standard regime for all monks, the emperor constructed a model monastery at Inden, only three miles from Aachen, to provide a base near the palace for his spiritual adviser Benedict of Aniane and a place of retreat for himself.[148] This close association between secular palace and holy monastic site illustrates Louis's institutionalisation of the notion that the palace was a place of purity and probity that represented the moral centre of the realm.

These ideologies and accusations took shape in a very particular political context. Louis's presentation of himself as a moral paragon was directed against not just his sisters, but also his father. Louis's open criticism of Charlemagne in the early years of his reign was intended to distance his regime from that of his father, and to give it a distinct personality. In 814 *missi* were sent throughout the empire, and with much fanfare announced that they had discovered oppression and corruption wherever they looked.[149] Though there is no consensus on the dating, it was arguably around this time that a new version of the *Royal Frankish Annals* was compiled, in which were included accounts of Charlemagne's military defeats which had been left judiciously unmentioned while the old emperor was alive.[150] Meanwhile, accusations of sexual licentiousness at Charles's court (implicitly aimed at the unmarried state of both the emperor and his daughters) found expression in highly political vision texts dating from the first decade after his death, one of which depicted the late emperor in purgatory having his genitals gnawed at by a beast.[151] The

---

[147] De Jong, '*Sacrum palatium*', esp. pp. 1247–51; M. de Jong, 'Charlemagne's Church', pp. 103–35.

[148] Ermold, *In honorem Hludowici*, pp. 93–7; Ardo, *Vita Sancti Benedicti abbatis Anianensis* [Life of Benedict], ed. G. Waitz and W. Wattenbach, *MGH SS* xv (Hanover, 1888), c. 35; selections trans. Dutton (ed.), *Carolingian Civilization*, pp. 176–98.

[149] *ARF, s.a.* 814; Thegan, *Gesta Hludowici imperatoris*, c. 13.

[150] R. Collins, 'The reviser revisited: another look at the alternative version of the *Annales regni francorum*', in A. Murray (ed.), *After Rome's Fall. Narrators and Sources of Early Medieval History* (Toronto, 1998), pp. 191–213; McKitterick, *Charlemagne: The Formation of a European Identity*, pp. 27–31.

[151] D. Traill (ed. and trans.), *Walahfrid Strabo's Visio Wettini: Text, Translation and Commentary* (Frankfurt, 1974); Dutton, *Politics of Dreaming*, pp. 63–5; D. Ganz, 'Charlemagne in Hell', *Florilegium* 17 (2002 for 2000), pp. 175–94. Einhard, *VK*, c. 19 refers to allegations of sexual misdemeanour at court.

irony of all this was that the man most responsible for establishing the political significance of the ruler's moral conduct had been none other than Charlemagne himself – Louis was not as different from his father as he perhaps liked to believe.

One reason that Louis felt the need to legitimise his rule so aggressively was that, even after he had purged the palace and got his feet under the table, there were still other Carolingians around with both a justifiable claim to power and a solid constituency of support. Chief among them was his nephew Bernard, king of Italy, who retained an independent power-base: some Italian charters from 814 refer to Bernard as king without making any mention of Louis.[152] Bernard was also an obstacle to Louis's own ambitions – the Astronomer hints that the emperor was disappointed not to have inherited direct control of Italy for himself.[153] Initially Louis kept his nephew close to him, having him appear at Aachen and perform other errands in the summers of 814, 815 and 816.[154] Relations seem to have become distinctly frostier, however, in the aftermath of the emperor's re-coronation by the pope at Rheims in October 816. Louis's wife Irmingard was also crowned on this occasion: a message was thus sent out about the exclusivity of the dynastic line directly descended from the emperor and his wife.[155] Louis may also have regarded this coronation as providing him with a new mandate that freed him from any obligations imposed on him by his father in 813. This had serious implications for Bernard, who was steadily being shunted into the role of outsider. Whether or not the 816 coronation started alarm bells ringing at the Italian court, the division plan which Louis proclaimed in 817 must have set off the red alert. This declaration, known as the *Ordinatio imperii* ('Ordering of the empire'), set forth a division of the empire between Louis's three sons. The youngest, Louis ('the German') was to receive a kingdom based on Bavaria and the middle son, Pippin, one focussed on Aquitaine. Lothar, the eldest, was to occupy a position of clear superiority in the Frankish heartlands and Italy, and also inherited the imperial title. The document contained a series of clauses on marriages, military campaigns

---

[152] Depreux, 'Das Königtum', p. 12. Bernard's position was also boosted by marriage in c.810–c.814.

[153] Astronomer, *Vita Hludowici imperatoris*, c. 20; Depreux, 'Das Königtum', pp. 8–9.

[154] Astronomer, *Vita Hludowici imperatoris*, cc. 23, 25, 26.

[155] Werner, 'Hludovicus augustus', pp. 38–40.

and other political matters on which the brothers were to cooperate, with the eldest to have the final say.[156] This was Louis's definitive statement on the shape of the family tree, its finality advertised with much beseeching of God's approval. King Bernard of Italy was not mentioned.

Because it envisaged Lothar as supervisor of the entire empire, in contrast to the traditional Frankish practice of equal division of power and territory between sons, the *Ordinatio* is often seen as evidence for the victory of a court party ideologically committed to the unity of the empire over another which argued for its division. However, the existence of such parties is not explicitly described in the sources, and in truth this perceived ideological dichotomy derives more from the preoccupations of historians living in an age of European fragmentation, the twentieth century, than from those of contemporaries. The practice of regnal division was a more or less uncontested norm which always coexisted in Frankish politics with a rhetoric of unity, whose broad Christian connotations cannot be reduced to a debate about the distribution of territory.[157] While the *Ordinatio* was innovative in its attempt formally to define the superiority of the eldest brother in terms of office as well as family, it differs in degree more than kind from Charlemagne's division plan of 806, which had granted, albeit less ostentatiously, a superior kingdom to Charles the Younger. There may also have been a similar, now lost, written plan promulgated in 813 to regulate relations between Louis the Pious and Bernard.[158] The *Ordinatio*'s novelties were driven less by ideology than by Louis's need to confront an age-old problem: how to forestall the almost inevitable outbreak of conflict among the ruler's ambitious adult sons. Such plans were not only for the future, but also affected political configurations at the time in which they were issued. By spelling out the disposition of the realm, Louis hoped to reassure his sons in their roles and to remove grounds for resentment

---

[156] *Ordinatio imperii*, *Capit.* I, cc. 4–8, 12–16.

[157] Kaschke, *Die karolingischen Reichsteilungen*, pp. 324–53; S. Patzold, 'Eine "loyale Palastrebellion" der "Reichseinheitspartei"? Zur "Divisio imperii" von 817 und zu den Ursachen des Aufstands gegen Ludwig den Frommen im Jahre 830', *Frühmittelalterliche Studien* 40 (2006), pp. 43–77. See also F.-R. Erkens, '*Divisio legitima* und *unitas imperii*: Teilungspraxis und Einheitsstreben bei der Thronfolge im Frankenreich', *DA* 52 (1996), pp. 423–85; K. H. Krüger, 'Herrschaftsnachfolge als Vater-Sohn-Konflikt', *Frühmittelalterliche Studien* 36 (2002), pp. 225–40.

[158] Fried, 'Elite und Ideologie', pp. 82–8.

and rebellion. But in this context, the most significant aspect of the *Ordinatio* was what it did not mention: the silence surrounding Bernard's status is deafening. His position as king of Italy, guaranteed by Charlemagne, was now suddenly and deliberately erased. Read as *Realpolitik*, one could interpret the imperial-unity language of the division not just as a projection for the next generation but as part of Louis's attempt to establish the idea of the empire as a single unit in the here and now – with him, and not his potential rival Bernard, as its ruler.

Bernard's response, as Louis must have expected, was to cross the Alps to negotiate, a move which the emperor readily interpreted as an act of rebellion.[159] Bernard was seized at Chalon, put on trial, condemned and blinded. Blinding was a Byzantine punishment reserved for usurpers, and in theory offered rulers a way of neutralising their enemies without risking the dishonour of killing them.[160] Unfortunately, if unsurprisingly, Bernard died of his injuries two days after having his eyes put out. Taking the opportunity to reel in the circle of potential heirs and tie it off even more tightly, Louis now also sent his young illegitimate brothers to monasteries. The restriction of royal power to legitimate male Carolingians born in the main line of descent was not a simply accepted rule: it had to be asserted and enforced constantly, often using violence or the threat of violence.

Bernard's 'rebellion' was arguably the result of Louis's aggression and insecurity. It was the culmination of an extended period of rivalry and manoeuvring within the ruling dynasty which went back to the deaths of Charlemagne's elder sons in 810–11. Such jostling for position at the political centre always had reverberations away from court as well, because royal figures built their power by winning the allegiance of aristocratic elites within their regional spheres of influence. Bernard was supported not only by magnates in Italy whose relationship with him gave them a vested interest in the continuation of his regime; but also by men as geographically distant as Bishop Theodulf of Orléans, one of Charlemagne's former advisers, who had been marginalised by Louis and therefore saw the rebellion as

---

[159] T. F. X. Noble, 'The revolt of King Bernard of Italy in 817: its causes and consequences', *Studi Medievali* 15 (1974), pp. 315–26; McKitterick, *History and Memory*, pp. 265–83.

[160] G. Bührer-Thierry, '"Just Anger" or "Vengeful Anger"? The punishment of blinding in the early medieval west', in B. Rosenwein (ed.), *Anger's Past. The Social Uses of an Emotion in the Middle Ages* (Ithaca, NY, 1998), pp. 75–91.

an opportunity for settling old scores.[161] Unfortunately for Theodulf and the other rebels, it was Louis the Pious who was doing most of the settling: Bernard's supporters all ended up either blinded or confined to monasteries. These dynastic machinations took place in parallel with the new ruler's continuation and intensification of Charlemagne's reform programme. Along with the standardisation of monastic life instigated by the inquisition of 817, the emperor held a series of councils in 816–17 which ruminated deeply on matters of monastic discipline.[162] That these and subsequent synods were all held at Louis's chief 'sacred palace' of Aachen, in contrast to the 813 councils which Charlemagne had called at points across the realm, is another indication of his desire to centralise the running of imperial affairs.[163]

The events and councils of 817 ended the first chapter of the reign. Louis must have been pleased with how things had worked out. He had removed a variety of actual and potential opponents, established himself as the political and spiritual leader of the empire and set his house in order for the future. However, political events unfolded in unpredictable ways. The death of Bernard was quickly followed by that of the empress Irmingard, an event of major significance. Louis had worked hard to reshape the royal family so that his sons by Irmingard would be regarded as the only Carolingians with a legitimate claim to the throne. Now, before the dust had had a chance to settle on his bloody achievements, the empress's death created the potential for renewed uncertainty in the configuration of the dynasty. A wise choice of new wife could, nevertheless, bring political advantages, at least in the short term. The choice he made, in 819, was a young noblewoman called Judith. The sources dwell on her youth and beauty, and suggest that she was chosen from a lineup at a kind of Miss (Carolingian) World brideshow. These claims may not be trustworthy, since the accounts were written some time later and use Judith's beauty to express a particular set of ideological and exegetical points that may not reflect the events of 819 at all.[164] At least as important to Louis as her physical appearance was Judith's

---

[161] J. L. Nelson, 'The Frankish kingdoms, 814–898: the west', in *NCMH* II, pp. 110–41, at pp. 113–15.

[162] *Conc.* II, nos. 39–40; McKitterick, *Frankish Kingdoms*, pp. 112–17.

[163] De Jong, 'Charlemagne's Church', p. 129.

[164] M. de Jong, 'Brideshows revisited: praise, slander and exegesis in the reign of the empress Judith', in L. Brubaker and J. M. H. Smith (eds.), *Gender in the Early Medieval World. East and West, 300–900* (Cambridge, 2004), pp. 257–77.

family and their extensive political connections east of the Rhine, particularly in Alemannia. The political organisation and culture of the empire's outlying regions had been gradually Frankified over the preceding few decades, and Louis's marriage to Judith gave him the influence to advance this process. The first appearance of counts in many parts of Alemannia can be dated to the period 817–20, a development which implies an intensive reorganisation of royal resources and political structures.[165] Louis's marriage to Judith and the fall of Bernard (who, remember, had allies in the region) must be seen as instrumental in this process, and it is no surprise that nobles from Alemannia, including the new empress's brothers and other relatives, subsequently became major players at court.[166] Royal intrusiveness was something to be desired by figures such as these, whose regional political careers were thereby catapulted into the big time. The marriage illustrates the interdependence of politics at court and those in the provinces, however great the geographical distance between them. With their networks of kin and contacts, queens could act as one important bridge between the two arenas, which is one reason why Carolingian rulers always married noblewomen from within the empire in preference to foreign princesses.[167]

Judith was to play an increasingly important role at court itself, and because of this was one of the main targets of the rebels who sought to depose Louis in the early 830s. However, there was no warning of the storm to come in the ruling dynasty in the early 820s, when the watchword was reconciliation. Charlemagne's cousins Wala and Adalhard and Louis's illegitimate half-brothers, all of whom had

---

[165] M. Borgolte, *Geschichte der Grafschaften Alemanniens in fränkischer Zeit* (Sigmaringen, 1984).

[166] For the significance of Bernard's fall for Louis's control of Alemannia see M. Borgolte, 'Die Alaholfingerurkunden. Zeugnisse vom Selbstverständnis einer adligen Verwandtengemeinschaft des frühen Mittelalters', in M. Borgolte, D. Geuenich and K. Schmid (eds.), *Subsidia Sangallensia* 1. *Materialien und Untersuchungen zu den Verbrüderungsbüchern und zu den älteren Urkunden des Stiftsarchivs St. Gallen* (St. Gallen, 1986), pp. 287–322.

[167] In this respect they were different from most other early medieval dynasties. See for example S. Hellmann, 'Die Heiraten der Karolinger', in S. Hellmann, *Ausgewählte Abhandlungen zur Historiographie und Geistesgeschichte des Mittelalters*, ed. by H. Beumann (Darmstadt, 1961), pp. 293–391; P. Stafford, *Queens, Concubines and Dowagers: the King's Wife in the Early Middle Ages* (London, 1983); S. MacLean, 'Queenship, nunneries and royal widowhood in Carolingian Europe', *P&P* 178 (2003), pp. 3–38.

earlier been cast into exile by the anxious emperor, were welcomed back at court and given prominent jobs. The process of reconciliation was capped in 822 at the palace of Attigny, where Louis performed a public penance to atone for his and his father's sins, including the death of Bernard. Past generations of historians regarded this as the pathetic gesture of a weak ruler giving in to the whisperings of religious advisers, but this is not how the contemporary sources presented it.[168] They suggest instead that it was an opportunity for Louis to portray himself as a new Theodosius, the great Roman emperor who had performed penance in 390, and to continue a well-established tradition of emperors organising the collective expiation of their own and their people's sins: if staged correctly, demonstrations of humility could project the ruler as the 'exalted servant' of God, and thus enhance his prestige.[169] If Louis's own sons felt threatened by their father's second marriage and the possibility of further offspring, he took steps to allay their fears: Lothar and Pippin were now granted wives and sent out to rule as kings in their own *regna* (Italy and Aquitaine, respectively), and the *Ordinatio imperii* was renewed. The early 820s also saw a rejuvenation of the emperor's circle of advisers after the deaths of many close counsellors in the period 814–22.[170] The birth of a new son, Charles 'the Bald', in 823 was a potential fly in the ointment and has often been seen, with hindsight, as sowing the seeds of conflict in the royal dynasty. However, contemporaries seem not to have regarded the birth as worthy of much comment, and Lothar even agreed to act as the boy's godfather. The fact that Charles was named after his grandfather suggests that the birth was integrated into Louis's programme of reconciliation, an attempt to make peace publicly with the memory of Charlemagne.[171]

---

[168] Astronomer, *Vita Hludowici imperatoris*, c. 35; *ARF, s.a.* 822.

[169] De Jong, 'Power and humility'; R. Deshman, 'The exalted servant: the ruler theology of the prayerbook of Charles the Bald', *Viator* 11 (1980), pp. 385–417; de Jong, *Penitential State*, pp. 122–31.

[170] Depreux, *Prosopographie*, pp. 48–9.

[171] K. H. Krüger, 'Neue Beobachtungen zur Datierung von Einhards Karlsvita', *Frühmittelalterliche Studien* 32 (1998), pp. 124–45 argues that the composition of Einhard's *Life of Charlemagne* should also be placed in this context. For the debate on the dating of Einhard's work, the following are important starting points: Innes and McKitterick, 'The writing of history', in McKitterick (ed.), *Carolingian Culture*, pp. 193–220; Tischler, *Einharts Vita Karoli*; McKitterick, *Charlemagne: The Formation of a European Identity*, pp. 11–14.

Contemporary flatterers like Ermold still knew that the way to praise Louis was to tell him that he was greater than his father.[172] From what we know about Louis's activities during the first half of the 820s, there is little sign that he would have had much cause to disagree. The *Royal Frankish Annals* for this period is dominated by news of successful campaigns on the Breton, Spanish and Slav frontiers prosecuted by Louis and his sons. Although, as we have seen, he was not interested in extending the empire's territory, the emperor did enhance Frankish influence among the Danes by intervening in a dynastic dispute on the side of King Harald Klak, who accepted baptism before the wall paintings at Ingelheim with his family and followers and allowed Louis to send missionaries among his people.[173] The most ostentatious demonstration of Louis's self-assurance during the earlier 820s is the great capitulary known as the *Admonitio ad omnes regni ordines* ('Admonition to all orders of the realm') issued at some point in the period 823–5. This document was a grand statement on the nature of rulership which spelled out the roles of all the empire's office-holders and placed them in a clear hierarchy descending from the emperor, while at the same time emphasising their solidarity with him – the ruler and his representatives were characterised as sharing a common responsibility for the good governance of the realm.[174] In its ambitious all-encompassing vision of society and wide definition of the nature of political power, this statement (like the *Admonitio generalis* of 789 with which it often circulated) epitomised the basic principles of Carolingian government and is manifestly the product of a period of supreme royal confidence.

KINGSHIP AND 'SUBKINGSHIP'

Working out how Louis got from this point to the crisis of the early 830s is not straightforward because the sources for the 820s are much fewer than for the decades on either side, making it difficult to trace political events in detail. Historians have often compensated

---

[172] Ermold, *In honorem Hludowici*, pp. 62–6.
[173] S. Coupland, 'From poachers to gamekeepers: Scandinavian warlords and Carolingian kings', *EME* 7 (1998), pp. 85–114; Wood, *Missionary Life*, pp. 123–41; J. Palmer, 'Rimbert's *Vita Anskarii* and Scandinavian mission in the ninth century', *Journal of Ecclesiastical History* 55 (2004), pp. 235–56.
[174] *Capit.* 1, no. 150; O. Guillot, 'Une "ordinatio" méconnue. Le Capitulaire de 823–825', in Godman and Collins (eds.), *Charlemagne's Heir*, pp. 455–86.

by projecting onto the period an image of instability, with factions at court lining up behind different members of the royal family and the emperor increasingly vulnerable to the corrupting influence of the bishops who, in a grotesque inversion of Attigny, would in 833 orchestrate another penance designed to deprive him definitively of his throne. The roots of these processes have been detected in the text of the *Admonitio* itself. In elaborating his conception of rulership as a shared *ministerium*, Louis not only expected counts and bishops to check up on each other, but also proffered the possibility that he himself might be held to account for the neglect of public affairs.[175] Here, some scholars have detected the concession of a starry-eyed king selling himself down the river and allowing his powerful monarchy to devolve into an episcopal theocracy.[176] This is a rather too constitutional way of looking at the matter. As we have already seen, the idea of office-holding as a *ministerium*, that is as a moral responsibility to be shouldered by all those entrusted with bishoprics, abbeys and counties, had been seeping into the consciousness of the Frankish elite for some decades, and in the *Admonitio* of 823–5 it only reached its fullest and most refined expression. Ultimately, this way of imagining the Carolingian empire does not really help us comprehend how and why some members of the political elite signed up to armed revolt only a few years later. To understand the crucial preconditions for the rebellions, we must instead try to evaluate the positions of the people who led them: the emperor's sons.

As we have already seen, the management of relationships and political expectations within the ruling dynasty was essential to the maintenance of stability within the empire, and to this end rulers sometimes issued formal statements of their children's responsibilities, as in 806 and 817. This created a very precarious tightrope for kings to walk, since they had to empower their sons at the same time as restraining them. They did so by making them kings too. Charlemagne had had his younger sons Pippin and Louis anointed as kings in 781, while they were still infants, and sent (with guardians) to act as rulers in Italy and Aquitaine respectively. Louis the Pious acted equally quickly once he came to power in 814, sending his eldest son Lothar to rule Bavaria and his second, Pippin, to Aquitaine; this was modified in 817 when Lothar was shifted to Italy to make room for

---

[175] *Capit.* I, no. 150, c. 15; Guillot, 'Une "ordinatio" méconnue', pp. 481–2.
[176] The characterisation is that of de Jong, '*Sacrum palatium*', p. 1246.

Louis the German, the third son, who was eventually despatched to Bavaria in 825.[177] Rulers expected their sons to establish themselves by immersing themselves in the *regna* assigned to them and building up connections among the indigenous aristocracy. To this end they were usually married to a noblewoman from a locally influential family as quickly as possible (Lothar in 821, Pippin in 822), and they were given lands which they could use to bestow patronage and gain influence.[178] 'Subkings', as they are generally known in the modern literature, also established their own palaces and operated a regional political system on the model of their father's.[179] When Louis the Pious organised his *missatica* in 825, no *missi* were assigned to Bavaria, Aquitaine or Italy, the *regna* where his sons were ruling as subkings.[180] This underlines the sons' relative autonomy, manifest in their ability to raise armies and sometimes to issue charters. At the same time, it reminds us of the regional nature of the empire, which was polycentric in a way that was not the case with centre/periphery empires like, say, the British. Because the *regna* retained their individual identities within the empire, and because its rulers' influence rippled out in concentric circles from the areas where they spent most of their time, they ruled different parts of the empire in different ways. While regions close to the Carolingian heartlands in northern France and the Rhineland could be controlled directly, *missi* tended to have a greater role in intermediate zones, and the furthest *regna* were those most often delegated to subkings, who therefore had a crucial part to play in binding the geographical peripheries of the realm to the political centre.[181]

The ways in which they did so can be partly understood by thinking of them as regional middle-men: thus we have examples of capitularies issued jointly by Lothar and his father for Italy; and we can find plentiful examples in the narrative sources from the reigns of

---

[177] Astronomer, *Vita Hludowici imperatoris*, cc. 24, 29.
[178] Astronomer, *Vita Hludowici imperatoris*, cc. 6, 17 for lands held by Louis the Pious as subking. E. J. Goldberg, *Struggle for Empire. Kingship and Conflict under Louis the German, 817–876* (Ithaca, NY, and London, 2006), pp. 75–85 elucidates the techniques used by Louis the German to increase his entourage in the 830s.
[179] On subkings see J. Jarnut, 'Ludwig der Fromme, Lothar I und das Regnum Italiae', in Godman and Collins (eds.), *Charlemagne's Heir*, pp. 349–62; R. Collins, 'Pippin I and the kingdom of Aquitaine', in Godman and Collins (eds.), *Charlemagne's Heir*, pp. 363–89; Kasten, *Königssöhne und Königsherrschaft*.
[180] *Capit.* I, no. 151.
[181] Werner, 'Missus–marchio–comes' is a classic discussion of these zones.

both Charlemagne and Louis the Pious of subkings mounting military campaigns on their fathers' direct orders and reporting back to them on the outcome.[182] However, the modern appellation 'subking' disguises the fact that there was no formal hierarchy of rulers in contemporary thought. A king was a king. Ermold describes the majesty and formality of Pippin of Aquitaine's court, crammed with courtiers prostrating themselves before the throne, in exactly the same terms as he describes Louis the Pious's.[183] The equivalence between them is also implicit in Bishop Jonas of Orléans's handbook on kingship composed for Pippin in the early 830s, which summarised a set of precepts on the same subject concocted for Louis the Pious at Paris in 829.[184] The reason that 'subkings' had to obey their fathers was not because they were a different kind of ruler, but exactly because they were their fathers' sons. The basis of paternal authority was moral and familial, authorised not by constitutional theories but by the Old Testament's fifth commandment: 'honour your father and your mother'.[185] This is why Ermold the Black and the Astronomer do not talk about the young Louis the Pious's relationship with Charlemagne in terms of a king obeying an emperor, but instead repeatedly stress that he was 'Charles's son'; why the sources try to establish the inferiority of Bernard of Italy's position by labelling him as 'Louis's nephew'; and why the *Ordinatio imperii*, even as it superimposes concepts of formal office onto family relationships, still describes Lothar's superiority over his younger brothers as a kind of pseudo-parenthood.[186]

The moral language of familial seniority was ubiquitous, and for the most part successful in bolstering the distribution of power within the royal family. This distribution was also crucial in 'Carolingianising' the political landscape of the empire.[187] The narrative sources

---

[182] Astronomer, *Vita Hludowici imperatoris*, cc. 6, 36, 38, 40; Ermold, *In honorem Hludowici*, pp. 46–50; Kasten, *Königssöhne und Königsherrschaft*, pp. 272–377; M. Geiselhart, *Die Kapitulariengesetzgebung Lothars I. in Italien* (Frankfurt, 2002), pp. 7–16, 247–50.

[183] Ermold, *Ad Pippinum regem*, ed. E. Faral, *Ermold le Noir. Poème sur Louis le Pieux* (with French trans.) (Paris, 1964), pp. 220–32.

[184] Jonas, *De institutione regia*; *Conc.* II, no. 50.

[185] Exodus 20:2–17; Deuteronomy 5:6–21.

[186] Ermold, *In honorem Hludowici*, pp. 21, 32; Astronomer, *Vita Hludowici imperatoris*, cc. 12, 14, 23, 29; *Ordinatio imperii*, *Capit.* I, c. 10; Paschasius, *Life of Wala*, II.17.1.

[187] For this expression, and the ideas behind this paragraph, see S. Airlie, *Carolingian Politics* (Oxford, forthcoming).

are much less interested in the administrative role of subkings as middle-men than they are in the kingliness of the younger generations. The Astronomer dwells on young Louis's clothing and outward behaviour: above all it was his comportment that marked him out as a king, and Charlemagne was anxious that '[no] outward matters should dishonour him'.[188] To 'dishonour' (*dehonestare*) was a stronger concept than simple embarrassment, and here carried overtones of loss of position or office: Louis's very status evidently depended on the kingliness of his behaviour. It was important that such performances of royalty were seen by the empire's elites. Just as the five-year-old Charles had been sent to represent his dynasty by meeting Pope Stephen in 753, so by propping his three-year-old son Louis on a horse and giving him a sword Charles fast-tracked him to adulthood and sent him to claim distant Aquitaine as a royal territory.[189] Along with the establishment of the palace system and the inculcation of new attitudes towards government in the minds of the ruling class, the despatching of young sons to the provinces was a critical component of the process by which the Frankish kingdom was turned into a Carolingian empire.

All these developments contributed, by the reign of Louis the Pious, to the emergence of new ways of representing rulership. Where eighth-century sources relentlessly stressed Charlemagne's dynamism and activity, the narratives of Louis's reign idealised the emperor as the still centre of the realm, receiving and dismissing subordinates and embassies, hunting in the royal forests after assemblies had finished, and despatching armies to the frontiers under the command of his sons. These steady rhythms also inform the idealisation of politics visible in the *Admonitio* of 823–5. Nevertheless, this platform of stability concealed a tectonic potential for friction: the more effectively the empire was restructured and defined as a family concern, the more efficiently disputes within the family would be translated into crisis across the empire. Louis's Achilles' heel was the very success of the transformation of Frankish politics engineered by him and his father since the start of the ninth century. In creating an elaborate political hierarchy defined in terms of honour and morality

---

[188] Astronomer, *Vita Hludowici imperatoris*, c. 6, trans. Cabaniss, *Son of Charlemagne*, p. 38.
[189] Astronomer, *Vita Hludowici imperatoris*, c. 4.

and articulated by oaths, they had made possible the effective government of an enormous continental empire. But by its own logic Louis's sons, as kings in their own right, had the potential to appropriate that same moral language to bid for control of the system for themselves, given the motivation and the right circumstances. Those circumstances presented themselves as a result of a series of events after 827.

REVOLT AND RECOVERY: DYNASTIC POLITICS 827–840

The roots of the crisis were found not in the palace, but hundreds of miles away on the southern and eastern frontiers. At an assembly in Aachen in early 828, reports were received of two major setbacks for the Franks. The Bulgars had wreaked havoc on the Pannonian frontier in the southeast, and in the Spanish March a rebellion supported by the Muslims ended with the devastation of the countryside around Barcelona and Girona.[190] For the former embarrassment the fall guy was Baldric, *dux* of Friuli, who was deprived of his *honores* for cowardice; for the latter, the patsies were Counts Hugh of Tours and Matfrid of Orléans, accused of delaying tactics when bringing reinforcements to the aid of Bernard of Septimania, count of Barcelona. In attempting to deprive these men of their public roles, Louis put the idea of *honores* as delegated offices to its first serious test. Hugh and Matfrid were particularly hard targets because, more so than Baldric, they had connections at court. Hugh was the leading member of a highly influential Alsatian family which was accustomed to a leading role in the empire. What's more, his daughter was married to Louis's eldest son Lothar.[191] Matfrid was if anything an even more formidable figure, who for most of the 820s was able to control access to Emperor Louis and was thus widely regarded as the second most influential person in the empire: a letter of Agobard, archbishop of Lyon, describes him in the mid-820s as being 'like a wall' between the king and his people, suggesting that his position was causing a certain amount of discomfort even before 828.[192]

---

[190] *ARF, s.a.* 827, 828.   [191] Depreux, *Prosopographie*, pp. 262–4.

[192] Depreux, *Prosopographie*, pp. 329–31; P. Depreux, 'Le Comte Matfrid d'Orléans (avant 815 – + 836)', *Bibliothèque de l'École des Chartes* 152 (1994), pp. 331–74; de Jong, *Penitential State*, pp. 143–4.

To try to humble men such as these might seem in retrospect an unwise move, but in truth Louis may have had little choice. Barcelona was a resonant city in his own career, ever since he had taken it for the Franks in a glorious campaign in 801. In the 820s this was still remembered as one of his greatest achievements – in his praise-poem to Louis, Ermold effectively collapsed the whole of the emperor's pre-814 career into an account of his siege of Barcelona.[193] His personal stake in the city's history made its fate a point of honour on which the emperor was required to act. By exercising the moral logic of office-holding to deprive the counts of their *honores*, Louis literally dis-honoured them. According to Thegan, Hugh was taunted as 'the Timid' by his followers, and was shamed into taking refuge in his house.[194] Adding insult to injury, their positions at court and their Neustrian counties were taken by Bernard of Septimania, the wronged hero of Barcelona, who was appointed to the influential position of chamberlain, and by his relatives. Contemporaries clearly regarded these moves as a test of the political system symbolised by the palace: the Astronomer, for example, associated the deposition of the two counts with an earthquake at Aachen that he evidently interpreted as a metaphor for unrest in the empire.[195] In 829, perhaps giddy with confidence after the removal of Hugh and Matfrid, the emperor flexed his muscles again by amending the *Ordinatio imperii* to provide a portion of the kingdom for Charles the Bald.[196] From this point on, Louis's problems only increased.

Exactly how and why has been a matter of much discussion among historians. In the broadest perspective, the rebellions against Louis the Pious were of a kind endemic in Frankish politics since at least the sixth century, a complex interplay between the ambitions of the ruler's adult sons, regional aristocratic politics, and unpredictable events. The specific dynamics which caused the emperor's bold gestures of 828–9 to flip over into open revolt are, however, less easy to discern. Traditional explanations characterise Louis as a passive figure at the mercy of competing court factions, one orchestrated by the empress Judith which pushed for a new division of the empire to favour her son Charles the Bald, and the other supporting Lothar

---

[193] Ermold, *In honorem Hludowici*, pp. 26–50.
[194] Thegan, *Gesta Hludowici imperatoris*, cc. 28, 55.
[195] Astronomer, *Vita Hludowici imperatoris*, c. 43.
[196] Thegan, *Gesta Hludowici imperatoris*, c. 35; *AX*, s.a. 829.

by standing up for the irrevocability of the *Ordinatio imperii*.[197] The problem with this reconstruction is that it relies too much on the evidence of highly polemical and aggressively gendered post-revolt sources designed to demonise the queen and justify the actions of the rebels.[198] It does not explain, for example, the motives of Pippin of Aquitaine for becoming involved in the revolt, since his territory was not affected by the grant of land to Charles the Bald in 829.[199] Nor does it square with Ermold's comment, written before the crisis, that Judith could be seen at court in the company of Hugh and Matfrid, her supposed enemies.[200]

If anything, the sources suggest that Louis was too aggressive rather than too passive. The royal activity generated by the tensions of 828–9 is indicated by a flurry of capitularies issued for the *missi*, who had clearly been sent out in droves.[201] These texts dwell on the need for the *missi* to check that each count was fulfilling his *ministerium*, to make sure that obligations to the king were being honoured, and to round up miscreants and bring them to the palace. Strikingly, they were also given licence to tamper with the make-up of the panels which helped decide the outcome of *placita* (formal dispute hearings). Inquisitions concerning royal lands were not to be decided by the usual witnesses but instead by those locals who were found to be 'better and truer'; *scabini* (judicial professionals, effectively permanent jurors) found to be dishonourable were to be replaced by people whom the *missi* regarded as better suited to decide cases; and there were repeated reminders that the ruler himself would hear the cases of those who 'refused to live in peace' and that he would decide in person 'what should be done about such men'.[202] The vagueness and menacing moralism of these prescriptions gives them the sinister ring of the political witch-hunt. It almost looks as if Louis's most trusted agents were being sent out as a pre-emptive strike to pick up those who were likely to oppose his interventionist manoeuvres.

---

[197] Boshof, *Ludwig*, pp. 129–34, 173–7, 182–91; B. Bigott, *Ludwig der Deutsche und die Reichskirche im ostfränkischen Reich (826–876)* (Husum, 2002), pp. 60–77, 116–18.

[198] E. Ward, 'Caesar's wife: the career of the empress Judith, 819–29', in Godman and Collins (eds.), *Charlemagne's Heir*, pp. 205–27; E. Ward, 'Agobard of Lyons and Paschasius Radbertus as critics of the empress Judith', *Studies in Church History* 27 (1990), pp. 15–25; de Jong, 'Brideshows revisited'; Patzold, 'Eine "loyale Palastrebellion"'.

[199] Collins, 'Pippin I', p. 377. [200] Ermold, *In honorem Hludowici*, p. 176.

[201] *Capit.* II, nos. 184–93. [202] *Capit.* II, no. 188, c. 2; no. 192, cc. 2, 7.

The main targets must have been the friends and supporters of Hugh and Matfrid, who had lost influence thanks to the two counts' disgrace. Not content with removing their public offices, Louis now went after them with guns blazing. Hugh's family power-base in Alsace was threatened by an apparent plan to install Charles the Bald as *dux* of the region.[203] Meanwhile, the *missi* were specifically instructed to solicit complaints about Matfrid and to invite people to denounce their association with him by revoking grants of land they had made to him.[204] The great power that the count of Orléans had recently enjoyed meant that dismantling the branches of his influence was a major task that could not be accomplished without a concerted effort. A subsequent edition of *De institutione laicali*, a handbook of advice for lay aristocrats dedicated to Matfrid by Jonas of Orléans, circulated with the count's name excised.[205] Matfrid, like Tassilo of Bavaria and Pippin 'the Hunchback' before him, had to be un-personed, erased from the approved political memory of the empire.[206]

This intrusive activity was instigated against a backdrop of famines and other natural disasters which were readily interpreted as signs of divine displeasure. God's wrath can only have seemed clearer given that the perpetrators of the setbacks on the frontiers in 827 had been non-Christians. The emperor himself shared this interpretation, and convened a series of reform councils in late 828 and early 829 to deliberate over the task of appeasing God.[207] Written records of these discussions were made, but only the proceedings of the great council of Paris survive. These reveal a lot of hand-wringing about the roles of different orders of society, including the ruler, in the correct management of the empire. Louis was a full participant in these deliberations. According to Paschasius Radbertus the emperor himself, together with the nobles, initiated the event as an enquiry into the causes of God's disfavour, and this is corroborated by contemporary letters.[208] He was not being brought to book by his bishops in some sort of proto-constitutional drama, as is often assumed, so much as engaging in an act of self-examination

---

[203] Hummer, *Politics and Power*, pp. 157–65.   [204] *Capit.* II, no. 188, c. 3.
[205] I. Schröder, 'Zur Überlieferung von *De institutione laicali* des Jonas von Orléans', *DA* 44 (1988), pp. 83–97 at pp. 89–92.
[206] On Tassilo and Pippin see above, Chapter 2, pp. 69–70, 78–9.
[207] *Conc.* II, no. 50.
[208] Paschasius, *Life of Wala* II.1; de Jong, *Penitential State*, pp. 170–6.

and collective expiation of a type that had been thought appropriate to the ruler of the Frankish empire at least since the reign of Charlemagne.[209] That said, the glowering mood is hard to ignore. Walahfrid's poem on the court written in 829 captured the atmosphere by, as we have seen, transforming the symbols of Aachen's prestige into gloomy tokens of decay.[210] Louis's court had always had room for a certain amount of 'admonition' aimed in the general direction of the ruler, as long as it was expressed formally and carefully, but there are signs that opinions were now being aired with increasing regularity and frankness. Influential nobles like Einhard and Wala composed booklets explaining where they thought things had gone wrong, and made them known at court.[211] Einhard went so far as to put critical echoes of the 829 synod into the mouth of a destructive demon called Wiggo (which some historians have interpreted as an abbreviated form of Ludwig – the vernacular equivalent of Louis).[212] Dormant recriminations were dredged up. In obliquely mentioning Louis in the same breath as Herod, the Bible's most famous child-killer, Walahfrid nodded slyly to the death of Bernard of Italy over a decade earlier.[213] He also noted that Pippin of Aquitaine was not present at court and voiced a concern that Louis the German's portion of the empire was too small. Louis the Pious had become over-confident in his ability to control the actions and fates of his sons and the leading aristocrats. The problem was that the atmosphere of self-examination and moral recrimination which he had deliberately fostered to justify his own actions early in his reign was sufficiently vague and moralistic to be appropriated in turn by his enemies.

Despite the sources' retrospective insistence that the grant of territory to Charles the Bald in 829 was the spark that lit the fuse of

---

[209] *Capit.* II, no. 185; de Jong, '*Ecclesia* and the early medieval polity', pp. 129–31; de Jong, *Penitential State*, esp. pp. 176–84.

[210] See above, p. 178.

[211] Paschasius, *Life of Wala* 1.2–3; Einhard, *Translatio et miracula sanctorum Marcellini et Petri* [*Translation and Miracles of Saints Marcellinus and Peter*], ed. G. Waitz, *MGH SS* XV.1 (Hanover, 1888), pp. 239–64, III.13, trans. Dutton, *Charlemagne's Courtier*, pp. 69–130.

[212] Einhard, *Translation and Miracles*, III.14. De Jong, *Penitential State*, pp. 161–3 rightly doubts the direct equation of Wiggo and Louis, though the choice of name is still striking.

[213] Fried, 'Elite und Ideologie', pp. 102–3.

rebellion, this does not seem to have been a major issue at the time.[214] Instead, the contemporary circumstances we have outlined suggest that the outrage of their aristocratic clients and supporters was probably the most important single factor in nudging Louis's sons over into open revolt. Kings could not afford to stand idly by when their most powerful supporters lost face: leaders have to be seen to lead. Hugh must have played a major role in winning his father-in-law Lothar over to the cause, and Pippin was made amenable to the idea through disillusion at his father's heavy-handed interference in Aquitaine.[215] The sons also stood to gain, of course, and the prospect of coming in from the empire's peripheries to stake claims at the political centre must have been very tempting. Open rebellion broke out in Lent 830 as the emperor led an army to the Breton frontier through territories controlled by Matfrid's friends.[216] Amidst a rhetorical attack on the court as riven with sorcery and adultery (a very similar discourse to the one which Louis himself had earlier deployed against his late father's regime), the emperor's two elder sons converged on Aachen. Bernard of Septimania, the deposed counts' nemesis, was picked up and removed from the palace. So too was the empress Judith, accused of illicit sexual relations with Bernard and hence of polluting the palace, the moral centre of the realm.

With the support of his third son Louis the German, who had remained detached from his brothers, Louis managed to out-grit his opponents, negotiate a compromise and make a full return to power. The peace was sealed in early 831 by a new division plan which relegated Lothar to Italy and bought off the other sons with portions of territory in Francia.[217] This document also contained a striking clause by which Louis reserved the right to change his mind about the details of the settlement – a far cry from the divinely inspired finality of 817 – and within months the emperor had upset his children again by forgiving and promoting Lothar. Pippin protested passively by refusing a summons to court, while Louis the German forced his father into military action by trying to take over Alemannia in 832. Louis's next move, the dispossession of Pippin in favour of Charles the

---

[214] Thegan, *Gesta Hludowici imperatoris*, c. 35.   [215] Collins, 'Pippin I', pp. 378–9.
[216] *AB*, s.a. 830. For detailed accounts of the rebellions see Boshof, *Ludwig*, pp. 192–210; Goldberg, *Struggle for Empire*, pp. 59–77; de Jong, *Penitential State*.
[217] *Capit.* II, no. 194.

Bald, showed how high-handed he had become in his management of his family. Responding to the emperor's capriciousness, the three sons made common cause and in 833 squared up to their father in Alsace – not coincidentally, Hugh's main stamping-ground. The emperor's men, stared out by the opposition, deserted: the place subsequently became known as the 'Field of Lies'.[218] Lothar began calling the shots and forced his father to perform penance at Soissons, a ritual which, in a sinister inversion of the voluntary penance he had undertaken at Attigny in 822, was held by the rebels to disqualify him from holding office – context was everything.[219] Louis resisted intense pressure to enter a monastery for long enough to be saved by renewed dissension among his sons. Lothar, eyes glazed over by memories of the superior role once promised him in the *Ordinatio imperii*, pushed for too much, triggering his brothers' disagreements and jealousies.[220] After a few months Louis the German again sprang his father from captivity and, rallying the emperor's supporters in the east, restored him to power. In 835 Louis was solemnly re-armed at St Denis in a public ritual intended to reverse his penance. Louis's first act was to depose and disgrace Archbishop Ebo of Rheims, who was accused of having masterminded the Soissons penance in 833. The two men had been childhood friends.

To attempt to depose an emperor permanently in this way was an act of breathtaking audacity. Virtually ever since, the emperor's humiliation at Soissons has been seen as the proof of Louis's weakness as a ruler, and even as the absolute nadir of Carolingian power.[221] Yet the accumulation of armed tension did not really spill over into open violence until 834, when Lothar and his supporters were pushed onto the back foot and had to fight a retreat.[222] The contest turned more on the protagonists' ability to win over a critical mass of elite support through argument, persuasion and intimidation. It is important to stress again that the language used against Louis by his opponents was not constitutional but familial and moral. The idea that a king should rule with equity and justice was a theme which became increasingly formalised through repetition in texts of this period: these were

---

[218] Thegan, *Gesta Hludowici imperatoris*, c. 42.
[219] De Jong, 'Power and humility'; de Jong, *Penitential State*, pp. 228–41.
[220] Nithard, *Historiarum Libri IV*, 1.4.   [221] Booker, *Past Convictions*.
[222] *AB, s.a.* 834; Thegan, *Gesta Hludowici imperatoris*, c. 52.

dangerously broad and flexible notions that became available to others to measure the ruler against. The accusations levelled against Louis in 833, recorded in a document that his opponents wished to be regarded as definitive, were couched in exactly this idiom.[223] His crimes included: having broken the *Ordinatio imperii* by instigating new divisions; having blinded Bernard of Italy; having organised a campaign in Lent; having tried people without due process (perhaps referring to Matfrid, Hugh and the inquisitions of 828–9); and having turned his sons into enemies instead of using paternal authority to keep the peace. Through these unjust actions (especially by changing the shape of the succession so often) he had compelled people to swear contradictory oaths that they could not keep, turning them into perjurers against their wills. They did not just accuse him of having been a bad father to his sons, but also went one better: above all (this was the first item on the charge-sheet), they denounced him as a bad son to his own father for having broken his 813 oath to protect his close relatives. These accusations were improvised attempts to rationalise what had happened. The rebels may have been throwing the book at Louis, but it was one they themselves were composing, spontaneously and conjecturally, not one that appealed to accepted legal justifications for rebellion.

Still, their list of accusations went entirely with the grain of Carolingian politics. Both sides used the same political codes to try to gain the moral high ground and justify their actions: this is why Lothar advertised his assumption of control after the Field of Lies by hunting and receiving ambassadors at the palace; and why Louis tried to undermine him by reminding him that he was his father; and why the emperor's deposition was articulated in the language of penance and sin, which had become the dominant idiom for talking about political responsibility.[224] These codes – the paternal authority of the ruler, the palace as the centre of the realm, the fundamental significance of oaths and the classification of political behaviour in terms of sin and virtue – were absolutely central symbols of the political system that the Carolingians had tried to establish. Louis's own rigorous management of the family tree since the 810s was intended to establish the notion that only his own sons could be regarded

---

[223] *Capit.* II, no. 197; de Jong, *Penitential State*, pp. 234–41 (and pp. 271–7 for a translation).
[224] Astronomer, *Vita Hludowici imperatoris*, cc. 45, 48, 49.

as legitimate kings, and it was he who had empowered them by overlaying the territories of the empire with a Carolingian dynastic template. This had worked: the fact that the aggrieved nobles turned to the emperor's sons to lead them is a sign of how much dynastic modes of thought had influenced them – theirs was a rebellion within the system, not against it. The structures of government were not, in other words, disintegrating. The problem was that they had become so refined and coherent that other Carolingians were able to manipulate the dominant political rhetoric to bid to take over the empire as a going concern. In this sense, Louis was a victim of his own success.

Clearly, though, he was a victim. Modern historians have thus generally been unwilling to countenance the possibility that he could ever have genuinely recovered from the political traumas of the early 830s. The absence of capitularies after 834 has been taken as an indication that he was a lame duck, playing out time until his death in 840. Yet, as Janet Nelson has argued, there are compelling reasons for rejecting this interpretation.[225] New appointments were made to restore peace in Neustria (where quarrels over Hugh and Matfrid's *honores* had turned into open war) and other trouble-spots. At court, Louis dismissed those he felt he could not rely on and then pulled up the drawbridge, giving the most important positions to his half-brothers and other close allies.[226] The coinage retained its value; and the emperor responded to the Danish raids which the rebellions had drawn in by renewing alliances across the frontiers to stabilise the situation. Lothar and his supporters were banished back to Italy, and there they stayed, only coming back in 839 with the emperor's permission. Charles the Bald's inheritance was finally forced through in Aquitaine after Pippin's death in 838. Although there was some opposition to this from Pippin's son, and then from Louis the German, these later rebellions never threatened to coalesce into an uprising as serious as those of the earlier 830s.[227] Charter evidence from east of the Rhine shows that the emperor managed to reassert his authority in the localities very successfully.[228] Louis's

[225] J. L. Nelson, 'The last years of Louis the Pious', in Godman and Collins (eds.), *Charlemagne's Heir*, pp. 147–59.
[226] Depreux, *Prosopographie*, pp. 52–3.
[227] J. L. Nelson, *Charles the Bald* (London and New York, 1992), pp. 92–101; Goldberg, *Struggle for Empire*, pp. 87–94.
[228] Innes, *State and Society*, pp. 202–7.

restoration of normal service suggests a certain tenacity and must be regarded as a notable success.

On the other hand, the smooth working of the system as it had been thought about in the 820s had been seriously disrupted. The memories of rebellion, and of Louis's high-handed unpredictability in its wake, did not just vanish. The bishops' slanders about the sexual licentiousness of the palace were still hanging in the air in 837, when Thegan felt compelled to counter them by re-erecting Louis's earlier persona as an unsmiling paragon of Christian self-control.[229] The routines of government may have returned to business as usual, but bitter rivalries had been created and hardened through being played out in an atmosphere of open confrontation. Although there had been little actual fighting, the connections between court factions and local elites meant that the royal family's distress had sent fault lines snaking out across the empire in every direction. These cracks in the aristocratic community were papered over but also, as we shall see in Chapter 8, saved up for the future. In view of what had happened, it was perhaps fitting that when Louis the Pious died on an island in the Rhine in June 840, he was once again campaigning against a rebellious son. Ironically, given his reputation for humourlessness, he reportedly died laughing.[230]

---

[229] See above, pp. 155–6.
[230] Astronomer, *Vita Hludowici imperatoris*, c. 64. On the authorial agendas at play in this anecdote see Tremp, 'Die letzten Worte'.

VILLAGES AND VILLAGERS, LAND AND LANDOWNERS

Afraid of meeting 'dog-headed men' on his travels in Scandinavia, the missionary Rimbert, some time in the middle of the ninth century, was moved to enquire of Abbot Ratramnus of Corbie whether such monstrous perversions of humanity had souls that could be saved. Ratramnus – a theological authority whose monastery had long-standing links with the Frankish mission in the north – replied that all the available information on contemporary Scandinavian societies pointed to familiar patterns of agrarian life: did not the Danes and Swedes follow laws, live in villages, farm the land, domesticate animals and indeed wear clothes similar to the Franks'? They therefore had souls; Rimbert's job was to save them for the true, Christian, God.[1] Ratramnus's exchange with Rimbert belongs in a long tradition of Roman and Frankish ethnographic fantasies about their northern neighbours which were intended to assert the normality of home society by vividly defining distant and not-so-distant neighbours as 'others'.[2] But rather than identifying, as was customary, monstrous peoples as agents of God's wrath or actors in Biblical

---

[1] Ratramnus of Corbie, *Epistolae*, ed. E. Perels, *MGH Epp.* VI (*Epp. Karolini aevi* IV) (Berlin, 1925), *Ep.* 12, pp. 155–7, and see Wood, *Missionary Life*, pp. 251–3.

[2] See I. Wood, 'Christians and pagans in ninth-century Scandinavia', in B. Sawyer, P. H. Sawyer and I. N. Wood (eds.), *The Christianization of Scandinavia* (Alingsås, 1987), pp. 36–67; Palmer, 'Defining paganism', at pp. 422–5; Dutton, *Charlemagne's Mustache*, pp. 46–7.

prophecies, here Ratramnus described the familiarity of the way of life of rural Scandinavia, regardless of the shape of its inhabitants' heads. These rural communities resembled those whose labours sustained Ratramnus and his monks in Francia, and so were ripe for conversion under the aegis of a Christian empire.

As so often, in imagining others distant from home Ratramnus and Rimbert reveal social assumptions that would have been much harder to voice in a discussion of their own society. Indeed, direct commentary on the structure of Frankish society by the spokespeople of the ruling elites of Church and court is rare. When such commentary did occur, it was theological in nature and ecclesiological in aim, designed to explicate the proper harmonious relationship between the different orders that made up Christian society. The first decades of the ninth century saw a series of attempts to apply to Carolingian society the theory of 'three orders of man' developed by Augustine and elaborated by other late antique churchmen. At Aachen in 802, for example, the three orders of clergy, laity and monks were each encouraged to meditate on their roles, as reflected in authoritative texts from canon law, secular law and the monastic rule.[3] A few decades later the monastic scholar Heiric of Auxerre, influenced by classical texts, inaugurated what was to become the dominant social theory of the Middle Ages by classifying society as made up of those who fight, those who pray and those who work.[4] Fascinating though it is, such theorising is primarily a part of intellectual history: early medieval social theories do not aim at the kind of understanding sought by modern historians.

The lack of recognisable social analysis in Carolingian sources has had important historiographical ramifications. Firstly, without useable contemporary comment as a starting point for debate, modern historians have tended to draw on chronologies and trajectories inherited from political history, and to equate periods of royal

---

[3] *AL, s.a.* 802.
[4] O. G. Oexle, 'Tria genera hominum. Zur Geschichte eines Deutungsschemas der sozialen Wirklichkeit in Antike und Mittelalter', in L. Fenske, *et al.* (eds.), *Institutionen, Gesellschaft und Kultur im Mittelalter. Festschrift Josef Fleckenstein* (Sigmaringen, 1984), pp. 483–99; D. Iogna-Prat, 'Le "Baptême" du schéma des trois ordres fonctionnels: l'apport de l'école d'Auxerre dans la seconde moitié du IXe siècle', *Annales ESC* 41/1 (1986), pp. 101–26. The classic discussion of post-Carolingian three orders theory is G. Duby, *The Three Orders: Feudal Society Imagined* (Chicago, 1982).

weakness with 'rising violence' or 'social breakdown'. These ideas are based on contemporary legislation, which exhibits a recurrent concern with protection for the poor, widows and orphans. But individual snippets of legislation should not be divorced from the context in which they were issued and taken as proof of more generalised 'abuses'. The complaints we find are standard, indeed stereotyped, with long precedents in Christian thought right across the late antique and early medieval worlds; they also tended to be voiced in times of political instability precisely because political instability was seen by the intellectual elite as a worrying manifestation of divine displeasure, and as such was likely to encourage social critique. Such concerns indicate, therefore, a louder volume of ideological conversation within the ruling class rather than actual social changes. One of the primary intentions of legislators was the inculcation of a distinctly Christian ethos amongst the 'powerful', to use their term for those who ruled. When legislation referred to the poor, it was to remind the powerful of their duty of protection in the context of a harmonious Christian social order – this was ideological posturing, not social analysis.[5] This is not to deny that kings could play a role in social change, particularly by destabilising local societies in which they intervened (as witnessed by the kind of tensions visible in the *Stellinga* revolt in Saxony in the 840s or, in a different form, by the century of endemic land litigation set in train by the Carolingian conquest of Alemannia).[6] But these developments were neither deliberately sought, nor had any direct connection with the aspirations declared in our more ideological texts.

A second, related, consequence of the lack of contemporary social analysis in our sources has been the tendency to slot the eighth and ninth centuries into existing grand narratives by importing models from either the Roman world or the high Middle Ages against which Carolingian developments can be measured. Interpretations of social history often debate where to place the Carolingian world in a linear

---

[5] On legislation as a genre of political communication, see Pössel, 'Authors and recipients'.

[6] *Stellinga*: E. Goldberg, 'Popular revolt, dynastic politics and aristocratic factionalism in the early middle ages: the Saxon Stellinga reconsidered', *Speculum* 70 (1995), pp. 467–501; Alemannia: M. Innes, 'Property, politics and the problem of the Carolingian state', in W. Pohl and V. Wieser (eds.), *Staat im frühen Mittelalter* (Vienna, 2009), pp. 299–313.

development 'from antiquity to feudalism'.[7] Thus for two early-twentieth-century pioneers, Alfons Dopsch and Henri Pirenne, in different ways the Carolingian period witnessed the end of an ancient economy and society and the beginning of the medieval. For Dopsch, impressed by the evidence for rural organisation and the development of estates, the Carolingian period created the social and economic foundations of the medieval countryside, on which later growth was built; for his near contemporary Pirenne, the Carolingian empire could be characterised as agrarian and land-locked, and its genesis seen as a direct result of the contraction of commerce and urban life.[8] Although their conclusions directly clashed, it is noteworthy that for both the central concern was to place the Carolingian era in a millennium-long transformation, not to understand its peculiarities and specificities on their own terms. Today it remains commonplace for studies of Carolingian and post-Carolingian Europe to be framed in terms of a debate over 'continuity' and 'change' that presumes that what we are really looking for is a point in history which marked the end of an 'ancient' social order and the beginning of the 'medieval'.[9]

One consequence of these historiographical problems is that potentially anachronistic categories of analysis are often imported into the eighth and ninth centuries from outside. Were, for example, Carolingian peasants 'slaves' or 'serfs'? Were Carolingian estates closer to their Roman forebears or to the medieval 'seigneurie'? Did Carolingian rural settlements resemble the Roman pattern or the villages of the high Middle Ages? Questions such as these can be useful if we are seeking to describe very long-term processes of change. But they are not the only questions, nor even the most fruitful.

---

[7] C. Wickham, 'The other transition: from the ancient world to feudalism', *P&P* 113 (1984), pp. 3–36, repr. in Wickham, *Land and Power*, pp. 7–42; Wickham, *Framing the Early Middle Ages*. For recent responses to Wickham's work, see the special issue of the *Journal of Agrarian Change* 9 (2009), edited by P. Sarris and J. Banaji: *Aristocrats, Peasants and the Transformation of Rural Society c.400–800*.

[8] A. Dopsch, *Economic and Social Foundations of European Civilisation* (New York and London, 1937; English trans. of 1923 German original); H. Pirenne, *Mohammed and Charlemagne* (London, 1939; English trans. of 1937 French original, published posthumously). See also below, Chapter 7.

[9] See for example C. Lauranson-Rosaz, *L'Auvergne et ses marges du VIIIe aux XIe siècles: La Fin du monde antique?* (Le Puy en Velay, 1987). For historiographical discussion and further references see Innes, 'Economies and societies in the early medieval west', in E. English and C. Lansing (eds.), *Companion to the Middle Ages* (Oxford, 2009), pp. 9–37.

Classifying Carolingian practices either as fossilised hangovers from antiquity or as embryonic versions of high medieval phenomena obscures their contemporary function and meaning, risks ignoring the human agents of change, and discounts the very likely possibility that society transformed not in a straight line but in a complex and discontinuous series of changes spanning half a millennium. It also rules out the possibility that the social structures of the fourth to tenth centuries might have had their own defining characteristics distinct from those of the preceding and succeeding periods.[10]

Another consequence is that there is no real consensus amongst historians on the social and economic dynamics of the Carolingian centuries. Those looking through high-medieval spectacles tend to talk about the ninth century as a time of relative stasis, with the end of the empire as the catalyst for massive and sudden change (the 'feudal revolution') in the tenth century that generated social structures familiar from the eleventh and twelfth.[11] Meanwhile, those interested in continuity with late antiquity normally focus on formal, institutional aspects (royal legislation, for example) rather than the inner workings of society. Neither view is much interested in analysing how Carolingian society functioned. Yet this state of affairs is not the result of any deficiency of evidence. Far from it: the deepening of source material from the Carolingian centuries, discussed in Chapter 1, means that for the very first time in European history it is possible for us to understand in detail the social relationships that animated the villages and hamlets of the eighth- and ninth-century countryside. The written evidence takes two forms: on the one hand charters, legal records mostly of land transfer and title, which survive in sufficient volume from the last decades of the eighth century onwards to allow us to peer into the small worlds of Carolingian villages; and on the other polyptychs, records of estate management, which proliferate in the ninth century. The documentary record, moreover, can be counterpointed with archaeology, in particular

---

[10] Innes, 'Economies and societies' argues for the distinctiveness of the early medieval west.

[11] G. Duby, *The Early Growth of the European Economy: Warriors and Peasants from the Seventh to the Twelfth Century* (Ithaca, NY, and London, 1974) (translation by H. B. Clarke of French original of 1973); T. N. Bisson, 'The "feudal" revolution', *P&P* 142 (1994), pp. 6–42, with subsequent debate in *P&P* 152 (1996), pp. 197–223, 155 (1997), pp. 177–225.

Figure 12. Reconstruction of the hilltop centre of a manorial estate (*curtis*) at
Miranduolo, Tuscany, where lords and peasants lived side by side: common in Italy,
far less so elsewhere. In its Carolingian phase Miranduolo was divided between a
fortified zone that housed the lord, and a group of peasant huts with an
unhierarchical material culture. Food storage huts in the fortified compound
indicate the rich diet of the elite.

the growing body of evidence from excavations of rural settlements
(see Figure 12).[12]

In marked contrast to the student of earlier centuries (including
the Roman period), the Carolingianist is thus in a fortunate position.
Rather than wrestling with isolated episodes gleaned from narratives
or spectral norms fleetingly glimpsed in law-codes, we have a rich

---

[12] For excellent recent syntheses see J.-P. Devroey, *Économie rurale et société dans
l'Europe franque (VI–IX siècles)* (Paris, 2003); Devroey, *Puissants et misérables: Système
social et monde paysan dans l'Europe des Francs (VI–IX siècles)* (Brussels, 2006); P.
Depreux, *Les Sociétés occidentales du milieu du VIe à la fin du IXe siècle* (Rennes,
2002); Wickham, *Framing the Early Middle Ages*; Innes, 'Economies and societies';
and Wickham, *The Inheritance of Rome: A History of Europe, 400–1000* (London,
2009).

body of evidence for the everyday dynamics of the countryside. The possibilities of this data are only just beginning to be appreciated, but we should also recognise the problems they present. For one thing, the geographical coverage of all three sources is very sporadic. Moreover, charters, polyptychs and archaeology by their very nature present radically different views of the countryside, and the relationship between them is not always easy to establish. Polyptychs, surveys in which kings and great churches documented the tenants and dues on their lands, present an image of carefully organised and centrally controlled great estates whose inhabitants were clearly divided into different classes; while the surviving charters, which mostly record transactions in which individual landowners transferred or occasionally disputed rights over land in the presence of their neighbours, show a more complex and fragmented grid of rights. Archaeology, meanwhile, is often integrated imperfectly with written sources. These observations about the sources and about the questions we should ask of them should be kept in mind as we proceed through this chapter. The next section deals with the village, the basic social unit of the Carolingian countryside. The two subsequent sections discuss rural landowners, village communities and their role in the social hierarchy. Next we explain one of the archetypal features of Carolingian economic organisation, namely the 'manorial system' found on the great estates of the king and the Church, and ask what we can learn from it about economic growth and stagnation. Finally we return to the village to look at how all of this fitted together and what it meant for the majority of the population by trying to understand if and how rural communities were able to resist the power of landlords, and how they saw their place in the great political hierarchies of the empire.

VILLAGES

Ratramnus's belief in the similarity of Frankish and Scandinavian societies rested on the fact that Scandinavians, like Franks, lived in villages. He used the Latin term *villa* to refer to these basic social units. The *villa* of the early Middle Ages differed radically from that of the Roman period, when the term generally refers to the rural residences of landowning elites, elaborate and often luxurious stone-built country houses which were also focal points for the organisation of land

and labour.[13] Poorer hamlets and farmsteads, often built of wood, are harder to identify and date, and as a consequence less well understood. It is nonetheless clear that the islands of conspicuous wealth that the *villa* represented dominated the rural economy and society of western Europe in the Roman era. In terms of administrative geography, *villas* shaped the estate units into which the countryside was divided. This rural landscape was, however, not to last: hence by the end of the sixth century the hagiographer and historian Gregory of Tours, himself a descendant of the *villa*-owning class, could use the term *villa* to denote an agglomeration of rural households – in other words, a village.[14]

The thickening of the documentary record in the course of the eighth century confirms the division of the countryside into a network of units built up of individual households, fields and other appendages. The degree to which habitation and human activity within these units was concentrated differed as a result of a variety of factors, first and foremost local topography. But right across Europe north of the Alps, rural society was divided into a grid of multi-household settlement units which were taking on an increasingly territorial definition. The degree to which these units had their own formal structures of organisation is inevitably cloudy, given the nature of our evidence, though judicial meetings of local landowners are well attested in the documentary record. Since the evidence gives little explicit sense of how communities were organised internally, and suggests that their layout varied considerably, some historians have seen the emergence of the village as a post-Carolingian phenomenon.[15] But while we should certainly accept that settlements changed over time (the idea of a timeless rural community is misleading), it would be a mistake to see the topographically and organisationally looser

---

[13] The standard work is J. Percival, *The Roman Villa* (London, 1976). Note that contemporary nomenclature was far more varied: *villa* has become a modern shorthand.

[14] M. Heinzelman, 'Villa d'après l'oeuvre de Grégoire de Tours', in E. Magnou-Nortier (ed.), *Aux sources de la gestion publique* I: *Enquête lexicographique sur fundus, villa, domus, mansus* (Lille, 1993) I, pp. 45–70; G. Halsall, *Settlement and Social Organisation: the Merovingian Region of Metz* (Cambridge, 1995).

[15] J. Chapelot and R. Fossier, *The Village and the House in the Middle Ages* (London, 1985). For some early medievalists' responses see the discussion on R. Fossier's paper ('Les Tendances de l'économie: stagnation ou croissance?') in *Settimane di Studio del Centro italiano di studi sull'alto medioevo* 27 (Spoleto, 1981), pp. 261–74, discussion at pp. 275–90.

settlements of the Carolingian period as fundamentally different from their more tightly structured successors.

North of the Alps, the Latin term *villa* was well established as the label for these settlement units. Polyptychs show great landowners detailing the dues expected from the rural population *villa* by *villa* and the charters, recording the transfer of individual pieces of property, show that landowners likewise conceptualised the countryside as a network of such units.[16] In Frankish Italy, terminology was more varied, but even here the grid of villages formed a basic mental map of the countryside.[17] Where habitation was fairly concentrated, *villa* could be used in a more restricted sense to refer to the primary area of residence at the core of the settlement. It could then be contrasted with the countryside beyond, the fields worked by the inhabitants and the surrounding landscape exploited more intermittently as pasture or woodland. These outlying areas, though legally and territorially dependent on the *villa*, were often referred to using a variety of other terms such as 'mark' (*marca*). A series of stories recorded in the *Annals of Fulda* give a clear sense of how these divisions structured village life in the Rhine valley, an area of nucleated settlement (i.e. containing concentrated villages). When a cattle plague hit the *villa* of Walahesheim, 'the dead animals were dragged daily from their stalls to the fields, where the village dogs tore up and devoured them' until they mysteriously gathered together and vanished. In the *villa* of Kempten, an evil spirit was blamed for fomenting bitter disputes among the inhabitants: bored with throwing stones and banging on walls, it spoke openly and spread accusations about theft so as to stir up feelings against one man, even causing houses to catch fire when his victim entered them: 'as a result the man was forced to live outside the *villa* in the fields with his wife and children, as all his kin feared to take him in'.[18] Just as at Walahesheim the inhabitants dealt with the disaster of dying livestock collectively, and their dogs were identified as belonging to the village, so the Kempten story indicates that the village was the basic unit for collective action: here

---

[16] Wickham, *Framing the Early Middle Ages*, pp. 280–93, 400–6, 465–514 synthesises material from across Europe.

[17] Costambeys, *Power and Patronage*, pp. 184–208; M. Costambeys, 'Settlement, taxation and the condition of the peasantry in post-Roman central Italy', *Journal of Agrarian Change* 9 (2009), pp. 92–119.

[18] *AF*, s.a. 878, 858. M. Innes is preparing an extended discussion of the Kempten story.

deep-rooted conflicts divided the community and were discussed and resolved by the village as a collectivity. Territorial boundaries articulated this identity, dividing the countryside into a network of villages. Thus when a flash flood hit Eschborn, not only did it uproot trees and vines, wash away foundations and hurl 'the draught animals and beasts with everything which was in the houses to destruction', it also swept corpses and coffins from their graves and washed them into the bounds of another village.[19]

Eschborn, Kempten and Walahesheim (see Map 7) in all probability lacked the degree of formal internal institutionalisation which was a hallmark of the high Middle Ages, but they had hierarchies and structures, as the ways in which the inhabitants of Kempten dealt with demonic trouble-making make clear. Legal documents show that disputes heard in these communities were debated in public meetings informed by the collective testimony of influential landowners, and where we can sometimes see a particular individual consistently serving as a 'chair', and often being the 'leading witness' for all local property transfers.[20] Very occasionally, charter scribes might give such individuals a formal title – judge (*iudex*) or hundredman (*centenarius*) – but such terms were not used consistently or frequently in the charters, nor were they explicitly linked to a particular locale or village.[21] Capitularies do make catch-all injunctions about 'hundredmen' and others, and constitutionally minded historians have as a result been tempted to see them as a particular class of local official, with consistent duties and reporting lines back to counts.[22] The charter evidence, however, shows a more informal system of local leadership in which counts operated not through institutional links but by seeking to draw local figures into patronage relationships. As we saw in Chapter 4, we should probably regard the capitularies' injunctions for these local leaders to swear oaths of office, hold courts and ensure the administration of justice as attempts to draw those able to exercise informal leadership within

---

[19] *AF*, s.a. 875.
[20] For an overview, see W. Davies, 'Local participation and legal ritual in early medieval law courts', in P. Coss (ed.), *The Moral World of the Law* (Cambridge, 2000), pp. 61–89.
[21] See Innes, *State and Society*, pp. 94–140.
[22] For example, Ganshof, *Frankish Institutions*; A. C. Murray, 'From Roman to Frankish Gaul: *centenae* and *centenarii* in the administration of the Merovingian kingdom', *Traditio* 44 (1988), pp. 59–100.

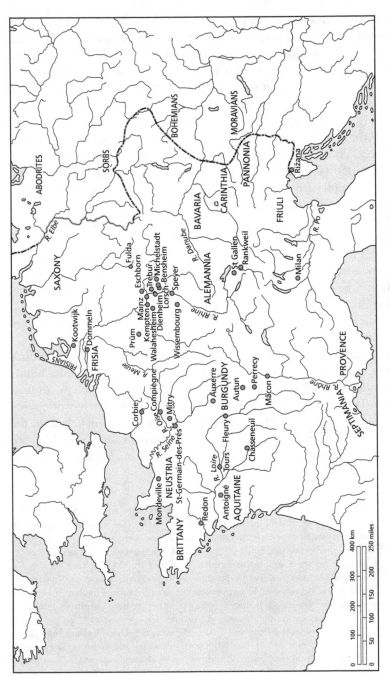

Map 7. Places mentioned in Chapter 5: 'Villages and villagers, land and landowners'

the community into the purview of the official hierarchies of the kingdom. It is only very occasionally that we see counts imposing an outsider in such positions, and the result was almost always tension. The Istrian landowners who met Charlemagne's *missi* (envoys) at Rižana in 804, for example, complained that the Frankish *dux* John had overturned their ornate local hierarchies by imposing instead 'his hundredmen'.[23] But such situations were exceptional and often, as at Rižana or with the career of the *escultaizo* Folkwine at Rankweil in the Alps, coincided with moments of political turmoil at strategically important locations. The norm is indicated instead by numerous examples from across the empire of locally pre-eminent men emerging to serve as the key intermediaries between villages and the official structures of rule.[24] Quite how locals referred to their 'headmen' we cannot be sure, although there are hints at vernacular terms (for example, *escultaizo* or *sculdahis*, ancestors of the modern German word *Schultheiss*). The titles used in capitularies and charters should be seen as generic labels, not formal designations of office, and the precise degree of influence and spheres of activity enjoyed by such men must have varied from area to area, depending on local tradition and political context.

A village was not a single unit of residence or agricultural exploitation: it was made up of an agglomeration of homes and other buildings, as our stories make clear. Both charters and polyptychs confirm this. The charters show landowners transferring rights over often tiny parcels of land – individual fields or plots – and also, on occasion, the household from which these parcels were cultivated, which might be called a courtyard (*curtis*) or a farm (*casalis, casata*), and might also

---

[23] C. Manaresi (ed.), *I placiti del regnum Italiae* I (Rome, 1955), no. 17. For full context, see H. Krahwinkler, *Friaul im Frühmittelalter. Geschichte einer Region vom Ende des fünften bis zum Ende des zehnten Jahrhunderts* (Vienna, 1992), pp. 199–243.

[24] For cases studies see Innes, *State and Society*, pp. 94–140; M. Innes, 'Practices of property in the Carolingian empire', in Davis and McCormick (eds.), *The Long Morning of Medieval Europe*, pp. 247–66; F. Bougard, 'Pierre de Niviano, dit le Spoletin, sculdassius, et le gouvernement du comté de Plaisance à l'époque carolingienne', *Journal des Savants* (1996), pp. 291–337. Istria: M. Innes, 'Framing the Carolingian economy', *Journal of Agrarian Change* 9 (2009), pp. 42–58, at pp. 42–6. Folkwine: P. Erhart and J. Kleindienst (eds.), *Urkundenlandschaft Rätiens* (Vienna, 2004), esp. pp. 83–90; M. Innes, 'Dossiers and archives: documents, landowners and power in Frankish society', in W. Brown *et al.* (eds.), *Documentary Culture*.

include a residence (*domus*).[25] The polyptychs, even though they show landlords organising extensive estates, show peasants living in restricted households – a marital couple, their children and perhaps their parents – and supporting themselves off the attached holding.[26] In the seventh and eighth centuries the vocabulary used to refer to these household-farms begins to show some standardisation, with *mansus* (manse) and its vernacular equivalents (*hoba, hufe*) increasingly used to refer to the 'standard family farm'. These units were not strictly surveyed assessments of agrarian output, but were based rather on a general sense of the norm that was appropriate for a peasant household. The origins of this nomenclature – and of the notion of a standardised household – probably lie in landlord initiatives: the settling of dependent peasants on planned estates, often 'new builds' on cleared land, a phenomenon we can trace as early as the seventh century and which was increasingly important in Carolingian times. Carolingian efforts to record and standardise the services expected from peasants on such great estates further encouraged its adoption, until *mansus* and its cognates became generic terms, as in the ninth-century estate inventories of the monastery of Fulda.[27]

The processes by which the early medieval countryside was pressed into this shape remain obscure. The reasons for the transition from late Roman *villa* units defined by ownership and management to

---

[25] F. Schwind, 'Beobachtungen zur inneren Struktur des Dorfes in karolingischer Zeit', in H. Jankuhn, *et al.* (eds.), *Das Dorf der Eisenzeit und des frühen Mittelalters* (Göttingen, 1977), pp. 444–93; D. Claude, 'Haus und Hof im Merowingerreich nach den erzählenden und urkundlichen Quellen', in H. Beck and H. Steuer (eds.), *Haus und Hof in ur- und frühgeschichtlichen Zeit* (Göttingen, 1997), pp. 321–34.

[26] D. Herlihy, *Medieval Households* (London, 1985), pp. 56–78; J. Bessmerny, 'Les Structures de la famille paysanne dans les villages de la Francie au IXe siècle', *Le Moyen Âge* 90 (1984), pp. 165–93.

[27] D. Herlihy, 'The Carolingian mansus', *EHR* 13 (1960), pp. 69–79; C.-E. Perrin, 'Observations sur la manse dans la region parisienne au début du IXe siècle', *Annales* 8 (1945), pp. 39–51; W. Schlesinger, 'Vorstudien zu einer Untersuchungen über die Hufe', 'Hufe und mansus im liber donationem des Klosters Weissenburgs', and 'Die Hufe im Frankenreich', in H. Patze and F. Schwind (eds.), *Ausgewählte Aufsätze von W. Schlesinger 1965–1979* (Sigmaringen, 1987), pp. 458–541, 543–85, 587–614. On seventh-century origins see now J. Banaji, 'Aristocracies, peasantries and the framing of the early middle ages', *Journal of Agrarian Change* 9 (2009), pp. 59–91, esp. 66–78; for Fulda see U. Weidinger, *Untersuchungen zur Wirtschaftsstruktur des Kloster Fulda in der Karolingerzeit* (Stuttgart, 1991), esp. pp. 23–54.

villages defined by collective action and shared territory are particularly shadowy, but the shift was complete north of the Alps by the time of our earliest documents in the seventh century, if not by the time of Gregory of Tours in the sixth; and even in Italy, although change was slower, by 800 at the latest the basic categories of social and economic activity had shifted in a similar direction. The physical reshaping of human settlement in the countryside that took place alongside these changes is apparent from the archaeology. Right across western Europe, Roman *villas*, even where they had survived the disruption of the fifth century, fell into disuse by the seventh.[28] North of the Alps, the vast majority of excavated rural settlements seem to have originated between the third and seventh centuries and continued developing into the Carolingian period, and often beyond. The archaeological record suggests, in other words, the emergence of a wholly new social order in the countryside in the late- and post-Roman eras. In many areas we cannot detect marked social differentiation between settlements, or indeed hard and fast status distinctions within settlements. In northern Gaul, for example, there are new forms of rural settlement and new building types in wood which suggest that groups of perhaps half a dozen households of roughly equal status were sharing the space.[29] In southern Gaul, Catalonia and parts of Italy, around the shores of the western Mediterranean, different patterns of change are evident. Roman *villas* persisted into the sixth century, some evolving into more modest centres of agrarian management. Elsewhere, new centres emerge in the settlement hierarchy: fortified centres on hilltops in both southern Gaul and Italy, for example. But most rural settlement in the western Mediterranean remained small-scale and relatively dispersed at the beginning of the Carolingian period, with village structures growing relatively slowly and late.[30]

[28] G. Ripoll and J. Arce, 'The transformation and end of Roman *villae* in the west (fourth–seventh centuries): problems and perspectives', in G. P. Brogiolo, N. Gautier and N. Christie (eds.), *Towns and their Territories from Late Antiquity to the Early Middle Ages* (Leiden, 2000), pp. 63–114; T. Lewit, '"Vanishing villas": what happened to elite rural habitation in the west in the fifth–sixth centuries?', *Journal of Roman Archaeology* 16 (2003), pp. 26–74; N. Christie (ed.), *Landscapes of Change: Rural Evolution in Late Antiquity* (Aldershot, 2004).

[29] P. Périn, 'The origins of the village in early medieval Gaul', in Christie (ed.), *Landscapes of Change*, pp. 255–78; Halsall, *Settlement and Social Organisation*.

[30] R. Francovich and R. Hodges, *Villa to Village* (London, 2003); Wickham, *Framing the Early Middle Ages*, pp. 481–95; Costambeys, 'Settlement, taxation and the

Excavated sites exhibit a number of important common characteristics that span the entire early medieval period across western
Europe. First and foremost was the almost complete dominance of
building in wood, other than for high-status structures like churches –
not for nothing was the scapegoated man at Kempten accused of
arson. There were two basic types of wooden structure. The larger
was a rectangular building, characteristically around 10–15 metres
long, supported by rows of wooden posts – these 'halls' were the
living-place for a household. Auxiliary buildings around them took
the form of smaller post-based structures built over a shallow pit, the
so-called *Grübenhaus, fonds de cabane* or 'sunken featured building'.[31]
These patterns reflect the social makeup of households based around
a marital couple and their immediate dependants, each holding its
own property. The alleged troublemaker at Kempten, for example,
lived in a household with his wife and children, separately from his
other kin in the *villa*, and tended and harvested his own fields even
when he was driven out to live in the mark. On many sites there
are clear indications of internal boundaries – fences and the like –
dividing rectangular 'halls' and their appendages from each other.
Narrative sources, legal evidence, and by the Carolingian period
charters, provide clear evidence that these internal boundaries were
widely understood as delimitations of private property: as is clear from
their role in bounding private and public space in the Kempten story,
fences and doorways were culturally significant locations as the points
at which household intersected with community. At Kootwijk in the
modern Netherlands, indeed, a fence neatly bisected one such plot,
marking out an area in which a second rectangular 'hall' and ancillary
structures were built, providing concrete evidence that property was
subdivided in the way indicated by charters and polyptychs.[32]

Such subdividing reflects the relative ease of erecting new wooden
structures, and this also made it possible for village topography to
respond to shifts in community life-cycles. As individuals reached

condition of the peasantry'; F. L. Cheyette, 'The disappearance of the ancient
landscape and the climatic anomaly of the early Middle Ages: a question to be
pursued', *EME* 16 (2008), pp. 127–65.

[31] The best archaeological discussion is H. Hamerow, *Early Medieval Settlements: the
Archaeology of Rural Communities in North-West Europe, 400–900* (Oxford, 2002),
pp. 12–50.

[32] Hamerow, *Early Medieval Settlements*, pp. 52–99; H. A. Heidinga, *Medieval Settlement and Economy North of the Lower Rhine* (Assen, 1987).

maturity, married and started households of their own, prospered or failed, inherited, and eventually died, the relative standing of the households within a village inevitably altered. New building was one way in which family and community could come to terms with the changing distribution of resources and social status. Perhaps related to this necessity of periodic rebuilding was the phenomenon of 'shifting settlement'. This is a particular characteristic of the very earliest, pre-Carolingian, early medieval centuries, and is best attested beyond the former Roman frontier in northern Germany and Scandinavia, where slightly different settlement forms and house types prevailed. The shape of many villages was determined by local topography as they strung along river terraces or beside roads, and as old buildings were abandoned and new constructed the central occupied zone of such villages might slowly – almost imperceptibly – move. One excavated settlement on the outskirts of modern Speyer, for example, worked its way half a kilometre along a terrace beside the Rhine between the fifth and ninth centuries.[33]

The sometimes scattered nature and shifting focus of settlements within a defined area should not be confused with nomadism, an economic strategy built round constant movement to tend herds, which was wholly alien to early medieval Europe west of the Carpathians.[34] Movements of a settlement 'core' within a wider area did, however, reflect a crucial characteristic of the early medieval rural economy: the relatively diverse and unspecialised economic strategies pursued by peasant households. The disappearance of the infrastructure of the Roman state dramatically changed the terms of aristocratic control in the countryside and relieved the pressures on peasant cultivators.[35] This is why skeletal data show the early medieval countryside populated by smaller livestock than had been the case in Roman times. This was not a simple matter of biological or technological regression. The impetus for economic specialisation, which encouraged

---

[33] H. Bernhard, 'Die frühmittelalterliche Siedlung von Speyer "Vogelgesang"', *Offa* 39 (1982), pp. 217–33.

[34] For this point and what follows see C. Wickham, 'Pastoralism and underdevelopment in the early middle ages', *Settimane di Studio del Centro italiano di studi sull'alto medioevo* 31 (Spoleto, 1983), pp. 401–55, repr. in Wickham, *Land and Power*, pp. 121–54.

[35] For a sense of just how fundamentally fiscal demands as mediated by landlords and local elites structured the Roman countryside, see T. Lewit, *Agricultural Production in the Roman Economy AD 200–400*, British Archaeological Reports International Series 568 (Oxford, 1991); J. Banaji, *Agrarian Change in Late Antiquity* (Oxford, 2001).

intensive stockbreeding of the type that had produced huge girths for specific purposes, was gone, and the use of livestock for agricultural work as well as for dairying and eventually slaughter made far more sense. Whereas in the Roman period agriculture often involved intensive concentration on a handful of crops ultimately destined for the tables of landlords or for sale at market to meet tax and rent demands, the early Middle Ages saw a diversification that altered the rural landscape. The margins of cultivation, waste and woods which might be used as pasture, hunting reserve or source of building materials increased in their importance.[36] In other words, as the pressures of intensified production abated in the immediately post-Roman period, cultivators adopted new strategies which involved a different relationship with the landscape, a relationship which began to change again from the seventh and eighth centuries as the impetus for intensification once again began.[37] The mark – the less densely exploited area on the margins of a settlement – thus stood in an economically symbiotic relationship with the houses and fields of the settlement core. Nonetheless, culturally and socially, the mark lay outside the sphere of normal public action and the collective gaze of the community, and so could serve as a wild and uncultivated 'other' against which the normal structure of village society defined itself. Just as Frankish writers could use the frozen north with its monstrous half-human, half-animal inhabitants to affirm the humanity of 'home' society, so for Frankish peasants (like the conflict-torn inhabitants of Kempten) the mark was the place to which to drive trouble-makers whose behaviour could be explained only by demonic possession.

The mobility of settlements remains a little-understood phenomenon. But, though it probably does mean that some villages had not yet acquired a permanent territorial focus, perhaps the most marked feature of Carolingian and post-Carolingian rural settlement

---

[36] Wickham, 'Pastoralism and underdevelopment'; C. Wickham, 'European forests in the early middle ages: landscape and land clearance', *Settimane di Studio del Centro italiano di studi sull'alto medioevo* 37 (Spoleto, 1989), pp. 479–548, repr. in Wickham, *Land and Power*, pp. 155–99. For skeletal data on livestock see B. Ward-Perkins, *The Fall of Rome and the End of Civilisation* (Oxford, 2005) p. 145, using it as evidence for 'decline'; cf. Hamerow, *Early Medieval Settlements*, pp. 146–7.

[37] M. Whittow, 'Decline and fall? Studying long term change in the east', in W. Bowden and L. Lavan (eds.), *Theory and Practice in Late Antique Archaeology* (Leiden, 2004), pp. 404–23; T. Lewit, 'Pigs, presses and pastoralism: farming in the fifth to seventh centuries', *EME* 17 (2009), pp. 77–91; R. Faith, 'Forces and relations of production in early medieval England', *Journal of Agrarian Change* 9 (2009), pp. 23–41.

was an increased stabilisation and nucleation of sites.[38] Even in Italy, where our data is much patchier, the concentration of peasant habitation into what we would recognise as villages (traditionally thought of as a post-Carolingian development) seems to begin in the late sixth and seventh centuries.[39] The crucial factor in this seems to have been the emergence of a static focal point (often a cemetery and church) around which habitation clustered. At Dommeln in the Netherlands, for example, a number of loosely related farmsteads and two- and three-household hamlets were replaced in the eighth century by a concentrated village with a clear internal hierarchy.[40] At a similar date at Mondeville in Normandy, the creation of a series of wooden structures in the cemetery – at first, 'grave-houses' over a single burial or group of burials – was followed by the building of a chapel associated with the cemetery and the stabilisation of the settlement.[41] Similar examples are known from Bavaria.[42] The building of churches in stone, increasingly common from the Carolingian period, created immovable focal points which helped to fix village identities not just physically, but also in the minds of their inhabitants. Churches and cemeteries were public spaces where meetings were held and legal actions took place, and where acts of community such as wakes for the dead were held.[43] The significance of this

---

[38] Hamerow, *Early Medieval Settlements*, pp. 52–124, and for a regional survey Halsall, *Settlement and Social Organisation*.

[39] R. Francovich, 'The beginnings of hilltop villages in early medieval Tuscany', in Davis and McCormick (eds.), *The Long Morning of Medieval Europe*, pp. 55–82; R. Francovich, 'Changing structures of settlement', in C. La Rocca (ed.), *Italy in the Early Middle Ages* (Oxford, 2002), pp. 144–67.

[40] F. Theuws, 'Landed property and manorial organisation in northern Austrasia: some considerations and a case study', in F. Theuws and N. Roymans (eds.), *Images of the Past. Studies on Ancient Societies in Northwestern Europe* (Amsterdam, 1991), pp. 299–407; Heidinga, *Medieval Settlement and Economy*.

[41] C. Lorren, 'Le Village de Saint-Martin de Mondeville de l'antiquité au haut moyen âge', in H. Atsma (ed.), *La Neustrie. Le Pays au nord de la Loire de 650 à 850*, Beihefte der Francia 16, 2 vols. (Sigmaringen, 1989), II, pp. 439–66.

[42] I. Stork, 'Zum Fortgang der Untersuchungen im frühmittelalterlichen Gräberfeld, Adelshof und Hofgrablege bei Lauchheim, Ostalbkreis', *Archäologische Ausgrabungen in Baden-Württemberg 1992*, pp. 231–9; F. Damminger, 'Dwellings, settlements and settlement patterns in Merovingian southwestern Germany and adjacent areas', in I. Wood (ed.), *Franks and Alamanni in the Merovingian Period* (Woodbridge, 1998), pp. 33–106; H. Dannheimer, 'Die frühmittelalterliche Siedlung bei Kirchheim', *Germania* 51 (1973), pp. 152–69.

[43] See M. Lauwers, 'Le Cimetière dans le Moyen Âge latin: Lieu sacré, saint et religieux', *Annales HSS* 54 (1999), pp. 1047–72, and pp. 110–11 above.

public space is also shown by its role in the playing out of conflict: Archbishop Hraban of Mainz, for example, had to deal with the disruption to sacred order caused when long-running feuds boiled over and led to bloody killings in that most public of places, the village church; while his friend Einhard dealt with a succession of convicted poachers, feuding peasants and eloping couples who came to the boundaries of his church at Michelstadt.[44] Whether such places acted as sites of consensus or conflict, these developments testify to the gradual coalescing of village society during the Carolingian age.

The stabilisation of rural settlement coincided with significant economic changes. There is clear archaeological evidence for more intensive arable exploitation and an increase in economic specialisation in the Carolingian period. Skeletal data suggest that livestock, whilst not matching the size of their Roman ancestors, were stock bred to a larger size than in Merovingian times, whilst faunal remains show a greater concentration on large-scale cereal cropping. There is also some evidence for expanded craft production: on the Rhine terrace near Speyer, for example, there were spinning and weaving workshops of a kind associated with 'women's work' in the written sources.[45] All of this implies a raised level of social organisation and a shift back towards the intensification of settlement and production that distinguishes the eighth and ninth centuries from the sixth and seventh. It also led to important shifts in the relationship between the settled 'core' of a territory and its immediate environment.[46]

LANDOWNING AND LANDOWNERS

To understand the dynamics behind these changes, we need to examine the effects of aristocratic and royal power at the level of the village. Here we can turn to the charter evidence, which survives in increasing quantities from the eighth and ninth centuries because monastic foundations were acquiring property and documenting their holdings

---

[44] Hrabanus Maurus, *Epistolae*, ed. E. Dümmler, *MGH Epp.* v (Berlin, 1898–9), pp. 380–533; Einhard, *Epistolae*, ed. K Hampe, *MGH Epp.* v (*Epp. Karolini aevi* III) (Berlin, 1898–9), pp. 105–42; nos. 16, 18, 25.

[45] Hamerow, *Early Medieval Settlements*, esp. pp. 125–90; Bernhard, 'Die frühmittelalterliche Siedlung'.

[46] C. Sonnlechner, 'The establishment of new units of production in Carolingian times: making early medieval sources relevant for environmental history', *Viator* 35 (2004), pp. 21–58.

on an unprecedented scale, meaning we have data-bases of dozens –
sometimes hundreds – of charters for village societies from Bavaria to
Brittany.[47] Although what they reveal varies from region to region
because of differences in social custom, landscape and aristocratic
power, they share a number of common characteristics. The basic
units of agrarian exploitation and property ownership were small and
fragmented: the property dealt with in the charter evidence typically
consisted of individual fields, plots, or occasionally farmsteads. Carefully used, the charter evidence reveals a social hierarchy with no
sharp or sudden discontinuities of status, in which small landowners
might scrape together a living from a handful of plots. The brothers
Ripwin and Giselhelm, for example, whose careers can be traced
in the late-eighth-century charters from Lorsch (a monastery in the
middle Rhine valley), owned around half a dozen such parcels. Most
of these holdings lay in the village of Bensheim, where the brothers often served as witnesses for their neighbours' transactions, and
where they had invested in clearing woodland to bring it under the
plough, but they also had individual plots in three other villages all
within a day's travel, in a pattern that is absolutely typical.[48]

The rich cache of charter evidence that documents Ripwin
and Giselhelm's careers allows us to see them as middling owner-
cultivators. The pair had poorer neighbours who owned only a couple of plots, and could not afford to make clearances, and richer
contacts who owned a dozen or more land parcels, some of them
farmed by unfree dependants. But within this broadly based and
inevitably unequal landowning class we do not find any landowners
distinguishing themselves from their peers with labels of social distinction or claims of legal privilege of the kind that structured late
Roman and high medieval society: the public office of count is the
only such distinction consistently advertised by charter scribes, and
was open only to a handful able to access and acquire royal patronage. This absence of overt status divisions within the landowning
class differentiates the early medieval centuries from the Roman and
high medieval worlds, and also from contemporary states elsewhere

---

[47] The pioneering case study was W. Davies, *Small Worlds: The Village Community
in Early Medieval Brittany* (London, 1988). See now C. Wickham, 'Rural society
in Carolingian Europe', in *NCMH* II, pp. 431–50; Wickham, *Framing the Early
Middle Ages*, esp. pp. 388–406.
[48] For this pair see Innes, *State and Society*, pp. 108, 147–52.

in Eurasia, where broader distinctions between producers and consumers of rent and tax are far clearer. In the absence of formal criteria of rank, tiny variations on the sliding scale of status within the community of landowners were revealed by precedence in public meetings, as reflected in the witness lists of charters. The modest status of Ripwin and Giselhelm is thus reflected by their regular appearances in witness lists; but the fact that they were not listed in prominent positions, and that they were frequently associated with a small group of higher-status individuals, points to the significance of patronage relationships within the community.

Even for those further up the social hierarchy than Ripwin and Giselhelm, landholding was made up of agglomerations of these small parcels interleaved with their neighbours' holdings. Among the outlying plots held by the brothers was one across the Rhine from their home in Bensheim, in the village of Dienheim. Dienheim was an important regional centre where several major churches had extensive interests; Ripwin and Giselhelm's entry into the patronage networks which centred on such places, clear from Ripwin's purchase of a horse in order to perform military service (a badge of high status, as we saw in earlier chapters), explains their interests here. Count Rupert, a member of the most powerful aristocratic family of the region, can be seen in our evidence levying tolls and sitting in judgement at Dienheim, his official role reinforced by dense networks of patronage evident in over a hundred charters from the years either side of 800. His family holdings here, however, essentially consisted of vineyards and plots little different from those held by Ripwin and Giselhelm, and although we have clear evidence of the scale of his family's wealth (a far-flung scattering of interests from Hesse and the Moselle valley down to the upper Rhine), there are only a handful of locations where more elaborate complexes can be seen. Even very important landowners like Rupert, then, built their influence on control of numerous units of a familiar type, without their being amalgamated into a different form of estate or landownership.[49] Whilst the archaeological and documentary evidence shows increasing concentration of aristocratic wealth in our period, distinguishing it from the immediately post-Roman centuries when landlord domination of peasants was relatively weak, this did not overturn the basic character of early medieval settlement and society.

[49] Innes, *State and Society*, pp. 61–5 and *passim*.

Charters can also tell us something about how land changed hands. Ecclesiastical archives sometimes preserve dossiers of title deeds handed over by early donors, from which we can get a sense of the frequency and nature of land exchanges. The hundreds of ninth- and tenth-century secular documents which existed in the Cluny archive in early modern times, when they were copied by antiquarians, consist of the fossilised remnants of dozens of such dossiers, typically consisting of bundles of between half a dozen and a dozen related documents, often annotated or physically connected to one another. Around half of these documents concern land sales, roughly evenly split between sales between kin and between neighbours, whilst written dowry agreements were also common.[50] In such material we find not a discrete and defined family plot held in trust by each generation in turn, but land parcels of varying sizes, from farms to fields to tiny plots, some clustered and some scattered, and normally held by an individual. In at least some cases, the transmission and division of property rights must have been affected by relationships within a kin-group as marriage, birth and death changed the demands and size of its constituent parts, and so the language of individual property described the distribution of resources within a family or a household. Certainly individuals transferring land beyond their immediate kin, for example by making a pious gift to the Church for the good of their souls, typically went out of their way to have their kin record their consent to the transaction (a practice endorsed in royal legislation), while a significant number of surviving land-disputes were brought by disinherited kin contesting a relative's decision to donate land. The donations to the west Frankish monastery of Fleury made in the will of the aristocrat Eccard of Mâcon, for example, were contested by kin who after his death seized the land in question 'as if it were inheritance'.[51] In other words, despite the fact that land was understood as individual property, and

---

[50] M. Innes, 'On the material culture of legal documents: charters and their preservation in the Cluny archive (9th–11th centuries)', in Brown, *et al.* (eds.), *Documentary Culture*. This kind of evidence is most common south of the Alps and Pyrenees: see e.g. A. Kosto, 'Laymen, clerics and documentary practices in the early middle ages: the example of Catalonia', *Speculum* 80 (2005), pp. 44–74; S. Gasparri and C. La Rocca (eds.), *Carte di famiglia. Strategie, rappresentazione e memoria del gruppo familiare di Totone di Campione, 721–877* (Rome, 2005); L. Feller, A. Gramain and F. Weber, *La Fortune de Karol. Marché de la terre et liens personnels dans les Abruzzes au haut moyen âge*, Collection de l'EFR 347 (Rome, 2005).

[51] M. Prou and A. Vidier (eds.), *Recueil des chartes de l'abbaye de Saint-Benoît-sur-Loire (Fleury)*, 2 vols. (Orleans and Paris, 1900–24), no. 25.

society as an agglomeration of conjugal households, cultural norms and social expectations to some extent limited individual control over property and made it a matter of family trust.

We should acknowledge that there were regional differences in the character of rural society: in Italy, for example, aristocrats were less wealthy than those north of the Alps, but at the same time enjoyed more formalised precedence over those who fell under their influence.[52] Likewise, political heartlands like the Moselle and Rhine valleys should be distinguished from 'peripheral' areas like Alemannia, Bavaria or Burgundy, which were dominated by regional aristocracies rather than the distant but powerful cliques of the court and so had a shallower social hierarchy. The Paris basin, as we shall see, was home to unusual forms of landholding that provide a notable exception to the norm. But even in royal heartlands like the middle Rhine valley, where the wooden halls of middling owner–cultivators like Ripwin and Giselhem were loomed over by monumental stone palaces and by the inherited interests of leading aristocratic families, and where, if anywhere, we would expect to find concentrations of wealth and formalised social hierarchies, landholding remained fragmented and social status a matter of subtle gradations among the community of free landowners.

That said, quantitative differences in the number of holdings did lead to qualitative differences in lifestyle. There is no evidence that Ripwin and Giselhelm possessed a dependent labour force of unfree peasants. As owner–cultivators, they may have engaged in short-term sub-letting, perhaps occasionally buying in labour at harvest time or even working in collaboration with kin and neighbours, but fundamentally they must have relied on their own labour and that of their kin to work their land. Their patron Count Rupert, on the other hand, dealt with peasant families who were an integral part of his landed properties. Peasant families like this, who worked the land-parcels owned by an aristocratic family, were typically unfree in status; free tenants remained rare even at the end of our period, and were in general rarer the further one travelled from the heartlands of the royal court and the imperial aristocracy in the Paris basin and the valleys of the Meuse, Moselle, Rhine and Po rivers.

[52] C. Wickham, 'Aristocratic power in eighth-century Lombard Italy', in A. C. Murray (ed.), *After Rome's Fall: Narrators and Sources of Early Medieval History* (Toronto, 1998), pp. 153–70; S. Gasparri, 'The aristocracy', in La Rocca (ed.), *Italy in the Early Middle Ages*, pp. 59–84.

But despite the existence of an unfree labour force on the estates of aristocratic families like Rupert's, it would be misleading to talk of a 'slave society' or a 'slave mode of production' in the Carolingian period. To translate the varied and often fuzzy early medieval terminology of unfreedom in terms of our concept of 'slavery' would be to prefer modern ideas and definitions to late antique and early medieval understandings of unfreedom and dependence. Even in the Roman period, the extensive use of slave gangs to exploit large estates – the classic case of a 'slave system' defined in economic terms – was confined to Italy, and in decline after the third century. Nonetheless, legal definitions of personal unfreedom – the possession of one human being by another – continued through late antiquity and into the early Middle Ages, in part because the classical discourse of freedom and slavery fed into the thought world of the early Christian Church.[53] One major problem for historians of early medieval society has been that the supposedly clear division between the legally free and the legally unfree was in practice blurred as varying degrees of subjection acquired their own labels and terminologies. Free and unfree were not absolute categories that related to clearly defined practices or conditions. It therefore makes more sense to think of a continuum of dependencies than a clear-cut divide.[54] For modern historians this continuum creates problems of interpretation, because it does not fit easily into our inherited grand narratives of transition 'from slavery to serfdom'. Faced with such a situation, rather than imposing the straitjacket of totalising categories on the evidence, we need to analyse the texture of rural society in the Carolingian period on its own terms, and try to tease out the complex interactions between legal status, economic function and social standing amongst the peasantry.

COMMUNITY AND MOBILITY

The pattern of scattered small-scale property units had important implications for social structure. Clearly, a lifestyle sustained by this type of landholding presupposed rhythms of residence and movement, vividly described in the ninth-century *Life* of the Saxon

[53] For the continuity of unfreedom in its socio-legal definition, see C. R. Whittaker, 'Circe's pigs: from slavery to serfdom in the Roman world', *Slavery and Abolition* 8 (1987), pp. 88–122 and on the discourse of slavery P. Garnsey, *Ideas of Slavery from Aristotle to Augustine* (Cambridge, 1996).

[54] See Rio, 'Freedom and unfreedom'.

noblewoman Liutberga.[55] Einhard's mocking description of the last Merovingians trundling around on an oxcart, even though they barely had estates to trundle between, implies similar expectations. This peripatetic lifestyle should not be seen as an economic necessity for aristocrats: it was not a case of behaving like the very hungry caterpillar, eating all an estate's resources before moving on to the next stop, since renders of food and livestock could easily be transported or stored. Although we lack the data to trace aristocratic itineraries in detail, the indications are that they were determined, like itinerant kingship, by political factors. Staying at a specific residence for winter, or to enjoy the hunting season, or to celebrate festivals like Lent and Easter, allowed links to be reforged with friends and neighbours, kin and clients. For adult male aristocrats at least, the demands of the king and the cares of office were further complicating factors, necessitating presence at the royal court, or on campaign, or involvement in the transmission of royal orders and the dispensation of royal justice.[56]

Structural mobility, however, was not confined to aristocratic elites: the patterns of landowning we have been investigating meant that it was a crucial aspect of social status at a local level too. Pioneering work on the charter evidence preserved at the monastery of Redon in Brittany, for example, has revealed how local landowners also moved around. While the majority of smallholders are generally encountered only in a single settlement and its immediate neighbours, the local standing of some individuals gave them a greater range, as they regularly appear as witnesses, guarantors or legal experts over a wider area.[57] Mobility of this type demonstrated a certain level of economic resource: it was only possible, after all, for those who were not tied into the daily routine of agricultural cultivation. Carolingian legislation, indeed, regulated the duration and frequency of public meetings so as to prevent smallholders who were summoned to them from suffering hardship.[58] Regular travel over these kinds of distances, moreover, presupposed ownership of horses, which were expensive and were therefore crucial badges of status. Indeed, prominent among the complaints of the inhabitants of Istria against their

---

[55] *Vita Liutbergae* [*Life of Liutberga*], ed. G. H. Pertz, *MGH SS* IV, pp. 158–64, trans. F. S. Paxton, *Anchoress and Abbess in Ninth-Century Saxony: the Lives of Liutbirga of Wendhausen and Hathumoda of Gandersheim* (Washington, DC, 2009).

[56] See below, Chapter 6.   [57] Davies, *Small Worlds*.

[58] For a survey see R. Hennebicque, '"Pauperes" et "paupertas" dans l'occident carolingien aux IXe et Xe siècles', *Revue du Nord* 50 (1968), pp. 167–87.

dux in 804 was that he had summoned them to the host, then taken the horses they had brought, given them to his own men and sent the Istrians home on foot, to the ridicule of their neighbours. In other words, entry onto the public stage of courts and meetings through which local society was organised was theoretically open to all, but in practice regular participation in the public business of the locality, crucial for those who sought to become involved in networks of favour and patronage, required a certain amount of modest wealth.

Possession of a horse was also a prerequisite for the performance of military service, the most significant public due demanded by the king and the most prestigious service one might perform on behalf of one's community. Military service was determined by precisely the bonds of patronage and obligation that structured rural society. That it could be viewed as both a duty and a right is clearest from the example of the Lombard kingdom, where the term *arimannus* and its Latin equivalent *exercitalis* (both literally mean 'army-man') denoted a free landowner who had the right to participate in the annual assembly of the army, which was at least as much a political gathering as a prelude to campaigning.[59] In the post-Roman centuries, liability for military service had come to imply not only freedom in law and from certain exactions by the state, but also an appreciable political and social status.[60] The Carolingian wars of expansion in the eighth century presented those who were liable with unprecedented opportunities to enhance their wealth and status on the wartrail, so that military service was both a goal for the socially aspiring, and an important element in patronage relationships.[61] The situation changed in the first decade of the ninth century, when (as we saw in Chapter 4) the end of expansion coincided with a spate of legislation placing the raising of the army in the hands of the royal *missi*.[62] That they were to draw up lists of those liable to serve suggests that participation in war had become less desirable: the opportunities for enrichment were fewer, and had given way to the needs of defence and consolidation.

---

[59] See S. Gasparri, 'Strutture militari e legami di dipendenza in Italia in età longobarda e carolingia', *Rivista storica italiana* 98 (1986), pp. 664–726.

[60] M. Innes, 'Land, freedom and the making of the early medieval west', *TRHS* 16 (2006), pp. 39–73.

[61] Cf. Innes, *State and Society*, pp. 143–53, and Halsall, *Warfare and Society*, pp. 71–110.

[62] See e.g. *Capit.* I, no. 48, cc. 1–2; no. 49, c. 3; no. 50, cc. 1, 9; no. 141, c. 27; Reuter, 'End of Carolingian military expansion'. See also above, Chapter 4, p. 170.

But while *ad hoc* patronage networks were therefore less reliable recruiters than they had been in the age of expansion, the obligation to participate continued to be based on generalised notions of a man's status and obligations, rather than on any direct relationship between service and landholding. The 'vassal' who held land in return for military service – an important prop in the traditional construction of 'feudalism' – is nowhere to be found in the Carolingian world.[63]

The central fact of the Carolingian countryside was thus the complex interaction between the steepening of the social hierarchy, leading to longer and more formal ties of patronage, on the one hand; and on the other a continued understanding of Frankish society as based on the community of free landowners acting collectively. Tensions between these two models surfaced in royal legislation, which was ostentatiously concerned with protection of the free poor whilst simultaneously attempting to formalise aristocratic power in terms of public office.[64] It is thus hardly surprising that it is from the Carolingian period that we also have the fullest attempts to formalise the public obligations of free landowners, for example the responsibility of all to fight in defence of their country (*patria*), first explicitly stated in ninth-century capitularies.[65] At the same time as their military obligations were more closely defined, peasants who armed themselves outside approved structures of authority were increasingly seen as acting illegitimately. In 859 when the 'common folk' between the Seine and Loire formed a sworn association (*coniuratio*) which 'stoutly resisted' the Vikings, the author of the *Annals of St Bertin* recorded the actions of their aristocratic overlords – who effortlessly (*facile*) butchered what was seen as an illegal and subversive association – with unhesitating approval.[66] What was at stake here and in similar cases was not the letter of the law, but the sometimes competing ways in which different social classes (the aristocracy and the wider free) defined their identities. Those who had organised themselves to fight the Vikings may have seen themselves as doing nothing other than defending the *patria* as stipulated by the law; but to the 'more powerful people' who killed them, their self-organisation was an affront

---

[63] See Susan Reynolds, *Fiefs and Vassals: the Medieval Evidence Reconsidered* (Oxford, 1996).

[64] See above, Chapter 4, pp. 182–93.

[65] See Reuter, 'End of Carolingian military expansion'.

[66] *AB, s.a.* 859. Innes, 'Economies and societies', pp. 27–9, comments on legitimate and illegitimate violence.

to a growing sense of social superiority which was endorsed by the ruling dynasty and which was partly expressed in terms of the right to bear arms and to participate in warfare.[67]

The picture sketched so far, of scattered and small-scale property interests, gradual but steepening social distinctions and considerable geographical mobility, contrasts with a received image of medieval communities as cohesive, inward-looking and tied together by common interests and kinship.[68] This image is simply incompatible with the patterns of public action revealed by our charters. The public meetings at which property transfers were enacted or disputes resolved were not 'village meetings'. Frequently, they took place in the same village as the property concerned, but where our charter evidence is dense enough we can discern public activity clustering around important regional sites which were also markets or administrative centres, and where high-status individuals were likely to be present: in Ripwin and Giselhelm's case, we have already seen their being pulled towards Dienheim, which was just such a centre. And although smallholders might be found witnessing transactions in their own villages more than elsewhere, their names typically appear associated with those of higher-status landowners who witnessed in several places. Moreover, although the Carolingian countryside was divided into a series of geographical units called *pagi* (singular: *pagus*), which had evolved from Roman administrative divisions and had clear territorial boundaries, the patterns of sociability and public action so visible in the charters do not correspond neatly to these units, nor to any visible subdivisions. Public activity which transcended the village was absolutely central to the social life of the Carolingian countryside: village affairs were not closed, but tied into the business of a wider locality. The 'culture of the public',

---

[67] See also below, Chapter 6.

[68] For the genesis and legacy of models of the unchanging village community see J. Burrow, 'The "village community" and the uses of history in late nineteenth-century England', in N. McKendrick (ed.), *Historical Perspectives: Studies in English Thought and Society in Honour of Sir J H Plumb* (Cambridge, 1974), pp. 255–84; R. Smith, 'Modernisation and the corporate village community: some sceptical reflections', in A. Baker and D. Gregory (eds.), *Explorations in Historical Geography* (Cambridge, 1984), pp. 140–79; S. Reynolds, *Kingdoms and Communities in Western Europe, 900–1300* (Oxford, 1997). For similar issues in a different historiographical tradition, F. Staab, 'A reconsideration of the ancestry of modern political liberty: the problem of the so-called King's Freemen (*Königsfreie*)', *Viator* 11 (1980), pp. 51–70.

which was a crucial legacy of Carolingian society from the Roman and post-Roman centuries, was defined by and tied up with these patterns of interaction, rather more than with the 'state' as a formal institution.[69]

None of this means that villages did not matter as formal structures: as we have seen, they (and not the *pagi*) were the basic units of society, in which fields and houses were located, to which demons and dogs belonged, and with which resident landowners were identified. Identification with a particular village emerges most clearly in our sources where we see villagers acting together, such as when collective testimony was needed on some matter of local knowledge, or where the village's boundaries needed defining. The increasing demands of king and God at a local level in the Carolingian period, indeed, encouraged these collectively expressed identities. The levying of tithe and the performance of 'public services' by the free population were organised on a village-by-village basis; similarly court cases show obligations towards landlords and rulers being resisted through such collective identities.[70] This indicates that we can see the village as the most basic of a series of interlocking tiers of public action. But just because villagers saw themselves as a community in some contexts, they did not always present a united front or act in the interests of all. At Kempten, as we saw, conflict and petty jealousies threatened to spiral out of control when one man and his wife were driven out of their home in the village core and forced to live in the fields. They had kin in the village, but these were afraid to take the scapegoated couple into their households because of the anger of the community as a whole and the family's need to continue social intercourse with their neighbours. This story shows how our ideas about social consensus, community identity and kin loyalty are ideals which in practice were compromised by circumstance and which were often in competition with each other. Kinship was a compelling bond so far as it overlapped with interests in property, but when the harvest had to be gathered and stored, it was no match for the urgent demands of community. And community, as the couple cast into

---

[69] For the 'culture of the public' see Wickham, *Inheritance of Rome*, esp. Chapter 23; for its definition in our centuries see Innes, *State and Society*, pp. 94–111; Innes, 'Dossiers and archives'.

[70] See e.g. Innes, *State and Society*, pp. 94–140, and for legal resistance Nelson, 'Dispute settlement'.

the fields beyond Kempten and their family inside the village could surely remind us were we able to ask them, can also be a euphemism for a small world of suspicion, discord and oppression.

LANDLORDS AND MANORS

Scattered smallholdings remained the dominant form of landholding right through our period, even for aristocrats. Nonetheless, in the course of the eighth and ninth centuries a new form of organisation becomes evident in the countryside: the manor. Sometimes termed 'bipartite estates', manors rested on a twofold division of the land: most was divided into individual plots of a familiar type, from which dependent peasant households supported themselves in return for rent, but a central area was set aside, its produce directly bound for the landlord. This 'demesne' or reserve was worked by the dependent peasantry, who performed fixed labour services or corvées (such as working in the lord's field a certain number of days a week, or performing other 'higher status' duties such as transporting goods, running errands or meeting public obligations on his behalf). The spread of this system on royal and ecclesiastical land is documented in the polyptychs – written documents (of which over two dozen survive from the ninth century) recording in minute detail the rent and service owed by peasants on ecclesiastical and royal estates.

The origin of the polyptychs is intimately tied up with the origins of this more intensive system of rural exploitation as a whole. Polyptychs, as records of estate management, help us trace the emergence of manorial organisation on royal land in the heartlands of the Merovingian kingdom in the Paris basin in the seventh century, and its slow export in the eighth and ninth as an aspect of the political and social expansion of the Frankish world under the Carolingians.[71] But in origin they are linked to the activities of rulers, and in reading them we have to remind ourselves that the distinction between public obligations and private estate management was far from clear

---

[71] See e.g. Devroey, *Puissants et misérables*; A. Verhulst, *The Carolingian Economy* (Cambridge, 2002); A. Verhulst, *Rural and Urban Aspects of Early Medieval Northwest Europe* (Aldershot, 1992); J.-P. Devroey, *Études sur le grand domaine carolingien* (Aldershot, 1993); Y. Morimoto, *Études sur l'économie rurale du haut moyen âge: historiographie, régime domanial, polyptyques carolingiens* (Paris, 2008).

cut, not least as the polyptychs recorded practice on royal and ecclesiastical domains which were political creations, and were treated by
the Carolingians as state resources.[72]

The term 'polyptych' was used to refer to lists of dues and obligations owed to the state in the Roman and immediately post-Roman
periods. A series of documents from the sixth and seventh centuries,
dealing with payments made to bishops, reveals the complex evolution that had taken place by the Carolingian era.[73] While landlords
had always played a central role in collecting such dues from the
peasantry before passing them on to the state, royal grants of immunity received by great churches turned them into islands of fiscal and
jurisdictional independence and allowed them to hold on to these
revenues in return for other services to the king and kingdom.[74]
Documentary practices once associated with public tax collection
thus survived through the seventh century, when actual royal tax
collection disappeared, on the estates of large churches and other
privileged landowners. The likely existence of a continuous documentary tradition connecting Roman practices of land-registration
and tax-assessment to the Carolingian polyptychs does not, therefore,
mean that the two forms of documentation had identical functions.
Indeed, the polyptychs' detailed surveying of agricultural resources,
household by household, and their recording of the specific rents
and services owed by dependent peasants to a landowner, would
have had no place in the tax-lists documenting dues to Roman
rulers and their immediate barbarian successors. By the same token,
the compilers of these Carolingian surveys detailed the public dues
and services owed by the dependent peasantry simply because such
demands were by now thoroughly integrated into practices of estate
management, often as fossilised custom.

[72] For a reading of the polyptychs that sees them too unproblematically as evidence
for the direct continuity into the early Middle Ages of some of the apparatus
of Roman government see J. Durliat, *Les Finances publiques de Dioclétien aux
Carolingiens (284–889)*. Beihefte der Francia 21 (Sigmaringen, 1990); but note the
convincing criticisms of C. Wickham, 'The fall of Rome will not take place', in
Little and Rosenwein (eds.), *Debating the Middle Ages*, pp. 45–57.
[73] W. Goffart, 'Merovingian polyptychs: reflections on two recent publications',
Francia 9 (1982), pp. 55–77, esp. pp. 65–8; repr. in W. Goffart, *Rome's Fall and After*
(London, 1989), pp. 233–53; S. Sato, 'The Merovingian accounting documents
of Tours: form and function', *EME* 9/2 (2003), pp. 143–61.
[74] On immunities, see Fouracre, 'Eternal light'; Rosenwein, *Negotiating Space*.

From the time of Pippin III on, as the Carolingians sought to utilise 'excess' church land, estate surveys of a fairly rudimentary type, listing the extent of ecclesiastical holdings, were compiled. It was on these practices that the Carolingian court drew when, in the years around 800, it began to insist on the systematic surveying of royal estates so as to ensure that they were exploited to their maximum potential; this example was subsequently adopted by the great churches of the empire as they sought to meet their dues to God and king. The distribution of the surviving polyptychs – all ninth century or later, all documenting royal or major ecclesiastical estates – is thus scarcely an accident. The production of polyptychs was a response to royal initiatives, and polpytychs closely followed templates promoted by the court, for example in *De villis* ('Concerning estates'), a capitulary outlining the duties of the steward of a model royal estate, and the closely related *Brevium exempla* ('Brief examples'), which consisted of actual surveys of specific estates produced to demonstrate the application of the template in practice.[75] As *De villis* made clear, this surveying activity was designed to ensure that estate-stewards operated with the interests of their royal masters in mind; its rapid application to ecclesiastical estates, again encouraged by the court, underlines the extent to which church land was understood as a public resource whose proper use was a responsibility of kings as well as the churchmen who administered it.

The manors which dominated the polyptychs of major churches such as the abbeys of St-Germain-des-Prés or Prüm rested on two central developments: the creation of a 'home farm' or demesne for the lord, and the imposition of corvées on the dependent peasantry to cultivate this reserve. Neither can be seen as standing in direct continuity with Roman forms of estate management.[76] The emergence in the seventh-century Paris basin of these new forms of estate on the lands of the Merovingian kings and their favoured churches should thus be seen as a conscious initiative, undertaken to support a new

---

[75] *Capitulare de villis*, Capit. I, no. 32, pp. 82–91; *Brevium exempla*, Capit. I, no. 128, pp. 250–6; both trans. Loyn and Percival, *Reign of Charlemagne*, pp. 65–73 and 98–105 respectively. W. Metz, *Das Karolingische Reichsgut* (Berlin, 1960) remains the fundamental analysis of this material; see now McKitterick, *Charlemagne: The Formation of a European Identity*, pp. 149–54.

[76] Cf. Banaji, 'Aristocracies, peasantries', and P. Sarris, 'The origins of the manorial economy: new insights from Late Antiquity', *EHR* 119 (2004), pp. 279–311.

political system centred for the first time on a single, sedentary, court establishment. It was an initiative which was possible only because its authors enjoyed political control and could lay claim to public rights inherited from the late Roman state, in particular to force the peasantry to labour on public works, and the title to large blocks of land from which demesnes could be created. A product of specific circumstances, this form of organisation was therefore neither natural nor 'normal'. The subsequent spread of the system from the Paris basin to a few other political heartlands, primarily in the north-east of the Frankish world, was likewise a reflection of expanding royal power under the Carolingians.

The generally fragmented patterns of landholding we have been discussing meant that the combination of factors necessary for the creation of manorial estates was difficult to realise, which explains why they did not become widespread very quickly. The investment of considerable resources in the clearance of wood or uncultivated land on a substantial scale was often necessary to create the discrete blocks of uninterrupted property necessary for manorialisation. Here, king and Church enjoyed a key strategic advantage, in that land of this kind – not only wooded land – was defined legally as *forestum* (forest), title to which lay ultimately in the hands of the king; and vast swathes of forest were subsequently granted to favoured churches under the Carolingians. These fairly abstract rights over large tracts of land might be transformed into manorial 'new build', particularly by churches which as large-scale institutional landowners had the resources to support the necessary investment, but also by the top tier of aristocratic families. A trend towards the foundation of separate aristocratic residences, centred on a hall or a church-and-hall complex and often distant from the hustle and bustle of village life, is visible in both archaeological and documentary sources of the seventh and eighth centuries, and encouraged the creation of discrete complexes of family property: it is typically at such sites that manorial structures are most clearly visible on aristocratic land.[77] Remarkable excavations in an area where we have good charter evidence have helped us see just such a process in the Dommeln region of the modern Netherlands. Here, in the first half of the eighth century, local elites aligning themselves with Charles Martel were able to transform

---

[77] On aristocratic residences see also below, Chapter 6.

the landscape through the systematic creation of new estate centres on cleared lands.[78]

The impact of these changes on peasant society remains little understood, partly because, as we saw at the beginning of this chapter, debate about Carolingian society has been conducted with reference to the serfdom of the twelfth century, and has therefore been overly concerned with whether or not manors hastened the transition from free to unfree by blurring the line between one and the other.[79] But as we have already noted, these categories were never as clear-cut as is sometimes made out. In fact, we cannot assume that manorialisation significantly altered the texture of peasant society. The Prüm polyptych, for example, contains clear indications of regional or local customs: horizontal bonds of community among the peasantry were arguably as important as monastic lordship in shaping the manorial economy and society here.[80] In the rare documents that allow a glimpse of the peasantry on manorial estates, we see familiar structures of local testimony and public meetings being deployed to process co-operation and competition within the community. For example, in the case of the scapegoated man at Kempten the community of tenant peasants dealt collectively with allegations of theft and wrongdoing before staging legal and religious rituals (an ordeal of hot iron and an exorcism); similarly, in 857 a complex dispute over possession of land within the immunity of St Martin's at Tours was resolved through a series of public meetings at which the testimony of local 'good men' (*boni homines*) and dependent peasants (*coloni*) was used to decide between conflicting written documents; and around 900 jurors (*scabini*) and a judge drawn from the peasant *familia* of an estate owned by the monastery of Gorze watched two of their fellows undertake the ordeal of hot iron in an attempt to prove that a particular holding was family 'inheritance'

---

[78] See Theuws, 'Landed property'; Costambeys, 'An aristocratic community'.

[79] For useful analysis and a variety of views see H.-W. Goetz, 'Serfdom and the beginnings of a "seigneurial system" in Carolingian Europe', *EME* 2 (1993), pp. 29–51; W. Davies, 'On servile status in the early Middle Ages', in M. Bush (ed.), *Serfdom and Slavery* (London, 1996), pp. 225–46; P. Bonnassie, *From Slavery to Feudalism in Southwest Europe*, trans. J. Birrell (Cambridge, 1991); P. Freedman, *The Origins of Peasant Servitude in Medieval Catalonia* (Cambridge, 1991).

[80] This is the basic thesis of L. Kuchenbuch, *Bäuerliche Gesellschaft und Klosterherrschaft im 9. Jht. Studien zur Sozialstruktur der Familia der Abtei Prüm* (Wiesbaden, 1978).

rather than a part of the abbey's reserve or demesne.[81] Landlords are visible primarily as a possible source of discipline where things were not resolved through these local agencies. Charlemagne's biographer Einhard, for example, intervened in a number of cases where local conflict escalated into violent feud, and the landlord's representative, rather than aggrieved kin, were to exercise rights of vengeance and impose physical punishment.[82] It is probably mistaken, therefore, to draw too strong a contrast between the workings of the 'public courts' used by free landowners and 'private justice' of the great estates. Dependent peasants could, indeed, bring certain cases against their landlords before public courts, especially those that concerned landownership or personal freedom.[83] Free tenants enjoyed access to public courts and meetings, and the prestigious services frequently expected from them – notably military service – placed them side by side with free landowners of good standing in the performance of public dues. On occasion, there are hints at the kind of bonds that could arise: a court case of *c*.820, for example, shows a free landowner called into the royal host entrusting his property to a dependent peasant on a nearby royal estate.[84]

Horizontal links of this kind were common precisely because bonds of association and kinship among the peasantry crossed tenurial boundaries, giving the lie to a view of manorial estates as discrete blocks controlling huge tracts of the countryside. In fact, where we have relatively full transmission of the charter evidence alongside the polyptychs, these estates begin to look much less solid. Estate surveys from Prüm in the Ardennes and Wissembourg in Alsace suggest that some estates – particularly those which rested on large-scale campaigns of clearance in marginal areas such as the Ardennes – were huge contiguous blocks of property, but in the more densely populated and intensively cultivated Moselle and Rhine valleys the abbeys' estates nestled alongside those of other landowners. In the immediate

---

[81] See Nelson, 'Dispute settlement', at pp. 56–9 (and pp. 248–50 for the Latin text); A. d'Herbomez (ed.), *Cartulaire de l'abbaye de Gorze*. Mettensia 2 (Paris, 1898), no. 78 (whose date is probably either 896 or 916).

[82] Einhard, *Epp.* 16, 25, 48. On legislation and lordship see also above, Chapter 4, p. 190.

[83] See for example the run of west Frankish cases discussed by Nelson, 'Dispute settlement', and Innes, 'Dossiers and archives' on the remarkable Perrecy dossier.

[84] *UBMR*, no. 53.

vicinity of the palace of Trebur in the Rhine valley, the rich charter evidence shows no private property or peasant-proprietors, but
beyond this area dependent peasants whose dues are listed in the surviving polyptych lived in villages where there was extensive private
landholding, and were interleaved with free peasant proprietors and
aristocratic estates.[85]

Manors are often seen as the real motors of social and economic
change in the Carolingian countryside. Yet manorialisation was not
an all-encompassing process sweeping all else aside and creating a
new rural landscape, but a strategy that was viable only where the
creation of a significant demesne and the provision of a labour-
force was possible. The presence of manors was the major difference
between the countryside of the seventh and the ninth centuries, but
their distribution was uneven, and they tended to cluster in those
political heartlands where the Carolingian kings and their favoured
churches enjoyed extensive landholdings, and which were also the
homelands to the top tiers of the aristocracy. Geographically and
socially, manors were anything but closed worlds, and their impact
on the economies and societies of the Carolingian world must be
understood in terms of their interaction with existing social forms.

THE PROBLEM OF ECONOMIC GROWTH

All of these issues also play a role in debates about whether the Carolingian period witnessed economic growth or stagnation.[86] Thanks
to the impression of systematic organisation gained from the polyptychs, some historians have seen the manor as a model of economic
efficiency and so a motor of economic development. For their opponents, however, big was not necessarily beautiful: manorial structures
were conservative, shackling rural producers to the demands of landlords and limiting their ability to participate in networks of exchange.

---

[85] See *Das Prümer Urbar*, ed. I. Schwab (Düsseldorf, 1983) with L. Kuchenbuch,
*Bäuerliche Gesellschaft und Klosterherrschaft im 9. Jht. Studien zur Sozialstruktur der
Familia der Abtei Prüm*. Vierteljahrsschrift für Sozial- und Wirtschaftgeschichte
Beihefte 66 (Wiesbaden, 1978); *Liber possessionum Wizenburgensis*, ed. C. Dette
(Mainz, 1987); and for the royal estates around Trebur, M. Gockel, *Karolingische
Königshöfe am Mittelrhein* (Göttingen, 1970).
[86] For a range of views see G. Duby, *Rural Economy and Country Life in the Medieval
West* (Los Angeles, CA, 1968); Fossier, 'Les Tendances de l'économie: stagnation
ou croissance?'; Verhulst, *Carolingian Economy*. See also below, Chapter 7.

But, as is the case with most set-pieces, the contours of this debate may tell us less about historical realities than the ideological and intellectual predilections of modern academics, here working in the last third of the twentieth century when ideological controversy raged over the relative merits of direct economic management by state elites and small-scale private enterprise.

There certainly are clear indications within the polyptychs that the systems of production pursued on the estates of the great churches succeeded not only in meeting the imperatives of generosity imposed on abbatial and episcopal tables by the Carolingian political system, but also in generating significant surpluses that were actively marketed. Careful study of the services demanded from the dependent peasantry on the estates of St Germain and Prüm, for example, has shown a complex system whereby certain privileged groups were required to oversee the transport of local surpluses by boat or cart, some to central points within the abbeys' holdings where it could be redistributed to feed the monks and their guests, but some to major markets for sale.[87] A series of royal privileges allowing the foundation of markets at central points within ecclesiastical estates, climaxing in the middle decades of the ninth century in west Francia and the tenth century in the east, illustrate how the infrastructure created by these systems of redistribution could stimulate exchange.[88] Perhaps more significantly still, the granting of formal privileges to license specialised 'markets' perhaps indicates a step change. We know that before the ninth century there were some seasonal fairs at major centres such as St Denis, which were the visible peaks of 'market-type' activity in a countryside where most exchange remained embedded within wider patterns of social interaction, buying and selling going on at regular public meetings which had a wide range of functions ranging from legal hearings to feasts and hunts. Such a state of affairs is typical of a world in which the economy was not yet understood

---

[87] J.-P. Devroey, 'Les Services de transport à l'abbaye de Prüm au ixe siècle', *Revue du Nord* 61 (1979), pp. 543–69; Devroey, 'Un monastère dans l'économie d'échanges: les services de transport à l'abbaye de St-Germain-des-Prés au ixe siècle', *Annales ESC* 39 (1984), pp. 570–89; both repr. in his *Études sur le grand domaine carolingien*.

[88] F. Hardt-Friedrichs, 'Markt, Münze und Zoll im ostfränkischen Reich bis zum Ende der Ottonen', *Blätter für deutsche Landesgeschichte* 116 (1980), pp. 1–32; W. Bleiber, 'Grundherrschaft und Markt zwischen Loire und Rhein während des 9. Jahrhunderts: Untersuchungen zu ihrem wechselseitigen Verhältnis', *Jahrbuch für Wirtschaftgeschichte* 3 (1982), pp. 105–35.

as a separate sphere of activity with its own rules and processes; and against such a backdrop the creation of recognised and recognisable markets more distinct from the generality of social intercourse constitutes an important shift.[89]

Royal demands also played an important role in this process.[90] Those free peasants who oversaw the transport of surpluses typically had relatively light obligations in respect of corvée labour on the lord's reserve, but were responsible for meeting many of the public obligations owed by their lord to the king, carrying goods or messages at the king's command or taking customary gifts of produce to royal palaces. On the estates of the abbey of Wissembourg, for example, certain groups of free peasants were required to carry stone and building materials for the upkeep of specific royal estates, and it was at these centres that regional markets developed. Systems of redistribution within estates, the need to meet the demands of kings for produce and services from those estates, and the emergence of broader exchange networks were thus thoroughly intertwined.

We will explain all this in more detail in Chapter 7. But for now it is important to underline that these developments were not the result of a conscious economic policy aimed at encouraging exchange: the primary aim of ecclesiastical and royal estate-management was the creation of a stable and predictable flow of goods and rent, not at what we would recognise as economic growth. Indeed, the economics of ecclesiastical and royal estates may have been far less centralised than is implied by the polyptychs and capitularies, with real agency resting in the hands of the bailiffs and stewards who were responsible for individual estate-complexes. Whilst the great polyptychs of ecclesiastical institutions like St Germain (in Paris) or Prüm (in the Ardennes) might encourage us to think of abbots and bishops hatching economic masterplans, the practical impact of estate surveys was at a more local level, and it is on this local level that we can see documents used in practice. Record keeping of this kind, of course, was a way of preventing estate managers enriching themselves at their lords' expense, and the documentary and literary evidence repeatedly hints at the influence of such figures, and the fuzzy boundaries between the interests of landlord and steward. But not all local agency should be seen in terms of corruption. Stewards and bailiffs, where we can

---

[89] See below, Chapter 7.
[90] Innes, 'Framing the Carolingian economy', and below, Chapter 7.

identify them, were drawn from influential landowning families and therefore had the contacts and knowledge to react to threats and opportunities far more effectively than distant landowners. Indeed, they were encouraged to show initiative: in *De villis*, for example, it was the steward who was responsible for the marketing of any produce that remained once the immediate needs of his estate and the demands of his royal lord had been met.[91] Above all, though, we should remember that those lordly demands were seen as more significant than the money raised through selling surplus. After all, ecclesiastical and royal estates were the primary sources of funding for both Carolingian kingship and the Carolingian renaissance: huge resources were consumed by the building and provisioning of palaces and churches, the production of luxury manuscripts, and the dispensing of patronage.

But for all that production for the market was not the primary aim of manorial economies, such initiatives were only possible because manors were producing considerable surpluses. Economies of scale played a part in this. Improvements in agricultural technology – the diffusion of iron ploughs or water mills – depended not on a heroic history of new inventions, but on the slow diffusion of practices which required significant investment. Similarly, the adoption of field rotations and new crops was far easier to effect on a carefully managed and extensive demesne than it was on scattered smallholdings, reflected in archaeological evidence for greater concentration on large-scale cereal cultivation on some Carolingian sites.[92] But some eighth- and ninth-century developments worked equally to the benefit of smaller landowners, such as the slow move towards some specialised cultivation. This should not be seen as a sweeping change from subsistence to cash-cropping: peasants and landowners continued to pursue a mixed agrarian strategy aimed at supplying their own households, cultivating a variety of crops, and raising livestock which supplied labour and non-food produce (wool, candles, leather) rather than being specially bred for meat. But in the eighth and particularly the ninth centuries, there is increasing evidence for specialised production for the market: the cultivation of vineyards,

---

[91] *Capitulare de villis*; on personnel see Metz, *Das Karolingische Reichsgut*.
[92] See Hamerow, *Early Medieval Settlements*, pp. 125–90, on the archaeological evidence for greater concentration on heavy cereal cropping.

or olive groves, or chestnuts.[93] Female labour might be especially important, too, engaging in the small-time baking of bread or weaving of cloth to serve nearby towns and their markets.[94] Such practices were suited to owner-cultivators, requiring as they did the careful tending of relatively small-scale units of land, and the making of small adjustments to the household economy; indeed, this kind of 'market gardening' was particularly suited to land not under the plough.

Manorial estates, then, were not closed systems, and formed an integral part of the world we have been describing, providing opportunities for all sectors of local society. The fact that *De villis* enjoined that dependent peasants not 'waste time' at the markets which they visited on behalf of their landlords shows the interlinking of these ostensibly different parts of the rural economy. Yet this was not just a world of growing opportunities. Even in an agrarian economy, the higher level of economic complexity implied by this evidence for specialisation and exchange involves a higher level of potential risk. The economic changes we have been discussing therefore help us understand why in our narrative sources we repeatedly read of dearth, famine and harvest failures. Even allowing for the occasionally overblown Biblical rhetoric of these reports, their frequency is striking: over the ninth century as a whole it has been calculated that we find a report of a famine or food shortage for one year in four, a much higher incidence than for the immediately preceding and succeeding periods.[95]

We should not rush to generalise these into a picture of widespread crisis. Most shortages were local in their geographical impact, and differentiated in their social impact. When in 806, for example, we find Charlemagne ordering counts and other holders of royal estates to use their surplus food to feed those affected by shortages, and to

---

[93] Vineyards: F. Staab, 'Agrarwissenschaft und Grundherrschaft. Zum Weinbau der Klöster im Frühmittelalter', in A. Gerlich (ed.), *Weinbau, Weinhandel und Weinkultur*. Geschichtliche Landeskunde, 40 (Stuttgart, 1993), pp. 1–48. Chestnuts: C. J. Wickham, *The Mountains and the City: the Tuscan Appennines in the Early Middle Ages* (Oxford, 1988); see also the papers in *Olio e Vino in Alto Medioevo*, Settimane di Studio del Centro italiano di studi sull'alto medioevo 54 (Spoleto, 2007).

[94] *AF*, s.a. 873.

[95] F. Curschmann, *Hungersnote im Mittelalter* (Leipzig, 1900); Dutton, *Charlemagne's Mustache*, pp. 169–88; Dutton, 'Observations on early medieval weather in general, bloody rain in particular', in Davies and McCormick (eds.), *The Long Morning of Medieval Europe*, pp. 167–80.

urge others to follow their example, leading a programme of alms-giving, fasting and prayer designed to appease an angry God, we realise that shortages were a product of social organisation as much as of natural disaster.[96] These were not the inevitable crises of a sub-sistence economy where hunger was endemic, but the consequence of a particular system of production. The creation of a landscape in which the pockets of habitation were more densely peopled, and elites sustained more lavish tables, involved the creation of more complex systems of exchange and redistribution involving manors and markets. These changes were sustained without any significant technological breakthrough, in an agrarian landscape still exploited by the labour of man and beast. They therefore benefited the ruling class, and left the peasantry increasingly exposed to relatively small climatic variations and meteorological misfortunes.[97]

THE POWERFUL AND THE POOR: SOCIAL CONFLICT IN THE CAROLINGIAN COUNTRYSIDE

The vivid impression left by the reports of these recurrent crises has deeply influenced modern perceptions of social change in the ninth-century countryside: accounts of agrarian crisis have encouraged some historians to see the Carolingian countryside as undergoing a fundamental social transformation, with a hard-pressed peasantry forced into ever-greater dependence on aristocratic and ecclesiastical landlords. Yet the idea that the ninth century saw the 'decline of the free peasantry' does not necessarily stand up to sustained examina-tion. Much of the evidence for peasant impoverishment comes from capitularies and church councils, which contain a range of injunc-tions intended to prevent oppression of 'the poor'. The practices condemned range from price-fixing in times of scarcity to manip-ulation of the processes of the law, for example ruining peasants by legal filibustering that necessitated their attendance at distant and expensive court-hearings and prevented them cultivating their land. But as we saw in the introduction to this chapter, these repeated

---

[96] See A. Verhulst, 'Karolingische Agrarpolitik. Das *Capitulare de Villis* und die Hungersnöte von 792/93 und 805/06', *Zeitschrift für Agrargeschichte und Agrar-soziologie* 13 (1965), pp. 175–89, repr. in Verhulst, *Rural and Urban Aspects*.

[97] For climatic issues see now M. McCormick, P. Dutton and J. Mayewski, 'Vol-canoes and the climate forcing of Carolingian Europe AD 750–950', *Speculum* 82 (2007), pp. 865–96.

exhortations were more ideological than descriptive: protection of
the poor had long been established in Christian thought as a crucial
duty of the powerful, and much Carolingian legislation of this ilk has
an almost timeless quality.[98] The practices condemned can therefore
be seen not as new problems, but rather as age-old practices becoming more visible because of a more assertive royal power issuing more
legislation (see Figure 13).

Historians, therefore, may have been too ready to read legislation offering protection to 'the poor' (*pauperes*) as a direct response
to the changing status of peasant–proprietors. In Carolingian usage,
'poverty' was defined not in economic, but in social terms: the
'poor' were the opposite of the 'powerful'.[99] Hence, royal protection of the poor cannot be seen as a matter of 'social welfare': kings
were attempting to educate their ruling elite in the proper exercise
of Christian power.[100] Ritual performances ostentatiously demonstrating care of the poor thus became an inextricable aspect of the
exercise of power: alms-giving could be understood as giving justice, while the capitularies asked judges to hear the cases of the poor
first rather than making them wait. Honouring the poor here was
meant to demonstrate that those exercising power did so legitimately,
and shows the powerful responding to royal exhortations to see their
position as a God-given ministry, rooted in charity. What this actually meant for individual 'paupers' is very hard to pin down: the
poor almost always appear in our sources as an anonymous mass. But
those paupers we do meet are typically indigent cousins or country priests having to juggle their pastoral responsibilities with the
necessity of farming if they are to eat, figures dangling precariously
at the end of those hierarchies of patronage and obligation which

[98] See above, pp. 224–5. See also E. Müller-Mertens, *Karl der Große, Ludwig der
Fromme und die Freien. Wer waren die* liberi homines *der karolingischen Kapitularien
(742/3–832)? Ein Beitrag zur Sozialgeschichte und Sozialpolitik des Frankenreiches.*
Forschungen zur mittelalterlichen Geschichte 10 (Berlin, 1963); W. Ullman,
'Public welfare and social legislation in the early medieval councils', *Studies in
Church History* 7 (1971), pp. 1–39; C. Humfress, 'Poverty and Roman law', in R.
Osborne and M. Atkins (eds.), *Poverty in the Roman World* (Cambridge, 2006),
pp. 183–203.

[99] K. Bosl, '*Potens* und *pauper.* Begriffsgeschichtliche Studien zur gesellschaftlichen
Differenzierung im frühen Mittelalter und zur "Pauperismus" des Hochmittel-
alters', in K. Bosl, *Frühformen der Gesellschaft in mittelalterlichen Welt* (Munich and
Vienna, 1964), pp. 106–34.

[100] J. Wollasch, 'Gemeinschaftsbewußtsein und soziale Leistung im Mittelalter',
Frühmittelalterliche Studien 9 (1975), pp. 61–77.

Figure 13. King as lawgiver, from the *Golden Psalter* of St Gallen, completed at the monastery of St Gallen in the 880s. Illustrating Psalm 17, King David is portrayed as a Carolingian king sitting in judgement, looking towards the hand of God, and pointing with his staff at vanquished foes, and with his finger at the righteous.

radiated from aristocratic elites. Indeed, the discourse of alms-giving and protecting the poor could even be used to describe the care shown by aristocrats for their retinues, patrons for their clients, and the influential for their less powerful kin.[101] In the context of a political system which allowed a favoured few to make and lose fortunes with dizzying speed, this discourse insisted on the essential social

---

[101] See e.g. Dhuoda, *Liber manualis*, ed. and trans. M. Thiébaux, *Dhuoda: Handbook for her Warrior Son* (Cambridge, 1998); also trans. C. Neel, *Handbook for William: a Carolingian Woman's Counsel for her Son* (London, NE, 1991), III.10 and IV.9 and Einhard, *Epistolae*, which also make liberal use of the language of poverty to mobilise patronage. See also Innes, 'Practices of property', pp. 259–62.

solidarity of the stars of court politics with those kin and neighbours who had not been so fortunate, but whose continuing support was vital. The charter evidence suggests a similar picture, with a greater concentration of landowning in the hands of the great churches and a handful of favoured aristocratic families steepening the gradient between the poor and the powerful, but not sweeping aside the basic structures of landownership. Even in the last decades of the ninth century and the first of the tenth, patterns of charter witnessing and court hearings continued to conform to familiar patterns, resting on the participation of a community of free landowners in public meetings which might be dominated by a local elite but were open to all. Even well-to-do peasants were still able to maintain a foothold in the world of public courts, and so attempt to mobilise the patronage through which local politics was effected; they may appear to us as a passive and manipulated audience, but they were still on the stage witnessing and swearing on oath.

Nonetheless, a series of court cases from diverse regions does show increasing pressure on the very lowest strata of the free peasantry, especially where they became implicated in great estates increasingly organised on manorial lines. In 828, for example, peasants (*coloni*) from the villa of Antoigné made a 70-km trip to the royal palace of Chasseneuil to complain about the demands made by the advocate responsible for running the villa, only for their landlord, the abbey of Cormery, to produce an estate survey confirming the validity of the demands being made; whilst in 861 free peasants from the villa of Mitry travelled 60 km along with wives and children to the royal palace of Compiègne to defend their free status against the monk Deodatus, who managed this estate for their landlord, the abbey of St Denis, and had been demanding onerous 'inferior services' normally expected from the unfree.[102] In Italy a complex parchment trail preserved by the cathedral church of San Ambrogio in Milan shows the ways in which an ecclesiastical landlord might use its power and control of the written record to outmanoeuvre dependent peasants on its estates over successive generations.[103] That the surviving documents tend to show peasants losing and ecclesiastical landlords

---

[102] See the discussion of Nelson, 'Dispute settlement'; for the documents B. Guérard (ed.), *Polyptyque de l'Abbé Irminon* (Paris, 1844), 2 vols., II, appendix 9, and G. Tessier, *et al.* (eds.), *Recueil des actes de Charles II le Chauve*, 3 vols. (Paris, 1943–55) II, no. 228.

[103] R. Balzaretti, 'The monastery of Sant'Ambrogio and dispute settlement in early medieval Milan', *EME* 3 (1994), pp. 1–18.

winning is no surprise: after all, their preservation is dependent on ecclesiastical archives. Aristocratic landowners kept careful records too, as is demonstrated by a remarkable dossier preserved at the estate of Perrecy in Burgundy, which shows the local agents who managed Perrecy and two other local estates on behalf of their aristocratic lords pursuing individual peasants and utilising the public courts of Autun and its hinterland to establish documentary proofs of their unfree status.[104] Yet this documentary haul also shows that peasants on aristocratic and ecclesiastical estates continued to enjoy access to public courts. And it would be wrong to assume that landlord pressure on the peasantry in these and other ninth-century documents, backed up by public documentation and local courts, was a wholly new development: the chronological horizons of our documentary evidence are determined by processes of transmission and preservation which mean that we simply have no comparable documentation from an earlier period.[105]

These cases may help us understand the central plank of Carolingian legislation regarding the *pauperes*, the free but powerless: the insistence of rulers that their access to public courts should not be impeded. Capitularies, indeed, not only guaranteed this access to public justice, but also reserved cases of personal freedom or property ownership to counts' courts.[106] Once there, we should not assume that peasants always and automatically lost: in fact, imperial judgements from the reign of Louis the Pious show that when and where it was possible to appeal to the king, the depredations of landlords might be resisted or reversed.[107] Even where peasants did not win in local courts, the pressure of public opinion and factional politics might force landlords to make concessions. For example, in 856 a dispute over the status of one Uadaruft was settled through a carefully choreographed though opaque compromise in which Uadaruft publicly acknowledged he was unfree, only for Abbot Grimald of St Gallen immediately to free him in return for a gift of land.[108] In the end, the surviving cases, which show both predatory landlord power

---

[104] Prou and Vidier (eds.), *Recueil . . . Saint-Benoît-sur-Loire*, nos. 9–13, 16–17; Innes, 'Practices of property', pp. 252–6.

[105] See above, Chapter 1, pp. 16–17, 26–9.

[106] On the legislation see Müller-Mertens, *Karl der Große, Ludwig der Fromme und die Freien*; Hennebicque, '"Pauperes" et "paupertas"'.

[107] See *Formulae imperiales*, ed. K. Zeumer, *MGH Formulae Merovingici et Karolini Aevi* (Hanover, 1886), pp. 285–328, nos. 9, 51.

[108] H. Wartmann (ed.), *Urkundenbuch der Abtei St. Gallen* II (Zürich, 1866), no. 446.

and the continuing ability of peasants to defend their rights at public meetings, reveal pressure on the margins of free landowning society rather than structural transformation. Carolingian peasants still had chances to put their case, for even the most powerful of landlords still had to work through publicly acceptable norms, and the factional politics of locality and kingdom meant that the powerful never quite had local courts wholly in their pockets. It was the establishment of formal seigneurial rights, some economic and some jurisdictional, that entrapped the free peasantry in a new world of servitude, and this was a process of the post-Carolingian centuries; we should not read it back into the Carolingian world.[109]

CONCLUSION: COMMUNITY AND CONFLICT

The Carolingian countryside was, as we have seen, a complex patchwork of properties, villages and scattered interests. In most respects it does not conform to the stereotypical image of the medieval lord dominating the peasants living in the shadow of their stone residences and subjecting them to punitive and capricious demands. In fact, elite residences were typically sited away from the primary agglomerations of rural settlement: powerful aristocrats distanced themselves from the hustle and bustle of village life and the demands of agrarian cultivation, and did not intervene directly in rural settlements, nor dirty their hands with the nitty-gritty of estate management. Aristocratic influence on village life was generally indirect, as they increasingly invested in gifts to churches which, as we saw earlier, could help give focus to rural settlements and made landlords' power visible but absent.[110] Villages were tied into the patronage networks that made the empire tick via well-connected local priests and estate managers who were, as we have seen, members of rural communities themselves rather than agents imposed from outside. The ability of such figures to connect indirectly with earthly and heavenly courts offered aid and protection for villagers in their struggle with the exigencies of rural life. Yet that struggle did not mean that the peasantry could not sometimes organise themselves, resist landlord pressure and access public courts. Despite the growing gap between rich and poor

---

[109] See especially Freedman, *Origins of Peasant Servitude*, pp. 1–25.
[110] See above, p. 240.

in the Carolingian world, even the 'powerless' could sometimes still act with a degree of autonomy.

But the growing role of churches and churchyards in the Carolingian period symbolises the changes that were taking place in the texture of rural society. The propagation of church 'reform' helped to tie these small worlds into the great religious and political hierarchies of the empire by reclaiming local churches as constituent cells of an overarching imperial Church. A final visit to the conflict-ridden settlement of Kempten demonstrates exactly how these connections worked. At Kempten, the misfortunes affecting the community as a whole were believed to be a punishment meted out by God for the wrongdoings of one individual, and so it was resolved that he should be put to death. At this point, 'priests and deacons with relics and crosses' were despatched by the bishop to bring peace and to drive out the wicked spirit that had stirred up trouble. As mediators between the village and wider Christian society, the representatives of the imperial Church here sought to reshape community justice so that it might fit more easily with contemporary ideologies of 'peace, unity and concord among the Christian people'. But the attempted exorcism was only a partial success: while the priests were reciting the litany and sprinkling holy water in the house where the demon had been most active, he 'threw stones at men coming there from the *villa* and wounded them', and once they had left he claimed that one of the priests had slept with the daughter of the steward of the villa. The demon, hiding under the robes of the corrupt priest whom he now controlled, had thus been protected from the holy rites designed to drive him out, and continued to spread mischief and arson for three years, bringing disaster to the inhabitants and leading to the abandonment of the settlement.[111]

Here we see a clear sense of the village as not just a social, but a spiritual community, afflicted by common misfortunes and dealt with by God, by demons, and by the institutional Church, as a moral unit. Social relationships between villagers were tied up with this sense of spiritual solidarity and shared responsibility. But this community domain of social action was neither self-sufficient nor wholly controlled by villagers; it was also the forum through which the village as a collectivity negotiated with the agencies of imperial rule. Thus the initial attempt to deal with the activities of the demon through

[111] *AF, s.a.* 858.

secular self-help, when it threatened to escalate into a scandalous offence against the moral and social order through the killing of the demon's victim, was ended by the intervention of the church hierarchy in the person of the local bishop. However, this second, external and ecclesiastical, attempt to purify the social life of the village also failed. It failed because – according to the demon – those individuals who were the intermediaries between village society and the world of aristocrats and bishops, the priest and the bailiff, were the ultimate cause of the village's misfortune: it was the corrupt priest who had inflicted demonic disorder on the villagers, his double-dealing encapsulated by his illicit sexual activity with the bailiff's daughter which delivered him into the demon's power.

Narratives like the Kempten story were carefully crafted and consciously deployed by their authors. But within this narrative it is difficult not to hear the dim echo of class conflict articulated in village gossip about the double-dealings and improper conduct of the representatives of aristocratic and ecclesiastical authorities, and ultimately of imperial rule, within the village. As told in the *Annals of Fulda* this is a tale designed to underline the importance of the strict standards inculcated by Carolingian reformers if local priests were to live up to their ministry. The Carolingian reform in both Church and kingdom encouraged such claims. Defining aristocratic and ecclesiastical rule in terms of hierarchies of devolved ministry meant that those individuals who did not conduct themselves as the agents of a Christian empire ought to be brought to book: hence the repetition of this village gossip by the compiler of our annals. In this tale, then, we see the village as a community, and one whose definition was tightened by villagers' shared experience of dealing with those figures who connected them to the hierarchy of Church and court. It turns on a series of complex interactions between horizontal bonds among villagers, and the vertical ties binding the village to the aristocratic and ecclesiastical rulers of the Christian empire. In voicing the ambivalences and tensions that arose from these interactions between community and hierarchy, it takes us to the heart of Carolingian society.

6

ELITE SOCIETY

We saw in the previous chapter that it is possible to say a surprising amount about the nature and dynamics of peasant life and rural society in the Carolingian age. Yet social class is relative, and it is not possible to study the poor and the powerless without discussing their relationship with the social elite. This is especially so when dealing with a world where power depended ultimately on control over land (see Map 8), and where much of what we know about the lower orders comes to us in texts written by and for members of a landed aristocracy. Although they made up only a very small percentage of the population, wealthy aristocrats' ability to leave a lasting mark on the written record means that they loom disproportionately large in our sources. Yet their impact on contemporary politics and society was also disproportionate, meaning that the study of elite society opens up to us a wide window onto various important aspects of the Carolingian world.

While the existence of an elite grouping that we can call aristocratic is clear from even the most perfunctory reading of the Carolingian sources, attempts to understand the workings of aristocratic society and the nature of aristocratic power have consistently proved controversial. For much of the nineteenth and twentieth centuries, historical research concentrated on the formal identification of this elite, focussing on questions of its origins, continuity, and definition, and as a result anxiously debating the appropriateness or not

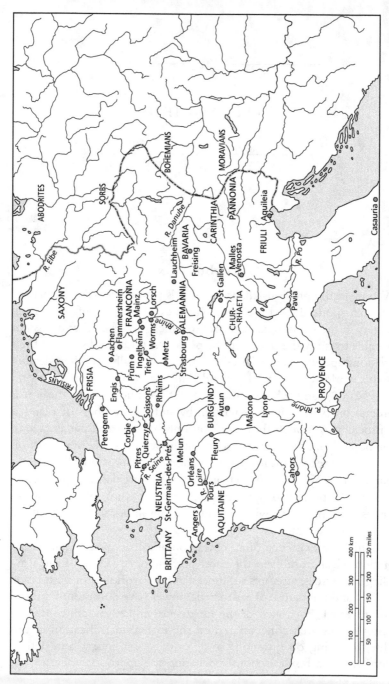

Map 8. Places mentioned in Chapter 6: 'Elite society'

of the terminology of 'nobility' and 'aristocracy'.[1] Such scholarship privileged certain questions: what was the relationship between early medieval elites and their predecessors, the ruling classes of the Roman empire and its barbarian neighbours? What effect did the rise and then fall of the Carolingians have on the great families of the Frankish world? To what extent did these families form a closed, separate caste, possessing a special legal status and even rights to rule which were in origin independent of kings? And to what extent did they survive the demise of the Carolingians with their social position intact? These issues made sense in a Europe where the fabric of the *ancien régime*, with its formal structures of noble privilege, was still fresh in the memory.[2]

In the second half of the twentieth century, the emergence of new research traditions, particularly in Germany, seemed to offer the hope of providing definitive answers to these hitherto almost intractable questions, and of moving the debate forward.[3] Detailed study of the careers and connections of individuals distinguished by their holding of high office and wielding of political power was championed as a potential key to unlocking the structure of early medieval elites. Prosopography, as this approach is known, served to place ties of kinship centre stage. The results tended to suggest that Carolingian elites were organised into broad and extensive 'clans' in which maternal relations were as important as paternal, and that the post-Carolingian period produced more narrowly focussed patrilineal 'lineages', in which succession passed from father to son; questions about the continuity of elites could thus be rephrased, as the issue became one of how families maintained their position by changing their internal structures. In its methodology, however, medieval prosopography tends to privilege kinship as an explanation for events, even as it reveals such ties to be multi-layered and fluid. It must be remembered that the aristocratic clans which populate the Carolingian world as described by modern historians are reconstructions whose names – Rupertiners, Widonids, Conradines and the like – were

<hr />

[1] T. Reuter, 'The medieval nobility in twentieth-century historiography', in M. Bentley (ed.), *Companion to Historiography* (London, 1997), pp. 177–202.

[2] Cf. R. W. Southern, *The Making of the Middle Ages* (London, 1953), p. 15.

[3] The essays edited and translated by Reuter (ed.), *The Medieval Nobility* offer a good taste of this stage of the debate; see T. N. Bisson, 'Nobility and family in France: a review essay', *French Historical Studies* 16 (1990), pp. 597–613, for a discussion of the distinctive French traditions, rooted in regional history.

almost all coined by historians rather than by contemporary medieval writers. Such groups may well have felt the bonds of their kinship keenly, but this needs to be demonstrated from the evidence and not just assumed.

Rather than seeking to join in these venerable debates about family continuity and political change, this chapter echoes more recent approaches by focussing on the mechanisms by which aristocratic power and status were constructed and exercised, and the consequent political role of the aristocracy. It begins by outlining the practices which marked out the Carolingian aristocracy as an identifiable social group in our sources, distinguished by military leadership, hunting, control of high offices, and particular forms of conspicuous consumption. It was through these strategies of distinction that the aristocracy projected and maintained its position as the dominant class within Carolingian society.[4] Aristocratic status came from participation in these forms of collective activity, which together formed a template of proper behaviour. Because this status was a matter of claiming membership of a group, it was rooted in the demonstration of the archetypical characteristics of that group; as a result, contemporaries did not delineate any precise economic or legal boundary for aristocracy, and nor can we.[5] Cultural codes and modes of conduct, patterns of residence and movement, can be analysed as contributing to these characteristic forms of activity. After discussing these features of the early medieval elite we will see how those behaviours related to their mentality and morality, especially the problems presented by a warrior lifestyle to those living in a world of Christian *correctio*. Next we return to kinship and family before concluding with the political role of the aristocracy.

We shall see that, although clearly identifiable, the aristocracy was not a completely closed caste, and social mobility both upwards and downwards was possible. Neither was it monolithic, socially or in its political behaviour. Although this discussion concentrates on the secular elite with some glances at their ecclesiastical cousins, it also emphasises divisions within that elite, stressing the existence of different layers within aristocratic society, and the interaction between

[4] See W. Pohl, 'Telling the difference: signs of ethnic identity', in W. Pohl and H. Reimitz (eds.), *Strategies of Distinction. The Construction of Ethnic Communities, 300–800*. Transformation of the Roman World 2 (Leiden, 1998), pp. 17–69.

[5] This insight owes much to recent work by Christina Pössel: C. Pössel, 'Authors and recipients'.

horizontal bonds – which might be rooted in regional origin or political participation as well as kinship – and vertical ties of patronage within it. Aristocratic status rested, of course, on control of resources: land and labour, obviously, but also networks of kin, clients and friends who both provided and expected support, through whom power could be exercised and as a result of which high office might be awarded. But it was legitimated by an unquestioned social dominance: there was no way of conceiving of the social hierarchy other than in terms of the markers of descent, office-holding, and participation in feasting, hunting and warfare which declared aristocratic status.

ARISTOCRATIC IDENTITY: VOCABULARY, APPEARANCE AND LIFESTYLE

Our sources use a rich and varied vocabulary to refer to those special characteristics which distinguished the elite. 'Noble' (*nobilis*), in origin a Latin term designating those of high social status, could apply to a wide spectrum of people: in its broadest definition, it simply denoted somebody who was not a nobody.[6] It is therefore not quite synonymous with the modern term 'aristocracy' – understood as a ruling elite sustained by the inheritance of land and formally empowered with political command – though it certainly overlapped with it. Nobility tended to refer to something slightly different, involving a person's character. To describe someone as 'noble' – in the sense of morally superior, truthful or of good character – depended on the context: witnesses to a charter might appear as such at the gathering where the document was issued, as the dominant figures in that particular locality, but might not in comparison with the magnates who routinely attended the royal court.[7] As Louis the Pious's biographer Thegan noted, denigrating his contemporary Archbishop Ebo of Rheims, true nobility was ingrained through descent and upbringing: he contrasted it with the distinction between free and unfree

---

[6] Reuter (ed.), *The Medieval Nobility*, pp. 1–16; H.-W. Goetz, '"Nobilis". Der Adel im Selbstverständnis der Karolingerzeit', *Vierteljahrsschrift für Sozial- und Wirtschaftsgeschichte* 70 (1983), pp. 153–91; T. Reuter, 'Nobles and others: the social and cultural expression of power relations in the Middle Ages', in Reuter, *Medieval Polities and Modern Mentalities*, pp. 111–26.

[7] For these relative values, see Innes, *State and Society*, pp. 83–4.

that was defined in written law.[8] 'Noble' was not however the commonest term used to describe the politically powerful in a kingdom,
for whom our sources tend to use either the titles of office – duke
(*dux*), count (*comes*), marcher lord/superior count (*marchio*) – or a
looser vocabulary that described the exalted status of a group relative
to the rest: the '(more) powerful' (*potentes, potentiores*), the 'illustrious'
(*illustres*), the 'best' (*optimates*) or the 'near' (*proceres*: near to the king,
that is). The latter designation in particular demonstrates the connection in the contemporary mind between this elite and kingship. The
proceres exhibited what German historians have termed *Königsnähe*:
a closeness not only to the king but also to the king's court, which
was the forum in which kingdom-wide politics were played out.[9]

Three points deserve to be emphasised about this vocabulary. First,
as already noted, it was not merely descriptive, but it imbued the
powerful with particular qualities, implying moral distinction: 'the
best', and so on. Second, it was a matter of subjective claim, not
objective judgement: being described as noble or powerful did not
rest on fulfilling a checklist of acknowledged criteria, but on social
pre-eminence and so participation in high-level politics. As we saw in
Chapter 5, the Carolingian aristocracy did not enjoy the formal legal
privileges that had gone with membership of the Roman senate, nor
did it cultivate the minute but carefully regulated hierarchy of honorifics that defined social status in the Roman world; similar systems,
and the sharp definitions they encouraged, were to emerge in later
medieval and *ancien régime* Europe, but not in the early Middle Ages.[10]
Third, this was primarily a vocabulary of collective action: we tend to
meet aristocrats in groups, designated as the *nobiles, potentes, proceres*
or *optimates*: it was through acting together that aristocrats defined
their social identity and came to perceive themselves as morally better than other social groups. This sense of collective superiority is
revealed in the insults that members of the aristocracy used against
their enemies. Low birth was just about the most damning thing
one could be accused of, for those of low birth could not be trusted

---

[8] Thegan, *Gesta Hludovici*, c. 20, trans. Dutton, *Carolingian Civilization*, pp. 165–6.
[9] S. Airlie, 'The aristocracy', in *NCMH* II, pp. 431–50, esp. pp. 448–50 for the
    different layers within the aristocracy.
[10] P. Garnsey, *Social Status and Legal Privilege in the Roman Empire* (Oxford, 1970);
    M. L. Bush, *Rich Noble, Poor Noble* (Manchester, 1988), pp. 30–42; S. Clark, *State
    and Status. The Rise of the State and Aristocratic Power in Western Europe* (Toronto,
    1995), pp. 129–54. See also above, Chapter 5, pp. 242–3.

to behave honourably: writing in the 840s, the worst insult Nithard could level at his peers who had not kept faith but turned traitor was that they had behaved 'like peasants'.[11] Disruption of the 'correct' social order was abhorrent. Charlemagne claimed, according to a letter written in 796 by his adviser Alcuin to King Offa of Mercia, that someone who killed his lord was 'worse than a pagan'.[12] A century later, the monk Abbo of St-Germain-des-Prés could think of no better way to show his revulsion at the predations of the Vikings than by describing their impact in the Paris area in terms of social inversion: 'serf became free, freeman became serf'.[13]

Social identities were not absolute, but had to be constantly reinforced and maintained. Legal practice recognised the social fact that aristocrats needed to be handled differently, and punished according to different norms, from their inferiors.[14] This superiority could be reinforced with violence – indeed this was only proper in the view of an eighth-century author who stated that someone who had 'acted against his lord' deserved death and even torture.[15] An even more striking incident is recorded in the *Annals of St Bertin* for 859: 'Some of the common people living between the Seine and the Loire formed a sworn association amongst themselves and fought bravely against the Danes on the Seine. But because their association had been made without due consideration, they were easily slain by our more powerful people.'[16] The actions of these 'more powerful people' had legal sanction: royal capitularies sought to legislate against such horizontal social solidarities, aiming thus to reinforce

---

[11] Nithard, *Historiarum Libri IV*, II.3, trans. Scholz, *Carolingian Chronicles*, p. 144; see also Thegan, *Gesta Hludowici imperatoris*, c. 44, pp. 232–8, trans. Dutton, *Carolingian Civilization*, pp. 170–3, and *AF*, *s.a.* 887; this point is noted by J. L. Nelson, 'Public *Histories* and private history in the work of Nithard', *Speculum* 50 (1985), pp. 251–93, at p. 272, repr. in Nelson, *Politics and Ritual in Early Medieval Europe* (London, 1986), pp. 195–237.

[12] *EHD* no. 198; Alcuin, *Ep.* 101, pp. 146–7.

[13] Abbo of St-Germain-des-Prés, *Bella Parisiacae urbis*, ed. H. Waquet, *Abbon. Le Siège de Paris par les Normands* (Paris, 1942), pp. 30–1, ll. 184–5: 'Efficitur servus liber, liber quoque servus / Vermaque fit dominus, contra dominos quoque verma.' This text is translated by N. Dass, *Viking Attacks on Paris* (Dudley, MA, 2007).

[14] See Capitulary for Aachen, 802–3, *Capit.* I, no. 77, c. 12, p. 171, trans. Loyn and Percival, *The Reign of Charlemagne*, pp. 82–4.

[15] *LHF*, c. 43, trans. Fouracre and Gerberding, *Late Merovingian France*, p. 88. The context is royal-aristocratic politics, but the comment is offered as stating a matter of principle.

[16] *AB*, *s.a.* 859, p. 80, trans. Nelson, p. 89.

the vertical obligations of sworn fidelity to a lord. For the Frankish aristocracy, apparently, threatening a lord's authority really was worse than being a pagan, and it could merit punishment by death.

The expression of this sense of aristocratic 'betterness' was therefore not simply confined to the terminology of written sources. However, concerted outbursts of violence against the less powerful such as that in 859 are rare in the written record. On a more everyday level, elite status had to be made visible in the ways that nobles looked and behaved. Although our sources provide very few detailed physical descriptions of Carolingian nobles, it is clear that lay aristocrats carried visual markers that set them apart from the rest of society. Most significant of these was the *cingulum militare*, the military belt. The importance of this item had its roots in the later Roman empire, when the belt stood for the holding of public office. In the Carolingian period it was equally symbolic, as illustrated by descriptions of kings and nobles who removed their belts. When Louis the Pious was deposed by bishops loyal to his sons in 833, he was made to remove his military belt and place it on the altar of the church in Soissons.[17] The gesture was echoed almost exactly forty years later by his grandson Charles the Fat, who astonished a royal assembly by throwing down his *cingulum* in a fit of contrition after rebelling against his father: his intention was to show his complete submission, and thus to throw himself on the king's mercy.[18] These rulers' sword belts symbolised their secular status. As usual, examples featuring kings are the best attested. However, in this respect kings were very much part of a common culture with the secular aristocracy: when Lothar wished to exile Count Odo of Orléans during the rebellion of 830, his first move was formally to disarm him.[19] Ninth-century provisions for the undertaking of public penance, a punishment considered appropriate for sins which had caused disruption on the political stage, regularly

---

[17] De Jong, 'Power and humility'; and see above, Chapter 4, pp. 218–19.

[18] *AB, s.a.* 873, p. 191; on the events of 873, see J. L. Nelson, 'A tale of two princes: politics, text and ideology in a Carolingian annal', *Studies in Medieval and Renaissance History* 10 (1988), pp. 103–40, repr. in Nelson, *Rulers and Ruling Families in Early Medieval Europe: Alfred, Charles the Bald and Others* (Aldershot, 1999), and S. MacLean, 'Ritual, misunderstanding and the contest for meaning: representations of the disrupted royal assembly at Frankfurt (873)', in B. Weiler and S. MacLean (eds.), *Representations of Power in Medieval Germany* (Turnhout, 2006), pp. 97–120.

[19] Astronomer, *Vita Hludowici imperatoris*, c. 45.

demanded that the penitent should set aside marriage, public office and the *cingulum*.[20] These three things constituted the essential badges of secular elite status, and the consistency of these regulations suggests that they were thought to define the lay aristocracy as a distinct and visible group.

High social status was also associated with other pieces of equipment that are often met alongside the *cingulum* in contemporary references to noble gear. The sword was an equally significant item of aristocratic equipment. The kings who cast aside their belts in 833 and 873 did likewise with their weapons. An apocryphal story from the later ninth century relates how Louis the Pious used to make regular gifts to his personal servants of all his clothing except for his sword and belt, and in the very rare ninth-century fresco at Malles Venosta in the Italian Alps, the lay patron of the church is depicted holding a sword (see Figure 14).[21]

The extent to which aristocrats identified with their weapons is underlined by the fact that they frequently gave them names, and sometimes had these names inscribed along with their own on the blades.[22] More broadly, capitularies demanded that men who were to serve in the army should be properly equipped with appropriate weaponry, armour and horses.[23] Weapons were not monopolised by the ruling class and could denote status at multiple social levels: in the mid-eighth century, the Lombard king Aistulf stipulated that each man who held seven or more peasant farms (*casae massariciae*) should have a horse, mail coat, shield and lance, while those without tenant

---

[20] K. Leyser, 'Early medieval canon law and the beginning of knighthood', in K. Leyser (ed. T. Reuter), *Communications and Power in Medieval Europe. The Carolingian and Ottonian Centuries* (London and Rio Grande, OH, 1984), pp. 51–71; M. de Jong, 'What was public about public penance? *Poenitentia publica* and justice in the Carolingian world', *La giustizia nell'alto medioevo (secoli IX–XI)*, Settimane 44 (Spoleto, 1997), pp. 863–902.

[21] Notker, *Gesta* 2.21. For Malles Venosta, see J. Beckwith, *Early Medieval Art* (London, 1969), p. 26.

[22] *ARF*, s.a. 799, trans. Scholz, *Carolingian Chronicles*, p. 78; P. Geary, 'Germanic tradition and royal ideology in the ninth century: the *visio Karoli Magni*', *Frühmittelalterliche Studien* 21 (1987), pp. 274–94, repr. in Geary, *Living with the Dead in the Early Middle Ages* (Ithaca, NY, and London, 1994), pp. 49–76, at pp. 67–71.

[23] See e.g. Charlemagne's *Capitulare Aquisgranense* [Capitulary for Aachen], *a.802–3*, *Capit.* I, no. 77, c. 9; *Duplex capitulare missorum in Theodonis villa datum* [Double capitulary of Thionville for the *missi*], *a.805*, *Capit.* I, no. 44, c. 6, both trans. Dutton, *Carolingian Civilization*, pp. 80, 83.

Figure 14. A nobleman, fresco in church of San Benedetto, Malles
Venosta, South Tyrol. Lying on an important Alpine route, this church contains a
set of frescoes generally thought to date from the Carolingian period. This secular
nobleman's clothing recalls pictures of aristocrats in manuscripts and underlines the
centrality of the sword to their social identity.

farms should still be able to furnish themselves with horse, shield and
lance, and those who could not afford a horse should possess a shield
and bow and arrows.[24] In so legislating, moreover, Aistulf was simply
setting minimum standards. Even in the Lombard kingdom, some
aristocrats could afford to equip not only themselves but also their
retinues in some style; all the more so, then, were the highest ranks

---

[24] *Leges Ahistulfi*, cc. 2–3; see also *Leges Ratchis* [Laws of Ratchis], ed. F. Beyerle,
Leges langobardorum, 643–866. Die Gesetze der Langobarden (Weimar, 1947; repr.
Witzenhausen, 1962), pp. 194–204, c. 4, both trans. Fischer-Drew, *The Lombard
Laws*.

of the generally wealthier Carolingian elite able to arm themselves and their men lavishly. The greater the quantity of horses, arms and armour, with all the status these implied, the greater the impact when they were taken away. Charles the Fat knew very well the degree of public humiliation and loss of status that he was inflicting on the noble followers of the illegitimate Carolingian rebel Hugh when in 885 he had them 'stripped of their horses, arms and clothing, and [they] scarcely escaped naked'.[25]

Since the early medieval peasantry could also bear arms, it was not the fact of owning weapons that was crucial so much as their quality. Good-quality swords, horses and armour were expensive, and as such they were symbols which actively distinguished rich nobles from members of less powerful social groups. This is illustrated by a story from Paschasius Radbertus's *Epitaphium Arsenii* (written in the mid-ninth century) which relates an encounter between Charlemagne's cousin Wala and a 'countryman' (*ruricola*). This yokel was wearing a belt and arms which Wala (because he was being tested by the king) offered to exchange for his own superior set. Unsurprisingly, the rustic enthusiastically agreed: the difference in quality between them was obvious.[26] This sort of military gear could help to reinforce social boundaries within the ranks of the nobility, as well as between nobles and non-nobles. Above all, these were secular items. Monks and clergy often came from the same noble families as did the lay elite; these men rubbed shoulders at the great assemblies of the realm, and they shared the same in-bred sense of superiority. But those aristocrats who entered the religious life had their own clothes, implements and identifiers of rank. By the late eighth century, surrendering the sword and belt on the altar was central to the ritual by which young lay aristocrats became monks.[27] According to the Astronomer it was only in the reign of Louis the Pious that bishops and clerics 'gave up belts with golden baldrics and jewelled knives, exquisite garments

---

[25] *AF*, s.a. 885, p. 98; S. MacLean, *Kingship and Politics in the Late Ninth Century: Charles the Fat and the End of the Carolingian Empire* (Cambridge, 2003), p. 151; R. Le Jan, 'Frankish giving of arms and rituals of power: continuity and change in the Carolingian period', in Theuws and Nelson (eds.), *Rituals of Power*, pp. 281–309, at pp. 286–7.

[26] Paschasius, *Epitaphium Arsenii* [*Life of Wala*], 1.6; Leyser, 'Early medieval canon law', p. 57; M. Innes, '"A place of discipline": Carolingian courts and aristocratic youth', in C. Cubitt (ed.), *Court Culture in the Early Middle Ages* (Turnhout, 2003), pp. 59–76.

[27] Le Jan, 'Frankish giving of arms', pp. 298–9.

and boots with spurs. Louis thought it a monstrosity that men of the clerical order should aspire to these items of worldly glory' (though the fact that he claimed this was a new development shows that some clerics at least did not consider their vocation to be inconsistent with packing iron).[28] These were also badges of exclusively male noble status: while Charlemagne made sure his sons learned to use weapons in fighting, riding and hunting, his daughters were schooled in the archetypal feminine occupations of weaving and making textiles.[29] The formal bestowing of sword and belt on adolescents played a role in structuring the life-cycle of the male aristocrat. This was not a new practice in the eighth and ninth centuries, but from the Carolingian period it seems to have become the main rite of passage for boys into adulthood, replacing Merovingian milestones such as hair-cutting or shaving the beard (indeed, beards and well-groomed hair were probably another sign of elite distinction, to judge from contemporary manuscript illuminations).[30] In other words, possession of the *cingulum militare* and the sword not only distinguished the aristocracy as an elite group, but also served to construct differences of age, status and gender within that group.

The humiliation of Hugh's followers in 885 also highlights the importance of clothing as a symbol of status. Einhard's description of the habits of Charlemagne's Aachen implies that clerical members of the court had a kind of uniform to denote their status, and it may be that lay courtiers' clothing likewise indicated their identity.[31] Easter was a time of renewal in the rituals of the Christian calendar, and scattered references in the sources suggest that the king and the nobles in his entourage marked this with a symbolic bath and a donning of new clothes.[32] Clothing here was used to symbolise spiritual rebirth, and to reinforce aristocratic group identity. What did these men

---

[28] Astronomer, *Vita Hludowici imperatoris*, c. 6; Leyser, 'Early medieval canon law', p. 56.

[29] Einhard, *VK*, c. 19, trans. Dutton, *Charlemagne's Courtier*, p. 28.

[30] Le Jan, 'Frankish giving of arms', pp. 284–5; Dutton, *Charlemagne's Mustache*, pp. 39–41.

[31] Einhard, *VK*, c. 26, trans. Dutton, *Charlemagne's Courtier*, p. 33; J. L. Nelson, 'Was Charlemagne's court a courtly society?', in C. Cubitt (ed.), *Court Culture in the Earlier Middle Ages* (Turnhout, 2003), pp. 39–57, at p. 47.

[32] J. L. Nelson, 'Ninth-century knighthood: the evidence of Nithard', in C. Harper-Bill, C. Holdsworth and J. L. Nelson (eds.), *Studies in Medieval History Presented to R. Allen Brown* (Woodbridge, 1989), pp. 255–66, repr. in Nelson, *Frankish World*, pp. 75–87, pp. 85–7.

actually wear? Both Einhard and Notker provide descriptions of the everyday clothing of the Franks: shoes with long laces, a linen shirt, cloth leggings or trousers and a cloak which hung long at the back and front, but short at the sides.[33] Aristocratic women, on the other hand, wore wide-sleeved tunics, often held at the waist with belts and covered with a mantle, and elaborate jewels and pendants which attracted comment from court poets.[34] By 'the Franks', Einhard and Notker meant Frankish aristocrats, and it is clear that the clothing of nobles distinguished them from the poor. Theodulf, bishop of Orléans in the reign of Charlemagne, wrote that to disguise oneself as a peasant the requisite items were a hood, a loose garment, a basic linen shirt and leggings made of strips of cloth, as well as a knife (not a sword) at one's side.[35] This was not so different in style from the outfit described by Einhard and Notker, but the difference in quality must have been obvious: Ermold the Black, albeit with some poetic licence, describes the brightly coloured clothing of courtiers as a source of wonder to onlookers.[36]

The dress of the male lay elite varied from region to region. The best-known example is the outfit which the very young Louis the Pious, as king of Aquitaine, is described as wearing on a trip to meet his father: a round mantle, long-sleeved shirt, full trousers and spurred boots were recognised as the attire of the Basques of his sub-kingdom.[37] To the Franks, with their tight trousers and linen shirts, this must have appeared a fairly outlandish get-up. Such differences were not merely a question of fashion, but helped to reinforce perceptions of difference within and between elites: visible cultural differences such as those expressed in clothing could help to buttress regional political identities, a significant fact in the politically fragmented west of the post-Roman period where elite landowning groups emphasised ethnic identity as one means to legitimate their domination of particular regions.[38] Hence the biographer of Pope Hadrian specifically reports of defectors to Rome from the Lombard

---

[33] Einhard, *VK*, c. 23, trans. Dutton, *Charlemagne's Courtier*, p. 31; Notker, *Gesta*, 1.34, trans. Ganz, p. 84.

[34] P. Riché, *Daily Life in the World of Charlemagne*, trans. J. A. McNamara (Liverpool, 1978), pp. 162–3.

[35] Theodulf, *Carmina* 17, ed. Dümmler, p. 472; Riché, *Daily Life*, pp. 161–2.

[36] Ermold, *In honorem Hludowici*, p. 212. Cf. Notker, *Gesta*, 2.14 for kings disapproving of fancy clothing.

[37] Astronomer, *Vita Hludowici imperatoris*, c. 4.2.   [38] See Innes, 'Land, freedom'.

duchy of Spoleto at the time of Charlemagne's invasion of Italy that they were 'shaved Roman-fashion'.[39] Elites defined themselves not simply against social inferiors, but also against other groups within the aristocracy. The social world experienced by inhabitants of the Carolingian empire was deeply conditioned by all these outward signs of status, identity and distinction. The translation of clothing, weaponry and bearing into a code of social hierarchy was internalised implicitly and unconsciously, if not always unquestioningly.

Status could thus be worn, ridden or carried: but it could also be owned, flaunted and consumed.[40] Wills left by Count Eberhard of Friuli (*d*.863–4) and his wife Gisela, and by Count Eccard of Autun (*d*.876), bequeathed to their heirs numerous pieces of armour and weaponry which were clearly of no practical use, including several swords decorated with gold and silver. They were passed on because they 'embodied their owner's social identity', symbolising the status which defined their holders as nobles.[41] Gisela's and Eberhard's children were also given large drinking and serving vessels, which symbolised the role of the noble as a feast-giver, an entertainer to his or her followers.[42] This was so fundamental an aspect of elite culture that it was frequently parodied in the ninth century. Notker of St Gallen lampoons the nobility's desire for exotic foodstuffs and feasting at several points in his idiosyncratic biography of Charlemagne: one memorable tale tells of a bishop who was so consumed by the urge to possess unusual luxuries that he was tricked into paying three pounds of silver for a mouse stuffed with spices, believing it to be an eastern delicacy.[43] Notker wrote with an agenda and a sharp wit,

---

[39] *LP* I, p. 495, trans. Davis, *Lives of the Eighth-Century Popes*, p. 137.

[40] For these expressions see R. Fleming, 'Lords and labour', in W. Davies (ed.), *From the Vikings to the Normans* (Oxford, 2003), pp. 107–37.

[41] P. Schramm and F. Mütherich, *Denkmale der deutschen Könige und Kaiser*, 2nd edn (Munich, 1981), pp. 93–4 (Eberhard's will); Prou and Vidier (eds.), *Receuil . . . Saint-Benoît-sur-Loire* I, p. 64 (Eccard's will). C. La Rocca and L. Provero, 'The dead and their gifts. The will of Eberhard, count of Friuli, and his wife Gisela, daughter of Louis the Pious (863–864)', in Theuws and Nelson (eds.), *Rituals of Power*, pp. 225–80, at p. 250.

[42] La Rocca and Provero, 'The dead and their gifts', pp. 251–3; see J. L. Nelson, 'Carolingian royal ritual', in D. Cannadine and S. Price (eds.), *Rituals of Royalty. Power and Ceremonial in Traditional Societies* (Cambridge, 1987), pp. 137–80, pp. 166–72 on royal feasts, and p. 174 for the food consumed at a royal commemoration at St Denis.

[43] Notker, *Gesta*, 1.16, trans. Ganz, pp. 66–7.

and so we have to doubt the literal accuracy of his anecdotes. But whether or not they could really tell an unusual snack from a spicy rodent, the rich tastes of such people had implications for how their social status was expressed. For one thing, their better diet probably made them taller and healthier than the poor, a conclusion supported by skeletal data.[44] Contemporary observers sometimes lingered on the impressive physical attributes of high-status males, as did Ermold when describing Pippin of Aquitaine, the son of Louis the Pious, and were also capable (like the author of the *Liber historiae francorum*) of equating lack of physique with a shortage of intelligence and moral fibre.[45] As we shall see in Chapter 7, the way that elite landowners filled their groaning tables made direct demands on peasant labour, meaning that their social status was underlined not just by the quantity, quality and variety of the food they consumed, but also by the process through which they acquired it.[46]

As far as displays of status are concerned, consumption is rarely more conspicuous than when it is made concrete in buildings. Yet aristocratic residences remain frustratingly poorly understood: we know surprisingly little about where the aristocracy lived, and still less about how houses and households articulated the status of their owners. Our difficulties in finding aristocratic residences both on the ground and in texts is partly a result of looking for the wrong things in the wrong places. A tendency to focus on kinship as the central determinant of aristocratic identity has led historians to imagine the early medieval aristocracy in ways similar to those in which their better-attested high medieval counterparts have been viewed. Thus early medieval aristocratic families are sometimes thought of as having identified themselves with a particular 'seat', which served as a fixed centre of lordship and which gradually became fortified. But these assumptions wrongly set up the aristocracy of the central Middle Ages as some kind of 'ideal form' which its predecessors strove to reach. In fact, not only have attempts to find fortified aristocratic strongholds in the Merovingian and Carolingian sources utterly failed, but there is no sign (as we saw in Chapter 5) that aristocratic residences were the nuclei of early medieval villages. Both Roman and high medieval

---

[44] Reuter, 'Nobles and others', pp. 116–17.
[45] Ermold, *In honorem Hludowici*, pp. 219–21; *LHF*, c. 4,8 trans. Fouracre and Gerberding, *Late Merovingian France*, p. 92.
[46] See below, Chapter 7, pp. 332–6.

aristocracies lived in structures that, while very different from each other, are nonetheless instantly recognisable archaeologically as elite dwellings, and were described as such in our written sources. That we can find few references in texts to, and scant archaeological traces of, specifically secular, aristocratic, structures between the sixth and tenth centuries is therefore significant: it must suggest that neither the identity nor the status of aristocratic families in this period depended on association with a stable central place.[47]

Evidence for rural construction in the sixth and seventh centuries shows a marked shift away from late Roman styles of residence, at all levels. The late Roman elite's villas of stone and brick were abandoned in the fifth century in the frontier provinces of northern Gaul, and in the sixth in the western Mediterranean. Rural settlement, whether village or isolated dwelling, became typified instead by rectangular wooden 'halls', which show some variation in length (the norm was 10–15 metres but some reached 25–30 metres) but no surviving signs, at that date, of structural elaboration: in other words, landowning elites lived in bigger, and presumably better decorated, versions of the same dwellings inhabited by the owner–cultivators who were now also their neighbours. The abandonment of stone building traditions must relate to the diminished resources of post-Roman elites. Our texts emphasise not buildings but clothing adorned with treasures as visible demonstrations of status. Improved networks of exchange in the Carolingian period catered for aristocratic demands for exotica such as 'robes made of pheasant-skins surrounded with silk; or of the necks, backs and tails of peacocks in their first plumage'.[48] Presumably the material wealth so evident in our wills was also used to adorn residences with exotic wall-hangings and fabulous tableware, making them fitting backdrops for the necessary conviviality, the bestowing of favour and the disciplining of subordinates that took place when the lord was present. Treasures – heirlooms around which stories collected, giving them a cultural biography, such as swords passed on from generation to generation which commemorated the daring deeds of forebears – also

[47] On defensibility, R. Samson, 'The Merovingian nobleman's house: castle or villa', *Journal of Medieval History* 13 (1987), pp. 287–315 is key. On family centres see Airlie, 'The aristocracy' in *NCMH* II, p. 436.

[48] Notker, *Gesta*, 2.17, trans. Ganz, pp. 110–11. Wickham, *Framing the Early Middle Ages*, pp. 201–2, notes that moveables were used to set apart aristocratic households.

functioned as objects of identity.[49] This preference for investment in forms of consumption which could be worn or carried belonged to a world where being powerful involved regular movement, seeing and being seen by clients and patrons: scattered landholdings, with their vibrant communities of free peasants, could not be ruled as mere adjuncts of aristocratic seats. Conspicuous consumption of a mobile kind rather than huge investment in stone and wood made sense in a world where what mattered were not rights of property or jurisdiction attached to a particular centre, but the presence of the powerful.

Exclusive focus on the countryside, encouraged by a doomed search for aristocratic 'seats' as fixed centres of rural lordship, can distort our understanding of aristocratic lives. The Roman elite had moved periodically between the country and the city, in a lifestyle articulated by the rhetorical opposition between cultivated leisure and public business, *otium* and *negotium*. Yet post-Roman aristocrats too were clearly active in cities – the charter evidence, for example, shows counts holding public courts there, and where it is thick enough can give an impression of the hustle and bustle of business being done publicly among the local elite.[50] In contrast to the Romans, we know very little about where they stayed when they were in town. Here, again, charters can help: in those from Mainz, we can see the great churchman and scholar Hraban Maur owning an expensive town-house, built in stone and bought with gold and horses, while rights over major city churches like St Lambert's were subdivided between upwards of twenty aristocratic patrons.[51] Townhouses were visible to more people than were rural dwellings and so had an important role in demonstrating status. Hraban's family town house jutted out into the 'public street', and there is archaeological and documentary evidence for its neighbours having imposing stone frontages, while Adrevald of Fleury describes the count of Orléans

---

[49] M. Hardt, *Gold und Herrschaft: die Schätze europäischer Könige und Fürsten im ersten Jahrtausend* (Berlin, 2004).

[50] Innes, 'Practices of property', pp. 246–66; Wickham, *Framing the Early Middle Ages*, pp. 208–13.

[51] *UBF* 177 (Hraban) and see also *UBF* 2 (gold and horses) and *CL* 1966–7, 1969–72, 1974. St Lambert's has been analysed well by M. Gockel, *Karolingische Königshöfe am Mittelrhein* (Göttingen, 1970), pp. 238–58, and is discussed briefly in Innes 'People, places and power', pp. 397–437, at p. 409.

residing in a two-storey residence.[52] These hints are all that our written sources reveal of the appearance of aristocrats' town-houses: what is lacking is more archaeological data, and here we draw a blank north of the Alps. It is in Italy that we find substantial evidence of a variegated urban architecture, including simple wooden structures, but also buildings in stone, brick and mortar, some of them with multiple rooms, stairs to upper storeys, and frequently reworked facades. Yet even Italian cities include areas that look to have been abandoned, and often given over to agriculture, in the early Middle Ages. So we have to imagine the 'unpacking' of space within cities, with large tracts of open ground and gardens often separating clusters of domestic buildings, sometimes enclosed by fences.[53] It is likely that cities in Francia as well as Italy developed this kind of patchwork urban landscape in the post-Roman centuries. Where these residential clusters included churches, they should be seen as demonstrating not the exclusion of the laity from cities dominated by bishops and their priests, but the engagement of local property owners in the patronage of religious buildings that were associated particularly with their families, and helped to declare their status.[54]

Aristocrats' associations with churches were becoming important in our period in the countryside just as much as in cities. The foundation of rural churches was just beginning in the seventh century, and accelerated in the eighth.[55] They were often staffed by family members, and remained under the influence of their founding family. Even the smallest churches could double as family mausolea, places where past and present fused as ancestors were commemorated in prayer; women often dominated such foundations, since they took the lead in preserving family identity by cultivating the remembrance of their menfolk.[56] Aristocratic church foundation was also an

---

[52] See L. Falck, *Mainz im frühen und hohen Mittelalter (Mitte 5. Jht. bis 1244)* (Düsseldorf, 1972). For Count Raho of Orléans, see Adrevald of Fleury, *Miracula Sancti Benedicti*, ed. O. Holder-Egger, *MGH SS* xv, pp. 474–97, at pp. 486–7.

[53] For Italian cities in this period, see Wickham, *Framing the Early Middle Ages*, pp. 644–56.

[54] Cf. K. Böhner, 'Urban and rural settlement in the Frankish kingdom', in M. W. Barley (ed.), *European Towns: Their Archaeology and Early History* (London, 1977), pp. 185–207.

[55] S. Wood, *The Proprietary Church in the Early Medieval West* (Oxford, 2006), pp. 16–32, 67–79. See also above, Chapter 5, pp. 239–41.

[56] R. Le Jan, 'Convents, violence, and competition for power in seventh-century Francia', in de Jong and Theuws with van Rhijn (eds.), *Topographies of Power*, pp. 243–69.

important factor in changing burial patterns. There are a number of examples where small groups of high-status burials were consciously marked out: east of the Rhine by new or reused barrows, presumably serving a family and its clients; more commonly elsewhere by increasingly elaborate structures that might eventually become chapels or churches.[57] These sites, central to the cultivation of family identity, should not be seen as solely ecclesiastical in their rationale. In the seventh and eighth centuries, the distinction between an aristocratic residence and a family monastery remained blurred at best, as members of the founding family enjoyed proprietorial rights which could entitle them to hospitality, especially from the nieces and daughters, widowed mothers and dowager aunts, who often cared for such sites. As a result, these structures could become recognised political centres which, in times of internal strife, were deliberately targeted by rival families with acts of violence.[58]

Foundation of such churches could involve building in stone for the first time since Roman times, or the appropriation of former Roman villa sites, as at a series of places in the Moselle valley, and accordingly had an impact on the rural as well as the urban landscape.[59] Like their urban houses and churches, rural churches, and particularly family monasteries, offered hospitality to kinsmen and women and thus helped to define complex extended kin-groups, whose elite status was associated with these sites of power. But not all monasteries had such an exclusive relationship with a single kin-structure: the largest institutions enjoyed patronage from a wide range of sources. Some were granted royal protection, coupled with new rights of immunity – enriched through royal as well as aristocratic patronage, they grew rapidly, housing hundreds of monks and dwarfing even the most lavish secular households. Their growth could in turn affect smaller-scale monastic enterprises, which, especially in the late eighth and earlier ninth centuries, were sometimes handed over to them by aristocratic families who were anxious to buy into the new level of commemoration and intercession offered by these

[57] K. Böhner, *Das Grab eines fränkischen Herren aus Morken im Rheinland* (Cologne, 1959); H. W. Böhme, *Germanische Grabfunde des 4. und 5. Jahrhunderts zwischen Elbe und Loire*. 2 vols. (Munich, 1974).

[58] Le Jan, 'Convents, violence, and competition for power'.

[59] K. Bowes, 'Early Christian archaeology: a state of the field', *Religion Compass* 2/4 (2008), pp. 575–619; E. James, *The Merovingian Archaeology of South-West Gaul*. BAR supplementary series, 25 (Oxford, 1977); G. P. Fehring, *The Archaeology of Medieval Germany: an Introduction*, trans. R. Samson (London, 1991).

'powerhouses of prayer'.[60] This had significant implications for the role of aristocratic women: unable to perform the mass or participate fully in acts of commemorative prayer, their place in the ninth-century church was more marginal than it had been, as nunneries were rarer and less central to the circuits of power, and women's role as guardians of family memory was increasingly tied to their educative responsibilities as wives and mothers.[61] At the same time, although Carolingian insistence on royal protection of the greatest monasteries significantly reduced the opportunities for formal family control of monastic centres, families maintained the informal links expressed through their patronage, in which boys given into divine service as child oblates increasingly came to act as bridges between monastery and family.[62] Ninth-century monasteries thus remained important points in aristocratic itineraries and anchors of family identity, even where they no longer responded exclusively to the concerns of a single family or kin-group.

Given these changes, it is no surprise that new forms of aristocratic residence do begin to emerge in our evidence for the eighth- and particularly the ninth-century countryside. Where previously aristocratic halls had simply been larger versions of the dwellings of the peasantry, from this time we begin to see in the countryside structures that more obviously declare the elite status of their occupiers. The proliferation of 'hall plus church' complexes, or occasionally of isolated halls, physically set apart from villages and other settlements, is striking. At Lauchheim in central Germany, for example, the process of separation was gradual: as the eighth century progressed, one plot in the settlement became increasingly dominant, the hall there rebuilt as part of a bigger compound containing a number of burials, enclosed by fences taking in a large area and increasing the physical distance between this residence and the rest of the settlement.[63] This kind of redevelopment indicates a level of power and resource that

---

[60] De Jong, 'Carolingian monasticism'; Brown, *Rise of Western Christendom*, pp. 219–24.

[61] J. M. H. Smith, 'The problem of female sanctity in Carolingian Europe *c.*750–920', *P&P* 146 (1995), pp. 3–37; M. Innes, 'Keeping it in the family: women and aristocratic memory *c.*700–1200', in E. van Houts (ed.), *Medieval Memories: Men, Women and the Past 700–1300* (London, 2001), pp. 17–35.

[62] On oblation, see M. de Jong, *In Samuel's Image. Child Oblation in the Early Medieval West* (Leiden and New York, 1996).

[63] See Damminger, 'Dwellings, settlements and settlement patterns', pp. 33–88; Stork, 'Zum Fortgang der Untersuchungen'.

could in some cases support the construction of purpose-built residences on new sites, distant from lower-status dwellings: the family of
Hraban Maur, for example, were in the second half of the eighth century able to build from scratch a structure of this kind, complete with
a small family church, which may have eclipsed their town-house at
Mainz as their principal residence.[64] An important intellectual figure
in the mid-ninth century, Hraban (abbot of Fulda 822–42, archbishop
of Mainz 847–56) belonged to a significant aristocratic family in the
middle Rhine region, where Ripwin and Giselhelm (discussed in
Chapter 5) also held their estates (see Map 9). As the map suggests,
we have fairly comprehensive information about this family's landholdings. Hofheim was the 'family seat', where the church founded
by Hraban's father (and dedicated to Boniface, Fulda's patron) became
something like a family mausoleum. Yet like other local worthies,
the family's holdings were relatively dispersed across the region. As
well as the house in Mainz, they had considerable interests west of
the Rhine, and were careful to cultivate their relationship with Fulda
some distance to the north-east. Through sites such as Hofheim, the
physical imprint of aristocratic power on the countryside becomes
evident for the first time since Roman times. The scale of investment
in these complexes, and their political importance, is clear at Petegem
in the Scheldt valley: here an eighth-century compound centred on
a church and associated cemetery was redeveloped in stone in the
ninth century, newly focussed on a rectangular hall with a tiled
roof. Petegem was an important point in local aristocratic networks,
where counts and bishops held meetings; hence Charles the Bald
lodged there when he was attempting to rally support in the area.[65]

These sites show no signs of fortification, no obvious need to
respond to contemporary threats from internal conflict or Viking
activity. The driving force behind their development was the display
of elite status, not concerns about defensibility. Even at Petegem,
where the site was defined by a seven-metre wide ditch, the function
of this boundary marker was to demarcate a space that was significant
in cultural and legal terms, rather than militarily; these priorities

---

[64] Innes, *State and Society*, p. 67, n. 49.
[65] G. Tessier, *et al.* (eds.), *Recueil des actes*, no. 274. On Petegem see C. Loveluck,
'Rural settlement hierarchy in the age of Charlemagne', in Story (ed.), *Charlemagne*, pp. 230–58, at pp. 237–8, 250; D. Callebaut, 'Résidences fortifiées et
centres administratifs dans la vallée de l'Escaut (ixe–xie siècle)', in D. Demolon,
H. Galinié and F. Verhaeghe (eds.), *Archéologie des villes dans le Nord-Ouest de
l'Europe (viie–viiie siècle)* (Douai, 1994), pp. 93–112, at pp. 95–7.

Map 9. Landholdings of Hraban Maur's family

found parallels at royal palaces, which were not built as defensive (or offensive) strongholds.[66] The archaeological evidence argues against the idea of a restructuring of the countryside around aristocratic strongholds: where a clause in Charles the Bald's Edict of Pîtres (864) commands the tearing down of unauthorised fortifications, it is by no means clear that these were residences.[67] References to similar structures in the narrative sources of the later ninth century often make them sound more like field fortifications, put up quickly and temporarily against an imminent threat.[68]

The most important influence on the development of aristocratic residences was the example provided by royal buildings.[69] One distinctive feature of the architecture of Carolingian kingship was the second storey, which provided a secluded but still public space for receiving petitioners and taking counsel, functions which complemented those of the great halls at palace sites like Ingelheim, and the open air spaces favoured for royal assemblies; the use of upper-storey space in this manner was a departure from late antique precedents where rulers met their subjects and counsellors in ground-floor chambers.[70] Second storeys are attested both at royal palaces and at centres of royal estates, where kings and their entourages might stay while passing through a locality.[71] They were safer, of course, when constructed in stone: the collapse of wooden porticoes at Aachen while Louis the Pious was processing through them, or in the smaller rural centre at Flammersheim when Louis the German was surrounded by a 'throng' of subjects, threatened the health of king and kingdom.[72] Buildings for royalty might also be constructed by important abbots and bishops as a way of ingratiating themselves with kings: thus Archbishop Leidrad of Lyon built a residence for the use of kings when they visited his city, and a magnificent and still surviving building was added at the gateway to the abbey

---

[66] See above, Chapter 4, pp. 175–6.
[67] *Edictum Pistense* [Edict of Pîtres], ed. V. Krause, *Capit.* II, no. 273, p. 328; for the archaeology see Loveluck, 'Rural settlement', pp. 239–40.
[68] E.g. *AF*, *s.a.* 880, trans. Reuter, p. 90; *AV*, *s.a.* 885, trans. Dutton, p. 510.
[69] At Petegem, the stone hall complex closely resembles those described in polyptychs serving royal estates, as noted by Loveluck, 'Rural settlement', pp. 237–9.
[70] The following sentences are heavily indebted to de Jong, 'Charlemagne's balcony'.
[71] See e.g. Notker, *Gesta*, 1.30; *Brevium exempla*, trans. Dutton, *Carolingian Civilization*, pp. 85–7.
[72] *ARF*, *s.a.* 817, trans. Scholz, p. 102, *AF*, *s.a.* 870, trans. Reuter, p. 62.

of Lorsch when, under Louis the German, it became a centre of royal representation.[73] Against this backdrop, the use of two-storeyed residences by aristocrats in the late ninth century – evident in a series of asides in our narrative accounts – should be understood in terms of aristocratic emulation of an originally royal idiom.[74] At Engis in modern Belgium, an early-eighth-century complex was rebuilt in stone in the ninth century, with the reconstructed church facing a lavish hall. These structures are strongly reminiscent of the Lorsch gatehouse and the descriptions of royal estate centres, and a document of 885 shows that this was a royal centre linked with hunting rights in a nearby forest, now granted out to members of a crucial aristocratic network in this highly contested region.[75]

The similarity of royal and aristocratic buildings is not surprising, for, as the Engis case suggests, the two overlapped. Royal estate centres were run by stewards recruited from the ranks of local landed elites, and where their careers can be traced royal estate managers often seem to have worked in areas where they also had family interests: Odo, one of the crucial political figures of the civil wars of the 830s when he served as count of Orléans, began his career running the royal palace at Ingelheim, which adjoined his family estates.[76] Royal estates were visible manifestations of royal power in the landscape, even when kings were not at home; but they were also home to ambitious aristocrats the year round, and provided lodgings for those rushing to and from court on royal business.[77] Hence

---

[73] For Leidrad of Lyon's royal house, see Leidrad, *Epistolae*, ed. E. Dümmler, *MGH Epp.* IV (*Epp. Karolini aevi* II) (Berlin, 1895), pp. 542–4, *Epistola ad Carolum*, no. 30. For the Lorsch gatehouse see W. Jacobsen, 'Die Lorscher Torhalle. Zum Problem ihrer Deutung und Datierung', *Jahrbuch des Zentralinstituts für Kunstgeschichte* I (1985), pp. 9–77; Innes, 'Kings, monks and patrons'. See also Figure 4a in Chapter 3 above.

[74] *Contra* Innes, 'People, places and power', assuming that it points to proto-castles/fortifications.

[75] Loveluck, 'Rural settlement', p. 238; J. Witwrouw, 'Le Centre domanial du haut moyen âge du Thier d'Olne à Engis/Hermalle-sous-Huy', *Bulletin de Liaison de l'Association Française d'Archéologie Mérovingienne* 23 (1999), pp. 105–8.

[76] For this and other examples, see S. Airlie, *The Political Behaviour of Secular Magnates in Francia, 829–79*, unpublished D.Phil. thesis, University of Oxford (1985); Airlie, 'The palace of memory'.

[77] Airlie, 'Palace of memory'; Airlie, 'Bonds of power and bonds of association in the court circle of Louis the Pious', in Godman and Collins (eds.), *Charlemagne's Heir*, pp. 191–204. See Einhard, *Translation and Miracles*, IV.7, trans. Dutton, *Charlemagne's Courtier*, pp. 115–17, for an example of a royal official stopping off at a royal villa.

aristocratic property complexes are often found around the fringes of royal estates, which suggests that aristocrats may have lived near to the residences of kings: Charles the Fat consciously encouraged this in the areas where he spent most of his time, Alemannia and Italy.[78] Bishops and other nobles (including Einhard) are also known to have had town houses in Aachen and Pavia, two of the principal royal centres of Francia and Italy.[79] All this points to a relatively regular proximity of kings and aristocrats, forming an important nodal point which sustained the identity of the aristocratic political community. The treatise 'On the Governance of the Palace', written by Adalhard of Corbie in the early ninth century and revised by Archbishop Hincmar of Rheims in 882, underlines the importance of this link by describing the various forms of interaction between different levels of aristocrat at assemblies and at the palace more generally.[80]

At Aachen, the doorway to the imperial private chambers was where courtiers loitered awaiting a chance to press their cases. From there, a series of walkways and balconies – where the privileged might access the emperor, but which were visible to all – provided linkages to the major ceremonial spaces of the church and audience hall. Meanwhile, in the surrounding buildings less formal codes of sociability held sway: here the great officers of the court maintained their own dwellings to which visitors and the lesser members of the court – styled 'servants' by Hincmar – might be invited, regaled with gossip and honoured with gifts.[81] Aristocratic households would have had similar, if less complex, arrangements of space: the attention paid to external markers – fences and ditches, and at several sites metalled tracks leading to the central building on a site – underlines the extent to which aristocratic power was seen as something exercised publicly, made manifest in visible activity and outdoor meetings. By the ninth century, not only were royal palaces and estates significant elements in aristocratic patterns of residence and movement, they also provided influential models for the conception and spatial organisation of aristocratic authority itself.

---

[78] Airlie, *Political Behaviour*, p. 198; MacLean, *Kingship and Politics*, pp. 89–90, 94–6.
[79] Nelson, 'Aachen as a place of power'; D. A. Bullough, 'Urban change in early medieval Italy: the example of Pavia', *PBSR* 34 (1966), pp. 82–130.
[80] Hincmar, *De ordine palatii*, c. 27, trans. Dutton, *Carolingian Civilization*, p. 527.
[81] See e.g. Einhard, *Translation and Miracles*, I.I, trans. Dutton, *Charlemagne's Courtier*, p. 70.

ARISTOCRATIC BEHAVIOUR: UPBRINGING,
MORALITY AND CULTURE

These hierarchies of space mattered because they defined social relationships and social identities. The 'servants' mentioned by Hincmar, for example, were probably not menial workers, but rather young or lesser-ranking nobles who did not yet hold formal offices. This brings us to the importance of the royal court (as well as the households of great nobles) as a forum for the socialisation of junior aristocrats.[82] In its heyday the Merovingian royal court had performed precisely this function, as the letters of Bishop Desiderius of Cahors, raised at the court of King Dagobert, attest.[83] The succession of minorities in the Merovingian royal line in the later seventh and early eighth centuries (discussed in Chapter 2) is likely to have diminished the role of the court in nurturing young nobles. Hincmar refers to these people as the *pueri*, the lads, and their career paths typically involved being sent to court to attend the king and his entourage in the hope of eventually making a good enough impression to be granted a good marriage, some land, an important office, or all three. The sorts of bonding activities in which they participated also helped to hone their martial abilities. Important among these was hunting, in which the Frankish aristocracy took great pride: Einhard claimed that 'there is hardly a people on earth who can rival the Franks in this skill'.[84] Hunting mattered also because it was something that kings and nobles did together; like feasting, it was a ritual that helped to express trust and consensus. It is not surprising that royal assemblies therefore often ended with a hunt.[85] 'The lads' were clearly also encouraged to engage in even riskier occupations. In 864 Young Charles, the son of Charles the Bald, was 'enjoying some horseplay with other young men of his own age' when one of his friends hit him on the head with a sword and 'penetrated almost as far as the brain, reaching from his left temple to his right cheekbone and jaw'.[86] Play-fighting with

---

[82] For this paragraph see Innes, 'A place of discipline'; Le Jan, 'Frankish giving of arms', pp. 282–5.

[83] Desiderius of Cahors, *Epistolae*, ed. W. Arndt, *MGH Epp.* III (*Epistolae Merovingici et Karolini aevi* I) (Berlin, 1892), pp. 191–214.

[84] Einhard, *VK*, c. 22, trans. Dutton, *Charlemagne's Courtier*, p. 30. Note also Hraban Maur's abridgement of the late Roman military manual by Vegetius, and his comments there on the importance of hunting as training for warfare: see Goldberg, *Struggle for Empire*, pp. 39–42.

[85] Nelson, 'Carolingian royal ritual'.

[86] *AB*, *s.a.* 864, p. 105, trans. Nelson, pp. 111–12; Regino, *Chronicle*, *s.a.* 870.

real weapons was a dangerous business, and Charles was by no means the only Carolingian to fall foul of such shenanigans. However, this was evidently not thought inappropriate behaviour for princes and budding secular aristocrats who would have to participate in warfare as adults. The abilities that these men acquired were impressive: Nithard describes spectacularly skilful war games organised by Louis the German and Charles the Bald during the civil wars, as part of which horsemen would charge at each other then wheel in feigned retreats, barely avoiding contact.[87]

Such skill could be nurtured by nobles' participation in the rituals and daily rough and tumble of the royal court, but sending off adolescents for 'finishing' in the house of a patron – often a relative or a godparent – remained the widely practised ideal.[88] Thus Einhard's letters show him acting as a guardian and patron for young men serving in his household, and taking an active role in negotiating marriages, securing the consent of both parties' kin and arranging the necessary bequests of property, when his charges moved on to establish households of their own.[89] Moreover, a figure like Einhard was a desirable patron precisely because he offered a point of contact with the royal court. Royal and aristocratic spheres of upbringing necessarily coexisted and overlapped.

Gaining access to the royal presence made it possible to catch the king's eye: one of Notker's stories concerns Isanbard, an aristocrat who had been disgraced and stripped of his offices until his bravery on the hunt, killing a ferocious beast which had wounded Charlemagne, led to his rehabilitation.[90] Aristocratic life, in a world of easily offended and jealously guarded honour, was not a risk-free activity, as Isanbard could attest. But bonds formed in youth, and rooted in royal and aristocratic households, were powerful, and could last for life.[91] The defining feature of these relationships was a kind of masculine honour. Although the son of Charles the Bald

---

[87] Nithard, *Historiarum Libri IV*, III.6, trans. Scholz, *Carolingian Chronicles*, p. 164.

[88] P. Stafford, 'Parents and children in the early middle ages', *EME* 10 (2001), pp. 257–71.

[89] Einhard, *Ep.* 62, trans. Dutton, *Charlemagne's Courtier*, p. 159; see also Innes, 'Practices of property', pp. 259–62; cf. T. Charles-Edwards, 'The distinction between land and moveable wealth in Anglo-Saxon England', in P. H. Sawyer (ed.), *Medieval Settlement: Continuity and Change* (London, 1976), pp. 180–7.

[90] Notker, *Gesta*, 2.8, trans. Ganz, pp. 93–4; see MacLean, *Kingship and Politics*, pp. 87–8, 217; M. Innes, 'Memory, orality and literacy in an early medieval society', *P&P* 158 (1998), pp. 3–36.

[91] Airlie, 'The aristocracy in the service of the state'.

who was maimed while playfighting never recovered, and was to die two years after his accident, it is significant that he and his peers tried to protect his assailant from punishment. Conversely, Count Hugh of Tours's failure to bring reinforcements to the imperial army on the Spanish March in 827 prompted opponents to castigate him as cowardly. Thegan's claim that Hugh was too scared to leave his house because of the taunts of his entourage shows how notions of honour were tied up with constructions of domestic and public space: Hugh's standing was undermined by his inability to control his own household, and his dishonour was complete because 'he almost never dared to put his feet out of doors' and cross the boundary from the domestic to the public sphere.[92] The urgency of these concerns reminds us that the categorisation of public offices in the vocabulary of 'honour' and 'dignity', which we discussed in Chapter 4, has to be taken extremely seriously.[93] Shared codes of honour mattered because entourages could be unruly and needed mastering, and the stories of Young Charles and Hugh confirm that the honour-bound aristocratic milieu was face-to-face, aggressive and macho: what one might expect, in fact, from a group which considered itself a warrior elite.[94]

Yet the martial elements of this identity do not tell the whole story. The training of young noblemen was not restricted to networking and male bonding, as shown by a handbook of advice written in the early 840s by the laywoman Dhuoda for her son William as he made his way at Charles the Bald's court. As well as expecting him to make useful contacts, Dhuoda hoped that William would cultivate wisdom and learn other virtues such as humility, patience and sobriety.[95] Self-restraint was itself part of the legitimate exercise of power. More formal aspects of education were also provided at court, as well as in monastic schools. An emphasis on the heavy moral responsibilities that accompanied the ability to rule followed from a

---

[92] Thegan, *Gesta Hludovici imperatoris*, cc. 28, 55, trans. Dutton, *Carolingian Civilization*, pp. 167, 175. On this story see Innes, 'He never even allowed his white teeth to be bared in laughter', at p. 153.

[93] See above, Chapter 4, p. 188.

[94] E. Goldberg, '"More devoted to the equipment of battle than the splendor of banquets": frontier kingship, martial ritual, and early knighthood at the court of Louis the German', *Viator* 30 (1999), pp. 41–78, esp. pp. 45–50.

[95] Dhuoda, *Liber manualis*, III.9, ed. and trans. Thiébaux, pp. 106–9; Innes, 'A place of discipline', p. 68.

political programme which saw all power as derived from God, and its wielders as responsible to God not only for their actions, but also for the souls of those in their care.

Those moral codes of conduct referred to by Dhuoda brought the lay nobility face to face with a potential contradiction in its position. Noble identity was bound up in family and military roles; yet how could sex and violence be squared with the rigours of Christianity? How, in short, could they save their souls? The paradox was still an irritant at the end of the ninth century to Notker of St Gallen, whose attempt to compare the piety of King Louis the German favourably with that of St Ambrose of Milan forced him to make telling caveats: 'Louis closely resembled the saint, except in such points as are necessary to an earthly commonwealth, as for instance marriage and the use of arms.'[96] These were troubling aspects of secular life which had a particular resonance during the violent expansion of the Carolingian empire in the second half of the eighth century, not all of which was directed at pagans. The sin of killing could be satisfied through penance, but that involved a surrender of arms, office and marriage which effectively emasculated and 'dis-nobled' the penitent.[97] This was not, however, a new problem, and a long intellectual tradition was available from which to construct solutions. For the Franks, a deep respect for the Old Testament coupled with the experience of expansionary warfare helped foster the idea that they were a new Israel, the chosen people of God.[98] Their successes thus became a fulfilment of the divine will on earth. This heavenly approval was not simply claimed, but actively canvassed. While on campaign against the Avars in 791, Charlemagne arranged for a three-day fast to be organised across the realm, in order to appease God before battle commenced.[99] In the second half of the ninth century, the problem of Franks fighting against Franks in civil war was even more traumatic. For this reason, Frankish writers were careful to deprive enemy kings of their legitimacy by labelling them as 'tyrants', while

---

[96] Notker, *Gesta*, 2.10, trans. Ganz, p. 98.
[97] J. M. H. Smith, 'Gender and ideology in the early Middle Ages', in R. N. Swanson (ed.), *Gender and Christian Religion, Studies in Church History* 14 (Woodbridge, 1998), pp. 51–73, at p. 61.
[98] Garrison, 'The Franks as the new Israel?'.
[99] *Epistolae variorum Karolo regnante*, ed. E. Dümmler, *MGH Epp.* IV (*Epp. Karolini aevi* II) (Berlin, 1895), no. 20, pp. 528–9, trans. King, *Charlemagne: Translated Sources*, pp. 309–10.

churchmen were often to be found with armies, orchestrating bless-
ings, penance and other rituals of collective expiation.[100] Pope John
VIII (872–82) was even ready to promise remission of sins to anyone
who came to defend Rome against the Muslims.[101]

It would be anachronistic to see this clerical language as a fig
leaf to legitimise violence and imperialism. The mentality of the
elite involved a genuine dichotomy in the core identities of men
who saw themselves as both warriors and true Christians. The deep
concern of some laymen for their own salvation is indicated by
the genre of instructional literature known as 'mirrors for princes'.
These books were composed by churchmen such as Archbishop
Paulinus of Aquileia, but they were actively sought by their lay recipients, in Paulinus's case Eric, count of nearby Friuli.[102] These tracts
addressed real concerns on the part of their recipients: Paulinus wrote
in response to Eric's fears about the dangers of being preoccupied
'in the business of warfare', while in another tract written in the
790s Alcuin aimed to demonstrate to Count Wido that his lay status
would not prevent him from getting to heaven.[103] The most ambitious such treatise, written by Bishop Jonas of Orléans for his local
count, Matfrid, presented itself as a guide for the 'lay institution',
offering a morality specifically tailored to the needs of those 'in the
married state'. Jonas was echoing a series of contemporary attempts
to define human society in terms suggested four hundred years earlier
by St Augustine, as being made up of three orders, each with their
special needs: the laity, defined by their married state; and monks and
priests, each of whom already had written rules which had recently

---

[100] J. L. Nelson, 'Violence in the Carolingian world and the ritualization of ninth-
century warfare', in G. Halsall (ed.), *Violence and Society in the Early Medieval West*
(Woodbridge, 1998), pp. 90–107; D. S. Bachrach, *Religion and the Conduct of War,
c.300–c.1215* (Woodbridge, 2003).

[101] John VIII, *Epistolae*, ed. E. Caspar, *MGH Epp.* VII (*Epp. Karolini aevi* V) (Berlin,
1928), nos. 41, 217, 246, pp. 39, 194, 214.

[102] See Paulinus of Aquileia, *Liber Exhortationis ad Hericum Comitem*, PL IC, cols.
197–282. On these tracts, see S. Airlie, 'The anxiety of sanctity: St Gerald of
Aurillac and his maker', *Journal of Ecclesiastical History* 43 (1992), pp. 372–95;
Smith, 'Gender and ideology', esp. pp. 60–5; H. H. Anton, *Fürstenspiegel und
Herrscherethos in der Karolingerzeit*, Bonner Historische Forschungen 32 (Bonn,
1968); R. Stone, 'Kings are different: Carolingian mirrors for princes and lay
morality', in F. Lachaud and L. Scordia (eds.), *Le Prince au miroir de la littérature
politique de l'Antiquité aux Lumières* (Rouen, 2007), pp. 69–86; T. F. X. Noble,
'Secular sanctity: forging an ethos for the Carolingian nobility', in Wormald and
Nelson (eds.), *Lay Intellectuals*, pp. 8–36.

[103] Alcuin, *De virtutibus et vitiis liber*, PL CI, cols. 613–38.

been approved by imperial authority.[104] The manuscript transmission of works like Jonas's and especially Alcuin's reflects their popularity, and at least some manuscripts were commissioned or owned by lay aristocrats: Eberhard of Friuli, for example, owned a copy of Alcuin's work.[105] That the messages of such tracts hit home is suggested by the writings of Charlemagne's biographer Einhard, a layman, who consistently called himself 'sinner' in his writings, reflecting a tendency to ponder acutely upon his own humility and worthlessness.[106] Later in the ninth century, we encounter a number of lay nobles who found the paradox impossible to live with and even tried to divest themselves of their secular status.[107]

There were limits to all this. Even churchmen like Notker, Alcuin and Jonas evidently recognised that sexual reproduction and warfare were essential to the survival of the Church and kingdom, and thus of God's chosen people. Restraint, not abstinence, was the core message of most handbooks. This was not, then, simply a case of the Church preaching to the laity. Rather, it reflects exchange between them, and a genuine piety which among at least some members of the secular aristocracy might have extended to a tendency to self-examination. Nevertheless, the strengthening of the institutional Church under the Carolingians (discussed in Chapter 3) firmed up the dividing line between ecclesiastical and secular elites. Priests and monks acquired a group identity through the conscious avoidance of the normal markers of aristocracy in lifestyle as well as dress and haircut: they were to avoid the polluting secularity of the hunt, not even riding behind it as spectators with their dogs, and to take care over their involvement in the lewd merriment of aristocratic feasting. Changing patterns of ecclesiastical recruitment reinforced these boundaries. By the ninth century, ecclesiastical leaders were overwhelmingly drawn from monasteries, having been given up by their parents as child oblates; brought up differently from their lay

---

[104] Jonas, *De institutione laicorum*, PL CVI, cols. 121–278.
[105] On the transmission of Alcuin, see D. Bullough, *Alcuin: Achievement and Reputation* (Leiden, 2003); P. Szarmach, 'A preliminary handlist of manuscripts containing Alcuin's *Liber de virtutibus et vitiis*', *Manuscripta* 25 (1981), pp. 131–40; on Jonas, see Schröder, 'Überlieferung'. On Eberhard see Kershaw, 'Eberhard of Friuli'.
[106] See J. M. H. Smith, 'Einhard: the sinner and the saints', *TRHS* 6th ser. 13 (2003), pp. 55–77.
[107] J. L. Nelson, 'Monks, secular men and masculinity, *c.* 900', in D. M. Hadley (ed.), *Masculinity in Medieval Europe* (London, 1999), pp. 121–42.

kinsmen, they acquired a distinct professional identity.[108] 'Career changes', when lay officeholders volunteered or were coerced into ecclesiastical roles – as was frequent in Merovingian Francia and was still possible in the reign of Charlemagne – became very rare thereafter.

Carolingian 'reform' may have encouraged the differentiation of ecclesiastical and secular elites, but this did not cut off the aristocracy from cultural developments. Far from it: there is good evidence for avid aristocratic consumption not only of 'self-help' manuals in the approved pieties of their day, but also of literate culture more generally. Stereotypes about a hard-drinking hard-fighting warrior elite are too simplistic.[109] The written works of lay people like Dhuoda, Einhard and Nithard, which are studded with classical and Biblical quotations, demonstrate that scholarly learning and the ability to write stylish Latin were not the exclusive preserve of a clerical elite, but a prized accomplishment of courtiers. Yet quite how many among the aristocracy were literate, and what kind of literacy they exhibited, remain matters open for debate. Modern concepts of literacy encourage us to connect the ability to read with the ability to write. But in the early Middle Ages the latter was seen as a craft for skilled manual workers. Einhard's portrait of Charlemagne keeping wax tablets under his pillow in his attempts to master the tricky art of writing, but eloquent in his Latin speech and ardently listening to Augustine's *City of God* read aloud over dinner, looks odd to our eyes, but should not lead us to underestimate the extent of the Frankish ruler's interest and involvement in literate culture.[110] Our understanding of literacy privileges a particular kind of reading, silent and individual, whose cultural dominance is a relatively recent historical phenomenon; in the early Middle Ages, this practice was associated with meditation on the hidden messages of a holy text.

Participation in a culture of books and intellectual debate was worth advertising. For example, among all the heavy weaponry and flashy drinking vessels, Eberhard and Gisela also bequeathed to their children several books, while Count Eccard of Mâcon also had a sizeable library, again showing an involvement with the latest debates

---

[108] De Jong, *In Samuel's Image.*
[109] McKitterick, *The Carolingians and the Written Word*, pp. 211–70.
[110] Einhard, *VK*, cc. 24–5, trans. Dutton, *Charlemagne's Courtier*, pp. 31–2; Dutton, *Charlemagne's Mustache*, pp. 69–92.

at centres like Auxerre.[111] The ability to demonstrate eloquence in Latin speech, and to appreciate the theological reading and public debates staged at court, were central accomplishments for any would-be political player.[112] Accomplished speech of this type was, of course, specific to the milieu of the royal court. In fact, there is some evidence that linguistic competence in Latin may have served as an important marker of social status. Certainly linguistic changes meant that by the ninth century the ability to speak Latin – which now required specialised tutoring – marked one out as an aristocrat. Differing degrees of Latinity also reinforced internal divisions within the aristocracy: this explains the famous oaths sworn by the followers of Charles the Bald and Louis the German at Strasbourg in 842, the earliest surviving instance of Old French and one of the earliest Old High German texts too.[113] Here, to affirm their alliance, a solemn Latin oath was drawn up; this was sworn in the 'Roman tongue', that is the Romance vernacular of western Francia, by the east Frankish king Louis the German and his followers, so that its meaning was transparent to their audience, the followers of the western king Charles the Bald; subsequently, Charles and his followers swore the oath in the 'Teutonic tongue' (*theudisca*), the Germanic vernacular of the eastern Franks. The texts of the oaths in both vernaculars survive; they seem to be phonetically inspired and easy-to-pronounce representations, designed for an audience unfamiliar with the sounds and structures of their respective languages.[114] The ceremony constituted a public guarantee by the two kings and their immediate retinues that they would stand by and protect the interests of those lesser aristocrats who had come to fight for their royal lords, men who would face political ruin if their leaders abandoned them. To these lower tiers of aristocratic society gathered at Strasbourg to listen to an alien king who had recently been an enemy, an oath sworn in the familiar language of the homeland, not the difficult and potentially slippery medium of courtly Latin, offered reassurance.

---

[111] See McKitterick, *The Carolingians and the Written Word*, pp. 245–50; Kershaw, 'Eberhard of Friuli'.

[112] Garrison, 'The emergence of Carolingian Latin literature'; M. de Jong, 'The empire as *ecclesia*: Hrabanus Maurus and biblical *historia* for rulers', in Hen and Innes (eds.), *The Uses of the Past*, pp. 191–226.

[113] Nithard, *Histories*, III, 5, trans. Scholz, pp. 162–3.

[114] See R. Wright, *A Sociophilological Study of Late Latin* (Turnhout, 2002), pp. 177–90.

ARISTOCRATIC FAMILIES

Although much of what we have discussed so far suggests an image of the aristocracy as a self-conscious class committed to acting in its own interests, we must remember that criss-crossing this class identity were equally important family solidarities. As we mentioned at the beginning of the chapter, a lot of research has been done on the origins and family structures of the Carolingian aristocracy. It used to be thought that the Carolingians effectively created the aristocracy which governed the empire, by empowering the families which had been their allies in seventh- and eighth-century Austrasia and boosting them on to a grander stage as friends of kings. However, through analysis of their naming patterns, it has been possible to show that powerful aristocratic families in the eighth century were often descended from individuals who were influential in the same regions in the immediate post-Roman period, long before the Carolingians became a serious dynastic proposition.[115] In other words, the Carolingians did not create the aristocracy, but emerged from it. This is why, after taking the throne, they had to work constantly to establish and reinforce their royal status.[116] They could not afford to treat influential noble families with impunity; equally, though, individual families needed to work within the Carolingian system to maintain their position in the social hierarchy.

Family identities often look impressively solid in the writings of modern historians, and this impression is only enhanced by these families' sheer size and wealth. The most important could control immense quantities of land spread across great distances. For example, the extent of the lands left to their children by Eberhard and his wife Gisela (a daughter of Louis the Pious) in 863–4 (see Map 10) shows the rewards of royal patronage: a family whose home-base was around the church of Cysoing in Flanders (an equivalent to Hraban's Hofheim) acquired possessions distributed across the empire, entailing associations with multiple kings.[117] As a consequence of this extensive wealth and influence, the identities of families like Eberhard's were not exclusively defined by their relationship to the royal court, but existed independently. One means of expressing this

---

[115] Werner, 'Important noble families'; for problems with the methodology see Airlie, 'The aristocracy', in *NCMH* II, pp. 437–8.

[116] Airlie, '*Semper fideles*?'.

[117] La Rocca and Provero, 'The dead and their gifts', pp. 245–9.

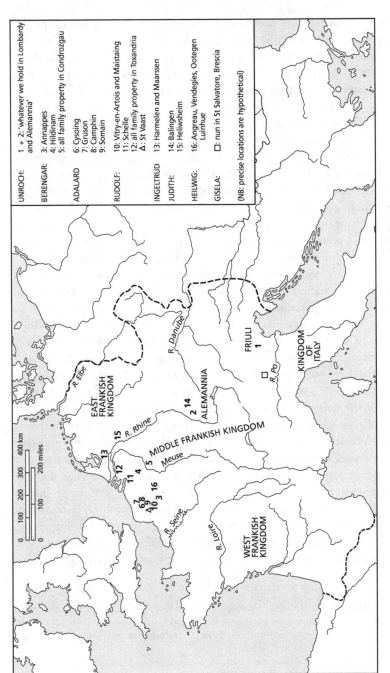

UNROCH: 1 + 2: 'whatever we hold in Lombardy and Alemannia'

BERENGAR: 3: Annappes
4: Hildinam
5: all family property in Condrozgau

ADALARD 6: Cysoing
7: Gruson
8: Camphin
9: Somain

RUDOLF: 10: Vitry-en-Artois and Maistaing
11: Schelle
12: all family property in Toxandria
△: St Vaast

INGELTRUD 13: Harmelen and Maarssen

JUDITH: 14: Balingen
15: Heliwsheim

HEILWIG: 16: Angreau, Vendegies, Ootegen Luinhue

GISELA: ☐: nun in St Salvatore, Brescia

(NB: precise locations are hypothetical)

Map 10. The lands in the will of Eberhard and Gisela of Friuli

identity was through names which recurred through generations and in a sense became family 'property': the names Charles and Louis, for instance, seem to have been monopolised by the Carolingians. Very occasionally we encounter families which were labelled by a collective name: the kin of the empress Engelberga, wife of Louis II of Italy, were referred to by an early-tenth-century writer corporately as the 'Supponids', after their most prominent male name, although it is far more normal to read of the 'associates' (*socii, propinqui*) of a named individual, a category which might encompass overlapping and mutually reinforcing bonds of kinship, friendship and lordship.[118] Aristocratic kindreds also expressed their sense of themselves by tracing their ancestry back to a single, sometimes mythical, ancestor who was sometimes a saint: in the case of the Carolingians, it was St Arnulf, a seventh-century bishop of Metz.[119] Many of these families thus invested emotionally in something like a cult of themselves.

Naming patterns suggest that the aristocracy enjoyed associations of an even greater range than the extensive landholdings of individual families. The personal links indicated by names have been taken to show the existence of vast kin-groups – extended clans – which have in turn often been seen as the fundamental building blocks of elite society. The largest repositories of names from this period are the *Libri memoriales* (memorial books), also known as 'Books of Confraternity', which were produced at monasteries across Europe to list the names used in liturgical ceremonies that were thought to benefit the souls of those named. They testify to the enormous size of the networks of prayer that formed around monastic communities. The two Carolingian-age confraternity books from St Gallen, for example, together contain some 14,932 names. The earlier was put together before 817 and includes names of members of thirty-one of the religious communities bound to St Gallen through confraternity agreements, both living and dead: on page 22 (pictured in Figure 15) the left-hand arcade has been labelled 'of the living' ('vivoru(m)'), the right-hand arcade 'of the dead' ('mortuor(um)'), though in both

---

[118] E. Hlawitschka, *Franken, Alemannen, Bayern und Burgunder in Oberitalien (774–962). Zum Verständnis der fränkischen Königsherrschaft in Italien* (Freiburg, 1960), pp. 299–309 (on the Supponids); MacLean, 'Queenship, nunneries', pp. 26–32 (on Engelberga and the Supponids).

[119] Thegan, *Gesta Hludovici imperatoris*, c. 1, p. 174, trans. Dutton, *Carolingian Civilization*, p. 159; see Fouracre, *Charles Martel*, pp. 33–4, 41–4.

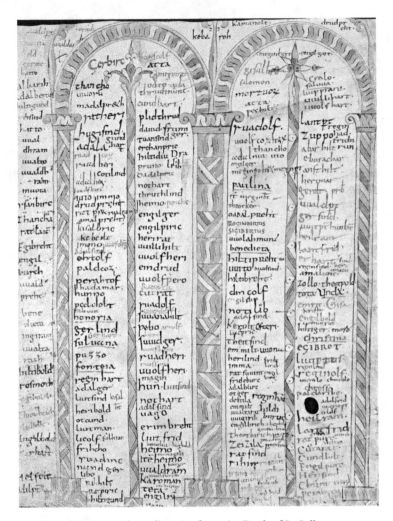

Figure 15. The earliest Confraternity Book of St Gallen.

the lists of names have outgrown the arcades. Careful work over
the last few decades has identified individual entries or groups of
entries, which may then sometimes be tied down to a specific date
or context, showing groups of aristocrats united in prayer. Scholars
have inferred that those found grouped in such a way, especially
those with similar name-elements, were related, and this has led to
the further hypothesis that family structure in the eighth and ninth

centuries was clan-based, with extensive bilateral ties pulling together individuals spread across the continent.[120]

The idea of the early medieval kin group as an extended network certainly helps to explain some aspects of the Carolingian high aristocracy, not least their extraordinary mobility. Even after the division of the empire in 843, which forced nobles to choose a single king to be their lord, well-connected aristocrats could still switch sides and move across regnal boundaries. A case in point is the career of Count Robert 'the Strong', a noble from the Worms region who was able to acquire important offices in west Francia thanks to his connections with the family of Charles the Bald's first queen, Ermentrude.[121] Robert's son Odo became king of west Francia in 888, and the Capetian dynasty which ruled west of the Rhine for centuries after 987 were his direct descendants: the ancestor figure of the greatest French medieval royal dynasty was therefore a Rhinelander. This highlights the impermanence of the internal frontiers which divide modern maps of the empire in the ninth century: men like Robert continued to perform on an imperial stage. Even after the disintegration of the empire in 888, such connections survived. Guy of Spoleto was able to make a credible, though ultimately unsuccessful, bid to become king of west Francia in 888, despite the fact that he had spent almost his entire political career in central Italy.[122] This mobility was possible partly because, as we have seen in the case of Eberhard, these great men held land scattered across different kingdoms; but extensive family links were also a pre-requisite.

Elite families could certainly conceive of themselves as extended groups for some purposes, therefore, but in other circumstances family identities could narrow quite sharply. In particular, claims to property were often expressed within a much smaller, even nuclear, family. This is illustrated by Dhuoda's handbook for her son which, listing the people William is to pray for, names only the relatives

---

[120] Reuter, 'Medieval nobility'; Airlie, 'The aristocracy', in *NCMH* II, pp. 433–40; G. Constable, 'The *Liber memorialis* of Remiremont', *Speculum* 48 (1972), pp. 260–77; H. Fichtenau, *Living in the Tenth Century* (Chicago, 1991), pp. 85–6.

[121] K. F. Werner, 'Untersuchungen zur Frühzeit des französischen Fürstentums', *Die Welt als Geschichte* 3–4 (1959), pp. 146–93; Nelson, *Charles the Bald*, pp. 130–1; Airlie, 'The aristocracy', in *NCMH* II, p. 435.

[122] *AV*, s.a. 888; S. Airlie, 'Review article: After empire. Recent work on the emergence of post-Carolingian kingdoms', *EME* 2 (1993), pp. 153–61.

of his father from whom he had inherited property.[123] Property and inheritance were similarly important in Italy in defining the narrower family unit.[124] When an annalist writing in Mainz in 883 wished to criticise the emperor (Charles the Fat) for attempting to dispossess Guy of Spoleto and his allies, the best way he could think of to underline the illegitimacy of this act was in terms of direct father–son inheritance: '[Charles] gave the benefices which they and their fathers and their grandfathers and their great-grandfathers had held to persons of much lower standing.'[125] These examples suggest that family identity could be defined as patrilinear and bound up with the ownership of inherited property.

The existence of these tighter 'practical' bonds within the wider array of 'official kin' points to the multi-layered and sometimes fluid nature of family structures amongst Carolingian elites.[126] Case-studies of the shifting political alignments of particular families suggest that individuals might privilege and play upon those ties of kinship connecting them to a well-placed figure at court in the hope of patronage and preferment, but that as the political situation changed they might realign themselves, stressing a different set of family ties to connect them with a different potential patron. Einhard and Thegan, for example, draw the kinship connections of Charlemagne's wife, Hildegard, differently, in ways which reflect the immediate political circumstances in which they wrote.[127] This fluidity was not based on confusion, but on the efforts of individuals to make the complex web of kin ties work for them. The sheer extent of the Carolingian empire, and its creation of a hierarchy within the aristocracy focussed on the court, worked integrally to shape the family structures of the aristocracy: the extensive and open-ended systems of kinship so evident in our sources was emphasised in a political context which put a premium on precisely those kinds of networks. The commonplace

---

[123] Dhuoda, *Liber manualis*, VIII.14, ed. and trans. Thiébaux, pp. 204–5; Innes, 'Keeping it in the family'. On inheritance see also above, Chapter 5, pp. 243–5.

[124] Costambeys, *Power and Patronage*, pp. 209–11.

[125] *AF*, s.a. 883, trans. Reuter, p. 95.

[126] This useful distinction comes from P. Bourdieu, *Outline of a Theory of Practice*, trans. R. Nice (Cambridge, 1977), pp. 33–8.

[127] R. Le Jan, 'Structures familiales et politiques au IXe siècle: un groupe familial de l'aristocratie franque', *Revue historique* 265 (1981), pp. 289–333; Le Jan, *Famille et pouvoir dans le monde franc, VIIIe–Xe siècles* (Paris, 1995), pp. 162–3. See Einhard, *VK*, c. 18; Thegan, *Gesta Hludowici imperatoris*, cc. 1–2, trans. Dutton, *Carolingian Civilization*, pp. 159–60.

that kinship was the basic social bond in early medieval society is true not because kin-groups were cohesive entities held together by overwhelming mutual obligation, but because ties with potential patrons and helpers could be activated and expressed by identifying and addressing those people as kin.

The fluidity of kinship ties has sometimes made it hard to map them on to patterns of property-owning and inheritance. Although the evidence for inheritance seems to point us in the direction of smaller family groups, as we have seen, the norms that governed these transfers are extremely elusive. Those set out in law codes tend to concern themselves with special classes of property or with exceptional cases, and were in any case of questionable practical application.[128] Documents that do reflect real cases – charters and records of dispute – nowhere explicitly state principles about inheritance. The run of two dozen or so surviving wills from the Frankish kingdoms, for example, continue to utilise the basic forms of the Roman will into the eighth century and invoke the rules of Roman law guaranteeing some heirs a stated minimum share; but they express no other norms. Admittedly, the sample of wills is exceptional: most of those that survive do so because their authors made a favoured church their principal heir.[129] Nonetheless, they do suggest a situation in which there was an expectation that an individual's property would be divided between heirs on their death, but that there was considerable room for negotiation over the nature of that division.

By the ninth century, indeed, even the Roman law structures that had characterised the earlier material disappear, and wills become agreements between an individual and his or her heirs concerning commemoration and charity: they are styled as, say, 'the alms of Eccard', and the beneficiaries and witnesses are bound together in their role as 'Eccard's almsmen', charged with ensuring the well-being of his soul through commemorative prayer. The best examples of this practice are those drawn up for Count Eccard of Mâcon *c.*863

---

[128] A. C. Murray, '*Pax et disciplina.* Roman public law and the Merovingian state', in K. Pennington, S. Chodorow and K. H. Kendall (eds.), *Proceedings of the Tenth International Congress of Medieval Canon Law* (Vatican City, 2001), pp. 269–85, repr. in T. F. X. Noble (ed.), *From Roman Provinces to Medieval Kingdoms* (New York and Abingdon, 2006), pp. 376–88.

[129] U. Nonn, 'Merowingische Testamente', *Archiv für Diplomatik* 18 (1972), pp. 1–129; Geary, *Aristocracy in Provence.*

and for Ercanfrida, the widow of Count Nithard of Trier, *c*.853.[130] In both cases, the pattern of bequests reflects ongoing associations between particular estates and individuals. Ercanfrida, for example, gave her major estate-complex to the monks at Prüm, who were to hold an annual feast there on her death day for the good of her soul and her husband's, while other estates were to go back to the closest descendants of those who gave them to Ercanfrida. Overall, such agreements present inheritance not as an abstract matter governed by formal rules, but as a practice rooted in personal relationships which generated emotional and moral claims: heirs were expected to link their receipt of a particular property to the commemoration of the ancestor from whom they received it.

These attitudes are not, it is true, directly documented in the records of property transfer that make up the bulk of the charter evidence – we would not expect them to be – but they are implicit in the commonplace acknowledgement of the wishes of previous owners in donation charters, and in the narrative strategies through which claims to property were made in court hearings. 'Inheritance' is then best understood as involving a claim to be acknowledged as kin and so to be included in the commemoration of the deceased and the redistribution of his or her property. Modern research on the charters, moreover, suggests that property was circulated within families not in a once-and-for-all deathbed drama of inheritance, but through a steady flow of grants between kin through the life-cycle: the centre-piece of Ercanfrida's will, indeed – the donation of her dower to Prüm – had already been ensured by a standard donation charter making no mention of her last will and testament. A family's central places, such as its church or churches, also helped to keep family properties concentrated: by granting one's lands to a church or monastery and then receiving them back as lifetime leases, the dangers of ever-increasing division and subdivision through inheritance could be sidestepped. The lands in question would theoretically belong to the institution in perpetuity, and so would always return intact to the control of the proprietary family of the institution as shorter-term arrangements (time-limited leases) ran their course.

---

[130] Eccard's will: Prou and Vidier (eds.), *Recueil Saint-Benoît-sur-Loire* I, no. 25, pp. 59–67; Ercanfrida's will: J. L. Nelson, 'The wary widow', in W. Davies and P. Fouracre (eds.), *Property and Power in the Early Middle Ages* (Cambridge, 1995), pp. 82–113.

There is also strong evidence for transferring land through purchase or exchange. In some parts of Europe, these types of transaction were just as common as donations as ways of circulating property within families, and between families and favoured institutions. Karol, son of Liutprand, built up a considerable estate through purchases in the Vico Teatino in central Italy between about 850 and 870, but perhaps over-reached himself, because his sons were forced to sell some of his estate to the monastery of Casauria, and then to lease it back for an annual rent.[131] Too strong a focus on formal division between kin effected at the deathbed of an individual thus misrepresents practices of property which rested on a continuum of exchange.[132]

ARISTOCRATIC RESOURCES AND RELATIONSHIPS: *HONORES*, BENEFICES AND LORDSHIP

Among the most significant indications of the flexibility of inheritance is the strong role played in surviving examples by women. Three of Eberhard and Gisela's daughters received land alongside their brothers, and they are among numbers of women whom we know to have had independent control over property, with all the social power that that implied. The crucial position of women in the process of augmenting and passing on a family's property was to some extent only natural. As brides, they contributed the dower or morning gift that was a part of the legitimate marriage procedure in most west European traditions. As wives and mothers, they produced the children who could legitimately share the family inheritance. As widows, they could often control at least a portion of the family patrimony in their own right. Since they were therefore linchpins in the ownership and transfer of property that was so crucial to a family's power and position, both in the aristocracy and below, it is no surprise that women were also the principal guardians of family identity, cultivating the remembrance of the deceased and transmitting ideas about the family's shape and status to future generations. Dhuoda's manual

---

[131] For differing interpretations of Karol's family's position, compare Feller, Gramain and Weber, *La Fortune de Karol*, pp. 93–115, with P. Cammarosano, 'Marché de la terre et mobilité sociale dans les Abruzzes aux ixe–xie siècles. À propos d'un livre récent', *Revue Historique* 310/2 (2008), pp. 369–82.

[132] Innes, 'Dossiers and archives'. For the well-documented example of the family of Toto of Campione, see Gasparri and La Rocca (eds.), *Carte di famiglia*.

is a notable example of the latter.[133] Similarly, Richgard, the wife of Charles the Fat, doggedly pursued the commemoration of her close natal kin and sought to restore its landed interests, which had been damaged in the royal scramble for Lotharingia in 869–70, through the control and clever manipulation of a series of nunneries.[134] In Italy too, Lombard law came to recognise female power over property in various circumstances, and the surviving charters not only reveal numbers of women – nuns, widows and mothers in particular – wielding this power, but also hint at the often decisive influence of personal relationships within the family in enhancing the power of women in particular cases.[135] Yet family identity was not the sole determinant of political allegiance. Despite their impressive size and power, noble families in the Carolingian period did not concertedly pursue their interests as indivisible units. Family members could and did fight against each other in the dynastic conflicts of the period. When (as we shall see in Chapter 8) Boso attempted to seize the throne in 879, for example, his brother Richard lined up with the Carolingians who opposed him. Conflict within, as well as between, families was very often what gave rulers like Charlemagne the opportunity to intervene in a locality and impose their power to adjudicate and govern.[136]

One of the reasons that aristocratic movement and lifestyle shaped itself round the royal court is that kings were a key source of patronage. *Honores* (offices such as that of count) were in the king's gift, and came to be seen as a vital part of a successful aristocratic career. As we saw in Chapter 4, the term itself indicates that office was thought of less in terms of abstract administrative competence than in the language of status rooted in shared codes of honourable behaviour. To gain an honour was quite literally to be honoured: in contemporary usage, it transformed a private individual into a public figure. *Honores* were also important resources for families, their attraction lying

---

[133] Geary, *Phantoms of Remembrance*, pp. 48–80; Innes, 'Keeping it in the family'.

[134] MacLean, 'Queenship, nunneries', pp. 20–6.

[135] M. Costambeys, 'Kinship, gender and property in Lombard Italy', in G. Ausenda, P. Delogu and C. Wickham (eds.), *The Langobards before the Frankish Conquest. An Ethnographic Perspective* (Woodbridge, 2009), pp. 69–94; see also Smith, *Europe after Rome*, pp. 121–2, 141–2; C. La Rocca, 'Pouvoirs des femmes, pouvoirs de la loi dans l'Italie lombarde', in S. Lebecq, A. Dierkens, R. Le Jan and J.-M. Sansterre (eds.), *Femmes et pouvoirs des femmes à Byzance et en Occident (VIIe–XIe siècles)* (Villeneuve-d'Ascq, 1999), pp. 37–50.

[136] Innes, *State and Society*, pp. 56, 180–2.

partly in the fact that they were secure: unlike the landed properties on which aristocratic power otherwise depended, they could not be dissipated through the vagaries of inheritance. Offices granted by the king helped members of the nobility to anchor their status: thus the Bavarian count Orendil, granting land to the church of Freising in 814, could ask the bishop to let it out to his son should he in turn come to exercise his father's ministry.[137]

The role of the *honor* as a crucial intersection in the relationship between aristocracy and king becomes even more important if it is seen as having become heritable in the ninth century. If *honores* could be passed on from one aristocrat to the next, then they were removed from the king's immediate power of patronage. Viewed in this way, the aristocratic *honor* has contributed to the idea that the second half of the ninth century saw a progressive weakening of royal power. There are, however, a number of problems with this theory. In the first place, it depends heavily on reading Charles the Bald's Capitulary of Quierzy (877) as recognising formally the heritability of *honores*. But the capitulary's stipulation that if any count died while the king was in Italy, his son was to succeed to his office, was in fact contingent and specific, not general, and was intended only to prevent Charles's son Louis redistributing offices while the king was away.[138] Secondly, the tendency for one or two families to dominate any given *honor* was not new in the ninth century, but a permanent and long-acknowledged fact of early medieval politics.[139] Nor was it necessarily detrimental to kings: as they well knew, it was precisely possession of local influence and pre-existing family connections that enabled individuals to exercise control of *honores* effectively. Where their backgrounds can be studied, it is therefore not surprising that many counts and other regional power-brokers in the reign of Charlemagne were in fact local aristocrats from families of long standing.[140] *Honores* such as countships were not levels in an abstract administrative 'state' hierarchy; rather, they were inseparably intertwined with the family and personal power of the aristocracy. Contemporaries accepted this implicitly. In 882, Hincmar of Rheims remarked nostalgically that the great office-holders of Louis the Pious's day were now all dead, but added: 'However, I do know

[137] Bitterauf (ed.), *Traditionen*, no. 313.   [138] Nelson, *Charles the Bald*, pp. 248–9.
[139] Airlie, 'The aristocracy' in *NCMH* II, p. 444.
[140] Innes, *State and Society*, pp. 180–95.

that sons were born to replace these fathers from their own families . . . May they seek not to be deficient in morals . . . thus they may
deservedly fill the places and positions of their fathers.'[141]
Nevertheless, the distribution of *honores* was an important element in royal patronage. Even if many such appointments went *de
facto* to the 'obvious' candidate, the desire for *honores* was one of the
key factors which kept noble ambitions focussed on the royal court
throughout the Carolingian period. Families might cultivate hopes
like those we have already seen Count Orendil expressing, but inheritance practices provided no firm basis for the formal transmission
of an office within the family: a count might have more than one
son, and collateral kin could not be excluded from the equation. The
kind of case which was advanced to lay claim to property, rooted in
an individual's moral and personal ties to the dead, might on occasion be used to make a claim to an *honor*. Dhuoda thus reminded
her son William of his status as the favoured heir of his uncle and
godfather, Theodoric, and expressed the hope that he would receive
honores from Charles the Bald.[142] But to remind a ruler of a moral
claim of this type was not to presume an automatic right. *Honores*
were acknowledged to be in the king's gift. Rulers, indeed, were
also capable of revoking *honores* and removing incumbents when circumstances permitted. When the obvious candidate for an *honor* was
young, this could be relatively straightforward, as in 868 when, a few
years after the death of Count Robert 'the Strong' of Angers, Charles
the Bald managed to remove his offices from the control of his young
son Odo and to hand them instead to another local potentate who
had been Robert's rival.[143] Exploitation of such local rivalries was an
essential weapon in the royal armoury, and the shunting of a given
office between members of two or three regionally powerful families is not an uncommon pattern. But kings could also engage in
much more forthright actions when circumstances allowed: witness
Louis the German's spectacular purge of leading members of the east
Frankish aristocracy in 861.[144]

---

[141] Hincmar, *De ordine palatii*, c. 37, trans. Dutton, *Carolingian Civilization*, p. 532.
[142] Dhuoda, *Liber manualis*, VIII.14–15, trans. Thiébaux, pp. 204–7; on this discourse
see Innes, 'Practices of property', p. 252, and note that Nithard, *Historiarum Libri
IV*, III, 2, trans. Scholz, p. 156, shows William was successful in mobilising this
argument.
[143] *AB*, s.a. 868, trans. Nelson, pp. 143–4.
[144] *AF*, s.a. 861; Goldberg, *Struggle for Empire*, pp. 267–9.

The power to revoke office also, however, depended in some measure on the ability of individual favourites to help the king remove those who had fallen from grace. A couple of years before his dispossession of Odo, Charles had attempted to revoke the offices of the rebellious Count Bernard by granting them to Robert himself; yet it emerged some time later that Robert had had considerable trouble in forcing Bernard off the turf which was supposedly now his, and so had failed to make good the king's gift.[145] Such 'aspirational' grants of offices or land certainly encouraged conflict between members of the elite, but this was because they were competing *for* royal favour and *honores*: such violence was an integral part of the Frankish political system under the Carolingians. It remained worthwhile to fight for royal patronage throughout our period: kings in the later ninth century had no more trouble distributing or revoking *honores* than had their predecessors. If aristocratic struggles over *honores* become more visible in our sources as the ninth century progresses, this is because kings intervened more often to revoke them. The late ninth century should not be seen, as it sometimes is, as an era in which public office was 'privatised', so much as one when aristocratic competition for royal favour increased in line with the political turmoil at the top.

Countships were not the only currency of royal patronage: estates could be granted out too, and these grants were likewise seen as *honores*.[146] Grants of land took a variety of forms. The Merovingians, like the other rulers of the post-Roman west, had rewarded loyal aristocrats with outright alienations of land, although, again as elsewhere, such gifts could be revoked by hook or by crook if the recipient or his heirs incurred the king's displeasure. Outright gifts of this kind were, however, avoided by the Carolingians until the 820s, when the practice was revived under Louis the Pious; they were then used sparingly, with a careful eye on the potential benefits and the need to conserve royal resources.[147] Far more common was a new form of

---

[145] *AB*, s.a. 864, 866, trans. Nelson, pp. 119, 131; see Nelson, *Charles the Bald*, pp. 211–12.

[146] See *AB*, s.a. 839, trans. Nelson p. 45, for 'honores consisting of benefices'.

[147] Thegan, *Gesta Hludowici imperatoris*, c. 10 notes the resumption, also evident in the charters. F. L. Ganshof, 'Note sur la concession d'alleux à des vassaux sous le règne de Louis le Pieux', in *Storiografia e Storia: Studi in onore di E. Dupré Theseider* (Rome, 1974), pp. 589–99 and D. Gladiß, 'Die Schenkungen der deutschen Könige zu privaten Eigen (800–1137)', *DA* 1 (1937), pp. 80–136, give lists. This practice and its use also deserve a special study: for a model contextualisation

gift, introduced under Pippin III, in which an estate was granted out to a favoured follower for his lifetime, but ultimately remained royal property: this was termed granting *in beneficium*, literally 'as a benefit', hence modern historians refer to the granting of 'benefices'. Based on the practice whereby a church might grant back to the family of a favoured patron rights over land which that patron had donated to it in a 'precarial grant', under the Carolingians grants of royal estates as benefices were a crucial integrative force, tying the many recipients of such royal patronage firmly into the Carolingian system. Indeed, royal grants of this kind were made not only out of fiscal estates, but also from church land, for under the settlement reached between the Frankish episcopate and the Carolingians in the 740s and subsequently renegotiated and reaffirmed, specific pieces of church land – those deemed 'excess' to immediate needs – could be granted out 'on the king's word' in this manner, so long as a token payment were made in recognition of the church's ultimate title: the process of Carolingian takeover characteristically involved the restructuring of familial patronage networks sustained by precarial grants as monasteries and bishoprics were integrated into a wider Frankish Church establishment working in partnership with the king.[148]

Holders of royal benefices have sometimes been thought of as a special group, bound to the king particularly tightly. It has seemed natural, moreover, to link them with those styled *vassi dominici* ('vassals of the lord [king]'), who are increasingly visible in our sources from the last decades of the eighth century.[149] It is then a small step to suggest that those who stood in such a special relationship with the king owed him a particular duty of military service. Taken together, the assumed linkages of benefice with vassal, and of vassal with military service, have produced a fairly narrow conception of the Carolingian royal vassal as a mainstay of the king's army; this figure has in turn been a major protagonist in arguments between historians over what some have called 'feudalism' (usually defined as a system in which grants of benefices were made with the specific

of its effects in one *regnum*, J. Martindale, 'The kingdom of Aquitaine and the dissolution of the Carolingian fisc', *Francia* 11 (1985), pp. 131–91.

[148] G. Constable, '*Nona et decima*: an aspect of the Carolingian economy', *Speculum* 35 (1960), pp. 224–50, usefully surveys this. On *precaria* and their fate, see Hummer, *Politics and Power*, pp. 76–104.

[149] On *vassi*, see W. Kienast, *Das fränkische Vassalität von den Hausmaiern bis zu Ludwig dem Kind und Karl dem Einfältigen* (Frankfurt, 1990), though note that the framework is anachronistic.

obligation on the beneficiary to perform military service for the grantor). But the sources for the Carolingian period offer little that really sustains this rather artificial construction. There is no firm proof either that those holding benefices were consistently thought of as vassals, or that those styled *vassi* always held benefices; nor is there any indication that military service was a particular requirement on those called *vassi*. Capitularies certainly required that they, like others enjoying royal favour, turned up on campaign when summoned, but they are also visible in documents, legislation and narratives performing a wide range of other functions for the king.[150]

Moreover, there is no evidence that Carolingian aristocrats were in turn granting out their own land in the form of benefices, or indeed calling their retainers 'vassals', on any meaningful scale. Of course, as we have seen, aristocratic households included bevies of young retainers, and ties of patronage formed within households continued to animate social relationships between landowners; but the documentary evidence shows that inheritance and exchange remained the dominant ways of acquiring land. If the granting of benefices by aristocrats to their followers remained rare, the terminology of aristocratic lordship also remained indistinct: beyond the end of the ninth century, aristocratic followings are said to be made up of *fideles* (faithful men) and other relatively vague and general terms.[151] There is simply no foundation for the notion that vassalage emerged in this period as a new form of lordship, characterised by tightly linked service and conditional tenure, and rapidly influencing an array of other relationships such as the obligations of bishops or counts to the king, or of peasants to landlords. The word 'vassal' (*vassus*), whatever its origins, simply became a replacement for the range of terms previously used to denote individuals bound into the service of the king. Its usage was spreading around 800, when landowners who might have spent part of their youth as servants or retainers in the royal household but who had subsequently returned to the countryside came systematically to be styled *vassi dominici*, and to be seen as royal representatives in their localities. This is not to say that all *vassi* held benefices: one commentator in 802 distinguished the 'poorer *vassi* from within the palace' from their counterparts who held benefices in the countryside.[152] The emergence of the *vassus* was ultimately a

---

[150] See Reynolds, *Fiefs and Vassals*.
[151] Le Jan, *Famille et pouvoir*, pp. 142–3 and 148–9.
[152] *AL*, s.a. 802, trans. King, *Charlemagne: Translated Sources*, pp. 144–5.

way to prolong bonds formed in the royal household, and to use them to project a direct relationship between the king and local landowning communities; it thus fits with a series of other developments in these decades.[153]

The high profile of benefices in our sources rests not on a direct link with royal service, but on the appetite of landowning elites for grants of royal and ecclesiastical land. A fragment of a register of royal rights in Rhaetia, high in the Alps, shows tiny bundles of royal land, some no more than large fields, granted out as benefices to well-placed sections of the local gentry, figures far too humble and distant from the world of court politics even to be referred to as *vassi dominici*, or to owe any special service to the king.[154] Although made in the king's name, these grants must normally have lain in the hands of counts and their subordinates. They helped to integrate landholders on this level into the political system by providing them with a particularly vital resource, because royal land transferred in this way was not passed on, and thereby fragmented, through inheritance. Those with access to the royal ear sought grants of benefices for their clients and retainers, as Einhard's letters, over a quarter of which involve such petitioning, vividly illustrate. The effective lord was one who could access the court to bid for the benefices and favours that helped to sustain his entourage. But in times of political upheaval benefices could be redistributed as a result of effective petitioning by one's enemies: for those on the fringes of aristocratic society, dependent on their relatives' goodwill and on a tiny benefice to keep them distinct from their less well-born neighbours, such changes of fortune could be disastrous. Hence the urgent need felt by families to hang onto benefices, evident in Hincmar of Rheims's account of the desperate struggle of the widow of Count Donatus of Melun to keep hold of a grant at Neuilly, or Einhard's description of an unnamed individual, who had been granted his father's benefice, though not his countship, as a recognition of his family name, but now was ill with gout, unable to do the emperor's bidding, and terrified of losing the estate which maintained his local standing.[155] Disaster could be averted only by the strength of ties of lordship at all levels. The ability

[153] On this see Innes, 'Charlemagne's government', and Chapter 4 above.
[154] E. Mayer-Marthaler and F. Perret (eds.), *Bündner Urkundenbuch* I (Chur, 1955), Anhang I, pp. 375–96.
[155] On Neuilly, see Hincmar of Rheims, *De villa Noviliaco*, ed. H. Mordek, 'Ein exemplarischer Rechtsstreit: Hinkmar von Reims und das Landgut Neuilly-Saint-Front', *Zeitschrift der Savigny-Stiftung für Rechtsgeschichte, Kanonistische*

to perform loyal service was balanced by the lord's ability to reward loyalty: both were matters of honour; and both worked as much between lesser landowners and their immediate superiors as between the high aristocracy and the king.

At the top of society, the nobility looked to the king for patronage and offices, while kings depended heavily on the support of influential aristocrats to rule effectively. In the absence of formal state structures as we would understand them today, this was inevitable. As we have seen, the power of the secular nobility did not derive from the Carolingian kings, but was rooted in a complex interplay of inherited family status, tenure of land, and possession of royal offices. The importance of the latter warns us not to understand the relationship between aristocrats and kings as mutually antagonistic, engaged in a zero-sum game in which the goal was to wrest as much power from the other as possible. When aristocratic groups did rebel, in the ninth century they almost always sought to replace one member of the Carolingian family with another. Much of the political violence of the period, while it may have destabilised the regime of this or that individual ruler, thus often worked within the system rather than against it.

Aristocratic power was legitimised by association with royal power; and royal power needed that of the nobility to operate effectively. But no one put it like this at the time. Rather, the most widespread metaphor that the Frankish elite used to conceptualise their political role was that of consensus. The Lombard king Liutprand issued his periodic additions and revisions of the Lombard code 'with the common counsel of the people', 'with all the people assisting', and 'after reviewing all the titles of the earlier edicts with the judges and the rest of our Lombard *fideles* [faithful men]'.[156] Equally, the ideal Frankish king was one who took advice from 'the people' (which meant the males of the high nobility), so images of good kingship from the period highlighted horizontal bonds between ruler and ruling class: Einhard, for example, depicted Charlemagne as sharing baths in the hot springs at Aachen with up to a hundred courtiers

---

Abteilung 83 (1997), pp. 86–112 at pp. 100–7; for Einhard, see Einhard, *Epp.* 27–8, trans. Dutton, *Charlemagne's Courtier*, p. 141; Innes, 'Practices of property', pp. 259–62 for discussion.

[156] *Leges Liutprandi*, pp. 99–182, prologues to the laws of the First Year, the Eighth Year and the Ninth Year, trans. Fischer-Drew, *The Lombard Laws*, pp. 146, 150, 153.

and bodyguards at a time.[157] Such apparently informal sociability was symbolic of good rulership: a king who relied too much on one group of advisers was a king who would encourage factionalism, discontent and strife.

This idea of consensus was not mere rhetoric: it was made real through the general assembly – a regular meeting with the king of those who mattered across the empire – supplemented with occasional regional gatherings of nobles with the ruler as he moved around his realm, and by meetings between the king and his inner circle of close advisers, many of whom would have been more or less permanent members of his entourage.[158] This was, of course, very far from being a democratic system of government. However, the pressing need for the ruler to demonstrate that he was open to advice, and to keep on side as many of the powerful groups among the elite as possible, meant that there must have been some level of genuine consultation at these assemblies.[159]

The discourse of consensus formed part of a relatively coherent set of ideas about the nature of the Carolingian political order and the position of the elite within it. An important capitulary issued by Louis the Pious c.825 conceives of the emperor's *ministerium*, his 'ministry' of rulership over the chosen people entrusted to him by God, as a collaborative venture. The emperor does not delegate power from a position of autocracy, but shares the very substance of his *ministerium* with the office-holders of the empire, in particular with bishops and counts.[160] This formulation of joint (but still hierarchical) power and responsibility was rooted in scripture, and fed into the Franks' perception of themselves as a new Israel, the chosen people of the Old Testament. Furthermore, while this view of the *ministerium* came to maturity as a keynote of royal ideology during the reign of Louis the Pious, it was based on ideas stretching back at least to Charlemagne's

---

[157] Einhard, *VK*, c. 22, trans. Dutton, *Charlemagne's Courtier*, p. 31.

[158] Hincmar, *De ordine palatii*, c. 30, trans. Dutton, *Carolingian Civilization*, p. 528. See above, Chapter 4, pp. 172–5.

[159] See J. L. Nelson, 'Legislation and consensus in the reign of Charles the Bald', in Wormald, Bullough and Collins (eds.), *Ideal and Reality*, pp. 202–27 repr. in Nelson, *Politics and Ritual in Early Medieval Europe* (London, 1985); J. L. Nelson, 'Kingship and empire in the Carolingian world', in McKitterick (ed.), *Carolingian Culture*, pp. 52–87; Pössel, 'Authors and recipients'; McKitterick, *Charlemagne: The Formation of a European Identity*, pp. 222–33; de Jong, *Penitential State*, Chapter 3.

[160] O. Guillot, 'Une "ordinatio" méconnue'. See above, Chapter 4, pp. 187–8.

Admonitio generalis of 789; and it was echoed in later texts such as Charles the Bald's Treaty of Coulaines of 843.[161] What we, looking in from outside, might describe as the mutual reliance of king and aristocracy, was to contemporaries wrapped up seamlessly into an ideology of elite participation in the running of the kingdom.

But we should not mistake this broad group identity as representing the absolute social or political solidarity of the ruling class. As we have seen in this chapter, the secular elite of the empire was by no means monolithic. A shared sense of social identity was important to the nobility, but it was cut across and modified by numerous other factors including gender, age and relative status. Nor did class consciousness ever translate into unity of political action. Even though the Carolingian period witnessed (as we saw in Chapter 5) a gradual increase in the affluence and social superiority of the wealthy, the aristocracy as a whole never acted as a single body in pursuit of distinct political aims. The political agendas of individuals were conditioned by specific and ever-changing circumstances, and animated by complex motives: the pursuit of *honores*, the desire to save face in the eyes of one's peers and followers, a feeling of having been excluded from royal patronage or from access to the king's inner circle, or indeed opportunism and the quest for personal gain. These imperatives could very well contribute to political instability (as we saw in Chapter 4, the dishonouring of high-powered counts by Louis the Pious was probably what pushed the emperors' sons into rebellion in 830), but they did so not because 'the aristocracy' saw any advantage in encouraging political crisis. Indeed, as shown by the angst-ridden account of the crisis of 840–2 by the lay noble Nithard, quite the opposite.[162]

The complex impact on aristocratic behaviour of the overlapping imperatives of individual ambition and collective identity can be illustrated by turning to a final contemporary scene which encapsulates many of the themes we have discussed in this chapter. A charter from December 839 recording a gift to the church of Freising in Bavaria

---

[161] See Noble, 'From brigandage to justice', pp. 49–75 on the *Admonitio generalis*; on Coulaines, see J. L. Nelson, 'The intellectual in politics: contexts, content and authorship in the Capitulary of Coulaines, November 843', in L. Smith and B. Ward (eds.), *Intellectual Life in the Middle Ages: Essays Presented to Margaret Gibson* (London, 1992), pp. 1–14, repr. in Nelson, *Frankish World*, pp. 155–68; Nelson, *Charles the Bald*, pp. 138–9.

[162] Nelson, 'Public *Histories*'.

provides a description of how the donor, Count Ratolt, made the gift in the courtyard of his house before a large entourage, 'while manfully girded with his sword'.[163] The occasion seems to have been a gathering of part of the east Frankish army, participation in which was essential to aristocrats' sense of who they were. The imminent danger of the campaign, coupled with what we have learned about elite lay religiosity in the ninth century, means that we should not doubt the scribe's claim that the count's generosity was motivated by a desire to save his own soul. But in this vivid image we also catch a whiff of the supreme confidence of men like Ratolt in their right to be powerful and to dominate others. His sword, house and entourage distinguished him not just because they were expensive and visually impressive but because, as we have seen, they were symbols that marked him out as a member of the secular ruling class – they represented his 'manliness'. Aristocratic status could not just be assumed, it had to be performed; and the audience on this occasion comprised not just the count's own men, but also the soldiers of the county who were gathered to serve under him, together with other local worthies and indeed the bishop of Freising himself. But such men saw no contradiction between on the one hand considering themselves part of an elite charged with governing the empire, and on the other the pursuit of their own ambitions. The campaign which Ratolt was preparing to join was organised by his lord Louis the German against the emperor, Louis the Pious, and was therefore part of what was generally regarded as a rebellion against the correct political order. By participating in this campaign, Ratolt was endorsing his lord's breaking of solemn oaths which had guaranteed the existing dynastic settlement only months earlier, and gambling that success would lead to his own advancement as the young Louis became increasingly powerful and able to dispense more glittering prizes to those he favoured. But for all his 'manliness', wealth and self-confidence, as Ratolt followed his lord west into rebellion, and even as he looked on while the old emperor fell ill and died, leaving the realm in a state of turmoil, he would most assuredly have regarded himself above all as a servant of kings.

---

[163] Bitterauf (ed.), *Die Traditionen*, no. 634; Goldberg, *Struggle for Empire*, pp. 92–3 (on whose interpretation this paragraph is based).

7

EXCHANGE AND TRADE: THE
CAROLINGIAN ECONOMY

INTRODUCTION: INTERPRETING THE CAROLINGIAN ECONOMY

Around 890, a team of scholars at the court of the Anglo-Saxon king
Alfred the Great undertook the translation of the fifth-century Latin
world history of Orosius into the written version of their vernacular
Old English language. Orosius's work, with its story of barbarian
invasions and Christian triumph, had an obvious message for readers
in Viking-age England, and Alfred's team translated freely: as a result,
when they came across Orosius's lengthy geographical descriptions of
Europe, they updated his very classical picture of northern and eastern Europe to reflect contemporary realities.[1] The detailed account
of the different peoples and groupings of the Baltic and southern
Scandinavia led into a series of digressions, recounting the tales told
to King Alfred by two travellers in the north, Ohthere and Wulfstan.
Ohthere claimed to Alfred that 'he lived the furthest north of all

---

[1] J. M. Bately (ed.), *The Old English Orosius* (Oxford, 1980), relevant sections repr.
and trans. in N. Lund (ed.), *Two Voyagers at the Court of King Alfred* (York, 1984),
and see Bately and A. Englert (eds.), *Ohthere's Voyages* (Roskilde, 2007). See also M.
Townend, *Language and History in Viking Age England: Linguistic Relations between
Speakers of Old English and Old Norse* (Turnhout, 2002), pp. 79–109; F. L. Michelet,
*Creation, Migration and Conquest. Imaginary Geography and the Sense of Space in Old
English Literature* (Oxford, 2006), pp. 115–62; S. Gilles, 'Territorial interpolations
in the Old English Orosius', in S. Gilles and S. Tomasch (eds.), *Text and Territory:
Geographical Imagination in the Middle Ages* (Philadelphia, PA, 1998), pp. 79–96;
M. Godden, 'The Anglo-Saxons and the Goths: rewriting the sack of Rome',
Anglo-Saxon England 31 (2002), pp. 47–68.

Northmen', and gave an account of his exploration around the modern Norwegian coast as far as Lapland and the White Sea. Ohthere's accounts of various groupings of *Beormas*, *Cwenas*, *Finnas* and *Norðmanna* distinguish them not in terms of ethnic origin but in terms of their land and their economy. The lands of the *Finnas*, for example, were described as 'waste', that is lacking agriculture, animal husbandry or permanent settlement: they were seasonal hunters, in contrast to the *Beormas*, whose territory was 'fully settled'.

But the scribe recording Ohthere's tale-telling was not solely interested in ethnographic and geographical detail: he focussed also on wealth and its exchange. Hence the almost palpable interest of the audience as they heard an account of riches rooted not in property rights over land and labour, but in control of livestock, some tame but most wild, and the collection of tribute: Ohthere told how he was 'a very rich man in those objects which their riches consist of, that is wild deer... he was among the first men of his land, but he had not more than twenty cattle, twenty sheep and twenty pigs, and little that he ploughed with horses'. The wealth of Ohthere's people, we are told, lay 'mostly in the tribute (*gafol*) that the *Finnas* pay them', which was carefully graded, with each different rank among the *Finnas* making specific gifts of animal skins, bird feathers and whale bones. These were destined to be exchanged, for Ohthere's account of his wealth and his relations with the neighbouring peoples naturally flowed into an account of a voyage down the Norwegian coast to the trading town (*port*) of Kaupang, and thence to Hedeby at the base of the Jutland peninsula, the nodal point of the trading routes of southern Scandinavia. From Ohthere's account of the trip to Hedeby, the scribe moved seamlessly on to an analogous account of the voyage of Wulfstan east from Hedeby to Truso, a major centre for exchange in the Baltic. Wulfstan's observation of the coastline and islands of the Baltic is enlivened by discussion of the customs of the peoples he encountered: the drinking habits, funeral rites and magical abilities of the *Este*.

Travellers' tales like those of Ohthere and Wulfstan have an obvious attraction and their survival reflects contemporary fascination with difference: by talking about the exotic practices of distant societies in the far north, where wealth could not be measured in familiar terms of landownership, and the dead were commemorated by drinking and games funded from their property, these stories defined the aristocratic Christian culture of the early medieval west against the otherness of its neighbours. But the adventures they describe also yield important insights into mechanisms of exchange. In this respect the accounts' omissions are as striking as the details carefully recounted. Both Ohthere's and Wulfstan's itineraries were situated in regard to Hedeby: the routes joining Hedeby to the coasts of north-western Europe and England did not need rehearsing, and Hedeby itself required no introduction. Despite their exoticism, Wulfstan's and Ohthere's accounts were therefore predicated on a body of common knowledge and a shared mental geography that implied routine seaborne contact between the societies around the North Sea. Ohthere, indeed, could refer without hesitation to Alfred as his lord (*hlaford*), and knew implicitly what gifts were appropriate to bring to his court.[2]

'Dark Age Argonauts'[3] like Ohthere and Wulfstan are frustratingly rare figures in the surviving record. The backdrop to their expeditions – the networks of exchange and communications around the North Sea glimpsed in the shadows of their accounts – has been fleshed out only in recent decades thanks to a dramatic increase in archaeological data, beginning at Hedeby in the 1930s but flowering in the 1960s and 1970s as the redevelopment of northern Europe's cities unearthed long inaccessible sites. This has revealed a well-established network of contacts between England, Francia and southern Scandinavia, and thus transformed our understanding of the economy of eighth- and ninth-century Europe. As this material first began to be synthesised in the 1980s, inherited views of the early medieval economy underwent the first stages of a sustained revision.

The beginnings of this process of rethinking primarily took the form of a dialogue with the work of the early-twentieth-century Belgian historian Henri Pirenne, and particularly his posthumously published masterpiece, *Mohammed and Charlemagne*. Pirenne argued that the long-distance trade networks which had long bound together the Mediterranean world survived the collapse of Roman power in the fifth-century west, only to fall victim to the rise of Islam, which meant that by the eighth century the Mediterranean was a religious frontier. This, he thought, marked the watershed between the ancient

---

[2] See D. Pratt, *The Political Thought of King Alfred the Great* (Cambridge, 2007), pp. 41, 117.
[3] The phrase is coined by R. Hodges, *Dark Age Economics: The Rebirth of Towns and Trade, 600–1000* (London, 1982).

and medieval worlds, with northwestern Europe, lacking cultural and economic contacts, forced to fall back on its own resources, thus precipitating the rise of the Carolingian empire – whence his famous dictum that 'without Mohammed Charlemagne would have been inconceivable'. For Pirenne, the Carolingian world had a rural and land-locked economy and it was the post-Carolingian period which saw the emergence of distinctively medieval trade networks and forms of town life.[4] Pirenne's perspective was resolutely but unconsciously that of a middle-class northwestern European at the height of the region's economic, cultural and political dominance in world affairs – his projection of that dominance into the distant past and his casting of Islam in the role of a rogue outsider destroying ancient civilisation hint at the prejudices of his own environment.[5] Although his view was not unchallenged – the contemporary German historian Alfons Dopsch wrote a monumental account of the social and economic foundations of medieval Europe that stressed the creativity of the Carolingian countryside rather than fluctuations in trade – the 'Pirenne thesis' maintained a dominant hold on understandings of the Carolingian economy throughout the twentieth century.[6]

The general outlines of Pirenne's chronology, with some modifications, still provide a useful starting point – the broad patterns of economic change in the post-Roman west are not at issue. Although different scholars would lay the emphasis in different places, few would dispute an outline chronology that has the systems of exchange that ensured the economic integration of the ancient Mediterranean, after a series of adjustments in the fifth and sixth centuries, finally collapsing at the end of the seventh; new connections around the North Sea emerging in the course of the seventh century, and growing in the late eighth and early ninth centuries, before undergoing a process of reorientation which enabled renewed growth in the tenth; and new networks emerging in the Mediterranean, too, in the late eighth and ninth centuries, which were likewise to lay the foundations for intensified activity thereafter. Yet the terms of the

---

[4] Pirenne, *Mohammed and Charlemagne*, p. 234; first published in French in 1937.
[5] On Pirenne, see B. Lyon, *Henri Pirenne: A Biographical and Intellectual Study* (Ghent, 1974); P. Delogu, 'Reading Pirenne again', in Hodges and Bowden (eds.), *The Sixth Century*, pp. 15–40.
[6] Dopsch, *Wirtschaftliche und soziale Grundlagen*; the English translation by Beard and Marshall (*Economic and Social Foundations of European Civilisation*) never achieved the same status as Pirenne's work.

Pirenne thesis are too often taken for granted, partly because it gives a role to urbanism that has provided a convenient framework for the spectacular archaeological finds of recent decades. Consequently, this data is often used to expand and modify, rather than question, Pirenne's model, and the result has been a generally pessimistic view of the actual level and vitality of trade and exchange in the eighth and ninth centuries.[7] Debates about trade and urbanism conducted in these terms tend, moreover, not to leave much room for study of the Carolingian economy in its own right, but rather see it as a transitional phase between the ancient and high medieval worlds.

The underlying argument of this chapter is that the Carolingian evidence should be examined on its own terms rather than viewed only in the light of Pirennian debates about long-term change. The debates that will concern us here deal with different characterisations of the Carolingian economy itself, and with different explanations for change. Broadly speaking, scholarly opinion can be plotted in relation to two central issues. The first concerns the driving motor of economic change: was it the creation of new trade routes and the emergence of trading settlements, or was it the productivity of the countryside and the production of surpluses? The second relates to the agents of change: rulers and elites, or relatively autonomous small and middling landowners? Nobody would disagree that economic change was ultimately conditioned by all of these things – by the interactions between trading networks and systems of agrarian production, and the dialectic between the wishes of kings and elites and the actions of their subjects and dependants. What is at issue is the nature of those interactions, and where we choose to lay the emphasis. Monumental books by Michael McCormick and Chris Wickham have shown just how complex and polyfocal was the early medieval economy of Europe, and revealed the dangers inherent in generalising from any one part to the whole.[8]

In what follows we will argue that the development of systems of exchange ultimately rested on the increased productivity of the Carolingian countryside, and the ability of a relatively broad landowning

---

[7] See Hodges, *Dark Age Economics*, expanded into a neo-Pirennian global model of the early medieval economy by R. Hodges and D. Whitehouse, *Mohammed, Charlemagne and the Origins of Europe* (London, 1983). See also Hodges, *Light in the Dark Ages: The Rise and Fall of San Vincenzo al Volturno* (London, 1997).

[8] McCormick, *Origins of the European Economy*; Wickham, *Framing the Early Middle Ages*.

class to seize on the possibilities created by the increasingly ambitious and extensive systems of redistribution developed by kings and their court elites. The networks of long-distance trade emerging from the archaeology may be spectacular, but even on the most optimistic assessment they can have accounted for only a tiny segment of the economy as a whole. And although many scholars have been tempted to imagine rulers like Charlemagne developing economic initiatives designed to promote urban growth and maximise exchange, such planning was wholly alien to a conservative worldview in which rulers strove to make their realm correspond to a divinely ordained order: we have no hint in our sources of the kind of strategic discussion and mobilisation that such 'policy-making' would have involved, nor even any real sense of the king and his advisers discussing economic exchange as a special form of activity which deserved promoting in its own right. The next section of the chapter develops these general points, explaining how we ought to conceptualise economic activity in the Carolingian era. The third, fourth and fifth sections then outline the rise and transformation of the North Sea trading network, explaining also the role of the Vikings. In the sixth section we turn south to Italy and the Mediterranean, before asking, in conclusion, whether there was such a thing as 'the Carolingian economy'.

MECHANISMS OF EXCHANGE

Another look at Ohthere's account of his activities reminds us of the great variety of mechanisms of exchange in the early Middle Ages, and cautions us to resist the instinct to think about the distant past in terms of the market forces familiar from the economics of the modern world.[9] The cargo taken by Ohthere to Kaupang and Hedeby, remember, was made up of the tribute he had received from the *Finnas*: 'Each pays according to his rank. The highest in rank has to pay fifteen marten skins, five reindeer skins, one bear skin

---

[9] The classic discussion remains K. Polanyi, 'The economy as instituted process', in Polanyi, C. Arensberg and H. Pearson (eds.), *Trade and Market in Early Empires* (Glencoe, IL, 1957), pp. 243–69; for subsequent reception, see S. C. Humphreys, 'History, economics, and anthropology: the work of Karl Polanyi', *History and Theory* 8 (1969), pp. 165–212; and for a medieval model W. I. Miller, 'Gift, sale, payment, raid: case studies in the negotiation and classification of exchange in medieval Iceland', *Speculum* 61 (1986), pp. 18–50.

and ten measures of feathers, and a jacket of bearskin or otterskin and two ship-ropes. Each of these must be sixty ells long, one made from whale-hide and the other from seal.'[10] These tributes were not part of a separate system operating alongside, but distinct from, market exchange of a kind familiar to us. Rather, they were part of a single multifaceted system of exchange, without which Ohthere's trading expedition to the markets of the great ports of southern Scandinavia would have been impossible. Ohthere is silent on the basis of his tributary relationship with the *Finnas*, but it clearly took a form of personal domination – lordship – based at least partly on the need for 'protection': that is, on the threat of force. But even his interactions with the *Finnas* were multi-stranded: as well as collecting tribute from them, we can also see hints of more straightforwardly 'economic' relations in his boasts about his herd of 600 'unsold' beasts (some of them 'decoy reindeer' used in hunting wild deer). In other words, not only was Ohthere selling onwards in the marketplace tribute acquired by what we would see today as 'extra-economic' mechanisms; he was also harvesting the fauna – by hunting walruses and taming reindeer – and exchanging at least some of the results with the *Finnas*, in the process helping them to make the next round of tribute payments.[11] Patterns of exchange were wrapped up in social relationships between groups and individuals, from which they cannot be separated, and market transactions that we would see as 'economic' were inextricably connected to 'extra-economic' forms of social obligation and political domination.

The interdependence of what to us look like quite different forms of exchange is underlined later in Ohthere's account. When Ohthere reached the land of the *Beormas* he stopped at the mouth of a great river: although there were extensive settlements beyond it, he did not dare to venture there. Our scribe explains Ohthere's reluctance with a spare phrase that he clearly expected his audience to understand immediately: going further was impossible 'on account of *unfriþ*'. The concept of *unfriþ* ('non-peace') signified not a state of formal enmity or dangerous hostility so much as, quite literally, an absence of *friþ*, that formal state of mutually recognised friendship which rested

[10] Lund (ed.), *Two Voyagers*, p. 20.
[11] Itinerant pastoralists like the *Finnas* are, as a rule, not economically self-sufficient but dependent on regular exchange with more settled peoples: see Wickham, 'Pastoralism and underdevelopment'.

on public agreements and allowed agreed processes of exchange.[12] The *Beormas* were strangers, not foes; Ohthere's non-relationship was different from the formal enmity of plundering and raiding which defined relations between other northern peoples, and also from the implicit violence underpinning the tributary subjection of the *Finnas*. Even more neutral and less personal forms of equal exchange – the activities from which our notion of 'trade' emerged – required the public acknowledgement of a state of formal trust, such as was lacking with the *Beormas*. Normally acquired through a visit to the local ruler, such recognition was a common requirement right across early medieval northwestern Europe. The earliest Frankish and Anglo-Saxon laws on merchants, for example, concern royal acknowledgement and the need for these strangers to advertise their special status, whilst the conclusion of peace between erstwhile enemies involved formal undertakings allowing the resumption of equal exchange and the end of plundering; in Carolingian times, these concerns are still evident in the special protection offered by the king to merchants from abroad, and the agreements reached between Franks and Vikings.[13]

Ohthere's account, of course, concerns a very different society from those of Carolingian Francia and Italy that are our primary concern – it would be misleading to develop a model from his testimony and impose it uncritically on the Carolingian evidence. But Ohthere is worth dwelling on because we lack comparable accounts of the systems of redistribution and exchange within the Carolingian world. In part, this absence shows that economic systems – some relatively sophisticated, as we saw in our discussion of rural society – were so deeply embedded within the social structure as to be taken as read. As a result historians of the Carolingian economy have tended to assume that the systems underpinning the circulation of wealth within Francia took forms familiar and natural to us. After all, the raw materials of Carolingian economic history seem to consist of apparently dry and neutral data, whether maps of the archaeological distribution of particular classes of pottery or finds of jewellery and metalwork from trading centres, royal documents relieving favoured

[12] C. Fell, '*Unfriþ*: an approach to a definition', *Saga-Book of the Viking Society for Northern Research* 21 (1982–3), pp. 85–100; N. Lund, 'Peace and non-peace in the Viking age', in J. E. Knirk (ed.), *Proceedings of the Tenth Viking Congress* (Oslo, 1987), pp. 255–69.

[13] P. Sawyer, 'Kings and merchants', in P. H. Sawyer and I. N. Wood (eds.), *Early Medieval Kingship* (Leeds, 1977), pp. 139–58.

churches of tolls and allowing them to establish mints and markets, or lists of dues required from peasants on royal and ecclesiastical land. For all their apparent neutrality, though, we should pause for thought before assuming that such data-sets should be explained solely in terms of phenomena that are familiar from our own experience, as the result of market-orientated economic exchange understood as having an independent logic outside of social relationships.

In fact, within the empire as on its northern fringe, there were a range of complementary and sometimes interlocking mechanisms at work simultaneously.[14] Tim Reuter memorably uncovered the regular flows of plunder and tribute that were such a central facet of Frankish political expansion. Eighth-century Frankish success then fuelled a flow of high-status gifts; kings like Charlemagne were able to control the distribution of the spoils of war, using them to forge bonds with neighbouring rulers such as Offa, but most importantly to reward the aristocrats who had effected conquest and to build up the institutional wealth of the imperial church. The end of expansion, of course, ended this primitive but effective system of redistribution, and in the ninth century both inter-Frankish conflict and more piecemeal patterns of frontier raiding and tribute gathering, notably in central Europe and northern Spain, offered poorer pickings, and encouraged a more intensive exploitation of internal resources.[15] Indeed, one model of political and economic change would see the Carolingians seizing the opportunity granted them by their eighth-century success, and attempting to reorientate their economy towards internal production in the ninth century – a model that would be supported by the evidence (introduced in Chapter 5) for the emergence of markets in the ninth- and tenth-century countryside.[16]

---

[14] The following section summarises an argument developed in Innes, 'Framing the Carolingian economy'.

[15] Reuter, 'Plunder and tribute', on which see J. L. Nelson, 'Charlemagne and the paradoxes of power', *Reuter Lecture* (University of Southampton, 2006). Reuter was responding to the plea of Philip Grierson for early medievalists to take seriously non-market systems of exchange: see P. Grierson, 'Commerce in the dark ages: a critique of the evidence', *TRHS* 9 (1959), pp. 123–40. For the impact of the most spectacular plunder, the Avar treasure, see Einhard, *VK*, c. 13; Alcuin, *Ep.* 100, trans. *EHD*, no. 197.

[16] Nelson, *Charles the Bald*, pp. 19–40; R. Hodges, 'Trade and market origins in the ninth century: an archaeological perspective on Anglo-Carolingian relations', in M. Gibson and J. Nelson (eds.), *Charles the Bald: Court and Kingdom* (2nd edn, Aldershot, 1990), pp. 213–33.

Nonetheless, there is also abundant evidence that redistributive social exchange continued to be a central mechanism of elite consumption; indeed, the thickening of evidence in the ninth century makes their centrality to aristocratic society even more visible for this period than for the age of conquest. Charlemagne's distributions of plunder were merely the visible tip of a far bigger iceberg, a system of exchange which bound together Frankish society. In order to understand the economic dynamics of Carolingian times, we need to look for the interaction between this system on the one hand, and the formal economy of market exchange on the other. The circulation of prized symbols of elite status – high-quality weaponry, lavish buckles and brooches – was probably the motor of the networks of sociable redistribution.[17] Such items were not commodities, that is anonymous objects whose value was standardised, for they had biographies and identities which rubbed off on their owners: swords, for example, had names, sometimes scratched into the blade, which were mnemonics for stories about former owners and daring deeds such as emerge in epic poetry surviving from our period, the 'Lay of Hildebrand' (*Hildebrandslied*) and the story of 'Walter Strongarm' (*Waltharius*).[18] Because of the cultural and social capital invested in this type of 'treasure', it was passed on face-to-face in personalised exchanges: after all, to pass on a weapon with which a forefather had killed countless foes, or a gift with which a king had shown favour to a relative, was to pass on a part of a family's identity. Exchanging such items through the impersonal mechanism of sale was potentially problematical, because their value lay not in the objects themselves but in the relationships they articulated and helped define.

This was not just a closed system of gift exchange which recycled treasure within a narrow elite: the necessity of generosity, and its

---

[17] See Le Jan, 'Frankish giving of arms'; C. Wickham, 'Rethinking the structure of the early medieval economy', in Davis and McCormick (eds.), *The Long Morning of Medieval Europe*, pp. 19–32. For theoretical perspectives see A. Appadurai (ed.), *The Social Life of Things. Commodities in Cultural Perspective* (Cambridge, 1986); A. Weiner, *Inalienable Possessions. The Paradox of Keeping-while-Giving* (Berkeley, CA, 1992).

[18] *Hildebrandslied* and *Waltharius*, ed. and trans. Knight Bostock, *Handbook on Old High German Literature*, pp. 44–7 and 259–80. On treasure and identity see M. Hardt, 'Royal treasures and representation in the early Middle Ages', in W. Pohl and H. Reimitz (eds.), *Strategies of Distinction. The Construction of Ethnic Communities, 300–800* (Leiden, 1998), pp. 255–80. On these texts see Innes, 'Teutons or Trojans?'.

increasing institutionalisation after the end of eighth-century expansion, meant that expectations about regular giving and receiving determined at least some of the objectives of manorial economies.[19] We have already seen how the royal assembly slowly mutated from the mustering of a war-host for its annual campaign into an organ of formal counsel-taking and decision-making in the second half of the eighth century. One result was that rulers like Charlemagne and Louis the Pious came to insist on being presented with 'annual gifts' from their leading subjects.[20] The loyalties and identities of the top tier of Carolingian society were thus shaped by a regular cycle of giving – and this cycle rested on a two-way flow of gifts, for kings might present robes and favours on such occasions as well as sharing time talking, feasting and hunting with their aristocracies. These imperatives had a direct impact on aristocratic estate management: for example, Einhard's letters apologising for late arrival and non-attendance at the assembly, and advising aristocrats on what to present, are accompanied by others ordering his stewards to have produce and goods ready to support his obligations to his royal master. Indeed, by the middle decades of the ninth century such obligations were so routinised that they might be recorded in the polyptychs alongside other duties and payments levied on the peasantry, whilst the 'gifts' expected from ecclesiastical institutions had been fixed in standardised 'tariffs' which might be renegotiated.[21]

These obligations of giving structured the relationships between kings, churches and aristocrats. Away from royal courts, on a more local level, systems of giving and receiving are harder to trace; nonetheless, there is little room for doubt that it was such mechanisms that allowed aristocrats and ecclesiastical institutions to build networks of support among the landowning classes, and indeed supplied contingents of properly armed and equipped soldiers for royal campaigns. There are, for example, some indications of significant change in the ways high-quality metalwork and weapons were produced between the seventh and ninth centuries: individual smiths, whose activities were earlier shaped by aristocratic, ecclesiastical and

---

[19] On manorial economies, see above, Chapter 5, pp. 252–8.
[20] See Reuter, 'Plunder and tribute', pp. 85–6; Nelson, 'The Lord's anointed', at p. 166.
[21] For standardised gifts and their renegotiation, see Innes, 'Framing the Carolingian economy', pp. 48–9; Innes, *State and Society*, pp. 159–62. See also Notker, *Gesta*, 2.21. On polyptychs see above, Chapter 5, pp. 252–4.

royal patronage, seem in the Carolingian period to be overshadowed by workshops embedded within the manorial economy. Although these indications must be carefully handled (since the nature of the surviving evidence shifts in the ninth century), the archaeological and documentary evidence for significant investment in iron production and workshops on many major Carolingian monastic sites, and the fact that certain types of swords were being given 'brand-names' by the end of the ninth century, is suggestive of larger-scale production leading to changes in patterns of distribution. These shifts again suggest that the social imperatives of the 'gift economy' played an increasingly important role in determining the workaday business of estate management and the organisation of production.[22]

The 'economic logic' of Carolingian landowners, then, was not simply a matter of profit-and-loss style calculation about the maximisation of production for the market. Indeed, we have no real evidence that Carolingian estates were run to return a profit, as we would define it; rather, they were social resources used to support their owners in meeting those obligations which came with their rank. As we saw in Chapter 6, demonstrating and maintaining social status, and developing political influence, were possible only through participation in a culture of elite display, hospitality and gift-giving, and estates were managed so as to facilitate these goals. Here more anecdotal sources, such as Einhard's letters, provide an invaluable context for the polyptychs: in them, as we have noted, Einhard instructs stewards to send cartloads of foodstuffs to nominated estates to feed himself, his retinue, and important guests, and chastises those who fail to send produce of adequate quality, while market exchange is wholly marginal.[23]

None of this is to deny that there were markets, and that both agrarian surpluses and the fruits of craft production could be bought

---

[22] On workshops, see F. Schwind, 'Zu karolingerzeitlichen Klöstern als Wirtschafts-organismen und Stätten handwerklicher Produktion', in L. Fenske, W. Rösener and T. Zotz (eds.), *Institutionen, Kultur und Gesellschaft im Mittelalter: Festschrift für Josef Fleckenstein zu seinem 65. Geburtstag* (Sigmaringen, 1984), pp. 101–23; R. Hodges, *San Vincenzo al Volturno 1. The Excavations 1980–1986, part 1* (London, 1993) and *San Vincenzo al Volturno 2. The Excavations 1980–1986, part 2* (London, 1995). For Carolingian weaponry, see S. Coupland, 'Carolingian arms and armour in the ninth century', *Viator* 29 (1990), pp. 29–50.

[23] See e.g. Einhard, *Epp.*, esp. 23, 24, 36, 37, 38, 54; and for discussion see Innes, 'Practices of property'.

and sold in the Carolingian period. But these forms of exchange cannot be automatically seen as the default mechanisms through which demands were met and to which production was geared. Those whose decisions determined the basic patterns of economic activity were motivated by other concerns, and adopted other strategies, than those which seem natural to us: markets had particular functions in a world where the culturally and ideologically dominant mechanisms of exchange were embedded in social relationships. After all, in practical terms large conglomerations of estates such as those revealed in the polyptychs or in Einhard's letters had their own internal mechanisms of redistribution and transportation, as we saw above; the demands of kings for gifts and obligations to attend court, to fight with an armed retinue and to perform other public services interacted with these internal mechanisms, and the resulting patterns of mobility might play an important role in determining the range of economic possibilities. Similarly, as Einhard's writings and letters show, when travelling to or from the king or undertaking official business the powerful might avail themselves of royal estates and their resources, just as De villis envisaged.[24] Carolingian kings, moreover, inherited from their Frankish and Roman predecessors a system of levying tolls on external trade, and on internal markets; and like them they also granted favoured subjects, and in particular great ecclesiastical institutions, privileges, most usually exemptions from the payment of tolls at particular places. Such privileges blurred the boundary between private and public resources: churches, after all, were so treated because they were a central part of the Frankish political system charged with public duties both religious and political, but a monastery or bishopric with the right to move half a dozen ships up and down a major river like the Po or the Seine could profit on the back of its public status.[25] The Carolingian economy was not like that of the Roman empire. The latter had been driven by a regular system of tax assessment and payment to support a standing army which effected large-scale transfers of wealth in state-minted coin and in provisions, and granted state franchises to those shipping vital supplies. By contrast, while Carolingian rulers and their agents might

---

[24] Einhard, Translation and Miracles describes his various journeys to and from Aachen. On De villis see above, Chapter 5, p. 254.

[25] For an encyclopaedic discussion of legislation on tolls and trade, see H. Siems, Handel und Wucher im Spiegel frühmittelalterliche Rechtsquellen (Hanover, 1992).

collect specific dues and demand particular services from all free men, there was no regular system of tax assessment or land inventorying, and no standing army or dedicated bureaucracy. Instead, the systems of obligation and privilege which bound together the aristocratic and ecclesiastical elites determined the basic structures of economic activity in our period.

The interaction of different spheres of economic activity and exchange can be illustrated by returning briefly to the capitularies. Carolingian legislation was particularly interested in establishing proper distinctions between the practices of gift-giving and the logic of the market, and policing the boundaries between them, and we need to understand these contemporary categories if we are to interpret the dynamics of social and economic change. Take the capitulary *De villis* which we introduced in Chapter 5. In its model of the ideal royal estate, markets play a role, with stewards enjoined to use them to ensure that food of a fitting quality was available when the king visited, and that there was sufficient seed and stock – but this role is clearly subsidiary, acting as a 'top up' to internal mechanisms of redistribution. *De villis* does recognise that stewards might maximise their estates' income by selling surplus produce, requiring that they render account of their sales each Easter, acquiring sufficient silver coin to send the appropriate payment to the palace. Here, not only was the market the destination for what remained after royal orders for the redistribution of produce had been met, and royal agents shown the appropriate hospitality: the payment of accounts in coin was also a mechanism for monitoring the activities of stewards. Market exchange, with its relatively impersonal standards of value, was useful in this context precisely because it removed some transactions from the web of local ties and personal obligations surrounding stewards, washing clean otherwise potentially sticky fingers – but it was not the ultimate goal of estate management.[26] If we are to understand the Carolingian economy we must take note of how these conceptually distinct mechanisms of exchange interlocked and overlapped, and realise that their operation resulted above all from the political interaction of kings, aristocrats and great churches.[27]

---

[26] *Capitulare de villis*, esp. c. 28.
[27] For more discussion of this theme, see Innes, 'Framing the Carolingian economy'; Innes, 'Practices of property'; Wickham, 'Rethinking the structure'; J. Moreland, 'Concepts of the early medieval economy', in Hansen and Wickham (eds.), *The Long Eighth Century*, pp. 1–34.

THE NORTH SEA ECONOMY

The archaeological discoveries of the past half-century leave little room for doubt over the scale of the long-distance exchange that these dynamics facilitated. Best known, because most spectacular, is the emergence by 700 of a network of dedicated economic centres serving the coastlines and estuaries of the North Sea, and its subsequent growth in the course of the eighth century and the first decades of the ninth. Excavations at sites such as Dorestad on the Rhine delta in the modern Netherlands, and Hamwic, the forerunner of Southampton on the south coast of England, have transformed our understanding of networks barely alluded to in our texts.[28] Perhaps the most striking feature of this network is its international nature: sites of an identical type become visible at very similar dates not only in Francia, but also in southern and eastern England and southern Scandinavia. In other words, we are dealing with the emergence of a regular system of shipborne exchange around the North Sea and its hinterland. These sites are sometimes referred to by archaeologists and historians as *wics*, on the basis of the common suffix shared by many of the Anglo-Saxon examples in particular, such as Hamwic and Ipswich. However, most discussion now uses the term 'emporium' (plural 'emporia') to describe these gateway sites dedicated to long-distance exchange (see Map 11).

Emerging in the decades around 700, the emporia of the North Sea were typically low-lying, serving sandy beaches in the estuaries of major rivers. The functions of these sites were resolutely economic: in addition to long-distance exchange, archaeology has indicated that they were also major centres for craft production and the secondary processing of raw materials from their hinterlands. They also remained noticeably distinct from the seats of cultural, social or

---

[28] On these developments, see Hodges, *Dark Age Economics*; M. Anderton (ed.), *Anglo-Saxon Trading Centres: Beyond the Emporia* (Glasgow, 1999); D. Hill and R. Cowie (eds.), *Wics: The Early Medieval Trading Centres of Northern Europe* (Sheffield, 2001); C. Scull, 'Urban centres in pre-Viking England?', in J. Hines (ed.), *The Anglo-Saxons from the Migration Period to the Eighth Century* (Woodbridge, 1997), pp. 269–310; H. Clarke and B. Ambrosiani (eds.), *Towns in the Viking Age* (London, 1995). For Frankish perspectives see R. Hodges, *Towns and Trade in the Age of Charlemagne* (London, 2000); A. Verhulst, *The Rise of Cities in North-West Europe* (Cambridge, 1999); Verhulst, *Carolingian Economy*. On cross-Channel connections more generally see Story, *Carolingian Connections*.

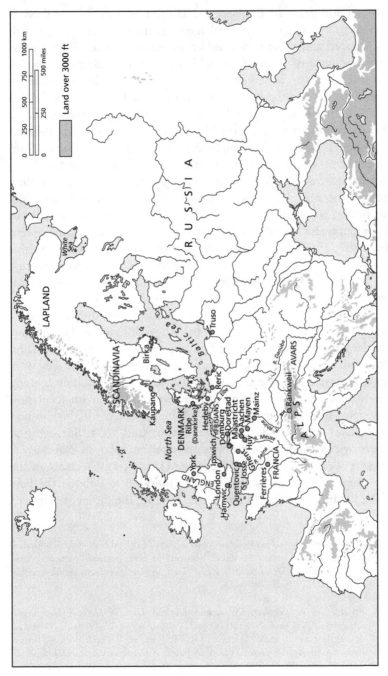

Map 11. Exchange and trade: the North Sea and the Baltic Sea (showing places mentioned in Chapter 7)

political authority, in England and Francia at least. While there is documentary evidence for royal agents at major Frankish sites such as Dorestad and Quentovic, and at the Anglo-Saxon centres, these were not seats of power from which the surrounding countryside was ruled, but specialised sites where the concentration of exchange demanded the presence of officials to ensure that lucrative royal rights to tolls on trade were upheld.[29] Similarly, while the religious needs of their populations were served by churches, they were not the sites of bishoprics. Normally undefended, they remained distinct from the remnants of major Roman centres, even where – as at London – they lay next door. This separation was primarily practical, enabling the creation of warehouses and jetties serving shallow beaches without having to negotiate difficult-to-clear and potentially dangerous Roman remains. But the fact that observers like Bede used a different vocabulary from the inherited Roman terminology to refer to this sort of extra-mural 'industrial estate' points to a consciousness that this network of economic sites was clearly identifiable and had its own distinct logic.[30]

That said, it would be a mistake to overstate the homogeneity of the North Sea emporia. First, they differed widely in size. The largest sites, the two main Frankish emporia of Quentovic and Dorestad, remain incompletely excavated precisely because they were huge. Dorestad at its height stretched at least three kilometres along the confluence of the Lek and the Kromme Rijn, with habitation clustering in a strip up to half a kilometre wide. Of this, around 30 hectares were excavated between 1967 and 1977. Surveying at Quentovic, whose site was only discovered in 1990, indicates a settlement of comparable size.[31] Compare Hamwic's 45 hectares, or the tiny emporium of just a few hectares founded at Ribe at the base of the Jutland peninsula in Denmark. Second, the differential impact

---

[29] *Gesta sanctorum patrum Fontanellensis coenobii* [Acts of the Abbots of St Wandrille], ed. F. Lohier and J. Laporte, Société de l'histoire de Normandie (Rouen and Paris, 1936), XII, 2, trans. *EHD*, no. 20; S. Kelly, 'Trading privileges from eighth-century England', *EME* I (1992), pp. 3–28.

[30] Bede, *HE* II.3.

[31] W. van Es and W. Verwers, *Excavations at Dorestad I. The Harbour, Hoogstraat I* (Amersfoort, 1980), and the short accessible summary in W. Verwers, 'Dorestad: a Carolingian town?', in B. Hobley and R. Hodges (eds.), *The Rebirth of Towns in the West, AD 700–1050* (London, 1988), pp. 52–6; on Quentovic, see D. Hill, *et al.*, 'Quentovic defined', *Antiquity* 61 (1990), pp. 51–8.

of the Roman past meant that emporia mapped on to very different topographies. Hence emporia fulfilled different functions in Francia, where the network of former Roman cities largely defined the geography of ecclesiastical authority and where continuity of activity and some economic specialisation can be seen on many such sites; England, where Roman cities were more or less wholly abandoned, but were sometimes revived by Romanising churchmen and rulers; and Scandinavia, where the Roman imprint was wholly lacking, meaning that emporia became seats of political power in a way that was impossible further south.[32]

These variations demonstrate that we are not dealing with the linking together of economies of roughly equivalent complexity and intensity.[33] The Frankish 'super-emporia' were conduits for the export of goods whose production was already a matter of specialisation and sophistication, thanks to significant 'home' demand fed through regional networks within the Frankish heartlands. The major Frankish exports – barrels of wine, top-quality pottery manufactured in the Rhineland workshops, millstones fashioned from Mayen quernstone – were thus produced neither initially nor primarily with a view to the potential of long-distance exchange. The best 'guesstimate' suggests that even at its height, the volume of fine tableware handled through Dorestad represented perhaps the cargo of a barge a week coming down the Rhine, or in other words a regular and routine supply but not a bulk trade – this was the selling on of excess products, not export-geared production.[34] The imports thus funded remain archaeologically far less visible. From the Scandinavian end, raw materials destined for Frankish workshops seem to dominate: amber, for example, is found in its raw form in staggering quantities at Dorestad, and we should add the kinds of goods mentioned by Ohthere, with ivory well attested archaeologically but furs inevitably invisible in the material record.[35] Anglo-Saxon exports are harder still to gauge, though textual evidence suggests that finished products rather than raw materials were dominant: cloaks of English and Frisian make were renowned, and fine cloth may have been

---

[32] For Scandinavian proto-towns as seats of royal power, see Rimbert, *Vita Anskarii* [*Life of Anskar*], ed. G. Waitz, *MGH SRG in usum scholarum separatim editi* LV (Hanover, 1884), cc. 19, 26, 27.

[33] Wickham, *Framing the Early Middle Ages*, pp. 794–819 emphasises the asymmetry of exchanges around the North Sea.

[34] See Verwers, 'Dorestad'.   [35] Hodges, *Dark Age Economics*, lists relevant finds.

the primary English export already, as in the later Middle Ages.[36]
Slaves, the most elusive commodity of all in the archaeological and
documentary record, were also an object of exchange, but the scale
and significance here was in all probability limited: these were not,
after all, agrarian regimes which rested on gang slavery, and in any
case the economy of the wartrail provided a ready supply of unfree
labour.[37]

The sheer size of sites like Dorestad must tell us something about
the increasing sophistication of internal systems of production and
distribution within northern Francia. Most interpretations of North
Sea trade, basing themselves on the emporia's likely political and economic benefits, tend to see royal agency behind these developments.
This view seems to sit well with sites like Hamwic, whose regular,
grid-like street plan is suggestive of planned foundation rather than
organic growth, and where there is evidence for the bulk transporting
of foodstuffs and other supplies from the surrounding countryside.
The clear archaeological horizon of the site c.700 fits with a political
context in which expansionist kings in Wessex – the Anglo-Saxon
kingdom in which Hamwic was situated – would have been interested in developing an outlet into the Channel. The site is later in its
history explicitly attested as being royal property.[38] But it would be a
mistake to generalise effortlessly from the specific case of Hamwic to
the North Sea economy as a whole. After all, Hamwic was founded
just as the networks of exchange which bound together the North
Sea were taking shape, but a generation or two after their beginning; Dorestad, by contrast, was an important site of long-distance
exchange already by the middle of the seventh century.[39] Hamwic
may represent a royal foundation, but one designed to give access

[36] Alcuin, *Ep.* 100, trans. *EHD*, no. 197. On Frisian cloaks, see also Notker, *Gesta*,
1.34. On the famous 'black stones', also discussed in Charlemagne's letter, see
now Story, *et al.*, 'Charlemagne's black marble', pp. 157–90.

[37] See above, Chapter 5, pp. 245–6; and cf. M. McCormick, 'New light on the
"dark ages": how the slave trade fuelled the Carolingian economy', *P&P* 177
(2002), pp. 17–54.

[38] On Hamwic, see A. D. Morton, *Excavations at Hamwic I* (London, 1992), pp. 20–
77, or more accessibly M. Brisbane, 'Hamwic (Saxon Southampton): an eighth
century port and production centre', in Hodges and Hobley (eds.), *The Rebirth of
Towns in the West*, pp. 101–8; on the political context, see B. Yorke, 'The Jutes of
Hampshire and Wight and the origins of Wessex', in S. Bassett (ed.), *The Origins
of Anglo-Saxon Kingdoms* (London and New York, 1989), pp. 84–96.

[39] On Merovingian Dorestad, see Wood, *Merovingian Kingdoms*, pp. 296–301.

to a North Sea economy that was already developing apace – this is why it should not be used as a template into which evidence from other sites can be slotted.

The evidence from Dorestad is particularly important in illuminating the process by which the emporia rose to prominence, for it gives us the best window on to the earliest phase of the North Sea network. Here, in the crucial period after the middle of the seventh century, when we have the first archaeological evidence for regular long-distance exchange, and the earliest written hints at the place's importance, Dorestad changed hands several times between the Franks and their pagan Frisian neighbours, with no detriment to the emporium's economic vitality; it was not until the 720s, decades later, that it lay unequivocally in Frankish hands.[40] The coin evidence, likewise, points to a picture of growing exchange that transcended political and religious frontiers. Seventh-century activity at Dorestad resulted in the presence of distinctive silver coins, pennies known to specialists as *sceattas*, which have a relatively wide distribution across northern Europe, from southern Scandinavia to coastal regions of England, Germany and the Netherlands. Unlike the other post-Roman coinages, the *sceattas* did not bear the name or device of any ruler, instead carrying symbols, some seemingly representing monsters and mythical figures; their distribution suggests that they were primarily minted to serve those involved in exchange around the coasts of the North Sea, and that most probably they originated in Frisia.[41] The role of the Frisians as middlemen connecting the coasts of the North Sea in the seventh century is well attested in the written sources. Frisia's economic vitality derived from its distinctive ecology and geography, with low-lying coastal marshes, shifting creeks and small islands of solid earth militating against agriculture and nurturing the inhabitants' expertise in navigation. This in turn prompted engagement with the exchanges that were intensifying along the river systems of the Frankish heartlands.[42] Seventh-century Dorestad was no more a creation of Frisian rulers than it was of the Franks. Its importance derived rather from its location on the river system

---

[40] See above, Chapter 2, pp. 48–9.
[41] On *sceattas* see Wood, *Merovingian Kingdoms*, pp. 299–303.
[42] On Frisia and the Frisians see S. Lebecq, *Marchands et navigateurs. Frisons du haut moyen âge* (Lille, 1983); D. Ellmers, 'The Frisian monopoly of coastal transport in the 6th to 8th centuries AD', in McGrail (ed.), *Maritime Celts, Frisians and Saxons*, pp. 91–2.

that was both a frontier between two kingdoms and a natural valve between two contrasting but potentially complementary economic systems.

The written sources suggest something approaching a Frisian monopoly on communication and exchange around the North Sea in the later seventh and early eighth centuries. In part, this was because the Frisians were ideally placed to dominate the routes that linked the North Sea coast of continental Europe to southern Scandinavia and eastern England (though we should note that 'Frisian' was sometimes used less as an ethnic label than as shorthand for 'expert sailor from the North Sea coast').[43] But these connections did not emerge in a vacuum. Archaeology, particularly in the rich evidence provided by the prized status symbols deposited as grave-goods right across sixth- and seventh-century northwestern Europe, suggests that artefacts and ideas travelled long distances around the Merovingian North Sea.[44] The circulation of such objects was not high volume, nor did it necessarily rest on trade as opposed to gift-giving and status emulation between ruling elites, encouraged by the experiences of exile and travel and the exchange of emissaries; seasonal 'beach markets', which have been canvassed as a potential mechanism for this level of exchange, inevitably remain hard to identify archaeologically.[45] By the later seventh century, the appearance of Frisian shipping in our written sources clearly marks a first step change: we read of emissaries, missionaries and pilgrims availing themselves of a nexus of predictable sailings from well-known points of departure, suggesting that by 700 at the latest the 'gift economy' around the North Sea was riding piggy-back on a system of regular communication and exchange.

[43] Cf I. Wood, 'The Channel from the 4th to the 7th centuries AD', and S. Lebecq, 'On the use of the word Frisian in the 6th to 10th centuries: some interpretations', both in McGrail (ed.), *Maritime Celts, Frisians and Saxons*, pp. 93–7 and 85–90 respectively.

[44] J. W. Huggett, 'Imported grave goods and the early Anglo-Saxon economy', *Medieval Archaeology* 32 (1988), pp. 63–96. The latter term is taken from Wood, *The Merovingian North Sea.*

[45] M. Carver, 'Pre-Viking traffic in the North Sea', in McGrail (ed.), *Maritime Celts, Frisians and Saxons*, pp. 117–25. For 'beach markets' see Hodges, *Dark Age Economics*, and for one possible example, certainly in use in the Viking age, see D. Griffiths, R. Philpott and G. Egan (eds.), *Meols. The Archaeology of the North Wirral Coast* (Oxford, 2007).

A second phase rapidly followed, marked by the expansion and planned development of existing nodal points, and also the creation of new sites designed to serve the growing activity around the North Sea. The former phenomenon is best represented by activity in the excavated 'harbour area' at Dorestad, where a series of large wooden warehouses and workshops served by wooden walkways over the beach and jetties leading into the river was constructed *c.*675–725, with a wooden roadway parallel to the course of the river behind them. Beyond that was a zone between 100 and 500 metres deep made up of individual households, wooden 'halls' and their ancillaries constructed in a manner identical to that of any rural site. The latter phenomenon – construction of new sites – is exemplified (as we have seen) by Hamwic. Its logic, however, is most vividly illustrated by Ribe, founded close by the settlement of Danekirke. Danekirke had been inhabited since the second century by a population whose economy was rooted in agriculture, but whose elite inhabitants were increasingly importing lavish status symbols in the sixth and seventh centuries, presumably on a relatively *ad hoc* basis as travellers and seafarers passed this high-status coastal site. The foundation of Ribe *c.*700 was designed to institutionalise and make routine these connections.[46]

The crucial development shared by both old and new sites was the emergence of widespread craft production; these were no longer simply ports of trade, but also places where raw materials from the immediate hinterland, and from trading partners, were processed to be sold on. A relatively similar array of activities (though with different emphases) is witnessed at all excavated sites – not only manufacturing through metalworking and glassworking, but also secondary services such as basket-weaving, boat-building and textile-working. Although the emporia were thus centres of production, this activity was quite scattered and seems to have been organised on the level of the individual household. The populations attracted by the

[46] On Danekirke, see H. J. Hansen, 'Dankirke: affluence in late Iron Age Denmark', in K. Randsborg (ed.), *The Birth of Europe. Archaeology and Social Development in the First Millennium AD* (Rome, 1989), pp. 123–8; for context see B. Ambrosiani and H. Clarke (eds.), *Developments around the Baltic and the North Sea in the Viking Age* (Stockholm, 1994), and for the connections between economics and politics in Denmark in this period U. Näsman, 'Exchange and politics: the eighth–early ninth century in Denmark', in Hansen and Wickham (eds.), *The Long Eighth Century*, pp. 35–68.

potential of such activities grew to significant levels relatively rapidly: in their heyday in the late eighth and early ninth century, major emporia supported resident populations of several thousand, which may sound modest to us but puts them on a par with any other contemporary aggregation in western Europe barring Rome. At peak times, these numbers would have swelled, and the need to cope with this seasonal demand probably explains why there is also good evidence for intensive farming at Dorestad, particularly in the outer sectors of residence; estates in the hinterland of major emporia were also engaged in marketing foodstuffs.[47] Increasing knowledge of the range of activities carried out in the emporia, and the infrastructure which supported sizeable artisanal populations, has led some scholars to stress the concentration of production and the reciprocal relationship this created with the surrounding countryside as the basic functions of the emporia.[48] After all, in Francia the continued use of some former Roman sites as seats of authority encouraged similar, if smaller-scale, concentrations of production, as at Cologne, and an environment structured by aristocratic wealth and excellent river connections meant that some aggregations of craft production could even spring up from nothing at nodal points in local patterns of communications, as at Huy or Maastricht.[49] But Dorestad or Quentovic differed from such sites not only quantitatively, but qualitatively: they were not defined by or tied to patterns of ecclesiastical and political power. If we are to account for their significance and size then these local economic interactions must take centre stage, but we cannot forget that a centre like Dorestad could not have grown and prospered without long-distance seaborne trade. It was their role as valves for the import and export of raw materials and manufactures that encouraged the growth there of production and secondary activity in trades such as shipbuilding, woodworking and butchering. Without the network of exchange off which they fed,

---

[47] A. Morton, 'Hamwic in its context', in Anderton (ed.), *Anglo-Saxon Trading Centres*, pp. 48–62.

[48] For example P. Blinkhorn, 'Of cabbages and kings: production, trade, and consumption in Middle-Saxon England', in Anderton (ed.), *Anglo-Saxon Trading Centres*, pp. 4–23.

[49] See S. Schütte, 'Continuity problems and authority structures in Cologne', in G. Ausenda (ed.), *After Empire: Towards an Ethnology of Europe's Barbarians* (San Marino, 1995), pp. 163–76; F. Theuws, 'Maastricht as a centre of power in the early Middle Ages', in De Jong and Theuws with van Rhijn (eds.), *Topographies of Power*, pp. 155–216, esp. pp. 200–5.

the emporia would not have been viable settlements on this scale or at these sites. The Frankish emporia were within their kingdoms, but not exactly *of* their kingdoms – this dual identity, and their simultaneous existence in two overlapping universes, was what made them what they were.

THE TRANSFORMATION OF THE EMPORIA: THE NINTH CENTURY

These processes (of rising elite-driven production in the interior leading to expanding external exchange) underwrote the boom in the emporia revealed by the archaeological record for the second half of the eighth century and the first three decades of the ninth. The real puzzle is explaining why they faltered in the succeeding half-century. For falter they did: by the end of the ninth century, Dorestad, Hamwic and Quentovic were drastically less active as centres of trade or production. Past generations of scholars working primarily from written sources were understandably tempted to explain these economic changes in terms of a generalised stereotype of ninth-century chaos and destruction, and pointed the finger squarely at a combination of aristocratic infighting and Viking raiding. But this view is incompatible with the recent findings of archaeologists. The cataclysmic view places a heavy weight on the mention of Viking raids on Dorestad and Hamwic in the 830s: Dorestad, indeed, was raided four years running from 834 to 837. The archaeology, however, incomplete though it is, lacks 'destruction layers' such as might indicate the effects of burning or ravaging, and points instead to a gradual flattening out of activity slowly tipping into decline in the 830s. This pattern is confirmed by the distribution of coins minted at Dorestad and Quentovic, which both peak *c.*830, and gradually fade away, with no sign of dramatic discontinuity, thereafter.[50] At the height of production, Dorestad was minting far and away the greatest number of the sole denomination in circulation in the Carolingian empire, the *denarius*, which had a purchasing power, in 794, of twelve two-pound loaves of bread (see Figure 16). By Louis the Pious's reign the Carolingian government was able to exclude foreign coins from

---

[50] See S. Coupland, 'Trading places: Quentovic and Dorestad reassessed', *EME* 11 (2002), pp. 209–32; S. Coupland, 'Between the devil and the deep blue sea: hoards in ninth-century Frisia', in B. Cook and G. Williams (eds.), *Coinage and History in the North Sea World c.500–1250. Essays in Honour of Marion Archibald* (Leiden, 2006), pp. 241–66; Coupland, 'Money and coinage'.

Figure 16. Silver *denarius* minted at Dorestad (DORESTATVS), 814–18. All examples of this issue have on the obverse a bust of the emperor Louis the Pious crowned with a laurel wreath. On the reverse, other mints depicted a set of city gates: the image of a ship struck at Dorestad and Quentovic underlines the status of those places as important trading centres – emporia – in the North Sea–Channel economic network.

circulation, to ensure that new issues were minted to a single design throughout the empire, and to arrange for the swift withdrawal from circulation of demonetized issues.

The significance of Quentovic, meanwhile, continued even in the heyday of Viking activity in the Channel – the coins indicate that its plateau came later, around the middle decades of the ninth century, and that it was not extinct even in the tenth.[51] Major churches fought hard to maintain property complexes at Quentovic, through which the surpluses produced on their estates could be sold on: the significance of such arrangements is vividly illustrated by the lobbying undertaken by Abbot Lupus of Ferrières, eager to evict the aristocrats whom Charles the Bald had installed at the small cell at

---

[51] Coupland, 'Trading places' (though with a different interpretation from that presented here); J. C. Moesgaard, 'A survey of coin production and currency in Normandy, 864–945', in J. Graham-Campbell and G. Williams (eds.), *Silver Economy of the Viking Age* (Walnut Creek, CA, 2007), pp. 99–121.

St Josse, close by Quentovic, and return this property into the direct control of his abbey.[52]

These patterns of gradual change must be explained with reference to processes more complex and long-term than political conflict or Viking attack. At Dorestad, the changing face of the excavated harbour on the Kromme Rijn is suggestive (see Map 12). Here, cargoes were loaded and unloaded into a series of 'warehouses' constructed on long thin plots connected to the river by a series of wooden 'tracks' over the sand. These were constructed and repaired throughout the eighth and ninth century; the period of Dorestad's decline in particular saw their elaboration and extension, the longest exceeding 100 metres in length before the site's final abandonment. This hints at environmental change, with changing sea levels and the rapid silting of the river – itself perhaps a result of the intensive human activity along its banks – simply making Dorestad less and less attractive as a port. But it may also point to the changing nature of trade. It still remains unclear whether in Dorestad's heyday boats were normally 'beached' for unloading, or whether the extreme end of the wooden tracks served as something like a jetty, but it is possible that the extension of the wooden tracks was also an attempt to provide platforms for deeper draught vessels more suited to navigating direct across the open sea, and able to carry higher-volume cargo. Our knowledge of early medieval ships remains imperfect, but there are hints that a major development of the North Sea's 'Viking age' was a move away from the earlier reliance on coast-hugging transport, with accompanying changes in ship design.[53]

Whatever the case, it seems clear that the relative importance of the long-distance high-status exchange that the emporia served was declining by the second half of the ninth century, and that new networks better able to handle the regional marketing of bulk goods

---

[52] See S. Lebecq, 'The role of the monasteries in the systems of production and exchange of the Frankish world between the seventh and the beginning of the ninth centuries', in Hansen and Wickham (eds.), *The Long Eighth Century*, pp. 121–48. On Lupus's struggle to regain St Josse, see Lupus of Ferrières, *Epistolae*, ed. P. K. Marshall (Leipzig, 1984), nos. 19, 32, 36, 42, 43, 45, 49, 58, 62, 65, 82, 86. See also J. L. Nelson, 'England and the continent in the ninth century: II, Vikings and others', *TRHS* 6th ser. 13 (2003), pp. 1–28, for Quentovic.

[53] See for example O. Crumlin-Pedersen, *From Viking Ships to Hanseatic Cogs* (London, 1983). Carver, 'Pre-Viking traffic' points out the methodological problems in identifying sea-routes from this kind of evidence.

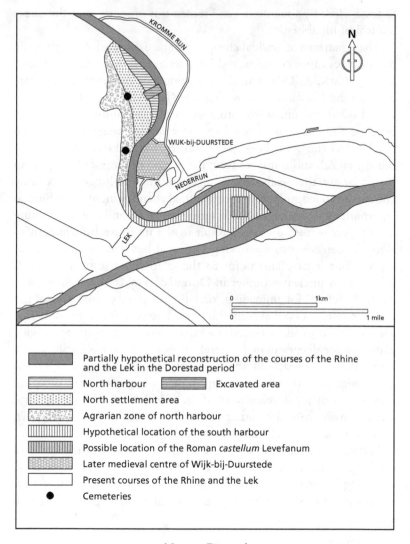

Map 12. Dorestad

were becoming the motor driving the economy. Here, in a sense, the emporia were almost victims of their own success: a site like Dorestad stimulated a significant degree of economic specialisation and secondary exchange in its hinterland, thanks to the demand it generated for foodstuffs, wood and other locally accessible raw materials, and its function as a market and centre of craft production. Already in its heyday, its sheer size was such that a number of secondary centres emerged nearby: smaller markets both on the coast (Dorestad was a significant sail of some 70 km up the Rhine delta from the open sea) as on the island of Domburg at the mouth of the Rhine, and inland too at the nodal points for the collection of produce from the countryside.[54] By the end of the ninth century, a series of sites in what had once been Dorestad's hinterland were emerging as new towns in their own right, smaller in scale but part of a dense network of local centres springing up along the major rivers of northwestern Europe, most fortified thanks to their attachment to a major centre of landlords' activity. Ghent, for example, grew up around a major monastery, and Bruges around an aristocratic centre.[55] Even in the late ninth century, long-distance trade had not disappeared, but now it took place in a series of market places that were defined by an increasingly dense pattern of local exchanges. The preceding two generations had seen a shift in the logic of the economy in northwest Europe, as the specialisation and local exchange encouraged by the success of the emporia became able to sustain dedicated centres better suited to the exchange of higher-volume but lower-value goods on a local level.

In Dorestad's hinterland, these changes must have caused some dislocation, even if only short-lived, which interacted with the disruption to long-distance exchange caused by Viking activity. Elsewhere in the Frankish heartlands, the rise of more deeply rooted regional markets may have been more seamless. Recent finds at Mainz, for example, demonstrate vividly how the early development of the North Sea economy could kickstart productive activity at a site several hundred kilometres down the Rhine, and eventually stimulate development of coherent systems of regional exchange. Mainz was a major Roman military site located at a strategically important point on the middle Rhine and had thus been an important communication nodal point in the fifth and sixth centuries. At some point in the early eighth century, a long section of the former Roman wall along the Rhine was demolished and a metalled 'public street' parallel to the river bank built, with long narrow plots leading off it serving as warehouses and workshops handling

54 W. van Es, 'Dorestad centred', in J. C. Besteman, J. M. Bos and H. A. Heidinga (eds.), *Medieval Archaeology in the Netherlands. Studies Presented to H. H. von Regteren Altena* (Assen and Maastricht, 1990), pp. 151–82, is an excellent analysis of the emporium's relationship to its hinterland.
55 See Verhulst, *The Rise of Cities*; and A. Verhulst, 'The origins of towns in the Low Countries and the Pirenne Thesis', *P&P* 122 (1989), pp. 3–35.

goods travelling along the river. Modern redevelopment in this area has unearthed a rich array of finds, indicative of intensive craft-production as well as the shipping onwards of materials from the city's hinterland: the distinctive metalwork produced here in the second half of the eighth century was distributed right across the eastern part of the Frankish world, and even as far as Birka and York.[56] This indicates a step change in the production and exchange of status-enhancing gifts at the site which directly parallels the changes taking place around the North Sea at the same time. This parallelism was no accident, and can indeed be seen as a matter of direct cause and effect: the wine exported through Dorestad was manufactured in the vineyards of the middle Rhine valley around Mainz, and transported downriver in barrels made of wood felled from the forests of the region.[57]

By the time we get to the ninth century we start to find descriptions of activities like the transport of grain on rafts down the Main, indicating the effects that this kind of demand could have on the local economy.[58] An annalist working in the entourage of the archbishop of Mainz was familiar enough with the role of the city as a regional market to retell sermonising stories of the moral dangers into which it was possible to fall by pursuing wealth too single-mindedly: not only was the archbishop an exemplar of holiness for turning over the produce of his estates to the common good in times of dearth, but miraculous punishments showed that using the Sabbath to undertake household-scale commercial work – baking bread to sell in the city – was a sin.[59] The plentiful documentation from the area shows that this activity was driven by landowners, not professional merchants: local landlords with extensive but not intimidating constellations of property are known to have owned warehouses on the Rhine-front, exporting corn and doubtless investing in craft production.[60] Coin finds in Mainz's hinterland, along with references to cash prices in charters and cash rents in polyptychs, indicate that by the ninth century this was a regional economy familiar with the use of coin. The shifting origins of these coins confirm the increasing coherence

---

[56] On the archaeology of Mainz, see E. Wamers, *Die frühmittelalterliche Lesefunde aus der Löhrstraße (Baustelle Hilton II) in Mainz* (Mainz, 1994). See also Falck, *Mainz im frühen und hohen Mittelalter.*

[57] Van Es and Verwers, *Excavations at Dorestad 1.*

[58] Einhard, *Translation and Miracles*, III.6.   [59] *AF, s.a.* 870.

[60] For references and discussion see Innes, *State and Society*, pp. 66–8, 96–8.

of these local networks and their gradual eclipsing of long-distance exchange. The relatively high percentage of issues from distant mints along the Rhine, notably Dorestad, in the later eighth and early ninth century gives way to a much more regionally focussed pattern by 900, with Mainz and neighbouring Rhineland mints accounting for over 80% of finds.[61] Although Mainz still had a 'Frisian quarter' of professional long-distance shippers operating up the Rhine, by 900 it was above all a leading regional market, and the connection to the Rhine delta and the North Sea certainly did not define or drive its activity.[62]

Full understanding of these transformations awaits more case-studies which can highlight regional differences: Mainz was, after all, a direct partner of Dorestad on a site central to natural networks of long-distance communication throughout our period, and is therefore not necessarily typical. Nonetheless, wherever we look similar processes can be discerned. Thus in Charles the Bald's west Frankish kingdom the second half of the ninth century saw major ecclesiastical institutions beginning to acquire royal privileges giving them the right to found new regular markets at specific estate-centres, and on occasion canvassing the king for the creation of new mints so as to allow their followers to acquire coin more easily, in a process which was to continue east of the Rhine in the tenth century.[63] A world where major landlords were seeking to establish markets conveniently sited to pass on the surpluses of their manorial economies, and working to secure a regular supply of coin, was a world which had been economically transformed.

THE VIKINGS AND THE FRANKISH ECONOMY

Although we have argued that the Vikings should not be seen as the primary reason for these changes, their role cannot be ignored altogether: after all, the new economic nodes of the decades around 900 were, unlike the emporia, typically defended by stone walls and

---

[61] For coin finds at Mainz, see Wamers, *Die frühmittelalterliche Lesefunde*; see also W. Hess, 'Geldwirtschaft am Mittelrhein in karolingischer Zeit', *Blätter für deutsche Landesgeschichte* 98 (1962), pp. 26–63; M. Blackburn, 'Coin circulation in Germany during the early Middle Ages: the evidence of single-finds', in B. Kluge (ed.), *Fernhandel und Geldwirtschaft* (Sigmaringen, 1993), pp. 37–54.

[62] For Frisians at Mainz see *AF* (Mainz continuation), *s.a.* 886.

[63] The best introduction is Nelson, *Charles the Bald*, pp. 19–40.

aristocratic entourages. Even Mainz saw the reconstruction of the city walls following the adventures of Godafrid III in the Rhine and Moselle valleys in the 880s, and the dangers of piracy and plundering must have played a role in shifting the balance away from long-distance exchange to local markets.[64] But the economic impact of Viking activity was a far more complex and subtle matter than the stereotype of wanton destruction would allow. Scandinavia was a crucial part of the North Sea economy served by the emporia, and the Scandinavian warlords who led Viking bands operated in a world where control of exchange was critical to the creation of political power. The rapid growth of the North Sea economy in the two or three generations immediately preceding the first references to Viking raiding in our written sources, in the years around 800, is striking, yet the relationship between the development of exchange and the onset of raiding remains little understood. The presence of Scandinavian warbands along the coasts and rivers of northwestern Europe, sometimes as allies and servants of Frankish kings, sometimes as enemies, points to a fundamental transformation of Scandinavian societies prompted by the gravitational pull of their Frankish neighbour.

Assessing the impact of Viking activity on these patterns of change is difficult because the relationship between trading and raiding remains poorly understood. The major problem here has been the polarised nature of Viking studies: until very recently specialists tended to divide into two camps, one investigating long-term economic and political connections and the other emphasising the short-term disruption wrought by ninth-century raiding, but both tending to draw general conclusions that lump together the diverse activities of different groups of Scandinavians.[65] The running and rerunning of somewhat moralistic arguments along these lines ('bad' vs 'not so bad') has become somewhat unhelpful, and it is only recently that new work has begun to help us reach a new understanding of how Frankish authors thought about the raiders, with polemical presentations of the Vikings as agents of God's wrath

---

[64] Note that the label 'Viking' is a modern term of art rather than a contemporary designation. Godafrid III's exploits are described in *AF*, *s.a.* 882–5.

[65] The debate was opened by P. H. Sawyer, *The Age of the Vikings* (London, 1962, 2nd edn London, 1971). See also P. Wormald, 'Viking studies: whence and whither?', in R. T. Farrell (ed.), *The Vikings* (Chichester, 1982), pp. 128–53; N. Lund, 'Allies of God or man? The Viking expansion in European perspective', *Viator* 20 (1989), pp. 45–59; Nelson, 'England and the continent'.

being selectively deployed as a means of criticising political opponents. These narratives were often highly coloured by Old Testament expectations which (carefully manipulated for maximum effect) cannot be taken at face value. Careful analysis of the careers, connections and motivations of Scandinavian leaders is the way to fuller understanding.[66]

By about 800, Carolingian military success in Saxony, along with the development of the North Sea economy, had brought Scandinavian rulers into increasingly direct contact with the Franks, and they sought to draw on the new opportunities afforded by this contact to stabilise their own positions. Control of systems of exchange, and particularly of the major emporia, was crucial for ambitious rulers anxious to establish royal claims and attract the armed followings that made them powerful: hence the Swedish king Anund seized Birka, driving out his rival, in order to make good his claims to royal status.[67] These patterns of internal conflict might impinge on Frankish interests. The Danish king Godafrid I, who had succeeded in establishing overlordship over much of the Jutland peninsula by 800, raided the emporium of Reric, situated on the Baltic coast in the territory of the Abodrites, precisely because it provided a valve between the Frankish world and the Baltic which bypassed the nearby Danish emporium at Hedeby. At Reric, archaeology helps show the real meaning of activities our sources refer to as 'raiding', revealing the relocation of a significant proportion of craft production previously carried out at Reric to Hedeby, which involved not only the forced removal of the artisan population but also the rerouting of networks of supply and distribution.[68] Godafrid's need to establish control over networks of exchange inevitably brought him into conflict with Charlemagne: not only did his activities harm the Abodrites (who were Frankish allies), but he also attempted to intervene in the networks stretching from Denmark down the coast to the rivers of the Frankish heartlands by mobilising a force of 200 ships and forcing the Frisians to offer him an annual tribute.[69] Although Frisia was politically part of

---

[66] See above all S. Coupland, 'The rod of God's wrath or the people of God's wrath? The Carolingian theology of the Viking invasions', *Journal of Ecclesiastical History* 42 (1991), pp. 535–54.

[67] Rimbert, *Vita Anskarii*, c. 19.

[68] See *ARF, s.a.* 808, 809; M. Müller-Wille, A. Tummuscheit and L. Hansen, *Frühstädtliche Zentren der Wikingerzeit und ihr Hinterland. Die Beispiele Ribe, Hedeby und Reric* (Göttingen, 2002).

[69] *ARF, s.a.* 810.

the Frankish realm, ecologically and geographically it was in many ways an extension of the Jutland peninsula to which it was closely tied economically – Godafrid's attempt to reduce it to tributary status was part and parcel of the strategies by which he had built and maintained his overlordship.

The stand-off between Charlemagne and Godafrid ended with the latter's death in 810 and the dissolution of his personal overlordship in the ensuing conflict between rival successors. Subsequent Frankish policy involved offering political support to Danish royal claimants as a means of avoiding potential conflict in the future. After the 820s this policy went hand in hand with attempts to convert Scandinavian rulers and their entourages, with the missionary bishop Anskar and his helpers acting as something like Frankish emissaries in Hedeby and Birka.[70] Frankish involvement seems to have prevented any individual royal recreating the kind of extensive overlordship enjoyed by Godafrid; this may, indeed, have been a conscious aim of Frankish policy.[71] But it also meant acknowledgement of the close ties between the Frisian coast and Denmark, for favoured Scandinavian leaders were not only given military backing when necessary, but were also allowed to have footholds on the Frisian coast as *honores* from the Frankish emperor, and thus to control the very area that Godafrid had been so keen to reduce to tributary status.[72]

Given the Frankish policy of selective intervention in Danish politics, it is scarcely an accident that the outbreak of open internal rivalry within the Carolingian family in the 830s coincided with the launching of raids by a series of would-be Scandinavian rulers. This was not simply the opportunistic taking of advantage of internal conflict among the Franks – endemic competition for power within southern Scandinavia spilled over as rival members of the royal family sought to acquire Frankish patronage, and by the 840s rival Carolingians were entering into alliances with different Scandinavian warlords. The

---

[70] Palmer, 'Rimbert's *Vita Anskarii*'; Wood, 'Christians and pagans'.

[71] Cf P. Heather, 'State formation in Europe in the first millennium AD', in B. Crawford (ed.), *Scotland in Dark Age Europe* (St Andrews, 1994), pp. 47–63; K. L. Maund, '"A turmoil of warring princes": political leadership in ninth-century Denmark', *Haskins Society Journal* 6 (1994), pp. 29–47; I. Garipzanov, 'Frontier identities: Carolingian frontier and *gens Danorum*', in I. H. Garipzanov, P. J. Geary and P. Urbanczyk (eds.), *Franks, Northmen, and Slavs: Identities and State Formation in Early Medieval Europe* (Turnhout, 2008), pp. 113–42.

[72] Coupland, 'From poachers to gamekeepers'.

reports of raids on emporia like Dorestad in the 830s, and on major Frankish political and ecclesiastical centres like Paris in the 840s, reflect responses to the disruption of these alliances caused by turmoil within Francia. Sailing on Dorestad, for example, was a means of attempting to impose tributary status and contest political control in a crucial region which was a real bone of contention between rival Scandinavian rulers and their Carolingian allies, and not (as our sources say) a straightforward matter of wanton destruction.

By the middle decades of the ninth century, Scandinavian warlords were a part of the Frankish system, seeking patronage and employment with which to gain renown, reward followers, and so augment their standing at home. Dorestad, for example, was granted to a succession of Scandinavians through the 840s, 850s and 860s, with only two documented raids, both the result of contests for Frankish patronage.[73] As poachers-turned-gamekeepers such figures were successful, but where Frankish patronage was not forthcoming or was withdrawn, raiding, and with it the ransoming of captives and levying of tribute, was the response. These developments must have had important implications for patterns of exchange. Scandinavian leaders and their followings were now receiving gifts and extracting tribute in Francia itself. Frankish status symbols were popular with Scandinavian warriors, as Notker noted, and are very much evident in the archaeology of ninth-century Scandinavia: their circulation now rested on patterns of gift and raid within Francia, whence they were carried home by returning warbands.[74]

At the same time, Viking activities and demands increased the liquidity of wealth within those areas of Francia where they were most active. The coin evidence from Charles the Bald's west Francia, for example, suggests a high volume of coinage in rapid circulation: major landowners, and particularly the Church, were required by Charles to raise large amounts of silver coin to enable him to pay tributes, and as a result there was significant pressure towards the greater monetisation of the rural economy.[75] What is more, much of the moveable wealth thus accumulated did not find its way back

---

[73] Coupland, 'From poachers to gamekeepers'; Coupland, 'Between the devil and the deep blue sea'.

[74] Notker, *Gesta*, 2.19; E. Wamers and M. Brandt (eds.), *Die Macht des Silbers: Karolingische Schätze im Norden* (Frankfurt, 2005).

[75] M. Metcalf, 'A sketch of the currency in the time of Charles the Bald', in M. T. Gibson and J. L. Nelson (eds.), *Charles the Bald: Court and Kingdom* (2nd edn,

to the Scandinavian homelands, but further stimulated the Frankish economy as Vikings sought to use it to acquire status-enhancing luxury goods. Hence the bewildering swiftness with which Vikings might alternate between plundering, demanding tribute, and buying and selling. In 882, for example, some Franks, seeing their leaders negotiating with a Viking leader, ventured without hesitation into the fortress they were besieging, 'some to trade, some to look around the defences', once the defenders had flung open the gates and raised a shield on high as a sign of peace.[76] Viking activities, then, not only encouraged the shifting of the old networks of long-distance exchange around the North Sea, but were also potent forces for the development of regional exchange within Frankish society.

ITALY AND THE MEDITERRANEAN ECONOMY

The emergence of long-distance exchange around the North Sea and the proliferation of rural markets in the Frankish heartlands have encouraged many archaeologists and historians to see northwestern Europe as the real economic dynamo of the Carolingian world. But for all the undoubted importance of the North Sea networks, we should beware generalising from them: unlike the Roman empire at its height, or later European colonial empires, the Carolingians did not sustain a core–periphery system whereby the economy of the heartlands dominated those around it. Even in the North Sea, demand and production in England and Scandinavia were never subordinated to Frankish needs, but drew on the possibilities inherent in long-distance exchange. Furthermore, these networks also remained relatively insulated from the Mediterranean economy. The seventh century had seen the final collapse of the long-distance exchange which had defined the Mediterranean economy in Roman times. Intimately tied to the demands of the state, this was essentially a system of franchises, where shippers who carried the annual convoy of supplies from surplus-producing provinces to the capital received

Aldershot, 1990), pp. 65–97; S. Coupland, 'The Frankish tribute payments to the Vikings and their consequences', *Francia* 26 (1999), pp. 57–75. For debates over the scale of coinage in circulation, see also P. Grierson, 'The volume of the Anglo-Saxon coinage', *Economic Historic Review* 20 (1967), pp. 153–60; Coupland, 'Money and coinage'.

[76] *AF* (Mainz continuation), *s.a.* 882.

fiscal and legal privileges giving them a crucial competitive advantage in conducting long-distance trade, which as a result rode 'piggy back' on state requisitions. The need to plug into the western end of these exchanges had exercised Merovingian kings in the sixth and early seventh centuries, prompting their recurrent interest in Marseille, the major valve between Frankish elites and the Mediterranean economy.[77] All this was in rapid decline by the second half of the seventh century, following Constantinople's loss of key shipping centres in Egypt and Syria. The final loss to the Muslims of Carthage in 698 seems to have precipitated the ultimate collapse of this trade, cutting off the trickle of communication still crossing diagonally from Constantinople to its most westerly province, and the slow drip of trade connected to this route, indicated by the presence of African amphorae in Rome and the Adriatic, petered out.[78]

The first half of the eighth century saw the nadir of long-distance exchange around the Mediterranean (see Map 13). It is precisely the contrast between this slump and the simultaneous emergence of the North Sea emporia which has encouraged Pirenne-inspired generalisations about a shifting economic balance northwards. Such a generalisation, however, does not take account of the persistence of less spectacular processes of regional exchange.[79] Take, for example, a treaty concluded in 715 between the men of Comacchio, a Byzantine outpost near the mouth of the river Po, and the Lombard king Liutprand: this regulated toll payments made by Comacchese ships as they plied their way up the Po, entering the Lombard kingdom at Mantua, and then if they wished, moving further still into the heart of the north Italian plain. This was not new trade (the treaty is said to confirm 'ancient custom'), nor was it high-volume – the carriers, after all, were referred to as 'soldiers' (*milites*), the standard

---

[77] See S. Loseby, 'Marseille and the Pirenne thesis I: Gregory of Tours, the Merovingian kings, and "un grand port"', in Hodges and Bowden (eds.), *The Sixth Century*, pp. 203–29.

[78] McCormick, *Origins of the European Economy*, Part I, for the best overview of the end of the ancient economy, emphasising the sixth-century plague; for Carthage as the final full stop, see M. Innes, *Introduction to Early Medieval Western Europe, 300–900. The Sword, the Plough and the Book* (London and New York, 2007), pp. 191–3.

[79] For a theoretical framework stressing the primacy of the latter in the pre-modern Mediterranean, see P. Horden and N. Purcell, *The Corrupting Sea: A Study of Mediterranean History* I (Oxford, 1999); P. Squatriti, 'Mohammed, the early medieval Mediterranean, and Charlemagne', *EME* 11 (2003), pp. 263–79.

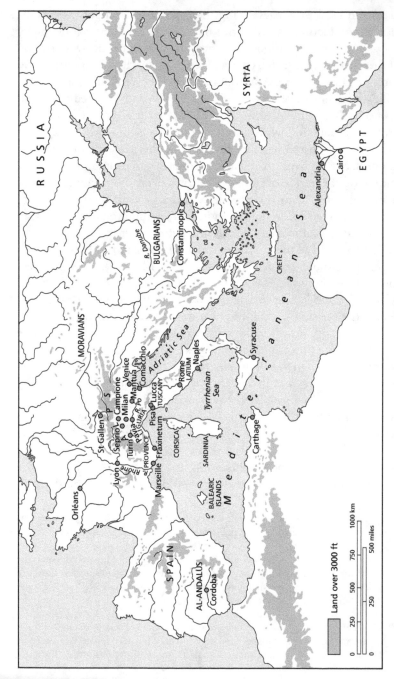

Map 13. Exchange and trade: the Mediterranean Sea (showing places mentioned in Chapter 7)

term for lesser landowners in Byzantine Italy. It rested primarily on the ready market in the cities of the Lombard kingdom for salt harvested from the mouth of the Po, supplemented by olive oil, fish sauce and on occasion pepper, suggesting that goods received from across the sea, presumably when emissaries were sent to and from Constantinople, might also be sold on. This network has left only a faint imprint in the archaeological record – it dealt, after all, with consumables – but the documents give a steady trickle of references to the presence in the interior of ships from Comacchio, trading and paying tolls right through our period.[80] In other words, the development of new long-distance exchange networks, which is such a dramatic feature of the Carolingian period, took place against a backdrop of existing regional connections served by the rivers and roads of the Italian peninsula, even after the remnants of post-Roman international trade had faded. Thus amongst the complaints voiced by the Istrians against their Frankish *dux* at Rižana in 804, which we looked at in Chapter 5, was his abuse of the requisitioned transport of state goods that they were expected to undertake along the Adriatic coastline and the rivers that connected with the interior.[81]

The archaeological and documentary evidence highlights the resolutely local horizons of northern Italy, where the basic social units were cities and their associated rural hinterlands.[82] These aspects of Italian society are illustrated by the career of the eighth-century landowner Toto, whose archive of two dozen original documents was kept at the church of St Zeno founded by his family at Campione

---

[80] Liutprand's *pactum* is edited by L. Hartmann, *Zur Wirtschaftsgeschichte Italiens im frühen Mittelalter* (Gotha, 1904); and for discussion see McCormick, *Origins of the European Economy*, pp. 117–18, 631–3, 778–9. On Comacchio, see S. Gelichi, 'The rise of an early medieval emporium and the economy of Italy in the late Longobard age', in *Annales. Series Historia et Sociologia* 18/2 (2008), pp. 319–36.

[81] See above, Chapter 5, p. 234.

[82] See Wickham, 'Aristocratic power', and for economic aspects R. Balzaretti, 'Cities and markets in early medieval Europe', in G. Ausenda (ed.), *After Empire. Towards an Ethnology of Europe's Barbarians* (San Marino, 1994), pp. 113–42; R. Balzaretti, 'Monasteries, towns and the countryside: reciprocal relationships in the archdiocese of Milan, 614–814', in G. P. Brogiolo, N. Gauthier and N. Christie (eds.), *Towns and Their Territories: Between Late Antiquity and the Early Middle Ages* (Leiden, 2000), pp. 235–57; R. Balzaretti, 'Cities, emporia and monasteries: local economies in the Po valley 700–875', in N. Christie and S. Loseby (eds.), *Towns in Transition. Urban Evolution in Late Antiquity and the Early Middle Ages* (Aldershot, 1996), pp. 213–34.

in the city-territory (*civitas*) of Seprio.[83] Toto's profile is fairly typical of the kind of figures evident from the documentary record, whose interests were more or less circumscribed to their home territory and its immediate neighbourhood: Toto dominated a number of villages around Seprio, and was also active in the far bigger and more important nearby city of Milan. These patterns of landholding and public activity, though not tied to just one city, were defined by local networks centred on major urban centres which were close at hand, in Toto's case Milan as well as Seprio. The result was a local economy resting on regular, unremarkable, flows whereby landowners like Toto could dominate the countryside, and consume its wealth, by involvement in local city life. Of course, not all Lombard landowners were of a comparable scale to Toto: there were bigger figures who benefited from royal patronage and were hence able to create more extensive aggregations of land. The Carolingian conquest strengthened this tendency, to such an extent that by the last decades of the ninth century the political class could divide into as few as two cohesive aristocratic constellations, each bound together by strong regional interests.[84] But even then patterns of redistribution based on the city remained the default, and the kind of extensive rural manorial economies which characterised the Frankish heartlands north of the Alps were largely absent.[85] One important result of these different social patterns was that Italian landowning was probably more implicated in local markets throughout our period: it is striking that, for all the apparent paucity of local coinages in the eighth and ninth century, Italian documents are far more conversant with coin as a standard of value and a mechanism of exchange than is the case north of the Alps. One of the documents in Toto's dossier, for example, records a landowner raising one *solidus*'s worth of gold, necessary to allow him to meet his obligations for the remainder of the year, guaranteed against some land, a transaction of a form more or less unknown north of the Alps. This indicates that liquid wealth was significant and that values were understood and expressed in abstract terms even at a relatively low social level; higher up the social scale,

---

[83] Gasparri and La Rocca (eds.), *Carte di famiglia*.

[84] Gasparri, 'The aristocracy'.

[85] Most prominent among the exceptions, which did develop manorial estates similar to those in northern Europe, are some of the larger monasteries: for the example of Farfa, see Costambeys, *Power and Patronage*.

there is good evidence for landowners holding significant reserves of moveable wealth, and paying prices of up to a hundred *solidi* for land.[86]

Despite significant differences between the north and central and southern Italy, the basic social parameters (a network of cities organically connected to the surrounding countryside) were common to most of the peninsula. Rome, notably, stood at the heart of a far-reaching system designed to maintain the city's food supply, resting on a mixture of imperial privileges and papal property claims.[87] The tying of the rich *latifundia* (estates) of Sicily to the city's needs had long encouraged regional exchange up the western Tyrrhenian coast, and even the papacy's loss of its Sicilian estates in the 720s and 730s did not end these connections.[88] In fact, the turning off of the regular flows of Sicilian surpluses to Rome ultimately encouraged not economic collapse, but the emergence of a series of more distinct and coherent regional economies. The papacy, for example, intensified its management of its properties and prerogatives in its immediate hinterland, Latium, with the development of a series of sites termed *domuscultae* in the written sources.[89] Newly excavated elite sites within early medieval Rome, such as the aristocratic residence found in the Forum of Nerva, witness a parallel shift, with local commodities like the fine pottery known as Forum Ware compensating for the lack of long-distance trade.[90] This, along with the programmes of building

---

[86] S. Gasparri, 'Mercanti o possessori? Profilo di un ceto dominante in un'età di transizione'; for coin and cash in Toto's documents see A. Rovelli, 'Economia monetaria e monete nel dossier di Campione', both in Gasparri and La Rocca (eds.), *Carte di famiglia*, pp. 157–78 and pp. 117–40 respectively; and for the general problems of coin use in eighth- and ninth-century Italy see A. Rovelli, 'Some considerations on the coinage of Lombard and Carolingian Italy', in Hansen and Wickham (eds.), *The Long Eighth Century*, pp. 195–223; A. Rovelli, 'Emissione e uso della moneta: le testimonianze scritte e archeologiche', *Settimane di Studio del Centro italiano di studi sull'alto medioevo* 48 (Spoleto, 2001), pp. 821–52; A. Rovelli, 'Coins and trade in early medieval Italy', *EME* 17 (2009), pp. 45–76.

[87] See M. Costambeys, 'Property, ideology and the territorial power of the papacy in the early Middle Ages', *EME* 9 (2000), pp. 367–96.

[88] Wickham, *Framing the Early Middle Ages*, pp. 736–41.

[89] On *domuscultae* see Francovich, 'Changing structures of settlement', at p. 163 (see also the glossary at p. 229); Costambeys, *Power and Patronage*, pp. 187–96.

[90] On the recent finds in Rome, see C. Wickham, 'Overview: production, distribution and demand, II', in Hansen and Wickham (eds.), *The Long Eighth Century*, pp. 345–77, at pp. 361–2. See also D. Whitehouse, '"Things that travelled": the surprising case of raw glass', *EME* 12 (2003), pp. 301–5 and M. McCormick,

in the city most extensively attested in the biographies written up in the 'Book of Pontiffs' (*Liber pontificalis*), illustrates how Rome stood at the hub of a complex infrastructure allowing investment in the fabric of the city, in part using the surpluses generated by the surrounding region.[91] With the ebbing away of imperial authority in the first decades of the eighth century, Rome became the main arena in which central Italian elites struggled for dominance: the integration of the hinterland and city is shown by the career of another Toto, this one duke of nearby Nepi, who raised a force from his city's rural hinterland, staged an invasion of Rome (staying at his townhouse for the duration), and confirmed his takeover by having his candidate made pope.[92]

These routine systems of redistribution centred on cities and their territories meant that when new long-distance connections did emerge in the later eighth and early ninth centuries, they could immediately plug into coherent and complex local economies. Michael McCormick's innovative study has transformed our understanding of the chronology of these new connections.[93] Assembling a huge range of data for the movement of people and goods around the Mediterranean, McCormick emphasises the limited and intermittent nature of inter-regional contacts in the first half of the eighth century, with some seaborne communication between Constantinople and its remaining Italian provinces, and a regular trickle of Islamic shipping hugging the north African coast. In the later eighth century, not only does the regularity and intensity of visible inter-regional connections increase, but a series of new axes of movement also emerge in both the archaeological and written records. Here, the last two or three decades of the eighth century appear to be particularly crucial. By 800, regular north–south links between Islamic north Africa, Sicily and Italy's Tyrrhenian coast had been established, taking in the islands of the western Mediterranean and reaching the coasts of western

---

'Complexity, chronology and context in the early medieval economy', *EME* 12 (2003), pp.307–23, and a number of the articles in Smith (ed.), *Early Medieval Rome and the Christian West*.

[91] For papal building, see T. F. X. Noble, 'Topography, celebration and power: the making of a papal Rome in the eighth and ninth centuries', in de Jong and Theuws with van Rhijn (eds.), *Topographies of Power*, pp. 45–92; Noble, 'Paradoxes and possibilities'; Goodson, *The Rome of Pope Paschal I*.

[92] *LP* I, pp. 468–71, trans. Davis, *Lives of the Eighth-Century Popes*, pp. 88–92.

[93] McCormick, *Origins of the European Economy*.

Spain and southern Gaul. Similar developments were taking place at the same time along Italy's Adriatic coast, which was increasingly tied into major routes across and around the Mediterranean. By the 860s the increasing activity around the hinterland of the Adriatic, and the connections made with the Danube river system and so with central and eastern Europe, helped stimulate the renewal of regular overland contacts between western Europe and Constantinople through the Balkan peninsula. The growth of communication and exchange here went hand in hand with the spread of Christianity to the Moravians and Bulgarians, and competition between the Franks and Byzantines for ecclesiastical and political influence.[94]

These new connections were based on the revival of long-distance trade, but it was a trade that followed a different logic from the state franchises of late antiquity. There is eye-catching evidence for the presence of oriental luxury goods – above all, silks and spices – in Carolingian Europe. All of these goods were status symbols, and the fashions underpinning their conspicuous consumption by Carolingian elites seem to have spread north from Italy. Thus in the 770s Pope Hadrian I made gifts of silk altar cloths and hangings to the churches of Rome as part of a systematic reshaping of the city, averaging over a hundred such gifts a year.[95] Silk – perhaps redolent of the holy city of Rome in the eyes of Carolingian courtiers – was soon avidly sought by the Carolingian aristocracy: thus in 793 Charlemagne 'repeatedly honoured' those Frankish aristocrats who had not been involved in Pippin the Hunchback's revolt with 'gold and silver and silk and many gifts'.[96] By the end of the ninth century, Notker of St Gallen could send up aristocratic taste for exotic vestments from beyond the sea, imagining Charlemagne celebrating a feast day surrounded by nobles who 'strutted in robes made of pheasant-skins and silk; or of the necks, backs and tails of peacocks in their first plumage. Some were decorated with purple- and lemon-coloured ribbons; some were wrapped round with otter-skins and some in ermine robes.' For Notker, such magnificence was the natural result of shopping in Italian markets – to explain the extravagance he goes

---

[94] For developments in central–eastern Europe see McCormick, *Origins of the European Economy*, pp. 548–62; and more generally F. Curta, *Southeastern Europe in the Middle Ages, 500–1250* (Cambridge, 2006).
[95] See for example *LP* I, p. 505, trans. Davis, *Lives of the Eighth-Century Popes*, p. 152.
[96] *AL, s.a.* 793.

on to mock, he adds that the court 'had just come from Pavia, whither the Venetians had carried all the wealth of the east from their territories beyond the sea'.[97] Spices, the other major oriental import, were used not only in the development of status-enhancing cuisine but also as incense to add mystery to liturgical ritual and, judging from the recipes for potions in Carolingian medical tracts, as drugs.[98] These goods were sucked into western Europe by the conspicuous consumption of Frankish elite society, not by the state-regulated commerce sometimes imagined.[99]

European exports are harder to track, in part because our written sources are less likely to discuss them, but the material available consistently points to furs and textiles, arms (especially highly prized Frankish swords) and slaves.[100] It is, inevitably, this last item that has aroused most attention, with McCormick in particular arguing that the selling on of European slaves in return for oriental luxuries was the basic motor driving the Carolingian economy in the Mediterranean and beyond.[101] There are, however, problems with such an emphasis, inevitably given the taciturn nature of our evidence. The eagerness of Islamic raiders and traders to acquire European slaves is clear from a remarkably rich seam of circumstantial evidence, anecdotes and asides in narrative sources and letters. Quite how this demand was routinely met is rather less clear. The best evidence is for slave-taking in central and eastern Europe (the origin of the term 'slave' in most modern European languages is the ethnonym 'Slav'), while the centre most consistently associated with slave exporting in our sources is Venice. Thus the disciples of the Byzantine missionary Methodius, active among the Moravian Slavs and their neighbours in the middle Danube, ended up being captured and taken to Venice, where they were redeemed just in time to prevent their sale as slaves.[102] But although some slaving took place in the Carolingian

[97] Notker, *Gesta*, 2.17, trans. Ganz, pp. 110–11; and see McCormick, *Origins of the European Economy*, pp. 719–26.

[98] McCormick, *Origins of the European Economy*, pp. 708–19.

[99] On aristocratic tastes see above, Chapter 6, pp. 284–5.

[100] McCormick, *Origins of the European Economy*, pp. 729–78.

[101] McCormick, *Origins of the European Economy*, pp. 761–8; McCormick, 'New light on the "dark ages"'.

[102] McCormick, *Origins of the European Economy*, pp. 766–7; *The* Vita *of Constantine and the* Vita *of Methodius*, ed. M. Kantor (Ann Arbor, MI, 1976), where Venice's nodal role in communications between Rome, Constantinople and central Europe is made clear.

realms, it is not at all clear that this was a sizeable trade. We certainly cannot see the economies of the Carolingian world as geared to or powered by slaving, nor is there any reason to believe that the Franks' defeated opponents found themselves sold beyond the sea, rather than taken hostage, ransomed or resettled.[103] Frankish participation in these networks was primarily indirect, as the Venetians and their suppliers around the edges of the Carolingian world shipped out the human traffic that allowed the import of oriental luxuries to Italian markets. True, by maintaining a demand for the export of European slaves these networks encouraged some merchants to work in Francia itself, hence the complaints of the Archbishop of Lyon in the 820s about the activities of Jewish merchants trading Christian slaves into Muslim hands.[104] But the major nodes of international trade in the Mediterranean lay on the fringes of Carolingian power, and operated independently of the Frankish kings.

The long-distance connections which made this series of exchanges possible were heroic in scope. The fascination they have inspired among many modern commentators was shared by some contemporaries, and gave rise to travellers' tales which parallel those of Ohthere and Wulfstan. Ibn Khurradadhbih, a high official under the Caliph al Mu'tamid, wrote his *Book of Routes and Kingdoms* in 885–6, describing the trading routes connecting the Caliphate with its neighbours. In it, he includes a famous discussion of a group of Jewish merchants he calls 'Radhanites' (*Radhaniyya*), who worked a series of long-distance routes transporting furs, swords and slaves from the shores of Francia into the Caliphate and beyond into the Indian Ocean and Asia.[105] Although texts of this type cannot be taken as journalistic travelogues, Ibn Khurradadhbih was not writing fiction, and there is indeed evidence for the presence of Jewish merchants involved in long-distance trade in Francia, where Louis the Pious had taken under his protection a group of Jewish merchants

---

[103] See e.g. A. J. Kosto, 'Hostages in the Carolingian world', *EME* 11 (2002), pp. 123–47.

[104] McCormick, *Origins of the European Economy*, p. 675; Agobard of Lyon's voluminous tracts against the Jews are edited by L. van Acker: *Agobardi Lugdunensis Opera Omnia*, CCCM 52 (Turnhout, 1981).

[105] Ibn Khurradadhbih, *Book of Routes and Kingdoms*, ed. M. J. de Goeje, *Bibliotheca geographorum arabicorum* 6 (Leiden, 1889), trans. R. S. Lopez and I. W. Raymond, *Medieval Trade in the Mediterranean World: Illustrative Documents* (London and New York, 1955), pp. 30–3; for discussion and bibliography, see McCormick, *Origins of the European Economy*, pp. 688–93.

operating out of Lyon.[106] This community probably represented the extremity of the network described by Ibn Khurradadhbih, for Lyon was ideally suited both to connect with the Frankish interior and, down the Rhône, with the Mediterranean. The Lyon merchants' activities also suggest that Ibn Khurradadhbih's description of the Radhanites working a single network and conducting direct transfers from Francia through the Caliphate as far as China should not be taken at face value; instead, we are probably dealing with a series of discrete interlocking segments, each served by a small community working from nodal points such as Lyon, Venice or Damascus.

Complex connections of this type are spectacular, but they should not distract our attention from the 'background noise' of regional exchange networks which they linked together, and without which they ultimately could not have operated. In Italy as in the North Sea zone the establishment of such local networks preceded and stimulated the crystallisation of new long-distance trade in the eighth century. In 750, for example, the Lombard King Aistulf was moved to issue legislation dealing with the military obligations of merchants (*negotiantes*) within his kingdom, who as a group were not only significant enough to elicit such legislation for the first time, but also diverse and numerous enough to be divided into three strata, and in 756 he sought to limit trade to 'legitimate' merchants licensed by the king. This attempt at regulation is a sure sign of growing exchange.[107] Documents from Lucca reveal some of the individuals to whom Aistulf's laws were addressed: here, people labelled as 'merchants' by charter scribes are seen serving as witnesses of local standing and good character in property disputes.[108] Such men were local landowners whose 'merchant' status, judging from the charters, was a subjective recognition that the balance of their activities, and their interest in buying and selling on goods, differed from that of their peers; they were doubtless engaged in the kind of regular expeditions up and down major rivers and roads, or along the coasts, practised by the 'soldiers' of Comacchio at the beginning of the century.

The priority of regional exchange in the development of trading networks is made clear by the history of the most important site in the

---

[106] *Formulae imperiales*, no. 31; McCormick, *Origins of the European Economy*, p. 772.
[107] *Leges Ahistulfi*, cc. 3, 4, 6.
[108] McCormick, *Origins of the European Economy*, pp. 630–1; see also Gasparri, 'Mercanti o possessori?', p. 169.

ninth-century Mediterranean, Venice. Human activity around the lagoons and islands of the Veneto had intensified in late antiquity, but it was during the eighth century, as Constantinople's authority over its remaining Italian possessions waned, that it emerged as a significant centre. The Veneto and its hinterland occupied an ecological and economic niche not unlike Frisia in the north, and by the middle decades of the eighth century Venice had become the Adriatic's major emporium, a southern counterpart to Dorestad. The example of Comacchio shows that Venice was not the only centre performing such a role, but it stood out thanks to its establishment of a near monopoly on the long-distance trade that connected the regional economies of the Adriatic to the Islamic southern shores of the Mediterranean. A series of rich coin hoards and stray finds from sites right across the Veneto, beginning in the second half of the eighth century, helps explain the supply of oriental luxuries that gave Venice a competitive advantage in catering for the tastes of the Carolingian elite.[109] By 862 the toll station at Mantua expected at least fifteen Venetian ships a year, making payments in pepper, cumin and linen as well as cash, and dwarfing Comacchio's trade.[110] Like Dorestad, Venice's initial success lay in bringing together a series of distinct local economies, but its subsequent rapid growth would not have been possible without the creation of a series of long-distance connections. An indication of the sophistication of the networks which sustained this kind of activity is given in the will of the *doge* ('leader') Justinian, which immediately stands out for its attention to moveable wealth, used as a means to fund trade. Justinian documents the resources currently invested in a voyage, on which he was awaiting a return, and land, unusually for this period, takes second place.[111]

Venice's political situation was also distinctive. Although, like the rest of the imperial possessions in north Italy, it fell under Carolingian rule in the second half of the eighth century, Venice had always been distant from the established centres of political power in the region, and run by Venetians rather than officials sent by any external authority. In the first decades of the ninth century, as Charlemagne was resisting the efforts of the Danish king Godafrid to establish

---

[109] See McCormick, *Origins of the European Economy*, pp. 361–9.
[110] McCormick, *Origins of the European Economy*, pp. 633–6.
[111] Justinian, *Testament a.828/9*, ed. L. Lanfranchi and B. Strina, *Ss. Ilario e Benedetto e Gregorio* (Venice, 1965), no. 2, p. 24.

overlordship in Frisia, he was also competing with Constantinople for the allegiance of Venice and its hinterland. Here, however, after inconclusive fighting involving the Byzantine fleet and various local parties allied to the Franks, Charlemagne conceded to Constantinople in return for formal recognition of his imperial title, selling out his allies within Venice in the process.[112] In fact, the authority he ceded was nominal and symbolic, for Venice remained essentially an independent actor from whom Constantinople might request naval help in Italian ventures, but whose assistance was always ultimately a matter of negotiation rather than command. With its umbilical ties to the markets of Italy, Venice remained *de facto* part of the Frankish system, its relations regulated by a series of treaties but its formal allegiance to Constantinople underlining its freedom from Carolingian political control.[113] That this relationship was agreeable to all parties underlines Venice's exceptional position, as a valve allowing the entry of oriental luxuries into the Carolingian economy. Its political independence underlay its continued success through the ninth century and beyond, allowing it to use the considerable maritime and mercantile resources already evident in the will of Justinian to secure its economic position. For all the structural similarities with Dorestad in its initial phase of growth, this combination of highly sophisticated economic infrastructure and formal political independence made Venice significantly different from anything to be found around the contemporary North Sea.

The growth of exchange on the other side of the Italian peninsula – in the area encompassing Italy's western coast, the major islands of Sicily, Sardinia and Corsica, and the northern African coast, as well as southern Gaul, western Spain and the Balearics – is harder to trace. In part, this is because exchange here did not fit the Venetian pattern of a single port monopolising long-distance routes through shipping, but grew more organically through the expansion of regional economies. Even Naples, the largest trading city on this side of the peninsula and like Venice an effectively independent duchy under nominal Byzantine sovereignty, could not establish an economic dominance to compare to Venice's in the Adriatic.[114] The

---

[112] The major source for these events is the *ARF*, *s.a.* 806–11.

[113] The earliest surviving treaty is from 22 February 840, though there may have been precedents.

[114] On Naples see P. Arthur, *Naples from Roman Town to City-state* (London, 2004).

creation of inter-regional links was closely tied to the process of political stabilisation in the Islamic world under the 'Abbasids, and the demand stimulated by wealthy political elites in Islamic Spain and Africa. Both had been profoundly affected by the conflicts over the nature of true leadership within the Islamic community which had convulsed the Umayyad Caliphate in the decades preceding the 'Abbasid *daw'la* or revolution of 750, with tensions erupting between the Islamised Berber tribes which had effected the conquest of these provinces in the decades around 700, and the Arab leaders and armies despatched to control and order them.[115] The position stabilised only in the second half of the eighth century: in Africa, the 'Abbasids recognised the dominance of a local dynasty, the Aghlabids, who were allowed to control the provincial governorship in return for an annual payment to the Caliph; in Spain, the Umayyad refugee 'Abd al-Rahman was able to establish an independent political system which he ruled as emir. Umayyad al-Andalus (as Islamic Spain was known) and Aghlabid Ifriqiya both stood on the fringes of the recast Islamic world, cut off from the major political conflicts and the flows of men and revenue that bound together the Middle Eastern heartlands of the Caliphate. The structure of Islamic politics, however, sustained systems for the redistribution of local wealth thanks to the imposition of a head-tax on non-believers, the right of the descendants of all participants in the initial Islamic conquest to an annual dole paid out of tax revenue, and the existence of salaried standing armies. All of these were powerful stimuli for the renewal of city life and the development of markets attuned to the demands of a secure political elite with significant disposable wealth.[116]

Against this backdrop, it is scarcely surprising to hear Theodulf of Orléans, *c.*780, marvelling at the wares of Narbonne: here the locals anxious to win Theodulf's favour offered eastern gems, Arab

---

[115] See P. Crone, *Slaves on Horses: The Evolution of the Islamic Polity* (Cambridge, 1980); H. Kennedy, *The Prophet and the Age of the Caliphates* (Harlow, 1986, 2nd edn 2004).

[116] H. Kennedy, 'Military pay and the economy of the early Islamic state', *Historical Research* 188 (2002), pp. 155–69; for early medieval Islamic cities the key discussion is H. Kennedy, 'From *polis* to *madina*: urban change in late antique and early Islamic Syria', *P&P* 106 (1985), pp. 3–27; for north Africa see M. Carver, 'Transitions to Islam', in N. Christie and S. Loseby (eds.), *Towns in Transition. Urban Evolution in Late Antiquity and the Early Middle Ages* (Aldershot, 1996), pp. 184–212.

gold coins, Andalusian silk and Cordoban leatherware.[117] Nor is it unexpected to find Islamic shipping making the short hop from the north African coast to Sicily, and then connecting via Naples, the major port of the Tyrrhenian Sea, to the regional economies of southern and central Italy and eventually the Ligurian coast. It was by this route, north from Africa up the Italian coast, that emissaries of the Caliph Harun al-Rashid reached Pisa and sought out Charlemagne in 801, offering him diplomatic gifts which included an elephant; Charlemagne then organised a convoy from Liguria to collect the gifts. These interactions may imply that sailings from northern Italy south to Africa were less regular than Islamic shipping making the reverse journey: Charlemagne's convoy had to be specially organised and it was also the occasion for the procuring of relics from St Cyprian's shrine at Carthage, an event which implies that travel here was anything but routine.[118] There is little reason to see regular Islamic shipping beyond Naples, perhaps even Sicily: most likely we are dealing with a series of interconnecting regional segments, not a single long-distance route.

The gradual integration of these regional economies, and the determination of Islamic rulers to establish control over them, emerged from a series of conflicts in the first decades of the ninth century. In 798–9 the Franks despatched a naval force to 'aid' the inhabitants of the Balearic Islands, notionally part of Islamic al-Andalus but now under attack from the rebellious governors of a number of coastal cities; the Frankish sources celebrate this successful intervention as a response to 'raiding' by 'Moorish pirates', resulting in the voluntary submission of the islanders.[119] The following decade sees western sources reporting near annual expeditions against Corsica, Sardinia and Sicily from al-Andalus and Africa, clearly aiming at political subjection but also generating a steady flow of tribute and plunder, not to mention saleable captives such as the five hundred Corsicans rescued when a Frankish fleet ambushed 'raiders'

[117] Theodulf, *Carmina* 28, ed. Dümmler, pp. 493–517, trans. Godman, *Poetry of the Carolingian Renaissance*, pp. 162–6.
[118] *ARF*, s.a. 801; Florus of Lyon, *Carmina*, ed. E. Dümmler, *MGH Poet. Latini aevi Karolini* II (Berlin, 1884), 13–14, pp. 544–6. On the elephant see Dutton, *Charlemagne's Mustache*, pp. 43–68.
[119] See *ARF*, s.a. 798–9; P. Guichard, 'Les Débuts de la piraterie andalouse en Méditerranée occidentale (798–813)', *Revue de l'Occident musulman* 35 (1983), pp. 55–76.

returning to Islamic Spain in 813.[120] The language of our sources, presenting Frankish initiatives in the islands as a matter of 'protection', may hide a reality of Frankish and Islamic fleets struggling to establish control over sea-lanes which were carrying a rapidly expanding regional trade: certainly, as the case of the Balearic Islands in 798–9 demonstrates, Frankish 'aid' could be a euphemism for the aggressive establishment of a military presence. The allegiance of these islands was suddenly becoming something which was more than nominal, and which mattered urgently. Whilst the fear of Islamic 'pirates' led to measures to ensure the defence of the coasts of southern Gaul and Italy – Bishop Claudius of Turin bemoaned the distractions of organising long coastal watches designed to provide early warning of raiders – this was certainly not one-way traffic.[121] In 828, for example, the counts of Tuscany were ordered to sail around Corsica and Sardinia to drive out 'pirates'; finding none, they headed south to Sicily and acquired pilots who could navigate them to Africa, where they raided several coastal settlements.[122]

The sudden appearance of 'pirates' and 'raiders' around the shores of the western Mediterranean is striking because it coincides fairly closely with the earliest Viking raiding around the North Sea. We should take care before assuming that such raids were wholly new, rather than being reported in the written sources for the first time: the growing prominence of the western Mediterranean in Frankish sources may simply reflect the novelty of Carolingian political ambitions in the area. There is, nonetheless, good reason for postulating an intensification of such expeditions in the first decades of the ninth century. This was, after all, the period in which a fleet from al-Andalus fought its way across the Mediterranean and, after briefly establishing itself in Alexandria, set about the conquest of Crete, thus creating a lucrative foothold over crucial sea-lanes in the eastern Mediterranean. This kind of predatory activity culminated with the Islamic conquest of Byzantine Sicily, which began with the capture of the island's south-western tip in 827 and continued until the fall of Syracuse, the provincial capital, in 878. This was

---

[120] *ARF, s.a.* 813, and see in general the year-by-year account in the *ARF* from 806 onwards.
[121] See M. Gorman, 'The commentary on Genesis of Claudius of Turin and Biblical studies under Louis the Pious', *Speculum* 72 (1997), pp. 279–329.
[122] *ARF, s.a.* 828; McCormick, *Origins of the European Economy*, p. 521.

no more a simplistic 'clash of civilisations' than was Viking activity in the North Sea. The initial campaign of 827, after all, had been aided and abetted by a rebellious former governor, by no means the first Byzantine official to seek support from the nearby Islamic garrisons of the north African coast, whilst the 'Islamic conquest' was carried out by a series of distinct and sometimes competing groups: Aghlabid fleets and garrisons jostling with adventurers and mercenaries from al-Andalus; local garrisons following their own leaders, sometimes in rebellion against their nominal superiors in Africa or their appointees as governors in Sicily itself; and individual groups of soldiers campaigning under their own steam, seeking out opportunities to plunder and raid, some even attempting to carve out dominions of their own on the Italian mainland in the 860s. Although the outcome was the economic integration of southern Sicily into a regional economy centred on north Africa and geared to the demands of the Islamic political elite there, this was not a war of territorial conquest but rather a predatory venture which absorbed the energies of a footloose and fluid Islamic military eager to enrich itself through plunder and tribute.[123] The implicit threats to Byzantine authority over its southern Italian possessions, allied to the increased volume of communication and connection around the Mediterranean, also meant that the ninth century saw an attempted reassertion of Byzantine political power in the region, with a degree of direct military and naval involvement not witnessed since the seventh century.[124]

The ninth-century Mediterranean therefore throws up similar problems of interpretation to the ninth-century North Sea, with the parallel growth of two apparently distinct, indeed conflicting, forms of exchange: trading and raiding. But whilst the narrative sources may dwell on armed conflict, it is clear from both archaeological and written evidence that this took place against a backdrop of rising prosperity and growing trade. The complexity of interactions so typical of the Viking age in the north is paralleled on a smaller scale by the group of Islamic warriors able to establish itself in a mountainous stronghold at Fraxinetum in Provence in the last decades of

---

[123] An up-to-date study of ninth-century Sicily is a desideratum: for an uncritical rehearsal of the sources, see A. Ahmed, *A History of Islamic Sicily* (Edinburgh, 1975).

[124] On the political context, see B. Kreutz, *Before the Normans: Southern Italy in the Ninth and Tenth Centuries* (Philadelphia, PA, 1996).

the ninth century and oscillate between raiding and plundering the vibrant trade of the Rhône valley and participating opportunistically in local political conflict.[125] Ultimately, however, the coastlines of southern Gaul and Italy stood on the edge of a zone of raiding and trading whose epicentre lay further south in Sicily. This reminds us that the differences between north and south are as important as the similarities. Whereas Viking activity in the North Sea was a response of emerging elites on the fringes of the Frankish empire to the gravitational pull exerted by the economy of northwestern Europe, the patterns of conflict in the ninth-century Mediterranean were the result of the efforts of political elites to seize control of rapidly growing regional economies at the point where the interests of three empires coincided, and to shape them to their own ends.

CONCLUSION: WAS THERE A CAROLINGIAN ECONOMY?

As we saw in the introduction to this chapter, the Carolingian economy has often been studied less for its own sake than for what it might tell us about the break between antiquity and the Middle Ages. Because of this subordination to debates about periodisation in European history, the Carolingian period tends to be presented in extreme terms, and usually as the proof that the post-Roman west was introverted and backward. Yet as we have seen, studying the evidence on its own terms reveals a much more complex picture. Arguments generalising from the evidence for traded luxuries or subsistence farming produce one-sided models, because elite exchange and marginal peasant production always coexisted (along with a spectrum of intervening possibilities) – the question is how to characterise the balance between them.[126] Most economic activity in the Carolingian era centred on agricultural production of the type described in Chapter 5. However, this was too orchestrated for us to dismiss it as purely subsistence production. For the most part, the resources to organise and benefit from concentrations of this kind of wealth lay with aristocratic landlords and large churches, and it was their activity that prompted growing regional exchange networks in the

[125] P. Sénac, *Musulmans et Sarrasins dans le sud de la Gaule du VIIIe au XIe siècle* (Paris, 1980).
[126] See Moreland, 'Concepts of the early medieval economy'.

seventh and eighth centuries. The need to provide for towns, which always remained significant forums for political action, especially but not only in Italy, provided another important stimulus.

These networks created surpluses that stimulated long-distance trade across the oceans; and the effects of that trade in turn encouraged the further development of regional exchange. Nonetheless, in the context of an overwhelmingly agrarian economy, long-distance trade played only a limited role in the overall picture of redistribution and exchange. This is why it is misleading to interpret major social and political shifts with reference to changes in patterns of trade. The argument, for example, that the North Sea economy was vital in funding the Carolingian renaissance, by creating an indirect connection with Middle Eastern gold and silver via the activities of Scandinavian traders travelling along the rivers of Russia, is hard to sustain – the segments that made up this disjointed snake of connections were relatively distinct, and the archaeology does not suggest that valuable resources flowed smoothly from one extreme to the other.[127] Other mechanisms existed for the circulation of wealth: the treasure of Europe was, largely, its own, inherited from antiquity and circulated by plunder, tribute-taking and gift exchange as well as by trade.

These considerations mean that it may even be misleading to write about 'the Carolingian economy' at all. The disjointedness of the trade route leading east from the North Sea was shared by the western Mediterranean and Adriatic networks we have considered in this chapter. These networks were not only internally discontinuous, but were effectively insulated from each other. Even at the level of individual rivers, differences can be found – this chapter has drawn much material from the very well-researched site of Dorestad on the Rhine, but were we to dwell instead on exchanges along the Meuse or Seine, significant differences would appear. Moreover, the flow of goods along these routes, and the local economic landscapes in which they were embedded, were not designed or controlled by any single central authority. The arteries of trade and exchange cut across

---

[127] See S. Bolin, 'Mohammed, Charlemagne and Ruric', *Scandinavian Economic History Review* 1 (1953), pp. 5–39; Hodges and Whitehouse, *Mohammed, Charlemagne and the Origins of Europe*, pp. 6–7. For archaeology see J. Callmer, 'Numismatics and archaeology', *Fornvännen* 75 (1980), pp. 203–12; S. Coupland, 'Carolingian coinage and Scandinavian silver', *Nordisk Numismatisk Årsskrift* (1985–86), pp. 11–32; Myhre, 'The archaeology of the early Viking age in Norway'.

political frontiers (internal and external) and, in both the North Sea and the Mediterranean, significantly predated the rise of Carolingian power. As these networks became increasingly profitable, rulers tried to profit from them by taking tolls and other dues, but even then there is nothing resembling 'economic policy' in the capitularies or other sources. Rather than thinking about a single 'Carolingian economy', it may therefore be preferable to imagine a series of distinct local and regional networks, overlapping and intersecting to various degrees, but lacking connection to any real central motor driving activity across the whole.

Yet even if we see the production and movement of goods as operating more or less independently of the political developments of the Carolingian period, we should not imagine that they were static. As we have seen, the ninth century witnessed gradual transformations in patterns of trade and exchange which, arguably, set the scene for the improved economic conditions of the central Middle Ages. The nature of those transformations by the end of our period is illustrated by the activities of the Viking leader Godafrid III in the 880s. Godafrid, on condition of accepting baptism, had been granted Frisia (and with it Dorestad) by Emperor Charles the Fat in 882, but in 885 was persuaded to pursue ambitions further inland. Contemporary texts portray him in fairly black-and-white terms as a treacherous rebel, but it is interesting that our best source describes him demanding control of wine-producing imperial estates in the middle Rhine.[128] Wine, rather than grain, was likely the most saleable agricultural product in this area, and played a major role in exchange along the rivers Seine, Meuse and Rhine.[129] Godafrid's Scandinavian predecessors, such as his namesake who had fought Charlemagne for control of Frisia in the first decade of the century, had been primarily concerned with controlling segments of the North Sea network and thus guaranteeing the opportunity to profit from long-distance exchange. Godafrid's ambitions, by contrast, suggest a desire to control not just the export but also the production of profitable goods from these Rhineland estates. This contrast illustrates again the declining significance of emporia like Dorestad and the rising economic importance of inland centres nearer the

---

[128] Regino, *Chronicle*, *s.a.* 885; see Coupland, 'From poachers to gamekeepers', pp. 108–12.
[129] Wickham, 'Overview', p. 355.

heartlands of the realm, and highlights the extent to which the North Sea network's centre of gravity had been drawn inland.

Things did not work out well for Godafrid: the emperor did not take kindly to his threats and, after tricking him into a meeting with his agents, had him and his followers murdered. Yet the fact that he tried to work his scam as an insider also indicates the extent to which that network's main players, Scandinavians and Franks, competed together for access to increasingly concentrated resources – not only had the northern trade routes become gradually more coherent, but so had the groups who sought to profit from them. Godafrid's identity was multi-faceted: detractors inevitably decried him as an invader, stressing his Scandinavian-ness, but he was also a Christian, a sworn follower of the emperor and the husband of a member of the Carolingian dynasty. Without doubt he saw himself as belonging to Frankish elite society, and his attempt to gain a foothold in one of the political and economic heartlands of the empire was probably motivated above all by a desire to cement that belonging. Membership of that society depended in large part on subscription to its social norms and the associated taste for ostentatious feasts, fancy clothes and exotic luxuries.[130] And above all, it was the demands and imperatives of the wealthy landowners who participated in such activities that drove the processes of exchange we have been describing. As the empire expanded and stabilised, drawing conquered (and even, as shown by the case of Godafrid, neighbouring) regional aristocracies into a shared political system, the growing coherence of the Frankish elite lent an increasing coherence to trade and exchange. The empire encouraged multi-regional landholding and fostered the growth of shared codes of conspicuous consumption among members of its ruling class, which in turn gave momentum to the dynamics we have sketched out in this chapter. There was a Carolingian economy, in other words, because there was a Carolingian empire.

---

[130] See above, Chapter 6, pp. 278–85.

8

SUSTAINING THE CAROLINGIAN EMPIRE: POLITICS AND GOVERNMENT, 840–888

The deposition of Louis the Pious in 833 was neither, we have seen, the definitive disaster of the emperor's own reign nor of the Carolingian empire writ large. Still, the Frankish political community was unmistakably shocked. The main protagonists harboured anxieties about what they had done: in a letter of 847, the emperor Lothar reflected almost disbelievingly on that time of conflict between him and his brothers as 'the work of the Devil through his agents'.[1] But even the traumas of the early 830s were eclipsed in the Frankish psyche by the three years of bloody civil war which followed the death of Louis the Pious in 840. Once again, his sons were at the heart of the matter. A loose alliance of Charles the Bald and Louis the German teamed up against Lothar and Pippin II of Aquitaine (the three kings' nephew who was hoping to dislodge Charles from the south-west and claim the kingdom of his father Pippin I, who had died in 838). As their armies ceaselessly roamed the empire in a game of armed chess whose top prize was control of the Carolingian heartlands in the north, a long series of armed stand-offs and skirmishes peaked at the bloody battle of Fontenoy in June 841. (See Map 14 for places mentioned in this chapter.) A man called Engelbert, who fought on Lothar's side, later wrote a poem lamenting the extreme violence and

---

[1] Leo IV, *Epistolae*, ed. A. de Hirsch-Gereuth, *MGH Epp.* v (*Epistolae Karolini aevi* III) (Berlin, 1898–9), no. 46.

Map 14. Places mentioned in Chapter 8: 'Sustaining the Carolingian empire: politics and government, 840–888'

horrifying implications of the battle: 'No slaughter was ever worse on any field of war . . . This battle is not worthy of praise, not fit to be sung.'[2]

Major pitched battles were rare in the early medieval period precisely because so much could hinge on their outcome; and recent history, even the dark days of the early 830s, provided few examples of noble Franks drawing swords in earnest against their comrades.[3] The Franks were thus stunned by the loss of aristocratic life at Fontenoy. Four decades later in a work written for the emperor Charles the Fat, Notker of St Gallen recoiled from even mentioning the name of the battle, so horrified was he that Christian blood had been spilled by Louis the German, Charles's father.[4] A few years before that, Pope John VIII had taunted the same Louis by reminding him of the 'still-damp fields of Fontenoy that he soaked with human blood in his youth'.[5] All four Carolingians survived the fighting and in this sense the battle was not decisive. However, victory for Charles and Louis gave them the edge and effectively undermined Lothar's prospects of winning the war as a whole. His forays into the western strongholds of Charles, and those of Louis in the east, became less and less convincing and he was forced to negotiate. The final seal was set on the truce in summer 843 by the famous Treaty of Verdun. This carefully planned division split the empire into three vertical strips, with Charles receiving the western portion, Lothar the middle, and Louis the eastern – Pippin II, like Pippin the Hunchback and Bernard of Italy before him, was airbrushed out of the family picture.[6]

Verdun represented an orderly conclusion to what had been a vicious and divisive conflict. This was not solely down to the shocking bloodshed of Fontenoy. The routine intimidation, bribery and betrayal that characterised the civil war are revealed by the detailed

---

[2] Engelbert, *Versus de bella quae fuit acta Fontaneto*, ed. E. Dümmler, *MGH Poet. Latini aevi Karolini* II (Berlin, 1884), pp. 138–9, trans. Dutton, *Carolingian Civilization*, pp. 332–3.

[3] For discussion of battles see Halsall, *Warfare and Society*, pp. 177–214; and the articles in B. Bachrach (ed.), *Journal of Medieval Military History* I (2003).

[4] Notker, *Gesta*, 2.11.

[5] *Johannes VIII. Papae Epistolae*, no. 7; E. J. Goldberg, *Struggle for Empire. Kingship and Conflict under Louis the German, 817–876* (Ithaca, 2006), p. 333 (whence the translation).

[6] On Pippin the Hunchback see above, Chapter 2, pp. 78–9; on Bernard of Italy, Chapter 4, pp. 202–5.

account composed by the lay noble Nithard, a disillusioned partisan of Charles the Bald whose mother was one of Charlemagne's
daughters.[7] The root cause of the war, and the reason for its atavistic
animosity, was fraternal rivalry. Even a casual glance at the Carolingian family tree reveals the extent to which fortune had favoured the
dynasty. Since 771 Charles and then Louis had been able to rule the
empire unencumbered by brothers to rival them; in 840, for the first
time in three generations, more than one royal son survived to fight
over their father's inheritance. The civil war of 840–3 resulted from
fraternal suspicions and ambitions which had simmered throughout
the 830s, and now erupted unrestrained by any consensus on how
power should be divided between members of the dynasty. The lack
of consensus was not inevitable – brothers, even royal brothers, do
sometimes get on with each other – but the preconditions for discord
had been created by the actions of the ageing Louis the Pious himself. Driven by Louis's desire to carve out a kingdom for Charles the
Bald, as well as his periodic need to punish his other sons for their
contumacy by restricting their future share in power and territory,
no fewer than five imperial division plans were promulgated between
829 and 839. This bred uncertainty in the minds of regional aristocracies shunted from pillar to post – which Carolingian should they
court as their future lord? The charge made against Louis in 833 –
that he had caused people to perjure themselves (and thus imperil
their souls) by swearing contradictory oaths – reveals the anxiety that
this dilemma created.[8] It also opened the way for conflict within the
dynasty. In the aftermath of the old emperor's death Lothar was able
to pitch a claim to the implementation of the *Ordinatio imperii* of 817,
which gave him a superior status; while partisans of Charles the Bald
such as Nithard believed that the most rightful division had been the
one made in 839, which endowed Charles with a large swathe of
territory, and that Lothar was breaking his oaths by attempting to

---

[7] On Nithard see above all Nelson, 'Public *Histories*'; and now S. Airlie, 'The world,
the text and the Carolingian: royal, aristocratic and masculine identities in Nithard's
Histories', in Nelson and Wormald (eds.), *Lay Intellectuals*, pp. 51–76. On the events
of the civil war see Nelson, *Charles the Bald*, pp. 105–31; A. Krah, *Die Entstehung
der 'potestas regia' im Westfrankenreich während der ersten Regierungsjahre Kaiser Karl II.
(840–877)* (Berlin, 2000); E. Screen, 'The importance of the emperor: Lothar I and
the Frankish civil war, 840–843', *EME* 12 (2003), pp. 25–51; Goldberg, *Struggle for
Empire*, pp. 86–116.

[8] See above, Chapter 4, pp. 218–19.

override it. The division plans of Louis's reign provided each contender with a more or less equal basis for arguing that his position
was legitimate and that the use of violence was therefore just.
The tone of most modern accounts of the decades between the
death of Louis the Pious and the disintegration of the empire in 888
is set by the fury of this internecine warfare. Historians used to write
the story of the post-840 period as an extended and dismal coda
to the disasters of Louis's reign, with familial conflict emblematic of
the centrifugal forces that are supposed to have spun the empire out
of the Carolingians' control. The root cause of the problems was
often diagnosed as territorial division itself: the change from a unified empire to a political landscape populated by multiple rulers was
regarded as symbolic of a tectonic shift in the underlying political
geology of the empire – a shift that led inexorably towards disintegration and collapse. Division and subdivision of territory, escalating
internal conflict, ever-weaker leadership in the face of Viking invasion, increasingly autonomous aristocratic power and rising disillu-
sionment with the ruling dynasty are the notes which form the bass
line in this version of history. Even the Carolingians' nicknames have
been held against them, the idea being that men known as Louis
the Stammerer and Charles the Fat must have been laughable figures
(despite the fact that most of these nicknames are not contemporary –
all we know about Charles the Fat's appearance is that he was tall
and blond).[9] Posterity has therefore seen in the years 840–88 not the
high period of the Carolingian empire but rather the birth-pangs of
nascent kingdom-nations such as France and Germany, ready to burst
out of an anachronistic imperial straitjacket on a trajectory towards
their modern destinies.

This view of the 'decline and fall of the Carolingian empire'
is underpinned by some problematic assumptions that are arguably
rooted as much in nineteenth- and twentieth-century ideas about historical processes as in the contemporary sources. Take as an example
the Treaty of Verdun, which is still regarded as the founding document of the kingdoms of France and Germany – put succinctly,
'the birth-certificate of Europe'.[10] Regardless of this metaphor's
undoubted resonance, we have to query whether it helps us understand history as it was experienced by ninth-century political figures.

---

[9] Notker, *Gesta*, 1.34; Goldberg, *Struggle for Empire*, p. 44.
[10] Riché, *The Carolingians*, p. 168.

They did not know how things would eventually turn out, so how can we properly explain their behaviour by reference to what only we know happened in their future? That the treaty would ultimately turn out to seem particularly significant should not be allowed to colour our judgement too much. As far as contemporaries were concerned, the Treaty of Verdun represented neither a disintegration of the empire nor an acknowledgement of proto-national sentiments, because such division had for centuries been the norm in Frankish politics and culture.[11] Even during the anomalous period of unity under Charlemagne and Louis the Pious the empire was more often than not, as we have seen, split into pieces controlled by rulers' sons crowned as kings with full royal authority. The 843 frontiers were planned very precisely to provide an agreeable division of royal resources between the brothers and did not correspond to linguistic or cultural boundaries between Romance- and Germanic-speaking regions. High aristocrats retained interests across the empire. The dominant idiom of political discourse remained Frankishness, rather than French- or German-ness, until the eleventh century at least.[12] Verdun was, moreover, superseded many times before the ninth century was out. By the 870s Provence and parts of Burgundy had become appendages of the kingdom of Italy; while during the 880s west Francia was divided horizontally into northern and southern kingdoms. All these divisions, including Verdun, were effectively provisional: their contemporary significance was not national but dynastic. Louis the German and Charles the Bald may have been retrospectively cast as founders of nations, but in their own minds they were backwards-looking rulers whose ambitions were resolutely imperial. The mental horizons of these kings were defined by their desire to imitate the achievements of Charlemagne, not to create nation-states – their competition to appropriate his mantle was what led them to seek the imperial title (which helps explain why that title was seemingly more important to his descendants than it had been to Charlemagne himself). The aristocratic elite shared this perspective: provincial observers in the realm of Louis the German, for instance, thought of him not as a king of *Germania*, but (rather optimistically) as an 'emperor'.[13]

---

[11] Kaschke, *Die karolingischen Reichsteilungen.*   [12] Brühl, *Deutschland–Frankreich.*

[13] *Dipl. LG* 66; W. Hartmann, *Ludwig der Deutsche* (Darmstadt, 2002), p. 121. Louis never actually acquired the imperial title. See also W. Diebold, '*Nos quoque morem*

If we need to be aware of our own tendency to project modern nations back onto the medieval world, we also have to acknowledge the ambiguity of the sources on which traditional descriptions of decline and fall are based. Ninth-century reflections on the battle of Fontenoy serve to illustrate this point. The last great historian of the Carolingian age, Regino of Prüm, looked back from the early years of the tenth century and identified Fontenoy as one of the factors in the demise of the empire. So many nobles had been killed, he said, that 'thereafter [the Franks] were incapable not only of expanding the kingdom, but also of defending its frontiers'.[14] This clear statement seems to offer a pellucid window onto contemporary realities, all the more reliable since it tallies with the regret about Fontenoy expressed by other writers like Notker. Historians have invoked such reminiscences in support of a narrative of decline in which the battle illustrates the process of the Franks turning against each other to seek spoils of war that were no longer available from conquests beyond the frontiers. Yet Regino also reveals the problem with this interpretation by contradicting himself in his praise for King Karlmann of Bavaria (876–80) who, he says: 'added to and extended the borders of his kingdom with the sword'.[15] Evidently we have to be very careful with such texts, which present us with pointed authorial constructs rather than objectively reliable information. Long before Regino's day, the trauma of Fontenoy had become part of the social memory of the nobility, crystallising into an episode in a story that late-ninth-century Franks were accustomed to tell each other about themselves.[16] The battle brought aristocrats up against a contradiction in their professed values and self-perception as a Christian elite, and the only way to incorporate it into their sense of themselves was through extravagant regret. Major events like battles, won or lost,

---

illius imitari cupientes. Charles the Bald's evocation and imitation of Charlemagne', *Archiv für Kulturgeschichte* 75 (1993), pp. 271–300; Goldberg, *Struggle for Empire*, pp. 288–92.

[14] Regino, *Chronicle*, s.a. 841.

[15] Regino, *Chronicle*, s.a. 880. On Regino's narrative strategies see Airlie, 'Sad stories of the deaths of kings'. Louis the German's eldest son is referred to as Karlmann to distinguish him from his namesake, the son of Charles the Bald, who is referred to as Carloman.

[16] On later commemoration of Fontenoy see J. L. Nelson, 'The search for peace in a time of war: the Carolingian *Brüderkrieg*, 840–843', in J. Fried (ed.), *Träger und Instrumentarien des Friedens im hohen und späten Mittelalter* (Sigmaringen, 1996), pp. 87–114 at pp. 112–14.

could play a key role in creating and sustaining a group identity.[17] Late Carolingian reminiscences about Fontenoy give us an insight into the formation of a shared elite mentality, but this does not mean we can take them at face value as sources for the dwindling of the empire's political vitality.

By highlighting these sorts of problems and looking at the sources afresh, historians have begun in recent decades to evaluate later Carolingian history more positively.[18] A first step in this is to realise that the decline-and-fall narrative lacks an appreciation of political short-termism. While the temptation is strong to write history in terms of sweeping cinematic changes and trends, we have to remember that the actions of early medieval kings (like politicians in any era) were more often than not reactive, driven by short-term concerns rather than the long-term processes extrapolated by modern writers. Replacing the sources in their precise contemporary contexts can therefore open up wholly different interpretations from those traditionally offered. The empire did indeed disintegrate in 888, but we cannot let our knowledge of that fact contaminate our understanding of everything that came before – if we chose to finish our narrative only three years earlier in 885, when the whole of Charlemagne's realm was re-unified for the first time since 840, we could write a triumphant story of how the empire was regained rather than a tragedy about how it was lost. As we shall see, the causes of conflict in late-ninth-century politics, including the end of the empire itself, were not macro-historical processes or fundamental structural decay, but rather specific combinations of circumstances and events.

The context in which these events took place was nonetheless defined by Louis the Pious's death and the Treaty of Verdun. Where family rivalries under Charlemagne and Louis had tended to flare up between kings and their sons, after 843 the potential was opened up for conflicts to cut horizontally and diagonally across the family tree as well as vertically. The prospect of uncles allying with disaffected nephews against their fathers added a combustible element to the mix. This also had the effect of encouraging volatility and uncertainty among the aristocracy, marginalised members of which could now

---

[17] A. Gillett (ed.), *On Barbarian Identity: Critical Approaches to Ethnicity in the Early Middle Ages* (Turnhout, 2002).

[18] For example: J. Fried, *König Ludwig der Jüngere in seiner Zeit* (Lorsch, 1984); Nelson, *Charles the Bald*; MacLean, *Kingship and Politics*; Goldberg, *Struggle for Empire*.

look more easily outside their own kingdoms for royal support. Extra dimensions were added by armed encounters with outsiders such as Scandinavians and Slavs. The proliferation of kings in the two generations after Louis the Pious meant that the Frankish empire became polycentric in a way that it had not been for over a century. Yet the political horizons of kings transcended their own kingdoms: it was precisely their enduring sense that the empire as a whole still mattered which brought kings into conflict with each other, not the gradual solidifying of regional or national units which wished to opt out.

These dynamics did not inevitably undermine the power of the Carolingians, but they did confront the dynasty with a new set of challenges. Successful kingship in this context relied on the clever management of aristocratic interests and family rivalries, and the ability to respond imaginatively and effectively to unexpected events. The political history of the empire between 843 and the dismemberment of Carolingian hegemony in 888 is complex, and has no single narrative thread which can be easily followed. In this era of multiple kingdoms and kings, uneasily trying to defend their interests against their relatives, we will see that it was the relationships between rulers that defined the course of political events. By following the shifts in these relationships through the second half of the ninth century we will see in the rest of this chapter that although the political environment of the empire had changed along with its geography, this does not mean that kings were weaker, nor that the decline and fall of the dynasty had become inevitable. Indeed, we shall see that the end of Carolingian hegemony, and of the Frankish empire, was the outcome of a particular set of circumstances that only played out the way they did precisely because the Carolingians had been so successful.

Throughout this analysis we must bear in mind a crucial change in the pattern of the sources.[19] The narratives that help us understand the reigns of Charlemagne and Louis the Pious were almost all written, before 830 at least, by people close to and generally sympathetic to those rulers. After that date, however, fuller narratives begin to appear which are much more likely to be openly critical of Carolingian rulers. This was partly a consequence of the splitting of the empire into kingdoms which developed their own historiographical traditions (the *Annals of Fulda* cover the politics of the east

---

[19] See also above, Chapter 1, pp. 22–3.

Frankish kingdom, the *Annals of St Bertin* the west), and partly down
to the effects of the Carolingian *correctio*, with its particular interest in written history. This multiplying of argumentative narratives
is incredibly useful for the historian, but by their very nature these
sources tell a less triumphalist story than the text on which they are
modelled, namely the *Royal Frankish Annals*. We should not read this
change of tone as a straightforward indication of political change.
These annals dwell above all on the conflict between the descendants of Louis the Pious, and consequently this period is sometimes
written off as chaotic. As we shall see, this is too simple. Although
inter-Carolingian conflict was indeed the driving force of politics, it
was governed by a series of implicit codes and norms which affected
and limited what kings could get away with, and which shaped the
events which led to the ultimate disintegration of the empire.

FRATERNAL LOVE, 843–877

Although the actual text of the Treaty of Verdun has not survived, we
can reconstruct its territorial provisions quite accurately. Despite the
fact that it was conceived as a peace-treaty to end a burst of conflict,
the division it enshrined proved to be one of the Carolingian era's
most enduring and successful settlements. Louis the German and
Charles the Bald ruled their portions until their deaths in 876 and
877 respectively; and although Lothar died in 855, his sons Lothar II
(*d.*869) and Emperor Louis II of Italy (*d.*875) ensured similar continuity in his realms.[20] The shape of the family tree thus suggests, in
retrospect, a certain stability. The longevity of this generation was
underpinned by a novel mechanism designed to ease the tensions
inherent in the new dynastic configuration. Harmony was to be
maintained not by the *Ordinatio imperii*'s vision of a superior emperor
acting as overlord, but rather through a system of regular summits
between rulers to discuss issues of mutual concern and neutralise disputes. About seventy such meetings are known to have taken place
between 843 and 887, and the proceedings of a few survive in the
form of jointly issued treaties or capitularies.[21]

---

[20] A third son, Charles of Provence, died young in 863.
[21] For these figures see Brühl, *Deutschland–Frankreich*, pp. 359–61; the classic
work on the subject is R. Schneider, *Brüdergemeine und Schwurfreundschaft:
der Auflösungsprozess des Karlingerreiches im Spiegel der Caritas-Terminologie in den
Verträgen der karlingischen Teilkönige des 9. Jahrhunderts* (Lübeck, 1964).

Some of these documents reveal the practicalities of inter-kingdom diplomacy through their attempts to settle disputes thrown up in the course of events. However, these meetings were not just forums for the micro-management of cross-border relations, but also had the cumulative effect of reinforcing a particular way of thinking about politics. Just as the power of junior Carolingian kings was regulated by a discourse about filial responsibility towards their fathers, so the sons of Louis the Pious established a rhetoric of fraternal love as the basis for the post-Verdun political order.[22] This ideology was repeated consistently in texts like the Treaty of Meersen negotiated by all three kings in 847, which self-consciously echoed landmark definitions of political order including the *Divisio regnorum* (806) and the Treaty of Coulaines (843).[23] The familial spirit supposedly captured by the meeting at Meersen is encapsulated in its opening statement: 'concerning the peace, concord and harmony of the three brother-kings: that they should be united by true and not false bonds of love'.[24] This was an understandable way of soothing the moral wounds of those who had lived through the civil wars, and it was this way of thinking that must have informed Lothar's regret about family conflict expressed in the letter of 847 with which we began this chapter. The ideology of brotherly love had thus fully matured a long time before its most famous and striking exposition in a letter of 871 from Louis II of Italy to Basil I of Byzantium. In this angry response to various belittling rebukes, Louis took a pot-shot at the youth of his counterpart's dynasty by arguing that the western empire was a unified whole rather than a collection of kingdoms (and that he himself was therefore a proper emperor) precisely because all of its rulers were of common blood.[25] Competition between Frankish kings, in this view, was aimed at transferring power within the political system rather than undermining or transforming the system *per se*. This discourse turned conflict between individual Carolingians into an opportunity for rehearsing the dynastic status of the family as a whole, and it played an important role in shaping

---

[22] On filial duty see above, Chapter 4, pp. 210–11.
[23] Nelson, *Charles the Bald*, p. 150, n. 81.   [24] *Capit.* II, no. 204, c. 1.
[25] *Epistola ad Basilium I.*, ed. W. Henze, *MGH Epp.* VII (*Epp. Karolini aevi* V) (Berlin, 1928), pp. 386–94; Fanning, 'Imperial diplomacy'. Christian unity was also used as a way of minimising the significance of regnal boundaries: see for example Hincmar, *De divortio Lotharii*, p. 236.

the political mentality of the elite in the second half of the ninth century.[26]

Nonetheless, whatever arguments were made about the meaning of conflict, conflict there most certainly was. Even the most rigorous diplomatic procedures and powerful dynastic ideologies were not enough to erase the suspicion engendered by the conflicts of 840–3. Lothar appears not to have given up on his aspiration to turn his imperial title into concrete superiority over his brothers. In an overtly political move in 844 he got Pope Sergius II to appoint his ally (and uncle) Bishop Drogo of Metz as papal vicar north of the Alps with rights to intervene in the Church across all three kingdoms. Although in practice Drogo was never really able to put these powers into effect, Lothar's actions caused Louis and Charles to maintain their alliance, suspicious of their elder brother's intentions. The air of mutual hostility heightened in 846 when Lothar's daughter married one of Charles's vassals without her father's consent, leading to the accusation that she had been kidnapped.[27] Louis and Charles immediately denied all knowledge – which in itself reveals the high political impact of the incident – and a meeting was convened at Meersen in 847 to sort out the problems between the brothers. The text of this treaty reflects contemporary circumstances by condemning 'abductions', and echoes aristocratic anxieties of the 830s and early 840s by stressing the need for nobles to remain faithful to one lord.[28] In the following year Lothar attempted to lure Louis away from Charles with an appeal to their full brotherhood, and in doing so perhaps insinuated that Charles's paternity was suspect: the language of fraternal love could be manipulated to subvert the political *status quo* as well as to support it.[29]

Meanwhile, the emperor tried to undermine Charles further by supporting the efforts of his nephew Pippin II to assert himself in Aquitaine. Charles's enormous difficulties in the south-west of his kingdom and on the Spanish March interacted with a steady escalation in attacks on the west Frankish realm by Viking raiders, who had been drawn into Frankish politics (often as mercenaries) by

---

[26] On the aristocracy's internalisation of this discourse see S. Airlie, 'Les Élites en 888 et après, ou comment pense-t-on la crise carolingienne?', in F. Bougard, L. Feller and R. Le Jan (eds.), *Les Élites au haut Moyen Âge. Crises et renouvellements* (Turnhout, 2006), pp. 425–37.

[27] *AF, s.a.* 846.

[28] *Capit.* II, no. 204; Nelson, *Charles the Bald*, pp. 149–50.   [29] *AF, s.a.* 848.

the conflicts of Louis the Pious's reign and its aftermath, and had now begun to overwinter on the continent (see Map 15). All early medieval kings were faced with the need to pursue a constant effort to maintain influence in distant regions of their kingdoms, but this was especially true in the immediate aftermath of Verdun, when rulers had to establish themselves in realms which had not previously existed as stand-alone units, and where their influence might be patchy. The presence of armed Scandinavians made this problem even more intractable. Viking bands scored some notable successes in this period, taking advantage of the turmoil caused by the civil war to occupy parts of Brittany and Frisia, but in general were more interested in seizing moveable wealth to bolster their positions back home in Scandinavia than in bringing down Frankish rulers.[30] Indeed, Frankish rulers could benefit from their raids. In 847–8 a Viking siege of Bordeaux, one of Pippin II's strongholds, provided Charles the Bald with an opportunity to demonstrate his kingly credentials to the Aquitanians. By appearing on the scene and attacking the besiegers he appears to have won over the majority of the south-western nobility, who formally submitted to his authority shortly afterwards. The real loser here was Pippin, whose previously effective local regime was fatally undermined – no more charters or coins bear his name after 848. Pippin's perfectly legitimate claim to royal status was finally snuffed out in 852, when he was apprehended and 'un-personed' by being confined to a monastery. The presence of pagan Scandinavians was therefore crucial in enabling Charles the Bald to wrest control of the peripheries of his realm away from his nephew and thus counteract his brother's attempts to undermine him.[31]

The politics of the middle and eastern kingdoms in the later 840s were likewise dominated by events at the fringes of their rulers' power. For all the trouble Charles had in Aquitaine, Lothar endured similar problems in Provence in 845, where he had to put down a major revolt; while Viking raids on Frisia, the trading nexus in the north of his realm, intensified at the same time.[32] Muslim raids on Italy reached a high point with an attack on Rome in 846, which forced Lothar to make a trip (his last) south of the Alps in 847 and made the Romans ever keener for imperial protection. The

---

[30] On the Vikings see also above, Chapter 7, pp. 353–8.
[31] Nelson, *Charles the Bald*, pp. 154–5.   [32] *AB*, s.a. 845; *AF*, s.a. 845.

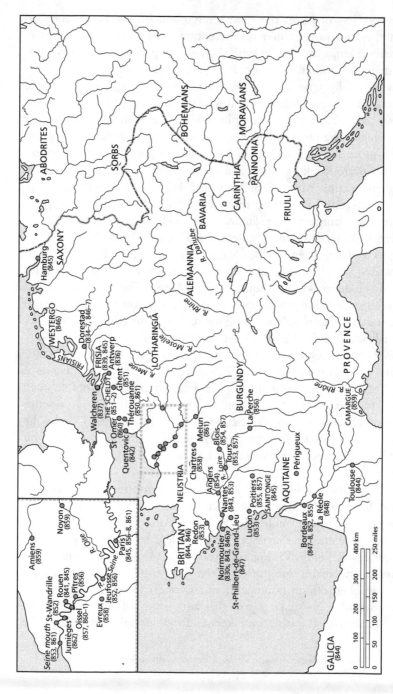

Map 15. Viking raids, c.835 to 863. The earliest attacks were mostly restricted to the Atlantic coastline; those further east were often associated with dynastic conflict within Scandinavia.

repercussions of these events left a permanent mark on the topography of Rome, where Pope Leo IV (847–55) effected the construction of the so-called Leonine Walls, partly at Frankish expense, to prevent a repeat.[33] Louis the German, meanwhile, spent much of the first decade after Verdun attempting to reconcile himself with members of the east Frankish nobility who had opposed him during the civil war and trying to enforce client status upon the Slavic peoples across his eastern frontier. These peoples, whose traditional subjection to Frankish rulers had been loosened by the conflict of 840–3, offered a stern military and political test for Louis, especially at times when he was distracted by affairs in the west or south of his kingdom.[34] For all these rulers, taming the peripheries of their realms was a necessity not simply to maintain the stability of the frontiers and to make their kingdoms cohere into rulable wholes, but also to reduce their vulnerability to the intrigues of their relatives while their backs were turned.

The general atmosphere of tension was eased somewhat in 849, when Charles and Lothar publicly recognised each other's positions and resolved to remain at peace. This time the rhetoric of fraternal solidarity was cemented through ostentatious political action, as Charles consulted Lothar over the imprisonment of the latter's old ally Pippin II in 852 and the two kings indulged in some joint campaigning against the Vikings.[35] The year 852 was also one of consolidation for Louis, who reinforced his control of the east Frankish realm by consecrating the new palace chapel at Frankfurt to the Virgin Mary, in imitation of Aachen, and then going on a regal itineration through Saxony.[36] However, it was now Louis's turn to be marginalised by his brothers. This realignment in the Carolingian diplomatic landscape led almost immediately to new patterns of conflict. Louis's strength in east Francia encouraged him to start negotiations with some of the leading men of the middle kingdom, presumably pitching a claim to succeed the ageing Lothar, now approaching the relatively advanced

---

[33] See B. Ward-Perkins, *From Classical Antiquity to the Middle Ages. Urban Public Building in Northern and Central Italy AD 300–850* (Oxford, 1984), pp. 195–6. On the Muslim raids see also above, Chapter 7, pp. 372–5.

[34] E. J. Goldberg, 'Ludwig der Deutsche und Mähren: Eine Studie zu karolingischen Grenzkriegen im Osten', in W. Hartmann (ed.), *Ludwig der Deutsche und seine Zeit* (Darmstadt, 2004), pp. 67–94; Goldberg, *Struggle for Empire*, pp. 119–46.

[35] *AB*, s.a. 852, 853; Nelson, *Charles the Bald*, p. 162.

[36] *AF*, s.a. 852; Reuter, *Germany in the Early Middle Ages*, pp. 85–91.

age of sixty.[37] Louis's predatory ambitions in the west also found a receptive audience in Aquitaine, where erstwhile partisans of Pippin II were once more disillusioned with the intrusive presence of Charles the Bald and had sent word that they would be amenable to the prospect of the eastern king taking over from the 'tyrant'.[38] In response, Charles encouraged the Bulgars to make trouble on his brother's eastern flank.[39] Louis was not deterred. After conspicuously absenting himself from a meeting with his brothers in early 854, he sent his nineteen-year-old son Louis the Younger to take over Aquitaine with a large army.[40] The invasion seems to have faltered almost immediately: Louis arrived in Aquitaine to find that only the kin of Gauzbert, a nobleman who had been decapitated for treason by Charles in the previous year, were pleased to see him. He therefore decided the whole thing was 'pointless' and went home.[41] This is, however, reported by an annalist writing with hindsight: the fact that Louis stayed in Aquitaine for about six months suggests that his invasion was a far more serious proposition than the sources let on.[42]

The death of Lothar in 855 upset the balance of power in the empire in a new way. For the first time, the eldest Carolingian and the emperor were not the same person, which undermined one informal point of stability.[43] The old emperor was succeeded by his three sons: the eldest Louis II as emperor and ruler of Italy, where he had been more or less autonomous since 844; Lothar II in Middle Francia (subsequently called Lotharingia, after him); and Charles in Provence and the Rhône valley. Charles of Provence was ill and his regime was neither well established nor long lived – he suffered badly from epilepsy and died in 863.[44] Competition between the other two sons dovetailed naturally with the ongoing stand-off between their uncles, and each sought to further his interests by allying with one or other of them. The combination of proclaimed peaceful confraternity and underlying tension which had characterised the period 843–55 was thus replaced by an even more complex inter-generational version of the same thing.

[37] *AF*, s.a. 852.
[38] *AB*, s.a. 853, p. 67; *AF*, s.a. 853; Martindale, 'The kingdom of Aquitaine'.
[39] *AB*, s.a. 853.   [40] *AF*, s.a. 854.   [41] *AF*, s.a. 854.
[42] Goldberg, *Struggle for Empire*, pp. 234–42.   [43] Nelson, *Charles the Bald*, p. 180.
[44] *AB*, s.a. 855, 856, 858, 859, 861, 863.

The first serious disturbance of this uneasy dynastic balance came at the end of 858, when Louis the German again launched an invasion of his brother's west Frankish kingdom. This time, Louis came in person and through an overwhelming display of military force almost made it stick: by early 859 Charles's support was in disarray and he only retained his throne thanks to the steadfast support of his bishops, who resisted pressure to legitimise the invader as king in the west. Charles's recovery from a position of apparent desperation shows no little political skill.[45] At the same time, it has to be noted that Louis had come very close to reuniting a huge swathe of his grandfather's empire. Nonetheless, as usual in Frankish politics, the causes of this confrontation cannot be reduced to an equation balancing the ambitions of inherently antagonistic 'strong' and 'weak' kings. The roots of Louis's invasion are to be found on the western frontier of the realm, where influential nobles led by Count Robert 'the Strong' of Angers (who was originally from the Rhineland) became resentful of the power of Charles's son Louis the Stammerer, who had been made (sub)king of Neustria under the sponsorship of the Breton *dux* Erispoë. These antagonisms combined with renewed unrest in Aquitaine, increasing Viking pressure on the Seine, and hostility to Charles's aggressive raising of money to pay off the Scandinavians. It was thus not royal weakness which caused the rebellion: if anything, the problem was that Charles, in an attempt to deal with a range of problems at once, had been too interventionist.[46] The combination of dynastic rivalry, cross-frontier politics and the jockeying for position of powerful regional aristocrats that precipitated the crisis of 858 was typical of the chemistry that catalysed much ninth-century dynastic history.

The invasions of 854 and 858 highlight two key features of later Carolingian politics. Firstly, the fact that these annexations were even attempted reminds us of just how much we are still dealing in this period with kings who retained a determinedly imperial political horizon, rather than with rulers of proto-nations either side of the Rhine. Kings like Louis and Charles still wanted to emulate Charlemagne by re-creating the empire, a mode of thought that exacerbated the endemic instability of the multicentric post-843 political landscape, where noble grievances in one area could have a major

[45] Nelson, *Charles the Bald*, pp. 181–96; Goldberg, *Struggle for Empire*, pp. 248–62.
[46] Nelson, *Charles the Bald*, pp. 181–6; Smith, *Province and Empire*, pp. 100–6.

influence on the ambitions of kings hundreds of miles away. The degree of instability was, however, tempered by the fact that the Aquitanians sought not to displace the ruling dynasty, but merely to replace one Carolingian with another. Such inter-kingdom tensions could threaten the power of individual rulers; yet paradoxically reinforced the hegemony of the dynasty as a whole by translating into action the notion that only an adult male full-born member of the Carolingian family could be a legitimate king. The extent to which the concept of Carolingian dynastic hegemony had been internalised by the Frankish elite of the mid-ninth century is further illustrated by the Lotharingian magnates' asking Louis the German – the empire's senior ruler – to approve the succession of his nephew Lothar II.[47] Secondly, these events grant us another insight into contemporary political norms. Louis's ambition to acquire the traditional family heartlands in west Francia was long standing and well known: only trouble on the eastern frontier had prevented him from taking up another invitation to invade in 856.[48] However, even driving ambition backed with the appropriate means and opportunity could not be pursued by riding roughshod over contemporary expectations about the correct behaviour of rulers. The moral gymnastics performed by Louis to justify his campaign of 858 are recorded in the so-called *Annals of Fulda*, which detail how he anxiously weighed up the need to liberate the west Franks from their 'tyrant' ruler against the wickedness of attacking his brother and the danger of appearing to his own people as though he were motivated by self-aggrandisement.[49] This public hand-wringing was evidently self-serving and designed to pre-empt potential accusations of tyranny against Louis himself, but it is still worth noting that he thought it necessary at all. Haunted as they were by the terrible memory of Fontenoy, the discourse of family love was taken seriously by Louis the German and by his subjects. Kings could not attack each other without justification. The late-ninth-century political order was threaded with political discourses that had a restraining influence on how the mighty pursued their ambitions – it was not a free-for-all.

Mistrust remained between the two brothers until peace was finally brokered in June 860 with the help of their nephew Lothar II. By now, however, Lothar himself was setting the political agenda by virtue of his divorce case, which dominated the course of dynastic

[47] *AF*, s.a. 855.   [48] *AB*, s.a. 856.   [49] *AF*, s.a. 858.

politics throughout the 860s.[50] As a young man, Lothar had had a relationship with a noblewoman called Waldrada who bore him a son named Hugh and two daughters.[51] Then, in late 855, he put Waldrada aside and married Theutberga, an aristocrat whose family connections brought him control of some of the major routes to Italy.[52] The aim was clearly to establish his influence in the south of Lotharingia at the start of his reign. Early in 860, Lothar divorced Theutberga at a synod in Aachen, using against her as justification a now-familiar litany of unlikely sexual accusations including incest, sodomy, conception through witchcraft, and abortion.[53] It is plausible that the king's primary motives were personal; that he did not like Theutberga, and genuinely loved Waldrada. At the same time, the political value of his marriage to Theutberga had decreased as Lothar's relationship with his brother and southern neighbour Louis II of Italy improved. In any case, the responses of Lothar's Carolingian relatives to the divorce quickly elevated the scandal from the royal bedchamber into a matter of empire-wide significance. Ideas about marriage were not yet cast in stone and Lothar sought to manipulate them in order to legitimise his divorce. But Louis the German and Charles the Bald were equally active in their attempts to keep Lothar married to Theutberga, motivated in part by a desire to obstruct the potential for Waldrada's son Hugh to be retrospectively identified as a legitimate heir. In these politically charged circumstances, Lothar's attempt to deploy against his wife the discourse of sexual sin, developed in the reigns of Charlemagne and Louis the Pious and now a well-established political code, backfired. His claim that he was unable to control the ardour of his own youthful body, a strategy intended to position him as a victim, was quickly taken up by his enemies and used against him.

The prominence of the political stage on which these arguments were aired helped to solidify and institutionalise even further the connection between the moral/sexual behaviour of the king's close family and the legitimacy of his power. This link was reflected in a guidebook on rulership by the Irish scholar Sedulius Scottus, prob- ably written for Charles the Bald in 869, which stressed that: 'A

---

[50] For what follows, see Nelson, *Charles the Bald*, pp. 198–201, 215–20; Airlie, 'Private bodies'; Goldberg, *Struggle for Empire*, pp. 292–5.
[51] Regino, *Chronicle, s.a.* 864.   [52] Nelson, *Charles the Bald*, p. 198.
[53] See above, Chapter 3, pp. 81–2.

pious and wise king fulfils his office of ruling in three ways. First he ought to rule himself. . . secondly his own wife, his children and his household, and thirdly the people entrusted to him.'[54] Sedulius here unmistakably nodded to the issues of royal self-control raised by Lothar's divorce. The scandal lent force to anxieties about the behaviour of women in particular, and therefore had particular implications for the role of the queen. The bandying-about of slurs about the behaviour of both Waldrada and Theutberga drew on a deep well of stereotypes about the disruptiveness of female sexuality that had been sharpened by the accusations made against Judith in the crisis of Louis the Pious's reign. Female power was traditionally idealised in terms of domesticity. Hincmar's *De ordine palatii*, for instance, defines the queen's role in terms of controlling the provisioning of the palace, and by extension access to the king.[55] Around the middle of the ninth century this began to change in subtle but important ways: the first ceremonies for the inauguration of queens were written, royal women became increasingly associated with specific forms of political authority associated with the control of nunneries, and royal couples became more careful about clearly establishing the propriety of their marriages.[56] These developments combined to give royal women a more defined political role and to harden expectations about their conduct. The flurries of heated rhetoric generated by Lothar's divorce case did not evaporate into thin air before they had left an enduring imprint on these aspects of dynastic politics.

Lothar, buoyed by the support of his brother the emperor, might have hoped to get his way at the cost of only minor territorial concessions. If so, he reckoned without the intervention of Pope Nicholas I, who sought to flex his muscles by denying the validity of the divorce and excommunicating Waldrada and the Lotharingian archbishops who had supported their king. Nicholas's stance was reactive and

---

[54] Sedulius, *Liber de rectoribus Christianis*, ed. S. Hellman, *Sedulius Scottus* (Munich, 1906), c. 5, trans. Dutton, *Carolingian Civilization*, p. 384. On date and audience see especially N. Staubach, *Rex Christianus: Hofkultur und Herrscherpropaganda im Reich Karls des Kahlen II: Die Grundlegung der 'religion royale'* (Cologne, 1993), pp. 109, 112, 176–81. On Sedulius see now P. J. E. Kershaw, 'English history and Irish readers in the Frankish world', in D. Ganz and P. Fouracre (eds.), *Frankland. The Franks and the World of Early Medieval Europe. Essays in Honour of Dame Jinty Nelson* (Manchester, 2008), pp. 126–51.

[55] Hincmar, *De ordine palatii*, c. 22.

[56] J. L. Nelson, 'Early medieval rites of queen-making and the shaping of medieval queenship', in A. J. Duggan (ed.), *Queens and Queenship in Medieval Europe* (Woodbridge, 1997), pp. 301–15; MacLean, 'Queenship, nunneries'.

opportunist rather than coherent and ideological – he was not constructing a test-case for the clashes between popes and emperors
that took place in the very different political landscape of the late
eleventh century. Institutionally and politically, the authority of the
mid-ninth-century papacy was not much greater than it had been
in the days of Stephen II and Leo III. Nonetheless, the pope's position provided an external point of reference that could be used as
a moral prop by Lothar's opponents. Bolstered by Nicholas's intervention, relations between Charles the Bald and Louis the German
began to hinge on their respective relationships with their troubled
nephew. The three kings met together on as many as sixteen occasions between 862 and 868. Although the uncles' specific intentions
and positions were constantly shifting in subtle ways according to
circumstance, in general Charles supported Theutberga and aggressively opposed Lothar's actions; while Louis tried to win concessions
from Lothar through diplomacy and conditional offers of support.[57]
The aim of both was to make inroads into the political heartlands of
Lotharingia. After about 865 Louis and Charles seem to have found
more common ground. In summer 868 they met in Metz and agreed
to divide Lotharingia and Italy between them if their nephews should
die heirless.[58] That this meeting took place in Lothar's kingdom, but
in his absence, underlines just how far his power had been undermined by the consequences of his divorce case. The death of Nicholas
I in 867 seemed to offer a ray of hope to Lothar, who travelled to
petition Hadrian II, the new pontiff, in 869. Hadrian, swayed in part
by the influence of Louis II and the empress Engelberga, gave the
king the answer he wanted: his excommunication was lifted, and a
council would convene to look again at the marriage. Yet the gods
of historical irony did not look favourably on Lothar II. No sooner
had he set off home with this victory under his belt than he caught
a fever in the sweltering Italian summer and died before he had even
made it as far as the Alps. He was buried in Piacenza, aged only
thirty-four.

Charles the Bald reacted fastest to the news. Taking advantage
of the fact that his brother was ill, he had himself crowned king
of Lotharingia on 9 September in Metz. Charles actively exploited
the dynastic resonances of the middle kingdom's topography: Metz

[57] Charles: *AB, s.a.* 861, 863, 864, 866. Louis: *AB, s.a.* 860, 862, 863, 867; *AF, s.a.*
863; *Dipl. Loth II* 34.
[58] *Capit.* II, no. 245.

housed the special dead of the Carolingian dynasty including St Arnulf and Louis the Pious. A compilation of Carolingian texts including Einhard's *Life of Charlemagne* and the *Royal Frankish Annals* produced to mark the occasion implicitly constructed the event as the triumphant culmination of dynastic history; the elite circle which produced it was evidently receptive to the ideological claims radiating from Charles's entourage.[59] Charles reinforced his position in the middle kingdom shortly afterwards when, following the death of his first wife, he married Richildis, sister of the powerful Lotharingian aristocrat Boso and niece of Theutberga.[60] However, Louis's return to health early in 870 enabled him to win over important members of the Lotharingian aristocracy and forced Charles to negotiate with him in accordance with the oaths they had made at Metz in 868. The outcome was an east–west split of Lotharingia enshrined in the Treaty of Meersen, which was as meticulously planned as the division of Verdun.[61] Unlike Verdun, though, the build-up to the Meersen agreement had been contained within the norms of dynastic politics (diplomacy, formal negotiation, veiled threats and courting of aristocratic power-brokers) rather than breaking out into open violence.

Meersen handed to Louis and Charles on a plate much of what they had been angling after for the previous decade. But before they had a chance to rest on their laurels, in the early 870s an old problem reappeared with a vengeance: the ambitions of ageing rulers' adult sons. Charles had had six sons in all. The eldest, Louis the Stammerer, had been closely controlled since rebelling against his father in 862 upon reaching the age of majority (fifteen). After this revolt, which was in part driven by the young king's desire to settle old scores in Neustria dating from the unrest of 858, Louis seems to have been kept on a pretty tight leash and caused his father no major trouble, and in 867 he installed as king in Aquitaine under close supervision.[62] Four of Louis's brothers died in childhood or young adulthood. By the early 870s, therefore, Charles's only other adult son was Carloman, whom he had tonsured into the religious life at the age of five. This was a highly unusual career for a legitimate male Carolingian – Charles's aggressive pruning of the family tree reveals his concern at the potential trouble that his brood of sons could pose him later in life. Until 869 Carloman seems to have been content with his lot, which included control of a series of

---

[59] Reimitz, 'Ein fränkisches Geschichtsbuch'.   [60] *AB*, *s.a.* 869.
[61] *AB*, *s.a.* 870.   [62] Nelson, *Charles the Bald*, pp. 204, 210–11, 231–2.

important and wealthy monasteries. However, Charles the Bald's expansion of his kingdom through the annexation of Lotharingia opened new horizons and reactivated Carloman's secular ambitions. At the same time the king's remarriage threatened to produce more sons and further marginalise Carloman's prospects. For the forgotten prince it was now or never. Carloman instigated a major rebellion in Lotharingia. Although his platform was formed by the ecclesiastical resources bequeathed by his father, the aim was to advertise the casting-aside of his religious status and to establish the validity of his claim to a throne. His rebellion lasted, on and off, until 873, sustained by some very powerful Lotharingian backers. So severe was the threat that Charles finally resorted to an act of breath-taking brutality, blinding his son to snuff out permanently his claim to a throne. Louis the Pious had been criticised heavily for blinding (and killing) his nephew Bernard of Italy in 818. To risk the opprobrium which opponents would attach to the infliction of a similar penalty on his own son shows just how high Charles felt the stakes to be.[63]

One reason for the great threat posed by Carloman's rising was that it threatened to play into the hands of Louis the German, who was a natural ally of the rebels owing to the fraternal suspicion that had been restored by the death of Lothar II. Louis, however, had his own problems. His sons had been active politically since the 840s, and during the 850s were given informal influence within defined areas of the east Frankish kingdom: Karlmann in Bavaria and the south-eastern marches; Louis the Younger in Saxony and Franconia; and Charles the Fat in Alemannia. These arrangements were shored up by arranged marriages with women of the local aristocracy, and sealed with a formal division plan promulgated in 865.[64] (See Maps 16 a, b and c for the ninth-century divisions of the empire.) Just as Charles the Bald had come up with a novel measure to minimise the inherent dangers of dynastic politics (the tonsuring of Carloman), so Louis improvised to prevent rebellions by refusing to crown his sons as kings. Louis and Charles were poachers

---

[63] On Carloman's rebellion see Nelson, 'A tale of two princes'; Nelson, *Charles the Bald*, pp. 226–31.

[64] *AF*, s.a. 865; Notker Balbulus, *Erchanberti breviarium continuatio*, ed. G. Pertz, *MGH SS* II (Hanover, 1829), pp. 329–30; M. Borgolte, 'Karl III. und Neudingen. Zum Problem der Nachfolgeregelung Ludwigs des Deutschen', *Zeitschrift für die Geschichte des Oberrheins* 125 (1977), pp. 21–55; Reuter, *Germany in the Early Middle Ages*, pp. 72–3.

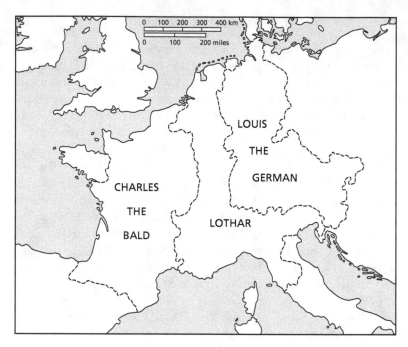

Map 16a. Ninth-century divisions: The partition of Verdun, 843

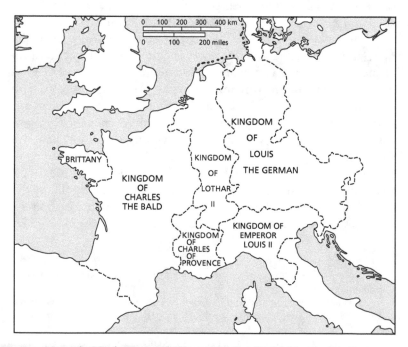

Map 16b. Ninth-century divisions: The Carolingian kingdoms in 855

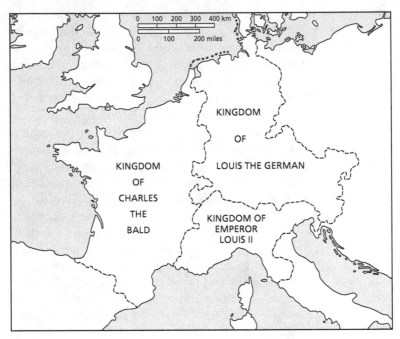

Map 16c. Ninth-century divisions: The partition of Meersen, 870. These maps of territorial divisions show that each was provisional, because designed around the configuration of the dynasty at that moment. Care was taken to accord kings equivalent shares of rights and resources. Between 870 and the end of the empire in 888 these kingdoms were reconfigured again as one king after another died.

turned gamekeepers whose memories of the 830s made them wise to the ambitions of their own sons. Unfortunately for them, such constitutional niceties did not carry decisive weight – a century of Carolingian history had taught the sons of kings that they were kings themselves, whether they were given the title formally or not. During the 860s, Louis, like his brother, endured sporadic defiance from his sons, but this coalesced into a more serious rebellion which lasted, in phases, from 871 to 874.[65] The main problem was a suspicion on the part of the two younger sons that the 865 plan was being modified to the benefit of Karlmann, the eldest, who seems to have been their mother's favourite.[66] Again, the potency of the rebels was amplified by their trans-empire horizons: they took advantage of the king's troubles with the Moravians on his eastern frontier by

[65] Goldberg, *Struggle for Empire*, pp. 304–34.   [66] *AB*, *s.a.* 870; *AF*, *s.a.* 871.

turning west to make common cause with their uncle Charles the Bald. Ultimately the pressure got too much for Charles the Fat, who submitted to his father at an assembly in early 873 with an extravagant display of penitential contrition that astonished the various annalists who recorded it.[67] Louis the Younger was only temporarily cowed by this turn of events, and went on to mount a final rebellion in 874.

All of these revolts on both sides of the Rhine were driven by exactly the same basic dynamics as the rebellions of the sons of Charlemagne and Louis the Pious decades earlier. Now, as then, princely ambition was fired by aristocratic discontent: Karlmann's rebellion of the early 860s was supported by marginalised factions on the eastern frontier, while the men who underwrote Carloman's bid for power were big fish motivated by the desire to avoid losing influence by being swept into a bigger pond through Charles the Bald's absorption of Lotharingia. As ever, a healthy dose of fraternal rivalry hindered kings' attempts to impose lasting family settlements. Just as Lothar's claims to superiority had raised the hackles on his brothers' necks in the early 830s, so Karlmann's seniority was the sticking point in Louis the German's attempts to keep a lid on relations between his sons. The language of rebellion was also unchanged. In an act that deliberately echoed the atmosphere of 829, Louis the Younger launched his revolt in 874 by insinuating that a series of famines, unusually harsh winters and a plague of locusts were signs of his father having lost God's favour.[68] Contemporaries clearly understood Louis's code: the author of the so-called *Annals of Fulda* (an anonymous churchman working in the circle of the archbishop of Mainz) explicitly reminisced about the rebellions against Louis the Pious when describing the 874 uprising. More importantly, Louis the German also understood the code and responded accordingly by complementing his mobilisation of force with an ostentatious display of penitential behaviour. By retreating from secular affairs to pray at the monastery of Fulda during Lent and Easter, and by ordering prayers for his father from all the churches of the kingdom, he not only showed that he too was troubled by the suggestion of divine wrath against his regime, but also engaged with the criticism levelled against him by his son and thus sought to undermine the basis of his

---

[67] *AB, s.a.* 873; *AF, s.a.* 873; *AX, s.a.* 873; MacLean, 'Ritual, misunderstanding and the contest for meaning'.

[68] On 829 see above, Chapter 4, pp. 213–18.

rebellion.[69] Kings like Louis the German and Louis the Younger participated in the same moral and familial discourses that had been used by Charlemagne and Louis the Pious for negotiating and disputing the distribution of power within the royal family.

It is clear that part of the reason for all these revolts was the acquisition and partitioning of Lotharingia in 870, which laid before the ambitious junior Carolingians the prospect of lands rich in estates, palaces and political resources. For their fathers, Louis the German and Charles the Bald, a crucial safety valve was presented by the situation south of the Alps where the prospect of acquiring the realm of their nephew Louis II of Italy became a real possibility in the years around 870. Louis II had been established as king of Italy by his father around 840, and was crowned emperor by Pope Sergius II in 844. Louis's spirited defence of his imperial status in the face of Byzantine ridicule has already been mentioned.[70] However, the fact that a west Frankish source refers to him as 'emperor *of* Italy' illustrates how the imperial title had become primarily an honour reserved for the ruler of that kingdom.[71] Although the prestige of the title made it desirable to many ninth-century kings, it had ceased to correspond to any concrete notion of superiority such as that spelled out in the *Ordinatio imperii* – arguably, the imperial crown had become more important to the political identity of the popes, who held it out as an incentive to win powerful Carolingian backers against their local rivals, than it was to the Carolingians themselves. As in the reign of Charlemagne himself, this was a model of authority with a largely Italian resonance.[72] In the wider world of Frankish politics, the title was simply one reference point among many that could be deployed in the non-stop competition for power.

Louis is much less well studied than his northern relatives, and the absence of major narrative sources for his reign means that the history of Italy in this period is relatively opaque. Nonetheless, he is generally regarded as one of the more stable and successful of the Carolingian rulers.[73] His marriage to Engelberga, the scion of an extremely

---

[69] *AF*, s.a. 874; Goldberg, *Struggle for Empire*, pp. 320–1.
[70] See above, p. 389.
[71] *AB*, s.a. 866; H. Zimmermann, '*Imperatores Italiae*', in H. Beumann (ed.), *Historische Forschungen für Walter Schlesinger* (Cologne and Vienna, 1974), pp. 379–99.
[72] See above, Chapter 4, pp. 167–70.
[73] See F. Bougard, 'La Cour et le gouvernement de Louis II (840–875)', in Le Jan (ed.), *La Royauté et les élites*.

influential aristocratic family, contributed to a very strong hand in north Italian politics.[74] He inspired little major unrest, responded effectively to Muslim incursions around Rome, and managed to gain influence and territories north of the Alps through judicious diplomatic interventions. He was, however, sonless, which helps account for the absence of rebellions against him. His great ambition, to incorporate the south of the peninsula with its patchwork of Muslim, Lombard and Byzantine interests, ultimately failed, and in 871 led to a period in captivity at the tender mercies of the Lombard duke of Benevento.[75] It seems to have been this crisis, which inspired rumours that he had been killed, that caused Louis to begin negotiating with his uncles over his succession. Louis the German emerged from this bout of diplomacy clutching the ace, securing in return for concessions in Lotharingia a guarantee of the Italian throne for his eldest son Karlmann. However, the length and nature of the negotiations created doubts about Louis the German's entitlement in the minds of some of Italy's most important power-brokers, including Pope John VIII, who was also disillusioned by his handling of the evangelisation of the Moravians. This meant that when Louis II died in 875, Charles the Bald also found an aristocratic constituency that favoured his succession. Reacting quickest to his nephew's death, Charles crossed the Alps with an army, scared off Karlmann and his brother, and persuaded John VIII to accept him as king.[76] This success inaugurated a five-year period of largely absentee kingship within Italy, which saw the aristocracy split between rival east and west Frankish claims. Charles the Bald succeeded in getting himself made emperor before his death in 877, after which Karlmann finally got his hands on the Italian crown for an equally brief period ended by a stroke in 879.[77]

The quarrels between the descendants of Louis the Pious that characterised the period 840–77 were bewilderingly complex and, to modern eyes, seem to have been the defining feature of the era. Yet, as we have seen, these conflicts and rebellions were expressed and executed within commonly understood and consciously fostered discourses of familial and moral obligation. The rulers of this generation

---

[74] C. E. Odegaard, 'The empress Engelberge', *Speculum* 26 (1951), pp. 77–103.
[75] *AB*, s.a. 871; Regino, *Chronicle*, s.a. 871. See Kreutz, *Before the Normans*.
[76] *AB*, s.a. 875; *AF*, s.a. 875.
[77] On these events see S. MacLean, '"After his death a great tribulation came to Italy . . . " Dynastic politics and aristocratic factions after the death of Louis II, c.870–c.890', *Millennium Jahrbuch* 4 (2007), pp. 239–60.

cannot be seen simply as land-grabbing despots dragging the empire into terminal political chaos, for they were part of a political order defined by strong codes of personal and political propriety. Because invasions and revolts were justified by loud claims and counter-claims about the protagonists' adherence to these codes, every act of aggression translated the rhetoric of Carolingian family hegemony into public political action in which leading aristocrats also participated. Even as the power of an individual Carolingian was expanded at the expense of another, the exclusive king-worthiness of the dynasty as a whole was reaffirmed. It is significant that of the many rebellions against rulers in this period, not a single one since the 780s had been led by a non-Carolingian – the aim of all these risings was to replace one Carolingian with another.[78] The never-ending sequence of family quarrels in the post-Louis the Pious generation did not, in other words, represent a disintegration of the political order because these quarrels were themselves an integral part *of* that order. To gain a more rounded sense of its shape, we must now consider the nature of later-ninth-century royal government.

GOVERNMENT AND RESOURCES

Despite the fact that the Frankish kingdoms in the second half of the ninth century were fractions of the massive empire governed by Charlemagne and Louis the Pious, the techniques and structures of government remained largely the same. The capitulary tradition was maintained in both Louis II's Italy and Charles the Bald's west Francia at levels comparable to the output of Louis the Pious.[79] *Missi* were organised in west Francia in a similar way to earlier in the century: in the Capitulary of Servais (853), for example, Charles the Bald defined twelve *missatica* to be visited by pairs of *missi* armed with instructions to do justice to the oppressed and to hunt down wrongdoers. Charles's demand that his *missi* should possess copies of 'the capitularies of our grandfather and father' (probably a reference to Ansegisus's collection) not only highlights continuity in the governmental practice and institutional memory of the political centre, but also shows the central role that written instructions were meant to play in the centre's communication with its regional agents.[80] The

---

[78] Airlie, '*Semper fideles?*'.   [79] Nelson, 'Legislation and consensus'.
[80] *Capit.* II, no. 260; Nelson, *Charles the Bald*, pp. 167–8, 326; Nelson, 'Literacy in Carolingian government'. On Ansegisus see above, Chapter 4, pp. 183–4.

undiminished ambition of Carolingian government comes through clearly in Charles the Bald's famous capitularies issued at Pîtres (864) and Quierzy (877), by which he sought to micro-manage manifold aspects of his realm including coinage, administration of estates, weights and measures, military service and the construction of unauthorised fortifications.[81] As ever with this sort of prescriptive material it is very hard to measure effectiveness – but it is at least suggestive that the evidence of coin-finds proves that a coinage reform ordered in 864 was carried out exactly as ordered.[82]

By contrast, no capitularies survive from the east Frankish kingdoms. This absence has favoured an interpretation of the eastern kings as old-fashioned warlords whose power was less sophisticated than that of the literate west Frankish and Italian rulers, being based primarily on the acquisition and redistribution of plunder from the Slavs. Although there is some truth in this, the contrast should not be drawn too starkly. We know that the east Frankish kings and many of their officials could in fact read Latin, and in charters and other documents we meet the full range of court and provincial officials found in the other Carolingian kingdoms. From stray references in the annals, we can also infer that Louis the German and his sons sometimes made pronouncements of exactly the type found in capitularies; but that these were delivered orally, not written down. This was a different political culture, but not necessarily an inferior or less effective one: again, it is revealing that silver pennies minted at Mainz under Louis were manufactured at exactly the weight prescribed by Charlemagne (1.67 grams).[83] This detail illustrates how much the strength of east Frankish kingship was built on Louis's wholesale importation of the full panoply of Carolingian methods and structures of government (including *missi*, counts and oaths of loyalty) into areas which had little previous experience of them.[84]

The royal palace sat at the fulcrum of these structures, as the focal point of Carolingian efforts to maintain the sense of a political community which would align royal and noble interests and mobilise the regional power of important aristocrats on behalf of the king. The regular itineraries of the later Carolingian kings around their palaces and estates were crucial in establishing the idea of their kingdoms as

---

[81] *Capit.* II, nos. 273, 281–2.   [82] Nelson, *Charles the Bald*, p. 33.
[83] K. F. Morrison, *Carolingian Coinage* (New York, 1967), pp. 88–9, 124–5, 172; Goldberg, *Struggle for Empire*, p. 205.
[84] Goldberg, *Struggle for Empire*, pp. 186–230.

units. In 852, for example, Louis the German covered nearly 1,000 miles in three months to advertise his authority by holding assemblies and settling disputes in every territory of his realm.[85] This sort of circuit was unusual; royal itineraries were not ceaseless, but were punctuated by stops, often quite long, at favoured palaces and estates. The east Frankish kings actually spent most of their time on the axis between Regensburg and Frankfurt, rarely travelling into the northern regions like Saxony: over 50% of Louis's surviving charters whose place of enactment is recorded were issued at one of these two palaces.[86] Similarly, Italian kings resided for the most part in the estates of the Po valley, while the west Frankish rulers' presence was felt most heavily in the Seine–Oise–Meuse area, and much less so in the northwest or southeast. Each kingdom therefore had a heartland which experienced royal government more intensively than less-visited outlying areas, whose own regulation was often delegated to a junior Carolingian or regional middleman.[87]

At the core of these heartlands stood the rulers' main residences – magnificent embodiments of royal majesty that served as the forum for the enactment of governmental business at regular assemblies, and as permanent reminders of the king's power when he was absent. The centrality of palaces like Aachen and Ingelheim in the political imagination of the Frankish elite had, as we saw in Chapter 4, underpinned the regimes of Charlemagne and Louis the Pious.[88] After 843 these archetypal royal monuments were clustered disproportionately in the middle kingdom of Lothar, so the other Carolingians responded by developing their own versions of them. Charles the Bald (see Figure 17) developed Compiègne on the Oise as his key residence, his 'Carlopolis'. In dedicating the palace chapel to the Virgin Mary in 877, the king dwelt on its similarities to the Mother of God chapel at Aachen and stated that his purpose was 'to imitate the pattern set by [Charlemagne] and by other kings and emperors, namely our predecessors'.[89] Frankfurt – regarded by at least one contemporary as 'the chief seat of the [eastern] kingdom' – performed a similar role

---

[85] *AF*, s.a. 852; Goldberg, *Struggle for Empire*, p. 164.
[86] Goldberg, *Struggle for Empire*, p. 224.
[87] Werner, 'Missus–marchio–comes'. Cf above, Chapter 4, pp. 171–8.
[88] See Chapter 4, pp. 172–8.
[89] Tessier, *et al.* (eds.), *Recueil des actes*, no. 425, trans. Nelson, *Charles the Bald*, p. 247. For the term 'Carlopolis' see D. Lohrmann, 'Trois palais royaux de la vallée de l'Oise d'après les travaux des érudits mauristes: Compiègne, Choisy-au-Bac et Quierzy', *Francia* 4 (1976), pp. 121–40.

Figure 17. Portrait of Charles the Bald from the *Codex aureus* of St Emmeram. One
of five surviving portraits of Charles, this illumination is taken from a gospel book
composed around 870. Although there are reasons to believe that the image
represents what Charles really looked like, the presentation is clearly stylised in
order to underline the divine and Biblical sources of legitimacy to which the
Carolingians laid claim.

as a neo-Aachen in the realm of Louis the German, while Sélestat in Alsace, the design of whose buildings was closely modelled on Aachen, did the same thing for Charles the Fat.[90] Architecturally and ideologically these palaces represented the ongoing renewal and reinvention of the Carolingian order, recalibrated to fit the new political landscape of the post-Verdun era.

Although the stages on which they operated were somewhat scaled down, the fundamental political rhythms represented by the palace system of government remained basically unchanged from the previous generation. Kings like Louis the German and Charles the Bald usually held at least one general assembly a year, supplemented by smaller meetings with important advisers.[91] As well as opportunities to discuss events and plans, these gatherings served the wider purpose of bringing the political community together in one place and reinforcing a sense of its continuous existence.[92] Communal activities such as hunting and feasting helped to establish this sense of belonging while ceremonial crown-wearings and other ritualised demonstrations of majesty simultaneously emphasised the special separateness of the king from his magnates.[93] The ties established between aristocrats and kings at such gatherings were tended in between times through the distribution of royal patronage. The flow of charters did not abate – where Louis the Pious issued around 500 extant charters, Charles the Bald is known to have distributed about 450; Louis the German 170; and Charles the Fat, in a much shorter reign, approximately the same number. Far from impoverishing the king, patronage was an important means of gaining local influence, helping to strengthen bonds of mutual obligation with the aristocrats on whom the government of the kingdom depended, and thus to overcome the problems of enormous geographical distance. The Carolingian family itself continued to function as a valuable resource for bridging

---

[90] Regino, *Chronicle*, s.a. 876; Zotz, 'Carolingian tradition'; MacLean, *Kingship and Politics*, pp. 187–9; T. Zotz, 'Ludwig der Deutsche und seine Pfalzen: Königliche Herrschaftspraxis in der Formierungsphase des ostfränkischen Reiches', in W. Hartmann (ed.), *Ludwig der Deutsche und seine Zeit* (Darmstadt, 2004), pp. 27–46.

[91] Nelson, *Charles the Bald*, pp. 45–50; Goldberg, *Struggle for Empire*, pp. 226–9.

[92] T. Reuter, 'Assembly politics in western Europe from the eighth century to the twelfth', in Linehan and Nelson (eds.), *The Medieval World*, pp. 432–50; repr. in Reuter, *Medieval Polities and Modern Mentalities*, pp. 193–216.

[93] Nelson, 'The Lord's anointed'; Goldberg, *Struggle for Empire*, pp. 187–200. For salutary methodological caveats see P. Buc, *The Dangers of Ritual* (Princeton, NJ, 2001).

the distance between political centre and periphery. The generation after 840 was well provided for with royal sons to install as subkings in far-off realms – the fact that these sons mounted so many rebellions in the 860s and 870s is backhanded testimony to how successfully they had been integrated into the political landscape and given a direct stake in the Carolingian polity through being able to establish relationships with powerful local aristocrats. Through the deployment of such classic methods of Carolingian government, the rulers of the post-843 realms sought to mould strong kingdoms from collections of *regna* whose elites were not necessarily used to thinking of themselves as connected. There was nothing new in this. Although it is beguilingly logical to imagine that the Frankish kingdoms had been definitively 'created' by 840, and that they subsequently unravelled, in truth state formation was a never-ending process – all early medieval polities had to be constantly renewed and reinvented in the imaginations of their inhabitants. The fact that one of the most important ninth-century kingdoms, Lotharingia, was a complete novelty with no historical antecedent highlights the Carolingians' success in persuading the ruling class to invest themselves in their definition of the political order.

The basic continuity of regional elite society is attested by shifting patterns of patronage visible in charters issued by the aristocracy for major royal churches such as Lorsch in the Rhineland and Freising in Bavaria. If the burst of giving to these institutions in the reign of Charlemagne reflects the turmoil created by the imposition of a new political regime, the gradual decrease in numbers of charters surviving thereafter suggests the absence of further social disruption on anything like the same scale.[94] At the same time, these documents do reveal a fundamental shift in the shape of Carolingian politics after 843, namely the narrowing of the distance between regional elites and kings. Records of dispute settlement (*placita*) involving Freising under Charlemagne and Louis the Pious demonstrate that the interests of these rulers were almost always represented by trusted *missi* like Archbishop Arn of Salzburg. In the second half of the ninth century, by contrast, all surviving *placita* bar three were presided over by a king in person.[95] The contraction of the social and geographical distance between rulers and their noble elites was a feature of the

---

[94] Innes, *State and Society*, pp. 42–3; Brown, *Unjust Seizure*, pp. 186–200.
[95] Brown, *Unjust Seizure*, pp. 187–8.

smaller kingdoms of the era, and helped to regularise and cement the political structures that glued them together.

The shrinking of the political stage on which individual rulers operated also presented them with some novel challenges. Resources were inevitably squeezed: in 856 Lothar II complained that the 'diminution of the kingdom' had forced his father to take lands from the Church.[96] Another structural problem resided in the fact that aristocrats often retained landed interests and family connections across more than one kingdom, a phenomenon that blurred internal frontiers and created opportunities, as we have seen, for magnates to court neighbouring kings when disaffected with their own. As kingdoms got smaller and the number of kings increased, more nobles became accustomed to the benefits of *Königsnähe* (access to the king). This meant that when a realm like Lotharingia was threatened with absorption, as it was in 869–70, its aristocratic elites were all the more prepared to resist the threat to their influence by inciting or joining a rebellion.

The evolving political geography of the empire not only brought kings and aristocrats closer together but also dragged the frontiers of the realm nearer to its political centres. The status of his relationship with the Breton leaders thus became a key consideration for Charles the Bald in his attempts to rule Neustria, as was the situation on the Spanish March for his control of Aquitaine. Breton involvement in the chain of events leading to Louis the German's invasion of west Francia in 858 shows how important management of the frontier was.[97] In the east, the Slavic Moravian polity presented an equally sustained problem. By about 870 it had emerged as a major central European empire with a developed aristocratic culture and military infrastructure. Moravian power was made concrete in a series of major fortifications including the imposing fortress at Mikulčice, whose 24 acres were defended by 10-foot thick stone-faced walls.[98] The formidable nature of the threat they posed forced the east Frankish kings into a series of close-run military campaigns and turned the evangelisation of the Slavs into a pressing issue for Louis the German, who struggled to resist Byzantine attempts to drag the Moravians under the sway of Constantinople.[99] But the influence

---

[96] *Dipl. Lothar II* 34.   [97] Smith, '*Fines imperii*'; and see above, pp. 395–6.
[98] Goldberg, *Struggle for Empire*, pp. 244–5.
[99] Goldberg, *Struggle for Empire*, pp. 300–1, 319–20.

ran both ways. Although neither the Slav polities nor Brittany were ever formally incorporated into the empire, Frankish pressure nevertheless contributed to their state formation. Cross-frontier relations could be close (as we saw with Erispoë of Brittany's association with the young Louis the Stammerer), and the Frankish kingdoms thus provided political models for neighbouring rulers. Carolingian kings also engaged in active interference, which accelerated the development of aristocratic hierarchies beyond the frontiers and could encourage political centralisation by providing support for particular leaders or factions.[100] For the Franks, particularly the east Franks, the frontiers remained sources of wealth as well as of instability: a document written between 844 and 862 at the court of Louis the German catalogues the fortresses of various Slavic peoples, and was probably intended to help with the calculation of regularised tribute payments to the east Frankish ruler.[101]

The same dynamics can also be seen at work in Denmark and other parts of Scandinavia, and had a role in the beginnings of the Viking raids, as we saw in Chapter 7. We will return to the Vikings here only to outline their impact on later-ninth-century Frankish politics. The danger to Frankish kings from Scandinavian raiders certainly became very significant in the second half of the ninth century. Viking bands began overwintering in Francia during the troubles of the early 840s and the semi-permanent bases they established, combined with their skill in a surprising variety of types of warfare, made them a serious military proposition. Unlike the Bretons or the Slavs, they were able to penetrate deep into the heart of the empire. The Scandinavians were also well informed and had an uncanny ability to turn up at times of political unrest to gain some advantage. The threat was magnified after 879, when the raiding bands returned in huge numbers and displayed a finely honed ability to coordinate their activities with each other. Sources from both sides of the Channel refer to this megaforce as the 'Great Army' and several annalists describe it as wreaking havoc in the years until it was forced to retreat by a famine in 892. Viking atrocity may have been exaggerated by contemporaries, but we should not over-compensate for this – Scandinavian raids had a major impact in late-ninth-century Europe (see Maps 17 and 18).[102]

---

[100] Smith, *Province and Empire*; Heather, 'State formation'; Innes, 'Franks and Slavs'.
[101] Goldberg, *Struggle for Empire*, pp. 135–7. For a different emphasis see Reuter, 'Plunder and tribute'.
[102] For recent discussion see Nelson, 'England and the continent'.

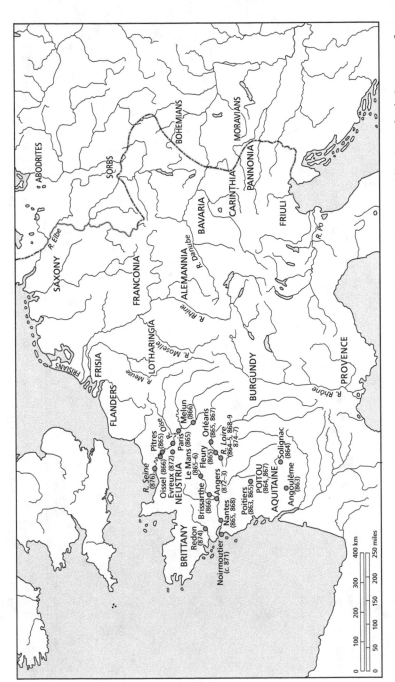

Map 17. Viking raids, 863–77. Attacks were fewer in this period, which, not coincidentally, saw intense raiding in England. One reason for the relative peace was the success of the defensive measures implemented by Charles the Bald.

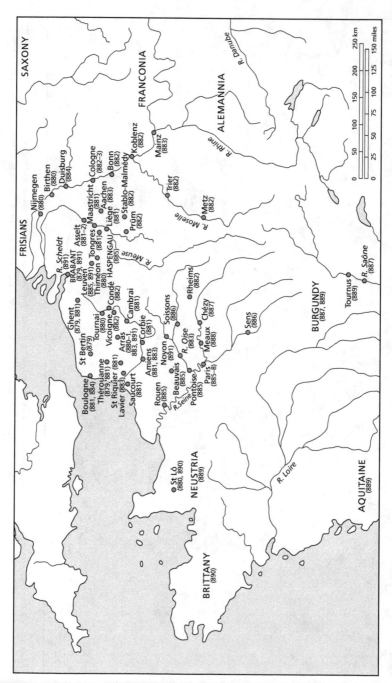

Map 18. Viking raids, 879–91. This era saw more intensive raiding than ever before between the Seine and Rhine. Although the Vikings reportedly sacked Carolingian palaces, Frankish leaders nonetheless scored some notable victories of their own.

Nonetheless, the precise nature of that impact cannot be reduced to a drive towards catastrophe. If we look past the hyperbole of the sources, we see that Frankish armies actually won more battles than they lost against the Vikings, giving the lie to the notion that Carolingian military efficiency withered on the vine after the end of expansion.[103] Strategies developed by Charles the Bald (including the paying of ransoms, the baptism and incorporation of Viking leaders into the empire, and the building of fortified bridges) succeeded in effectively removing the Vikings from Francia for over a decade from the mid-860s.[104] Although the sources, written from a theological perspective, portrayed them as alien and monolithic elements in Frankish politics, and above all as agents of God's wrath, Vikings and Slavs alike were frequently utilised as allies by aristocratic rebels, and by one Carolingian against another: at times, bands of Scandinavian mercenaries can be found on both sides of internal Carolingian disputes.[105] This was true even of the 'Great Army', which was altogether less coherent in its aims and organisation than contemporary authors were inclined to admit.[106] The Vikings were less a source of menace than refuge for some, like the Frankish noblewoman Engeltrude who, under pressure from Pope Nicholas I to return to her discarded husband, retorted that she would rather 'go to the Northmen' than comply.[107] These outsiders were thus a complicating factor in Carolingian politics, but their aim was to profit from the Frankish kingdoms, not to bring them down. In their guise as allies of various Frankish kings, Scandinavian warbands became integral to the conduct of politics in the second half of the ninth century.

The geography of the empire after 843 therefore presented the rulers of the new kingdoms with a series of challenges that constantly threatened to undermine their power. The evidence does not, however, suggest that these kings were structurally weaker than Charlemagne or Louis the Pious. Despite the squeeze on resources

---

[103] S. Coupland, 'The Carolingian army and the struggle against the Vikings', *Viator* 35 (2004), pp. 49–70.

[104] Nelson, *Charles the Bald*, pp. 206–13.

[105] Nelson, *Charles the Bald*, pp. 205–7; on the sources see above all Coupland, 'The rod of God's wrath'. In general see P. Sawyer (ed.), *The Oxford Illustrated History of the Vikings* (Oxford, 1997).

[106] R. Abels, 'Alfred the Great, the *micel hæthen here* and the Viking threat', in T. Reuter (ed.), *Alfred the Great: Papers from the Eleventh-Centenary Conferences* (Aldershot, 2003), pp. 265–79.

[107] Hincmar, *De divortio*, p. 244.

they were still able to find sources of revenue to underpin their authority. Some of these were new (the taxes raised by Charles the Bald to pay off the Vikings and those extracted by Louis the German from the eastern parts of his kingdom); while others drew on traditional structures to siphon some of the profits of late-ninth-century commerce and agrarian production into royal coffers.[108] The granting of immunity and protection to wealthy monasteries and churches, some of them controlled by members of the ruling dynasty, continued to provide points of interface and influence between the court and regional elites. Such privileges brought with them the expectation that the churches concerned would, as a charter of Louis the German put it, enter the king's 'power and lordship'.[109] Rulers were eminently capable of translating these resources into political power. They raised armies as effectively as had their predecessors, utilising the same structures of aristocratic lordship: in 858, Louis the German was able to put three armies into the field at the same time, and in 886 it was still possible for Charles the Fat to attack the Vikings in Paris with a huge army drawn from all corners of the empire, persuading them to fight far from their homelands.[110] The authority that these rulers wielded over the elites of their kingdoms is also clear from their ability to punish royal agents who had fallen from favour. Charles the Bald did not shirk from executing even powerful aristocrats like Bernard of Septimania (the villain of the first rebellion against Louis the Pious) in 844 and the Aquitanian Gauzbert in 853.[111] Similarly, in 861 Louis the German managed to reconfigure the balance of power among the east Frankish aristocracy by dispossessing a very influential group of nobles centred on Count Ernest, 'the chief among all his leading men'.[112] The Carolingians could not afford to inflict such extreme punishments on powerful men on a regular basis, but kings could evidently still make or break aristocratic careers.[113] In fact, the later Carolingians arguably had a greater

---

[108] Nelson, *Charles the Bald*, pp. 19–40; Innes, *State and Society*, pp. 156–9; Goldberg, *Struggle for Empire*, pp. 205–6. See also above, Chapter 7.

[109] *Dipl. LG* 71; Goldberg, *Struggle for Empire*, p. 215.

[110] S. MacLean, 'Charles the Fat and the Viking Great Army: the military explanation for the end of the Carolingian empire', *War Studies Journal* 3 (1998), pp. 74–95; MacLean, *Kingship and Politics*, pp. 55–64.

[111] *AB*, s.a. 844, p. 47; Regino, *Chronicle*, s.a. 860.   [112] *AF*, s.a. 861.

[113] For more examples see Nelson, *Charles the Bald*, pp. 202, 211–12; A. Krah, *Absetzungsverfahren als Spiegelbild von Königsmacht. Untersuchungen zum Kräfteverhältnis*

ability to remove counts and other agents from their *honores* than had Charlemagne and Louis the Pious. Whereas (as we saw in Chapter 4) the latter's attempts to dismiss two counts in 828 had led to his own deposition, Louis the German's ejection of Ernest testifies to the increasing efficacy of the Carolingians' claims that their agents could be treated as accountable officials. The ideologies underpinning such claims were, as we saw, still in their infancy in the capitularies of the early ninth century. By its end they had become so ingrained that observers were beginning to claim the king's right to appoint and dismiss officials as fundamental to definitions of royal power itself.[114] The political structures of the empire after 843 were, in short, somewhat altered but not weakened. To understand why it disintegrated, we must look elsewhere, and turn back to the vagaries of political events.

THE END OF THE EMPIRE, 877–888

If the fortunes of the Carolingian empire had a turning point, it came neither in 814 nor in 843, but rather in 875. Between 875 and 884 no fewer than eight reigning Carolingians died, an unprecedented rate of loss, at the end of which only one man was left standing. The impact of these deaths was felt well beyond the ruling family itself because any royal succession created tensions within the kingdom as aristocrats and neighbouring rulers jostled to reposition themselves, and eight in nine years was an unheard-of frequency for such flashpoints. Decline from this point was still not inevitable, but this stunning series of body-blows to the dynasty must have led some to wonder whether divine favour had deserted the ruling house. With this in mind the period has aptly been described as the crisis of the Carolingian empire.[115]

Amidst this complex dynastic dance there was one cuckoo in the nest. In 879, Count Boso of Vienne had himself made king by the leading churchmen and aristocrats of Provence, in the hope of ultimately taking over the whole west Frankish realm. Boso was an establishment figure: his usurpation was built on his status as one of

zwischen Königtum und Adel im Karolingerreich und seinen Nachfolgestaaten (Aalen, 1987).
[114] Regino, *Chronicle*, *s.a.* 876; Notker, *Gesta*, 2.11.
[115] Airlie, 'Les Élites en 888', pp. 426–7.

the empire's greatest nobles, a man of wide-reaching connections and influence who had held a series of high offices. In dynastic terms, though, Boso was emphatically an outsider, the first non-Carolingian to lead a rebellion since the 780s, and the first successfully to become king since the removal of the last Merovingian in 751. Wisely, Boso attempted to play his hand within the Carolingian system. He was married to the daughter of Louis II and Engelberga, and his sister was Richildis, Charles the Bald's second wife. Boso played up these Carolingian connections in an attempt to demonstrate his legitimacy. In doing so, he paid a backhanded compliment to the enduring vitality of the idea that legitimate kingship meant Carolingian kingship: Boso wanted to be a member of the club, not to shut it down.[116] Nevertheless, he was plainly an outsider according to the rules of succession that the Carolingians had spent over a century trying to establish. His usurpation was therefore sensational, and represented a genuine challenge to the dynastic hegemony.

Boso's motivation was not principle but rather opportunism. After 876, the sons of Louis the German concerned themselves mainly with internal consolidation and renegotiating their father's territorial division.[117] Only in 879, after Karlmann was paralysed by a stroke, did the brothers come into open conflict with each other, as Louis the Younger tried to push his claims to Bavaria.[118] Relations with the west Frankish cousins were more fraught. Karlmann was much occupied with pursuing his claim to Italy against Charles the Bald. Charles's imperial ambitions were not, however, directed exclusively south of the Alps. In 876, on hearing of his brother's death, he mounted a major invasion of east Francia, only to be thwarted in spectacular and decisive manner on the field of battle at Andernach by Louis the Younger. After Fontenoy as before, open battle between Carolingians was rare, so Andernach struck contemporaries as an event of singular importance.[119] Louis's victory guaranteed his possession of crucial resources in Lotharingia, including Aachen, and gave him a platform on which to build one of the more impressive

---

[116] See S. Airlie, 'The nearly men: Boso of Vienne and Arnulf of Bavaria', in A. Duggan (ed.), Nobles and Nobility in Medieval Europe (Woodbridge, 2000), pp. 25–41; S. MacLean, 'The Carolingian response to the revolt of Boso, 879–87', EME 10 (2001), pp. 21–48.

[117] Regino, Chronicle, s.a. 877.   [118] AF, s.a. 879, 880.

[119] AF, s.a. 876; AB, s.a. 876; Regino, Chronicle, s.a. 876.

regimes of the ninth century.[120] By about 877, then, the distribution of power in the reconfigured empire had been fought over and more or less settled by the next generation of kings. The reign of Charles's son Louis the Stammerer (877–9) in west Francia sowed the seeds of further conflict. Louis was not a particularly 'bad' king. In fact, he showed great military and political vigour in dealing with his aristocracy and the papacy, and in mobilising efforts against the Vikings on the Loire. The problem was his rapidly declining health, and the fact that his two sons were still minors. The king roped in Louis the Younger to underwrite their succession, but the uncertainty of the situation meant that the west Frankish political community was already forming into factions ready to push their own agendas when Louis died in April 879 at the age of only thirty-three. In the aftermath of the king's death, the realm broke down into near civil war for several months. One group of aristocrats supported the succession of the eldest son Louis III while another, fearing that this outcome would leave them politically marginalised, tried to force a division of the kingdom between Louis and his brother, Carloman II.[121] To make matters worse, the Vikings based in England heard about the unrest, and returned to the continent in greater numbers than had been seen there for over a decade (the so-called Great Army).[122] This specific set of circumstances meant that west Francia was deprived of clear leadership, and it was this power vacuum which gave Boso the opportunity to pitch his claim.

Out of conflict, however, was born cooperation. The crisis of 879–80 seems to have shocked the Carolingians into action. Louis the Younger, Charles the Fat, Louis III and Carloman II joined forces in 880 to hound Boso out of his stronghold in Provence and southern Burgundy, and his support crumbled instantly. At the same time, recognising the fact that none of them had a legitimate heir, the four swore oaths to guarantee their future successions to each others' kingdoms, and settled an array of territorial disputes which had been thrown up by the rapidly changing political landscape of the previous decade. Accordingly, in marked contrast to the later 870s,

---

[120] Fried, *König Ludwig.*
[121] K. F. Werner, 'Gauzlin von Saint-Denis und die westfränkische Reichsteilung von Amiens (März 880). Ein Beitrag zur Vorgeschichte von Odos Königtum', *DA* 35 (1979), pp. 395–462; MacLean, 'Carolingian response'.
[122] *AV, s.a.* 879.

the first half of the 880s was a time of effective Carolingian political cooperation.[123] Contemporary authors were full of optimism for the future of the empire and its ruling dynasty. In 881 Notker of St Gallen referred to Louis III and Carloman as 'the hope of Europe', and was not embarrassed to flatter Charles the Fat that he was an even greater ruler than Charlemagne himself.[124] In the period after 880 these four kings scored some significant successes: victories were won over the Vikings, notably by Louis III, and Charles the Fat acquired the imperial title from the pope in 881. But the four men still lacked even a single legitimate heir between them, and fate intervened before any of them had a chance to procreate further. In 882 Louis the Younger and Louis III both died unexpectedly and prematurely: the former through illness, the latter a victim of youthful indiscretion as he chased a girl into a house on horseback and sustained a fatal injury from the doorframe. In 884 the slapstick mortality continued as Carloman fell foul of a freak hunting accident; he and his brother, Notker's 'hope of Europe', had thus both succumbed to death by misadventure before the age of twenty. Even now, with the options dwindling, the power-brokers of the empire's regions remained locked into a Carolingian mindset: rather than go it alone, the nobles of each of the kingdoms that had lost its ruler summoned Charles the Fat, the only legitimate male Carolingian adult left, to be their king. In 885, the empire of Charlemagne and Louis the Pious was therefore reunited for the first time since 840.

Charles is usually seen as a peculiarly weak king, pushing vainly against a historical tide that was relentlessly sweeping the empire away to make room for the kingdoms of France and Germany. This, however, is a caricature that draws primarily on sources written by the emperor's enemies. In truth he was an energetic, competent and relatively successful ruler. His record against the Vikings was no worse or better than his predecessors', and his ceaseless circuits of the empire to deal with rebellions, shore up noble support, and obtain recognition of his bastard son Bernard as a legitimate heir were enough to convince regional bigwigs to continue regarding themselves as imperial agents.[125] (See Map 19.) His itinerary was partly a matter of necessity: Charles began as king of Alemannia, but gradually acquired

[123] MacLean, 'Carolingian response'.
[124] Notker, *Erchanberti breviarium continuatio*, p. 330.
[125] MacLean, *Kingship and Politics*, pp. 81–122.

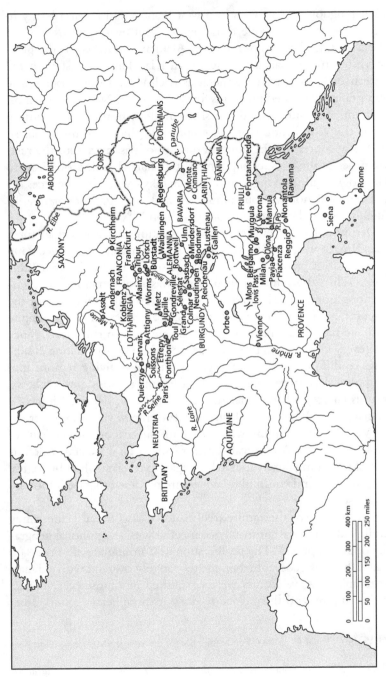

Map 19. Places on the itineraries of Charles the Fat (876–88)

other kingdoms. His forays into west Francia and Bavaria testify to a genuine attempt to rule those regions, but even towards the end of his reign his heartlands remained Alemannia and Italy – the place he visited more than any other was Pavia. The contrast with the pattern of Charlemagne's itineraries is clear, and this geographical shift gradually created problems for the emperor. Nevertheless, most contemporary authors did not share modern historians' pessimism about the reunification of the empire. Regino of Prüm's analysis explicitly contrasted the political turmoil of past ages with the relative peace of the 880s, concluding that '[Charles] understood how to take hold of all the kingdoms of the Franks (which his predecessors had acquired not without bloodshed and with great effort) easily, quickly and without conflict or opposition.'[126]

Despite Charles's efforts, the reunification lasted less than three years. In November 887, the emperor was deposed in a palace coup by Arnulf of Carinthia, the illegitimate son of his late brother Karlmann. This, the empire's final crisis, was rooted neither in disintegrating political structures nor in the personal weaknesses of the emperor, but rather in the logic of dynastic politics itself. The empire was, and had always been, too big for one man to rule alone. Since 781, every Carolingian ruler had depended on his sons acting as subkings to diffuse access to the dynasty and tie outlying regions into the political centre. Charles's lack of legitimate sons and nephews, and his failure to have Bernard accepted as heir, deprived him of a crucial political resource. Meanwhile, the emperor's age and increasing Viking activity in the west turned the succession into an issue of resolute urgency. A political system focussed on a particular definition of the ruling family inevitably began to unravel when biological happenstance and youthful misadventure rendered that definition no longer sustainable.

The wilting of the family tree mattered also because the ruling family's identity was intimately connected with the political geography of the empire.[127] The proliferation of Carolingians after the 840s meant that this geography became thoroughly overlaid with a dynastic template. Royal courts were established in almost every corner of the empire, and this helped to draw its peripheral regions closer

---

[126] Regino, *Chronicle*, s.a. 888. For a translation of this text see MacLean, *History and Politics*.

[127] On Carolingian politics as a dynastic system see above all Airlie, *Carolingian Politics*.

to the political centre. By the 870s regional magnates in all parts of the empire had (as we saw earlier) become accustomed to the nearby presence of a Carolingian king, and kings were therefore able to rule relatively intensively. When this tide of Carolingians washed back out again in the late 870s and early 880s, the picture it left in its wake was inverted. Regional elites were quite suddenly deprived of access to the dynasty as Carolingians started to die in quick succession and royal courts grew ever more distant. The most striking illustration of the political centre's drift to the geographical periphery is the reign of Charles the Fat, who despite his movement and energy mainly ruled the empire from his own power-bases in Alemannia and Italy and never visited Aachen, even having its relic collection relocated to his court.[128] The elites of the empire's traditional heartlands thus began to feel excluded from the centres of power.[129] In a world where the operation of politics depended on personal patronage, on favours and friendship, and on seeing and being seen, this was a very significant development.

This combination of problems left Charles running to stand still. Concerns about the future spiked when he fell ill at the end of 886, and potential successors began to jostle for position. Prominent among them was Arnulf, who was the most powerful and experienced of the illegitimate Carolingians, but who had been systematically ignored by his uncle as a candidate to share in the succession after a rebellion in 883–4. In late 887, Arnulf felt he had no option but to mount a coup, and at an assembly in Tribur he confronted the sick emperor with a display of force and deposed him. His motives were no different from those of numerous Carolingian rebels of decades and centuries past: like Pippin the Hunchback in 792, the sons of Louis the Pious in the 830s, or even Charles the Fat himself in 871–3, Arnulf was the son of a king, an adult with his own power base and an ageing ruler blocking his path to the throne. When men like this felt themselves being marginalised, their pride and need to prove themselves to their followers forced them into action. For Arnulf in 887, as for Bernard of Italy in 817 or Pippin II of Aquitaine in the 840s, honour dictated that the only way was forwards. For Charles the Fat, middle-aged, sick and heirless, it all ended in tears. Deserted by his men, he was sent back to Alemannia and allowed a few estates as a pension by Arnulf. Charles sent his nemesis the relic of the

---

[128] MacLean, *Kingship and Politics*, pp. 157–8.
[129] Innes, 'People, places and power'.

True Cross on which he had once sworn loyalty to him, 'so that he might be reminded of his oaths and not behave so cruelly and barbarously to him. Arnulf is said to have shed tears at the sight.'[130] The permanence of the coup was sealed six weeks later in January 888 when Charles died of natural causes before he had a chance to make a Louis-the-Pious-style comeback.

If Arnulf's motives have to be understood within the traditional framework of inter-generational Frankish dynastic politics, there was nonetheless one crucial factor distinguishing his status: he was illegitimate. The idea that nobody other than a legitimate-born Carolingian male could be a king had been repeatedly asserted throughout the late eighth and ninth centuries, and at times backed up by force and intimidation. Boso's usurpation aside, this ideology had helped sustain the dynastic *status quo* for over a century, strengthened, not weakened, by the types of political action and discourse that, as we have seen, characterised the history of the empire after 840. In 887–8, however, there were no legitimate adult Carolingians left to turn to.[131] The success of Arnulf's coup therefore meant that all bets were off. His decision to restrict his ambitions to the east Frankish kingdom allowed female-line, illegitimate and non-Carolingians to push a claim for kingship elsewhere if they had enough backing. The political landscape that emerged from the dust settling on Arnulf's coup was thus populated by a new set of rulers who had made their careers as high aristocrats in the 870s and 880s: Odo, count of Paris became king in west Francia; the *marchiones* (margraves) Berengar of Friuli and Guy of Spoleto were crowned as rival rulers of Italy; Rudolf became king in Transjurane Burgundy; and Count Ramnulf of Poitiers reportedly made a pitch to rule in Aquitaine.[132] These men were not representatives of a 'rising aristocracy' that had become increasingly powerful at the expense of their kings. They were trusted agents of kings like Charles the Bald and Charles the Fat, who had empowered them as a means of ruling their extensive

---

[130] *AF* (Mainz continuation), *s.a.* 887, p. 103. On this and other such episodes see M. Becher, 'Cum lacrimis et gemitu. Vom Weinen der Sieger und der Besiegten im frühen und hohen Mittelalter', in G. Althoff (ed.), *Formen und Funktionen öffentlicher Kommunikation im Früh- und Hochmittelalter* (Stuttgart, 2001), pp. 25–52.

[131] Louis the Stammerer's posthumously born third son Charles 'the Straightforward' (or 'Simple') had a claim, but was still very young.

[132] *AF*, *s.a.* 888.

kingdoms. Their seizure of power in 888 was not a triumphant act of usurpation based on national or class consciousness – rather, it was an attempt to meet the pressing need for leadership in *regna* where the deposition and death of Charles the Fat had created an intolerable power vacuum.[133] What else could they do?

These men were not related to each other in any meaningful way. They sought to establish their own dynasties in their own kingdoms, and in competition with each other – the sense of corporate family rule that since 843 had helped bind together the various Frankish kingdoms simply vanished. The dynastic monopoly was over. The new kings' support-bases were factional and equivalent, and wearing a crown was not enough to convince all their peers that they had acquired the aura of royal majesty – even more than the Carolingians, they were open to challenges from any political opponent who felt he was strong enough. Little wonder a contemporary annalist labelled them *reguli*, 'kinglets'.[134] Regino of Prüm offered the most persuasive summary:

After his [Charles the Fat's] death the kingdoms which had obeyed his authority, just as though a legitimate heir were lacking, dissolved into separate parts and, without waiting for their natural lord, each decided to create a king from its own guts. This was the cause of great wars; not because the Franks lacked leaders who by nobility, courage and wisdom were capable of ruling the kingdoms, but rather because the equality of descent, authority and power increased the discord among them; none so outshone the others that the rest deigned to submit to his rule.[135]

Not just in retrospect, but also to contemporaries like Regino, 888 represented an ending. The dynasty had been so successful in Carolingianising the empire that the shattering of its monopoly on kingship was translated instantly onto the political landscape of the Frankish kingdoms – the crisis of the family became the crisis of the empire.[136]

---

[133] Airlie, 'The nearly men'.   [134] *AF*, *s.a.* 888, p. 115.

[135] Regino, *Chronicle*, *s.a.* 888. On Regino as a historian of the end of the empire see Airlie, 'Sad stories of the deaths of kings'; MacLean, *History and Politics*, pp. 1–60, and S. MacLean, 'Insinuation, censorship and the struggle for late Carolingian Lotharingia in Regino of Prüm's *Chronicle*', *EHR* 124 (2009), pp. 1–28.

[136] Airlie, 'Les Élites'; Airlie, *Carolingian Politics*.

9

EPILOGUE

Equipped as we are with perfect hindsight, modern historians are instinctively inclined to look for beginnings and endings. The urge to impose ordered narratives on the disorder of the past is hard to resist, and thus the story of the Carolingian empire is often told (as indeed it is in this book) as one with an identifiable beginning, middle and end. Introducing this book, we justified our selection and definition of a specifically 'Carolingian' period. By way of conclusion, we can return to the place of the Carolingian era in the bigger picture of European history, and remind ourselves of the tension in all historical explanation between the ideas of abrupt change and continuous development.

In the longer narratives of European history from which our ideas about the origins of modern nations are constructed, the Carolingian period is seen above all as an age of beginnings: of the hierarchical social structures often packaged together as 'feudalism'; of medieval concepts of empire; of the political geography and concept of Europe itself. The details of all this are of course contested, but although few historians now would be as confident and categorical in their arguments as were those who identified Charles Martel as the inventor of vassalage and hence feudalism, a Carolingian template still seems to most to form an essential substructure of central medieval political culture.[1] The Carolingian empire may have fallen in 888, but

---

[1] See above, Chapter 2, pp. 44–51 on Charles Martel; and for a sophisticated modern interpretation of the Carolingian legacy and the creation of medieval Europe see

the grand narratives of the present day often assign it a privileged position in the foundation of the future.

There are methodological grounds for distrusting the pursuit of what Marc Bloch sceptically described as 'the idol of origins'.[2] But even if we disregard such doubts, there remain good reasons to be wary of overestimating the significance of the Carolingians in the shaping of European history. As we have seen, the sources that emphasise the novelty and scope of the dynasty's reach were, in the main, themselves written within the ambit of the royal courts. To all intents and purposes, the story of the origins of Carolingian hegemony is a story told by the Carolingians themselves. Contemporary claims about the epoch-making character of the alliance between the new Frankish rulers and the papacy, as we saw at the beginning of this book, were not neutral observations of a page turning in the course of history, but political arguments made in real time, emerging from the controversies and insecurities of the later eighth century. The same can be said of texts discussing events like the battle of Tertry in 687, retrospectively identified by Carolingian sympathisers as the point at which the dynasty's power began to eclipse that of the kings they later displaced. The baggage hung by modern historians on these dates (and on others like 800 and 843) owes much to the repetitive and insistent rhetoric of reform and renewal deployed by writers surrounding the Carolingian rulers. When Einhard depicted the last Merovingians as straggly haired rustics trundling round the countryside in ox-carts, his aim above all was to sharpen his readers' sense of difference between past and present, and hence to mask the continuities between the two eras. The novelty of Carolingian social and political structures was deliberately exaggerated from the start, and amplified further in the echo-chamber of historical tradition. We might even argue, as some have, that the eighth and ninth centuries should be seen more as an age of endings than beginnings, representing the last gasp of the post-Roman age and its increasingly irrelevant ideas about empire and political unity rather than the template for the disjointed European map of the central Middle Ages.[3]

R. Bartlett, *The Making of Europe: Conquest, Colonization and Cultural Change, 950–1350* (London, 1993), esp. pp. 269–70, 285–6.

[2] M. Bloch, *The Historian's Craft*, ed. P. Burke (Manchester, 1992), pp. 24–9.

[3] Sullivan 'The Carolingian age'.

Posterity thus envisages the Carolingian world teetering precariously on the fulcrum between the late antique past and the medieval future, and, based on what they believe about its economy, or its rural life, or its aristocracy, historians are frequently tempted to venture arguments about which way it tilted. In this book we have attempted to avoid these debates about long-term continuity and change, and to ask instead what the contemporary sources can tell us about the Carolingian period on its own terms. This has revealed a great deal of economic and social diversity within the empire, and a distinct lack of the political centralisation looked for by earlier generations of historians. Judged by modern standards, the empire's rulers might seem structurally weak: they did not have the capability to reach efficiently into the households and pockets of local elites, nor even to dictate very effectively the legal norms that held sway in comital courtrooms. As we have seen, power derived ultimately from the land and people controlled by the great and the good of the kingdom rather than from any state machinery or impositions from above. Yet somehow these kings were able to gather large armies, to mount campaigns of conquest, and to hold the resulting empire together for nearly a century and a half. To understand this we have to embrace the unusualness of contemporary discourse. Eighth- and ninth-century kings regarded themselves as propagators of *correctio* – to rule (*regere*) was to correct (*corrigere*), according to the influential early medieval etymologist Isidore of Seville, who saw an essential truth implicit in the similarity of the words.[4] Kings were persuaders, not dictators. The impact of the 'Carolingian project' resided not so much in the coercive capabilities of its architects as in its attractiveness to regional elites, who saw the opportunities for personal advancement that could come from buying in (a calculation that was probably made more instinctive by the shared cultural assumptions of post-Roman elites across the west).[5] Imperial ideology stressed unity, but also allowed regional identities and local political traditions to survive. Thus it was that the elites of annexed territories such as Italy and Bavaria could be successfully co-opted as allies; and that well before the end of the ninth century, even the Saxons,

---

[4] Isidore, *Etymologiae* IX.3.4, ed. and trans. Barney, *et al.*, p. 200.
[5] P. Fouracre, 'Cultural conformity and social conservatism in early medieval Europe', *History Workshop Journal* 33 (1992), pp. 152–61.

Charlemagne's most implacable enemies, were commemorating him as a great Christian ruler. The forces that held the Carolingian empire together emanated as much from below as from above – it worked because most of its powerful inhabitants believed that it existed and that it mattered.

When we try to make sense of the dense blizzards of texts produced in the reigns of rulers like Charlemagne, Louis the Pious and Charles the Bald, we should therefore keep in mind that the early Middle Ages was a distinct historical period and avoid anachronistic comparisons with high medieval administrative kingship or the structured power of the Roman state. Instead, our sources make most sense as reflections of a sustained attempt to create and maintain new patterns of elite mentality. This should not be taken to mean that Carolingian rule was only an abstract concept. These patterns of thought demonstrably shaped elite action, and their effects were far from intangible. As we have seen, they underpinned a patronage system that bound local elites and even rural village communities into increasingly hierarchical relationships with the political centre, reinforced the importance of office and royal service to aristocratic careers, strengthened the tradition of corporate episcopal action, and articulated a sprawling political system that encompassed an entire European empire. The world described in this book was not a new social and political order created from nothing, but it can be said at least to have constituted a comprehensive re-imagining of the existing building blocks of early medieval society. This structure lasted for over a century, and aligned the interests of the landed elite with strong kingship – it was the sudden removal of Carolingian rule in the dynastic crisis of the 880s, not the gradual decay of putative institutions, that caused it to unravel at the end of the ninth century.

For all that the dynastic upheavals of 888 created, as we saw at the end of Chapter 8, the sense of an ending in the minds of Carolingian authors, many features of ninth-century society and political culture survived. There was no major disruption in the character of society at the end of the ninth century, just as there had not been in the middle of the eighth. The insidious social changes often held to underpin the supposed fragility of later-ninth-century politics – particularly the concept of a 'rising' aristocracy holding increasingly concentrated properties and exercising ever-firmer control over the inhabitants of their localities – are, contrary to what one might suspect from a casual reading of the secondary literature, almost impossible to identify in the sources.[6] Carolingian hegemony had had an impact on the shape of the political landscape, creating nodal points around rural palaces and favoured rich monasteries, but the essential features of this landscape long outlasted the dynasty and persisted at least until the early eleventh century, when the transformation of Frankish social relations was symbolised by the increasing domination of the castle.[7] Historians have recently expended much ink on debating whether this happened quickly, around the millennium, in a 'feudal revolution', or whether it was the result of a long evolution driven by the dynamics of the post-Carolingian world. This is not the place for a detailed analysis of the debate.[8] However, it does serve to highlight the fact that it is only really with reference to the mid-eleventh century that we can begin to talk confidently about the emergence of a new social landscape that we might call 'high medieval'. Characterised by castles and lords, knights and chivalry, cities and merchants and the rise of administrative kingship, this is the classical Middle Ages familiar from Hollywood and the historical novel, and though all of its features may have had clear Carolingian antecedents, in sum they constituted a new type of society. Underlying the emergence of this new Middle Ages was the economic improvement of the tenth century and the increasingly complex society that evolved as a consequence. In the Carolingian era, social and political power was rooted ultimately in land and patronage, but by the eleventh and twelfth centuries the rising importance of alternative sources of power such as cities, mercantile activity and universities had created a world of smaller, intensively governed polities in which the old-style imperial aristocracy no longer had the field to themselves. This is the fundamental shift that marks the evolution of early medieval Europe

[6] For pertinent comments see now F. Mazel, 'Des familles de l'aristocratie locale en leurs territoires: France de l'ouest, du IXe au XIe siècle', in P. Depreux, F. Bougard and R. Le Jan (eds.), *Les Élites et leurs espaces. Mobilité, rayonnement, domination (du VIe au XIe siècle)* (Turnhout, 2007), pp. 361–98; A. Rio, 'High and low: ties of dependence in the Frankish kingdoms', *TRHS* 6th ser., 18 (2008), pp. 43–68. See above, Chapter 5.

[7] See H. Hummer, 'Reform and lordship in Alsace at the turn of the millennium', in W. C. Brown and P. Górecki (eds.), *Conflict in Medieval Europe: Changing Perspectives on Society and Culture* (Aldershot, 2003), pp. 69–84; for the Carolingians and monasteries, see Costambeys, *Power and Patronage*, pp. 52–3.

[8] For an introduction to the issues and further references see S. MacLean, 'Apocalypse and revolution: Europe around the year 1000', *EME* 15 (2007), pp. 86–106.

into the high Middle Ages – placed in this context, the end of the Carolingian empire in 888 does not seem as significant as we might assume.[9]

Similar conclusions could be drawn from a survey of the highest political level, where the horizons of Europe's rulers remained defined by the old borders of the Frankish empire for generations to come: tenth- and eleventh-century kings still thought of themselves as successors of Charlemagne rather than founders of proto-nation-states. Some of these kings were even *bona fide* Carolingians. Charles 'the Straightforward' (traditionally, 'the Simple'), Louis the Stammerer's third son who had been too young to pitch a claim in 888, ruled west of the Rhine in the period 898–923, and his descendants did likewise from 936 until 987. In the eastern kingdom, Carolingian kings reigned until 911, and in Italy too descent from Charlemagne proved an effective argument for would-be kings until at least the 950s. Nor was there any fundamental shift in the methods or styles of power at the highest level: all the post-888 rulers, even those unrelated to the Carolingians, attempted to rule using the symbolic idioms, political language and (to a lesser extent) written instruments of their predecessors.

Yet these dynastic changes mattered profoundly because, as we saw at the end of Chapter 8, they were intimately connected with the political geography of the empire. Arnulf's illegitimacy gave licence to powerful magnates across the empire to try to have themselves recognised as kings whether they could claim Carolingian ancestry or not. Possession of Carolingian blood was no longer held out as the exclusive touchstone of royal legitimacy. The decades after 888 were therefore characterised not by conflict within a single dynasty, but by conflicts between (would-be) dynasties. The uncertainty bred by this situation meant that while post-888 kings may have presented themselves as continuing the legacy of Charlemagne and tried to mould themselves to his model, their power was in fact more fragile than their predecessors': powerful rebels, rather than seeking to ally themselves with a relative of the ruler, were now more likely to make a bid to seize the throne themselves. Consequently, while kings can be found fighting other kings in most eras of the early Middle Ages,

---

[9] See P. Fouracre, 'Marmoutier and its serfs in the eleventh century', *TRHS* 15 (2005), pp. 29–49; P. Fouracre, 'Space, culture and kingdoms in early medieval Europe', in Linehan and Nelson (eds.), *The Medieval World*, pp. 366–80.

the political violence of the first generations after 888 had a different character to that of the high Carolingian period. As we saw earlier, the history of the 840s and 850s was one of kings based in traditional royal heartlands struggling to control the peripheries of their kingdoms.[10] A measure of how things had changed is that the story of the 890s is rather one of kings whose power-bases lay at the edges of the Frankish kingdoms struggling to take control of the heartlands, often by force of arms. Kings Berengar of Friuli (888–924) and Guy of Spoleto (888–94) fought for control of the royal estates of the Po valley in northern Italy; King Odo (888–98), whose main power-base was in Neustria and the Breton March, expended much energy trying to assert himself in the east and south of his kingdom; and Arnulf's son King Zwentibald found it almost impossible to take command of the traditional levers of power in Lotharingia, leading to a struggle that eventually provoked his murder. Kings like Charles the Bald and Charles the Fat had ruled by trying to balance the interests and ambitions of various factions and groups among the high nobility; kings like Odo and Berengar were themselves not much more than leaders of individual factions.[11]

In all of the post-888 kingdoms, it therefore took some time for more or less stable dynasties to establish themselves, and where they succeeded they did so on new terms. In Italy Berengar and Guy, important servants of the late Carolingians, both had themselves declared king and spent the early 890s engaged in an armed struggle for supremacy. The lack of consensus on royal legitimacy in Italy meant that kings' regimes were constantly under threat of rebellion and usurpation, and no new dynasty was able to establish itself with lasting success until the invasion of the Saxon king of east Francia, Otto I (936–73), in the 950s.[12] The first Ottonian ruler of east Francia itself, Otto's father Henry I, did not become king until 919, and even then only slowly established his authority through a willingness to recognise the independent power of the regional dukes. Henry was a magnate who acquired the throne after prospering politically during the minority of Arnulf's son Louis the Child (900–11) and the fragile regime of Conrad I (911–19), another aristocrat-turned-king: his success was in helping the other dukes to forget, or to overlook,

---

[10] See above, Chapter 8, pp. 391–5.   [11] MacLean, 'After his death'.
[12] G. Sergi, 'The kingdom of Italy', in Reuter (ed.), *The New Cambridge Medieval History* III, pp. 346–71.

the fact of their social equality with him and to start to think of his family as royal.[13] In the west, the throne fluctuated between the relatives of Odo and those of Charles the Straightforward. Yet the fact that Odo had been able to integrate the lands of the Carolingian kings in Neustria and Francia with his own family properties meant that the power of the tenth-century Carolingians was heavily compromised. They could still rule, but not in the same way as had their ancestors in the ninth century. Finally, in 987 the throne was taken over definitively by Odo's descendants, known to posterity as the Capetians, and they kept it until 1328. The removal in 888 of the dynastic hegemony that the Carolingians established therefore did have direct and important effects on the way that politics was conducted. The end of the Carolingian empire might not have entailed radical social or structural changes – but it mattered. The Europe that emerged in the tenth century was the same but different. This Europe still thought of itself as Frankish and continued to look backwards to the Carolingians for its sense of itself – but the shape of its politics had subtly and significantly changed.

Ultimately, any attempt to unpick what the Carolingian world bequeathed to the future from what it received from the past must raise as many questions as answers. Seeing in the empire a direct revival of Rome, a prelude to the classical Middle Ages of the high medieval period or a prototype for the European Union does not really do justice to what was specific about the eighth and ninth centuries. Instead we have to acknowledge that the history of the Carolingian world presents us with astonishing ambition, failed experiments and a number of open questions and seeming contradictions. Powerful but fragile, coherent but fragmented, culturally conservative but politically volatile – the paradoxes of the Carolingian empire reveal the distinctive features of the early Middle Ages as a whole.

---

[13] Reuter, *Germany in the Early Middle Ages*, pp. 137–47.

BIBLIOGRAPHY

———————— · ————————

Volumes of charters (and hence also some other series like Capitularia and Concilia) are to be found under the editor's name.

There are separate entries for those individual capitularies which are cited frequently.

I. PRINTED PRIMARY SOURCES

Abbo of St-Germain-des-Prés, *Bella Parisiacae urbis*, ed. H. Waquet, *Abbon. Le Siège de Paris par les Normands* (Paris, 1942); extract trans. Dutton (ed.), *Carolingian Civilization*, pp. 514–16; full trans. N. Dass, *Viking Attacks on Paris* (Dudley, MA, 2007).

Acts of the Council of Pavia, ed. G. Waitz, *MGH SRL* (Hanover, 1878), pp. 189–91.

Actus pontificum Cennomannis in urbe degentium, ed. G. Busson and A. Ledru, Archives historiques du Maine 2 (Le Mans, 1902).

Admonitio generalis, ed. A. Boretius, *Capit.* I, no. 22, pp. 52–62; trans. King, *Charlemagne: Translated Sources*, pp. 209–20.

Admonitio ad omnes regni ordines, ed. A. Boretius, *Capit.* I, no. 150, pp. 303–7.

Adrevald of Fleury, *Miracula Sancti Benedicti*, ed. O. Holder-Egger, *MGH SS* xv, pp. 474–97.

Æcerbot, ed. and trans. G. Storms, *Anglo-Saxon Magic* (The Hague, 1948), pp. 173–4.

Agnellus, *Liber pontificalis ecclesiae Ravennatis*, ed. D. M. Deliyannis, *CCCM*, 199 (Turnhout, 2006); trans. D. M. Deliyannis, *Agnellus of Ravenna. The Book of Pontiffs of the Church of Ravenna* (Washington, DC, 2004).

Agobard of Lyon, *De Antiphonario*, in *Agobardi Lugdunensis opera omnia*, ed. L. van Acker, *CCCM* 52 (Turnhout, 1981), pp. 335–51.

Alcuin, *De virtutibus et vitiis liber*, *PL* CI, cols. 613–38.
—, *Epistolae*, ed. E. Dümmler, *MGH Epp.* IV (*Epp.* Karolini aevi II) (Berlin, 1895), pp. 1–493; trans. S. Allott, *Alcuin of York: His Life and Letters* (York, 1974).
—, *Vita Willibrordi*, ed. W. Levison, *MGH SRM* VII (Hanover, 1920), pp. 81–141; trans. Talbot, *Anglo-Saxon Missionaries*, repr. in Noble and Head, *Soldiers of Christ*, pp. 189–211.
Altfrid, *Vita Liudgeri*, ed. W. Diekamp, *Die Vitae Sancti Liudgeri* (Münster, 1881); selections trans. Whitelock, *EHD*, no. 160, pp. 787–90.
Amalarius of Metz, *De officiis*, ed. J. Hanssens, *Amalarii opera liturgica omnia* II, Studi e Testi 138–40 (Vatican City, 1948–50), pp. 13–543.
Anglo-Saxon Chronicle, trans. Whitelock, *EHD*, no. 1.
Annales Alamannici, ed. G. H. Pertz, *MGH SS* I (Hanover, 1826), pp. 22–60.
Annales Bertiniani [Annals of St Bertin], ed. F. Grat, J. Vielliard, S. Clémencet and L. Levillain (Paris, 1964); trans. J. L. Nelson, *The Annals of Saint-Bertin* (Manchester, 1991).
Annales Cambriae, ed. and trans. D. N. Dumville, *Annales Cambriae, AD 682–954, texts A–C in parallel* (Cambridge, 2002).
Annales Fuldenses, ed. B. de Simson, *MGH SRG in usum scholarum separatim editi* IX (Hanover, 1891); trans. T. Reuter, *The Annals of Fulda* (Manchester, 1992).
Annales Guelferbytani, ed. G. H. Pertz, *MGH SS* I (Hanover, 1826), pp. 23–31, 40–6.
Annales Laubacenses, ed. G. H. Pertz, *MGH SS* I (Hanover, 1826), pp. 7–15.
Annales Laureshamenses [Annals of Lorsch], ed. G. H. Pertz, *MGH SS* I (Hanover, 1826), pp. 22–39; selections trans. King, *Charlemagne: Translated Sources*, pp. 137–45.
Annales Mettenses priores, ed. B. von Simson, *MGH SRG in usum scholarum separatim editi* X (Hanover and Leipzig, 1905); Section 1 (to 725) trans. P. Fouracre and R. Gerberding, *Late Merovingian France. History and Hagiography 640–720* (Manchester, 1996), pp. 330–70.
Annales Nazariani, ed. G. H. Pertz, *MGH SS* I (Hanover, 1826), pp. 23–31, 40–4.
Annales Petaviani, ed. G. H. Pertz, *MGH SS* I (Hanover, 1826), pp. 7–18.
Annales regni francorum [Royal Frankish Annals], ed. F. Kurze, *MGH SRG in usum scholarum separatim editi* VI (Hanover, 1895), trans. B. Scholz, *Carolingian Chronicles* (Ann Arbor, MI, 1970).
Annales Sancti Amandi, ed. G. H. Pertz, *MGH SS* I (Hanover, 1826), pp. 6–14.
Annales Tiliani, ed. G. H. Pertz, *MGH SS* I (Hanover, 1826), pp. 6–8, 219–24.
Annales Vedastini [Annals of St Vaast], ed. B. von Simson, *Annales Xantenses et Annales Vedastini, MGH SRG in usum scholarum separatim editi* XII

(Hanover and Leipzig, 1909); extract (*a*.844–62) trans. Dutton (ed.), *Carolingian Civilization*, pp. 347–50.

Annales Xantenses [Annals of Xanten], ed. B. von Simson, *Annales Xantenses et Annales Vedastini, MGH SRG in usum scholarum separatim editi* XII (Hanover and Leipzig, 1909); extract (*a*.882–6) trans. Dutton (ed.), *Carolingian Civilization*, pp. 507–12.

Ardo, *Vita Sancti Benedicti abbatis Anianensis* [Life of Benedict], ed. G. Waitz and W. Wattenbach, *MGH SS* xv (Hanover, 1888); selections trans. Dutton (ed.), *Carolingian Civilization*, pp. 176–98.

Astronomer, *Vita Hludowici imperatoris*, ed. E. Tremp, *Astronomus. Das Leben Kaiser Ludwigs, MGH SRG in usum scholarum separatim editi* LXIV (Hanover, 1995); trans. A. Cabaniss, *Son of Charlemagne: A Contemporary Life of Louis the Pious* (Syracuse, NY, 1961).

Barlow, C. W. (ed. and trans.), *Iberian Fathers* I: *Martin of Braga, Paschasius of Dumium, Leander of Seville* (Washington, DC, 1969).

Bately, J. M. (ed.), *The Old English Orosius* (Oxford, 1980), extracts trans. in N. Lund (ed.), *Two Voyagers at the Court of King Alfred* (York, 1984).

Bede, *Continuation*. See *Continuation* of Bede.

—, *Epistola ad Egbertum* [Letter to Egbert], ed. C. Plummer, *Venerabilis Baedae opera historica* (Oxford, 1896), pp. 405–23; trans. Whitelock, *EHD*, no. 170, pp. 799–810.

—, *Historia ecclesiastica gentis anglorum*, ed. C. Plummer, *Venerabilis Baedae opera historica* (Oxford, 1896); ed. and trans. B. Colgrave and R. A. B. Mynors, *Bede's Ecclesiastical History of the English People*, Oxford Medieval Texts (Oxford, 1969).

—, *Vita Cuthberti*, ed. and trans. B. Colgrave, *Two Lives of Saint Cuthbert. A Life by an Anonymous Monk of Lindisfarne and Bede's Prose Life* (Cambridge, 1940).

Beowulf, ed. E. van K. Dobbie, *Beowulf and Judith*. Anglo-Saxon Poetic Records 4 (New York and London, 1953); trans. R. M. Liuzza, *Beowulf* (Peterborough, ON, 2000).

Beyer, H., Eltester, L., and Goerz, A. (eds.), *Urkundenbuch zur Geschichte der jetzt die Preußischen regierungsbezirke Coblenz und Trier bildenden mittelrheinischen Territorien*, I: *Von den ältesten Zeiten bis zum Jahre 1169* (Koblenz, 1860).

Bitterauf, T. (ed.), *Die Traditionen des Hochstifts Freising* I (Munich, 1905).

Böhmer, J. F., and Mühlbacher, E., *Regesta imperii* I, 2nd edn (Innsbruck, 1908).

Boniface, *Epistolae*, ed. M. Tangl, *Die Briefe des Heiligen Bonifatius und Lullus, MGH Epp. selectae* I (Berlin, 1916); selected letters trans. E. Emerton, *The Letters of Saint Boniface* (New York, 1940); Talbot, *Anglo-Saxon Missionaries*; Hillgarth, *Christianity and Paganism*.

Boretius, A., and Krause, V. (eds.), *Capitularia regum francorum, MGH Leges sectio* III, 2 vols. (Hanover, 1883–97). Selections trans. in Dutton (ed.), *Carolingian Civilization*, pp. 65–92, 501–2; D. Herlihy, *A History of*

Feudalism (London, 1970); King, *Charlemagne: Translated Sources*, pp. 202–68; Loyn and Percival, *Reign of Charlemagne*, pp. 46–105.

Bouchard, C. B. (ed.), *The Cartulary of Flavigny, 717–1113* (Cambridge, MA, 1991).

Brevium exempla, ed. A. Boretius, *Capit.* I, no. 128, pp. 250–6; trans. Loyn and Percival, *Reign of Charlemagne*, pp. 98–105; Dutton (ed.), *Carolingian Civilization*, pp. 85–7.

Bruckner, A. (ed.), *Regesta Alsatiae*, I. *Quellenband* (Strasbourg, 1949).

Bruckner, A., Marichal, R., *et al.* (eds.), *Chartae latinae antiquiores. Facsimile Edition of the Latin Charters prior to the Ninth Century*, 49 vols. (Olten and Lausanne, 1954–1998).

Caesarius of Arles, *Sermones*, ed. G. Morin, 2 vols., *CCSL* 103–4 (Turnhout, 1953).

Capitulare Aquisgranense [Capitulary for Aachen], *a.802–3*, ed. A. Boretius, *Capit.* I, no. 77, pp. 170–2; trans. Loyn and Percival, *The Reign of Charlemagne*, pp. 82–4; part also trans. in Dutton (ed.), *Carolingian Civilization*, p. 83.

Capitulare missorum generale [Programmatic Capitulary], *a.802* ed. A. Boretius, *Capit.* I, nos. 33–4, pp. 91–102; trans. King, *Charlemagne: Translated Sources*, pp. 233–42.

Capitulare de villis, ed. A. Boretius, *Capit.* I, no. 32, pp. 82–91; trans. Loyn and Percival, *Reign of Charlemagne*, pp. 65–73.

Capitularia regum francorum. See Boretius, A., and Krause, V. (eds.).

Carmen de synodo Ticinensi, ed. L. Bethmann, *MGH SRL* (Hanover, 1878), pp. 189–91.

Cavallo, G., Nicolaj, G., *et al.* (eds.), *Chartae latinae antiquiores. Facsimile Edition of the Latin Charters*, 2nd ser.: *Ninth Century*, 63 vols., in progress (Olten and Lausanne, 1997–).

Chartae latinae antiquiores. See Bruckner, A., *et al.*, and Cavallo, G., *et al.*

Chevrier, G., and Chaume, M. (eds.), *Chartes et documents de St Benigne de Dijon* (Dijon, 1943).

Chronicle of Ireland, trans. T. Charles-Edwards, *The Chronicle of Ireland*, 3 vols. (Liverpool, 2006).

Chronicon Moissiacense, ed. G. Pertz, *MGH SS* I (Hanover, 1829), pp. 282–313; extracts trans. in King, *Charlemagne: Translated Sources*, pp. 145–9.

Clausula de unctione Pippini Regis, ed. B. Krusch, *MGH SRM* I (Hanover, 1885); trans. B. Pullan, *Sources for the History of Medieval Europe from the Mid-Eighth to the Mid-Thirteenth Century* (Oxford, 1966), pp. 7–8; repr. in Dutton, *Carolingian Civilization*, pp. 13–14.

Cockayne, G. O. (ed.), *Leechdoms, Wortcunning, and Starcraft of Early England*, 3 vols. Rolls Series 35, reprint rev. C. Singer (London, 1961).

Codex epistolaris Carolinus, ed. W. Gundlach, *MGH Epp.* III (*Epistolae merovingici et karolini aevi* I) (Berlin, 1892), pp. 476–657; selections trans. and summarised in King, *Charlemagne: Translated Sources*, pp. 268–307.

Codice diplomatico longobardo. See Schiaparelli, L., *et al.* (eds.).

Colgrave, B. (trans.), *The Life of Bishop Wilfrid by Eddius Stephanus* (Cambridge, 1927; repr. 1985).

Concilia Galliae a.314–a.506, ed. C. Munier, *CCSL* 148 (Turnhout, 1953).

Concilia Galliae a.511–695, ed. C. de Clercq, *CCSL* 148A (Turnhout, 1963).

Continuation of Bede, *Historia Ecclesiastica,* ed. and trans. B. Colgrave and R. A. B. Mynors, *Bede's Ecclesiastical History of the English People,* Oxford Medieval Texts (Oxford, 1969), pp. 572–7; trans. Whitelock, *EHD,* no. 5, pp. 285–6.

Conventus episcoporum at ripas Danubii (a.796), in *Conc.* II/1, no. 20, pp. 172–6.

Corpus consuetudinum monasticarum (Siegburg, 1963–).

Council of Laodicea, PL LXVII, cols. 165–70.

Desiderius of Cahors, *Epistolae,* ed. W. Arndt, *MGH Epp.* III *(Epistolae Merovingici et Karolini aevi* I) (Berlin, 1892), pp. 191–214.

d'Herbomez, A. (ed.), *Cartulaire de l'abbaye de Gorze. MS 826 de la Bibliothèque de Metz.* Mettensia 2 (Paris, 1898).

Dhuoda, *Liber manualis,* ed. and trans. M. Thiébaux, *Dhuoda: Handbook for her Warrior Son* (Cambridge, 1998); also trans. C. Neel, *Handbook for William: a Carolingian Woman's Counsel for her Son* (London, NE, 1991).

Diplomata Karolinorum I. See Mühlbacher, *et al.* (eds.).

Divisio regnorum, ed. A. Boretius, *Capit.* I, no. 45, pp. 126–30; trans. Loyn and Percival, *Reign of Charlemagne,* pp. 91–6.

Dumville, D. N. (ed.), *Annales Cambriae,* AD *682–954, texts A–C in parallel* (Cambridge, 2002).

Duplex capitulare missorum in Theodonis villa datum [Double capitulary of Thionville for the *missi*], *a.805,* ed. A. Boretius, *Capit.* I, nos. 43–4, pp. 120–6; trans. King, *Charlemagne: Translated Sources,* pp. 86–90; extract trans. Dutton, *Carolingian Civilization,* p. 80.

Edictum Pistense [Edict of Pîtres], ed. V. Krause, *Capit.* II, no. 273, pp. 332–7.

Eigil, *Vita Sturmi,* ed. G. Pertz, *MGH SS* II (Hanover, 1829), pp. 365–77; trans. Talbot, *Anglo-Saxon Missionaries,* repr. in Noble and Head, *Soldiers of Christ,* pp. 165–87.

Einhard, *Epistolae,* ed. K. Hampe, *MGH Epp.* V *(Epp. Karolini aevi* III) (Berlin, 1898–9), pp. 105–42; trans. Dutton (ed.), *Charlemagne's Courtier,* pp. 131–63.

—, *Translatio et miracula sanctorum Marcellini et Petri* [*Translation and Miracles of Saints Marcellinus and Peter*], ed. G. Waitz, *MGH SS* XV.1 (Hanover, 1888), pp. 239–64; trans. Dutton (ed.), *Charlemagne's Courtier,* pp. 69–130.

—, *Vita Karoli,* ed. O. Holder-Egger, *MGH SRG* XXV (Hanover, 1911); trans. Dutton (ed.), *Charlemagne's Courtier,* and D. Ganz, *Two Lives of Charlemagne* (Harmondsworth, 2008).

Engelbert, *Versus de bella quae fuit acta Fontaneto*, ed. E. Dümmler, *MGH Poet. Latini aevi Karolini* II (Berlin, 1884), pp. 138–9; trans. Dutton, *Carolingian Civilization*, pp. 332–3.

English Historical Documents (EHD). See Whitelock, D. (ed.).

Epistola ad Basilium I., ed. W. Henze, *MGH Epp.* VII (*Epp. Karolini aevi* V) (Berlin, 1928), pp. 386–94.

Epistola de litteris colendis [On cultivating letters], ed. A. Boretius, *Capit.* I, no. 29, pp. 78–9; trans. King, *Charlemagne: Translated Sources*, pp. 232–3.

Epistolae aevi Merowingici collectae no. 18, ed. W. Gundlach, *MGH Epp.* III (*Epp. Merovingici et Karolini aevi* I) (Berlin, 1892), pp. 434–68.

Epistolae variorum Karolo regnante, ed. E. Dümmler, *MGH Epp.* IV (*Epp. Karolini aevi* II) (Berlin, 1895), pp. 494–567.

Erchanbert, *Breviarium regum francorum annis 715–827*, ed. G. Pertz, *MGH SS* II (Hanover, 1829), p. 328.

Erhart, P., and Kleindienst, J. (eds.), *Urkundenlandschaft Rätiens* (Vienna, 2004).

Ermenric of Ellwangen, *Epistola ad Grimaldum Abbatem*, ed. E. Dümmler, *MGH Epp.* V (*Epp. karolini aevi* III) (Berlin, 1899), pp. 534–79.

Ermold, *Ad eundem Pippinum*, ed. E. Faral, *Ermold le Noir. Poème sur Louis le Pieux* (with French trans.) (Paris, 1964), pp. 202–19.

—, *Ad Pippinum Regem*, ed. E. Faral, *Ermold le Noir. Poème sur Louis le Pieux* (with French trans.) (Paris, 1964), pp. 220–32.

—, *In Honorem Hludowici*, ed. E. Faral, *Ermold le Noir. Poème sur Louis le Pieux* (with French trans.) (Paris, 1964), pp. 2–201; extracts trans. in Godman, *Poetry of the Carolingian Renaissance* (London, 1985), pp. 250–7.

Expositio antiquae liturgiae Gallicanae, ed. E. Ratcliff, Henry Bradshaw Society 98 (London, 1971), pp. 3–16, trans. J. N. Hillgarth, *Christianity and Paganism 350–750* (Philadelphia, PA, 1986), pp. 186–92.

Faral, E. (ed.), *Ermold le Noir. Poème sur Louis le Pieux* (with French trans.) (Paris, 1964).

Flodoard of Rheims, *Historia Remensis ecclesiae*, ed. J. Heller and G. Waitz, *MGH SS* XIII (Hanover, 1881), pp. 405–599; trans. S. Fanning and B. S. Bachrach, *The Annals of Flodoard of Rheims, 991–966* (Peterborough, ON, 2004).

Florus of Lyon, *Adversus Amalarium*, PL 119, cols. 71–80.

—, *Carmina*, ed. E. Dümmler, *MGH Poet. Latini aevi Karolini* II (Berlin, 1884), pp. 507–66.

Formulae imperiales, ed. K. Zeumer, *MGH Formulae Merovingici et Karolini Aevi* (Hanover, 1886), pp. 285–328.

Fredegar, *Chronicle*, ed. and trans. J. M. Wallace-Hadrill, *The Fourth Book of the Chronicle of Fredegar with its Continuations* (London, 1960).

—, *Continuationes*, ed. and trans. J. M. Wallace-Hadrill, *The Fourth Book of the Chronicle of Fredegar with its Continuations* (London, 1960).

Frothar of Toul, *Letters*, ed. K. Hampe, *MGH Ep.* V (*Epp. Karolini aevi* III) (Berlin, 1899), pp. 275–98; French trans. M. Parisse and J. Barbier,

La Correspondance d'un évêque carolingien: Frothaire de Toul (ca. 813–847). Avec les lettres de Theuthilde, abbesse de Remiremont (Paris, 1998).

Fulrad of Saint-Denis, *Testament*, ed. M. Tangl, 'Das Testament Fulrads von Saint-Denis', *Das Mittelalter in Quellenkunde und Diplomatik. Ausgewählte Schriften*, Forschungen zur mittelalterliche Geschichte 12 (Graz, 1966), pp. 540–81.

Gesta sanctorum patrum Fontanellensis coenobii [Acts of the Abbots of St Wandrille], ed. F. Lohier and J. Laporte, Société de l'histoire de Normandie (Rouen and Paris, 1936).

Glockner, K. (ed.), *Codex Laureshamensis*, Arbeiten der historischen Kommission für den Volksstaat Hessen 3. 3 vols. (Darmstadt, 1929–36).

Guérard, B. (ed.), *Polyptyque de l'Abbé Irminon* (Paris, 1844), 2 vols.

Heidrich, I. (ed.), *Die Urkunden der Arnulfinger* (Bad Münstereifel, 2001).

Hildebrandslied, ed. and trans. Knight Bostock, *Handbook on Old High German Literature*, pp. 44–7.

Hincmar of Rheims, *Capitula episcoporum*, ed. R. Pokorny and M. Stratmann, *MGH Capitula episcoporum* II (Hanover, 1995), pp. 1–89.

—, *Capitula quibus de rebus magistri et decani singulas ecclesias inquirire*, PL CXXV, cols. 777–92.

—, *Collectio de ecclesiis et capellis*, ed. M. Stratmann, *MGH Fontes iuris germanici antiqui* XIV (Hanover, 1990).

—, *De divortio Lotharii regis et Theutbergae reginae*, ed. L. Böhringer, *MGH Concilia* IV, supp. 1 (Hanover, 1992).

—, *De ordine palatii* [On the Governance of the Palace], ed. T. Gross and R. Schieffer, *MGH Fontes iuris germanici antiqui* III (Hanover, 1980); trans. D. Herlihy, *A History of Feudalism* (London, 1970), pp. 209–27 and repr. in Dutton (ed.), *Carolingian Civilization*, pp. 516–32.

—, *De villa Noviliaco*, ed. H. Mordek, 'Ein exemplarischer Rechtsstreit: Hinkmar von Reims und das Landgut Neuilly-Saint-Front', *Zeitschrift der Savigny-Stiftung für Rechtsgeschichte Kanonistische Abteilung* 83 (1997), pp. 86–112.

—, *Vita Remigii episcopi Remensis*, ed. B. Krusch, *MGH SRM* III (Hanover, 1896), pp. 239–349, trans. D. Herlihy, *A History of Feudalism* (London, 1970), pp. 122–4.

Hrabanus Maurus, *De institutione clericorum libri tres. Studien und Edition*, ed. D. Zimpel (Frankfurt, 1996).

—, *De rerum naturis*, PL III, cols. 9–614.

—, *Epistolae*, ed. E. Dümmler, *MGH Epp.* V *(Epp. Karolini aevi* III*)* (Berlin, 1898–9), pp. 380–533.

—, *Homiliae*, PL CX, cols. 9–470.

Ibn Khurradadhbih, *Book of Routes and Kingdoms*, ed. M. J. de Goeje, *Bibliotheca geographorum arabicorum* 6 (Leiden, 1889); trans. R. S. Lopez and I. W. Raymond, *Medieval Trade in the Mediterranean World: Illustrative Documents* (London and New York, 1955), pp. 30–3.

Indiculus superstitionum et paganiarum, ed. R. Rau, *Briefe des Bonifatius; Willibalds Leben des Bonifatius* (Darmstadt, 1968), pp. 444–8; trans. J. T. McNeill and H. A. Gamer (eds.), *Medieval Handbooks of Penance* (New York, 1990), pp. 419–21, and repr. in Dutton (ed.), *Carolingian Civilization*, pp. 3–4.

Ine, *Laws*, ed. F. Liebermann, *Die Gesetze der Angelsachsen*, 3 vols. (Halle, 1903–16); trans. F. L. Attenborough, *The Laws of the Earliest English Kings* (Cambridge, 1922; repr. 2000), pp. 36–61.

Isidore of Seville, *Etymologiae*, ed. and trans. S. A. Barney, *et al.*, *The Etymologies of Isidore of Seville* (Cambridge, 2006).

John VIII, *Epistolae*, ed. E. Caspar, *MGH Epp.* VII (*Epp. Karolini aevi* V) (Berlin, 1928), pp. 1–333; no. 7 trans. E. J. Goldberg, *Struggle for Empire. Kingship and Conflict under Louis the German, 817–876* (Ithaca,NY, and London, 2006), p. 333.

Jonas, *Vita Columbani*, ed. B. Krusch, *MGH SRM* IV (Hanover, 1902), pp. 1–152; trans. E. Peters, *Monks, Bishops and Pagans* (Philadelphia, PA, 1975), pp. 75–113.

Jonas of Orléans, *De institutione laicorum*, *PL* CVI, cols. 121–278.

—, *De institutione regia*, ed. J. Reviron, *Les Idées politico-religieuses d'un évêque du* IXe *siècle: Jonas d'Orléans et son* De institutione regia (Paris, 1930), pp. 119–94.

Justinian, *Testament a.828/9*, ed. L. Lanfranchi and B. Strina, *Ss. Ilario e Benedetto e Gregorio* (Venice, 1965), no. 2, p. 24.

Karolus magnus et Leo papa [Paderborn Epic], ed. E. Dümmler, *MGH Poet.* I (Berlin, 1881), pp. 366–79; partial trans. in Godman, *Poetry of the Carolingian Renaissance*, pp. 197–207.

Kehr, P. (ed.), *Die Urkunden Ludwigs des Deutschen, Karlmanns und Ludwigs des Jüngeren. MGH Diplomata Regum Germanie ex stirpe Karolinorum* I (Berlin, 1934).

Knight Bostock, J., *A Handbook on Old High German Literature*, 2nd edn rev. K. King and D. McLintock (Oxford, 1976).

Kölzer, T., with Hartmann, M., and Stieldorf, A. (eds.), *Die Urkunden der Merowinger, MGH Diplomata regum francorum e stirpe Merovingica*, 2 vols. (Hanover, 2001).

Krusch, B., 'Chronologica regum francorum stirpis Merovingicae', *MGH SRM* VII (Hanover, 1920), pp. 468–516.

Leges Ahistulfi [Laws of Aistulf], ed. F. Beyerle, *Leges langobardorum, 643–866. Die Gesetze der Langobarden* (Weimar, 1947; repr. Witzenhausen, 1962), pp. 194–204; trans. Fischer-Drew, *The Lombard Laws*.

Leges Liutprandi, ed. F. Beyerle, *Leges langobardorum, 643–866. Die Gesetze der Langobarden* (Weimar, 1947; repr. Witzenhausen, 1962), pp. 99–182; trans. Fischer-Drew, *The Lombard Laws*.

Leges Ratchis [Laws of Ratchis], ed. F. Beyerle, *Leges langobardorum, 643–866. Die Gesetze der Langobarden* (Weimar, 1947; repr. Witzenhausen, 1962), pp. 183–93; trans. Fischer-Drew, *The Lombard Laws*.

Leidrad, *Epistolae*, ed. E. Dümmler, *MGH Epp.* IV *(Epp. Karolini aevi* II*)* (Berlin, 1895), pp. 539–46.

Leo IV, *Epistolae*, ed. A. de Hirsch-Gereuth, *MGH Epp.* V *(Epistolae Karolini aevi* III) (Berlin, 1898–9), pp. 585–612.

Liber de episcopis Mettensibus (Gesta episcoporum Mettensium), PL, 163, cols. 579–614; and ed. G. Pertz, *MGH SS* II (Hanover, 1829), pp. 260–8.

Liber historiae francorum, ed. B. Krusch, *MGH SRM* II (Hanover, 1888), pp. 241–328; trans. B. S. Bachrach, *Liber historiae francorum* (Lawrence, KS, 1973).

Liber pontificalis, ed. L. Duchesne, *Le Liber pontificalis. Texte, introduction et commentaire*, 2 vols. (Paris, 1886 and 1892); amplified 3 vol. edn ed. C. Vogel (Paris, 1955–7); trans. in three books by R. Davis, *The Book of Pontiffs* (Liber pontificalis), rev. edn (Liverpool, 2000); *The Lives of the Eighth-Century Popes* (Liber pontificalis) (Liverpool, 1992); *The Lives of the Ninth-Century Popes* (Liber pontificalis) (Liverpool, 1995).

Liber possessionum Wizenburgensis, ed. C. Dette (Mainz, 1987).

Libri Carolini. See *Opus Caroli regis.*

Liutprand, *Pactum*, ed. L. Hartmann, *Zur Wirtschaftsgeschichte Italiens im frühen Mittelalter* (Gotha, 1904).

Lull, *Epistolae.* See Boniface, *Epistolae.*

Lupus of Ferrières, *Epistolae*, ed. P. K. Marshall (Leipzig, 1984); trans. G. W. Regenos, *The Letters of Lupus of Ferrières* (The Hague, 1966).

Manaresi, C. (ed.), *I placiti del regnum Italiae*, 3 vols. (Rome, 1955–60).

Mango, C., and Scott, R., with Greatrex, G. (trans.), *The Chronicle of Theophanes Confessor. Byzantine and Near Eastern History AD 284–813* (Oxford, 1997).

Martin of Braga, *De correctione rusticorum (On the correction of the rustics)*, ed. and trans. Barlow, *Iberian Fathers.*

Mayer-Marthaler, E., and Perret, F. (eds.), *Bündner Urkundenbuch* I (Chur, 1955).

Mühlbacher, E., *et al.* (eds.), *Die Urkunden der Karolinger* I: *Die Urkunden Pippins, Karlmanns und Karls des Großen. MGH Diplomata Karolinorum* I (Hanover, 1906).

Nithard, *Historiarum Libri IV*, ed. P. Lauer, *Histoire des fils de Louis le Pieux* (Paris, 1926); trans. B. Scholz, *Carolingian Chronicles* (Ann Arbor, MI, 1970).

Noble, T. F. X., and Head, T., *Soldiers of Christ. Saints and Saints' Lives from Late Antiquity and the Early Middle Ages* (University Park, PA, 1995).

Northern Annals, ed. T. Arnold, *Symeonis monachi opera omnia*, 2 vols., Rolls Series 75 (London, 1882–5), II, pp. 30–66; trans Whitelock, *EHD*, no. 3(a), pp. 264–76.

Notitia de servitio monasteriorum (a.819), ed. P. Becker, *CCM* I (Siegburg, 1963), pp. 493–9.

Notker Balbulus, *Erchanberti breviarium continuatio*, ed. G. Pertz, *MGH SS* II (Hanover, 1829), pp. 329–30.

—, *Gesta Karoli magni imperatoris*, ed. H. F. Haefele, *MGH SRG* n.s. 12 (Berlin, 1959); trans. D. Ganz, *Two Lives of Charlemagne* (Harmondsworth, 2008), and by L. Thorpe, *Einhard and Notker the Stammerer: Two Lives of Charlemagne* (Harmondsworth, 1969).

Opus Caroli regis contra synodum (Libri Carolini), ed. A. Freeman with P. Meyvaert, *MGH Concilia* II, suppl. 1 (Hanover, 1998).

Ordinatio imperii, ed. A. Boretius, *Capit.* I, no. 136, pp. 270–3; trans. Dutton (ed.), *Carolingian Civilization*, pp. 199–204.

Pactus legis Salicae, ed. K. A. Eckhardt, *MGH Legum sectio* I, *Leges Nationum Germanicarum* IV (Hanover, 1962); trans. K. Fischer-Drew, *The Laws of the Salian Franks* (Philadelphia, PA, 1991).

Paderborn Epic. See *Karolus magnus et Leo papa*.

Pardessus, J. M., *Diplomata, chartae, epistolae, leges ad res Gallo-Francicas spectantia*, 2 vols. (Paris, 1843–9; repr. Aalen 1969).

Paschasius Radbertus, *De corpore et sanguine Domini*, ed. B. Paulus, *CCCM* 16 (Turnhout, 1969); trans. G. E. McCracken, *Early Medieval Theology* (Philadelphia, PA, 1957), pp. 94–108.

—, *Epitaphium Arsenii* [*Life of Wala*], ed. E. Dümmler, *Abhandlungen der kaiserlichen Akademie der Wissenschaften zu Berlin, phil.-hist. Klasse* (1900), trans. A. Cabaniss, *Charlemagne's Cousins. Contemporary Lives of Adalard and Wala* (New York, 1967).

—, *Vita Sancti Adalhardi*, ed. Dom. J. Mabillon, *PL* CXX, 1507–1556c; trans. A. Cabaniss, *Charlemagne's Cousins: Contemporary Lives of Adalard and Wala* (New York, 1967).

Paul the Deacon, *Historia langobardorum*, ed. L. Bethmann and G. Waitz, *MGH SRL* (Hanover, 1878), pp. 12–187; trans. W. D. Foulke, *History of the Langobards by Paul the Deacon* (Philadelphia, 1907).

Pauli continuatio cassinese, ed. G. Waitz, *MGH SRL* (Hanover, 1878), pp. 198–200.

Pauli continuatio tertia, ed. G. Waitz, *MGH SRL* (Hanover, 1878), pp. 203–16.

Paulinus of Aquileia, *Liber Exhortationis ad Hericum Comitem*, PL IC, cols. 197–282.

Planctus de obitu Karoli, ed. E. Dümmler, *MGH Poet. Latini Aevi Karolini* I, pp. 435–6; trans. Dutton, *Carolingian Civilization*, pp. 157–9.

Prou, M., and Vidier, A. (eds.), *Recueil des chartes de l'abbaye de Saint-Benoît-sur-Loire (Fleury)*, 2 vols. (Orleans and Paris, 1900–24).

Prümer Urbar, Das, ed. I. Schwab (Düsseldorf, 1983).

Ratramnus of Corbie, *De corpore et sanguine Domini*, PL CXXI, cols. 169–70; trans. G. E. McCracken, *Early Medieval Theology* (Philadelphia, PA, 1957), pp. 118–47.

—, *Epistolae*, ed. E. Perels, *MGH Epp.* VI (*Epp. Karolini aevi* IV) (Berlin, 1925), *Epistolae variorum*, nos. 8–13, pp. 149–58; no. 12 trans. Dutton, *Carolingian Civilization*, pp. 452–5.

Regino of Prüm, *Chronicon*, ed. F. Kurze, *MGH SRG* 50 (Hanover, 1890); trans. MacLean, *History and Politics*.

Rimbert, *Vita Anskarii*, ed. G. Waitz, *MGH SRG in usum scholarum separatim editi* LV (Hanover, 1884); trans. C. H. Robinson, *Anskar, The Apostle of the North, 801–865* (London, 1921), repr. in Dutton, *Carolingian Civilization*, pp. 409–51.

Sancti Bonifatii et Lulli Epistolae. See Boniface, *Epistolae.*

Schiaparelli, L., Brühl, C., and Zielinski, H. (eds.), *Codice diplomatico longobardo.* 5 vols. Fonti per la storia d'Italia 62–6 (Rome, 1929–86).

Schieffer, T., *Die Urkunden Lothars I und Lothars II. MGH Diplomata Karolinorum* III (Berlin, 1966).

Schlosser, H. D. (ed.), *Althochdeutsche Literatur* (Frankfurt, 1970).

Sedulius, *Liber de rectoribus Christianis*, ed. S. Hellman, *Sedulius Scottus* (Munich, 1906); trans. E. G. Doyle, *Sedulius Scottus. On Christian Rulers and the Poems* (New York, 1983), extracts trans. Dutton, *Carolingian Civilization*, pp. 374–86.

Stengel, E. E. (ed.), *Urkundenbuch der Kloster Fulda*, Veröffentlichungen der historischen Kommission für Hessen und Waldeck 19 (Marburg, 1936).

Stephen of Ripon, *Vita Wilfridi*, ed. and trans. B. Colgrave, *The Life of Bishop Wilfrid by Eddius Stephanus* (Cambridge, 1927; repr. 1985).

Tacitus, *Germania*, trans. A. R. Birley, *Agricola and Germany* (Oxford, 2009); J. B. Rives, *Germania* (Oxford, 1999); H. W. Benario, *Germany* (Warminster, 1999); M. Hutton, *Agricola, Germania, Dialogus* (London, 1970).

Tangl, M. (ed.), 'Das Testament Fulrads von Saint-Denis', *Das Mittelalter in Quellenkunde und Diplomatik. Ausgewählte Schriften*, Forschungen zur mittelalterliche Geschichte 12 (Graz, 1966), pp. 540–81.

Tessier, G., *et al.* (eds.), *Recueil des actes de Charles II le Chauve*, 3 vols. (Paris, 1943–55).

Thegan, *Gesta Hludowici imperatoris*, ed. E. Tremp, *Die Taten Kaiser Ludwigs, MGH SRG in usum scholarum separatim editi* LXIV (Hanover, 1995); trans. P. Dutton, Thegan, *Life of Louis the Pious*, in Dutton, *Carolingian Civilization*, pp. 159–76.

Theodemar of Monte Cassino, *Letter to Charlemagne*, ed. K. Hallinger and M. Wegener, *CCM* I (Siegburg, 1963), pp. 157–75; ed. E. Dümmler, *MGH Epp.* IV (*Epp. Kar. aev.* II), (Berlin, 1895), no. 13, pp. 509–14.

Theodulf, *Carmina*, ed. E. Dümmler, *MGH Poet.* I (*Poet. Karolini Aevi* I) (Hanover, 1881), pp. 437–581; selections trans. Godman, *Poetry of the Carolingian Renaissance*, and Dutton, *Carolingian Civilization*, pp. 100–6.

Theophanes, *Chronographia*, ed. C. de Boor, 2 vols. (Leipzig, 1883–5), trans. C. Mango and R. Scott with G. Greatrex, *The Chronicle of Theophanes Confessor. Byzantine and Near Eastern History* AD *284–813* (Oxford, 1997).

Thietmar of Merseburg, *Chronicon*, ed. R. Holtzmann, *MGH SRG*, n.s. IX (Berlin, 1935), trans. D. Warner, *Ottonian Germany: The Chronicon of Thietmar of Merseburg* (Manchester, 2001).

Visio Baronti, ed. W. Levison, *MGH SRM* V (Hanover, 1910), pp. 386–94, trans. J. Hillgarth, *Christianity and Paganism*, pp. 195–204.

Visio Fursei [Vision of Fursa], ed. C. Carozzi, *Le Voyage de l'âme dans l'audelà*, Collection de l'EFR 189 (Rome, 1994), p. 691.

Vita Amandi, ed. B. Krusch, *MGH SRM* v (Hanover, 1910), pp. 428–49; trans. Hillgarth, *Christianity and Paganism*, pp. 139–48.

Vita Audoini episcopi Rotomagensis, ed. W. Levison, *MGH SRG* v (Hanover, 1910), pp. 536–67; trans. P. Fouracre and R. Gerberding, 'Life of Audoin', *Late Merovingian France. History and Hagiography 640–720* (Manchester, 1996), pp. 133–65.

Vita *of Constantine and the* Vita *of Methodius, The*, ed. M. Kantor (Ann Arbor, MI, 1976).

Vita Eligii, ed. B. Krusch, *MGH SRG* iv (Hanover, 1902), pp. 634–761.

Vita Lebuini, ed. A. Hofmeister, *MGH SS* xxx.2 (Leipzig, 1934), pp. 789–95; trans. Talbot, *Anglo-Saxon Missionaries*.

Vita Liutbergae [*Life of Liutberga*], ed. G. H. Pertz, *MGH SS* iv, pp. 158–64, trans. F. S. Paxton, *Anchoress and Abbess in Ninth-Century Saxony: the Lives of Liutbirga of Wendhausen and Hathumoda of Gandersheim* (Washington, DC, 2009).

Vita Vulframni, ed. W. Levison, *MGH SRM* v (Hanover, 1910), pp. 657–73.

Vita Willehadi, ed. A. Poncelet, *De sancto Willehado primo Bremensis episcopo et inferioris Saxoniae apostolo*, Acta Sanctorum (Brussels, 1910), 3 November, pp. 842–6; trans. Noble and Head, *Soldiers of Christ*, pp. 279–91.

Vita Willehadi, ed. A. Röpke, *Das Leben des heiligen Willehad* (Bremen, 1982); trans. Noble and Head, *Soldiers of Christ*, pp. 279–91.

Waltharius, ed. and trans. Knight Bostock, *Handbook on Old High German Literature*, pp. 259–80.

Wampach, C. (ed.), *Geschichte der Grundherrschaft Echternach im Frühmittelalter* 1.2: *Quellenband* (Luxembourg, 1930).

Warner, D. (trans.), *Ottonian Germany: The Chronicon of Thietmar of Merseburg* (Manchester, 2001).

Wartmann, H. (ed.), *Urkundenbuch der Abtei St. Gallen* ii (Zürich, 1866).

Werminghoff, A. (ed.), *Concilia aevi Karolini* ii.1 and ii.2 (Hanover, 1906–8).

Whitelock, D., *English Historical Documents*, 2nd edn (London and New York, 1979), i: *c.500–1042*.

Willibald, *Vita Bonifatii*, ed. W. Levison, *MGH SRG in usum scholarum separatim editi* lvii (Hanover, 1905); trans. Talbot, *Anglo-Saxon Missionaries*, repr. in Noble and Head, *Soldiers of Christ*, pp. 107–40.

2. SECONDARY SOURCES

Abels, R., 'Alfred the Great, the *micel hæthen here* and the Viking threat', in T. Reuter (ed.), *Alfred the Great: Papers from the Eleventh-Centenary Conferences* (Aldershot, 2003), pp. 265–79.

Ahmed, A., *A History of Islamic Sicily* (Edinburgh, 1975).

Airlie, S., 'The anxiety of sanctity: St Gerald of Aurillac and his maker', *Journal of Ecclesiastical History* 43 (1992), pp. 372–95.

—, 'The aristocracy', in *NCMH* II, pp. 431–50.

—, 'The aristocracy in the service of the state in the Carolingian period', in Airlie, Pohl and Reimitz (eds.), *Staat im frühen Mittelalter*, pp. 92–111.

—, 'Bonds of power and bonds of association in the court circle of Louis the Pious', in Godman and Collins (eds.), *Charlemagne's Heir*, pp. 191–204.

—, *Carolingian Politics* (Oxford, forthcoming).

—, 'Charlemagne and the aristocracy: captains and kings', in Story (ed.), *Charlemagne*, pp. 90–102.

—, 'Les Élites en 888 et après, ou comment pense-t-on la crise carolingienne?', in F. Bougard, L. Feller and R. Le Jan (eds.), *Les Élites au haut Moyen Âge. Crises et renouvellements* (Turnhout, 2006), pp. 425–37.

—, '"For it is written in the law": Ansegis and the writing of Carolingian royal authority', in S. Baxter, *et al.* (eds.), *Early Medieval Studies in Memory of Patrick Wormald* (Aldershot, 2009), pp. 219–36.

—, 'Narratives of triumph and rituals of submission: Charlemagne's mastering of Bavaria', *TRHS* 6th ser. 9 (1999), pp. 93–119.

—, 'The nearly men: Boso of Vienne and Arnulf of Bavaria', in A. Duggan (ed.), *Nobles and Nobility in Medieval Europe* (Woodbridge, 2000), pp. 25–41.

—, 'The palace of memory: the Carolingian court as political centre', in S. R. Jones, R. Marks and A. J. Minnis (eds.), *Courts and Regions in Medieval Europe* (York, 2000), pp. 1–20.

—, *The Political Behaviour of Secular Magnates in Francia, 829–79*, unpublished D. Phil. thesis, University of Oxford (1985).

—, 'Private bodies and the body politic in the divorce case of Lothar II', *P&P* 161 (1998), pp. 3–38.

—, 'Review article: After empire. Recent work on the emergence of post-Carolingian kingdoms', *EME* 2 (1993), pp. 153–61.

—, '"Sad stories of the deaths of kings": narrative patterns and structures of authority in Regino of Prüm's *Chronicle*', in E. M. Tyler and R. Balzaretti (eds.), *Narrative and History in the Early Medieval West* (Turnhout, 2006), pp. 105–31.

—, '*Semper fideles?* Loyauté envers les carolingiens comme constituant de l'identité aristocratique', in Le Jan (ed.), *La Royauté et les élites*, pp. 129–43.

—, 'Talking heads: assemblies in early medieval Germany', in P. S. Barnwell and M. Mostert (eds.), *Political Assemblies in the Earlier Middle Ages* (Turnhout, 2003), pp. 29–46.

—, 'Towards a Carolingian aristocracy', in Becher and Jarnut (eds.), *Der Dynastiewechsel von 751*, pp. 109–28.

—, 'The world, the text and the Carolingian: royal, aristocratic and masculine identities in Nithard's *Histories*', in Nelson and Wormald (eds.), *Lay Intellectuals*, pp. 51–76.

Airlie, S., Pohl, W., and Reimitz, H. (eds.), *Staat im frühen Mittelalter. Forschungen zur Geschichte des Mittelalters* 11 (Vienna, 2006).

Alberi, M., 'The evolution of Alcuin's concept of the *Imperium Christianum*', in Hill and Swan (eds.), *The Community*, pp. 3–17.

Allott, S., *Alcuin of York – his Life and Letters* (York, 1974).

Althoff, G., *Otto III* (Darmstadt, 1996), trans. P. J. Jestice, *Otto III* (University Park, PA, 2003).

Althoff, G., and Wollasch, J., 'Bleiben die *Libri Memoriales* stumm? Eine Erwiderung auf H. Hoffmann', *Deutsches Archiv für Erforschung des Mittelalters* 56 (2000), pp. 33–53.

Ambrosiani, B., and Clarke, H. (eds.), *Developments around the Baltic and the North Sea in the Viking Age* (Stockholm, 1994).

Anderton, M. (ed.), *Anglo-Saxon Trading Centres: Beyond the Emporia* (Glasgow, 1999).

Angenendt, A., *Das Frühmittelalter. Die abendländische Christenheit von 400 bis 900* (Stuttgart, 1990).

—, 'Theologie und Liturgie der mittelalterlichen Totenmemoria', in K. Schmid and J. Wollasch (eds.), *Memoria. Der geschichtliche Zeugniswert des liturgischen Gedenkens im Mittelalter* (Munich, 1984), pp. 80–199.

Anton, H. H., *Fürstenspiegel und Herrscherethos in der Karolingerzeit*, Bonner Historische Forschungen 32 (Bonn, 1968).

Appadurai, A. (ed.), *The Social Life of Things. Commodities in Cultural Perspective* (Cambridge, 1986).

Arnold, J., *Belief and Unbelief in Medieval Europe* (London, 2005).

Arthur, P., *Naples from Roman Town to City-state* (London, 2004).

Attenborough, F. L. (trans.), *The Laws of the Earliest English Kings* (Cambridge, 1922; repr. 2000).

Bachrach, B., 'Charles Martel, mounted shock combat, the stirrup and feudalism', *Studies in Medieval and Renaissance History* 7 (1970), pp. 49–75.

Bachrach, B. (ed.), *Journal of Medieval Military History* 1 (2003).

Bachrach, D. S., *Religion and the Conduct of War, c.300–c.1215* (Woodbridge, 2003).

Bailey, R. N., 'St Wilfrid, Ripon and Hexham', *American Early Medieval Studies* 1 (1990), pp. 3–25.

Balzaretti, R., 'Cities, emporia and monasteries: local economies in the Po valley 700–875', in N. Christie and S. Loseby (eds.), *Towns in Transition. Urban Evolution in Late Antiquity and the Early Middle Ages* (Aldershot, 1996), pp. 213–34.

—, 'Cities and markets in early medieval Europe', in G. Ausenda (ed.), *After Empire. Towards an Ethnology of Europe's Barbarians* (San Marino, 1994), pp. 113–42.

—, 'Monasteries, towns and the countryside: reciprocal relationships in the archdiocese of Milan, 614–814', in G. P. Brogiolo, N. Gauthier and

N. Christie (eds.), *Towns and Their Territories: Between Late Antiquity and the Early Middle Ages* (Leiden, 2000), pp. 235–57.

—, 'The monastery of Sant'Ambrogio and dispute settlement in early medieval Milan', *EME* 3 (1994), pp. 1–18.

Banaji, J., *Agrarian Change in Late Antiquity* (Oxford, 2001).

—, 'Aristocracies, peasantries and the framing of the early middle ages', *Journal of Agrarian Change* 9 (2009), pp. 59–91.

Banniard, M., 'Language and communication in Carolingian Europe', in *NCMH* II, pp. 695–708.

Barbero, A., *Charlemagne: Father of a Continent* (Berkeley, 2004).

Barford, P. M., *The Early Slavs. Culture and Society in Early Medieval Eastern Europe* (London, 2001).

Barthélemy, D., 'La Chevalerie carolingienne: prélude au xie siècle', in Le Jan (ed.), *La Royauté et les élites*, pp. 159–75.

—, 'Debate. The "Feudal Revolution"', *P&P* 152 (1996), pp. 196–205.

—, 'Modern mythologies of medieval chivalry', in Linehan and Nelson (eds.), *The Medieval World*, pp. 214–28.

Bartlett, R., *The Making of Europe: Conquest, Colonization and Cultural Change, 950–1350* (London, 1993).

—, 'Reflections on paganism and christianity in medieval Europe', *PBA* 101 (1998), pp. 55–76.

Bately, J. M., and A. Englert (eds.), *Ohthere's Voyages* (Roskilde, 2007).

Becher, M., *Charlemagne* (New Haven, CT, and London, 2003).

—, '*Cum lacrimis et gemitu*. Vom Weinen der Sieger und der Besiegten im frühen und hohen Mittelalter', in G. Althoff (ed.), *Formen und Funktionen öffentlicher Kommunikation im Früh- und Hochmittelalter* (Stuttgart, 2001), pp. 25–52.

—, 'Drogo und die Königserhebung Pippins', *Frühmittelalterliche Studien* 23 (1989), pp. 131–53.

—, *Eid und Herrschaft: Untersuchungen zum Herrscherethos Karls des Großen* (Sigmaringen, 1993).

—, 'Die Kaiserkrönung im Jahr 800. Eine Streitfrage zwischen Karl dem Großen und Papst Leo III.', *Rheinische Vierteljahrblätter* 66 (2002), pp. 1–38.

—, 'Neue Überlieferungen zum Geburtsdatum Karls des Großen', *Francia* 19 (1992), pp. 37–60.

Becher, M., and Jarnut, J. (eds.), *Der Dynastiewechsel von 751. Vorgeschichte, Legitimationsstrategien und Erinnerung* (Münster, 2004).

Beckwith, J., *Early Medieval Art* (London, 1969).

Bernhard, H., 'Die frühmittelalterliche Siedlung von Speyer "Vogelgesang"', *Offa* 39 (1982), pp. 217–33.

Berto, A., *Testi storici e poetici dell'Italia carolingia* (Padua, 2002).

Bessmerny, J., 'Les structures de la famille paysanne dans les villages de la Francie au ixe siècle', *Le Moyen Âge* 90 (1984), pp. 165–93.

Bigott, B., *Ludwig der Deutsche und die Reichskirche im ostfränkischen Reich (826–876)* (Husum, 2002).

Bischoff, B., *Latin Palaeography. Antiquity and the Middle Ages*, trans. D. Ó Cróinín and D. Ganz (Cambridge, 1990).

Bisson, T. N., 'The "feudal" revolution', *P&P* 142 (1994), pp. 6–42; 'Reply', *P&P* 155 (1997), pp. 208–25.

—, 'Nobility and family in France: a review essay', *French Historical Studies* 16 (1990), pp. 597–613.

—, 'La Terre et les hommes: a programme fulfilled?', *French History* 14 (2000), pp. 322–45.

Bjork, R. E., and Niles, J. D. (eds.), *A Beowulf Handbook* (Lincoln, NE, 1997).

Blackburn, M., 'Coin circulation in Germany during the early Middle Ages: the evidence of single-finds', in B. Kluge (ed.), *Fernhandel und Geldwirtschaft* (Sigmaringen, 1993), pp. 37–54.

Blair, J., *The Church in Anglo-Saxon Society* (Oxford, 2005).

Bleiber, W., 'Grundherrschaft und Markt zwischen Loire und Rhein während des 9. Jahrhunderts: Untersuchungen zu ihrem wechselseitigen Verhältnis', *Jahrbuch für Wirtschaftgeschichte* 3 (1982), pp. 105–35.

Blinkhorn, P., 'Of cabbages and kings: production, trade, and consumption in Middle-Saxon England', in Anderton (ed.), *Anglo-Saxon Trading Centres*, pp. 4–23.

Bloch, M., *The Historian's Craft*, ed. P. Burke (Manchester, 1992).

Bloch, M. E., 'The resurrection of the house among the Zafimaniry of Madagascar', in J. Carsten and S. Hugh-Jones (eds.), *About the House: Levi-Strauss and Beyond* (Cambridge, 1995), pp. 69–83.

Böhme, H.W., *Germanische Grabfunde des 4. und 5. Jahrhunderts zwischen Elbe und Loire*. 2 vols. (Munich, 1974).

Böhner, K., *Das Grab eines fränkischen Herren aus Morken im Rheinland* (Cologne, 1959).

—, 'Urban and rural settlement in the Frankish kingdom', in M. W. Barley (ed.), *European Towns: Their Archaeology and Early History* (London, 1977), pp. 185–207.

Bois, G., *The Transformation of the Year 1000: The Village of Lournand from Antiquity to Feudalism*, trans. J. Birrell (Cambridge, 1992).

Bolin, S., 'Mohammed, Charlemagne and Ruric', *Scandinavian Economic History Review* 1 (1953), pp. 5–39.

Bonnassie, P., *From Slavery to Feudalism in Southwest Europe*, trans. J. Birrell (Cambridge, 1991).

Booker, C., 'The demanding drama of Louis the Pious', *Comitatus: A Journal of Medieval and Renaissance Studies* 34 (2003), pp. 170–5.

—, *Past Convictions: the Penance of Louis the Pious and the Decline of the Carolingians* (Philadelphia, PA, 2009).

Borgolte, M., 'Die Alaholfingerurkunden. Zeugnisse vom Selbstverständnis einer adligen Verwandtengemeinschaft des frühen Mittelalters', in M. Borgolte, D. Geuenich and K. Schmid (eds.), *Subsidia Sangallensia* I. *Materialien und Untersuchungen zu den Verbrüderungsbüchern und zu den älteren Urkunden des Stiftsarchivs St. Gallen* (St. Gallen, 1986), pp. 287–322.

—, *Geschichte der Grafschaften Alemanniens in fränkischer Zeit* (Sigmaringen, 1984).

—, 'Karl III. und Neudingen. Zum Problem der Nachfolgeregelung Ludwigs des Deutschen', *Zeitschrift für die Geschichte des Oberrheins* 125 (1977), pp. 21–55.

Boshof, E., *Ludwig der Fromme* (Darmstadt, 1996).

Bosl, K., '*Potens* und *pauper*. Begriffsgeschichtliche Studien zur gesellschaftlichen Differenzierung im frühen Mittelalter und zur "Pauperismus" des Hochmittelalters', in Bosl, *Frühformen der Gesellschaft in mittelalterlichen Welt* (Munich and Vienna, 1964), pp. 106–34.

Boudriot, W., *Die altgermanische Religion* (Bonn, 1928).

Bougard, F., 'La Cour et le gouvernement de Louis II (840–875)', in Le Jan (ed.), *La Royauté et les élites*, pp. 249–67.

—, 'Pierre de Niviano, dit le Spoletin, sculdassius, et le gourvernement du comté de Plaisance à l'époque carolingienne', *Journal des Savants* (1996), pp. 291–337.

Bourdieu, P., *Distinction: A Social Critique of the Judgement of Taste*, trans. R. Nice (London, 1984).

—, *Outline of a Theory of Practice*, trans. R. Nice (Cambridge, 1977).

Bowes, K., 'Early Christian archaeology: a state of the field', *Religion Compass* 2/4 (2008), pp. 575–619.

Braune, W., *et al.*, *Althochdeutsches Lesebuch* (Tübingen, 1958).

Braunfels, W., *Monasteries of Western Europe. The Architecture of the Orders*, trans. A. Laing (London, 1972).

Brisbane, M., 'Hamwic (Saxon Southampton): an eighth century port and production centre', in R. Hodges and B. Hobley (eds.), *The Rebirth of Towns in the West, AD 750–1050* (London, 1988), pp. 101–8.

Brown, G., 'Introduction: the Carolingian Renaissance', in McKitterick (ed.), *Carolingian Culture*, pp. 1–51.

Brown, P., *Body and Society. Men, Women and Sexual Renunciation in Early Christianity* (New York, 1988).

—, *The End of the Ancient Other World: Death and Afterlife between Late Antiquity and the Early Middle Ages*, Tanner Lectures (New Haven, CT, 1996).

—, *The Rise of Western Christendom*, 2nd edn (Oxford, 2003).

—, 'Vers la naissance du purgatoire. Amnistie et pénitence dans le christianisme occidental de l'Antiquité tardive au Haut Moyen Âge', *Annales HSS* 6 (1997), pp. 1247–61.

Brown, W., 'On the *Gesta municipalia* and the public validation of documents in Frankish Europe', in Brown, *et al.* (eds.), *Documentary Culture*.

—, 'The idea of empire in Carolingian Bavaria', in Weiler and MacLean (eds.), *Representations of Power*, pp. 37–55.

—, 'Lay people and documents in the Frankish formula collections', in Brown, *et al.* (eds.), *Documentary Culture*.

—, *Unjust Seizure: Conflict, Interest and Authority in an Early Medieval Society* (Ithaca, NY, 2001).

Brown, W., Costambeys, M., Innes, M., and Kosto, A. (eds.), *Documentary Culture and the Laity in the Early Middle Ages* (forthcoming).

Brubaker, L., and Smith, J. M. H. (eds.), *Gender in the Early Medieval World. East and West, 300–900* (Cambridge, 2004).

Brühl, C., *Deutschland–Frankreich. Die Geburt zweier Völker*, 2nd edn (Cologne and Vienna, 1995).

Brunner, K., *Oppositionelle Gruppen im Karolingerreich* (Vienna, 1979).

Buc, P., *The Dangers of Ritual* (Princeton, NJ, 2001).

Bührer-Thierry, G., '"Just Anger" or "Vengeful Anger"? The punishment of blinding in the early medieval west', in B. Rosenwein (ed.), *Anger's Past. The Social Uses of an Emotion in the Middle Ages* (Ithaca, NY, 1998), pp. 75–91.

Bullimore, K., 'Folcwin of Rankweil: the world of a Carolingian local official', *EME* 13 (2005), pp. 43–77.

Bullough, D., *The Age of Charlemagne* (London, 1965).

—, 'Alcuin', *DNB, s.n.*

—, *Alcuin: Achievement and Reputation* (Leiden, 2003).

—, '*Aula renovata*: the Carolingian court before the Aachen palace', *PBA* 71 (1985), pp. 267–301, repr. in Bullough, *Carolingian Renewal*, pp. 123–60.

—, *Carolingian Renewal: Sources and Heritage* (Manchester 1991).

—, 'Charlemagne's men of God: Alcuin, Hildebald and Arn', in Story (ed.), *Charlemagne*, pp. 136–50.

—, 'Urban change in early medieval Italy: the example of Pavia', *PBSR* 34 (1966), pp. 82–130.

—, 'What has Ingeld to do with Lindisfarne?', *Anglo-Saxon England* 22 (1993), pp. 93–125.

Burrow, J., 'The "village community" and the uses of history in late nineteenth-century England', in N. McKendrick (ed.), *Historical Perspectives: Studies in English Thought and Society in Honour of Sir J H Plumb* (Cambridge, 1974), pp. 255–84.

Bush, M. L., *Rich Noble, Poor Noble* (Manchester, 1988).

Caciola, N., 'Wraiths, revenants and ritual in medieval culture', *P&P* 152 (1996), pp. 3–45.

Callebaut, D., 'Résidences fortifiées et centres administratifs dans la vallée de l'Escaut (ixe–xie siècle)', in D. Demolon, H. Galinié and F. Verhaeghe (eds.), *Archéologie des villes dans le Nord-Ouest de l'Europe (VIIe–VIIIe siècle)*, Actes du IVe Congrès d'Archéologie Médiévale (Douai, 1994), pp. 93–112.

Callmer, J., 'Numismatics and archaeology', *Fornvännen* 75 (1980), pp. 203–12.

Cameron, A., *The Later Roman Empire* (London, 1993).

Cammarosano, P., 'Marché de la terre et mobilité sociale dans les Abruzzes aux IXe–XIe siècles. À propos d'un livre récent', *Revue Historique* 310/2 (2008), pp. 369–82.

Carroll, C. J., 'The bishoprics of Saxony in the first century after Christianization', *EME* 8 (1999), pp. 219–45.

Carsten, J., and Hugh-Jones, S. (eds.), *About the House: Lévi-Strauss and Beyond* (Cambridge, 1995).

Carver, M., 'Pre-Viking traffic in the North Sea', in McGrail (ed.), *Maritime Celts, Frisians and Saxons*, pp. 117–25.

—, *Sutton Hoo: Burial Ground of Kings?* (Philadelphia, PA, 1998).

—, 'Transitions to Islam', in N. Christie and S. Loseby (eds.), *Towns in Transition. Urban Evolution in Late Antiquity and the Early Middle Ages* (Aldershot, 1996), pp. 184–212.

Castagnetti, A., *L'organizzazione del territorio rurale nel medioevo. Circoscrizioni ecclesiastiche e civile nella 'Langobardia' e nella 'Romania'* (Turin, 1970).

Chandler, C. J., 'Between court and counts: Carolingian Catalonia and the aprisio grant, 778–897', *EME* 11/1 (2002), pp. 19–44.

Chapelot, J., and Fossier, R., *The Village and the House in the Middle Ages* (London, 1985).

Charles-Edwards, T., 'The distinction between land and moveable wealth in Anglo-Saxon England', in P. H. Sawyer (ed.), *Medieval Settlement: Continuity and Change* (London, 1976), pp. 180–7.

—, *Early Christian Ireland* (Cambridge, 2000).

Cheyette, F. L., 'The disappearance of the ancient landscape and the climatic anomaly of the early Middle Ages: a question to be pursued', *EME* 16 (2008), pp. 127–65.

Chiesa, P. (ed.), *Paolo Diacono. Uno scrittore fra tradizione longobarda e rinnovamento carolingio* (Università di Udine, 2000).

Christie, N. (ed.), *Landscapes of Change: Rural Evolution in Late Antiquity* (Aldershot, 2004).

Clark, S., *State and Status. The Rise of the State and Aristocratic Power in Western Europe* (Toronto, 1995).

Clarke, H., and Ambrosiani, B. (eds.), *Towns in the Viking Age* (London, 1995).

Classen, P., 'Karl der Große und die Thronfolge im Frankenreich', in *Festschrift für Hermann Heimpel* (Göttingen, 1972), III, pp. 109–34.

Claude, D., 'Haus und Hof im Merowingerreich nach den erzählenden und urkundlichen Quellen', in H. Beck and H. Steuer (eds.), *Haus und Hof in ur- und frühgeschichtlichen Zeit* (Göttingen, 1997), pp. 321–34.

Claussen, M., *The Reform of the Frankish Church. Chrodegang of Metz and the Regula canonicorum in the Eighth Century* (Cambridge, 2004).

Coates-Stephens, R., 'Byzantine building patronage in post-Reconquest Rome', in M. Ghilardi, *et al.* (eds.), *Les Cités de l'Italie tardo-antique (IVe–VIe siècle)* (Rome), pp. 149–66.

—, 'Dark Age Architecture in Rome', *PBSR* 65 (1997), pp. 177–232.

Collins, R., *Charlemagne* (Basingstoke, 1998).

—, 'Charlemagne and his critics, 814–29', in Le Jan (ed.), *La Royauté et les élites*, pp. 193–211.

—, 'Charlemagne's imperial coronation and the Annals of Lorsch', in Story (ed.), *Charlemagne*, pp. 52–70.

—, 'Deception and misrepresentation in early eighth-century Frankish historiography: two case studies', in J. Jarnut, U. Nonn and M. Richter (eds.), *Karl Martell in seiner Zeit*, Beihefte der Francia 37 (Sigmaringen, 1994), pp. 227–47.

—, *Early Medieval Spain: Unity in Diversity, 400–1000* (2nd edn, Basingstoke, 1995).

—, *Fredegar*, Authors of the Middle Ages 13 (Aldershot, 1996).

—, 'Pippin I and the kingdom of Aquitaine', in Godman and Collins (eds.), *Charlemagne's Heir*, pp. 363–89.

—, 'Pippin III as mayor of the palace: the evidence', in Becher and Jarnut (eds.), *Der Dynastiewechsel von 751*, pp. 75–91.

—, 'The reviser revisited: another look at the alternative version of the *Annales regni francorum*', in A. Murray (ed.), *After Rome's Fall. Narrators and Sources of Early Medieval History* (Toronto, 1998), pp. 191–213.

—, *Visigothic Spain, 409–711* (Oxford, 2004).

Constable, G., 'The *Liber memorialis* of Remiremont', *Speculum* 48 (1972), pp. 260–77.

—, *Monastic Tithes from their Origins to the Twelfth Century* (Cambridge, MA, 1964).

—, '*Nona et decima*: an aspect of the Carolingian economy', *Speculum* 35 (1960), pp. 224–50.

Contreni, J. J., 'Dícuil', *DNB, s.n.*

Cooper, K., 'Ventriloquism and the miraculous: conversion, preaching, and the martyr exemplum in late antiquity', in K. Cooper and J. Gregory (eds.), *Signs, Wonders, Miracles. Representations of Divine Power in the Life of the Church*, Studies in Church History 41 (Woodbridge, 2005), pp. 22–45.

Corradini, R., Diesenberger, M., and Reimitz, H. (eds.), *The Construction of Communities in the Early Middle Ages* (Leiden and Boston, 2003).

Corradini, R., Meens, R., Pössel, C., and Shaw, P. (eds.), *Texts and Identities in the Early Middle Ages* (Vienna, 2006).

Costambeys, M., 'An aristocratic community on the northern Frankish frontier', *EME* 3/1 (1994), pp. 39–62.

—, 'Burial topography and the power of the Church in fifth- and sixth-century Rome', *PBSR* 69 (2001), pp. 169–89.

—, 'Disputes and courts in Lombard and Carolingian central Italy', *EME* 15 (2007), pp. 265–89.

—, 'Kinship, gender and property in Lombard Italy', in G. Ausenda, P. Delogu and C. Wickham (eds.), *The Langobards before the Frankish Conquest. An Ethnographic Perspective* (Woodbridge, 2009), pp. 69–94.

—, 'The laity, the clergy, the scribes and their archives: the documentary record of eighth- and ninth-century Italy', in Brown, *et al.* (eds.), *Documentary Culture*.

—, *Power and Patronage in Early Medieval Italy: Local Society, Italian Politics and the Abbey of Farfa, c.700–900* (Cambridge, 2007).

—, 'Property, ideology and the territorial power of the papacy in the early Middle Ages', *EME* 9 (2000), pp. 367–96.

—, 'Settlement, taxation and the condition of the peasantry in post-Roman central Italy', *Journal of Agrarian Change* 9 (2009), pp. 92–119.

—, 'Willibrord', *Oxford Dictionary of National Biography, s.n.*

Costambeys, M., and Leyser, C., 'To be the neighbour of St Stephen: patronage, martyr cult and Roman monasteries, *c.*600–900', in K. Cooper and J. Hillner (eds.), *Religion, Dynasty and Patronage in Early Christian Rome, 300–900* (Cambridge, 2007), pp. 262–87.

Coupland, S., 'Between the devil and the deep blue sea: hoards in ninth-century Frisia', in B. Cook and G. Williams (eds.), *Coinage and History in the North Sea World c.500–1250. Essays in Honour of Marion Archibald* (Leiden, 2006), pp. 241–66.

—, 'Carolingian arms and armour in the ninth century', *Viator* 29 (1990), pp. 29–50.

—, 'The Carolingian army and the struggle against the Vikings', *Viator* 35 (2004), pp. 49–70.

—, 'Carolingian coinage and Scandinavian silver', *Nordisk Numismatisk Årsskrift* (1985–86), pp. 11–32.

—, 'Charlemagne's coinage: ideology and the economy', in Story (ed.), *Charlemagne*, pp. 211–29.

—, 'The Frankish tribute payments to the Vikings and their consequences', *Francia* 26 (1999), pp. 57–75.

—, 'From poachers to gamekeepers: Scandinavian warlords and Carolingian kings', *EME* 7 (1998), pp. 85–114.

—, 'Money and coinage under Louis the Pious', *Francia* 17/1 (1990), pp. 23–54.

—, 'The rod of God's wrath or the people of God's wrath? The Carolingian theology of the Viking invasions', *Journal of Ecclesiastical History* 42 (1991), pp. 535–54.

—, 'Trading places: Quentovic and Dorestad reassessed', *EME* 11 (2002), pp. 209–32.

Crone, P., *Meccan Trade and the Rise of Islam* (Princeton, NJ, 1987).

—, *Slaves on Horses: The Evolution of the Islamic Polity* (Cambridge, 1980).

Crumlin-Pedersen, O., *From Viking Ships to Hanseatic Cogs* (London, 1983).

Curschmann, F., *Hungersnote im Mittelalter* (Leipzig, 1900).

Curta, F., *Southeastern Europe in the Middle Ages, 500–1250* (Cambridge, 2006).

Damminger, F., 'Dwellings, settlements and settlement patterns in Merovingian southwestern Germany and adjacent areas', in I. Wood (ed.), *Franks and Alamanni in the Merovingian Period* (Woodbridge, 1998), pp. 33–106.

Dannheimer, H., 'Die frühmittelalterliche Siedlung bei Kirchheim', *Germania* 51 (1973), pp. 152–69.

Davies, W., 'Local participation and legal ritual in early medieval law courts', in P. Coss (ed.), *The Moral World of the Law* (Cambridge, 2000), pp. 61–89.

—, 'On servile status in the early Middle Ages', in M. Bush (ed.), *Serfdom and Slavery* (London, 1996), pp. 225–46.

—, *Small Worlds: The Village Community in Early Medieval Brittany* (London, 1988).

Davies, W., and Fouracre, P. (eds.), *The Settlement of Disputes in Early Medieval Europe* (Cambridge, 1986).

Davis, J., *Land and Family in Pisticci* (Cambridge, 1974).

Davis, J. R., and McCormick, M., 'The early Middle Ages: Europe's long morning', in Davis and McCormick (eds.), *The Long Morning of Medieval Europe*, pp. 1–10.

Davis, J. R., and McCormick, M. (eds.), *The Long Morning of Medieval Europe. New Directions in Early Medieval Studies* (Aldershot, 2008).

Davis, R., *The Book of Pontiffs* (Liber pontificalis), rev. edn (Liverpool, 2000).

—, *The Lives of the Eighth-Century Popes* (Liber pontificalis) (Liverpool, 1992).

—, *The Lives of the Ninth-Century Popes* (Liber pontificalis) (Liverpool, 1995).

Déléage, A., *La Vie économique et sociale de la Bourgogne dans le haut moyen âge* (Mâcon, 1941).

Delogu, P., 'Reading Pirenne again', in Hodges and Bowden (eds.), *The Sixth Century*, pp. 15–40.

Depreux, P., 'Le Comte Matfrid d'Orléans (avant 815 – + 836)', *Bibliothèque de l'École des Chartes* 152 (1994), pp. 331–74.

—, 'Das Königtum Bernhards von Italien und sein Verhältnis zum Kaisertum', *QFIAB* 72 (1992), pp. 1–25.

—, 'Louis le Pieux reconsidéré? À propos des travaux récents consacrés à l'héritier de Charlemagne et à son règne', *Francia* 21 (1994), pp. 181–212.

—, 'La *Pietas* comme principe de gouvernement d'après le *Poème sur Louis le Pieux* d'Ermold le Noir', in Hill and Swan (eds.), *The Community*, pp. 201–24.

—, *Prosopographie de l'entourage de Louis le Pieux (781–840)* (Sigmaringen, 1997).

—, *Les Sociétés occidentales du milieu du VIe à la fin du IXe siècle* (Rennes, 2002).

Deshman, R., 'The exalted servant: the ruler theology of the prayerbook of Charles the Bald', *Viator* 11 (1980), pp. 385–417.

Devroey, J.-P., *Économie rurale et société dans l'Europe franque (VI–IX siècles)* (Paris, 2003).

—, *Études sur le grand domaine carolingien* (Aldershot, 1993).

—, 'Un monastère dans l'économie d'échanges: les services de transport à l'abbaye de St-Germain-des-Prés au IXe siècle', *Annales ESC* 39 (1984), pp. 570–89, repr. in Devroey, *Études sur le grand domaine carolingien*.

—, *Puissants et misérables: Système social et monde paysan dans l'Europe des Francs (VI–IX siècles)* (Brussels, 2006).

—, 'Les Services de transport à l'abbaye de Prüm au IXe siècle', *Revue du Nord* 61 (1979), pp. 543–69, repr. in Devroey, *Études sur le grand domaine carolingien*.

Diebold, W., '*Nos quoque morem illius imitari cupientes*. Charles the Bald's evocation and imitation of Charlemagne', *Archiv für Kulturgeschichte* 75 (1993), pp. 271–300.

Dierkens, A., 'Autour de la tombe de Charlemagne: considérations sur les sépultures et les funérailles des souverains carolingiens et des membres de leur famille', *Byzantion* 61 (1991), pp. 156–80.

Doll, A., 'Das Pirminskloster Hornbach. Gründung und Verfassungs-entwicklung bis Anfang des 12. Jahrhunderts', *Archiv für mittelrheinische Kirchengeschichte* 5 (1953), pp. 108–42.

Dopsch, A., *Wirtschaftliche und soziale Grundlagen der europäischen Kultur-entwicklung aus der Zeit von Cäsar bis auf Karl den Großen* (Vienna, 1918–20); 2nd edn (Vienna, 1923–4), trans. M. G. Beard and N. Marshall, *Economic and Social Foundations of European Civilisation* (New York and London, 1937).

Duby, G., *Guerriers et paysans, VII–XIIe siècle: premier essor de l'économie européenne* (Paris, 1973), trans. H. B. Clarke, *The Early Growth of the European Economy: Warriors and Peasants from the Seventh to the Twelfth Century* (Ithaca, NY, and London, 1974).

—, *Rural Economy and Country Life in the Medieval West* (Los Angeles, CA, 1968).

—, *The Three Orders: Feudal Society Imagined* (Chicago, 1982).

Durliat, J., *Les Finances publiques de Dioclétien aux Carolingiens (284–889)*. Beihefte der Francia 21 (Sigmaringen, 1990).

Dutton, P. E., *Charlemagne's Mustache and Other Cultural Clusters of a Dark Age* (New York, 2004).

—, 'Observations on early medieval weather in general, bloody rain in particular', in Davis and McCormick (eds.), *The Long Morning of Medieval Europe*, pp. 167–80.

—, *The Politics of Dreaming in the Carolingian Empire* (Lincoln, NE, 1994).

Dutton, P. E. (ed.), *Carolingian Civilization: a Reader*, 2nd edn (Peterborough, ON, 2004).

—, *Charlemagne's Courtier. The Complete Einhard* (Peterborough, ON, 1998).

Dutton, P., and Kessler, H. L., *The Poetry and Painting of the First Bible of Charles the Bald* (Ann Arbor, MI, 1997).

Edwards, C., 'German vernacular literature: a survey', in McKitterick (ed.), *Carolingian Culture*, pp. 141–70.

Effros, B., *Merovingian Mortuary Archaeology and the Making of the Early Middle Ages* (Berkeley and London, 2003).

Ellmers, D., 'The Frisian monopoly of coastal transport in the 6th to 8th centuries AD', in McGrail (ed.), *Maritime Celts, Frisians and Saxons*, pp. 91–2.

Endemann, T., *Markturkunde und Markt in Frankreich und Burgund vom 9. bis 11. Jahrhundert* (Constance, 1964).

Enright, M. J., *Iona, Tara, and Soissons: the Origin of the Royal Anointing Ritual* (Berlin and New York, 1985).

Erhart, P., and Kleindienst, J. (eds.), *Urkundenlandschaft Rätiens* (Vienna, 2004).

Erkens, F.-R., '*Divisio legitima* und *unitas imperii*: Teilungspraxis und Einheitsstreben bei der Thronfolge im Frankenreich', *DA* 52 (1996), pp. 423–85.

Es, W. van, 'Dorestad centred', in J. C. Besteman, J. M. Bos and H. A. Heidinga (eds.), *Medieval Archaeology in the Netherlands. Studies Presented to H. H. von Regteren Altena* (Assen and Maastricht, 1990), pp. 151–82.

Es, W. van, and Verwers, W., *Excavations at Dorestad I. The Harbour, Hoogstraat I* (Amersfoort, 1980).

Esmonde Cleary, A. S., *The Ending of Roman Britain* (London, 1989).

Everett, N., *Literacy in Lombard Italy, c.568–774* (Cambridge, 2003).

Ewig, E., 'Studien zur merowingischen Dynastie', *Frühmittelalterliche Studien* 8 (1974), pp. 15–59.

Faith, R., 'Forces and relations of production in early medieval England', *Journal of Agrarian Change* 9 (2009), pp. 23–41.

Falck, L., *Mainz im frühen und hohen Mittelalter (Mitte 5. Jht. bis 1244)* (Düsseldorf, 1972).

Fanning, S., 'Imperial diplomacy between Francia and Byzantium: the letter of Louis II to Basil I in 871', *Cithara* 34 (1994), pp. 3–15.

Fasoli, G., *I Re d'Italia (888–962)* (Florence, 1949).

Fehring, G. P., *The Archaeology of Medieval Germany: an Introduction*, trans. R. Samson (London, 1991).

—, *Die Stadtkirche St. Dionysius in Esslingen a.N.: Archäologie und Baugeschichte* (Stuttgart, 1995).

Fell, C., '*Unfriþ*: an approach to a definition', *Saga-Book of the Viking Society for Northern Research* 21 (1982–3), pp. 85–100.

Feller, L., *Les Abruzzes médiévales. Territoire, économie et société en Italie centrale du IXe au XIIe siècle*. Bibliothèque des Écoles Françaises d'Athènes et de Rome 300 (Rome, 1998).

Feller, L., Gramain, A., and Weber, F., *La Fortune de Karol. Marché de la terre et liens personnels dans les Abruzzes au haut moyen âge*, Collection de l'EFR 347 (Rome, 2005).

Ferry, J., and Costambeys, M., *Historians of Ninth-Century Italy* (Liverpool, forthcoming).

Fichtenau, H., *Living in the Tenth Century* (Chicago, 1991).

Fischer-Drew, K., *The Laws of the Salian Franks* (Philadelphia, PA, 1991).

—, *The Lombard Laws* (Philadelphia, PA, 1973).

Fleming, R., 'Lords and labour', in W. Davies (ed.), *From the Vikings to the Normans* (Oxford, 2003), pp. 107–37.

Fletcher, R., *The Conversion of Europe: From Paganism to Christianity, 371–1386* (London, 1997).

Flint, V., *The Rise of Magic in Early Medieval Europe* (Oxford, 1991).

Folz, R., *The Coronation of Charlemagne, 25 December 800* (London, 1974).

Fossier, R., *Enfance de l'Europe*, 2 vols. (Paris, 1982).

—, 'Les Tendances de l'économie: stagnation ou croissance?', *Settimane di Studio del Centro italiano di studi sull'alto medioevo* 27 (Spoleto, 1981), pp. 261–74.

Fouracre, P., *The Age of Charles Martel* (Harlow, 2000).

—, 'Carolingian justice: the rhetoric of improvement and contexts of abuse', *Settimane di Studio del Centro italiano di studi sull'alto medioevo* 42 (Spoleto, 1995), pp. 771–803.

—, 'Conflict, power and legitimation in Francia in the late seventh and early eighth centuries', in I. Alfonso, H. Kennedy and J. Escalona (eds.), *Building Legitimacy: Political Discourses and Forms of Legitimacy in Medieval Societies*, The Medieval Mediterranean: Peoples, Economies and Cultures 400–1500 53 (Leiden, 2004), pp. 3–26.

—, 'The context of the OHG *Ludwigslied*', *Medium Aevum* 54 (1985), pp. 97–103.

—, 'Cultural conformity and social conservatism in early medieval Europe', *History Workshop Journal* 33 (1992), pp. 152–61.

—, 'Eternal light and earthly needs: practical aspects of the development of Frankish immunities', in W. Davies and P. Fouracre (eds.), *Property and Power in the Early Middle Ages* (Cambridge, 1995), pp. 53–81.

—, 'The long shadow of the Merovingians', in Story (ed.), *Charlemagne*, pp. 5–21.

—, 'Marmoutier and its serfs in the eleventh century', *TRHS* 15 (2005), pp. 29–49.

—, 'Merovingian history and Merovingian hagiography', *P&P* 127 (1990), pp. 3–38.

—, 'The origins of the Carolingian attempt to regulate the cult of saints', in J. Howard-Johnston and P. A. Hayward (eds.), *The Cult of Saints in Late Antiquity and the Middle Ages. Essays on the Contribution of Peter Brown* (Oxford, 1999), pp. 143–66.

—, 'Space, culture and kingdoms in early medieval Europe', in Linehan and Nelson (eds.), *The Medieval World*, pp. 366–80.

—, 'The work of Audoenus of Rouen and Eligius of Noyon in extending episcopal influence from the town to the country in seventh-century Neustria', *Studies in Church History* 16 (1979), pp. 77–91.

Fouracre, P., and Gerberding, R., *Late Merovingian France: History and Hagiography, 640–720* (Manchester and New York, 1996).

France, J., 'The composition and raising of the armies of Charlemagne', *Journal of Medieval Military History* 1 (2002), pp. 61–82.

Francovich, R., 'The beginnings of hilltop villages in early medieval Tuscany', in Davis and McCormick (eds.), *The Long Morning of Medieval Europe*, pp. 55–82.

—, 'Changing structures of settlement', in C. La Rocca (ed.), *Italy in the Early Middle Ages* (Oxford, 2002), pp. 144–67.

Francovich, R., and Hodges, R., *Villa to Village* (London, 2003).

Freedman, P., *The Origins of Peasant Servitude in Medieval Catalonia* (Cambridge, 1991).

Fried, J., 'Elite und Ideologie, oder die Nachfolgeordnung Karls des Großen vom Jahre 813', in Le Jan (ed.), *La Royauté et les élites*, pp. 71–109.

—, 'Der karolingische Herrschaftsverband im 9. Jahrhundert zwischen "Kirche" und "Königshaus"', *HZ* 235 (1982), pp. 1–43.

—, *König Ludwig der Jüngere in seiner Zeit* (Lorsch, 1984).

—, 'Papst Leo III. besucht Karl den Großen in Paderborn oder Einhards Schweigen', *HZ* 272 (2001), pp. 281–326.

Gabriele, M., and Stuckey, J. (eds.), *The Legend of Charlemagne in the Middle Ages. Power, Faith and Crusade* (New York, 2008).

Gaffney, V., Patterson, H., and Roberts, P., 'Forum novum (Vescovio): a new study of the town and bishopric', in H. Patterson (ed.), *Bridging the Tiber: Approaches to Regional Archaeology in the Middle Tiber Valley* (London, 2004), pp. 237–48.

Ganshof, F. L., *The Carolingians and the Frankish Monarchy* (London, 1971).

—, 'Charlemagne's failure', in Ganshof, *The Carolingians and the Frankish Monarchy*, pp. 256–60.

—, 'Charlemagne's programme of imperial government', in Ganshof, *The Carolingians and the Frankish Monarchy*, pp. 55–85.

—, *Frankish Institutions under Charlemagne* (Providence, RI, 1968).

—, 'The last period of Charlemagne's reign: a study in decomposition', in Ganshof, *The Carolingians and the Frankish Monarchy*, pp. 240–55.

—, 'Louis the Pious reconsidered', in Ganshof, *The Carolingians and the Frankish Monarchy*, pp. 261–72.

—, 'Note sur la concession d'alleux à des vassaux sous le règne de Louis le Pieux', in *Storiografia e Storia: Studi in onore di E. Dupré Theseider* (Rome, 1974), pp. 589–99.

Ganz, D., 'Book production in the Carolingian empire and the spread of Carolingian minuscule', in *NCMH* II, pp. 786–808.

—, 'Charlemagne in Hell', *Florilegium* 17 (2002 for 2000), pp. 175–94.

—, 'Dúngal', *DNB*, *s.n.*

—, *Einhard* (forthcoming).

—, 'Einhard's Charlemagne: the characterization of greatness', in Story (ed.), *Charlemagne*, pp. 38–51.

—, 'The *Epitaphium Arsenii* and opposition to Louis the Pious', in Godman and Collins (eds.), *Charlemagne's Heir*, pp. 537–50.

—, 'Theology and the organisation of thought', in *NCMH* II (Cambridge, 1995), pp. 758–85.

—, *Two Lives of Charlemagne* (Harmondsworth, 2008).

Ganz, D., and Goffart, W., 'Charters earlier than 800 from French collections', *Speculum* 65 (1990), pp. 906–32.

Garipzanov, I. H., 'The Carolingian abbreviation of Bede's World Chronicle and Carolingian imperial "genealogy"', *Hortus Artium Medievalium* (2005), pp. 291–7.

—, 'Communication of authority in Carolingian titles', *Viator* 36 (2005), pp. 41–82.

—, 'Frontier identities: Carolingian frontier and *gens Danorum*', in I. H. Garipzanov, P. J. Geary and P. Urbanczyk (eds.), *Franks, Northmen, and Slavs: Identities and State Formation in Early Medieval Europe* (Turnhout, 2008), pp. 113–42.

—, *The Symbolic Language of Authority in the Carolingian World, c.751–877* (Leiden and Boston, 2008).

Garnsey, P., *Ideas of Slavery from Aristotle to Augustine* (Cambridge, 1996).

—, *Social Status and Legal Privilege in the Roman Empire* (Oxford, 1970).

Garrison, M., 'The emergence of Carolingian Latin literature and the court of Charlemagne (780–814)', in McKitterick (ed.), *Carolingian Culture*, pp. 111–40.

—, 'The Franks as the new Israel? Education for an identity from Pippin to Charlemagne', in Hen and Innes (eds.), *Uses of the Past*, pp. 114–61.

—, 'Fridugisus', *DNB*, *s.n.*

—, 'Joseph Scottus', *DNB*, *s.n.*

—, 'Quid Hinieldus cum Christo?', in K. O'Brien O'Keefe and A. Orchard (eds.), *Latin Learning and English Lore: Studies in Anglo-Saxon Literature for Michael Lapidge*, 2 vols. (Toronto, 2005), I, pp. 237–59.

Gasparri, S., 'The aristocracy', in La Rocca (ed.), *Italy in the Early Middle Ages* (Oxford, 2002), pp. 59–84.

—, 'Mercanti o possessori? Profilo di un ceto dominante in un'età di transizione', in Gasparri and La Rocca (eds.), *Carte di famiglia*, pp. 157–78.

—, 'Roma e i longobardi', in *Roma nell'alto medioevo*, Settimane di Studio del Centro italiano di studi sull'alto medioevo 48 (Spoleto, 2001), pp. 219–47.

—, 'Strutture militari e legami di dipendenza in Italia in età longobarda e carolingia', *Rivista storica italiana* 98 (1986), pp. 664–726.

Gasparri, S., and La Rocca, C. (eds.), *Carte di famiglia. Strategie, rappresentazione e memoria del gruppo familiare di Totone di Campione, 721–877* (Rome, 2005).

Geary, P., *Aristocracy in Provence. The Rhône Basin at the Dawn of the Carolingian Age* (Stuttgart, 1985).

—, 'Exchange and interaction between the living and the dead in early medieval society', in Geary, *Living with the Dead in the Early Middle Ages* (Ithaca, NY, and London, 1994), pp. 77–94.

—, 'Germanic tradition and royal ideology in the ninth century: the *visio Karoli Magni*', *Frühmittelalterliche Studien* 21 (1987), pp. 274–94, repr. in Geary, *Living with the Dead in the Early Middle Ages* (Ithaca, NY, and London, 1994), pp. 49–76.

—, *The Myth of Nations* (Princeton, NJ, 2002).

—, *Phantoms of Remembrance: Memory and Oblivion at the End of the First Millennium* (Princeton, NJ, 1994).

Geiselhart, M., *Die Kapitulariengesetzgebung Lothars I. in Italien* (Frankfurt, 2002).

Gelichi, S., 'The rise of an early medieval emporium and the economy of Italy in the late Longobard age', in *Annales. Series Historia et Sociologia* 18/2 (2008), pp. 319–36.

Gerberding, R., *The Rise of the Carolingians and the* Liber historiae francorum (Oxford, 1987).

Geuenich, D., 'A survey of the early medieval confraternity books from the continent', in D. Rollason (ed.), *The Durham* Liber Vitae *and its Context* (Woodbridge, 2004), pp. 141–7.

Gilles, S., 'Territorial interpolations in the Old English Orosius', in S. Gilles and S. Tomasch (eds.), *Text and Territory: Geographical Imagination in the Middle Ages* (Philadelphia, PA, 1998).

Gillett, A. (ed.), *On Barbarian Identity: Critical Approaches to Ethnicity in the Early Middle Ages* (Turnhout, 2002).

Gladiß, D., 'Die Schenkungen der deutschen Könige zu privaten Eigen (800–1137), *DA* 1 (1937), pp. 80–136.

Gobry, I., *Histoire des rois de France: Louis Ier, Premier successeur de Charlemagne* (Paris, 2002).

Gockel, M., *Karolingische Königshöfe am Mittelrhein* (Göttingen, 1970).

Godden, M., 'The Anglo-Saxons and the Goths: rewriting the sack of Rome', *Anglo-Saxon England* 31 (2002), pp. 47–68.

Godman, P., *Poetry of the Carolingian Renaissance* (London, 1985).

—, *Poets and emperors: Frankish Politics and Carolingian Poetry* (Oxford, 1987).

Godman, P., and Collins, R. (eds.), *Charlemagne's Heir: New Perspectives on the Reign of Louis the Pious* (Oxford, 1990).

Godman, P., Jarnut, J., and Johanek, P. (eds.), *Am Vorabend der Kaiserkrönung: das Epos "Karolus Magnus et Leo papa" und der Papstbesuch in Paderborn 799* (Berlin, 2002).

Goetz, H.-W., '"Nobilis". Der Adel im Selbstverständnis der Karolingerzeit', *Vierteljahresschrift für Sozial- und Wirtschaftsgeschichte* 70 (1983), pp. 153–91.

—, '*Regnum*: zum politischen Denken der Karolingerzeit', *Zeitschrift der Savigny-Stiftung für Rechtsgeschichte, Germanistische Abteilung* 104 (1987), pp. 110–89.

—, 'Serfdom and the beginnings of a "seigneurial system" in Carolingian Europe', *EME* 2 (1993), pp. 29–51.

—, 'Social and military institutions', in *NCMH* II, pp. 451–80.

—, 'Die Wahrnehmung von "Staat" und "Herrschaft" im frühen Mittelalter', in Airlie, Pohl and Reimitz (eds.), *Staat im frühen Mittelalter*, pp. 39–58.

Goffart, W., 'The Fredegar problem reconsidered', *Speculum* 38 (1963), pp. 206–41.

—, 'Merovingian polyptychs: reflections on two recent publications', *Francia* 9 (1982), pp. 55–77; repr. in Goffart, *Rome's Fall and After* (London, 1989), pp. 233–53.

—, 'Old and new in Merovingian taxation', in Goffart, *Rome's Fall and After* (London, 1989), pp. 213–31.

—, 'Paul the Deacon's *Gesta episcoporum Mettensium* and the early design for Charlemagne's succession', *Traditio* 42 (1986), pp. 53–87.

Goldberg, E. J., 'Ludwig der Deutsche und Mähren: Eine Studie zu karolingischen Grenzkriegen im Osten', in W. Hartmann (ed.), *Ludwig der Deutsche und seine Zeit* (Darmstadt, 2004), pp. 67–94.

—, '"More devoted to the equipment of battle than the splendor of banquets": frontier kingship, martial ritual, and early knighthood at the court of Louis the German', *Viator* 30 (1999), pp. 41–78.

—, 'Popular revolt, dynastic politics and aristocratic factionalism in the early middle ages: the Saxon Stellinga reconsidered', *Speculum* 70 (1995), pp. 467–501.

—, *Struggle for Empire. Kingship and Conflict under Louis the German, 817–876* (Ithaca, NY, and London, 2006).

Goodson, C., *The Rome of Pope Paschal I. Papal Power, Urban Renovation, Church Rebuilding and Relic Translation, 817–824* (Cambridge, 2010).

Gorman, M., 'The commentary on Genesis of Claudius of Turin and Biblical studies under Louis the Pious', *Speculum* 72 (1997), pp. 279–329.

Grant, L., *Abbot Suger of St-Denis: Church and State in Early Twelfth-Century France* (London, 1998).

Green, D. H., and Siegmund, F. (eds.), *The Continental Saxons from the Migration Period to the Tenth Century: an Ethnographic Perspective* (Woodbridge, 2003).

Grierson, P., 'Commerce in the dark ages: a critique of the evidence', *TRHS* 9 (1959), pp. 123–40.

—, 'The volume of the Anglo-Saxon coinage', *Economic Historic Review* 20 (1967), pp. 153–60.

Griffiths, D., Philpott, R., and Egan, G. (eds.), *Meols. The Archaeology of the North Wirral Coast* (Oxford, 2007).

Guichard, P., 'Les Débuts de la piraterie andalouse en Méditerranée occidentale (798–813)', *Revue de l'Occident musulman* 35 (1983), pp. 55–76.

Guillot, O., 'Une "ordinatio" méconnue. Le Capitulaire de 823–825', in Godman and Collins (eds.), *Charlemagne's Heir*, pp. 455–86.

Haldon, J., and Brubaker, L., *Byzantium in the Iconoclast Era, c.680–850* (Cambridge, 2010).

Halphen, L., *Charlemagne et l'empire carolingien* (Paris, 1947), trans. G. de Nie, *Charlemagne and the Carolingian Empire* (Amsterdam, 1977).

Halsall, G., *Barbarian Migrations and the Roman West, 376–568* (Cambridge, 2007).

—, 'Burial ritual and Merovingian society', in Hill and Swan (eds.), *The Community*, pp. 325–38.

—, 'Female status and power in early Merovingian central Austrasia: the burial evidence', *Early Medieval Europe* 5/1 (1996), pp. 1–24.

—, *Settlement and Social Organisation: the Merovingian Region of Metz* (Cambridge, 1995).

—, *Warfare and Society in the Barbarian West* (London and New York, 2003).

Halsall, G. (ed.), *Humour, History and Politics in Late Antiquity and the Early Middle Ages* (Cambridge, 2002).

Hamerow, H., *Early Medieval Settlements: the Archaeology of Rural Communities in North-West Europe, 400–900* (Oxford, 2002).

Hamilton, S., 'Early medieval rulers and their modern biographers', *EME* 9 (2000), pp. 247–60.

—, 'The unique favour of penance: the Church and the people c.800–c.1100', in Linehan and Nelson (eds.), *The Medieval World*, pp. 229–45.

Hammer, C. I., *From Ducatus to Regnum: Ruling Bavaria under the Merovingians and Early Carolingians* (Turnhout, 2007).

Handley, M. A., *Death, Society and Culture: Inscriptions and Epitaphs in Gaul and Spain, AD 300–750* (Oxford, 2003).

Hannig, J., 'Zentralle Kontrolle und regionale Machtbalance. Beobachtungen zum System der karolingischen Königsboten am Beispiel des Mittelrheingebietes', *Archiv für Kulturgeschichte* 66 (1984), pp. 1–46.

—, 'Zur Funktion der karolingischen *missi dominici* in Bayern und in den südöstlichen Grenzgebieten', *Zeitschrift der Savigny-Stiftung für Rechtsgeschichte, Germanistische Abteilung* 101 (1984), pp. 256–300.

Hansen, H. J., 'Danekirke: affluence in late Iron Age Denmark', in K. Randsborg (ed.), *The Birth of Europe. Archaeology and Social Development in the First Millennium AD* (Rome, 1989), pp. 123–8.

Hansen, I. L., and C. J. Wickham (eds.), *The Long Eighth Century. Production, Distribution and Demand* (Leiden, 2000).

Hardt, M., *Gold und Herrschaft: die Schätze europäischer Könige und Fürsten im ersten Jahrtausend* (Berlin, 2004).

—, 'Royal treasures and representation in the early Middle Ages', in W. Pohl and H. Reimitz (eds.), *Strategies of Distinction. The Construction of Ethnic Communities, 300–800* (Leiden, 1998), pp. 255–80.

Hardt-Friedrichs, F., 'Markt, Münze und Zoll im ostfränkischen Reich bis zum Ende der Ottonen', *Blätter für deutsche Landesgeschichte* 116 (1980), pp. 1–32.

Hartmann, L., *Zur Wirtschaftsgeschichte Italiens im frühen Mittelalter* (Gotha, 1904).

Hartmann, W., *Ludwig der Deutsche* (Darmstadt, 2002).

Heather, P., 'Frankish imperialism and Slavic society', in P. Urbańczyk (ed.), *The Origins of Central Europe* (Warsaw, 1997), pp. 171–90.

—, 'State formation in Europe in the first millennium AD', in B. Crawford (ed.), *Scotland in Dark Age Europe* (St Andrews, 1994), pp. 47–63.

Heather, P., and Matthews, J., *The Goths in the Fourth Century* (Liverpool, 1991).

Heidinga, H. A., *Medieval Settlement and Economy North of the Lower Rhine* (Assen, 1987).

Heinzelman, M., 'Villa d'après l'oeuvre de Grégoire de Tours', in E. Magnou-Nortier (ed.), *Aux sources de la gestion publique* I: *Enquête lexicographique sur fundus, villa, domus, mansus* (Lille, 1993), pp. 45–70.

Hellmann, S., 'Die Heiraten der Karolinger', in S. Hellmann, *Ausgewählte Abhandlungen zur Historiographie und Geistesgeschichte des Mittelalters*, ed. by H. Beumann (Darmstadt, 1961), pp. 293–391.

Hemming, J., 'Strong rulers – weak economy? Rome, the Carolingians, and the archaeology of slavery in the first millennium AD', in Davis and McCormick, *The Long Morning of Medieval Europe*, pp. 33–54.

Hen, Y., 'The Annals of Metz and the Merovingian past', in Hen and Innes (eds.), *Uses of the Past*, pp. 175–90.

—, 'The Christianisation of kingship', in Becher and Jarnut (eds.), *Der Dynastiewechsel von 751*, pp. 163–77.

—, *Culture and Religion in Merovingian Gaul* (Leiden, 1995).

—, 'Knowledge of canon law among rural priests', *Journal of Theological Studies* 50 (1999), pp. 117–34.

—, *The Royal Patronage of Liturgy in Frankish Gaul to the Death of Charles the Bald (877)*, Henry Bradshaw Society Subsidia 3 (London, 2001).

—, 'The structure and aims of the *Visio Baronti*', *Journal of Theological Studies*, n.s. 47 (1996), pp. 477–97.

Hen, Y., and Innes, M. (eds.), *The Uses of the Past in the Early Middle Ages* (Cambridge, 2000).

Hennebicque, R., '"Pauperes" et "paupertas" dans l'occident carolingien aux IXe et Xe siècles', *Revue du Nord* 50 (1968), pp. 167–87.

Hennebicque-Le Jan, R., 'Prosopographica neustrica. Les Agents du roi en Neustrie de 639 à 840', in H. Atsma (ed.), *La Neustrie: les pays au nord de la Loire de 650 à 850*, Beihefte der Francia, 16, 2 vols. (Sigmaringen, 1989), I, pp. 231–69.

Herlihy, D., 'The Carolingian mansus', *EHR* 13 (1960), pp. 69–79.

—, 'Church property on the European continent, 701–1200', *Speculum* 36 (1961), pp. 81–105.

—, *A History of Feudalism* (London, 1970).

—, *Medieval Households* (London, 1985).

Herren, M., 'The *De imagine Tetrici* of Walafrid Strabo: edition and translation', *The Journal of Medieval Latin* 1 (1991), pp. 118–39.

—, 'Walafrid Strabo's *De imagine Tetrici*: an interpretation', in R. North and T. Hofstra (eds.), *Latin Culture and Medieval Germanic Europe* (Groningen, 1992), pp. 25–41.

Herrin, J., *The Formation of Christendom* (Oxford, 1987).

Hess, W., 'Geldwirtschaft am Mittelrhein in karolingischer Zeit', *Blätter für deutsche Landesgeschichte* 98 (1962), pp. 26–63.

Hill, D., *et al.*, 'Quentovic defined', *Antiquity* 61 (1990), pp. 51–8.

Hill, D., and Cowie, R. (eds.), *Wics: The Early Medieval Trading Centres of Northern Europe* (Sheffield, 2001).

Hill, J., and Swan, M. (eds.), *The Community, the Family and the Saint: Patterns of Power in Early Medieval Europe: Selected Proceedings of the International Medieval Congress, University of Leeds, 4–7 July 1994, 10–13 July 1995* (Turnhout, 1998).

Hillgarth, J., *Christianity and Paganism, 350–750. The Conversion of Western Europe* (Philadelphia, PA, 1986).

Hlawitschka, E., *Franken, Alemannen, Bayern und Burgunder in Oberitalien (774–962). Zum Verständnis der fränkischen Königsherrschaft in Italien* (Freiburg, 1960).

Hodges, R., *Dark Age Economics: The Rebirth of Towns and Trade, 600–1000* (London, 1982).

—, *Light in the Dark Ages: The Rise and Fall of San Vincenzo al Volturno* (London, 1997).

—, *San Vincenzo al Volturno 1. The Excavations 1980–1986, part 1* (London, 1993).

—, *San Vincenzo al Volturno 2. The Excavations 1980–1986, part 2* (London, 1995).

—, *Towns and Trade in the Age of Charlemagne* (London, 2000).

—, 'Trade and market origins in the ninth century: an archaeological perspective on Anglo-Carolingian relations', in M. Gibson and J. Nelson (eds.), *Charles the Bald: Court and Kingdom* (2nd edn, 1990), pp. 213–33.

Hodges, R., and Bowden, W. (eds.), *The Sixth Century. Production, Distribution and Demand* (Leiden, 1998).

Hodges, R., and Whitehouse, D., *Mohammed, Charlemagne and the Origins of Europe* (London, 1983).

Horden, P., and Purcell, N., *The Corrupting Sea: A Study of Mediterranean History* 1 (Oxford, 1999).

Huggett, J. W., 'Imported grave goods and the early Anglo-Saxon economy', *Medieval Archaeology* 32 (1988), pp. 63–96.

Humfress, C., 'Poverty and Roman law', in R. Osborne and M. Atkins (eds.), *Poverty in the Roman World* (Cambridge, 2006), pp. 183–203.

Hummer, H., *Politics and Power in Early Medieval Europe: Alsace and the Frankish Realm, 600–1000* (Cambridge, 2005).

—, 'The production and preservation of documents in Francia: the evidence of cartularies', in Brown, *et al.* (eds.), *Documentary Culture.*

—, 'Reform and lordship in Alsace at the turn of the millennium', in W. C. Brown and P. Górecki (eds.), *Conflict in Medieval Europe: Changing Perspectives on Society and Culture* (Aldershot, 2003), pp. 69–84.

Humphreys, S. C., 'History, economics, and anthropology: the work of Karl Polanyi', *History and Theory* 8 (1969), pp. 165–212.

Hvass, S., 'Rural settlements in Denmark in the first millennium AD', in K. Randsborg (ed.), *The Birth of Europe* (Rome, 1989), pp. 91–9.

Innes, M., 'Charlemagne's government', in Story (ed.), *Charlemagne*, pp. 71–89.

—, 'Charlemagne's will: piety, politics and the imperial succession', *EHR* 112 (1997), pp. 833–55.

—, 'Danelaw identities: ethnicity, regionalism and political allegiance', in D. M. Hadley and J. D. Richards (eds.), *Cultures in Contact: Scandinavian Settlement in England in the Ninth and Tenth Centuries* (Turnhout, 2000), pp. 65–88.

—, 'Dossiers and archives: documents, landowners and power in Frankish society', in Brown, *et al.* (eds.), *Documentary Culture.*

—, 'Economies and societies in the early medieval west', in E. English and C. Lansing (eds.), *Companion to the Middle Ages* (Oxford, 2009), pp. 9–37.

—, 'Framing the Carolingian economy', *Journal of Agrarian Change* 9 (2009), pp. 42–58.

—, 'Franks and Slavs, 700–1000: European expansion before the millennium', *EME* 6 (1997), pp. 201–14.

—, '"He never even allowed his white teeth to be bared in laughter": the politics of humour in the Carolingian renaissance', in Halsall (ed.), *Humour, History and Politics*, pp. 131–56.

—, *Introduction to Early Medieval Western Europe, 300–900. The Sword, the Plough and the Book* (London and New York, 2007).

—, 'Keeping it in the family: women and aristocratic memory *c.*700–1200', in E. van Houts (ed.), *Medieval Memories: Men, Women and the Past 700–1300* (London, 2001), pp. 17–35.

—, 'Kings, monks and patrons: political identities and the abbey of Lorsch', in Le Jan (ed.), *La Royauté et les élites*, pp. 301–24.

—, 'Land, freedom and the making of the early medieval west', *TRHS* 16 (2006), pp. 39–73.

—, 'On the material culture of legal documents: charters and their preservation in the Cluny archive (9th–11th centuries)', in Brown, *et al.* (eds.), *Documentary Culture.*

—, 'Memory, orality and literacy in an early medieval society', *P&P* 158 (1998), pp. 3–36.

—, 'People, places and power in the Carolingian world: a microcosm', in de Jong and Theuws with van Rhijn (eds.), *Topographies of Power*, pp. 397–437.

—, '"A place of discipline": Carolingian courts and aristocratic youth', in C. Cubitt (ed.), *Court Culture in the Early Middle Ages* (Turnhout, 2003), pp. 59–76.

—, 'Practices of property in the Carolingian empire', in Davis and McCormick (eds.), *The Long Morning of Medieval Europe*, pp. 246–66.

—, 'Property, politics and the problem of the Carolingian state', in W. Pohl and V. Wieser (eds.), *Staat im frühen Mittelalter* (Vienna, 2009), pp. 299–313.

—, *State and Society in the Early Middle Ages: The Middle Rhine Valley, 400–1000* (Cambridge, 2000).

—, 'Teutons or Trojans? The Carolingians and the Germanic past', in Hen and Innes (eds.), *Uses of the Past*, pp. 227–49.

Innes, M., and McKitterick, R., 'The writing of history', in McKitterick (ed.), *Carolingian Culture*, pp. 193–220.

Iogna-Prat, D., 'Le "Baptême" du schéma des trois ordres fonctionnels: l'apport de l'école d'Auxerre dans la seconde moitié du ixe siècle', *Annales ESC* 41/1 (1986), pp. 101–26.

—, 'The dead in the celestial bookkeeping of the Cluniac monks', in Little and Rosenwein (eds.), *Debating the Middle Ages*, pp. 340–62.

Jacobsen, W., 'Die Lorscher Torhalle. Zum Problem ihrer Deutung und Datierung', *Jahrbuch des Zentralinstituts für Kunstgeschichte* 1 (1985), pp. 9–77.

James, E., *The Merovingian Archaeology of South-West Gaul*. BAR supplementary series 25 (Oxford, 1977).

Jankuhn, H., *et al.* (eds.), *Das Dorf der Eisenzeit und des frühen Mittelalters* (Göttingen, 1977).

Janssen, W., 'Dorf und Dorfformen des 7.-12. Jhts. im Lichte neuer Ausgrabungen in Mittel- und Nordeuropa', in Jankuhn, *et al.* (eds.), *Das Dorf der Eisenzeit*, pp. 285–356.

Jarnut, J., 'Die Adoption Pippins durch König Liutprand', in J. Jarnut, U. Nonn and M. Richter (eds.), *Karl Martell in seiner Zeit* (Sigmaringen, 1994), pp. 217–26.

—, 'Ein Bruderkampf und seine Folgen: die Krise des Frankenreiches (768–771)', in G. Jenal and S. Haarländer (eds.), *Herrschaft, Kirche, Kultur: Beiträge zur Geschichte des Mittelalters. Festschrift für Friedrich Prinz zu seinem 65. Geburtstag* (Stuttgart, 1993), pp. 165–76.

—, 'Ludwig der Fromme, Lothar I und das Regnum Italiae', in Godman and Collins (eds.), *Charlemagne's Heir*, pp. 349–62.

—, 'Untersuchungen zur Herkunft Swanahilds, der Gattin Karl Martells', *Zeitschrift für bayerische Landesgeschichte* 40 (1977), pp. 254–9.

Jong, M. de, 'Brideshows revisited: praise, slander and exegesis in the reign of the empress Judith', in Brubaker and Smith (eds.), *Gender in the Early Medieval World*, pp. 257–77.

—, 'Carolingian monasticism: the power of prayer', in *NCMH* II, pp. 622–53.

—, 'Charlemagne's balcony: the solarium in ninth-century narratives', in Davis and McCormick (eds.), *The Long Morning of Medieval Europe*, pp. 277–90.

—, 'Charlemagne's Church', in Story (ed.), *Charlemagne*, pp. 103–35.

—, '*Ecclesia* and the early medieval polity', in Airlie, Pohl and Reimitz (eds.), *Staat im Frühmittelalter*, pp. 113–32.

—, 'The empire as *ecclesia*: Hrabanus Maurus and biblical *historia* for rulers', in Hen and Innes (eds.), *Uses of the Past*, pp. 191–226.

—, *In Samuel's Image. Child Oblation in the Early Medieval West* (Leiden and New York, 1996).

—, 'Monastic prisoners or opting out? Political coercion and honour in the Frankish kingdoms', in de Jong and Theuws with van Rhijn (eds.), *Topographies of Power*, pp. 291–328.

—, *The Penitential State: Authority and Atonement in the Age of Louis the Pious, 814–840* (Cambridge, 2009).

—, 'Power and humility in Carolingian society: the public penance of Louis the Pious', *EME* 1 (1992), pp. 29–52.

—, 'Religion', in R. McKitterick (ed.), *The Early Middle Ages: Europe 400–1000. The Short Oxford History of Europe* (Oxford, 2001), pp. 131–66.

—, '*Sacrum palatium et ecclesia*. L'Autorité religieuse royale sous les carolingiens (790–840)', *Annales. HSS* 58 (2003), pp. 1243–69.

—, 'To the limits of kinship: anti-incest legislation in the early medieval west (500–900)', in J. Bremmer (ed.), *From Sappho to De Sade: Moments in the History of Sexuality* (London and New York, 1989), pp. 36–59.

—, 'Transformations of penance', in Theuws and Nelson (eds.), *Rituals of Power*, pp. 184–224.

—, 'What was public about public penance? *Poenitentia publica* and justice in the Carolingian world', *La giustitia nell'alto medioevo (secoli IX–XI)*, Settimane di Studio del Centro italiano di studi sull'alto medioevo 44 (Spoleto, 1997), pp. 863–902.

Jong, M. de, and Theuws, F. with Rhijn, C. van (eds.), *Topographies of Power in the Early Middle Ages* (Leiden, Boston, MA, and Cologne, 2001).

Jorns, W., 'Zullestein. Ein Beitrag zur Kontinuität von Bauwerken', in *Deutsche Königpfalzen: Beiträge zu ihrer historischen und archäologischen Erforschung* III, Veröffentlichungen des Max-Planck-Institutes für Geschichte II (Göttingen, 1979), pp. 111–35.

Kaschke, S., *Die karolingischen Reichsteilungen bis 831. Herrschaftspraxis und Normvorstellungen in zeitgenössischer Sicht* (Hamburg, 2006).

Kasten, B., *Adalhard von Corbie: die Biographie eines karolingischen Politikers und Klostervorstehers* (Düsseldorf, 1986).

—, *Königssohne und Königsherrschaft. Untersuchungen zur Teilhabe am Reich in der Merowinger- und Karolingerzeit, MGH* Schriften XLIV (Hanover, 1997).

Kelly, S., 'Trading privileges from eighth-century England', *EME* 1 (1992), pp. 3–28.

Kennedy, H., 'From *polis* to *madina*: urban change in late antique and early Islamic Syria', *P&P* 106 (1985), pp. 3–27.

—, 'Military pay and the economy of the early Islamic state', *Historical Research* 188 (2002), pp. 155–69.

—, *Muslim Spain and Portugal: A Political History of Al-Andalus* (London, 1996).

—, *The Prophet and the Age of the Caliphates* (Harlow, 1986, 2nd edn 2004).

Kershaw, P., 'Eberhard of Friuli, a Carolingian lay intellectual', in Wormald and Nelson (eds.), *Lay Intellectuals*, pp. 77–105.

—, 'Laughter after Babel's fall: misunderstanding and miscommunication in the ninth-century west', in Halsall (ed.), *Humour, History and Politics*, pp. 179–202.

—, 'English history and Irish readers in the Frankish world', in D. Ganz and P. Fouracre (eds.), *Frankland. The Franks and the World of Early Medieval Europe. Essays in Honour of Dame Jinty Nelson* (Manchester, 2008), pp. 126–51.

Kienast, W., *Das fränkische Vassalität von den Hausmaiern bis zu Ludwig dem Kind und Karl dem Einfältigen* (Frankfurt, 1990).

King, P. D., *Charlemagne: Translated Sources* (Kendal, 1987).

Kirby, D. P. (ed.), *Saint Wilfrid at Hexham* (Newcastle-upon-Tyne, 1974).

Knowles, D., *Great Historical Enterprises* (London, 1963).

Kosto, A. J., 'Hostages in the Carolingian world', *EME* 11 (2002), pp. 123–47.

—, 'Laymen, clerics and documentary practices in the early middle ages: the example of Catalonia', *Speculum* 80 (2005), pp. 44–74.

Koziol, G., 'Is Robert I in Hell?', *EME* 14 (2006), pp. 233–67.

Krah, A., *Absetzungsverfahren als Spiegelbild von Königsmacht. Untersuchungen zum Kräfteverhältnis zwischen Königtum und Adel im Karolingerreich und seinen Nachfolgestaaten* (Aalen, 1987).

—, *Die Entstehung der 'potestas regia' im Westfrankenreich während der ersten Regierungsjahre Kaiser Karl II. (840–877)* (Berlin, 2000).

Krahwinkler, H., *Friaul im Frühmittelalter. Geschichte einer Region vom Ende des fünften bis zum Ende des zehnten Jahrhunderts* (Vienna, 1992).

Kreutz, B., *Before the Normans: Southern Italy in the Ninth and Tenth Centuries* (Philadelphia, PA, 1991).

Krüger, K. H., 'Herrschaftsnachfolge als Vater-Sohn-Konflikt', *Frühmittelalterliche Studien* 36 (2002), pp. 225–40.

—, 'Neue Beobachtungen zur Datierung von Einhards Karlsvita', *Frühmittelalterliche Studien* 32 (1998), pp. 124–45.

Kuchenbuch, L., *Bäuerliche Gesellschaft und Klosterherrschaft im 9. Jht. Studien zur Sozialstruktur der Familia der Abtei Prüm.* Vierteljahrsschrift für Sozial- und Wirtschaftsgeschichte Beihefte 66 (Wiesbaden, 1978).

La Rocca, C., 'Le elites, chiese e sepolture familiari tra vIIIe e IXe secolo in Italia settentrionale', in Depreux, Bougard and Le Jan (eds.), *Les Élites et leurs espaces*, pp. 259–71.

—, 'La legge e la pratica. Potere e rapporti sociali nell'Italia dell'vIII secolo', in C. Bertelli and G. P. Brogiolo (eds.), *Il futuro dei Longobardi. L'Italia e la costruzione dell'Europa di Carlo Magno* (Brescia, 2000), pp. 45–69.

—, 'Pouvoirs des femmes, pouvoirs de la loi dans l'Italie lombarde', in S. Lebecq, A. Dierkens, R. Le Jan and J.-M. Sansterre (eds.), *Femmes et pouvoirs des femmes à Byzance et en Occident (vIIe–xIe siècles)* (Villeneuved'Ascq, 1999), pp. 37–50.

—, 'Segni di distinzione. Dai corredi funerari alle donazioni "post obitum" nel regno longobardo', in L. Paroli (ed.), *L'Italia centro-settentrionale in età longobarda* (Florence, 1997), pp. 31–54.

La Rocca, C. (ed.), *Italy in the Early Middle Ages, 476–1000.* The Short Oxford History of Italy (Oxford, 2002).

La Rocca, C., and Provero, L., 'The dead and their gifts. The will of Eberhard, count of Friuli, and his wife Gisela, daughter of Louis the Pious (863–864)', in Theuws and Nelson (eds.), *Rituals of Power*, pp. 225–80.

Ladner, G., *The Idea of Reform: Its Impact on Christian Thought and Action in the Age of the Fathers* (Cambridge, MA, 1959).

Lanfranchi, L., and Strina, B., *Ss. Ilario e Benedetto e Gregorio* (Venice, 1965).

Lange, W., *Texte zur Bekehrungsgeschichte* (Tübingen, 1962).

Larrington, C., 'The psychology of emotion and study of the medieval period', *EME* 10/2 (2001), pp. 251–6.

Lauranson-Rosaz, C., *L'Auvergne et ses marges du vIIIe aux xIe siècles: La Fin du monde antique?* (Le Puy en Velay, 1987).

Lauwers, M., 'Le Cimetière dans le Moyen Âge latin: Lieu sacré, saint et religieux', *Annales HSS* 54 (1999), pp. 1047–72.

Le Jan, R., 'Convents, violence, and competition for power in seventh-century Francia', in de Jong and Theuws with van Rhijn (eds.), *Topographies of Power*, pp. 243–69.

—, *Famille et pouvoir dans le monde franc, vIIIe–xe siècles* (Paris, 1995).

—, 'Frankish giving of arms and rituals of power: continuity and change in the Carolingian period', in Theuws and Nelson (eds.), *Rituals of Power*, pp. 281–309.

—, 'Die Sakralität der Merowinger oder: Mehrdeutigkeiten der Geschichtsschreibung', in Airlie, Pohl and Reimitz (eds.), *Staat im frühen Mittelalter*, pp. 73–92.

—, 'Structures familiales et politiques au IXe siècle: un groupe familial de l'aristocratie franque', *Revue historique* 265 (1981), pp. 289–333.

Le Jan, R. (ed.), *La Royauté et les élites dans l'Europe carolingienne (du début du IXe siècle aux environs de 920)*, Centre de l'Europe du Nord-Ouest 17 (Lille, 1998).

Lebecq, S., *Marchands et navigateurs. Frisons du haut moyen âge* (Lille, 1983).

—, 'On the use of the word Frisian in the 6th to 10th centuries: some interpretations', in McGrail (ed.), *Maritime Celts, Frisians and Saxons*, pp. 85–90.

—, 'The role of the monasteries in the systems of production and exchange of the Frankish world between the seventh and the beginning of the ninth centuries', in Hansen and Wickham (eds.), *The Long Eighth Century*, pp. 121–48.

Levison, W., *England and the Continent in the Eighth Century* (Oxford, 1946).

Lewit, T., *Agricultural Production in the Roman Economy AD 200–400*, British Archaeological Reports International Series 568 (Oxford, 1991).

—, 'Pigs, presses and pastoralism: farming in the fifth to seventh centuries', *EME* 17 (2009), pp. 77–91.

—, '"Vanishing villas": what happened to elite rural habitation in the west in the fifth–sixth centuries?', *Journal of Roman Archaeology* 16 (2003), pp. 26–74.

Leyser, K., 'Concepts of Europe in the early and high middle ages', *P&P* 137, pp. 25–47, repr. in Leyser, *Communications and Power in Medieval Europe: The Carolingian and Ottonian Centuries* (London, 1994), pp. 1–18.

—, 'Early medieval canon law and the beginning of knighthood', in K. Leyser (ed. T. Reuter), *Communications and Power in Medieval Europe. The Carolingian and Ottonian Centuries* (London and Rio Grande, OH, 1984), pp. 51–71, first published in L. Fenske, W. Rösener and T. Zotz (eds.), *Institutionen, Kultur und Gesellschaft im Mittelalter. Festschrift für Josef Fleckenstein zu seinem 65. Geburtstag* (Sigmaringen, 1984), pp. 549–66.

Linehan, P., and J. L. Nelson (eds.), *The Medieval World* (London, 2001).

Little, L. K., and Rosenwein, B. H. (eds.), *Debating the Middle Ages. Issues and Readings* (Oxford, 1998).

Lobbedey, U., 'Carolingian royal palaces: the state of research from an architectural historian's viewpoint', in C. Cubitt (ed.), *Court Culture in the Early Middle Ages* (Turnhout, 2003), pp. 129–54.

Lohrmann, D., 'Trois palais royaux de la vallée de l'Oise d'après les travaux des érudits mauristes: Compiègne, Choisy-au-Bac et Quierzy', *Francia* 4 (1976), pp. 121–40.

Lopez, R. S., and Raymond, I. W., *Medieval Trade in the Mediterranean World: Illustrative Documents* (London and New York, 1955).

Lorren, C., 'Le Village de Saint-Martin de Mondeville de l'antiquité au haut moyen âge', in H. Atsma (ed.), *La Neustrie. Le Pays au nord de la Loire de 650 à 850*, Beihefte der Francia 16, 2 vols. (Sigmaringen, 1989), II, pp. 439–66.

Loseby, S., 'Marseille and the Pirenne thesis I: Gregory of Tours, the Merovingian kings, and "un grand port"', in Hodges and Bowden (eds.), *The Sixth Century*, pp. 203–29.

—, 'Marseille and the Pirenne thesis II: "ville morte"', in Hansen and Wickham (eds.), *The Long Eighth Century*, pp. 167–94.

Loveluck, C., 'Rural settlement hierarchy in the age of Charlemagne', in Story (ed.), *Charlemagne*, pp. 230–58.

Loyn, H. R., and Percival, J., *The Reign of Charlemagne: Documents on Carolingian Government and Administration* (London, 1975).

Lund, N., 'Allies of God or man? The Viking expansion in European perspective', *Viator* 20 (1989), pp. 45–59.

—, 'Peace and non-peace in the Viking age', in J. E. Knirk (ed.), *Proceedings of the Tenth Viking Congress* (Oslo, 1987), pp. 255–69.

Lund, N. (ed.), *Two Voyagers at the Court of King Alfred* (York, 1984).

Lynch, J., *Godparents and Kinship in Early Medieval Europe* (Princeton, NJ, 1986).

Lyon, B., *Henri Pirenne: A Biographical and Intellectual Study* (Ghent, 1974).

MacCulloch, D., *Reformation. Europe's House Divided, 1490–1700* (London, 2003).

MacLean, S., '"After his death a great tribulation came to Italy . . ." Dynastic politics and aristocratic factions after the death of Louis II, *c.*870–*c.*890', *Millennium Jahrbuch* 4 (2007), pp. 239–60.

—, 'Apocalypse and revolution: Europe around the year 1000', *EME* 15 (2007), pp. 86–106.

—, 'The Carolingian response to the revolt of Boso, 879–87', *EME* 10 (2001), pp. 21–48.

—, 'Charles the Fat and the Viking Great Army: the military explanation for the end of the Carolingian empire', *War Studies Journal* 3 (1998), pp. 74–95.

—, *History and Politics in Late Carolingian and Ottonian Europe: the Chronicle of Regino of Prüm and Adalbert of Magdeburg* (Manchester, 2009).

—, 'Insinuation, censorship and the struggle for late Carolingian Lotharingia in Regino of Prüm's *Chronicle*', *EHR* 124 (2009), pp. 1–28.

—, *Kingship and Politics in the Late Ninth Century: Charles the Fat and the End of the Carolingian Empire* (Cambridge, 2003).

—, 'Queenship, nunneries and royal widowhood in Carolingian Europe', *P&P* 178 (2003), pp. 3–38.

—, 'Ritual, misunderstanding and the contest for meaning: representations of the disrupted royal assembly at Frankfurt (873)', in B. Weiler and S. MacLean (eds.), *Representations of Power in Medieval Germany* (Turnhout, 2006), pp. 97–120.

Macy, G., 'Was there a "Church" in the Middle Ages?', in R. Swanson (ed.), *Unity and Diversity in the Church*, Studies in Church History 52 (Oxford, 1996), pp. 107–16.

Magdalino, P., 'The distance of the past in early medieval Byzantium (VII–X centuries)', in *Ideologie e pratiche del reimpiego nell'alto medioevo*, Settimane di Studio del Centro italiano di studi sull'alto medioevo 46 (Spoleto, 1999), I, pp. 115–46.

Manacorda, F., *Ricerche sugli inizii della dominazione dei Carolingi in Italia* (Rome, 1968).

Marenbon, J., 'Candidus', *DNB*, *s.n.*

Markus, R., *Gregory the Great and his World* (Cambridge, 1997).

Martindale, J., 'The kingdom of Aquitaine and the dissolution of the Carolingian fisc', *Francia* 11 (1985), pp. 131–91.

Matthew, H. C. G., Harrison, B. H., and Goldman, L., *et al.* (eds.), *Oxford Dictionary of National Biography* (Oxford, 2004).

Matthews, J. F., *Western Aristocracies and the Imperial Court, 364–425* (Oxford, 1975).

Maund, K. L., '"A turmoil of warring princes": political leadership in ninth-century Denmark', *Haskins Society Journal* 6 (1994), pp. 29–47.

Mayr-Harting, H., 'Charlemagne, the Saxons and the imperial coronation of 800', *EHR* 111 (1996), pp. 1113–33.

—, *The Coming of Christianity to Anglo-Saxon England* (3rd edn, London, 1991).

—, 'Two abbots in politics: Wala of Corbie and Bernard of Clairvaux', *TRHS* 5th ser. 40 (1990), pp. 217–37.

Mazel, F., 'Des familles de l'aristocratie locale en leurs territories: France de l'ouest, du IXe au XIe siècle', in P. Depreux, F. Bougard and R. Le Jan (eds.), *Les Élites et leurs espaces. Mobilité, rayonnement, domination (du VIe au XIe siècle)* (Turnhout, 2007), pp. 361–98.

McClendon, C., *The Imperial Abbey of Farfa* (New Haven, CT, 1987).

McCormick, M., 'Complexity, chronology and context in the early medieval economy', *EME* 12 (2003), pp. 307–23.

—, 'Molecular Middle Ages: early medieval economic history in the 21st century', in Davis and McCormick (eds.), *The Long Morning of Medieval Europe*, pp. 83–98.

—, 'New light on the "dark ages": how the slave trade fuelled the Carolingian economy', *P&P* 177 (2002), pp. 17–54.

—, *Origins of the European Economy. Communications and Commerce AD 600–900* (Cambridge, 2001).

—, 'Pippin III, the embassy of Caliph al Mansur, and the Mediterranean World', in Becher and Jarnut (eds.), *Der Dynastiewechsel von 751*, pp. 221–41.

—, 'Textes, images et iconoclasme dans le cadre des relations entre Byzance et l'occident', *Testo e immagine nell'alto medioevo*, Settimane di Studio del Centro italiano di studi sull'alto medioevo 41 (Spoleto, 1994), pp. 95–162.

—, 'Toward a molecular history of the Justinianic pandemic', in L. K. Little (ed.), *Plague and the End of Antiquity. The Pandemic of 541–750* (Cambridge, 2007), pp. 290–312.

McCormick, M., P. Dutton and J. Mayewski, 'Volcanoes and the climate forcing of Carolingian Europe AD 750–950', *Speculum* 82 (2007), pp. 865–96.

McGrail, S. (ed.), *Maritime Celts, Frisians and Saxons* (London, 1990).

McKeon, P., *Hincmar of Laon and Carolingian Politics* (Urbana, IL, 1978).

McKitterick, R., *Anglo-Saxon Missionaries in Germany: Personal Connections and Local Influences*, Vaughan Paper 36 (Brixworth, 1991), repr. in McKitterick, *Books, Scribes and Learning in the Frankish Kingdoms, 6th–9th Centuries* (Aldershot, 1994).

—, 'Carolingian book production: some problems', *The Library*, 6th ser., 12 (1990), pp. 1–33, repr. in McKitterick, *Books, Scribes and Learning in the Frankish Kingdoms, 6th–9th Centuries* (Aldershot, 1994).

— (ed.), *Carolingian Culture: Emulation and Innovation* (Cambridge, 1994).

—, 'The Carolingian renaissance of culture and learning', in Story (ed.), *Charlemagne*, pp. 151–166.

—, *The Carolingians and the Written Word* (Cambridge, 1989).

—, *Charlemagne: The Formation of a European Identity* (Cambridge, 2008).

—, 'Constructing the past in the early Middle Ages: the case of the Royal Frankish Annals', *TRHS* 6th ser. 7 (1999), pp. 101–29.

—, *The Frankish Church and the Carolingian Reforms, 789–895* (London, 1977).

—, *The Frankish Kingdoms under the Carolingians, 751–987* (London and New York, 1983).

—, *History and Memory in the Carolingian World* (Cambridge, 2004).

—, 'Paul the Deacon and the Franks', *EME* 8 (1999), pp. 319–39.

—, *Perceptions of the Past in the Early Middle Ages* (Notre Dame, IN, 2006).

—, 'Political ideology in Carolingian historiography', in Hen and Innes (eds.), *Uses of the Past*, pp. 162–74.

—, 'Script and book production', in McKitterick (ed.), *Carolingian Culture*, pp. 221–247.

—, 'Some Carolingian law-books and their function', in B. Tierney and P. Linehan (eds.), *Authority and Power. Studies in Medieval Law and Government Presented to Walter Ullman* (Cambridge, 1984), pp. 13–27, repr. in McKitterick, *Books, Scribes and Learning in the Frankish Kingdoms, 6th–9th Centuries* (Aldershot, 1994).

—, 'Unity and diversity in the Carolingian church', in R. Swanson (ed.), *Unity and Diversity in the Church*, Studies in Church History 32 (Oxford, 1996), pp. 59–82.

—, 'Zur Herstellung von Kapitularien: Die Arbeit des Leges-Skriptoriums', *Mitteilungen des Instituts für Österreichische Geschichtsforschung* 101 (1993), pp. 3–16.

McKitterick, R. (ed.), *The New Cambridge Medieval History*, II *c.700–c.900* (Cambridge, 1995).

McLaughlin, M., *Consorting with Saints: Prayer for the Dead in Early Medieval France* (Ithaca, NY, and London, 1994).

McNamara, J., 'A legacy of miracles: hagiography and nunneries in Merovingian Gaul', in J. Kirshner and S. Wemple (eds.), *Women of the Medieval World. Essays in Honour of John H. Mundy* (Oxford, 1985), pp. 36–52.

McNeill, J. T., and Gamer, H. A. (eds.), *Medieval Handbooks of Penance* (New York, 1990).

Meaney, A., 'Magic', in M. Lapidge, *et al.* (eds.), *The Blackwell Encyclopedia of Anglo-Saxon England* (Oxford, 1999), pp. 298–9.

Meens, R., 'The frequency and nature of early medieval penance', in P. Biller and A. Minns (eds.), *Handling Sin: Confession in the Middle Ages* (Woodbridge, 1998), pp. 35–61.

Metcalf, M., 'A sketch of the currency in the time of Charles the Bald', in M. T. Gibson and J. L. Nelson (eds.), *Charles the Bald: Court and Kingdom* (2nd edn, Aldershot, 1991), pp. 65–97.

Metz, W., *Das Karolingische Reichsgut* (Berlin, 1960).

Meulengracht Sørensen, P., 'Religions old and new', in Sawyer (ed.), *The Oxford Illustrated History of the Vikings*, pp. 202–24.

Michelet, F. L., *Creation, Migration and Conquest. Imaginary Geography and the Sense of Space in Old English Literature* (Oxford, 2006).

Miller, M., 'Final stages in the construction of the Harleian *Annales Cambriae*', *Journal of Celtic Studies* 4 (2004), pp. 205–11.

Miller, W. I., 'Gift, sale, payment, raid: case studies in the negotiation and classification of exchange in medieval Iceland', *Speculum* 61 (1986), pp. 18–50.

Moesgaard, J. C., 'A survey of coin production and currency in Normandy, 864–945', in J. Graham-Campbell and G. Williams (eds.), *Silver Economy of the Viking Age* (Walnut Creek, CA, 2007), pp. 99–121.

Moore, R. I., 'Literacy and the making of heresy *c.*1000–*c.*1150', in P. Biller and A. Hudson (eds.), *Heresy and Literacy, 1000–1530* (Cambridge, 1994), pp. 19–37, repr. in Little and Rosenwein (eds.), *Debating the Middle Ages*, pp. 163–75.

Mordek, H., 'Ein exemplarischer Rechtstreit: Hinkmar von Reims und das Landgut Neuilly-Saint-Front', *Zeitschrift der Savigny-Stiftung für Rechtsgeschichte, Kanonistische Abteilung* 83 (1997), pp. 86–112.

Moreland, J., 'Concepts of the early medieval economy', in Hansen and Wickham (eds.), *The Long Eighth Century*, pp. 1–34.

Morimoto, Y., *Études sur l'économie rurale du haut moyen âge: historiographie, régime domanial, polyptyques carolingiens* (Paris, 2008).

Morrison, K. F., *Carolingian Coinage* (New York, 1967).

Morrissey, R. J., *Charlemagne and France: A Thousand Years of Mythology* (Notre Dame, IN, 2003).

Morton, A. D., *Excavations at Hamwic I* (London, 1992).

Morton, A., 'Hamwic in its context', in Anderton (ed.), *Anglo-Saxon Trading Centres*, pp. 48–62.

Müller-Mertens, E., *Karl der Große, Ludwig der Fromme und die Freien. Wer waren die* liberi homines *der karolingischen Kapitularien (742/3–832)? Ein Beitrag zur Sozialgeschichte und Sozialpolitik des Frankenreiches*, Forschungen zur mittelalterlichen Geschichte 10 (Berlin, 1963).

Müller-Wille, M., 'Fremdgut und Import östlicher Provenienz in Schleswig-Holstein (9.-12. Jahrhundert)', *Bericht der römisch-germanischen Kommission* 69 (1988), pp. 740–83.

Müller-Wille, M., Tummuscheit. A., and Hansen, L., *Frühstädtliche Zentren der Wikingerzeit und ihr Hinterland. Die Beispiele Ribe, Hedeby und Reric* (Göttingen, 2002).

Murray, A. C., 'From Roman to Frankish Gaul: *centenae* and *centenarii* in the administration of the Merovingian kingdom', *Traditio* 44 (1988), pp. 59–100.

—, '*Pax et disciplina*. Roman public law and the Merovingian state', in K. Pennington, S. Chodorow and K. H. Kendall (eds.), *Proceedings of the Tenth International Congress of Medieval Canon Law* (Vatican City, 2001), pp. 269–85, repr. in T. F. X. Noble (ed.), *From Roman Provinces to Medieval Kingdoms* (New York and Abingdon, 2006), pp. 376–88.

Myhre, B., 'The archaeology of the early Viking age in Norway', in H. B. Clarke, M. Ní Mhaonaigh and R. Ó Floinn (eds.), *Ireland and Scandinavia in the Early Viking Age* (Dublin, 1998), pp. 3–36.

Näsman, U., 'Exchange and politics: the eighth–early ninth century in Denmark', in Hansen and Wickham (eds.), *The Long Eighth Century*, pp. 35–68.

Nehlsen, H., 'Zur Aktualität und Effektivität germanischer Rechtsaufzeichnungen', in P. Classen (ed.), *Recht und Schrift im Mittelalter* (Sigmaringen, 1977), pp. 449–502.

Nehlsen-von Stryck, K., *Die boni homines des frühen Mittelalters unter besonderer Berücksichtigung der fränkischen Quellen*, Freiburger Rechtsgeschichtlichen Abhandlungen 2 (Berlin, 1981).

Nelson, J. L., 'Aachen as a place of power', in de Jong and Theuws with van Rhijn (eds.), *Topographies of Power*, pp. 217–41.

—, 'Bertrada', in Becher and Jarnut (eds.), *Der Dynastiewechsel von 751*, pp. 93–108.

—, 'Carolingian royal funerals', in Theuws and Nelson (eds.), *Rituals of Power*, pp. 131–84.

—, 'Carolingian royal ritual', in D. Cannadine and S. Price (eds.), *Rituals of Royalty. Power and Ceremonial in Traditional Societies* (Cambridge, 1987), pp. 137–80.

—, 'Charlemagne's church at Aachen', *History Today* (Jan. 1998), pp. 62–3.

—, 'Charlemagne and empire', in Davis and McCormick (eds.), *The Long Morning of Medieval Europe*, pp. 223–34.

—, 'Charlemagne the man', in Story (ed.), *Charlemagne*, pp. 22–37.

—, 'Charlemagne and the paradoxes of power', *Reuter Lecture* (University of Southampton, 2006).

—, 'Charlemagne: pater optimus?', in Godman, Jarnut and Johanek (eds.), *Am Vorabend der Kaiserkrönung*, pp. 271–83.

—, *Charles the Bald* (London and New York, 1992).

—, 'Charles le Chauve et les utilisations du savoir', in D. Iogna-Prat, C. Jeudy and G. Lobrichon (eds.), *L'École carolingienne d'Auxerre* (Paris, 1991), pp. 37–54, repr. as no. VII in Nelson, *Rulers and Ruling Families*.

— 'The Church's military service in the ninth century: a contemporary comparative view?', in W. J. Shiels (ed.), *The Church and War, Studies in Church History* 20 (1983), pp. 15–30, repr. in Nelson, *Politics and Ritual*, pp. 117–32.

—, 'La Cour impériale de Charlemagne', in R. Le Jan (ed.), *La Royauté*, pp.177–91; repr. in Nelson, *Rulers and Ruling Families*.

—, 'Dispute settlement in Carolingian west Francia', in Davies and Fouracre (eds.), *Settlement of Disputes*, pp. 45–64.

—, 'Early medieval rites of queen-making and the shaping of medieval queenship', in Anne J. Duggan (ed.), *Queens and Queenship in Medieval Europe* (Woodbridge, 1997), pp. 301–15.

—, 'England and the continent in the ninth century: II, Vikings and others', *TRHS* 6th ser. 13 (2003), pp. 1–28.

—, 'The Frankish kingdoms, 814–898: the west', in *NCMH* II, pp. 110–41.

—, *The Frankish World, 750–900* (London, 1996).

—, 'Gender and genre in women historians', in J.-P. Genet (ed.), *L'Historiographie médiévale en Europe*, Éditions du CNRS (Paris, 1991), pp. 149–63, repr. in Nelson, *Frankish World*, pp. 183–97.

—, 'Gendering courts in the early medieval west', in Brubaker and Smith (eds.), *Gender in the Early Medieval World*, pp. 185–97.

—, 'The intellectual in politics: contexts, content and authorship in the Capitulary of Coulaines, November 843', in L. Smith and B. Ward (eds.), *Intellectual Life in the Middle Ages: Essays Presented to Margaret Gibson* (London, 1992), pp. 1–14, repr. in Nelson, *The Frankish World*, pp. 155–68.

—, 'Kingship and empire in the Carolingian world', in McKitterick (ed.), *Carolingian Culture*, pp. 52–87.

—, 'Kingship, law and liturgy in the political thought of Hincmar of Rheims', *EHR* 92 (1977), pp. 241–79.

—, 'The last years of Louis the Pious', in Godman and Collins (eds.), *Charlemagne's Heir*, pp. 147–59.

—, 'Legislation and consensus in the reign of Charles the Bald', in P. Wormald, D. Bullough and R. Collins (eds.), *Ideal and Reality in Frankish and Anglo-Saxon Society* (Oxford, 1983), pp. 202–27; repr. in Nelson, *Politics and Ritual*.

—, 'Literacy in Carolingian government', in R. McKitterick (ed.), *The Uses of Literacy in Early Medieval Europe* (Cambridge, 1990), pp. 258–96.

—, 'The Lord's anointed and the people's choice: Carolingian royal ritual', in D. Cannadine and S. Price (eds.), *Rituals of Royalty* (Cambridge, 1987), pp. 137–80; repr. in Nelson, *Frankish World*, pp. 99–131.

—, 'Making a difference in eighth-century politics: the daughters of Desiderius', in A. C. Murray (ed.), *After Rome's Fall: Narrators and Sources of Early Medieval History. Essays presented to Walter Goffart* (Toronto, 1998), pp. 171–90.

—, 'Monks, secular men and masculinity, *c*.900', in D. M. Hadley (ed.), *Masculinity in Medieval Europe* (London, 1999), pp. 121–42.

—, 'Ninth-century knighthood: the evidence of Nithard', in C. Harper-Bill, C. Holdsworth and J. L. Nelson (eds.), *Studies in Medieval History Presented to R. Allen Brown* (Woodbridge, 1989), pp. 255–66, repr. in Nelson, *Frankish World*, pp. 75–87.

—, *Opposition to Charlemagne* (German Historical Institute, London, 2008).

—, *Politics and Ritual in Early Medieval Europe* (London, 1986).

—, 'Public *Histories* and private history in the work of Nithard', *Speculum* 50 (1985), pp. 251–93, repr. in Nelson, *Politics and Ritual*, pp. 195–237.

—, 'Queens as Jezebels: Brunhild and Balthild in Merovingian history', in D. Baker (ed.), *Medieval Women: Essays Dedicated and Presented to Professor Rosalind M. T. Hill*, Studies in Church History: Subsidia 1 (Oxford, 1978), pp. 31–77, repr. in Nelson, *Politics and Ritual*, pp. 1–48, and in Little and Rosenwein (eds.), *Debating the Middle Ages*, pp. 219–53.

—, 'Rewriting the history of the Franks', in Nelson, *Frankish World*, pp. 169–83.

—, *Rulers and Ruling Families in Early Medieval Europe: Alfred, Charles the Bald and Others* (Aldershot, 1999).

—, 'The search for peace in a time of war: the Carolingian *Brüderkrieg*, 840–843', in J. Fried (ed.), *Träger und Instrumentarien des Friedens im hohen und späten Mittelalter* (Sigmaringen, 1996), pp. 87–114.

—, 'A tale of two princes: politics, text and ideology in a Carolingian annal', *Studies in Medieval and Renaissance History* 10 (1988), pp. 103–40; repr. in Nelson, *Rulers and Ruling Families*.

—, 'Violence in the Carolingian world and the ritualization of ninth-century warfare', in G. Halsall (ed.), *Violence and Society in the Early Medieval West* (Woodbridge, 1998), pp. 90–107.

—, 'The voice of Charlemagne', in R. Gameson and H. Leyser (eds.), *Belief and Culture in the Middle Ages: Studies Presented to Henry Mayr-Harting* (Oxford, 2001), pp. 76–88.

—, 'The wary widow', in W. Davies and P. Fouracre (eds.), *Property and Power in the Early Middle Ages* (Cambridge, 1995), pp. 82–113.

—, 'Was Charlemagne's court a courtly society?', in C. Cubitt (ed.), *Court Culture in the Earlier Middle Ages* (Turnhout, 2003), pp. 39–57.

—, 'Why are there so many different accounts of Charlemagne's imperial coronation?', in Nelson, *Courts, Elites and Gendered Power in the Early Middle Ages: Charlemagne and Others* (Aldershot, 2007), no. XII.

—, 'Women at the court of Charlemagne: a case of Monstrous Regiment?', in J. C. Parsons (ed.), *Medieval Queenship* (New York, 1993), pp. 43–61, repr. in Nelson, *Frankish World*, pp. 223–42.

Noble, T. F. X., 'From brigandage to justice: Charlemagne, 785–794', in C. M. Chazelle (ed.), *Literacy, Politics, and Artistic Innovation in the Early Medieval West* (Lanham, MD, 1992), pp. 49–76.

—, *Images, Iconoclasm and the Carolingians* (Philadelphia, PA, 2009).

—, 'Louis the Pious and his piety reconsidered', *Revue Belge* 58 (1980), pp. 297–316.

—, 'Lupus of Ferrières in his Carolingian context', in A. C. Murray (ed.), *Rome's Fall and after. Narrators and Sources of Early Medieval History* (Toronto, 1998), pp. 232–250.

—, 'The monastic ideal as a model for empire: the case of Louis the Pious', *Revue Bénédictine* 86 (1976), pp. 235–50.

—, 'Paradoxes and possibilities in the sources for Roman society in the early middle ages', in Smith (ed.), *Early Medieval Rome and the Christian West*, pp. 55–83.

—, *The Republic of St Peter. The Birth of the Papal State, 680–825* (Philadelphia, PA, 1984).

—, 'The revolt of King Bernard of Italy in 817: its causes and consequences', *Studi Medievali* 15 (1974), pp. 315–26.

—, 'Secular sanctity: forging an ethos for the Carolingian nobility', in Wormald and Nelson (eds.), *Lay Intellectuals*, pp. 8–36.

—, 'Topography, celebration and power: the making of a papal Rome in the eighth and ninth centuries', in de Jong and Theuws with van Rhijn (eds.), *Topographies of Power*, pp. 45–92.

Nonn, U., 'Merowingische Testamente', *Archiv für Diplomatik* 18 (1972), pp. 1–129.

Odegaard, C. E., 'The empress Engelberge', *Speculum* 26 (1951), pp. 77–103.

Oexle, O. G., '*Coniuratio* und Gilde im frühen Mittelalter', in B. Schwineköper (ed.), *Gilden und Zünfte: kaufmännische und gewerbliche Genossenschaften im frühen und hohen Mittelalter* (Sigmaringen, 1985), pp. 151–213.

—, 'Tria genera hominum. Zur Geschichte eines Deutungsschemas der sozialen Wirklichkeit in Antike und Mittelalter', in L. Fenske, *et al.* (eds.), *Institutionen, Gesellschaft und Kultur im Mittelalter. Festschrift Josef Fleckenstein* (Sigmaringen, 1984), pp. 483–99.

Olio e Vino in Alto Medioevo, Settimane di Studio del Centro italiano di studi sull'alto medioevo 54 (Spoleto, 2007).

Orchard, A., *A Critical Companion to 'Beowulf'* (Woodbridge, 2004).

Palmer, J., 'Defining paganism in the Carolingian world', *EME* 15 (2007), pp. 402–25.

—, 'Rimbert's *Vita Anskarii* and Scandinavian mission in the ninth century', *Journal of Ecclesiastical History* 55 (2004), pp. 235–56.

—, 'The "vigorous rule" of Bishop Lull: between Bonifatian mission and Carolingian church control', *EME* 13/3 (2005), pp. 249–76.

Patze, H., and Schwind, F. (eds.), *Ausgewählte Aufsätze von W. Schlesinger 1965–1979* (Sigmaringen, 1987).

Patzold, S., 'Die Bischöfe im karolingischen Staat. Praktisches Wissen über die politische Ordnung im Frankenreich des 9. Jahrhunderts', in Airlie, Pohl and Reimitz (eds.), *Staat im frühen Mittelalter*, pp. 133–62.

—, 'Eine "loyale Palastrebellion" der "Reichseinheitspartei"? Zur "Divisio imperii" von 817 und zu den Ursachen des Aufstands gegen Ludwig den Frommen im Jahre 830', *Frühmittelalterliche Studien* 40 (2006), pp. 43–77.

—, 'Redéfinir l'office épiscopal: les évêques francs face à la crise des années 820/30', in F. Bougard, L. Feller and R. Le Jan (eds.), *Les Élites au haut Moyen Âge. Crises et renouvellements* (Turnhout, 2006), pp. 337–59.

Paxton, F. S., *Christianizing Death: The Creation of a Ritual Process in Early Medieval Europe* (Ithaca and London, 1990).

Pearson, K. L. R., *Conflicting Loyalties in Early Medieval Bavaria: a View of Socio-Political Interaction, 680–900* (Aldershot, 1999).

Percival, J., *The Roman Villa* (London, 1976).

Périn, P., 'The origins of the village in early medieval Gaul', in Christie (ed.), *Landscapes of Change*, pp. 255–78.

Perrin, C.-E., 'Observations sur la manse dans la region parisienne au début du ixe siècle', *Annales* 8 (1945), pp. 39–51.

Peters, E., *Monks, Bishops and Pagans* (Philadelphia, PA, 1975).

—, *The Shadow King. Rex inutilis in Medieval Law and Literature, 751–1327* (New Haven, CT, 1970).

Petersohn, J., 'Saint-Denis – Westminster – Aachen. Die Karls-Translatio von 1165 und ihre Vorbilder', *Deutsches Archiv für Erforschung des Mittelalters* 31 (1975), pp. 420–54.

Pirenne, H., *Mahomet et Charlemagne* (Brussels, 1937), trans. B. Miall, *Mohammed and Charlemagne* (London, 1939).

Pizarro, J. M., *Writing Ravenna. The Liber pontificalis of Andreas Agnellus* (Ann Arbor, MI, 1995).

Plassmann, A., 'Mittelalterliche *origines gentium*. Paulus Diaconus als Beispiel', *QFIAB* 87 (2007), pp. 1–35.

Pohl, W., 'Paolo Diacono e la costruzione dell'identità longobarda', in P. Chiesa (ed.), *Paolo Diacono. Uno scrittore fra tradizione longobarda e rinnovamento carolingio* (Udine, 2000), pp. 413–26.

—, 'Das Papsttum und die Langobarden', in Becher and Jarnut (eds.), *Der Dynastiewechsel von 751*, pp. 145–61.

—, 'Paulus Diaconus und die "Historia langobardorum": Text und Tradition', in A. Scharer and G. Scheibelreiter (eds.), *Historiographie im frühen Mittelalter*, Veröffentlichungen des Instituts für Österreichische Geschichtsforschung 32 (Vienna and Munich, 1994), pp. 375–405.

—, 'Staat und Herrschaft im Frühmittelalter: Überlegungen zum Forschungsstand', in S. Airlie, W. Pohl and H. Reimitz (eds.), *Staat im Frühen Mittelalter*, pp. 9–38.

—, 'Telling the difference: signs of ethnic identity', in W. Pohl and H. Reimitz (eds.), *Strategies of Distinction. The Construction of Ethnic Communities, 300–800*. Transformation of the Roman World 2 (Leiden, 1998), pp. 17–69.

Pohl, W., and Reimitz, H. (eds.), *Grenze und Differenz im frühen Mittelalter*, Denkschriften (Österreichische Akademie der Wissenschaften. Philosophisch-Historische Klasse). Forschungen zur Geschichte des Mittelalters 1 (Vienna, 2000).

—, *Strategies of Distinction. The Construction of Ethnic Communities, 300–800*. Transformation of the Roman World 2 (Leiden, 1998).

Pohl, W., Wood, I., and Reimitz, H. (eds.), *The Transformation of Frontiers from Late Antiquity to the Carolingians* (Leiden, Boston and Cologne, 2001).

Polanyi, K., 'The economy as instituted process', in K. Polanyi, C. Arensberg and H. Pearson (eds.), *Trade and Market in Early Empires* (Glencoe, IL, 1957), pp. 243–69.

Pössel, C., 'Authors and recipients of Carolingian Capitularies, 779–829', in R. Corradini, R. Meens, C. Pössel and P. Shaw (eds.), *Texts and Identities in the Early Middle Ages* (Vienna, 2006), pp. 253–74.

Pratt, D., *The Political Thought of King Alfred the Great* (Cambridge, 2007).

Raaijmakers, J., 'Memory and identity: the *Annales necrologici* of Fulda', in R. Corradini, R. Meens, C. Pössel and P. Shaw (eds.), *Texts and Identities in the Early Middle Ages*, Forschungen zur Geschichte des Mittelalters 12 (Vienna, 2006), pp. 303–22.

Reimitz, H., 'The art of truth. Historiography and identity in the Frankish world', in R. Corradini, R. Meens, C. Pössel and P. Shaw (eds.), *Texts and Identities in the Early Middle Ages* (Vienna, 2006), pp. 87–104.

—, 'Conversion and control: the establishment of liturgical frontiers in Carolingian Pannonia', in Pohl, Wood and Reimitz (eds.), *Transformation of Frontiers*, pp. 188–207.

—, 'Ein fränkisches Geschichtsbuch aus Saint-Amand und der Codex Vindobonensis palat. 473', in C. Egger and H. Weigl (eds.), *Text-Schrift-Codex. Quellenkundliche Arbeiten aus dem Institut für Österreichische Geschichtsforschung*, MIÖG Ergänzungsband 35 (Vienna and Munich, 2000), pp. 34–90.

Reuter, T., 'Assembly politics in western Europe from the eighth century to the twelfth', in Linehan and Nelson (eds.), *The Medieval World*, pp. 432–50; repr. in Reuter, *Medieval Polities and Modern Mentalities*, pp. 193–216.

—, 'Carolingian and Ottonian warfare', in M. Keen (ed.), *Medieval Warfare: A History* (Oxford, 1999), pp. 13–35.

—, 'Charlemagne and the world beyond the Rhine', in Story (ed.), *Charlemagne*, pp. 183–94.

—, 'Debate. The "Feudal Revolution"', *P&P* 155 (1997), pp. 177–95.

—, 'The end of Carolingian military expansion', in Godman and Collins (eds.), *Charlemagne's Heir*, pp. 391–405; repr. in Reuter, *Medieval Polities and Modern Mentalities*, pp. 251–67.

—, *Germany in the Early Middle Ages 800–1056* (London and New York, 1991).

—, 'The medieval nobility in twentieth-century historiography', in M. Bentley (ed.), *Companion to Historiography* (London, 1997), pp. 177–202.

—, *Medieval Polities and Modern Mentalities*, ed. J. L. Nelson (Cambridge, 2006).

—, 'Nobles and others: the social and cultural expression of power relations in the Middle Ages', in Reuter, *Medieval Polities and Modern Mentalities*, pp. 111–26.

—, 'Plunder and tribute in the Carolingian empire', *TRHS* 5th ser. 35 (1985), pp. 75–94; repr. in Reuter, *Medieval Polities and Modern Mentalities*, pp. 321–50.

Reuter, T. (ed.), *The Medieval Nobility: Studies on the Ruling Classes of France and Germany from the Sixth to the Twelfth Century* (Amsterdam, 1979).

—, *The New Cambridge Medieval History*, III: *c.900–c.1024* (Cambridge, 1999).

Reynolds, R., 'The organisation, law and liturgy of the western church, 700–900', in *NCMH* II, pp. 587–621.

Reynolds, S., *Fiefs and Vassals: the Medieval Evidence Reconsidered* (Oxford, 1996).

—, *Kingdoms and Communities in Western Europe, 900–1300* (Oxford, 1997).

Rhijn, C. van, *Shepherds of the Lord. Priests and Episcopal Statutes in the Carolingian Period* (Turnhout, 2007).

Rhijn, C. van, and Saan, M., 'Correcting sinners, correcting texts: a context for the *Paenitentiale pseudo-Theodori*', *EME* 14/1 (2006), pp. 23–40.

Riché, P., *Les Carolingiens: une famille qui fit l'Europe* (Paris, 1983), trans. M. I. Allen, *The Carolingians: A Family who Forged Europe* (Philadelphia, PA, 1993).

—, *Daily Life in the World of Charlemagne*, trans. J. A. McNamara (Liverpool, 1978).

Rio, A., *The Formularies of Angers and Marculf: Two Merovingian Legal Handbooks* (Liverpool, 2008).

— 'Freedom and unfreedom in early medieval Francia: the evidence of the legal formularies', *P&P* 193 (2006), pp. 7–40.

—, 'High and low: ties of dependence in the Frankish kingdoms', *TRHS* 6th ser., 18 (2008), pp. 43–68.

—, *Legal Practice and the Written Word in the Early Middle Ages: Frankish Formulae, c.500–1000* (Cambridge, 2009).

Ripoll, G., and Arce, J., 'The transformation and end of Roman *villae* in the west (fourth–seventh centuries): problems and perspectives', in G. P.

Brogiolo, N. Gautier and N. Christie (eds.), *Towns and their Territories from Late Antiquity to the Early Middle Ages* (Leiden, 2000), pp. 63–114.

Rösener, W. (ed.), *Strukturen der Grundherrschaft im frühen Mittelalter*, VMPIG 92 (Göttingen, 1989).

Rosenwein, B. H., 'The family politics of Berengar I, king of Italy (888–924)', *Speculum* 71 (1996), pp. 247–89.

—, *Negotiating Space: Power, Restraint and Privileges of Immunity in Early Medieval Europe* (Manchester, 1999).

Rouche, M., 'Géographie rurale du royaume de Charles le Chauve', in J. L. Nelson and M. Gibson, *Charles the Bald: Court and Kingdom* (2nd edn, Aldershot, 1991), pp. 189–202.

Rovelli, A., 'Coins and trade in early medieval Italy', *EME* 17 (2009), pp. 45–76.

—, 'Economia monetaria e monete nel dossier di Campione', in Gasparri and La Rocca (eds.), *Carte di famiglia*, pp. 117–40.

—, 'Emissione e uso della moneta: le testimonianze scritte e archeologiche', *Settimane di Studio del Centro italiano di studi sull'alto medioevo* 48 (Spoleto, 2001), pp. 821–52.

—, 'Some considerations on the coinage of Lombard and Carolingian Italy', in Hansen and Wickham (eds.), *The Long Eighth Century*, pp. 195–223.

Rubin, M., *Corpus Christi: the Eucharist in Late Medieval Culture* (Cambridge, 1991).

Samson, R., 'Carolingian palaces and the poverty of ideology', in M. Locock (ed.), *Meaningful Architecture: Social Interpretations of Buildings* (Aldershot, 1994) pp. 99–131.

—, 'The Merovingian nobleman's house: castle or villa', *Journal of Medieval History* 13 (1987), pp 287–315.

Sarris, P., *Economy and Society in the Age of Justinian* (Cambridge, 2007).

—, 'The origins of the manorial economy: new insights from Late Antiquity', *EHR* 119 (2004), pp. 279–311.

Sarris, P., and Banaji, J. (eds.), *Aristocrats, Peasants and the Transformation of Rural Society c.400–800*, special issue of the *Journal of Agrarian Change* 9.1 (2009), pp. 1–153.

Sato, S., 'The Merovingian accounting documents of Tours: form and function', *EME* 9/2 (2003), pp. 143–61.

Sawyer, P. H., *The Age of the Vikings* (London, 1962, 2nd edn 1971).

—, 'Kings and merchants', in P. H. Sawyer and I. N. Wood (eds.), *Early Medieval Kingship* (Leeds, 1977), pp. 139–58.

Sawyer, P. (ed.), *The Oxford Illustrated History of the Vikings* (Oxford, 1997).

Scharf, I., 'Studien zur Smaragdus und Jonas', *Deutsches Archiv für Erforschung des Mittelalters* 17 (1961), pp. 333–84.

Schieffer, R., 'Charlemagne and Rome', in Smith (ed.), *Early Medieval Rome and the Christian West*, pp. 279–95.

—, '"Die folgenschwerste Tat des ganzen Mittelalters"? Aspekte des wissenschaftlichen Urteils über den Dynastiewechsel von 751', in Becher and Jarnut (eds.), *Der Dynastiewechsel von 751*, pp. 1–14.

—, 'Ludwig "der Fromme"'. Zur Entstehung eines karolingischen Herrscherbeinamens', *Frühmittelalterliche Studien* 16 (1982), pp. 58–73.

Schlesinger, W., 'Die Hufe im Frankenreich', in Patze and Schwind (eds.), *Ausgewählte Aufsätze von W. Schlesinger*, pp. 587–614.

—, 'Hufe und mansus im liber donationem des Klosters Weissenburgs', in Patze and Schwind (eds.), *Ausgewählte Aufsätze von W. Schlesinger*, pp. 543–85.

—, 'Vorstudien zu einer Untersuchungen über die Hufe', in Patze and Schwind (eds.), *Ausgewählte Aufsätze von W. Schlesinger*, pp. 458–541.

Schmidt-Weigand, R., 'Das Dorf nach den Stammesrechten des Kontinents', in Jankuhn, *et al.* (eds.), *Das Dorf der Eisenzeit*, pp. 408–43.

Schmitt, J., *Untersuchungen zu den Liberi Homines der Karolingerzeit* (Frankfurt, 1977).

Schmitz, G., 'The capitulary legislation of Louis the Pious', in Godman and Collins (eds.), *Charlemagne's Heir*, pp. 425–36.

Schneider, R., *Brüdergemeine und Schwurfreundschaft: der Auflösungsprozess des Karlingerreiches im Spiegel der Caritas-Terminologie in den Verträgen der karlingischen Teilkönige des 9. Jahrhunderts* (Lübeck, 1964).

Scholz, B., *Carolingian Chronicles* (Ann Arbor, MI, 1970).

Schramm, P., and Mütherich, F., *Denkmale der deutschen Könige und Kaiser*, 2nd edn (Munich, 1981).

Schröder, I., 'Zur Überlieferung von *De institutione laicali* des Jonas von Orléans', *DA* 44 (1988), pp. 83–97.

Schüssler, H., 'Die fränkische Reichsteilung von Vieux-Poitiers (742) und die Reform der Kirche in den Teilreichen Karlmanns und Pippins', *Francia* 13 (1985), pp. 45–111.

Schütte, S., 'Continuity problems and authority structures in Cologne', in G. Ausenda (ed.), *After Empire: Towards an Ethnology of Europe's Barbarians* (San Marino, 1995), pp. 163–76.

Schwind, F., 'Beobachtungen zur inneren Struktur des Dorfes in karolingischer Zeit', in Jankuhn, *et al.* (eds.), *Das Dorf der Eisenzeit*, pp. 444–93.

—, 'Zu karolingerzeitlichen Klöstern als Wirtschaftsorganismen und Stätten handwerklicher Produktion', in L. Fenske, W. Rösener and T. Zotz (eds.), *Institutionen, Kultur und Gesellschaft im Mittelalter: Festschrift für Josef Fleckenstein zu seinem 65. Geburtstag* (Sigmaringen, 1984), pp. 101–23.

Screen, E., 'The importance of the emperor: Lothar I and the Frankish civil war, 840–843', *EME* 12 (2003), pp. 25–51.

Scull, C., 'Urban centres in pre-Viking England?', in J. Hines (ed.), *The Anglo-Saxons from the Migration Period to the Eighth Century* (Woodbridge, 1997), pp. 269–310.

Sénac, P., *Musulmans et Sarrasins dans le sud de la Gaule du VIIIe au XIe siècle* (Paris, 1980).

Sennis, A., 'The power of time: looking at the past in medieval monasteries', in A. Müller and K. Stöber (eds.), *Self-Representation of Medieval*

Religious Communities: the British Isles in Context, Vita Regularis, Abhandlungen 40 (Münster, 2009), pp. 307–26.

Sergi, G., 'The kingdom of Italy', in Reuter (ed.), *The New Cambridge Medieval History*, III, pp. 346–71.

Shanzer, D., 'Dating the baptism of Clovis: the Bishop of Vienne vs the Bishop of Tours', *EME* 7 (1998), pp. 29–57.

Siems, H., *Handel und Wucher im Spiegel frühmittelalterliche Rechtsquellen* (Hanover, 1992).

Słupecki, L., *Slavonic Pagan Sanctuaries* (Warsaw, 1994).

Smith, J. M. H., 'Einhard: the sinner and the saints', *TRHS* 6th ser. 13 (2003), pp. 55–77.

—, *Europe after Rome: A New Cultural History* (Oxford, 2005).

—, '*Fines imperii*: the Marches', in *NCMH* II, pp. 169–89.

—, 'Gender and ideology in the early Middle Ages', in R. N. Swanson (ed.), *Gender and Christian Religion*, Studies in Church History 14 (Woodbridge, 1998), pp. 51–73.

—, 'A hagiographer at work: Hucbald and the library at Saint-Amand', *Revue bénédictine* 106 (1996), pp. 151–71.

—, 'Old saints, new cults: Roman relics in Carolingian Francia', in Smith (ed.), *Early Medieval Rome and the Christian West*, pp. 317–39.

—, 'The problem of female sanctity in Carolingian Europe *c*.750–920', *P&P* 146 (1995), pp. 3–37.

—, *Province and Empire. Brittany and the Carolingians* (Cambridge, 1992).

Smith, J. M. H. (ed.), *Early Medieval Rome and the Christian West: Essays in Honour of Donald A. Bullough* (Leiden and Boston, 2000).

Smith, R., 'Modernisation and the corporate village community: some sceptical reflections', in A. Baker and D. Gregory (eds.), *Explorations in Historical Geography* (Cambridge, 1984), pp. 140–79.

Sonnlechner, C., 'The establishment of new units of production in Carolingian times: making early medieval sources relevant for environmental history', *Viator* 35 (2004), pp. 21–58.

Sot, M., 'Le *Liber de episcopis Mettensibus* dans l'histoire du genre "Gesta episcoporum"', in P. Chiesa (ed.), *Paolo Diacono. Uno scrittore fra tradizione longobarda e rinnovamento carolingio* (Udine, 2000), pp. 527–50.

Southern, R. W., *The Making of the Middle Ages* (London, 1953).

Sprandel, R., 'Gerichtsorganisation und Sozialstruktur Mainfrankens im früheren Mittelalter', *Jahrbuch für fränkische Landesforschung* 38 (1978), pp. 7–38.

Squatriti, P., 'Mohammed, the early medieval Mediterranean, and Charlemagne', *EME* 11 (2003), pp. 263–79.

Staab, F., 'Agrarwissenschaft und Grundherrschaft. Zum Weinbau der Klöster im Frühmittelalter', in A. Gerlich (ed.), *Weinbau, Weinhandel und Weinkultur*. Geschichtliche Landeskunde 40 (Stuttgart, 1993), pp. 1–48.

—, 'A reconsideration of the ancestry of modern political liberty: the problem of the so-called King's Freemen (*Königsfreie*)', *Viator* 11 (1980), pp. 51–70.

—, *Untersuchungen zur Gesellschaft am Mittelrhein in der Karolingerzeit*, Geschichtliche Landeskunde 11 (Wiesbaden, 1975).

Stafford, P., 'The Anglo-Saxon Chronicles, identity and the making of England', *Haskins Society Journal* 19 (2008), pp. 28–50.

—, 'Parents and children in the early middle ages', *EME* 10 (2001), pp. 257–71.

—, *Queens, Concubines and Dowagers: the King's Wife in the Early Middle Ages* (London, 1983).

Stancliffe, C., 'Cuthbert and the polarity between pastor and solitary', in G. Bonner, D. Rollason and C. Stancliffe (eds.), *St Cuthbert, his Cult and his Community to AD 1200* (Woodbridge, 1989), pp. 21–44.

—, 'Kings who opted out', in P. Wormald (ed.), *Ideal and Reality in Frankish and Anglo-Saxon Society* (Oxford, 1983), pp. 154–76.

Stanley, E. G., *The Search for Anglo-Saxon Paganism* (Cambridge, 1975).

Stansbury, M., 'Early medieval biblical commentaries, their writers and readers', *Frühmittelalterliche Studien* 33 (1999), pp. 49–82.

Staubach, N., *Rex Christianus: Hofkultur und Herrscherpropaganda im Reich Karls des Kahlen II: Die Grundlegung der 'religion royale'* (Cologne, 1993).

Stengel, E. E. (ed.), *Urkundenbuch der Kloster Fulda*, Veröffentlichungen der historischen Kommission für Hessen und Waldeck 19 (Marburg, 1936).

Stoclet, A., *Autour de Fulrad de Saint-Denis (v.710–784)* (Geneva, 1993).

Stone, R., 'Kings are different: Carolingian mirrors for princes and lay morality', in F. Lachaud and L. Scordia (eds.), *Le Prince au miroir de la littérature politique de l'Antiquité aux Lumières* (Rouen, 2007), pp. 69–86.

Stork, I., 'Zum Fortgang der Untersuchungen im frühmittelalterlichen Gräberfeld, Adelshof und Hofgrablege bei Lauchheim, Ostalbkreis', *Archäologische Ausgrabungen in Baden-Württemberg 1992* (Stuttgart, 1993), pp. 231–9.

Störmer, W., *Adelsgruppen im früh- und hochmittelalterlichen Bayern.* Studien zur Bayerischen Verfassungs- und Sozialgeschichte 4 (Munich, 1972).

Storms, G., *Anglo-Saxon Magic* (The Hague, 1948).

Story, J., *Carolingian Connections: Anglo-Saxon England and Carolingian Francia, c.750–870* (Aldershot, 2003).

—, 'Cathwulf, kingship and the royal abbey of Saint-Denis', *Speculum* 74 (1999), pp. 1–21.

—, 'Charlemagne and the Anglo-Saxons', in Story (ed.), *Charlemagne*, pp. 195–210.

—, 'Introduction: Charlemagne's Reputation', in Story (ed.), *Charlemagne*, pp. 1–4.

Story, J. (ed.), *Charlemagne: Empire and Society* (Manchester and New York, 2005).

Story, J., *et al.*, 'Charlemagne's black marble: the origins of the epitaph of Pope Hadrian I', *PBSR* 73 (2005), pp. 157–90.

Sullivan, R., 'The Carolingian age: Reflections on its place in the history of the Middle Ages', *Speculum* 64 (1989), pp. 267–306.

Szarmach, P., 'A preliminary handlist of manuscripts containing Alcuin's *Liber de virtutibus et vitiis*', *Manuscripta* 25 (1981), pp. 131–40.

Talbot, C. H., *Anglo-Saxon Missionaries in Germany* (London, 1954).

Thacker, A., 'In search of saints: the English Church and the cult of Roman apostles and martyrs in the seventh and eighth centuries', in Smith (ed.), *Early Medieval Rome and the Christian West*, pp. 247–77.

—, 'Wilfrid', *Oxford Dictionary of National Biography*, s.n.

Theuws, F., 'Landed property and manorial organisation in northern Austrasia: some considerations and a case study', in F. Theuws and N. Roymans (eds.), *Images of the Past. Studies on Ancient Societies in Northwestern Europe* (Amsterdam, 1991), pp. 299–407.

—, 'Maastricht as a centre of power in the early Middle Ages', in de Jong and Theuws with van Rhijn (eds.), *Topographies of Power*, pp. 155–216.

Theuws, F., and Nelson, J. L. (eds.), *Rituals of Power: From Late Antiquity to the Early Middle Ages* (Leiden, 2000).

Thurlemann, F., 'Die Bedeutung der Aachener Theoderich-Statue für Karl den Großen (801) und bei Walahfried Strabo (829). Materialien zu einer Semiotik visueller Objekte im frühen Mittelalter', *Archiv für Kulturgeschichte* 59 (1977), pp. 24–65.

Tischler, M., *Einharts Vita Karoli. Studien zur Entstehung, Überlieferung und Rezeption, MGH Schriften* 48, 2 vols. (Hanover, 2001).

Tolkien, J. R. R., 'Beowulf: the monsters and the critics', *PBA* 22 (1936) 1–53; repr. in J. R. R. Tolkien, *The Monsters and the Critics and Other Essays* (London, 1983).

Toubert, P., 'The Carolingian moment (eighth–tenth century)', in A. Burguiere, *et al.* (eds.), *A History of the Family* (Cambridge, 1996), pp. 379–406.

—, *Les Structures du Latium médiéval: Le Latium méridional et la Sabine du IXe siècle à la fin du XIIe siècle*, 2 vols., Bibliothèque des Écoles Françaises d'Athènes et de Rome 221 (Rome, 1973).

Townend, M., *Language and History in Viking Age England: Linguistic Relations between Speakers of Old English and Old Norse* (Turnhout, 2002).

Traill, D. (ed. and trans.), *Walahfrid Strabo's Visio Wettini: Text, Translation and Commentary* (Frankfurt, 1974).

Treffort, C., *L'Église carolingienne et la mort* (Lyon, 1996).

Tremp, E., 'Die letzten Worte des frommen Kaisers Ludwig. Von Sinn und Unsinn heutiger Textedition', *DA* 48 (1992), pp. 17–36.

Ullman, W., 'Public welfare and social legislation in the early medieval councils', *Studies in Church History* 7 (1971), pp. 1–39.

Verhulst, A., *The Carolingian Economy* (Cambridge, 2002).

—, 'La Genèse du regime domanial classique en France au haut moyen âge', *Settimane di Studio del Centro italiano di studi sull'alto medioevo* 13 (1966), pp. 135–60, repr. in Verhulst, *Rural and Urban Aspects*.

—, 'Karolingische Agrarpolitik. Das *Capitulare de Villis* und die Hungersnöte von 792/93 und 805/06', *Zeitschrift für Agrargeschichte und Agrarsoziologie* 13 (1965), pp. 175–89, repr. in Verhulst, *Rural and Urban Aspects*.

—, 'The origins of towns in the Low Countries and the Pirenne Thesis', *P&P* 122 (1989), pp. 3–35.

—, *The Rise of Cities in North-West Europe* (Cambridge, 1999).

—, *Rural and Urban Aspects of Early Medieval Northwest Europe* (Aldershot, 1992).

Vermes, G., *The Changing Faces of Jesus* (London, 2001).

—, *Jesus the Jew. A Historian's Reading of the Gospels*, 5th edn (London, 1994).

—, *Jesus and the World of Judaism* (Philadelphia, PA, 1984).

Verwers, W., 'Dorestad: a Carolingian town?', in B. Hobley and R. Hodges (eds.), *The Rebirth of Towns in the West, AD 700–1050* (London, 1988), pp. 52–6.

Wallace-Hadrill, J. M., *The Barbarian West, 400–1000* (London, 1952).

—, *The Frankish Church* (Oxford, 1983).

Wallach, L., *Alcuin and Charlemagne*, 2nd edn (Ithaca, NY, 1968).

Wamers, E., *Die frühmittelalterliche Lesefunde aus der Löhrstraße (Baustelle Hilton II) in Mainz* (Mainz, 1994).

Wamers, E., and Brandt, M. (eds.), *Die Macht des Silbers: Karolingische Schätze im Norden* (Frankfurt, 2005).

Ward, E., 'Agobard of Lyons and Paschasius Radbertus as critics of the empress Judith', *Studies in Church History* 27 (1990), pp. 15–25.

—, 'Caesar's wife: the career of the empress Judith, 819–29', in Godman and Collins (eds.), *Charlemagne's Heir*, pp. 205–27.

Ward-Perkins, B., *The Fall of Rome and the End of Civilization* (Oxford, 2005).

—, *From Classical Antiquity to the Middle Ages. Urban Public Building in Northern and Central Italy AD 300–850* (Oxford, 1984).

Watkins, C., 'Sin, penance and purgatory in the Anglo-Norman realm', *P&P* 175 (2002), pp. 3–33.

Weidinger, U., *Untersuchungen zur Wirtschaftsstruktur des Kloster Fulda in der Karolingerzeit* (Stuttgart, 1991).

Weiler, B., and MacLean, S. (eds.), *Representations of Power in Medieval Germany, 800–1500* (Turnhout, 2006).

Weiner, A., *Inalienable Possessions. The Paradox of Keeping-while-Giving* (Berkeley, CA, 1992).

Weinrich, L., *Wala. Graf, Mönch und Rebell. Die Biographie eines Karolingers* (Lübeck, 1963).

Werner, K. F., 'Gauzlin von Saint-Denis und die westfränkische Reichsteilung von Amiens (März 880). Ein Beitrag zur Vorgeschichte von Odos Königtum', *DA* 35 (1979), pp. 395–462.

—, 'Hludovicus Augustus: gouverner l'empire chrétien – idées et réalités', in Godman and Collins (eds.), *Charlemagne's Heir*, pp. 3–123.

—, 'Important noble families in the kingdom of Charlemagne', trans. in Reuter (ed.), *The Medieval Nobility*, pp. 137–202, first published in W. Braunfels and P. E. Schramm (eds.), *Karl der Große: Lebenswerk und Nachleben*, 4 vols. (Düsseldorf, 1967).

—, 'Missus–marchio–comes: entre l'administration centrale et l'administration locale de l'empire carolingien', in W. Paravicini and K. F. Werner (eds.), *Histoire comparée de l'administration (IVe–XVIIIe siècle)* (Sigmaringen, Munich and Zurich, 1980), pp. 191–239.

—, 'Untersuchungen zur Frühzeit des französischen Fürstentums', *Die Welt als Geschichte* 3–4 (1959), pp. 146–93.

West, C., *Upper Lotharingia and Champagne, c.850–c.1100*, unpublished PhD thesis (Cambridge, 2007).

White, S. D., 'Debate. The "Feudal Revolution"', *P&P* 152 (1996), pp. 205–23.

Whitehouse, D., '"Things that travelled": the surprising case of raw glass', *EME* 12 (2003), pp. 301–5.

Whittaker, C. R., 'Circe's pigs: from slavery to serfdom in the Roman world', *Slavery and Abolition* 8 (1987), pp. 88–122.

Whittow, M., 'Decline and fall? Studying long term change in the east', in W. Bowden and L. Lavan (eds.), *Theory and Practice in Late Antique Archaeology* (Leiden, 2004), pp. 404–23.

Wickham, C., 'Aristocratic power in eighth-century Lombard Italy', in A. C. Murray (ed.), *After Rome's Fall: Narrators and Sources of Early Medieval History* (Toronto, 1998), pp. 153–70.

—, 'Debate: the Feudal Revolution', *P&P* 155 (1997), pp. 196–207.

—, *Early Medieval Italy. Central Power and Local Society, 400–1000* (London and Basingstoke, 1981).

—, 'European forests in the early middle ages: landscape and land clearance', *Settimane di Studio del Centro italiano di studi sull'alto medioevo* 37 (Spoleto, 1989), pp. 479–548, repr. in Wickham, *Land and Power*, pp. 155–99.

—, 'The fall of Rome will not take place', in Little and Rosenwein (eds.), *Debating the Middle Ages*, pp. 45–57, first published as 'La Chute de Rome n'aura pas lieu', *Le Moyen Âge* 99 (1983), pp. 107–26.

—, 'Le forme del feudalesimo', *Settimane di Studio del Centro Italiano di Studi sull'Alto Medioevo* 47 (2000), pp. 15–51.

—, *Framing the Early Middle Ages: Europe and the Mediterranean, 400–800* (Oxford, 2005).

—, *The Inheritance of Rome: A History of Europe, 400–1000* (London, 2009).

—, *Land and Power. Studies in Italian and European Social History, 400–1200* (London, 1994).

—, *The Mountains and the City: the Tuscan Appennines in the Early Middle Ages* (Oxford, 1988).

—, 'Ninth-century Byzantium through western eyes', in L. Brubaker (ed.), *Byzantium in the Ninth Century: Dead or Alive?* (Aldershot, 1998), pp. 245–56.

—, 'The other transition: from the ancient world to feudalism', *P&P* 113 (1984), pp. 3–36, repr. in Wickham, *Land and Power*, pp. 7–42.

—, 'Overview: production, distribution and demand, II', in Hansen and Wickham (eds.), *The Long Eighth Century*, pp. 345–77.

—, 'Pastoralism and underdevelopment in the early middle ages', *Settimane di Studio del Centro italiano di studi sull'alto medioevo* 31 (Spoleto, 1983), pp. 401–55, repr. in Wickham, *Land and Power*, pp. 121–54.

—, 'Rethinking the structure of the early medieval economy', in Davis and McCormick (eds.), *The Long Morning of Medieval Europe*, pp. 19–32.

—, 'Rural society in Carolingian Europe', in *NCMH* II, pp. 431–50.

Widdowson, M., 'Merovingian partitions: a genealogical charter?', *EME* 17 (2009), pp. 1–22.

Witwrouw, J., 'Le Centre domanial du haut moyen âge du Thier d'Olne à Engis/Hermalle-sous-Huy', *Bulletin de Liaison de l'Association Française d'Archéologie Mérovingienne* 23 (1999), pp. 105–8.

Wolfram, H., 'The creation of the Carolingian frontier system, c.800', in Pohl, Wood and Reimitz (eds.), *Transformation of Frontiers*, pp. 233–45.

Wollasch, J., 'Gemeinschaftsbewußtsein und soziale Leistung im Mittelalter', *Frühmittelalterliche Studien* 9 (1975), pp. 61–77.

Wood, I. N., 'Before or after mission. Social relations across the middle and lower Rhine in the seventh and eighth centuries', in Hansen and Wickham (eds.), *The Long Eighth Century*, pp. 149–66.

—, 'Beyond satraps and ostriches: political and social structures of the Saxons in the early Carolingian period', in D. H. Green and F. Siegmund (eds.), *The Continental Saxons from the Migration Period to the Tenth Century: An Ethnographic Perspective* (Rochester, NY, 2003), pp. 271–97.

—, 'The bloodfeud of the Franks: a historiographical legend', *Early Medieval Europe* 14 (2006), pp. 489–504.

—, 'Boniface', *Oxford Dictionary of National Biography, s.n.*

—, 'The Channel from the 4th to the 7th centuries AD', in McGrail (ed.), *Maritime Celts, Frisians and Saxons*, pp. 93–7.

—, 'Christians and pagans in ninth-century Scandinavia', in B. Sawyer, P. H. Sawyer and I. N. Wood (eds.), *The Christianization of Scandinavia* (Alingsås, 1987), pp. 36–67.

—, 'Deconstructing the Merovingian family', in R. Corradini, M. Diesenberger and H. Reimitz (eds.), *The Construction of Communities in the Early Middle Ages* (Leiden and Boston, 2003), pp. 149–71.

—, 'John Michael Wallace-Hadrill, 1916–85', *Proceedings of the British Academy* 124 (2004), pp. 333–55.

—, *The Merovingian Kingdoms, 450–751* (London, 1994).

—, *The Merovingian North Sea* (Alingsås, 1983).

—, 'Missionaries and the Christian frontier', in Pohl, Wood and Reimitz (eds.), *Transformation of Frontiers*, pp. 209–18.

—, *The Missionary Life: Saints and the Evangelisation of Europe, 400–1050* (Harlow, 2001).

—, 'Pagan religion and superstitions east of the Rhine from the fifth to the ninth century', in G. Ausenda (ed.), *After Empire* (Woodbridge, 1995), pp. 253–68.

—, 'Saint-Wandrille and its hagiography', in I. N. Wood and G. A. Loud (eds.), *Church and Chronicle in the Middle Ages* (London, 1991), pp. 1–15.

Wood, S., *The Proprietary Church in the Medieval West* (Oxford, 2006).

Woolf, S., 'Europe and its historians', *Contemporary European History* 12 (2003), pp. 323–37.

Wormald, P., '*Lex scripta* and *verbum regis*: legislation and Germanic kingship from Euric to Cnut', in P. H. Sawyer and I. N. Wood (eds.), *Early Medieval Kingship* (Leeds, 1977), pp. 105–38.

—, *The Making of English Law: King Alfred to the Twelfth Century*, I: *Legislation and its Limits* (Oxford, 1999).

—, 'Pre-modern "state" and "nation": definite or indefinite?', in Airlie, Pohl and Reimitz (eds.), *Staat im frühen Mittelalter*, pp. 179–89.

—, 'Viking studies: whence and whither?', in R. T. Farrell (ed.), *The Vikings* (Chichester, 1982), pp. 128–53.

Wormald, P., and Nelson, J. (eds.), *Lay Intellectuals in the Carolingian World* (Cambridge, 2007).

Wormald, P., Bullough, D., and Collins, R. (eds.), *Ideal and Reality in Frankish and Anglo-Saxon Society* (Oxford, 1983).

Wright, R., *A Sociophilological Study of Late Latin* (Turnhout, 2002).

Wurnburger, A. (ed.), *Über eine ungedruckte Kanonensammlung aus dem 8. Jahrhundert* (Munich, 1890).

Yorke, B., 'The Jutes of Hampshire and Wight and the origins of Wessex', in S. Bassett, *The Origins of Anglo-Saxon Kingdoms* (London and New York, 1989), pp. 84–96.

Zeddies, N., 'Bonifatius und die zwei nützliche Rebellen: die Häretiker Adelbert und Clemens', *Ordnung und Aufruhr im Mittelalter: historische und juristische Studien zur Rebellion*, Ius Commune. Sonderheft 70 (Frankfurt, 1995).

Zelzer, K., 'Von Benedikt zu Hildemar. Zu Textgestalt und Textgeschichte der *Regula Benedicti* auf ihrem Weg zur Alleingeltung', *Frühmittelalterliche Studien* 23 (1989), pp. 112–30.

Zimmermann, H., '*Imperatores Italiae*', in H. Beumann (ed.), *Historische Forschungen für Walter Schlesinger* (Cologne and Vienna, 1974), pp. 379–99.

Zotz, T., 'In Amt und Würden. Zur Eigenart "offizieller" Positionen im früheren Mittelalter', *Tel Aviver Jahrbuch für deutsche Geschichte* 22 (1993), pp. 1–23.

—, 'Carolingian tradition and Ottonian–Salian innovation: comparative observations on Palatine policy in the empire', in A. Duggan (ed.), *Kings and Kingship in Medieval Europe* (London, 1993), pp. 69–100.

—, 'Ludwig der Deutsche und seine Pfalzen: Königliche Herrschaftspraxis in der Formierungsphase des ostfränkischen Reiches', in W. Hartmann (ed.), *Ludwig der Deutsche und seine Zeit* (Darmstadt, 2004), pp. 27–46.

INDEX

CPSIA information can be obtained
at www.ICGtesting.com
Printed in the USA
LVHW050402130723
752245LV00003B/40

9 780521 564946